Series: Digital Sovereignty and Human-Centric AI

1. Artificial Intelligence in Context of Digital Sovereignty
   Sanjay Misra, Petter Kvalvik, Bjørn Axel Gran, Kai Morgan Kjolerbakken, Aida Omerovic, Nadia Saad Noori (Editors), 2026

Series: Digital Sovereignty and Human-Centric AI

Artificial Intelligence in Context of Digital Sovereignty

Editors

Sanjay Misra
Sr. Scientist, Department of Digital Sovereignty
Institute for Energy Technology, Halden, Norway

Petter Kvalvik
Sr. Scientist, Head of Department of Digital Sovereignty
Institute for Energy Technology, Halden, Norway

Bjørn Axel Gran
Vice President, Institute for Energy Technology
Halden, Norway

Kai Morgan Kjølerbakken
Head, Department of Applied Data Science
Institute for Energy Technology, Halden, Norway

Aida Omerovic
Senior Scientist, SINTEF Digital
Oslo, Norway

Nadia Saad Noori
Associate Professor
Department of Information Communication Technology
Universitetet i Agder, (UiA), Grimstad, Norway

Routledge
Taylor & Francis Group
NEW YORK AND LONDON

First published 2026
by Routledge
605 Third Avenue, New York, NY 10158

and by Routledge
4 Park Square, Milton Park, Abingdon, Oxon, OX14 4RN

Routledge is an imprint of the Taylor & Francis Group, an informa business

Library of Congress Cataloging-in-Publication Data
A catalog record for this title has been requested

ISBN: 978-1-032-94550-7 (hbk)
ISBN: 978-1-032-94753-2 (pbk)
ISBN: 978-1-003-58158-1 (ebk)

DOI: 10.1201/9781003581581

Typeset in Times New Roman
by Prime Publishing Services

Preface

Introduction

As artificial intelligence becomes deeply embedded in the infrastructure of modern societies, the question of digital sovereignty has moved from the margins of policy debates to the centre of national and international agendas. It is no longer sufficient to explore what AI can do; we must also examine who controls it, how it is governed, and to whose benefit it is deployed. Digital sovereignty is not simply a matter of technology ownership or data localisation; it is about securing the capacity to act independently, ethically, and transparently in the digital realm.

Artificial intelligence, when aligned with sovereign principles, has the potential to support democratic values, protect privacy, and advance public interests across sectors. However, without appropriate frameworks, AI can deepen dependencies on foreign technologies, centralise control in opaque infrastructures, and undermine the ability of states and communities to define their digital futures.

This book responds to these challenges by offering a timely, comprehensive exploration of the relationship between AI and digital sovereignty. Unlike other works that treat these subjects in isolation, this volume examines their intersections across technical systems, policy frameworks, ethical debates, and geopolitical contexts. Its interdisciplinary perspective brings together practical insights, conceptual tools, and case-based research that will benefit decision-makers, researchers, and practitioners alike.

By drawing on diverse global examples and addressing critical domains—from agriculture and healthcare to smart cities and cybersecurity—this book offers a grounded understanding of how sovereignty can be maintained, negotiated, and reimagined in AI-driven societies.

Organization of the Book

The volume is structured around sixteen chapters, each examining a unique aspect of how AI intersects with the principle and practice of digital sovereignty.

1. **Digital Sovereignty and Digital Transformation Extension for the Software Life Cycle Process with ISO/IEC/IEEE 12207:2017**
   This chapter presents a structured process model that integrates digital sovereignty principles into the AI software development lifecycle, offering guidance for

public and private sector organizations to align software engineering practices with sovereignty and transformation goals.

2. **Re-Conceptualizing Sovereignty: Distributed Digital Sovereignty and Artificial Intelligence, A New-Institutionalist Perspective and Socio-Technical Fields**
   A theoretical framework is introduced that treats digital sovereignty as a practice-specific and distributed concept. The chapter offers a typology to analyze how sovereignty is enacted across various AI-driven domains, using a socio-technical and institutional lens.
3. **Trustworthy AI in Safety-Critical Systems: Toward Robustness, Adversarial Resilience, and Uncertainty-Aware Intelligence**
   This chapter explores the design of robust AI systems in critical environments such as 6G networks and autonomous vehicles. It examines how uncertainty quantification and adversarial defense strategies contribute to trustworthy, sovereign AI deployment.
4. **Generative Artificial Intelligence and AI-enabled Archiving to Promote Digital Sovereignty in the Context of Core International Crimes**
   Through the lens of digital archiving for international justice, this chapter demonstrates how AI-enabled tools—such as transcription and semantic search—can be used to protect data integrity and privacy, supporting sovereignty in politically sensitive contexts.
5. **Secure and Collaborative Crop Disease Prediction with Federated Deep Learning: Safeguarding Data Sovereignty in Agriculture**
   Focusing on agricultural applications, this chapter shows how federated learning enables accurate crop disease prediction while ensuring that sensitive local data remains under the control of farmers and institutions.
6. **Rent-Seeking in AI Infrastructure: A Structural Threat to Digital Sovereignty and Cybersecurity**
   This chapter critiques the economic structures that allow dominant technology providers to restrict access, extract rents, and undermine state control. A strategic framework is proposed to reclaim autonomy and resilience in critical AI infrastructure.
7. **Enhancing Design Science Research Methodology with a Focus on Security (S-DSRM) and Data Sovereignty: A Proof-of-Concept Study**
   A new research methodology is introduced that embeds security and sovereignty into every stage of system design. Demonstrated through a healthcare prototype, it shows how privacy and compliance can be built into AI systems from the ground up.
8. **Safeguarding Digital Sovereignty with Privacy-Preserving Edge Computing: A Hybrid Deep Learning Framework**
   A federated, deep learning-based intrusion detection system is presented for use in mobile edge computing environments. The framework emphasizes speed, privacy, and adaptability—key pillars for maintaining digital sovereignty in distributed systems.
9. **A Semi-Automatic Pipeline Design to Enhance Document Accessibility, Digital Sovereignty, and Web Crawling**

This chapter outlines a pipeline that enhances the accessibility and discoverability of web documents while allowing institutions to retain control over content formatting and indexing, reinforcing sovereign control over digital information.

10. **Towards Digital Sovereignty in Africa: A Machine Learning Characterization of the Yoruba Language Alphabets Using Their Graphical Data Structures**
    By analyzing the graphical properties of African language scripts, this chapter proposes a set of metrics for character recognition that support the development of inclusive, locally grounded AI systems.
11. **Rethinking Data Sovereignty through Convivial AI**
    The concept of Convivial AI is introduced as a framework for participatory, community-centered AI development. Field experiments are used to illustrate how local knowledge and co-creation can support ethical and inclusive data governance.
12. **From Benefits to Ethics of Artificial Intelligence Applications Towards Industry 4.0 and Beyond**
    This chapter maps the benefits and risks of AI in industrial settings, paying particular attention to ethical tensions in automation, predictive maintenance, and cyber-physical systems.
13. **Data Governance in the Digital Era: How BRICS Nations Balance Sovereignty and Global Data Transfers**
    A comparative analysis of BRICS countries is provided, highlighting how each nation approaches digital sovereignty through policy frameworks, data localization, and AI governance in a multipolar digital landscape.
14. **European Digital Sovereignty in the Age of AI: Regulation, Infrastructure, and Democratic Legitimacy**
    This chapter examines the European Union's regulatory leadership and infrastructural efforts to establish digital sovereignty, emphasizing the need for deeper public engagement and coordination in AI governance.
15. **AI Governance for Digital Sovereignty in Smart City Surveillance**
    Surveillance systems in smart cities are critically analyzed for their impact on sovereignty and privacy. The chapter reviews governance strategies to ensure that smart city technologies remain transparent, accountable, and locally controlled.
16. **Digital Linguistic Sovereignty: The Exclusion of African Languages in Natural Language Processing**
    Highlighting systemic biases in mainstream AI models, this chapter calls attention to the exclusion of African languages in NLP and presents community-driven efforts to promote linguistic equity in digital systems.

Conclusion

This book offers a comprehensive exploration of how artificial intelligence intersects with the foundational questions of sovereignty in the digital age. It highlights both the opportunities and the risks AI presents, urging a rethink of how governance, infrastructure, ethics, and innovation must evolve together. The central message is clear: digital sovereignty is not just about protecting borders in cyberspace, it is about building systems that reflect the values, priorities, and identities of the communities they are meant to serve. As AI technologies become more embedded in public and private life, ensuring that they are developed and governed in public interest is emerging as a defining challenge for policymakers, technologists, and civil society alike.

More than a theoretical contribution, this volume offers tangible tools and pathways for shaping sovereign digital futures. From federated learning applications in agriculture to frameworks for AI governance, resilient infrastructure, and inclusive data practices, each chapter presents models, case studies, or methods with direct relevance for practitioners. Whether integrating sovereignty into the software lifecycle, safeguarding linguistic diversity in NLP, or confronting rent-seeking in AI infrastructure, the book translates complex challenges into practical strategies. In doing so, it equips readers with both the understanding and the means to act, making it a timely and valuable resource for those working to reclaim control over their digital ecosystems.

Sanjay Misra
Petter Kvalvik
Bjørn Axel Gran
Kai Morgan Kjolerbakken
Aida Omerovic
Nadia Saad Noori

Contents

CHAPTER

1

Digital Sovereignty and Digital Transformation Recommendations within ISO/IEC/IEEE 12207:2017 for AI Project Teams

Aida Stelter[1,3*(0000-0002-1935-6440)], **Martha Klare**[2*(0000-0001-6098-7917)], **Ulrike Lechner**[2(0000-0002-4286-3184)] **and John C. Eisenhauer**[3]

[1] University of Siegen
[2] University of the Bundeswehr Munich
[3] Detecon International GmbH

1.1 Introduction

The topic of strengthening technological sovereignty within the European Union has recently gained momentum. At the Minister Presidents' Conference in Berlin in March 2025, the connection between Artificial Intelligence (AI) and Digital Sovereignty was underscored by the following statement: "AI is one of the central cross-sectional and future technologies of the 21st century" (eGovernment, 2025).

Klare et al. (2022) have demonstrated that AI is a key technology for advancing Digital Sovereignty, illustrating how federated learning—a machine learning approach—can enhance data sovereignty. A growing consensus among researchers, including Vogt (2021), Wolf (2021), and others underscores the critical link between AI, Digital Sovereignty, and Digital Transformation in strengthening Europe's digital economy (Calderaro, 2022; Roberts et al., 2023).

This prompted us to further investigate the additional steps needed to strengthen Digital Sovereignty. Our latest publication examines the relationship between Digital Sovereignty, Digital Transformation, and the Software Life Cycle (Klare et al., 2025), aligning with Morl (2024), who highlights the link between these domains and the digital supply chain. We also emphasize the challenges of integrating emerging

*Corresponding authors: Aida.Stelter@uni-siegen.de; Martha.Klare@unibw.de

DOI: 10.1201/9781003581581-1

technologies such as AI into public administration (Stelter et al., 2020; Klare et al., 2024). Stelter et al. (2020) found that successful implementation depends not only on technological factors but also on the surrounding social and organizational context. Moreover, we observe that cognitive biases—particularly the status quo bias—can impede AI adoption within Digital Transformation initiatives (Oschinsky et al., 2023). Klare et al. (2024) further identified a lack of viable alternatives to English-language AI models among German development teams. These findings underscore the need for AI project teams to develop a more comprehensive understanding of Digital Sovereignty in the context of software production and related services.

We aim to underscore the importance of Digital Sovereignty throughout the software life cycle, particularly in the context of ongoing Digital Transformation. In doing so, we contribute our perspective on the intersection of AI, Digital Sovereignty, and Digital Transformation, focusing primarily on the viewpoints of: (1) public administration and (2) private organizations in Germany. Our inquiry is guided by the following research questions:

RQ1: *How can AI project teams enhance their digitally sovereignity amid rapid technological change?*

RQ2: *What process steps can AI project teams consider to integrate Digital Sovereignty and Digital Transformation measures within their software life cycle?*

Klare et al. (2025) found that organizations require clearer guidelines for incorporating Digital Sovereignty requirements into the Software Life Cycle. Many public and private sector organizations continue to grapple with how best to integrate AI across various stages of the software life cycle (Fountaine, 2019). A noticeable gap exists in structured, standardized frameworks to support decision-making aligned with the principles of AI, Digital Sovereignty, and Digital Transformation. As a result, the software they develop, procure, or retire may fail to meet sovereignty requirements. This lack of guidance presents significant challenges, particularly in relation to security, data protection, and compliance with national and international regulations.

This chapter is structured into key thematic sections: Section 2 outlines the methodology of Soft Design Science (SDSM). Section 3 presents the theoretical background, divided into three core areas: Digital Sovereignty, Digital Transformation, and the Software Life Cycle. Section 4 addresses how requirements related to AI, Digital Sovereignty, and Digital Transformation can be integrated into the software life cycle. Section 5 discusses the study's limitations, while the final section offers conclusions and outlines future research directions.

1.1.1 Contributions

This chapter aims to develop an artefact—the ISO 12207:2017 Extension—to assist AI project teams in addressing concerns related to Digital Sovereignty and Digital Transformation, and to support them in navigating challenges throughout the Software Life Cycle. The main contributions are:

- The artifact we present offers a structured approach to integrating Digital

Sovereignty and Digital Transformation requirements at each stage of the Software Life Cycle Process.

- To guide this development, we refer to ISO/IEC/IEEE 12207:2017, which encompasses the entire software life cycle. As organizations undergo digital evolution, their software systems must adapt to emerging challenges in data security, regulatory compliance, and sovereignty requirements (Tan et al., 2023).
- By adopting ISO/IEC/IEEE 12207:2017, we ensure a comprehensive and standardized approach to incorporating Digital Sovereignty and Digital Transformation measures.
- While other frameworks, like TOGAF, are available, we chose not to adopt them. ISO/IEC/IEEE 12207:2017 offers a more expansive understanding of the Software Life Cycle and is better suited to the needs of AI project teams and the ongoing transformation of organizations. As an internationally recognized standard encompassing processes from conception to decommissioning, it serves as an ideal guide for integrating these critical elements into organizational practice
- The Soft Design Science Methodology (SDSM), developed by Venable et al. (2017), integrates traditional design science with soft systems thinking. It emphasizes not only the construction of technical solutions but also the exploration of complex, real-world problems through stakeholder perspectives. This dual focus makes it particularly valuable for addressing socio-technical challenges such as digital sovereignty and digital transformation.

The Soft Design Science Methodology (SDSM), developed by Venable et al. (2017) integrates traditional design science with soft systems thinking. It emphasizes not only the construction of technical solutions but also the exploration of complex, real-world problems through stakeholder perspectives. This dual focus makes it particularly valuable for addressing socio-technical challenges such as digital sovereignty and transformation.

Methodically, we focus on research activity steps 3 through 8 of the Soft Design Science Methodology (SDSM), as the preceding steps have already been completed in Klare et al. (2025) (see Table 1.1).

Table 1.1. SDSM Activities

Research activity	**Real world or design thinking world?**
1. Learn about the specific problem	Real World
2. Inspire and create the general problem and general requirements	Design Thinking
3. Intuit and abduce the general solution	Design Thinking
4. Ex Ante Evaluation (General)	Design Thinking
5. Design specific solution for specific problem	Design Thinking
6. Ex Ante Evaluation (Specific)	Real World
7. Construct specific solution	Real World
8. Ex Post Evaluation	Real World

The concept of Digital Transformation is further supported by theoretical models such as the Technology Acceptance Model (TAM), developed by Davis (1989). TAM posits that the success of digital technologies depends significantly on users' perceptions of ease of use and perceived usefulness. These perceptions influence the adoption and integration of new technologies, highlighting the critical role of user engagement in the transformation process.

Digital Transformation is not merely a technological challenge, it is also an organizational and cultural one. According to Westerman et al. (2011), it requires new ways of thinking and working, fundamentally changing business operations and strategies. The transformation is multidimensional, deeply embedded in social, cultural, and economic contexts, and it involves significant technological, organizational, and strategic shifts. Only through such a comprehensive approach can organizations adapt to the increasingly interconnected digital landscape and ensure their continued relevance and competitiveness.

1.2.3 Software Life Cycle

In this book chapter, we define the "Software Life Cycle" as a process that includes the procurement, development, deployment, maintenance, and decommissioning of software within organizations.

According to Ortt and Smits (2015), the increasing complexity of global digital supply chains has directly influenced the development of software systems. In response to this complexity, various software development models have emerged. One of the earliest, the Waterfall Model, developed in the 1970s, follows a linear, sequential process with clearly defined phases (Boehm, 1976). Later, the Rapid Application Development (RAD) model emerged, focusing on iterative development, and incorporating user feedback (Martin, 1991). Agile methodologies, which emphasize flexibility, collaboration, and incremental delivery, have since gained significant traction (Highsmith, 2002).

The System Development Life Cycle (SDLC) provides a structured, phased approach to software development. However, traditional SDLC models, often rooted in systems engineering, tend to focus more on development and project management, while neglecting other crucial stages of the software life cycle.

As software systems have grown increasingly complex, it has become evident that additional methodologies are required. The expanding array of tools and processes has given rise to more holistic approaches that encompass the initiation, maintenance, and decommissioning phases. Product Lifecycle Management (PLM), for instance, was developed to oversee a product's entire lifespan—from conception to retirement (Stark, 2015). Similarly, Application Lifecycle Management (ALM) offers a framework for managing software systems throughout their entire life cycle, ensuring that applications are properly maintained, updated, and retired as needed (Boehm, 1976). These models emphasize the importance of continuous monitoring and evolution, moving beyond traditional approaches that often neglect post-development stages.

In the domain of Enterprise Architecture Management (EAM), additional life cycle phases have been proposed to align software development with strategic organizational objectives. Frameworks such as TOGAF (The Open Group Architecture Framework) define a series of phases—including vision, business architecture, governance, and architecture change management (The Open Group, 2018). These frameworks help organizations align IT systems with business strategies, by providing a structured approach to managing complex enterprise systems.

1.3 Guidance for Artificial Intelligence, Digital Sovereignty and Digital Transformation Requirements Within the Software Life Cycle Process

This study critically reflects on the survey results presented in Klare et al. (2025) and introduces a new artefact: the ISO 12207:2017 Extension (see Section 4.1). The ISO 12207:2017 standard offers guidance on how to incorporate Digital Sovereignty and Digital Transformation measures throughout the software life cycle. The basis for this extension lies in the recommendation blocks proposed by Klare et al. (2024), thereby building directly on the empirical data gathered in that study.

A key addition in this work is the evaluation of the ISO standard in the context of AI project teams, carried out via expert interviews (see Section 4.2). Through this evaluation, we aim to address a gap identified in the current standard by assessing the practical relevance of the 12207:2017 Extension for German AI project teams.

1.3.1 The ISO/IEC/IEEE 12207:2017 Extension

The ISO/IEC/IEEE 12207:2017 Extension introduces essential action blocks for integrating Digital Transformation and Digital Sovereignty considerations into the software life cycle (see Table 1.2). It provides procedural guidance to organizations seeking to implement sovereignty-related requirements in their software development and procurement processes.

Table 1.2 illustrates how the extension of ISO/IEC/IEEE 12207:2017 can be applied to systematically address Digital Sovereignty (DS) and Digital Transformation (DT) throughout the software life cycle. The standard offers a structured framework for organizations to embed corresponding requirements into existing software development processes. Its normative process groups—spanning Agreement and Organizational Project-Enabling, Technical Management and Technical—are enriched with content-based recommendations derived from key action blocks, including Independence, Resilience, Strategic Alignment, and IT Skills (BMWK, 2017).

The table outlines how these recommendation blocks can serve as inputs for individual processes. For example, independence is particularly relevant to procurement strategies and architectural definitions—for instance, by emphasizing the use of open-source or easily replaceable components. Resilience is primarily reflected in risk and quality management practices, aiming to reduce technological dependencies. Strategic *Alignment* and *IT Skills* are addressed mainly through project and personnel planning, supporting long-term technological capability.

Table 1.2. ISO/IEC/IEEE 12207:2017 Extension

Process group	Process	Explanation
Agreement	Acquisition	Incorporating the four recommendation blocks when preparing supply requests and agreements raises awareness and establishes clear links to strategic objectives. Explicit expectations for suppliers—e.g., the "Independence" recommendation block—should be clearly defined.
	Supply	Independence and Resilience considerations should be embedded in the supply strategy. These serve as explicit acceptance criteria.
Organizational project-enabling	Life Cycle Model Management	Policies can be defined here—for example, Human Resource Management requirements, training needs and specific skill-sets required for relevant software or integration practices.
	Human Resource Management	Training requirements for training and the development or acquisition of specific skills for relevant software can be considered across all activities within the process.
	Portfolio Management	Requirements from the recommendation blocks "Strategic Alignment", "Independence" and "Resilience" can be integrated into the Defined and Authorized Projects Activity.
	Quality Management	Risk Management considerations can serve as inputs for evaluating and executing corrective and preventive action activities
	Knowledge Management	The recommendation blocks "IT skills" and "Resilience" (focused on technical risk reduction) are particularly relevant.
Technical Management	Project Planning	Input from all recommendation blocks should inform the Project Definition activity, particularly in defining objectives and constraints, as well as in planning the acquisition of materials and enabling systems.
	Risk Management	Input from the "Resilience" recommendation block is particularly relevant for defining and monitoring risk.
	Quality Assurance	Recommendation blocks serve as inputs for evaluating the conformance of products and services to defined project-specific and organizational criteria.
Technical	Business or Mission Analysis	Concerns from the "Independence" recommendation block—particularly those related to Digital Sovereignty—can strengthen the evaluation of alternative solution classes.
	Stakeholder Needs and Requirements Definition	Recommendation blocks can serve as foundational sources for defining non-functional requirements at both organizational and project levels.
	Architecture Definition	Specifically, the recommendation blocks "Independence" and "Resilience" can inform the development of alternative architectures with a focus on features such as easily replaceable, or open-source components.

This extension supports organizations in embedding DS objectives early in software projects and securing them at the organizational level, a crucial step given growing dependence on global software supply chains.

1.3.2 Expert Interview Results

Between April and May 2025, we expanded our AI artifact database and conducted expert interviews to evaluate the ISO Extension. We interviewed ten German AI experts, each with a minimum of three years of professional experience in AI project teams across public and private sectors.

Our aim was to determine whether the measures proposed in the ISO/IEC/IEEE 12207:2017 Extension are already being implemented by AI project teams.

When asked whether they consider the independence of external suppliers in AI projects (see Figure 1.1), only 2 out of 10 participants responded affirmatively. None of the respondents reported using acceptance criteria to mitigate dependency on specific suppliers. Additionally, only 4 out of 10 indicated that they consider resilience in their AI projects.

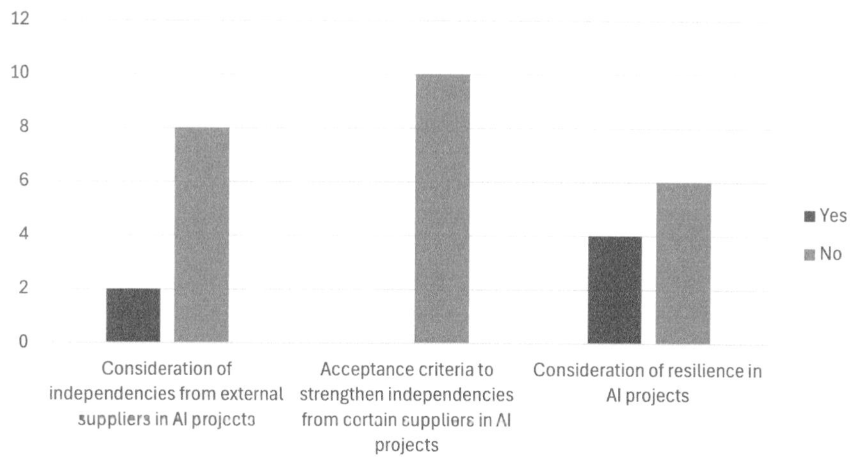

Figure 1.1. Expert interview results: Agreement.

These results suggest a clear need to strengthen the application of Agreement measures from the ISO/IEC/IEEE 12207:2017 Extension in AI project teams.

Within the category of Organizational Project Enabling (see Figure 1.2), respondents were asked whether they had established specific policies to mitigate excessive dependencies on particular external suppliers of hardware and software in the context of their AI projects. Only one respondent confirmed the existence of such guidelines, the remaining participants indicated that no such measures were in place.

Additionally, only two respondents reported having implemented initiatives within their AI projects explicitly aimed at enabling the replacement of hardware and software components. The remaining eight participants stated that no such measures were in place.

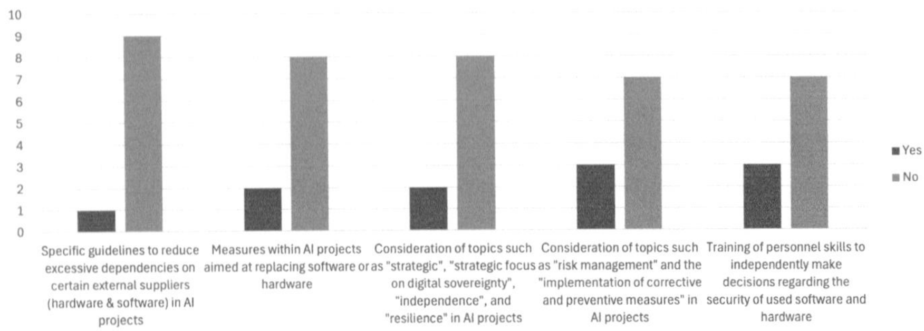

Figure 1.2. Expert interview results: Organizational project enabling.

Beyond the technical and procurement aspects, several responses also highlighted gaps in strategic and organizational practices relevant to AI project success. Only two respondents confirmed that their organizations had systematically considered topics such as "strategic", "strategic focus digital sovereignty", "independence", and "resilience" in the planning and prioritization of AI projects.

In the area of Quality Management, only three participants reported addressing "Risk Management" in conjunction with "Corrective and Preventive Measures" within their AI projects. Similarly, under Knowledge Management, only three organizations indicated that they had invested in developing the capabilities of their personnel to make independent and security-aware decisions regarding the software and hardware used in AI systems.

These results underscore the value of more strongly integrating measures from the second process, "Organizational project-enabling" of the ISO/IEC/IEEE 12207:2017 Extension into AI project teams.

In the third category, Technical Management (see Figure 1.3), respondents were asked whether they oversee the procurement of hardware and software during

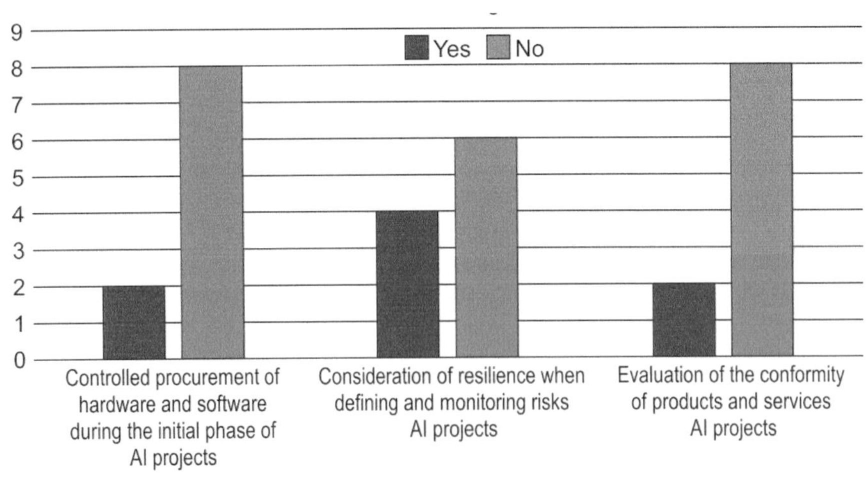

Figure 1.3. Expert interview results: Technical management.

the implementation phase of their AI projects. Only two respondents affirmed this practice.

Of particular interest was the finding that four out of ten participants reported that the concept of resilience is considered when defining and monitoring risks in AI projects. Finally, the interview study examined whether the compliance of products and services is assessed within AI projects. In this context, two out of ten respondents indicated that such evaluations are conducted.

These results indicate that the concept of *Resilience* already aligns with efforts associated with the third process step of the ISO/IEC/IEEE 12207:2017 extension: "Technical Management". However, these, measures—along with the other two elements referenced in Figure 1.3—remain expandable to more effectively support the achievement of Digital Sovereignty and Digital Transformation goals within AI project teams.

In the final category, Technical (see Figure 1.4), participants were asked whether they establish alternative solution approaches within AI projects to address issues related to security and self-determination. Two out of ten participants responded affirmatively. Regarding the existence of specific definitions for non-functional requirements exist in AI projects, two out of ten respondents indicated "yes," while the remaining participants answered "no". The final question in this category focused on the use of alternative architectures in AI projects. Three out of ten respondents confirmed that such architectures are employed.

These results again underline that the process "Technical" from ISO/IEC/IEEE 12207:2017 can be used in AI project teams to integrate Digital Sovereignty and Digital Transformation measures more intensively.

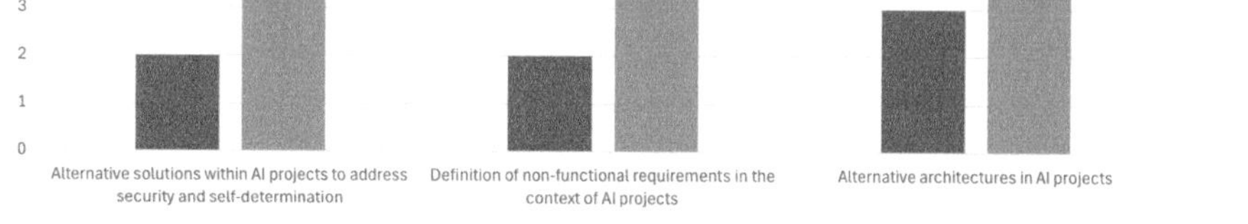

Figure 1.4. Expert interview results: Technical.

1.3.3 Implications and Discussions for Digital Sovereignty and Digital Transformation Measures in AI Project Teams

Measure 1: Introduce the Agreement Process Group more Strongly in AI AI Project Teams

This interview study shows that the Agreement process group is essential for the introduction of more Digital Sovereignty and Digital Transformation measures in AI project teams (see Figure 1.1). Most of the AI experts interviewed do not yet include the process group Agreement from ISO/IEC/IEEE 12207:2017 in their daily work.

With the ISO Extension, we advocate for the inclusion of preparatory measures in supply requests within AI project teams (see Table 1.2). Moreover, the development of a procurement strategy should incorporate Digital Sovereignty and Digital Transformation measures—such as considerations of independence, resilience, and acceptance criteria—which aligns with the empirical findings of Klare et al. (2025).

The results align with Brüsch et al. (2022), who advocate for a supply chain management strategy to support Digital Sovereignty in their research. Brüsch et al. (2022) propose the design of essential technologies for Digital Sovereignty, which also corresponds to the *Technical* process group within ISO/IEC/IEEE 12207:2017.

The literature-based evaluation further suggests the need to strengthen the linkage between measures from the Agreement and Technical process groups.

Measure 2: Introduce the Organizational Project Enabling Process Group more Strongly in AI Project Teams

The results of the interview study underline the need to introduce an Organizational Project Enabling Process, as only one person shares that guideline for enabling AI projects have already been introduced (see Figure 1.2).

As part of the ISO expansion, we have demonstrated that training requirements should be clearly defined to support the acquisition of specific competencies.These include risk management practices in the context of Digital Sovereignty and Digital Transformation as well as technical risk minimization through the evaluation of required software (see Table 1.2).

Skill development can be understood as a cyclical process involving the acquisition, application, and continuous updating of competencies. Seifried and Bertschek (2021) emphasize the importance of aligning this process with data sovereignty, technological sovereignty, and digital skill advancement.

The relevance of such competencies in the context of Digital Transformation is further emphasized by Vial (2021), who highlights the organizational and skill-based challenges companies encounter during digital transformation initiatives.

This underscores the need to more strongly integrate the Organizational Project Enabling process group into AI project teams.

Measure 3: Introduce the Technical Management Process Group more Strongly into AI Project Teams

The results of the interview study indicate that efforts to enhance *Resilience* are already evident within AI project teams. However, aspects such as the controlled procurement of software and hardware, as well as the conformity of products with respect to Digital Sovereignty and Digital Transformation, tend to receive comparatively less attention (see Figure 1.3).

The ISO extension supports the alignment of project definitions, risk monitoring and the design of product and service conformity through project- and organization-specific criteria (see Table 1.2).

Elements of the ISO extension are also reflected in the research by Glohr et al. (2022). Glohr et al. (2022), who advocate for Digital Sovereignty-oriented project management and call for organizational commitment to end-to-end digitization. Glohr (2022) integrates these these findings with the need for staff training, thereby addressing multiple process groups from the ISO extension: Technical Management, Organizational Project Enabling and Agreement.

Elements of the ISO extension are also reflected in the research by Božić (2023), who advocates for the integration of risk management into digital transformation. Božić emphasizes the importance of identifying and mitigating risks at an early stage to foster innovation and ensure business continuity.

However, the ISO extension places greater emphasis on supply chain considerations and life cycle processes. The literature evaluation suggests that the integration of measures as outlined in the Technical Management Process is often underrepresented in the publications reviewed.

Measure 4: Introduce the Technical process group more strongly in AI project teams

The interview study reveals that AI experts address few alternative solutions related to self-determination (see Figure 1.4).

The ISO extension calls for the development of alternative architectures within projects, the definition of non-functional requirements, and the consideration of alternative solutions related to security and independence (see Table 1.2).

Madiega (2020) challenges the assumptions embedded, in the technical process group, advocating instead for the design of innovation that explicitly incorporates Digital Sovereignty. This focus has yet to be adequately addressed within the current scope of the technical process group. In contrast, Smit et al. (2022) demonstrate how digital infrastructures can be adapted to enhance independence through a Digital Sovereignty lens. Similarly, Vial (2021) emphasizes that digital transformation processes must account for the broader implications of self-determination and independence in technological infrastructure—both of which are critical for maintaining control over digital assets.

At present, the ISO Extension remains primarily focused on procurement-related aspects and should be expanded to more comprehensively address these strategic dimensions.

At present, the ISO Extension remains primarily focused on procurement-related aspects to more comprehensively address these strategic dimensions.

According to ourfindings, the following process groups from the ISO/IEC/IEEE 12207:2017 extension are reflected in the practical literature: (1) Agreement, (2) Organizational Project-Enabling, (3) Technical Management, and (4) Technical. Based on the evaluation, the literature places a strong emphasis on the *Agreement* process group Agreement, while Technical Management receives comparatively limited attention. This suggests that the ISO/IEC/IEEE 12207:2017 extension may serve as a valuable framework for strengthening the implementation of Digital Sovereignty throughout the software life cycle. However, it remains necessary to consolidate existing standards such as ISO/IEC/IEEE 12207:2017 and expand the ISO extension to incorporate additional dimensions—such as innovation orientation.

1.4 Limitations

The proposed artefact is grounded in an empirical survey and expert interviews with experienced practitioners. While these sources offer valuable insights, the limited sample size reduces statistical generalizability. Additionally, the study does not fully account for potential response bias or interpretation errors due to the domain-specific nature of participants.

To enhance the robustness of future research, triangulation with other data sources, such as case studies or cross-sectoral comparisons, is recommended. Furthermore, although ISO/IEC/IEEE 12207:2017 provides a comprehensive basis, it has not been systematically evaluated for compatibility with other frameworks or industry-specific requirements. Broader validation across varying regulatory and sectoral contexts is required to assess the artefact's adaptability and practical relevance.

1.5 Conclusion and Outlook

Our primary contribution to this book is the development of an extension to the ISO/IEC/IEEE 12207:2017 standard, serving as guidance for organizations to integrate Digital Sovereignty (DS) and Digital Transformation (DT) considerations into software development processes. This extension was evaluated through empirical feedback from AI project teams. The findings indicate that DS and DT measures are not yet systematically applied in practice. Based on this, we recommend stronger integration of all four ISO-defined process groups within AI projects: (1) Agreement, (2) Organizational Project-Enabling, (3) Technical Management, and (4) Technical.

Our analysis of practitioner-oriented literature on digital sovereignty confirms that existing publications mostly reflect recommendations associated with the Agreement, Technical, and Organizational Project-Enabling process groups. In contrast, the Technical Management dimension remains significantly underrepresented, suggesting a research and practice gap.

The ISO/IEC/IEEE 12207:2017 extension makes a novel contribution by providing a structured framework for embedding DS into the software life cycle. It equips AI project teams with practical orientation for navigating the intersection of DS, AI, and DT, particularly relevant in environments characterized by rapid technological change. As digital transformation accelerates, the need for such structured approaches becomes critical to maintaining control, resilience, and regulatory alignment in software-intensive systems.

A key limitation of the current extension lies in its scope: it is specifically focused on the software life cycle and has not yet been tested in broader operational contexts. For future research, we recommend evaluating the extension through comparative application in practical projects, including cross-domain settings (e.g., healthcare, finance), benchmarking against established frameworks like TOGAF, and assessing its quantitative impact on project outcomes such as compliance, delivery timelines, and system robustness.

Acknowledgements

We thank all study participants, the partner Detecon International GmbH and the project LIONS that is funded by dtec.bw of the Research Center for Digitization and Technology of the Bundeswehr, financed by the EU, NextGenerationEU.

Use of AI-Assisted Tools

During the preparation of this work, the authors utilized AI-assisted tools such as Deep and ChatGPT to enhance English language accuracy, including spelling, grammar, and punctuation. The content generated or corrected by these tools was thoroughly reviewed, revised, and edited by the authors to ensure accuracy and originality. The authors accept full responsibility for the originality of the final content of this publication.

References

Bellanova, R., Carrapico, H., & Duez, D. (2022). Digital/sovereignty and European security integration: An introduction. *European Security*, 31(3), 337-355.

BMWK (Federal Ministry for Economic Affairs and Climate Action). (2017). Kompetenzen für eine digitale Souveränität. Berlin, URL: https://www.bmwk.de/Redaktion/DE/Publikationen/Studien/kompetenzen-fuer-eine-digitale-souveraenitaet.pdf?__blob=publicationFile&v=1 accessed on 2025-06-19.

Boehm, B.W. (1976). Software engineering: An overview. *ACM Computing Surveys*, 8(1), 1-40.

Božić, V. (2023). Integrated risk management and artificial intelligence. *Journal of AI*, 7(1), 63-80.

Brüsch, C., Menzi, C., & Mertes, Alexander. (2022). Digitale Verwaltung: Herausforderungen und Chancen neuer Trends für die Schweiz, ZHAW Zürcher Hochschule für Angewandte Wissenschaften, *ZHAW School of Management and Law*, 1-27, URL: https://assets.kpmg.com/content/dam/kpmgsites/ch/pdf/studie-digitale-verwaltung-2022.pdf. accessed on 2025-06-19.

Calderaro, A., & Blumfelde, S. (2022). Artificial intelligence and EU security: The false promise of digital sovereignty. *European Security*, 31(3), 415-434.

Couture, S., & Toupin, S. (2019). What does the notion of "sovereignty" mean when referring to the digital? *New Media & Society*, 21(10), 2305-2322.

Edler, J., Blind, K., Kroll, H., & Schubert, T. (2023). Technology sovereignty as an emerging frame for innovation policy. Defining rationales, ends and means. *Research Policy*, 52(6), 104765.

eGovernment. (2025). MPK: Digitale Souveränität durch KI, URL: https://www.egovernment.de/mpk-digitale-souveraenitaet-durch-ki-a/b0b795a494c9994c4e90ae412495c180/ accessed on 2025-03-20.

Floridi, L. (2020). The fight for digital sovereignty: What it is, and why it matters, especially for the EU. *Philosophy & Technology*, 33, 369-378.

Fountaine, T., McCarthy, B., & Saleh, T. (2019). Building the AI-powered organization. *Harvard Business Review*, 97(4), 62-73.

Glasze, G., Cattaruzza, A., Douzet, F., Dammann, F., Bertran, M.G. et al. (2023). Contested spatialities of digital sovereignty. *Geopolitics*, 28(2), 919-958.

Glohr, C., Schult, S. & Schulze-Hulitz, E. (2022). Zukunft gestalten: Erfolgsfaktoren zur Digitalisierung in der öffentlichen Verwaltung, Detecon International GmbH, 1-36, URL: https://www.detecon.com/drupal/sites/default/files/2023-08/Studie_ErfolgsfaktorenzurDigitalisierunginderoeffentlichenVerwaltung.pdf_accessed on 2025-06-19.

Heidebrecht, S. (2024). From market liberalism to public intervention: Digital sovereignty and changing European union digital single market governance. *JCMS: Journal of Common Market Studies*, 62(1), 205-223.

Highsmith, J. (2002). *Agile Software Development Ecosystems*. Addison-Wesley Professional. ISBN: 978-0-201-76043-9.

Hummel, P., Braun, M., Tretter, M., & Dabrock, P. (2021). Data sovereignty: A review. *Big Data & Society*, 8(1). DOI: 10.1007/978-3-658-33755-1.

ISO/IEC/IEEE 12207:2017 (2017). First edition 2017-11: ISO/IEC/IEEE International Standard – Systems and Software Engineering – Software Life Cycle Processes. IEEE.

Klare, M., & Lechner, U. (2023). Digital Sovereignty from the Perspective of IT Consultancy in Germany: A Model. ICSOB Companion, 1-14. URL: https://ceur-ws.org/Vol-3621/poster-paper5.pdf

Klare, M., Stelter, A., Hrestic, R. & Lechner, U. (2025). Digital sovereignty and digital transformation practice recommendation for the software life cycle process. *Procedia Computer Science*, 254, 221-229. DOI: 10.1016/j.procs.2025.02.081.

Klare, M., Verlande, L., Greiner, M. & Lechner, U. (2022). How Blockchain and Artificial Intelligence influence Digital Sovereignty. In: *European, Mediterranean, and Middle Eastern Conference on Information Systems* (pp. 3-16). Cham: Springer Nature Switzerland. DOI: https://doi.org/10.1007/978-3-031-30694-5_1

Klare, M., & Lechner, U. (2024). A reference model to strengthen digital sovereignty in companies. In: *ICSOB 2024*, 1-9. URL: https://ceur-ws.org/Vol-3921/phd-paper3.pdf

Madiega, T.A. (2020). Digital Sovereignty for Europe: Enhancing Strategic Autonomy in the Digital Field. EPRS: European Parliamentary Research Service. URL: https://www.europarl.europa.eu/RegData/etudes/BRIE/2020/651992/EPRS_BRI(2020)651992_EN.pdf_accessed on 2025-06-19.

Martin, J. (1991). *Rapid Application Development*. Macmillan Publishing Company.

Moerel, L., & Timmers, P. (2021). Reflections on digital sovereignty. *EU Cyber Direct, Research in Focus Series*, 1-33.

Musiani, F. (2022). Infrastructuring digital sovereignty: A research agenda for an infrastructure-based sociology of digital self-determination practices. *Information, Communication & Society*, 25(6), 785-800.

Oschinsky, F., Stelter, A. & Niehaves, B. (2021). Cognitive biases in the digital age – How resolving the status quo bias enables public-sector employees to overcome restraint. *Government Information Quarterly*, 38(8), 101611.

Pohle, J., & Thiel, T. (2020). Digital sovereignty. *Internet Policy Review*, 9(4), 2-19.

Roberts, H., Hine, E., & Floridi, L. (2023). Digital sovereignty, digital expansionism, and the prospects for global AI Governance. In: *Quo Vadis, Sovereignty? New Conceptual and Regulatory Boundaries in the Age of Digital China* (pp. 51-75). Cham: Springer Nature Switzerland.

Seifried, M. & Bertschek, I. (2021). Schwerpunktstudie Digitale Souveränität – Bestandsaufnahme und Handlungsfelder, Bundesministerium für Wirtschaft und Energie, URL: https://www.de.digital/DIGITAL/Redaktion/DE/Digitalisierungsindex/Publikationen/publikation-download-schwerpunkt-digitale-souveraenitaet-2021.pdf accessed on 2025-06-19.

Smith, S., Tyreman, M., Mischke, J., Ernst, P., Hazan, E., Novakm J. et al. (2022). *Securing Europe's Competitivenes*, McKinsey & Company, URL: https://www.mckinsey.com/~/

media/mckinsey/business%20functions/strategy%20and%20corporate%20finance/our%20insights/securing%20europes%20competitiveness%20addressing%20its%20technology%20gap/securing-europes-competitiveness-addressing-its-technology-gap-september-2022.pdf accessed on 2025-06-19.

Stark, J. (2015). *Product Lifecycle Management (Volume 1): 21st Century Paradigm for Product Realisation*. Springer. ISBN 978-3-319-17440-2.

Stelter, A., Kaping, C., Oschinsky, F.M., & Niehaves, B. (2020). Theoretical foundations on technology acceptance and usage in public administrations: investigating bounded acceptance and usage of new technology by employees. In: *Proceedings of the 21st Annual International Conference on Digital Government Research (dg.o '20)* (pp. 344-345). Association for Computing Machinery, New York, NY, USA.

Tan, K.L., Chi, C.H., & Lam, K.Y. (2023). Survey on digital sovereignty and identity: From digitization to digitalization. *ACM Computing Surveys*, 56(3), 1-36.

The Open Group (2018). TOGAF 9.2: The Open Group Architecture Framework. URL: https://www.opengroup.org/togaf-licensed-downloads accessed on 2025-06-19.

Venable, John R., Pries-Heje, Jan & Baskerville, Richard L. (2021). Choosing a design science research methodology. *ACIS 2017 Proceedings*, 112.

Vial, G. (2021). Understanding digital transformation: A review and a research agenda. Managing digital transformation (1st Edition, 13-66), Imprint Routledge.

Vogt, R. (2021). Digitale Souveränität und Künstliche Intelligenz für den Menschen. In: *Digitalisierung Souverän Gestalten: Innovative Impulse im Maschinenbau* (pp. 143-150). Springer Berlin Heidelberg.

Wolf, S. (2021). Künstliche Intelligenz–Digitale Souveränität fördern. *Sozialwirtschaft aktuell (SWa)*, 31(18), 1-3.

CHAPTER

2

A New-Institutionalist Perspective: Re-Thinking Digital Sovereignty as Distributed Digital Sovereignty and a Proposed Typology for Understanding Artificial Intelligence Across Socio-Technical Fields

Halvdan Haugsbakken(0000-0001-8980-1717)
Østfold University College

2.1 Introduction

Early political thinkers such as Hobbes (1962) conceived sovereignty through the Levia-than—a social contract and an institutional arrangement endowed with significant authority, designed to ensure order and protect individuals from risk. This reflected a monolithic, state-centered, and territorial understanding of sovereignty. In the 20th century, Schmitt (2008) challenged this conception by asserting that the sovereign is the one who can declare a state of exception. In this view, sovereignty overrides legal norms and principles, replacing them with a political order that, through claims of suspension and preservation, enables a form of absolute governance. Agamben (2005) expanded Schmitt's perspective; arguing that the state of exception has become a normalized condition in modern governance. This shift has profound consequences, as individuals may be reduced to what Agamben (2020) terms "bare life"—a biological existence stripped of all legal protections. At the turn of the 21st century, other political theorists proposed new approaches. Hardt and Negri (2000) contended that globalization has produced a deterritorialized form of sovereignty—a global power structure no longer confined to state borders, but instead materialized through transnational networks of states, multinational corporations, global

*Email: Halvdan.Haugsbakken@hiof.no

DOI: 10.1201/9781003581581-2

institutions, and military actors. In this configuration, the nation-state functions as a tool for advancing the interests of these global entities—a power structure they termed Empire. As a counterforce, Hardt and Negri (2004) introduced the concept of the Multitude—a decentralized collective subject with the political agency to challenge and resist the dynamics of global power. The discourse on sovereignty has evolved, with increasing emphasis is on digital sovereignty (Couture & Toupin, 2019). This shift is driven in part by the European Union (EU), a supranational institution actively engaged in digital policy-making processes (Floridi, 2020). As global technology companies consolidate their influence and digital transformation reshapes individuals and civil society, technology has become a subject of political interest. These developments have significantly impacted the academic research landscape, where digital sovereignty is framed through diverse theoretical lenses—ranging from political discourse (Pohle & Santaniello, 2024; Pohle & Voelsen, 2022) to individualistic perspectives (Couture & Toupin, 2019). Consequently, digital sovereignty remains conceptually fluid and not definitively defined. As a contribution to this evolving discourse, this chapter introduces the concept of distributed digital sovereignty. Drawing on New Institutionalism (DiMaggio & Powell, 1983; Meyer & Rowan, 1977; Scott, 1995) and field theory (Bourdieu & Wacquant, 1992; Fligstein & McAdam, 2012), it argues for a broader practice perspective on digital sovereignty. Digital Sovereignty is approached as a field-specific, practice-driven process in which legitimacy, control, and authority are continuously produced, claimed, and contested by actors across varied contexts. Rather than viewing sovereignty as state-centric or defined by a state of exception, this purpose emphasizes its enactment through ongoing struggles and practices within and across socio-technical domains. These tensions manifest in conflicting logics surrounding Artificial Intelligence (AI) and are embedded in socio-technical fields. To substantiate this argument, a typology is presented comprising nine socio-technical fields, each characterized by distinct institutional pillars and sources of legitimacy. These range from formal-legal authority to cultural and cognitive discourses that shape how actors assert and defend control. The proposed typology enables the operationalization of digital sovereignty for empirical research and practical application. Key contributions of this chapter include:

- A framework to grasp links between digital sovereignty and AI across contexts
- Theorizing a practice-based perspective on digital sovereignty and legitimacy

The chapter begins with a synthesis of key contributions and relevant scholarship from the expanding body of research on digital sovereignty. It then outlines foundational concepts from New Institutionalism, which serve as the analytical basis for the proposed concept of distributed digital sovereignty. The core—and largest—section of the chapter presents a typology of nine socio-technical fields, each linked to discourses on Artificial Intelligence (AI) and distinguished by specific institutional logics. This is followed by a discussion of the framework's contributions, after which its limitations are critically examined. The chapter concludes with a summary of key insights, accompanied by practical recommendations and actionable policy guidance.

2.2 Relevant Research on Digital Sovereignty

To position the proposed concept of distributed digital sovereignty and its accompanying typology, it is essential to examine how researchers have approached digital sovereignty and AI-related governance models. This exploration helps clarify how the present contribution complements or overlaps with existing discussions in the literature. Although Abraham (2013) offered an early contribution, the prevailing impression is that digital sovereignty has been interpreted in diverse ways—ranging from informatics-driven frameworks to security- and policy-oriented perspectives. This diversity underscores the limitations of relying on a single, universal definition. Research examining how a powerful actor—namely, the European Union (EU)—has embedded digital sovereignty into its policy frameworks and institutional governance discourses further illustrates this complexity (e.g., Bellanova et al., 2022; Broeders et al., 2023; Farrand & Carrapico, 2022; Floridi, 2020; Roberts et al., 2021). These studies challenge reductionist tendencies and instead reveal that when the European Union (EU) seeks to exercise control within European contexts, the resulting analyses are rich, empirically grounded, and context-sensitive—highlighting the complexity of underlying political and societal mechanisms. Moreover, this body of research demonstrates that digital sovereignty is frequently framed as a governance tool through which actors position themselves within geopolitical tensions—primarily to assert control, defend against external threats, and emphasize self-determination, independence, and autonomy (Fries et al., 2023). In such situated research, digital sovereignty exhibits a strong *polysemic* foundation, carrying multiple interpretations that acquire meaning depending on context. This observation is further strengthened by identifiable research streams that explore digital sovereignty, as displayed in Table 2.1.

2.2.1 Research Stream 1: Technical and Infrastructure Studies

The first stream can be characterized by a *technically oriented approach* to digital sovereignty. These studies focus on digital infrastructure, where sovereignty is closely tied to specific forms of control over technological systems—such as data centers, user interfaces, cloud services, open-source software, and network architectures. Rather than treating digital sovereignty as a geopolitical abstraction, this body of work integrates it with technological choices and system designs. As a result, digital sovereignty is frequently conceptualized in terms of technical capacity, architectural ownership, and design autonomy. Within this stream, several distinct research approaches emerge, each with a clear analytical orientation.

For example, some studies are grounded in computer science or informatics and conduct in-depth empirical investigations of infrastructure at various levels (Azevedo et al., 2025; Boeira et al., 2024; Haq et al., 2023; Sai & Tipper, 2024; Wessel et al., 2022). These studies seek to measure digital sovereignty or its outcomes using concrete technological indicators, assessing whether a given system supports control, independence, or technological self-sufficiency. Another set of studies is situated within the field of Human–Computer Interaction, placing greater emphasis on human-centric dimensions (Conradie & Nagel, 2022; Lawo, Neifer, Esau-Held, et al., 2023; Weinreuter et al., 2023. In these cases, the focus is often on design

Table 2.1. Key Research Streams (RS) on Digital Sovereignty (DS)

RS1: Technical and infrastructure	**RS2: Security and geopolitics**	**RS3: Regulatory and governance**
This stream examines how DS is related to technological infrastructure and design. Research focuses on control over data centers, cloud services, architecture, and user interfaces.	This stream examines DS in the context of security questions, focusing on national and European legitimacy, defense against external threats and geopolitics power struggles and tensions.	This stream explores how DS is negotiated through regulation and governance, focusing on legislation, political legitimacy, alliances, and power relations.
Key topics	**Key topics**	**Key topics**
• Control over infrastructure • Autonomy in technological development and design choices • HCI and individual user control • Measuring technical capacity and ownership • Use of STS and socio-technical perspectives	• Linked to questions of security and legitimacy • Security and threat management: EU vs. external actors • Tensions between EU member states and the EU • EU as a security actor and digital geopolitical player • EU as a defender of democracy	• Focus on regulation, legislation, and normative authority • Political legitimation: values, democracy, trust, and alliances • Discursive struggle: multiple understandings, common rhetoric • Critical analysis of political and institutional practices • EU regulatory frameworks: GDPR, DSA, DMA, EMFA, AI Act

choices that promote digital sovereignty at the user level—for instance by developing interfaces that enhance individual autonomy and control over personal data. A third approach adopts more sociotechnical perspectives, frequently drawing on established theoretical frameworks from Science and Technology Studies (STS) (Gordon, 2024; Klare et al., 2023; Musiani, 2022, Prasad, 2022; Rone, 2024). This body of research offers a nuanced and complex understanding of how digital sovereignty is articulated and practiced within concrete configurations where technology and society co-evolve. Through methods such as discourse analysis and practice-oriented studies, these scholars demonstrate how digital sovereignty acquires meaning and application within specific institutional, political, and technological settings. In sum, these contributions treat digital sovereignty as an abstract or isolated principle. Instead, they conceptualize it as a complex, materially embedded, and negotiated construct—shaped through technological development, design decisions, and usage contexts.

2.2.2 Research Stream 2: Security and Geopolitical Studies

The second research stream comprises security- and geopolitically-oriented studies. In this context, digital sovereignty is primarily associated with questions of security and various governance models or frameworks. Although Artificial Intelligence

(AI) is not always the central focus, a recurring theme is the robustness and effectiveness of these models in managing complex digital infrastructures. Several empirical studies link digital sovereignty to issues of legitimacy, control, and the management of both internal and external threats (Akcali Gur, 2022; Fries et al., 2023). These perspectives often lead to a broader problematization of the concept of sovereignty itself. On one hand, the concept is viewed as insufficient, given its varied interpretations across empirical contexts (Barrinha & Christou, 2022; Bellanova et al., 2022). On the other hand, efforts to assert control and legitimacy frequently generate tensions with competing priorities in the digital domain—particularly the protection of democratic rights (Hulkó et al., 2025; Leese, 2024). This tension has laid the groundwork for meta-studies (Bechara & Lechner, 2024; Bellanova et al., 2022) that seek to interrogate the very meaning of digital sovereignty, especially in relation to national security and technologically complex domains like quantum computing and advanced data processing.

Several studies emphasize the contradictory forces inherent in digital governance. For instance, research indicates that when the European Union (EU) assumes an active role in security matters, it contributes to redefining notions of European identity and security mean (Akcali Gur, 2022). This is particularly evident in efforts to control and develop digital infrastructure, where initiatives may not necessarily enhance technological control, but instead foster integration through multi-level governance levels and collaboration among member states (Akcali Gur, 2022). These contradictions are further explored in other studies. Some researchers argue that digital sovereignty functions as a symbolic discourse—one that generates multiple and often conflicting, interpretations of the concept (Adler-Nissen & Eggeling, 2024). In their study of the EU's Gaia-X project, Adler-Nissen and Eggeling (2024) argue that digital sovereignty encompasses security, economic, and democratic dimensions, which are not easily reconciled. Additional research focuses on the EU's cybersecurity strategies, analyzing how the EU attempts to justify and implement a vision of technological sovereignty, both internally and externally, to reinforce technological independence (Barrinha & Christou, 2022). Furthermore, some studies explicitly link digital sovereignty to open-source software and security, investigating how such strategies may support—or contradict—democratic control and related normative values (Farrand & Carrapico, 2022 A broader geopolitical perspective is adopted by scholars who situate these dynamics within the context of a multipolar world order (Haq et al., 2023; ten Oever et al., 2024).

2.2.3 Research Stream 3: Regulatory and Governance Studies

The third research stream can be described as regulatory and governance-oriented. This stream adopts critical perspectives that illuminate inconsistencies in digital sovereignty and governance models at multiple levels. This becomes apparent in in-depth normative and discourse-analytical approaches, which show how actors seek to position themselves and establish legitimacy within the digital domain (Donnelly et al., 2024). At a general level, this research suggests that claims to legitimacy are often tied to acts of symbolic positioning. In some cases, critical analyses reveal significant discrepancies between attempts at legitimation and what ultimately amounts to symbolic politics (Brännström, 2023), thereby limiting the tangible impact of digital sovereignty and governance initiatives. Some studies point to a trust deficit (Blancato & Carr, 2024), highlighting the absence of a shared understanding of what digital security entails. Building trust is not solely a matter of technical solutions; it also involves deeper disagreements over how control, power, and independence should be exercised. Scholars further examine how the EU seeks to assert normative ambitions through digital sovereignty—for instance, through direct content regulation of digital platforms and efforts to govern the public sphere (Flonk et al., 2024). Additional studies address shifts in power resulting from data concentration and digital dependencies, showing how state territorial control is being weakened, while the influence of technology companies grows and the position of citizens is undermined (Hesselman et al., 2020).

We also find studies that explore issues through what may be termed normative perspectives. This gives rise to broader analyses of strategic autonomy, control, and value-based governance, where digital sovereignty becomes anchored in questions related to human dignity, self-determination, and power relations (Gstrein, 2023). Here, some contributions focus on how digital sovereignty functions not only as an overarching normative ideal, but also as a rhetorical and delegating tool used in political struggles (Hoeffler & Mérand, 2024). This becomes evident in studies examining unexpected alliances or conflicts between technology companies and civil society actors (Heermann, 2024). Some research adopts a more technocratic approach by developing indexes and measurement tools, thereby linking digital sovereignty to technological strategy (Kaloudis, 2022). Others critically question the actual reach of EU policy and the rhetoric of digital sovereignty, asking whom this sovereignty truly serves and what it ultimately achieves (Kugler & Tavengerwei, 2024). These studies show a discrepancy between rhetorical ambitions and regulatory reality.

Also in this stream, a set of studies explores local levels and philosophical perspectives, examining how digital sovereignty is expressed in cities and local communities (Pierri & Lüning, 2023). In these cases, digital sovereignty—as discourse—takes on highly localized meanings and becomes embedded in democratic and municipal frameworks. Conversely, other studies adopt a meta-perspective, analyzing sovereignty as an expanding discourse that frequently contrasts with the multistakeholder model of internet governance (Pohle & Santaniello, 2024). This work maps how state actors are increasingly active in shaping and promoting national narratives of sovereignty, thereby shifting the balance of power in internet governance. The work of Pohle and Voelsen (2022) seeks to build analytical bridges between regulation, geopolitics, and technical infrastructure by conducting historical and theoretical analyses that demonstrate how both states and private actors attempt to reshape the internet through technical and political means to strengthen their power. Finally, we find work by Roberts (2024) that establishes a more philosophical orientation, distinguishing between descriptive and normative understandings of digital sovereignty. In sum, these studies show that digital sovereignty is not a stable legal category but is contested across multiple arenas.

2.2.3.1 Relating Distributed Digital Sovereignty and Typology to Research

To position the proposed concept of distributed digital sovereignty and typology, it is important to consider how it is similar to or extends with existing research on digital sovereignty and current AI governance models. To start with, however, it must be stressed that there are very few contributions that explicitly look at the connections between the mentioned items except for certain studies (e.g., Bentalha & Boukare, 2024; Calderaro & Blumfelde, 2022; Mügge, 2024; Roberts et al., 2023; Woods, 2023). On that note, the existing literature paints an overall picture of digital sovereignty that is clearly framed by context and disciplinary orientation. This leads to digital sovereignty being somewhat framed as being part of value conflicts and power relations, shaped between and betwixt regulatory ambitions and control over technology, indicating a single and universal definition. In contrast, the three dominant research streams—technological and infrastructural, security and geopolitics, and regulation and governance—offer instead distinct yet complementary insights. Each stream emphasizes different dimensions which are shaped by particular analytical lenses. The technological and infrastructural stream almost defines sovereignty primarily as control over infrastructure, system design, and data flows. It emphasizes measurable technical capacity and promotes governance models grounded in material and functional terms. By contrast, the security and geopolitics stream adopts what can be argued to be a state-centric perspective, presenting sovereignty as strategic autonomy and self-defense capacity in relation to either internal and external threats or a combination of these. This produces a type of instrumental logic of tensions and resilience. Finally, the regulation and governance stream takes very often on normative and discursive approaches, often inspired by critical political theory. Here, sovereignty is conceived primarily as a symbolic and value-based project, where legitimacy and political authority are central. The focus is on how actors seek to establish and defend control and value frameworks through law, norms, and rhetoric, which are often argued to be somewhat limited in range and practice.

The proposed typology aligns with elements from all three streams but introduces a distinctive analytical shift. Distributed digital sovereignty emphasizes a practice-based, field-sensitive approach that foregrounds institutional logics and context-specific manifestations of authority. It enables inquiry that goes beyond technical indicators by incorporating legitimacy claims, normative authority, and the particularities of institutional practice. For instance, the typology illustrates that legitimacy is not necessarily state-based, and that normative authority may be interpreted differently across fields. In this way, the typology functions as a complementary analytical tool that structures the relationship between politics, technology, and institutional practice. It aims to bridge AI discourses with empirical realities of governance, offering analytical traction where existing models remain too narrow or abstract. While the typology resonates with key themes across the three research streams, it also reveals certain blind spots in the existing literature. In particular, there remain relatively few contributions that apply an organizational sociological perspective combined with New Institutionalism or field theory. Thus, this chapter argues that there is a need for conceptual frameworks that can analyze how legitimacy, authority, and digital control are created and negotiated across socio-technical fields. Although various research streams suggest the presence of field-specific logics and tensions, these dynamics are rarely framed analytically in relation to institutional pillars, nor are they made explicit in terms of distinctive field configurations or legitimacy regimes. In addition, the analysis suggests that digital sovereignty remains a polysemous concept—flexible, contested, and often strategically employed across diverse settings. For these reasons, it becomes even more relevant to approach digital sovereignty as *distributed digital sovereignty*, with analytical emphasis on institutional variation, actor constellations, and competing claims to authority.

That being said, the proposed typology consisting of the socio-technological fields, which will be introduced later in the chapter, somehow aligns with elements from all three streams but can also be a valuable addition. This is foremost connected to the aspect that distributed digital sovereignty emphasizes a practice-based, field-sensitive approach that foregrounds institutional logics and context-specific manifestations of authority. It can perhaps enable inquiry that goes beyond technical indicators by incorporating legitimacy claims, normative authority, and the particularities of institutional practice. For instance, it can show that legitimacy is not necessarily state-based, and that normative authority may be interpreted differently across settings by different actors. In this way, the typology serves as a complementary analytical tool that structures the relationship between politics, technology, and institutional practice. It aims to bridge AI discourses with empirical realities of governance, offering analytical traction where existing models remain too narrow or abstract. While the typology resonates with key themes across the three research streams, it also has the potential to reveal certain blind spots in the existing literature. In particular, relatively few studies apply an organizational sociological perspective that integrates New Institutionalism or field theory. Thus, what this chapter argues for the development of conceptual frameworks capable of analyzing how legitimacy, authority, and digital control are produced and negotiated across socio-technical fields. Although various research streams suggest the presence of field-specific logics and tensions, these dynamics are rarely framed analytically in relation to institutional pillars, nor are they made explicit in terms of distinctive field configurations or legitimacy regimes. In addition, the foregoing presentation of digital sovereignty also suggests that digital sovereignty remains a polysemous concept—flexible, contested, and often strategically employed across diverse settings. For these reasons, it becomes even more relevant to approach digital sovereignty as distributed digital sovereignty, with analytical emphasis on institutional variation, actor constellations, and competing claims to authority.

2.3 A New-Institutionalist Approach to Digital Sovereignty

2.3.1 Rational Myths, Decoupling and Pillars

New-Institutionalism in organizational sociology emerged in the 1970s as a response to dominant paradigms within the social sciences. It was developed because earlier theoretical approaches understood institutional processes by using rational-choice models, assuming that actors were utility-maximizing in their motives and actions. Furthermore, early approaches were descriptive and historically oriented, lacking robust theoretical frameworks and focusing on formal structures. However, New-Institutionalism was first introduced by Meyer and Rowan (1977). In their important work, they argued that organizations did not adopt new structures or technologies to become efficient but rather to conform to existing institutional norms and expectations. They also introduced the notion of rational myths, which referred to shared beliefs about what constitutes rational and appropriate behavior. A key point in their theorizing is that adaptation to the existing environment leads to a process of internal decoupling within organizations, where formal structures are symbolically adopted without leading to real changes in actual practices and internal structures. Applying this to digital sovereignty, actors such as organizations may adopt AI policies not with the genuine aim of transforming internal practices, but rather to conform to dominant norms and claim legitimacy through symbolic actions. In this sense, adopting AI policies becomes a form of institutional posturing. For example, member states in the EU may formally align themselves with the AI Act, not to reform routines, but to signal compliance and gain recognition within the European field. Here, legitimacy is achieved through symbolic adaptation rather than real implementation.

New-Institutionalism has been subject to significant theorizing. Scott (1995) suggested that organizations tend to rest on three pillars that are argued to sustain the stability and meaning of social systems. This system shapes, among other things, how actors behave, justify their actions, and make sense of their environment. Addressing each of them, the first pillar, the regulative, refers to formal rules, laws, procedures, and sanctions (Scott, 1995). It is assumed that behavior is shaped and constrained by what is legally permitted or punishable. The pillar is grounded in legal and bureaucratic authority and essentially equates to regulatory power. An example can be the EU's AI Act. Here, digital sovereignty is framed as a type of legal control over data flows and digital platforms. The second, according to Scott (1995), is the normative pillar, which encompasses values, norms, and moral obligations, which are essentially what actors ought to do. It refers to socially accepted expectations, professional standards, and best practices. In this domain, digital sovereignty is less about control and more about legitimacy and moral authority. Digital sovereignty is about advancing normative commitments and exercising moral leadership in a given domain. An example might be the EU's value-driven technology agenda or its ethical guidelines for the development and deployment of AI in and across member states. The third one is the cognitive pillar (Scott, 1995). This pillar is about deeply internalized beliefs—those things perceived as natural, taken-for-granted, or self-evident among actors. These assumptions operate beneath the level of conscious reflection. Control and legitimacy in this domain are connected to symbolic and cultural authority. Here, one can argue, digital sovereignty works more as a form of symbolic control by shaping collective understandings of what is morally legitimate and appropriate. An example would be the widely held belief that digital sovereignty is inseparable from national security, or that critical infrastructure ought to be nationally controlled.

2.3.2 The Process of Institutional Isomorphism

A limitation with New-Institutionalism, at the time, however, was that it paid inadequate attention to the broader social and cultural contexts in which actors communicate and interact. This meant that the theoretical framework lacked the ability to explain how different actors exerted influence or asserted legitimacy within and across social spaces. This limitation was addressed by DiMaggio and Powell (1983), who, as a consequence, introduced organizational fields. They defined it as: "By a field we mean those organizations that, in the aggregate, constitute a recognized area of institutional life: key suppliers, resource and product consumers, regulatory agencies, and other organizations that produce similar services or products" (DiMaggio & Powell, 1983, p. 148). This implied that fields do not consist of a single actor but include several actors within an institutional ecosystem, implying a network of actors embedded in larger networks. Within a field, shared norms, practices, rules, and symbolic systems emerge, and the field itself only comes into being when actors begin to see themselves as part of a shared arena and when their actions become mutually dependent. Also, organizational fields are not formed randomly. Rather, they emerge through complex relational structures, evolving power balances, and sustained interaction over time.

Eventually, shared understandings of what constitutes legitimate practice or goals will then develop. DiMaggio and Powell (1983) argued further that as these dynamics take hold and materialize, an interesting paradox appears: organizations or institutions within the same field will become increasingly similar—a process DiMaggio and Powell called *institutional isomorphism*. In their influential paper, they identified three mechanisms of isomorphism: *coercive* isomorphism arises from political pressure or legal mandates. This typically happens when the state imposes new requirements that need to be adopted by other organizations, showing clearly how control is enacted. *Mimetic* isomorphism is a condition that occurs under uncertainty. It is an adoption that happens when organizations imitate others that are seen as successful or legitimate. *Normative* isomorphism is an adoption driven by processes of professionalization. It takes place when individuals with similar backgrounds and values import shared logics and practices into organizations. Together, these mechanisms explain why organizations often converge in structure and practice, meaning that institutional isomorphism can be seen as a model explaining the implications of change processes.

2.3.2.1 Fields and Institutional Logics

A limitation with organizational fields was the lack of attention to how fields operate as arenas of power and struggle. Bourdieu and Wacquant (1992) addressed this matter and contended that fields are structured spaces of positions in which actors compete over resources, influence, and the authority to define what counts as legitimate practice. Each field involves struggles over different types of capital—economic, cultural, social, and symbolic. The field's implicit rules (doxa) determine which forms of capital are valued and how legitimacy is constructed. This raises questions about what forms of capital give actors influence within a field and who holds the power to define normative and strategic agendas. A key extension of Bourdieu and Wacquant's theorizing is found in Fligstein and McAdam's (2012) concept of strategic action fields (SAFs), which is defined as: "A strategic action field is a constructed meso-level social order in which actors are attuned to and interact with one another based on shared understandings about the purposes of the field, relationships to others in the field (including who has power and why), and the rules governing legitimate action" (Fligstein & McAdam, 2012, p. 9).

In other words, they emphasized that fields are not static but are arenas of strategic interaction where actors continually interpret, adapt to, and try to influence one another. In fact, fields are dynamic and interconnected, and changes in one field can spill over into others—especially in periods of exogenous or endogenous crisis. Fields are actively constructed and maintained through social interaction and operate at the meso-level, between macro-level structures and micro-level agency. This makes them useful for analyzing mid-level dynamics, such as debates over AI governance. Strategic Action Fields are characterized by shared understandings of purpose, power relations, and legitimate forms of action. Typically, three kinds of actors are found in fields: incumbents, challengers, and governance units. These actors engage in strategic efforts to shape the field to their advantage by mobilizing resources, forming alliances, and interpreting rules and norms. As an extension, the concept of *institutional logics* was suggested, and it refers to the belief systems and organizing principles that shape and guide action within a given field (Thornton et al., 2012). These logics influence how actors interpret what counts as legitimate, rational, and appropriate behavior, and are deeply embedded in cultural and institutional structures. Moreover, fields might be governed by distinct logics.

2.3.2.2 An Approach to Distributed Digital Sovereignty

Then, to connect the outlined key concepts to digital sovereignty more firmly, this can create clarity to the proposed notion of distributed digital sovereignty. For a start, conventional approaches have conceptualized sovereignty as a static attribute of the nation-state, emphasizing monopoly over lawmaking and territorial control, leading to instrumental and deterministic approaches (Agnew, 2005). However, a New-Institutionalist lens would argue that sovereignty is to be established as a relational and processual phenomenon, which is shaped by norms, practices, and institutional arrangements across multiple levels and fields, moreover, which are not necessarily confined to the state apparatus (Schmidt, 2008). This perspective paves the way for a multilevel and field-sensitive perspective where conventional sovereignty or digital sovereignty is articulated and enacted through heterogeneous actors who are guided by diverse and overlapping logics. Rather than a hierarchical or binary attribute, sovereignty emerges as distributed and contingent—formed through the ongoing negotiation of authority, legitimacy, and control in various socio-technical domains (De Gregorio & Radu, 2022; Donnelly et al., 2024). Such a view allows for a flexible conceptualization of digital sovereignty, one that accounts for both public and private authority, infrastructural dependencies, and the situated character of rulemaking in digital environments (Azevedo et al., 2025; Floridi, 2020). Moreover, it can be argued that New-Institutionalism would put less emphasis on relying on technical or infrastructural reductions of digital sovereignty and also include social and cultural conditions. Instead, one shifts focus towards questions of governance, normative authority, and institutional power in diverse contexts (Blancato & Carr, 2024; Hulkó et al., 2025). Distributed digital sovereignty, in this view, can be grasped as a situated, relational, and institutionally embedded form of authority that is constantly (re)negotiated across legal, political, and technological domains and fields.

Based on the above, a definition is proposed. It is suggested that distributed digital sovereignty can be defined as the process by which control, authority, and legitimate governance over digital infrastructures, data, and technological practices are not concentrated in a single institutional, legal, or technical center, but is enacted, negotiated, and contested by a variety of actors across fields—including states, private companies, civil society organizations, technical standards bodies, and knowledge institutions. This definition emphasizes three key dimensions. First, it introduces a practice-oriented perspective: sovereignty is not simply enforced by a sovereign actor, but is produced through interactions among a multitude of actors seeking to claim legitimacy and exert influence. This calls for a heterogeneous and complex understanding. Second, it highlights the potential for multiple institutional logics to shape how sovereignty is understood and enacted in different contexts. Third, it recognizes that digital sovereignty is not only performed but also symbolically claimed—actors assert sovereignty as part of broader struggles over meaning, legitimacy, and access to resources. Perhaps most importantly, the definition underscores the need to connect sovereignty to the conditions of the digital age. It is inextricably tied to networks of technological systems, infrastructures, and socio-technical practices—where control, governance, and meaning-making unfold in a contested manner.

2.4 Typology of Socio-technological Fields in AI

This section presents the proposed typology (see Table 2.2). Drawing on central concepts in New-Institutionalism, the main goal is to demonstrate how legitimacy claims related to AI and digital sovereignty are formed, expressed, and contested across fields. The typology is assumed to consist of nine socio-technical fields, and it is argued that within each field, the practices and activities of actors are shaped by different institutional logics (DiMaggio & Powell, 1983; Fligstein & McAdam, 2012). Rather than assuming a fixed or state-centered definition of sovereignty, the aim is to show how legitimacy can be articulated through both formal mechanisms (such as legal authority or institutional mandates) and informal ones (such as shared norms, values, or taken-for-granted practices) (Scott, 1995; Thornton et al., 2012). These field-specific articulations of legitimacy often reflect tensions between competing ideas of control, responsibility, and authority. In that sense, the typology offers an empirical lens for understanding how digital sovereignty is enacted and negotiated in practice.

2.4.1 Sub-field 1: Technological Infrastructure and AI

The first field is called *Technological Infrastructure and AI*. This is a mature field where questions of digital sovereignty are made visible through the positioning of a range of actors—both large and small, public and private—who seek to assert legitimacy in relation to the infrastructures that enable the development and application of critical AI technologies. Such technologies include data centers, cloud-

Table 2.2. Table with overview of proposed socio-technical fields, pillars and core logics

No.	Field	Pillars	Core logics and tensions
1.	Technological Infrastructure	Regulative	State control vs. global platforms; infrastructural standards vs. dependency; autonomy vs. efficiency
2.	Data Governance	Regulative + Normative	Privacy vs. innovation; localization vs. flow; trust-building vs. extraction
3.	Ethics and Policy	Normative	Universal values vs. local norms; responsible AI vs. market interests; legitimacy vs. technical framing
4.	Science and Knowledge Production	Cognitive	Research autonomy vs. security; open vs. closed knowledge; centralization vs. diversity
5.	Education and Competence in AI	Normative + Cognitive	AI literacy vs. legacy digital skills; inclusion vs. specialization; public pedagogy vs. private influence
6.	Commercial Development	Regulative + Cognitive	Profit vs. ethics; platform power vs. national regulation; state support vs. market liberalism
7.	Cybersecurity	Regulative + Normative	Privacy vs. surveillance; openness vs. control; public-private co-dependence
8.	Work and Organizational Life	All three (R/N/C)	Automation vs. agency; flexibility vs. job security; organizational autonomy vs. platform dependency
9.	Civil Society and Culture	Normative + Cognitive	Individual rights vs. corporate control; cultural pluralism vs. algorithmic standardization; grassroots vs. state logic

based servers, semiconductor components and AI-specific chips, supercomputers, cloud platforms, and large language models. In other words, they encompass the full spectrum of infrastructure required to train, deploy, and access AI systems in practice. Currently, this critical infrastructure is highly concentrated in the hands of a small number of dominant actors, primarily American and Chinese tech giants (see Table 2.3). Indeed, these actors may be understood as incumbents—in a way, they are powerholders over critical technologies and hold massive institutional capital, where it can be argued that they have a strategic interest in maintaining existing structures and hierarchies. In contrast, this status is disputed by challengers through acts of formal mechanism or governance where the goal can be to redistribute control or create alternative infrastructure to reduce technological dependency. control. In a European context, this is can be articulated as a geopolitical issue, where public authorities such as the EU, seek to exercise regulatory power over AI critical infrastructure controlled by incumbents through implementing and enacting legal frameworks, procedures, and other legal instruments (Adler-Nissen & Eggeling, 2024; Musiani, 2022). One of the strongest examples showing such formal mechanisms in practice

Table 2.3. Table of actors in the subfield of technological infrastructure and AI

Region/ Country	Actor	Type of infrastructure	Ownership
USA	Amazon AWS	Cloud Platform	Private (US)
USA	OpenAI	Large Language Models (LLMs)	Private (US, with Microsoft investment)
USA	Google (DeepMind)	LLMs and Research	Private (US)
USA	NVIDIA	AI Chips (Hardware)	Private (US)
China	Alibaba Cloud	Cloud Platform	Private (China)
China	Baidu	LLMs and Cloud Services	Private (China)
China	Huawei	Cloud and Chips	State-linked (China)
Europe	Gaia-X	Data Infrastructure Framework	Consortium (EU-based)
Europe	LUMI Supercomputer	Supercomputer	State-supported (Finland/EU)
Middle East	G42 (UAE)	Cloud + LLM Training Capacity	Private-State Partnership (UAE)
India	AI4Bharat	Open Source LLMs + Gov Support	Public/Academic (India)
Canada	Mila (Quebec AI Institute)	AI Research Institute	Public/Academic (Canada)

is the EU's AI Act. On the other hand, these legal initiatives appear to be copied by other challengers who develop their own frameworks in other regions. For example, in 2024, India introduced the India AI Safety Institute (AISI), which is an initiative to ensure safe and ethical development and deployment of AI systems. For a longer period, Canada has worked with Bill C-27, the Artificial Intelligence and Data Act (AIDA). This is a legal framework that, among other things, introduces a risk-based framework inspired by the EU AI Act, particularly targeting areas involving high-impact applications. The focus is on accountability requirements, risk management, and control over high-impact AI systems. Such patterns clearly indicate a global surge and spread of frameworks to regulate key infrastructure, also showing isomorphic mechanisms at play.

However, the number of actors engaged in acts of claiming digital sovereignty creates a diversity of tensions, as they struggle over strategic positioning showing competing field logics. The most obvious field logic at play is the regulative one, as actors in control over governance structures seek to establish legitimacy through the creation of laws and rules that other major actors are expected to comply with. But the dynamics do not stop there: we also see the emergence of initiatives aimed at facilitating or developing alternative critical infrastructures that can serve as viable counterpoints to the dominant ones. Although Gaia-X is technically a framework (Adler-Nissen & Eggeling, 2024; Musiani, 2022) it has an ambition to support infrastructure grounded in European values such as openness, privacy, and security. While many other initiatives exist, they often generate coordination challenges and reveal conflicting logics. These frictions are not merely technical but reflect deeper normative disagreements over how digital infrastructures should be governed. For example, we see recurring tensions reflecting the logic between efficiency and autonomy: actors in control over global AI infrastructures can demand scale and investment, but local control or regional control can be a political and economic burden. Another recurring competing logic is the tension between openness and control (Pohle & Voelsen, 2022): while some actors push for openness and transparency, this often collides with institutional or state-based needs for oversight and state sovereignty. Therefore, such tensions manifest in the strategic interactions between incumbents, challengers, and governance actors, illustrating how distributed digital sovereignty is enacted and contested in practice and activities.

2.4.2 Sub-field 2: Data Governance and AI

The second field is called *Data Governance and AI*. This field overlaps with the first field in the typology, but it places greater emphasis on a particular object that actors today must care about: data; moreover, how different actors position themselves and claim legitimacy in relation to this resource, often said to be the "new oil." Here, legitimacy is constructed, negotiated, and established through the control, regulation, and administration of data—whether this concerns personal, commercial, or data tied to public infrastructure (De Gregorio & Radu, 2022; Gstrein, 2023). Again, digital sovereignty is expressed through the enactment of regulatory frameworks such as the EU's GDPR (General Data Protection Regulation) Act. We also observe patterns of isomorphism as actors beyond Europe begin constructing similar governance frameworks. For example, in 2020, Brazil implemented Lei Geral de Proteção de Dados Pessoais (LGPD), while India in 2023 established the Digital Personal Data Protection Act (DPDPA-2023). However, this field is not limited only to a regulatory pillar but also involves a normative dimension, as it evokes principles and values in culture and society (Floridi, 2020). This means that data holds both strategic and economic significance, meaning that issues such as privacy, data crossing, data flows, localization, frameworks, and public interest are central in discourses on digital sovereignty. The actors engaging in this field also consist of incumbents and challengers, meaning those who store data and those who regulate and define its value and permissible uses. Interestingly, a key driver is the high uncertainty surrounding how data is stored, who has access to it, and how trust can be established (Blancato & Carr, 2024; Hesselman et al., 2020), rendering a type of black box tech challenge. Tech companies make strong claims about their compliance with privacy laws and regulations, but in practice, it is difficult to verify these claims—especially in light of several scandals where data has leaked or been used without user consent (Floridi, 2020). But more importantly, its significance is markedly transformed with the rapid adoption of Generative AI, which has created more tension about how available and new data is understood, utilized, and governed (Roberts, 2024; Woods, 2023).

The importance of this field continues to grow, as data is now used in increasingly diverse ways—not least in the training of large language models (LLMs). This includes not only user-generated data, but intellectual property and cultural expressions such as music, books, images, and videos. Trust in the big tech companies comes under severe pressure when users discover that their own content—posted on social media platforms—is actively used by them to train algorithms, with considerable uncertainty about how this actually happens (Woods, 2023). This tension is further exacerbated when companies, on the one hand, claim to respect privacy and data protection, while on the other hand, overlook these concerns in the name of optimizing user experiences. This is utterly legal and ethical and gives rise to tension, as competing field logics come into conflict (Farrand & Carrapico, 2022). Some actors argue that privacy is a fundamental right, while others claim that innovation and data-driven business models require more flexible and less rigid regulatory frameworks—an argument often put forward by tech companies critical of regulations like the GDPR. Another key tension arises between national security and individual rights, especially in times of crisis when governments invoke a "state of exception" to bypass privacy protections and justify surveillance or intelligence activities (Hulkó et al., 2025). A further dimension of tension concerns the appropriate level of governance: should data sovereignty and regulation be situated at the national level, or is there a need for regional or continental frameworks—and how should these levels be harmonized? (Farrand & Carrapico, 2022; Gstrein, 2023). These tensions are not resolved by the discourse on digital sovereignty; rather, they are amplified, as data governance is deeply embedded in economic competition, ethical responsibility, and geopolitical strategy.

2.4.3 Sub-field 3: Ethics and Policy in AI

The third field is called *Ethics and Policy in AI*, which is also a mature field. It comprises many actors in a complex communication network and is primarily driven by a normative pillar that emphasizes the values, norms, and moral obligations that should guide actors' use of AI (Floridi, 2020; UNESCO, 2021). In other words, it addresses a value-based governance of technology, where digital systems should be regulated in accordance with societal values such as human rights and democratic principles (Gstrein, 2023). It is within this context that digital sovereignty is articulated—not in the narrow sense of legal or technological regulation, but as a matter of asserting legitimacy through negotiations and interactions over what should be done (De Gregorio & Radu, 2022; Farrand & Carrapico, 2022). Again, the field consists of many actors—large and small—including those working on ethical guidelines, technology companies, civil rights organizations, and academic institutions. The discourses in which they engage revolve around frameworks for AI, digital rights, and questions concerning responsible technology use. In many ways, this field overlaps with the previous field, and to some extent with the field of education, which I will address later. Its strength lies in the ability to articulate autonomous and value-driven aspects of AI technology, rather than focusing solely on control exercised by public authorities, private corporations, or transnational actors. Examples include national AI strategies, UNESCO's recommendations for the ethical use of AI, and similar principles articulated by the OECD (2019). What seems to drive this field forward is the rapid explosion of frameworks and initiatives aimed at isolating and rendering digital technology accountable. Many actors with AI expertise have developed their own ethical frameworks, typically articulated in policy documents and formalized principles. These frameworks often align with broader normative ideals such as democracy and human rights. A central question, then, is how different actors—by participating in the process of defining acceptable digital conduct—not only develop frameworks but also exercise a form of normative authority over what counts as appropriate technological practice. This can be understood as a type of normative digital sovereignty where actors seek to establish ethical standards within a given jurisdiction or population. In promoting European values, these actors simultaneously contribute to shaping global discourses on what constitutes responsible technology use in the domain of artificial intelligence.

This field, too, is characterized by field logics that generate persistent tensions. One of the most persistent tensions lies in balancing innovation with the imperative for regulation. Some argue that stringent ethical requirements may hamper technological progress and be a disadvantage for national industries developing AI (Hoffmann-Riem, 2020). Another central field logic relates to the question of who has the mandate to define the "right" ethical standards. Cultural and national differences frequently lead to divergent interpretations of what constitutes ethical AI. As a result, European ideals and values related to privacy, transparency, and human dignity may conflict with more market-driven or context-specific approaches found elsewhere in the world. This becomes evident when NGOs and advocacy groups are involved in policymaking, while other actors exert only peripheral or indirect influence. The consequence can be considerable variation in how ethical frameworks are institutionalized and enacted. Another dilemma relates to the tension between universal ethical principles and national sovereignty in the context of AI. On the one hand, many of the risks associated with AI—such as discrimination, surveillance, and manipulation—are transnational in character. On the other hand, these risks may clash with national and local interests, complicating efforts to establish common standards for what should be considered responsible AI use. This can result in a form of digital sovereignty that is unevenly distributed and shaped by asymmetrical power relations, geopolitical differences, and competing field logics.

2.4.4 Sub-field 4: Scientific and Knowledge in AI

The fourth field is called *Science and Knowledge in AI*. This field consists of actors who engage in networks of communities that can be described as a complex ecosystem of research, innovation, and knowledge production related to AI. They are positioned within networks of interlinked entities that include universities, public research institutions, private R&D labs, research councils, and organizations responsible for disseminating scientific knowledge to the broader public. In many ways, this field aligns with a cognitive value system. Legitimacy claims revolve around symbolic control and the cultural legitimacy to define what counts as legitimate AI research, implying an emphasis on informal mechanisms. In this sense, legitimacy is enacted through epistemological and infrastructural autonomy: who controls the knowledge, expertise, and technologies that shape the trajectory of AI. This includes not only those conducting basic or applied research but also those building institutions and human capacity (Fligstein & McAdam, 2012). The field can be can be considered a mature domain, operating across both national and international levels and reflecting a form of digital governance that transcends territorial and legal boundaries. At the same time, it is marked by geopolitical tensions—particularly concerning who funds research, who controls technological infrastructure, and who possesses the human capital required to lead in this space (König & Wenzelburger, 2020). Consequently, it has evolved into a site of resource struggles, characterized by strategic mobilization and complex positioning within a highly competitive environment.

While multiple field logics may coexist, a key driver is closely tied to those who either claim leadership or are ascribed such a role in advancing AI development—a status that itself becomes a form of capital, subject to differential valuation. Historically, AI research has been closely associated with specific technological hubs—often tied to elite universities—particularly within the U.S. context, such as those located in California and Seattle, which have long served as incumbents in the field. Increasingly, these research hubs are challenged by initiatives aiming to develop alternative research ecosystems, both nationally and internationally. In Europe, there are several initiatives; the European Laboratory for Learning and Intelligent Systems (ELLIS), created in 2018, is a research network consisting of more than 40 units belonging to 17 countries that aims to secure Europe's position in foundational AI research. Addressing national initiatives: In the Netherlands, the Innovation Center for Artificial Intelligence (ICAI) is a collaboration between universities, industry, and government. Italy has the Italian Institute of Artificial Intelligence for Industry (AI4I), established in 2024. This is a government-supported initiative that aims at strengthening research on industrial AI applications. If we look beyond Europe, the United Arab Emirates launched the regional effort Technology Innovation Institute (TII) in 2020. Such developments, however, exemplify what New-Institutionalism calls institutional entrepreneurship (DiMaggio, 1988), whereby actors mobilize resources and attempt to reshape an otherwise highly competitive field (Fligstein & McAdam, 2012). That said, we also observe discourses on how AI should be researched. Actors without access to key infrastructure often adopt human-centered approaches, focusing on the societal, institutional, and individual impacts of AI (Birhane, 2021). This contributes to the formation of field logics, often structured around tensions. One example is the divide between those advocating for open research and those linking AI development to security concerns. Openness—often upheld as a core academic value—may conflict with more strategic approaches that favor restricted dissemination due to concerns about national security or economic competitiveness (Zuboff, 2019). This raises the issue of whether researchers should publish breakthroughs or withhold them. Another field logic centers around the tension between centralized and decentralized research infrastructures. As research communities attempt to establish AI "flagships" or centers of excellence, this often leads to a concentration of resources, resulting in the marginalization of other research groups that may struggle to keep pace. Moreover, centers that attain prestigious status or are held in high esteem can evolve into bureaucratic and managerial entities, governed by short-term funding logics. As a result, they may prioritize educational mandates—such as the production of PhDs—over long-term research goals aimed at capacity building that benefits the broader field.

2.4.5 Sub-field 5: Educational and Competence in AI

The fifth field is *Education and Competence in AI.* It is related to the development of knowledge, skills, and expertise across society and the labor market, and connects to normative and cognitive aspects, implying that legitimacy is articulated through informal mechanisms. Here, digital sovereignty is legitimized and linked to the societal need to build and maintain human capital, which is essential for the use, governance, and innovation of AI (Miao & Cukurova, 2024; OECD, 2021). The field comprises a network of diverse actors operating within a complex ecosystem of education, lifelong learning, and workplace training. This entails engagement across educational institutions at all levels, as well as participation by national and intergovernmental organizations (European Commission, 2021).

The field assumes that both individuals and organizations possess the necessary competencies to lead, interpret, and develop AI in ways that support autonomy and democratic participation (Ng et al., 2021). It is not only about basic digital literacies, but also about citizens' capacity to actively participate and use AI in safe, responsible, and meaningful ways. In fact, competence in AI is necessary to engage in societal debates; moreover, it becomes critical in education and work life. Also, specialized knowledge is required; this applies to AI specialists, security experts, and data engineers, as well as ordinary workers and other groups who use technology in their daily work. At a broader level, a key driver is legitimacy that attempts to define what is the most relevant competence, which is now discussed under the umbrella term AI literacy (Biagini, 2025). This is evident as several actors are in the process of having either developed or are creating AI literacy frameworks. One example is UNESCO's framework, which has gained wide acceptance and serves as a model (Miao & Cukurova, 2024). This leads to a tendency toward isomorphism, resulting in both generic and complex AI literacy frameworks.

That said, underlying tensions reveal the presence of divergent field logics. One is straightforward – without a competent population, the use of the technology can be rendered useless. Investing in AI technologies makes little sense without the human capital necessary to utilize them, as such capital is essential to establishing the technology's foundational legitimacy Yet, tensions in this regard are readily observable. A central challenge lies in the inherent mismatch between different scales and interpretations of required competencies. This raises a critical question: are we referring to digital competence or AI literacy—and to which technologies should competence frameworks be aligned? One could argue that digital competence was developed for technologies dominant in an earlier era, whereas AI requires different types of expertise—raising the question of whether existing frameworks adequately address this shift (Caena & Redecker, 2019). Another tension often observed relates to the balance between simplification and actual complexity in application. Many AI frameworks are developed by interested organizations and through bureaucratic processes that emphasize generic skills and knowledge. This may contrast with perspectives from educational researchers, who argue that such frameworks fail to account for the situated, contextual, and practice-based dimensions of competence (Markauskaite & Goodyear, 2017). Another key tension lies between inclusion and expertise: some actors argue for the necessity of developing highly specialized competence to enable participation in technological innovations—thus asserting strategic control over digital competence. At the same time, there is strong normative pressure for digital inclusion, so that broader segments of the population—who might otherwise be excluded—can participate. Conversely, this can lead to a hierarchical model; the general population receives basic competence training, while a smaller group acquires specialized expertise. This raises a more ethical question: who has the authority to define the content and direction of education? Should technology companies—often promoting product-centered competencies and pre-defined modular knowledge and skills —define the agenda? Or should educational goals be anchored in broader pedagogical and civic aims? These tensions challenge the definition of competence as something situated, multidimensional, and normatively constructed—and simultaneously reveal that the education field is shaped by power struggles over legitimacy claims to define what constitutes the right kind of knowledge and skills needed.

2.4.6 Sub-field 6: Commercial AI Development

The sixth field is *Commercial AI Development.* It concerns an industry and market-based ecosystem composed of both small and large companies involved in AI development and implementation. This field operates at the intersection of the normative and cognitive pillars, while also extending into the regulative domain, meaning a combination of formal and informal mechanisms. It is characterized by a stratified and diverse power structure, where global technology giants coexist with startups, private enterprises, and, in some cases, state-initiated companies that develop software, design algorithms, build platforms, and deliver products and services. A key component is the financial infrastructure that supports technological advancement and entrepreneurship (Bria et al., 2025). It is a field that is embedded in the competitive economy that contributes to technological advancements, consisting of actors who design and own intellectual property and generate economic value through AI-driven innovation. Digital sovereignty in this context is about legitimacy over critical components, ownership of technological infrastructure and intellectual property, and the capacity to drive innovation (De Gregorio & Radu, 2022). This field overlaps with the first and second fields in the typology and exists in a state of ongoing tension with actors seeking to regulate infrastructures and data. Incumbents can be identified, typically concentrated in tech hubs. The dominant players are largely based in technology centers in the United States, particularly Silicon Valley, while similar concentrations exist in China. These actors hold power due to their economic capacity and extensive research and development divisions, enabling them to invest heavily in AI. As a result, they also shape global standards for platforms and digital ecosystems. Such factors grant them considerable legitimacy which closely ties them to market values and market dominance—giving them significant global influence (König & Wenzelburger, 2020).

It does not take long to identify field logics and tension. A central one can be the opposition between national control over key technologies and the interests of global technology companies. A recurring discourse concerns how AI is adapted to national interests—interests that frequently stand in contrast to how major technology companies conceptualize and implement these technologies. National priorities—as articulated, for example, within European contexts—do not necessarily align with the values held by the companies that develop and distribute them (Donnelly et al., 2024). An example is data privacy. Here, different values often conflict between national imperatives and the commercial goals of global tech giants, whose positions are often shaped by their own national and commercial environments. Further tensions arise between ethical regulation and commercial innovation. Small and medium-sized enterprises operating in national contexts can face difficulties complying with ethical standards, in part because it is resource-intensive to integrate such standards into existing infrastructures—unlike large corporations, which can often accommodate them with minimal disruption. Another tension can be between state intervention and market liberalism. While European economies have emphasized competition and minimal industrial intervention as drivers of AI-related growth, recent shifts reveal that some national economies now deploy state subsidies to foster domestic tech ecosystems (Bria et al., 2025). This tension becomes visible when larger EU member states are better positioned to provide financial support for AI initiatives than smaller countries, thereby introducing further asymmetries and challenges to realizing a unified European approach.

2.4.7 Sub-field 7: Cybersecurity in AI

The seventh field is called *Cybersecurity in AI*. It consists of a community of diverse actors who engage in protecting digital systems, networks, and data from unauthorized access, attacks, and damage, reflecting a mature field. This field can be understood as regulatory, though also having a normative dimension, suggesting an integration of formal and informal mechanisms. This field is important for enacting digital sovereignty, since an absence of effectively secured infrastructure can undermine autonomy and leave societies vulnerable to disruption and destabilization (De Gregorio & Radu, 2022). An inclusion of a wide range of actors makes it interesting—not only state institutions, but also non-state, public, private, small, and large actors—depicting a global character. However, there might be slight variation in practice. A key driver is the ongoing discourse and restructuring of multiple standards and understandings of what cybersecurity "is", and how such processes are connected to a global industry that develops services and supplies products (Carr, 2016). There also exist distinct conceptualizations of what "security" entails—for instance, cybersecurity, cyber defense, and cyber diplomacy. These standards, relate to increasingly deeper divides and restructuring across institutional structures. Historically, security responsibilities were divided between civil and military institutions: police authorities oversaw domestic affairs, while the military was tasked with defending external threats. Now, countries have developed their indigenous national cybersecurity strategies, which are often explicitly linked to digital sovereignty. The relevance of this connection becomes clearer when actors are forced to defend against both internal and external threats related to AI, such as cyberattacks, which paradoxically create technology dependency on tech giants that often supply the critical infrastructure. One approach actors use to claim legitimacy is by asserting that the infrastructure they protect must be robust and resilient. Thia often requires the formation of complex and collaborative alliances, resulting in layered formal and informal mechanisms, processes, and structures that must be carefully organized and administered. This dynamic gives rise to a notable tension: governments are increasingly required to collaborate with private actors who own and operate critical AI-related infrastructure. A mutually dependent relationship emerges, in which the state cannot merely exercise control, but must also coordinate and build trust with other central stakeholders, creating challenges.

Addressing field logics, we can find observable tensions. One such tension lies between privacy and security in the use of AI. On one hand, national security agencies seek to expand their mandates to gain access to data—often justified as necessary for combating crime and terrorism through AI. On the other hand, this collides with principles of privacy and civil rights. Importantly, sovereignty-based arguments are employed on both sides of the debate: security institutions claim that national autonomy, technological capability, and independence must not come at the expense of effective investigation—and that strong encryption should not shield criminal actors (Pohle & Thiel, 2021). In contrast, privacy advocates argue that encryption is essential to protect citizens from both domestic and foreign surveillance. Balancing these interests is challenging when it becomes evident that intelligence services have engaged in illegal surveillance of their own populations. For example, this has occurred in national intelligence agencies such as the NSA, GCHQ, and Chinese state authorities, which have monitored citizens' digital habits through advanced spy programs such as PRISM, TEMPORA, and the social credit system. These programs have collected data from big platforms such as Google and Facebook and conducted surveillance of users' online behavior such as searches, purchases, and social media activity. Such programs introduce a highly normative and moral question: who should control access to and use of the internet and AI? Another field logic emerges around the tension between openness and control. What rules should govern access to AI, and how should data be used to make decisions about individuals? Historically, Western democracies have advocated for an open and global internet, but increasing threats from cyberespionage, disinformation, and systemic attacks—amplified through AI—have led several governments to reconsider this stance. This could result in a shift away from a multi-stakeholder model toward a more state-centered field logic. This manifests in concrete policy decisions, such as the exclusion of foreign companies from national infrastructure projects, which has often been the case with Chinese tech companies.

2.4.8 Sub-field 8: Labor and Organizational Conditions in AI

The eighth field is *Labor and Organizational Conditions in AI*. This field concerns how digital sovereignty is legitimized within a communication network involving actors operating in the fields of labor and life organization. In many ways, this field addresses how AI affects labor, organizational practices, and leadership strategies.

In short, one can also argue that this field includes formal and informal mechanisms of digital sovereignty. This means we can explore how organizations respond to changes in their external environments, while simultaneously undergoing internal adjustments or being controlled or mimicking other organizations, reflecting isomorphic mechanisms (DiMaggio & Powell, 1983). There are several key issues that drive this field. For example, what are the legal frameworks and policies that define and regulate what counts as work and how it should be carried out? Alternatively, debates around automation are inevitably tied to this field—how can labor rights be safeguarded while making necessary changes so that they are in accordance with current technological advancements (Rani & Furrer, 2021)? Additionally, this raises questions about organizations' growing dependence on external technological infrastructures, such as cloud-based and proprietary software platforms, and how these systems interface with AI. For example, Amazon warehouses use automated management systems to control worker pace, while Uber's platform architecture governs driver behavior through algorithmic matching and ratings. In this context, what happens when new technologies are introduced: do employees have influence, or are they passive recipients? AI and data-driven decision-making systems change the conditions of the workplace. Where humans once made strategic decisions, we now see AI systems increasingly integrated into key organizational processes. Who, then, is in control—humans or machines? A concern in this debate is whether digital transformation empowers the workforce or leads to its marginalization. This also prompts questions about competence: what kinds of skills are needed in response to these technologies, and how should systems be designed to meet that demand? Another issue involves the proliferation of measurement tools and systems that track employee performance. Today, clearly defined metrics for work tasks are common, which raises questions about surveillance and new forms of control (Pasquale, 2015). This highlights an important ethical discussion: who controls the data-driven workflows, who has access to the data, who owns it—and who ultimately exercises control?

The above results in identifiable field logics that reflect underlying tensions. The most prominent is the tension between automation and the efficiency of human labor. On one hand, AI is frequently promoted as a tool for rationalizing and automating work processes, with the claim that machines can perform tasks significantly faster than humans. However, one should show caution here; it is not necessary that all technologies lead to efficiency in practice. Increasingly, AI appears to function as yet another digital layer added to an already complex work environment. This may lead to heightened complexity and additional decision points involving both humans and machines—potentially resulting in greater inefficiency rather than improved productivity. Another field logic concerns the tension between flexibility and job security. It is often argued that technology can work around the clock and complete tasks faster than humans, which in turn creates insecurity among workers. We increasingly observe that small and medium-sized tech companies in this field tend not to operate as traditional employers but rather position themselves as technology innovators. This leads to the redefinition of employment contracts—where workers are effectively freelancers—resulting in the erosion of welfare rights (Rani & Furrer, 2021). This development has altered the conditions for stable employment and access to social benefits. It is especially prevalent in sectors governed by platform logics, where business models have been redefined—particularly in the transport and tourism industries, such as Uber and Airbnb.

2.4.9 Sub-field 9: Civic and Culture in AI

The final field is *Civic and Cultural in AI*. At its core, this is a human-centered field that addresses the role of civil society, public discourse, and cultural identity in AI. The field consists of actors such as citizens, NGOs, activists, and local authorities that make legitimacy claims about values, rights, and cultural aspects. This field encompasses elements that range from formal to informal mechanisms but is likely to be dominated by normative and cognitive aspects. Drivers that engage actors are questions related to digital rights and activism. The field also embraces grassroots technology initiatives, such as open-source communities, decentralized infrastructure, and community-led digital education and programming. Another central concern is the preservation of language and cultural diversity in the digital sphere—and the need for AI to actively support such efforts. This is rooted in a broader understanding that digital transformation should not be a uniform and streamlined process, but one that aligns with democratic values and respects local cultures. As a result, a particular need for legitimacy arises—one tied to individual- and user-centered conceptions of digital sovereignty. The focus is on strengthening the individual's right to maintain control over their digital life. This vision partially contrasts with more state-centered interpretations of digital governance.

That said, there are multiple field logics expressed in the negotiations between actors. This is undoubtedly linked to the fact that one of the primary drivers here is not state institutions but grassroots initiatives and civil society organizations working for civil rights, suggesting a focus on value-driven tensions. One does not have to look far to see how individuals and larger actors mobilize to challenge the dominant position held by major tech companies in the AI landscape. A point of contention is how AI threatens intellectual property rights in popular culture. Many cultural workers report that their creations—books, films, images, and other forms of expression—are being used without their consent by tech companies to train their LLMs (Erdélyi & Goldsmith, 2018). This raises concerns similar to those seen when digital platforms took control of music and film distribution: the platforms gained disproportionate power and redirected revenue streams, leaving content creators with little income. Another related tension is how major tech firms often adopt a contradictory stance on privacy, operating under a kind of "state of exception" condition. On one hand, they claim to respect users' data and privacy, while on the other, they make exceptions to improve their products by using personal data to train their algorithms, as has been the case with Meta.

There are also examples of other tensions. One such logic emerges from the opposition between state-driven and citizen-driven interpretations of digital sovereignty. In authoritarian regimes, the rhetoric of digital sovereignty is often used to justify censorship and internet control. In contrast, democratic societies invoke the same concept to reinforce individual agency and control over personal data. Another tension is found in the relationship between local and global spheres. The internet is transnational, but data is increasingly subject to localization and national regulatory compliance. This has led to growing fears of "digital Balkanization," which could threaten the free flow of information and human expression (Gillespie, 2018). On one hand, we see European societies promoting privacy and pushing for the regulation of international platforms. On the other hand, there is a tension between cultural protection and digital market competition. Platforms tend to prioritize dominant languages and homogenized content, which has sparked concerns that this undermines both innovation and user choice. These debates are undeniably tied to content moderation, much of which is driven by algorithms and data-based decision-making.

2.5 Discussion

This analysis was inspired by an academic discourse. At the end of the 1990s and into the early 2000s, several influential texts began to reexamine sovereignty, theorizing it beyond its original boundaries. A central argument was that sovereignty somewhat changed face as a consequence of global processes. To a certain extent, sovereignty could be a new political order that had the power to suspend the legal apparatus through enacting or making decisions of "state of exception" (Agamben, 2005) and strip humans of all legal protection to "bare life" (Agamben, 2020). It could also exercise state power through certain intermediaries—actors operating through or alongside more powerful actors to pursue their own interests. This was called *Empire* (Hardt & Negri, 2000). That said, what this literature did not fully anticipate was the massive rise of digital technologies—later consolidated into platforms (Dijck et al., 2018)—and the ways in which data and AI systems would contribute to the emergence of what are now essentially tech oligopolies.

The above raises the question: What are the consequences of theorizing in this new landscape? Certain points can be indicated. First, it can be argued that sovereignty has not lost its relevance, but established interpretations, such as understanding it as a static and legal construct tied to the territorial authority of the nation-state, call for careful reconsideration and new theoretical directions. Second, one might consider that sovereignty becomes more flexible and takes on new connotations depending on which actors use the term and how it is framed theoretically as part of political contexts. Third, one may also argue that sovereignty is undergoing a form of dual restructuring, expressed through fragmentation and coordination processes. A clear indication of this aspect is the proliferation of parallel regulatory frameworks and standards for AI governance, which often resemble each other. While these may create splintering mechanisms within global governance efforts, they also create space for sovereignty to be increasingly embedded as part of regionalization processes. Fourth, and perhaps most notable, is how sovereignty can be argued to take on a more privatized meaning, as major technology companies effectively act as de facto regulators of their platforms, having large implications. This development compels both states and large non-state actors to accept hybrid models of public–private governance. Finally, sovereignty is becoming part of a broader normative struggle, in which it is linked to core societal values such as democracy, security, competition, and privacy. The prioritization of these values helps determine which boundaries are perceived as legitimate forms of control—an issue that has also been central in recent scholarship on digital sovereignty (e.g. Gordon, 2024; Klare et al., 2023; Prasad, 2022; Rone, 2024).

Based on the above arguments, one can argue that distributed digital sovereignty reflects a consequence of digitalization: sovereignty appears increasingly multifaceted and manifests across various domains, each with differing levels of complexity. This suggests that sovereignty has become highly context-dependent, thereby challenging more established understandings in the academic literature. Distributed digital sovereignty calls for a shift in focus—towards how sovereignty is actually produced, negotiated, and legitimized through practices and activities situated in specific contexts and initiated by a wide range of actors. The theoretical backdrop here touches on a classical issue in sociological theory: the relationship between agency and structure—that is, the tension between the capacity of actors to exercise agency, and the social structures that enable or constrain this capacity. Digital transformation has likely intensified this dynamic. Both individuals and institutional actors are increasingly engaged in questions of legitimacy and power within the digital realm. As more actors choose to act, make decisions, and seek to exert influence, questions of institutionalization arise—namely, how new practices become established, and how they challenge the position of already existing institutions or actors. Understanding these processes—how actors seek to establish new structures or disrupt entrenched ones—requires analysis at a more decentralized level. This, in turn, calls for mapping more of how the terrain of sovereignty actually takes shape in practice. Within this terrain, we find a plurality of change agents acting in pursuit of their own interests or forming alliances to gain legitimacy for their claims and solutions. When such mechanisms are at play, identifying the key actors becomes increasingly difficult. As a result, alternative analytical tools are needed to grasp the implications of digitalization processes and how they shape—and are shaped by—the ongoing struggles over sovereignty.

In this context, this is why the typology of the nine socio-technical fields was introduced. It should be emphasized that it is not a classification system, but rather an analytical tool that can be applied by both researchers and practitioners. The typology is intended to offer a way to examine how actors claim legitimacy as part of practice. These claims often unfold through recognizable tensions—dichotomies such as state versus individual, local versus global, or technical control versus democratic accountability (Fligstein & McAdam, 2012; Scott, 1995; Thornton et al., 2012). Such tensions drive practice and give sovereignty multiple faces. The typology enables comparisons across different fields, both empirically and analytically. It functions as a kind of "field map," illustrated in Figure 2.1—an entry point into a complex terrain—that can help us identify where power dynamics are playing out, or how sovereignty is being claimed or challenged in practice. This is important because the terrain itself is ambiguous, which implies that we need tools to interpret and make sense of it.

That said, the proposed typology is neither definitive nor exhaustive, but flexible. It must also be emphasized that it is not intended as a final version. It is entirely possible that there are additional fields beyond those identified, or that some may overlap in ways not fully captured here. There may also be hybrid formations

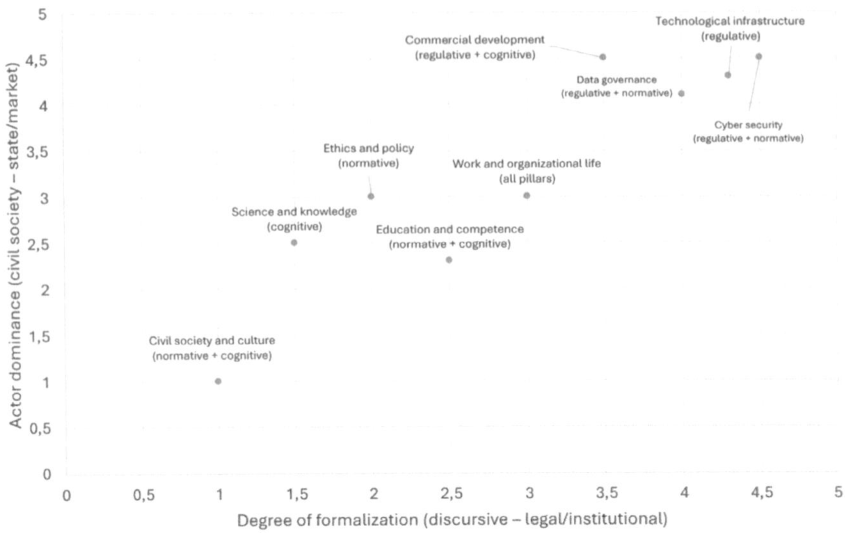

Figure 2.1. Field map of digital sovereignty across socio-technological fields.

or emerging configurations that call for further empirical work. If anything, this should be seen as an invitation for further research, implying that the objective behind this chapter becomes clear—to open an analytical trajectory for the study of digital sovereignty and connect it to New-Institutionalism (DiMaggio & Powell, 1983; Meyer & Rowan, 1977). Such an approach makes it possible to theorize digital sovereignty not only as an analytical construct, but also to empirically explore how it may form part of political strategies, for example. Thus, the core message is to offer the research community an additional analytical toolbox grounded in New-Institutional theory—a perspective that has, until now, been largely absent from studies of digital sovereignty. One of the key strengths of New-Institutionalism is its ability to problematize and unpack power structures in nuanced ways. This makes it a fruitful approach for understanding how control and legitimacy operate in the digital domain, serving as a complement to other frameworks.

2.6 Limitations

Like other research contributions, this analysis has its limitations, which we will highlight. First, this is foremost a theoretical and conceptual piece of work. It is not based on systematic empirical research aimed at measuring digital sovereignty. Second, the practical examples elaborated within the various socio-technical fields are mainly tied to European contexts, with some references to American and Chinese developments. This means that other cultural contexts are left out, and it is clear that if one accounts for how sovereignty discourses unfold there, a different geopolitical or cultural picture will obviously emerge. In addition, the framework has a geopolitical limitation in the sense that the typology brings forward transnational logics, but it does not analyze the deeper power-political asymmetries between regions or states.

Therefore, it is important to emphasize that other frameworks, such as digital value chains and the infrastructure dependencies model, produce insights that institutional approaches can only capture partially. Third, as indicated in the discussion, the definition of digital sovereignty employed here is not absolute, and this too can be seen as a limitation. It is possible that other types of social fields—or combinations thereof—are beginning to emerge beyond those identified here, and that they may develop into more mature or hybrid forms. This brings up an important point: the technological complexity and the pace of innovation may challenge the ability of field-based analyses to keep up with the consequences of new developments. This might be a black box issue, where technology and its effects run ahead of what institutional perspectives are able to grasp. This is a limitation the framework does not fully address. Fourth, it also implies that the definition of distributed digital sovereignty and the proposed typology do not sufficiently capture the implications of legal frameworks. New institutionalism mainly explains institutional logics and actor constellations but gives less attention to binding legal frameworks and formal jurisdiction. This means there may be limitations in how the analytical framework proposed can account for the effects of AI regulations.

2.7 Conclusion

This is a conceptual chapter where the goal has been to demonstrate that digital sovereignty is distributed across fields. This challenges a common understanding in which sovereignty is primarily tied to the nation-state's apparatus. Instead, it is proposed that sovereignty is produced, negotiated, and legitimized through practices carried out by actors within concrete contexts. To illustrate this, socio-technical fields were introduced, and AI was used as an example to show how legitimacy can be asserted differently. This led to the development of a framework that can enable comparative analysis and be applied by researchers and practitioners. Thus, the typology makes it possible to understand how digital sovereignty and claims to legitimacy take on different forms across contexts, meaning that it might contribute to making sense of the complexity of AI development more accessible.

As for future research challenges and actionable policy recommendations, certain areas stand out. Considering future research challenges first, the typology presented here is not final; it can and should be expanded. Future studies could further investigate the identified fields by drawing on organizational sociology and New Institutionalism. The hope is that this approach may open up a new analytical space for understanding the dynamics and processes through which digital sovereignty is articulated—and that it may serve as a contribution to existing ways of thinking about sovereignty. Regarding policy recommendations, one suggestion is that practitioners and policymakers apply the typology in a field-sensitive manner, rather than assuming that policy processes should follow a one-size-fits-all approach. Another important point is that governance frameworks need to accommodate overlapping and competing institutional logics, and facilitate arenas where different actors can negotiate issues related to AI governance. This is essential in order to avoid siloed policy-making and to prevent the establishment of impermeable boundaries between domains with shared interests. Such coordination is also necessary to ensure a more efficient use of resources. A further aspect is that practitioners and policymakers should not view digital sovereignty solely as a mechanism of state control and regulation. Rather, it should be understood as a distributed process that also involves civil society and technology providers—who must likewise be considered responsible and accountable actors in these processes.

Declaration of AI-Assisted Technologies

During the preparation of this work, the author utilized AI-assisted tools to enhance English language accuracy, including spelling, grammar, and punctuation. The content generated or corrected by these tools was thoroughly reviewed, revised, and edited by the authors to ensure accuracy and originality. The author accepts full responsibility for the originality of the final content of this chapter.

References

Abraham, S. (2013). The fight for digital sovereignty. *Economic and Political Weekly*, 48(42), 84-85.

Adler-Nissen, R., & Eggeling, K.A. (2024). The discursive struggle for digital sovereignty: Security, economy, rights and the cloud project Gaia-X. *Journal of Common Market Studies*, 62(4), 993-1011. https://doi.org/10.1111/jcms.13594

Agamben, G. (2005). *State of Exception*. University of Chicago Press.

Agamben, G. (2020). *Homo Sacer: Sovereign Power and Bare Life*. Stanford University Press.

Agnew, J. (2005). Sovereignty regimes: Territoriality and state authority in contemporary world politics. *Annals of the Association of American Geographers*, 95(2), 437-461. https://doi.org/10.1111/j.1467-8306.2005.00468.x

Akcali Gur, B. (2022). Cybersecurity, European digital sovereignty and the 5G rollout crisis. *Computer Law and Security Review*, 46, 105736. https://doi.org/10.1016/j.clsr.2022.105736

Azevedo, A., Scheid, E., Franco, M., Boeira, D., Zembruzki, L., & Granville, L. (2025). The role of network centralization in shaping digital sovereignty: An analysis under the DNS lens. *Int J Network Mgmt*, 35, e2309. https://doi.org/10.1002/nem.2309

Barrinha, A., & Christou, G. (2022). Speaking sovereignty: The EU in the cyber domain. *European Security*, 31(3), 356-376. https://doi.org/10.1080/09662839.2022.2102895

Bechara, J., & Lechner, U. (2024). Digital sovereignty and open-source software – A discussion paper. In: Phillipson, F., Eichler, G., Erfurth, C., Fahrnberger, G. (eds), *Innovations for Community Services. I4CS 2024. Communications in Computer and Information Science*, Vol 2109. Springer, Cham. https://doi.org/10.1007/978-3-031-60433-1_22

Bellanova, R., Carrapico, H., & Duez, D. (2022). Digital/sovereignty and European security integration: An introduction. *European Security*, 31(3), 337-355. https://doi.org/10.1080/09662839.2022.2101887

Bentalha, B., & Boukare, M. (2024). AI-driven territorial intelligence an integrated approach to enhancing digital sovereignty. In: *Generative AI and Implications for Ethics, Security, and Data Management* (pp. 231-261). https://doi.org/10.4018/979-8-3693-8557-9.ch008

Biagini, G. (2025). Towards an AI-literate future: A systematic literature review exploring education, ethics, and applications. *International Journal of Artificial Intelligence in Education*. https://doi.org/10.1007/s40593-025-00466-w

Birhane, A. (2021). Algorithmic injustice: A relational ethics approach. *Patterns*, 2(2), 100205. https://doi.org/https://doi.org/10.1016/j.patter.2021.100205

Blancato, F.G., & Carr, M. (2024). The trust deficit. EU bargaining for access and control over cloud infrastructures. *Journal of European Public Policy*. https://doi.org/10.1080/13501763.2024.2441418

Boeira, D.F.F., Scheid, E.J., Franco, M.F., Zembruzki, L., & Granville, L.Z. (2024). Traffic centralization and digital sovereignty: An analysis under the lens of DNS servers. In: *2024 IEEE Network Operations and Management Symposium (NOMS)* (pp. 1–9). IEEE. https://doi.org/10.1109/NOMS59830.2024.10575700.

Bourdieu, P., & Wacquant, L.J.D. (1992). *An Invitation to Reflexive Sociology*, University of Chicago Press.

Bria, F., Timmers, P., & Gernone, F. (2025). *EuroStack – A European Alternative for Digital Sovereignty*. Bertelsmann Stiftung.

Broeders, D., Cristiano, F., & Kaminska, M. (2023). In search of digital sovereignty and strategic autonomy: Normative power Europe to the test of its geopolitical ambitions. *Journal of Common Market Studies*, 61(5), 1261-1280. https://doi.org/10.1111/jcms.13462

Brännström, L. (2023). Global inequality and the EU international law position on cross-border data flows. *Nordic Journal of International Law*, 92(1), 119-137. https://doi.org/10.1163/15718107-bja10059

Caena, F., & Redecker, C. (2019). Aligning teacher competence frameworks to 21st century challenges: The case for the European Digital Competence Framework for Educators. *European Journal of Education*, 54(3), 356-369. https://doi.org/https://doi.org/10.1111/ejed.12345

Calderaro, A., & Blumfelde, S. (2022). Artificial intelligence and EU security: The false promise of digital sovereignty? *European Security*, 31(3), 415-434. https://doi.org/10.1080/09662839.2022.2101885

Carr, M. (2016). Public-private partnerships in national cyber-security strategies. *International Affairs*, 92, 43-62. https://doi.org/10.1111/1468-2346.12504

Conradie, N.H., & Nagel, S.K. (2022). Digital sovereignty and smart wearables: Three moral calculi for the distribution of legitimate control over the digital. *Journal of Responsible Technology*, 12, 100053. https://doi.org/10.1016/j.jrt.2022.100053

Couture, S., & Toupin, S. (2019). What does the notion of "sovereignty" mean when referring to the digital? *New Media and Society*, 21(10), 2305-2322. https://doi.org/10.1177/1461444819865984

De Gregorio, G., & Radu, R. (2022). Digital constitutionalism in the new era of Internet governance. *International Journal of Law and Information Technology*, 30(1), 68-87. https://doi.org/10.1093/ijlit/eaac004

Dijck, J.V., Waal, M.D., & Poell, T. (2018). *The Platform Society: Public Values in a Connective World*. Oxford University Press.

DiMaggio, P. (1988). Interest and agency in institutional theory. In: L.G. Zucker (ed.), *Research on Institutional Patterns: Environment and Culture* (pp. 3-22). Ballinger Publishing Co.

DiMaggio, P., & Powell, W.W. (1983). The iron cage revisited – Institutional isomorphism and collective rationality in organizational fields. *American Sociological Review*, 48(2), 147-160.

Donnelly, S., Ríos Camacho, E., & Heidebrecht, S. (2024). Digital sovereignty as control: The regulation of digital finance in the European Union. *Journal of European Public Policy*, 31(8), 2226-2249. https://doi.org/10.1080/13501763.2023.2295520

Erdélyi, O.J., & Goldsmith, J. (2018). Regulating artificial intelligence: Proposal for a global solution. In: *Proceedings of the 2018 AAAI/ACM Conference on AI, Ethics, and Society (AIES '18)* (pp. 95-101). Association for Computing Machinery. https://doi.org/10.1145/3278721.3278731

European Commission. (2021). *Digital Education Action Plan 2021–2027: Resetting Education and Training for the Digital Age*. https://education.ec.europa.eu/focus-topics/digital-education/action-plan

Farrand, B., & Carrapico, H. (2022). Digital sovereignty and taking back control: From regulatory capitalism to regulatory mercantilism in EU cybersecurity. *European Security*, 31(3), 435-453. https://doi.org/10.1080/09662839.2022.2102896

Fligstein, N., & McAdam, D. (2012). *A Theory of Fields*. Oxford University Press.

Flonk, D., Jachtenfuchs, M., & Obendiek, A. (2024). Controlling internet content in the EU: Towards digital sovereignty. *Journal of European Public Policy*, 31(8), 2316-2342. https://doi.org/10.1080/13501763.2024.2309179

Floridi, L. (2020). The fight for digital sovereignty: What it is, and why it matters, especially for the EU. *Philosophy and Technology*, 33(3), 369-378. https://doi.org/10.1007/s13347-020-00423-6

Fries, I., Greiner, M., Hofmeier, M., Hrestic, R., Lechner, U., &Wendeborn, T. (2023). Towards a layer model for digital sovereignty: A holistic approach. In: Hämmerli, B., Helmbrecht, U., Hommel, W., Kunczik, L., Pickl, S. (eds), *Critical Information Infrastructures Security*. CRITIS 2022. Lecture Notes in Computer Science, Vol 13723. Springer, Cham. https://doi.org/10.1007/978-3-031-35190-7_9

Gillespie, Tarleton. (2018). *Custodians of the Internet: Platforms, Content Moderation, and the Hidden Decisions that Shape Social Media*. 10.12987/9780300235029.

Gordon, G. (2024). Digital sovereignty, digital infrastructures, and quantum horizons. *AI and Society*, 39(1), 125-137. https://doi.org/10.1007/s00146-023-01729-7

Gstrein, O.J. (2023). Data autonomy: Recalibrating strategic autonomy and digital sovereignty. *European Foreign Affairs Review*, 28(4), 379-396. https://doi.org/10.54648/eerr2023028

Haq, M.Y.M., Abhishta, A., Sommese, R., Jonker, M., & Nieuwenhuis, L.J.M.(2023). Assessing network operator actions to enhance digital sovereignty and strengthen network resilience: A longitudinal analysis during the Russia-Ukraine conflict. In: *2023 IEEE European Symposium on Security and Privacy Workshops (EuroS&PW)*. IEEE. https://doi.org/10.48550/arXiv.2305.17666

Hardt, M., & Negri, A. (2000). *Empire*. Harvard University Press.

Hardt, M., & Negri, A. (2004). *Multitude: War and Democracy in the Age of Empire*. The Penguin Press.

Heermann, M. (2024). Undermining lobbying coalitions: The interest group politics of EU copyright reform. *Journal of European Public Policy*, 31(8), 2287-2315. https://doi.org/10.1080/13501763.2023.2249948

Hesselman, C., Grosso, P., Holz, R., Kuipers, F., Xue, J.H., Jonker, M. et al., (2020). A responsible Internet to increase trust in the digital world. *Journal of Network and Systems Management*, 28(4), 882-922. https://doi.org/10.1007/s10922-020-09564-7

Hobbes, T. (1962). *Leviathan, or, The Matter, Forme and Power of a Commonwealth, Ecclesiasticall and Civil* (R.S. Peters & M. Oakeshott, eds). Collier Books; Collier Macmillan Publishers.

Hoeffler, C., & Mérand, F. (2024). Digital sovereignty, economic ideas, and the struggle over the digital markets act: A political-cultural approach. *Journal of European Public Policy*, 31(8), 2121-2146. https://doi.org/10.1080/13501763.2023.2294144

Hoffmann-Riem, W. (2020). Artificial intelligence as a challenge for law and regulation. In: Wischmeyer, T., Rademacher, T. (eds), *Regulating Artificial Intelligence*. Springer, Cham. https://doi.org/10.1007/978-3-030-32361-5_1

Hulkó, G., Kálmán, J., & Lapsánszky, A. (2025). The politics of digital sovereignty and the European Union's legislation: Navigating crises. *Frontiers in Political Science*, 7, 1548562. https://doi.org/10.3389/fpos.2025.1548562

Kaloudis, M. (2022). Sovereignty in the digital age – How can we measure digital sovereignty and support the Eu's action plan? *New Global Studies*, 16(3), 275-299. https://doi.org/10.1515/ngs-2021-0015

Klare, M., Verlande, L., Greiner, M., & Lechner, U. (2023). How blockchain and artificial intelligence influence digital sovereignty. In: Papadaki, M., Rupino da Cunha, P., Themistocleous, M., Christodoulou, K. (eds), *Information Systems*. EMCIS 2022. Lecture Notes in Business Information Processing, vol 464. Springer, Cham. https://doi.org/10.1007/978-3-031-30694-5_1

Kugler, K., & Tavengerwei, R. (2024). Navigating digital sovereignty: Implications for African Countries. *Global Trade and Customs Journal*, 19(7-8), 1-13.

König, P., & Wenzelburger, G. (2020). Opportunity for renewal or disruptive force? How artificial intelligence alters democratic politics. *Government Information Quarterly*, 37, 101489. https://doi.org/10.1016/j.giq.2020.101489

Lawo, D., Neifer, T., Esau-Held, M., & Stevens, G. (2023). Digital sovereignty: What it is and why it matters for HCI. In: *Extended Abstracts of the 2023 CHI Conference on Human Factors in Computing Systems (CHI EA '23)* (Article 85, pp. 1–7). Association for Computing Machinery. https://doi.org/10.1145/3544549.3585834

Leese, M. (2024). Staying in control of technology: Predictive policing, democracy, and digital sovereignty. *Democratization*, 31(5), 963-978. https://doi.org/10.1080/13510347.2023.2197217

Markauskaite, L., & Goodyear, P. (2017). *Epistemic Fluency and Professional Education: Innovation, Knowledgeable Action And Actionable Knowledge* (Vol. 14). Springer. https://doi.org/10.1007/978-94-007-4369-4.

Meyer, J.W., & Rowan, B. (1977). Institutionalized organizations - Formal-structures as myth and ceremony. *American Journal of Sociology*, 83(2), 340-363.

Miao, F., & Cukurova, M. (2024). *AI Competency Framework for Teachers*. UNESCO.

Musiani, F. (2022). Infrastructuring digital sovereignty: A research agenda for an infrastructure-based sociology of digital self-determination practices. *Information Communication and Society*, 25(6), 785-800. https://doi.org/10.1080/1369118X.2022.2049850

Mügge, D. (2024). EU AI sovereignty: For whom, to what end, and to whose benefit? *Journal of European Public Policy*, 31(8), 2200-2225. https://doi.org/10.1080/13501763.2024.2318475

Ng, D.T.K., Leung, J.K.L., Chu, S.K.W., & Qiao, M.S. (2021). Conceptualizing AI literacy: An exploratory review. *Computers and Education: Artificial Intelligence*, 2, 100041. https://doi.org/https://doi.org/10.1016/j.caeai.2021.100041

OECD. (2019). *Recommendation of the Council on Artificial Intelligence*. Organization for Economic Co-operation and Development.

OECD. (2021). *AI and the Future of Skills*. Volume 1 OECD Publishing.

Pasquale, F. (2015). *The Black Box Society: The Secret Algorithms that Control Money and Information*. Harvard University Press.

Pierri, P., & Lüning, E.C. (2023). A democratic approach to digital rights: Comparing perspectives on digital sovereignty on the city level. *International Journal of Communication*, 17, 3600-3618.

Pohle, J., & Santaniello, M. (2024). From multistakeholderism to digital sovereignty: Toward a new discursive order in internet governance? *Policy and Internet*, 16(4), 672-691. https://doi.org/10.1002/poi3.426

Pohle, J., & Thiel, T. (2020). Digital sovereignty. *Internet Policy Review*, 9(4). https://doi.org/10.14763/2020.4.1532

Pohle, J., & Voelsen, D. (2022). Centrality and power. The struggle over the techno-political configuration of the Internet and the global digital order. *Policy and Internet*, 14(1), 13-27. https://doi.org/10.1002/poi3.296

Prasad, R. (2022). People as data, data as oil: The digital sovereignty of the Indian state.

Information Communication and Society, 25(6), 801-815. https://doi.org/10.1080/1369118X.2022.2056498

Rani, U., & Furrer, M. (2021). Digital labour platforms and new forms of flexible work in developing countries: Algorithmic management of work and workers. *Competition & Change*, 25(2), 212-236. https://doi.org/10.1177/1024529420905187

Roberts, H. (2024). Digital sovereignty and artificial intelligence: A normative approach. *Ethics and Information Technology*, 26(4), 70. https://doi.org/10.1007/s10676-024-09810-5

Roberts, H., Cowls, J., Casolari, F., Morley, J., Taddeo, M., & Floridi, L. (2021). Safeguarding European values with digital sovereignty: An analysis of statements and policies. *Internet Policy Review*, 10(3). https://doi.org/10.14763/2021.3.1575

Roberts, H., Hine, E., & Floridi, L. (2023). Digital sovereignty, digital expansionism, and the prospects for global AI governance. In: Timoteo, M., Verri, B., Nanni, R. (eds), *Quo Vadis, Sovereignty? Philosophical Studies Series*, Vol 154. Springer, Cham. https://doi.org/10.1007/978-3-031-41566-1_4

Rone, J. (2024). 'The sovereign cloud' in Europe: Diverging nation state preferences and disputed institutional competences in the context of limited technological capabilities. *Journal of European Public Policy*, 31(8), 2343-2369. https://doi.org/10.1080/13501763.2024.2348618

Sai, K., & Tipper, D. (2024). Gauging public interest in the digital sovereignty domain: A social sensor analysis. In: *2024 IEEE International Symposium on Technology and Society (ISTAS)* (pp. 1-8). IEEE. https://doi.org/10.1109/ISTAS61960.2024.10732608

Schmidt, V.A. (2008). Discursive institutionalism: The explanatory power of ideas and discourse. *Annual Review of Political Science*, 11, 303-326. https://doi.org/https://doi.org/10.1146/annurev.polisci.11.060606.135342

Schmitt, C. (2008). *Political Theology II: The Myth of the Closure of any Political Theology*. Polity.

Scott, W.R. (1995). *Institutions and Organizations*. Sage.

ten Oever, N., Perarnaud, C., Kristoff, J., Müller, M., Resing, M.,Filasto, A., & Kanich, C. (2024). Sanctions and infrastructural ideologies: Assessing the material shaping of EU digital sovereignty in response to the war in Ukraine. *Policy and Internet*, 16(4), 692-710. https://doi.org/10.1002/poi3.422

Thornton, P.H., Ocasio, W., & Lounsbury, M. (2012). *The Institutional Logics Perspective: A New Approach to Culture, Structure, and Process*. Oxford University Press.

UNESCO. (2021). *Recommendation on the Ethics of Artificial Intelligence*. United Nations Educational, Scientific and Cultural Organization.

Weinreuter, M., Alpers, S., & Oberweis, A. (2023). Method for eliciting requirements in the area of digital sovereignty (MERDigS). In: Yang, X.S., Sherratt, R.S., Dey, N., Joshi, A. (eds), *Proceedings of Eighth International Congress on Information and Communication Technology*. ICICT 2023. Lecture Notes in Networks and Systems, Vol 693. Springer, Singapore. https://doi.org/10.1007/978-981-99-3243-6_76

Wessel, D., Claudy, S., Hanke, K., Herzog, C., Preiß, R., Wegner, C., & Heine, M. (2022). Prototypes for e-government websites to support the digital sovereignty of citizens. In: *Proceedings of Mensch und Computer 2022 (MuC '22)* (pp. 615-617). Association for Computing Machinery. https://doi.org/10.1145/3543758.3547514

Woods, Andrew Keane. (2023). Digital Sovereignty + Artificial Intelligence. In: Anupam Chander, and Haochen Sun (eds), *Data Sovereignty: From the Digital Silk Road to the Return of the State* (New York, 2023; online edn, Oxford Academic, 14 Dec. 2023), https://doi.org/10.1093/oso/9780197582794.003.0006.

Zuboff, S. (2019). *The Age of Surveillance Capitalism: The Fight for the Future at the New Frontier of Power*. Profile Books PublicAffairs.

CHAPTER
3

Trustworthy AI in Safety-Critical Systems: Toward Robustness, Adversarial Resilience, and Uncertainty-Aware Intelligence

Ferhat Ozgur Catak[*(0000-0002-2434-9966)] **and Jungwon Seo**[(0000-0001-8174-9352)]
[1] University of Stavanger, Rogaland, Norway

3.1 Introduction

With the continuous advancement of AI technology, its application has expanded from domains where errors carry relatively minor consequences to those where erroneous decisions may result in critical failures, safety hazards, or significant societal impacts. These high-stakes domains include 6G communication, autonomous driving, healthcare, and cyber defense (Abdel Hakeem et al., 2022; Begoli et al., 2019; Gao et al., 2021; Guembe et al., 2022, Kumar et al., 2025).

In the former case, even an imperfect recommendation typically remains preferable to a random choice, and the impact of mistakes is limited. In contrast, in high-stakes domains, the cost of a wrong decision can be severe or even catastrophic (Thudumu et al., 2020).

As AI becomes increasingly embedded in safety-critical systems, ensuring that these technologies are trustworthy is paramount. Trustworthy AI is characterized not only by high predictive performance, but also by robustness to unexpected scenarios, resilience to adversarial manipulation, and the ability to appropriately quantify and communicate uncertainty (Li et al., 2023, Abdar et al., 2021). In these contexts, the stakes are such that users and stakeholders must have confidence that AI systems will operate reliably, safely, and transparently.

At this stage, inadequate model performance is no longer the main obstacle to deploying AI in high-impact settings. Advances in training methodologies, data processing techniques, and hardware capabilities have enabled large-scale neural

*Corresponding author: f.ozgur.catak@uis.no

DOI: 10.1201/9781003581581-3

network models (e.g., large language models) to achieve human-level performance on many benchmark tasks (Jones, 2024). However, unlike traditional IT systems, AI research has historically prioritized improving model performance and expanding the diversity of tasks to which AI can be applied. Consequently, issues unique to AI, such as adversarial vulnerabilities and the quantification of predictive uncertainty, have received comparatively less attention (Pelekis et al., 2025, Biggio et al., 2018, Akhtar et al., 2018).

For example, consider a computer vision system for autonomous vehicles that achieves near-perfect accuracy on standard datasets. If a malicious actor were to place a carefully crafted sticker on a traffic sign the vehicle might make a dangerous misclassification, potentially leading to serious accidents (Eykholt et al., 2018). Similarly, in healthcare, an AI-based diagnostic system may provide predictions without quantifying its confidence, making it difficult to judge the reliability of its recommendations in ambiguous or novel cases (Begoli et al., 2019).

Framing AI robustness and uncertainty awareness within established ethical and regulatory paradigms is essential for safety-critical domains. 'Trustworthy AI' extends beyond algorithmic soundness to include adherence to principles such as beneficence, non-maleficence, justice, and respect for human autonomy (Cohen et al., 2020). In highly regulated areas, such as medical diagnosis, autonomous transport, or critical communications, developers must align the model behavior with domain-specific laws and guidelines. By explicitly mapping technical safeguards (i.e. robust training, uncertainty quantification) onto these frameworks, practitioners can demonstrate both ethical integrity and legal compliance. This ensures that trustworthy AI systems are not only technically resilient but also socially and legally accountable throughout their lifecycle—from design through deployment.

We introduce core methodologies for both attacking and defending AI models against adversarial threats drawing on prior work (Carlini and Wagner, 2017; Goodfellow et al., 2015), as well as techniques for understanding and quantifying model uncertainty. We discuss representative adversarial attack strategies and robust defense mechanisms and explain why uncertainty quantification is critical for deploying trustworthy AI in safety critical domains. Furthermore, we present case studies illustrating these concepts in practice, including adversarial attacks for spectrum sensing in 6G communication systems, and uncertainty quantification for large language model responses (Saad et al., 2020). Through these examples, we highlight practical challenges and solutions for enhancing the reliability and safety of modern AI systems.

To help readers from varied backgrounds, we briefly define several foundational concepts used throughout this chapter. An adversarial attack refers to a deliberate perturbation of input data crafted to induce erroneous model predictions. In response, adversarial defenses encompass strategies that harden models against these manipulations, ensuring reliable performance even under hostile perturbations (Yuan et al., 2019).

Equally important is uncertainty quantification, the process of estimating a model's confidence or the quality of its predictions. Techniques such as deep ensembles aggregate outputs from multiple independently trained networks to capture epistemic uncertainty. In contrast,the convex hull metric assesses how far a new feature representation lies outside the convex hull of training data, thereby signaling out-of-distribution risk. These methods provide calibrated confidence estimates that can trigger human review or safe-fail protocols when model certainty falls below prescribed thresholds.

The remainder of this chapter is organized as follows. Section 2 reviews the fundamental principles of adversarial attacks and defense strategies in AI models introducing key concepts and practical approaches to uncertainty quantification, and underscoring their importance for trustworthy AI deployment. Section 3 presents real-world case studies that illustrate the challenges and solutions associated with adversarial robustness and uncertainty quantification. Finally, Section 4 synthesizes the main findings and explores future directions for advancing reliable and ethical AI within the broader framework of trustworthiness. The contributions in this chapter are as follows:

- A comprehensive overview of adversarial attack strategies and robust defense mechanisms for AI models have been provided focussing on safety-critical applications.
- Key concepts and practical techniques have been introduced for uncertainty quantification in AI, emphasizing their importance for trustworthy system deployment.
- Two practical case studies (i.e. spectrum sensing in 6G communication systems and large language model responses on the MATH 500 dataset) have been presented to illustrate real-world challenges and solutions related to adversarial robustness and uncertainty quantification.

3.2 Background

This section reviews adversarial attacks and defenses, building on existing literature.

3.2.1 Adversarial Attacks

Adversarial attacks intentionally create perturbations imperceptible to humans yet are highly effective to induce erroneous predictions in deep neural networks. Formally, let $f\colon R^d \rightarrow Y$ be a classifier, $x \in R^d$ be a clean input with label y, and $\epsilon > 0$ a perturbation budget under a norm $| \cdot |_p$. An adversarial example is a point x^{adv} that satisfies

$$|x^{\text{adv}} - x|_p \leq \epsilon, \text{ and } f(x^{\text{adv}}) \neq y.$$

Notation 1: Throughout, $\nabla_x L(f(x), y)$ denotes the loss gradient with respect to the input, $\text{proj}_{B_p}(x, \epsilon)$ is the projection onto the p norm ball $B_p(x, \epsilon) = z \; |z - x|_p \leq \epsilon$, and $\text{sgn}(\cdot)$ is the element-wise sign function. Unless stated otherwise, we adopt the ℓ_∞ threat model.

3.2.1.1 Perturbation Norms and ℓ_p-Balls

Before looking at concrete attack algorithms, it helps to formalize the region in which an adversary is allowed to operate. Given a clean input $x \in R^d$, we say that an adversary is ϵ-bounded in the ℓ_p sense if every candidate adversarial point z must lie inside the ℓ_p-ball

$$B_p(x, \epsilon) = \{z \in R^d \mid \|z - x\|_p \leq \epsilon\}.$$

Any perturbation $\delta = z - x$ that remains in this set is called admissible. The choice of the norm p and the radius ϵ jointly determines how much freedom the attacker has.

The geometry of B_p changes with p: for $p = 2$ it is the familiar hypersphere; for $p = \infty$ it becomes an axis-aligned hypercube, each coordinate limited to $\pm\epsilon$; for $p = 1$ it assumes a diamond-shaped shape (an ℓ_1 octahedron in higher dimensions). Although these shapes look quite different, the conceptual role of the ball is the same: It encloses all inputs that are 'close enough' to x in the chosen measure. In two dimensions the difference is easy to imagine: a circle, a square and a diamond of the same 'radius' ϵ share the same center but enclose different areas.

Figure 3.1 translates the algebraic definition of $B_p(x, \epsilon)$ into three transparent shells in 3-D space. All balls share the same center x and radius $\epsilon = 1$, yet their geometry differs markedly: the ℓ_2 ball is a smooth sphere, the ℓ_∞ ball encloses the same center in a cube whose faces sit exactly ϵ units away in each coordinate direction, and the ℓ_1 ball forms an octahedron whose six tips touch the axes at distance ϵ. The arrows emphasize that, regardless of norm, the farthest an adversary may push x along any axis is still ϵ; what changes is the set of combined perturbations allowed when multiple coordinates vary simultaneously. Visualizing the shapes side-by-side makes it clear why "robust in ℓ_∞" is the strictest criterion: the cube fits entirely inside the sphere, which in turn fits inside the octahedron.

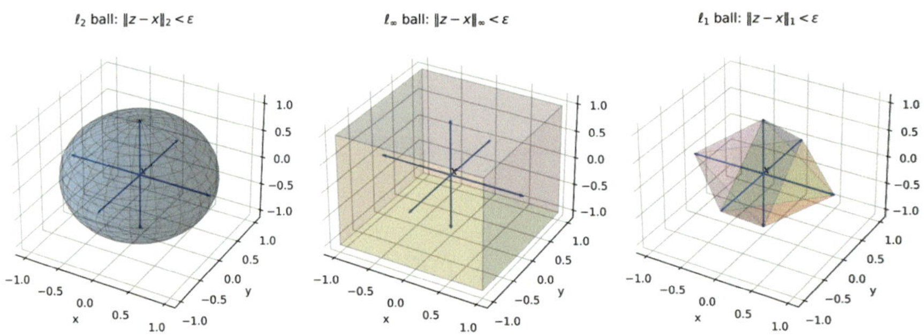

(a) ℓ_2 ball (b) ℓ_∞ ball (c) ℓ_1 ball

Figure 3.1. Three-dimensional visualization of ℓ_p admissible regions (centered at x with radius $\epsilon = 1$). Each ball illustrates how the same perturbation budget produces a sphere ($p = 2$), a cube ($p \to \infty$), or an octahedron ($p = 1$). Arrows indicate the maximum displacement along the coordinate axes.

If no limit were imposed, an adversary could trivially force misclassification by replacing x with any arbitrary image. Bounding the perturbation ensures two things: (1) the corrupted input remains perceptually or semantically similar to the original, so a human would still recognize it as the same object, and (2) the bound establishes a common threat model for researchers to compare defenses quantitatively. On 8-bit images that are rescaled to the unit interval, the community often uses $\epsilon = 255^{2}, 255^{4},$ or 255^{8} under the ℓ_∞ norm. These values correspond to perturbations of at most 2, 4, or 8 grey-levels per pixel and strike a balance between *imperceptibility* to humans and *attack success*. When switching to the ℓ_2 norm, one typically rescales the radius so that the *average* per-pixel change is similar; in practice an ℓ_2 radius of about 1.0 for a 32×32 image is roughly on par with $\epsilon = 8/255$ in ℓ_∞.

For a fixed ϵ, the ℓ_∞ ball is the smallest and the ℓ_1 ball the largest. Mathematically, $B_\infty(x, \epsilon) \subseteq B_2(x, \epsilon) \subseteq B_1(x, \epsilon)$. Robustness in ℓ_∞ therefore implies robustness in ℓ_2 and ℓ_1 at the same radius, but not vice-versa.

Many attacks generate adversarial examples through a sequence of small gradient steps. To ensure each intermediate point remains admissible, we apply the projector

$$\text{proj}_{B_p(x,\epsilon)}(z) = \arg\min_{u \in B_p(x,\epsilon)} \| u - z\|_2.$$

Closed-form projectors exist for $p \in \{1, 2, \infty\}$, and will appear in the pseudocode of later sections.

3.2.1.2 Fast Gradient Sign Method (FGSM)

Key idea (2015) (Goodfellow et al., 2015): linearize the loss locally and take a single step in the sign direction of the gradient.

$$x^{\text{adv}} = x + \epsilon \cdot \text{sgn}\,(\nabla_x \mathcal{L}(f(x), y)). \tag{1}$$

FGSM is computationally inexpensive (one forward–backward pass) but generally less effective against adversarially trained models.

Algorithm 3.1. FGSM Generation

```
Require: Clean input x, label y, model f, loss 𝓛, perturbation budget ϵ
g ← ∇_x 𝓛(f(x), y)                                 ▷ Back-propagation
x^adv ← x + ϵ, sgn(g)
return clip_[0,1]^d(x^adv)
```

Figure 3.2 offers both geometric and optimization perspectives on FGSM. Subfigure (a) depicts a three-dimensional quadratic loss bowl, with the clean input x lies on its surface. A single FGSM step of size ϵ, moves it to x_{adv} located at the edge of the admissible ℓ_∞ cube (only the $+x$ axis is shown for clarity). Panel (b) illustrates the same concept in two dimensions: level curves of the loss, a dashed ℓ_∞ square of radius ϵ, and two arrows—one indicating the raw gradient direction, the other the signed FGSM step. Together, the plots highlight that FGSM performs an axis-aligned move that maximizes the loss while adhering to the per-pixel budget.

3.2.1.3 Basic Iterative Method (BIM)/Iterative FGSM

Building on FGSM, the Basic Iterative Method (BIM), also called I-FGSM, applies multiple small FGSM steps and projects back into the allowed ℓ_∞ ball at each iteration. Introduced by Kurakin et al. (2018), it is defined as follows:

$$x_0^{\text{adv}} = x,\; x_{t+1}^{\text{adv}} = \text{Proj}_{B_\infty(x,\epsilon)}\,(x_t^{\text{adv}} + \alpha\,\text{sign}\,(\nabla_{x_t^{\text{adv}}} \mathcal{L}(f(x_t^{\text{adv}}), y))), \tag{2}$$

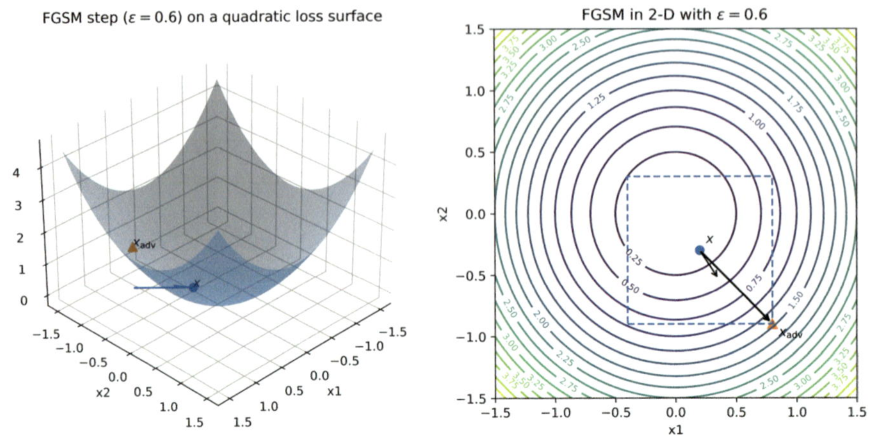

(a) 3-D loss surface (b) 2-D contour view

Figure 3.2. Illustration of a single FGSM step ($\epsilon = 0.6$) on a simple quadratic loss. The gradient arrow (thin) indicates the steepest ascent direction, while the thicker arrow shows the discretized sign (∇_L) step that lands exactly on the boundary of the ℓ_∞ ball.

where

$$\mathrm{Proj}_{B_\infty(x,\epsilon)}(z) = \min(\max(z, x - \epsilon), x + \epsilon)$$

clips each coordinate of z into the interval $[x_i - \epsilon, x_i + \epsilon]$. Typically, one chooses a small step size $\alpha << \epsilon$ and repeats it for T iterations, yielding a stronger attack than the single-step FGSM.

Algorithm 3.2. Basic Iterative Method (BIM)/I-FGSM

Require: Clean input x, label y, model f, loss $\mathcal{L}$, budget ϵ, step size α, iterations T
Ensure: Adversarial example x_T^{adv}

$x_0^{\mathrm{adv}} \leftarrow x$
for $t = 0, \ldots, T-1$ **do**
    $g \leftarrow \nabla_{x_t^{\mathrm{adv}}} \mathcal{L}(f(x_t^{\mathrm{adv}}), y)$
    $x' \leftarrow x_t^{\mathrm{adv}} + \alpha\, \mathrm{sign}(g)$
    $x_{t+1}^{\mathrm{adv}} \leftarrow \mathrm{Proj}_{\mathcal{B}_\infty(x,\epsilon)}(x')$
end for
return x_T^{adv}

Key points:

- By taking $T > 1$ small step of size α, BIM finds more precise adversarial perturbations than FGSM's one-step jump.
- The projection step ensures $\| x_t^{\mathrm{adv}} - x \|_\infty \leq \epsilon$ at every iteration.
- BIM often serves as a baseline for stronger attacks (e.g. PGD) and for evaluating robustness of defended models.

Figure 3.3 visualizes the Basic Iterative Method (BIM/I-FGSM) on the same quadratic loss surface used for the FGSM. Panel (a) shows the 3-D loss bowl, with the clean input x marked in blue. Each arrow represents one BIM step of size $\alpha = 0.15$, always moving along the sign of the gradient and then clipping back into the ℓ_∞ ball of radius $\epsilon = 0.6$. After $T = 4$ iterations the adversarial example $x_{\text{adv}}{}^T$ (red triangle) lies on the boundary of the admissible region. Panel (b) is the 2-D contour view: the dashed square indicates the same $_{\ell\infty}$ constraint around x, while the purple line shows the successive iterates converging to $x_{\text{adv}}{}^T$. Together, these plots highlight how BIM refines FGSM's single step jump into a sequence of smaller, cumulative perturbations that more precisely maximize the loss under the perturbation budget.

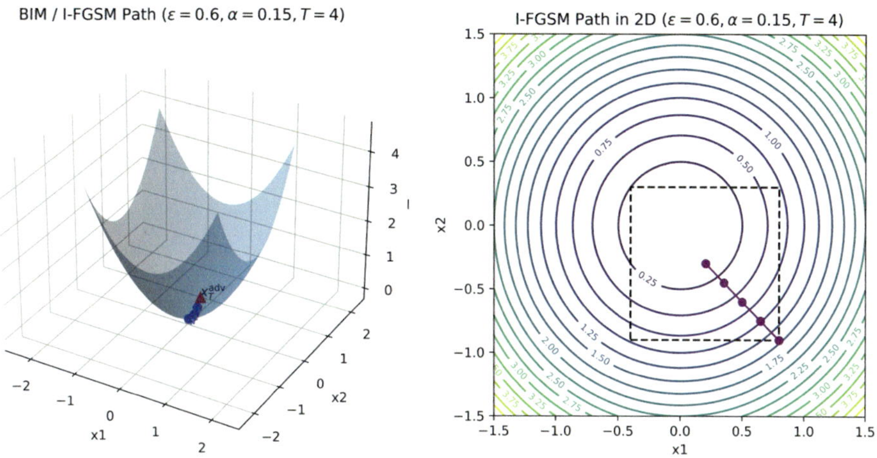

(a) 3-D BIM path

(b) 2-D contour path

Figure 3.3. Illustration of the BIM/I-FGSM algorithm on a simple quadratic loss. Starting from x, each step follows sign(∇_L) scaled by α, then projects into the ℓ_∞ ball ($\epsilon = 0.6$). (a) shows steps as arrows on the 3-D surface; (b) overlays the iterates on level curves with the admissible square.

3.2.1.4 Projected Gradient Descent (PGD)

PGD and extends the Basic Iterative Method by adding random restarts inside the perturbation ball, seeking the worst-case point under the same ℓ_∞ budget. At each restart, an initial $x_{\text{adv}0}$ is sampled uniformly from $B_{\infty(x,\,\epsilon)}$, followed by T iterations of optimization,

$$x_{t+1}^{\text{adv}} = \text{Proj}_{B\infty(x,\epsilon)}\,(x_t^{\text{adv}} + \alpha\ \text{sign}(\nabla_{x_t^{\text{adv}}}\mathcal{L}(f(x_t^{\text{adv}}), y))).$$

By repeating this process R times with different random starts and taking the example that maximizes the loss, PGD approximates the strongest first–order attack under the ℓ_∞ threat model (Madry et al., 2017). In practice, $R = 1$ already outperforms BIM, and modest $R \geq 5$ suffices to saturate many defenses.

Algorithm 3.3. Projected Gradient Descent (PGD)

Require: Clean input x, label y, model f, loss $\mathcal{L}$, budget ϵ, step size α, iterations T, restarts R

Ensure: Strong adversarial example $x^{\text{adv}}_{\text{best}}$

```
ℓ_max ← −∞
for r = 1, ..., R do
    Sample x_0^adv ~ U(B_∞(x, ε))
    for t = 0, ..., T − 1 do
        g ← ∇_{x_t^adv} L(f(x_t^adv), y)
        x' ← x_t^adv + α sign(g)
        x_{t+1}^adv ← Proj_{B_∞(x,ε)}(x')
    end for
    ℓ_r ← L(f(x_T^adv), y)
    if ℓ_r > ℓ_max then
        ℓ_max ← ℓ_r
        x_best^adv ← x_T^adv
    end if
end for
return x_best^adv
```

At each R random restart, PGD begins by sampling an initial point uniformly within the ℓ_∞-ball of radius ϵ around the clean input. Perform T iterations of gradient-sign ascent with step size α, projecting back into the admissible ball after each step to enforce the perturbation constraint. After completing T steps, it evaluates the loss; if this restart yields the highest loss observed so far, its endpoint becomes the current best adversarial example. By exploring multiple initializations, PGD approximates the worst-case perturbation within the same budget, making it a more powerful attack than single-start iterative methods.

Figure 3.4 visualizes a single PGD run with $R = 5$ random restarts. Panel (a) shows the 3-D loss surface: the blue dot is the chosen random start, and each magenta arrow is one PGD iteration, clipped back into the ℓ_∞ ball around x. The red triangle marks the final adversarial example from the restart that reached the highest loss. Panel (b) displays the same trajectory on 2-D level curves with the dashed square denoting the ℓ_∞ constraint. These plots illustrate how PGD leverages multiple initializations to escape local maxima and find a stronger attack than BIM or FGSM alone.

3.2.1.5 Momentum Iterative Method (MIM)

The Momentum Iterative Method (MIM) enhances BIM by accumulating a decayed sum of past gradients, allowing the attack to escape poor local maxima and improving both white-box strength and transferability to other models (Dong et al., 2018). At iteration t, MIM updates:

$$g_{t+1} = \mu g_t + \frac{(\nabla x_t^{\text{adv}} \mathcal{L})(f(x_t^{\text{adv}}), y)}{|\nabla x_t^{adv} \mathcal{L}(f(x_t^{adv}), y)|_1}, \quad x_{t+1}^{\text{adv}} = \text{Proj}_{B\infty(x,\epsilon)}!\,(x_t^{\text{adv}} + \alpha\, \text{sign}(g_{t+1})),$$

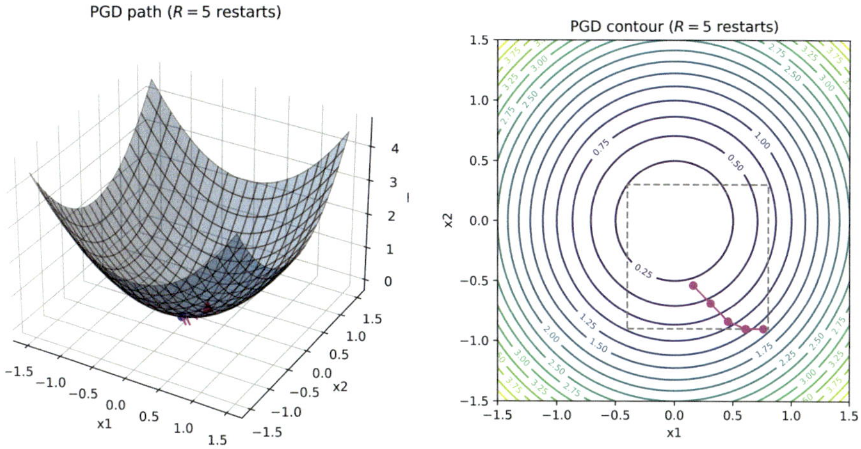

(a) 3-D PGD path

(b) 2-D contour PGD

Figure 3.4. Visualization of PGD with random restarts ($\epsilon = 0.6, \alpha = 0.15, T = 4, R = 5$). Multiple starting points are drawn, but only the trajectory yielding maximal final loss (magenta) is shown in each panel.

where $\mu \in [0,1)$ is the momentum decay (often 0.9), and the gradient is normalized by its ℓ_1-norm. This momentum term smooths the update direction over iterations, yielding more stable and transferable adversarial examples.

Algorithm 3.4. Momentum Iterative Method (MIM)

Require: Clean input x, label y, model f, loss $\mathcal{L}$, budget ϵ, step size α, momentum μ, iterations T

Ensure: Adversarial example x_T^{adv}

$x_0^{\text{adv}} \leftarrow x, \quad g_0 \leftarrow 0$

for $t = 0, \ldots, T-1$ **do**

  $u \leftarrow \nabla_{x_t^{\text{adv}}} \mathcal{L}(f(x_t^{\text{adv}}), y)$

  $u \leftarrow u / \|u\|_1$ ▷ Normalize by ℓ_1 norm

  $g_{t+1} \leftarrow \mu\, g_t + u$

  $x' \leftarrow x_t^{\text{adv}} + \alpha\, \text{sign}(g_{t+1})$

  $x_{t+1}^{\text{adv}} \leftarrow \text{Proj}_{\mathcal{B}_\infty(x,\epsilon)}(x')$

end for

return x_T^{adv}

Algorithm 3.4 describes the Momentum Iterative Method (MIM). Starting from the clean input, MIM maintains a momentum term g_t that accumulates a decayed, normalized gradient direction at each step. Specifically, it first computes the loss gradient u, normalizes it by its ℓ_1 norm, then updates the momentum via $g_{t+1} = \mu g_t + u$. The adversarial example is advanced by a signed step of size α along this momentum vector, followed by projection back into the ℓ_∞ ball of radius ϵ. By smoothing the update direction over iterations, MIM (with typical decay $\mu = 0.9$) yields more stable and highly transferable adversarial perturbations compared to standard iterative attacks.

Figure 3.5 demonstrates how MIM smooths and accelerates the attack trajectory compared to BIM. In panel (a), the 3-D loss surface shows the green line of successive iterates, beginning at the blue dot and ending at the red triangle after $T = 6$ steps.

Panel (b) projects these iterates onto level curves, with the dashed square indicating the ℓ_∞ region. The momentum term ($\mu = 0.9$) smooths the update direction, enabling the attack to build up velocity and reach higher-loss regions more quickly than standard iterative methods.

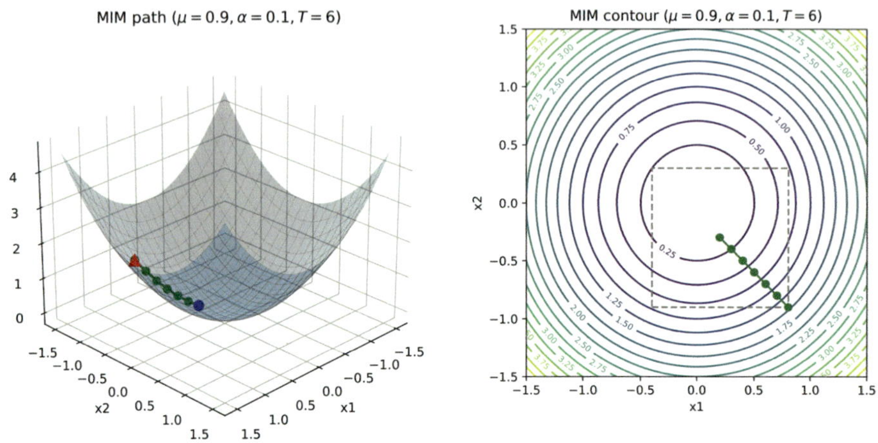

(a) 3-D MIM trajectory (b) 2-D contour MIM

Figure 3.5. Visualization of the Momentum Iterative Method (MIM) on a quadratic loss ($\epsilon = 0.6$, $\alpha = 0.1$, $\mu = 0.9$, $T = 6$). Both views show how momentum-guided updates (green) traverse directly toward high-loss regions under the ℓ_∞ constraint.

3.2.2 Mitigation Methods/Defense Mechanisms

To counteract adversarial attacks, several classes of defenses have been proposed:

3.2.2.1 Adversarial Training

In many safety-critical applications, a model's decision surface can exhibit intricate oscillations that an adversary can exploit with imperceptible perturbations. Adversarial training directly addresses this by teaching the model to withstand its own worst-case inputs (Goodfellow et al., 2015). At each training iteration, rather than minimizing the clean loss alone, one first searches (via an inner maximization) for a small perturbation that maximizes the loss and then updates the model parameters to correctly classify even this "hardest" example. Figure 3.6 shows the adversarial training-based defense pipeline steps.

Figure 3.6. Flowchart of the adversarial defense pipeline.

Formally, let θ denote the network parameters, and $f(x; \theta)$ its prediction on input x. The training objective becomes the saddle-point problem

$$\min_{\theta} E_{(x,y)\sim\mathbb{D}} \underbrace{[\max_{|\delta|p\leq\epsilon} \mathcal{L}(f(x+\delta;\theta),y)]}_{\text{inner (adversarial) loss}}.$$

Here, ϵ bounds the adversary's perturbation under an ℓ_p norm, ensuring that $x + \delta$ remains perceptually like the clean input. While the outer minimization adjusts θ to reduce risk, the inner maximization simulates the strongest possible attack within the allowed budget.

Key Steps in Adversarial Training

(1) *Inner maximization (attack generation):* Starting from $\boldsymbol{\delta}_0 = 0$, repeat K steps of projected gradient ascent:

$$\delta_{k+1} = \text{Proj}_{|\delta|p\leq\epsilon}(\delta_k + \alpha\,\text{sign}(\nabla_\delta \mathcal{L}(f(x+\delta_k;\theta), y))).$$

At the end, set the adversarial example $x^{\text{adv}} = x + \delta_K$.

(2) *Outer minimization (parameter update):* Replace each clean example with its adversarial counterpart, and perform a standard gradient step:

$$\theta \leftarrow \theta - \eta\nabla_\theta\left[\frac{1}{|B|}\sum_{(x^{\text{adv}},\,y)\in B} \mathcal{L}(f(x^{\text{adv}};\theta),y)\right].$$

Algorithm 3.5. Adversarial Training

Require: Dataset $\{(x_i, y_i)\}_{i=1}^{N}$, model $f(\cdot;\theta)$, loss $\mathcal{L}$, budget ϵ, inner steps K, inner step size α, outer rate η

for each minibatch $\mathcal{B} \subset \{1, \ldots, N\}$ **do**
  for each (x, y) in $\mathcal{B}$ **do**
    $\delta \leftarrow 0$
    for $k = 1$ to K **do**
      $g \leftarrow \nabla_\delta \mathcal{L}(f(x+\delta;\theta), y)$
      $\delta \leftarrow \text{Proj}_{\|\delta\|_p\leq\epsilon}(\delta + \alpha\,\text{sign}(g))$
    end for
    $x^{\text{adv}} \leftarrow x + \delta$
  end for
  $\theta \leftarrow \theta - \eta\nabla_\theta\left[\frac{1}{|\mathcal{B}|}\sum \mathcal{L}(f(x^{\text{adv}};\theta), y)\right]$
end for

Why Adversarial Training Works: By explicitly minimizing the highest loss reachable within an ℓ_p-ball around each training input, the network learns to "flatten" sharp peaks in its loss landscape. Intuitively, the model no longer relies on finely-tuned, high frequency wrinkles in the decision boundary but instead adopts smoother, more robust surfaces.

Illustrative Example: Figure 3.7 visualizes this effect on a toy 2-D classification task. Each panel shows contour regions of an illustrative loss surface, overlaid with the learned binary decision boundary (dashed line) and two clusters of sample points.

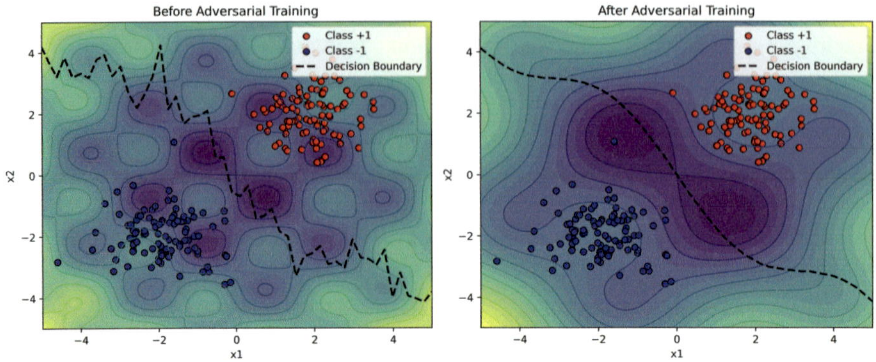

Figure 3.7. Toy binary classification boundary before (left) and after (right) adversarial training. Note how the minimax objective smooths out high-frequency oscillations in the decision surface.

- *Before Adversarial Training (left):* The boundary oscillates rapidly to carve out each class, yielding a highly non-linear, wiggly separator.
- *After Adversarial Training (right):* Those oscillations are smoothed away, producing a simpler curve that generalizes better under small input perturbations.

Trade-offs and Practical Tips: Adversarial training is among the most effective defenses against first-order attacks, but it incurs a computational cost roughly K-fold higher than standard training. Typical choices (i.e. ℓ_∞-threat, $K = 7$–10 steps, $\alpha = 2\epsilon/K$) strike a balance between robustness and training time. Recent advances (e.g. *fast adversarial training*) reduce this overhead by approximating or randomizing the inner maximization.

3.2.2.2 Defensive Distillation

Defensive distillation (Papernot and McDaniel, 2016) is a two-stage training scheme that transfers "dark knowledge" from a high-capacity teacher to a student model by leveraging softened class probabilities. Rather than exposing the student directly to hard one-hot labels, distillation uses the teacher's information on inter-class similarity, encoded in its temperature-scaled SoftMax outputs, to encourage smoother, more robust decision surfaces.

(1) Teacher Training: Train a teacher network f_T on the original dataset $\{(x_i, y_i)\}$ but replace the usual SoftMax with a high temperature $T \gg 1$. Let the teacher's logits be

$$z_T(x) = [z_{T,1}(x), \ldots, z_{T,C}(x)] \in R^C,$$

then its *soft labels* are

$$p_T(y = k \mid x) = \frac{\exp(z_{T,k}(x)/T)}{\sum_{j=1}^{C} \exp(z_{T,j}(x)/T)}.$$

A large T produces a "flatter" probability vector, revealing which classes the teacher considers similar.

(2) Student Training: Fix the teacher's parameters. The student network f_S is trained to minimize a weighted combination of two cross-entropies:

$$\mathcal{L}_{\text{distill}} = (1-\lambda)\underbrace{\left[-\sum_{k=1}^{C} y_k \log p_S(y=k \mid x; T=1)\right]}_{\text{hard-label loss}} + \lambda T^2 \underbrace{\left[-\sum_{k=1}^{c} p_T(y=k \mid x; T) \log p_S(y=k \mid x; T)\right]}_{\text{soft-label loss}}$$

where $p_S(\cdot \mid x; T)$ is the student's SoftMax at temperature T, and $\lambda \in [0, 1]$ balances the two terms. In practice one often sets $\lambda = 1$ during distillation, then discards the hard-label term.

Algorithm 3.6. Defensive Distillation

Require: Dataset $\{(x_i, y_i)\}_{i=1}^{N}$, temperatures $T \gg 1$, $\lambda \in [0,1]$, learning rate η

▷ Stage 1: Train teacher

Initialize teacher parameters θ_T
for each minibatch $\mathcal{B}$ **do**
  Compute logits $z_T(x)$, soft labels $p_T(y \mid x) = \text{softmax}(z_T(x)/T)$
  $\theta_T \leftarrow \theta_T - \eta \nabla_{\theta_T}\left[-\sum_{(x,y)\in\mathcal{B}} y^\top \log p_T(y \mid x)\right]$
end for

▷ Stage 2: Train student on teacher's soft labels

Initialize student parameters θ_S
for each minibatch $\mathcal{B}$ **do**
  $p_T(y \mid x)$ from fixed teacher
  Student's outputs: $q_{\text{hard}}(x) = \text{softmax}(z_S(x))$, $q_{\text{soft}}(x) = \text{softmax}(z_S(x)/T)$
  Compute loss

$$\mathcal{L} = (1-\lambda)\left[-y^\top \log q_{\text{hard}}(x)\right] + \lambda\left[-p_T(y \mid x)^\top \log q_{\text{soft}}(x)\right]$$

  $\theta_S \leftarrow \theta_S - \eta \nabla_{\theta_S}\mathcal{L}$
end for
return student parameters θ_S

Figure 3.8 summarizes this workflow. The upper pane shows the teacher's network producing temperature-scaled SoftMax outputs ("soft labels"). These, together with the original hard labels, feed into the distillation loss. The lower pane depicts the student model being trained to mimic both the teacher's softened distributions (at $T \gg 1$) and the ground-truth labels, then deploying a crisp SoftMax ($T = 1$) at inference.

By concentrating on the teacher's inter-class probability structure rather than only the hard labels, the student learns smoother gradients and decision surfaces, improving its resilience against small, gradient-based adversarial perturbations.

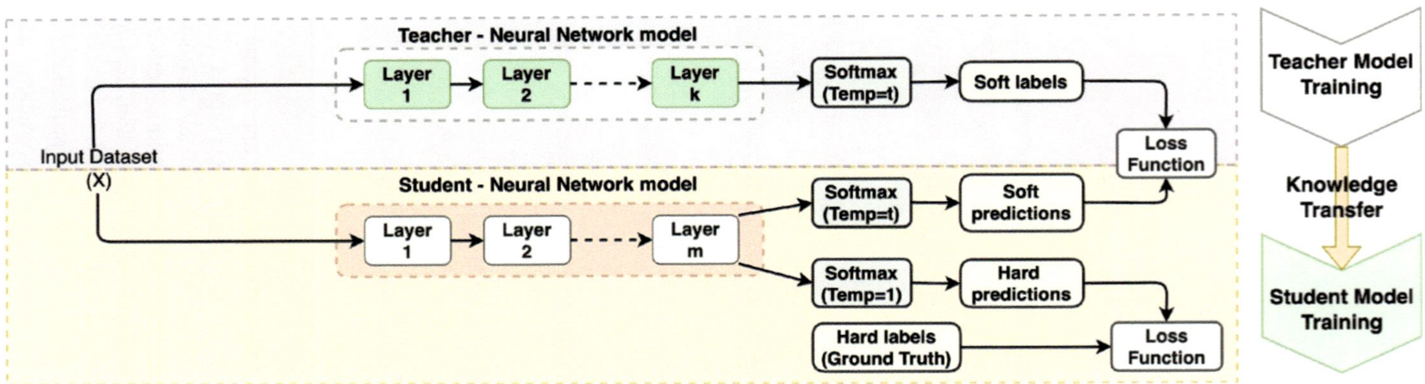

Figure 3.8. Defensive distillation: Knowledge flows from teacher logits through a high-temperature SoftMax to produce soft labels, which then guide student training alongside ground truth.

3.2.3 Uncertainty Quantification in Deep Learning

Modern deep neural networks achieve remarkable accuracy, but their deterministic point-estimate predictions often lack any measure of confidence. This subsection explores why uncertainty arises in deep learning, its sources and consequences, how to quantify it, and strategies to mitigate overconfidence.

3.2.3.1 Why Does Uncertainty Exist? Sources and Problems

Deep models face two fundamental types of uncertainties:

- **Aleatoric uncertainty (data noise):** Refers to the inherent randomness in the data generation process, such as sensor noise or label ambiguity. This type of uncertainty is irreducible and cannot be mitigated by collecting additional data.
- **Epistemic uncertainty (model uncertainty):** Stems from limited knowledge about the true data distribution or model parameters. It arises due to insufficient training data or imperfect model specification and can be reduced through additional data or improved priors.

Figure 3.9 illustrates a simple regression task designed to separate aleatoric (data) uncertainty from epistemic (model) uncertainty. The accompanying Python code first generates noisy observations of the sine function on $[-4,4]$ with heteroscedastic noise (higher variance for $x < 0$), and then defines a predictive mean $\sin(x)$. Aleatoric uncertainty is depicted by a semi-transparent band around the mean whose half-width $\sigma_a(x)$ matches the input-dependent noise level, while total uncertainty combines $\sigma_a(x)$ with an epistemic term $\sigma_e(x)$ that grows outside the training domain. Vertical dashed lines at $x = -4,0,4$ partition the input into four regions each labelled accordingly. This visualization highlights how a model's uncertainty decomposes into irreducible data noise and parameter uncertainty in regions with or without training data.

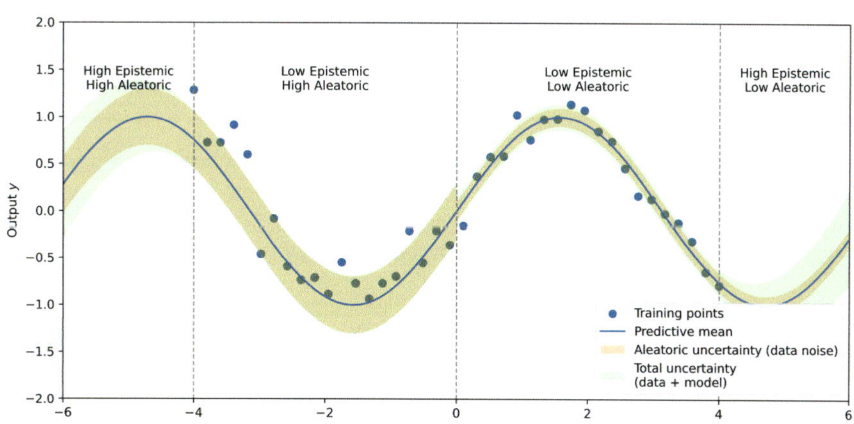

Figure 3.9. Regression example showing aleatoric versus epistemic uncertainty. The yellow line is the predictive mean, the lighter band shows input-dependent aleatoric uncertainty, and the darker band shows total uncertainty (aleatoric + epistemic). Vertical dashed lines delineate regions of high/low aleatoric and epistemic uncertainty.

Consequences of Ignoring Uncertainty

- *Overconfident errors:* Neural networks may assign high confidence (e.g., 99%) to incorrect predictions, undermining reliability and trust.
- *Poor calibration:* Predicted probabilities often fail to align with empirical accuracy, resulting in misleading risk assessments.
- *Unsafe deployment:* In high-stakes environments, unrecognized model ignorance can lead to catastrophic failures.

3.2.3.2 Measuring Uncertainty: Metrics and Diagnostics

Given an input x and a predictive distribution $p\ (y \mid x)$, common uncertainty metrics include:

Predictive entropy:

$$H\,[p(y \mid x)] = -\sum_{k=1}^{C} p\ (y = k \mid x) \log p\ (y = k \mid x)$$

Entropy quantifies the total uncertainty in a single forward pass. It is especially useful in classification tasks (e.g. image recognition, medical diagnosis) where one wishes to flag inputs whose class membership is intrinsically ambiguous.

Mutual information (capturing epistemic uncertainty):

$$MI\ (y, \theta \mid x) = H\,[E_\theta\, p\ (y \mid x, \theta)] - E_\theta\ [H\ [p\ (y \mid x, \theta)]]$$

By comparing the entropy of the ensemble-averaged prediction to the average entropy of each stochastic sample (e.g. MC-Dropout or deep ensemble member), MI isolates model uncertainty. It is best applied in safety-critical settings (autonomous vehicles, fault detection) to detect out-of-distribution or underexplored regions.

Expected calibration error (ECE): Partition predictions into M confidence bins B_m, then

$$\text{ECE} = \sum_{m=1}^{M} \frac{|B_m|}{N}\ |\text{acc}\ (B_m) - \text{conf}\ (B_m)|$$

ECE quantifies how closely reported confidence scores match observed empirical accuracy. It is widely employed to benchmark calibration techniques—such as temperature scaling and isotonic regression—particularly in tasks requiring reliable probability estimates, including risk scoring in healthcare.

Negative log-likelihood (NLL):

$$\text{NLL} = -\frac{1}{N}\sum_{i=1}^{N} \log p\ (y_i \mid x_i)$$

As a proper scoring rule, NLL rewards both accuracy and well-calibrated probabilities. It is the de facto loss for probabilistic regression and classification and is recommended when comparing different uncertainty-aware models on hold-out sets.

Brier Score:

$$\mathrm{BS} = \frac{1}{N}\sum_{i=1}^{N} | p(y \mid x_i) - y_i |_2^2$$

Equivalent to the mean squared error of predictive probabilities, the Brier score is interpretable and bounded in [0,1]. It is particularly popular in weather forecasting and ensemble learning contexts.

Predictive entropy excels at detecting inherently noisy inputs but conflates aleatoric and epistemic effects, making it less suitable when one needs to distinguish data noise from model ignorance. Mutual information, by isolating parameter uncertainty, is ideal for active learning and out-of-distribution detection, where one must identify samples that will most improve the model if labeled. ECE and Brier score focus on calibration: use them when the goal is to ensure that "80% confidence" truly corresponds to 80% accuracy—common in medical risk assessment or decision support. NLL remains the gold-standard objective for training and evaluating probabilistic models across both regression and classification settings.

Practical Diagnostics

- *Reliability diagrams:* Plot accuracy versus confidence across bins to visually inspect calibration.
- *Uncertainty-error curves:* Rank predictions by uncertainty and plot aggregate error on the top-*k*% most uncertain to assess how well uncertainty correlates with mistakes.
- *Coverage vs. width (regression):* For continuous outputs, plot the proportion of targets within predicted credible intervals versus interval width to evaluate interval sharpness and validity.

By carefully selecting and combining these metrics, practitioners can both diagnose and improve the trustworthiness of deep models in diverse applications.

3.2.3.3 Uncertainty Quantification

3.2.3.3.1 Monte Carlo Dropout (MC-Dropout)

Gal and Ghahramani (2016) showed that standard dropout can be reinterpreted as a variational approximation to a deep Gaussian process. If we keep dropout *active* at prediction time, each forward pass samples a different sub-network, yielding a draw from the approximate posterior over network weights.

Practical Implementation

(1) **Train as usual with dropout:** During training dropout layers are already employed—for example, Dropout(p = 0.5) applied after each dense or convolutional block.

(2) **Activate dropout at test time:** Instead of disabling dropout after training, retain it. Most frameworks (e.g., PyTorch, TensorFlow) allow overriding the model's 'eval ()' mode selectively for dropout layers—for example:

```
model. train() # enable dropout with torch.no_grad
(): preds = [] for _ in range(T):
```

logits = model(x) # each pass uses a new mask probs = SoftMax(logits) preds.append(probs)

(3) Aggregate predictions: After T stochastic passes you have $\{p_t\,(y \mid x)\}_{t=1}^{T}$. The *predictive mean*

$$\hat{p}\,(y \mid x) = \frac{1}{T}\sum_{t=1}^{T} \mid p_t(y \mid x)$$

serves as final class probabilities, reducing variance compared to a single pass.

(4) Compute uncertainty metrics:

- Total uncertainty (predictive entropy): $H\,[\hat{p}] = -\sum_k \widehat{p_k}\,\log \widehat{p_k}$
- Epistemic uncertainty (mutual information):

$$\mathrm{MI} = H\,[\hat{p}] - \frac{1}{T}\sum_{t=1}^{T} H\,[p_t] = H\left[\frac{1}{T}\sum_t p_t\right] - \frac{1}{T}\sum_t H\,[p_t]$$

In Algorithm 3.7, we begin by forcing the trained model's dropout layers to remain active at test time (line 1), so that each forward pass samples a different subset of the network's neurons. We then perform T stochastic passes (lines 3–6), where each pass implicitly draws a dropout mask m^t, computes the corresponding logits z_t, and converts them into class probabilities p_t via the SoftMax function. All T probability vectors are collected into the list P. After the loop, we compute the predictive mean p by averaging these T samples (line 8). The total uncertainty is measured by the entropy of p (line 9), capturing both data and model noise, while the average of the individual entropies (line 10) quantifies the expected aleatoric component. Finally, subtracting the average entropy from the total entropy yields the mutual information (line 11), which isolates epistemic uncertainty arising from model parameter variability. Together, these three outputs provide a complete uncertainty profile at prediction time.

Algorithm 3.7. Monte Carlo Dropout for Uncertainty

Require: input x, trained model $f(\cdot\,;\theta)$ with dropout, number of samples T
Ensure: predictive mean $\hat{p}$, total entropy $H[\hat{p}]$, epistemic MI

1: Set model to "train" mode for dropout layers only
2: Initialize accumulator $\mathcal{P} \leftarrow []$
3: **for** $t = 1$ to T **do**
4: Sample dropout masks m_t implicitly via forward pass
5: Compute logits $z_t = f(x; \theta \odot m_t)$
6: Compute softmax $p_t = \mathrm{softmax}(z_t)$
7: Append p_t to $\mathcal{P}$
8: **end for**
9: $\hat{p} \leftarrow \frac{1}{T}\sum_{p \in \mathcal{P}} p$ ▷ predictive mean
10: $H_{\mathrm{total}} \leftarrow -\sum_k \hat{p}_k \log \hat{p}_k$
11: $H_{\mathrm{avg}} \leftarrow \frac{1}{T}\sum_{p \in \mathcal{P}}\left(-\sum_k p_k \log p_k\right)$
12: $\mathrm{MI} \leftarrow H_{\mathrm{total}} - H_{\mathrm{avg}}$
13: **return** $\hat{p}$, H_{total}, MI

When to use MC-Dropout:

- *Resource-aware approximate Bayesian inference:* No changes to training, only T extra forward passes at test time.
- *Active learning:* Select inputs with high MI for labeling to reduce epistemic uncertainty.
- *Out-of-distribution detection:* Points with unusually large total entropy or MI often lie far from the training manifold.

By leveraging test-time stochasticity, MC-Dropout provides a lightweight yet effective mechanism to quantify both aleatoric and epistemic uncertainty in deep networks. Figure 3.10 show an example from MNIST dataset.

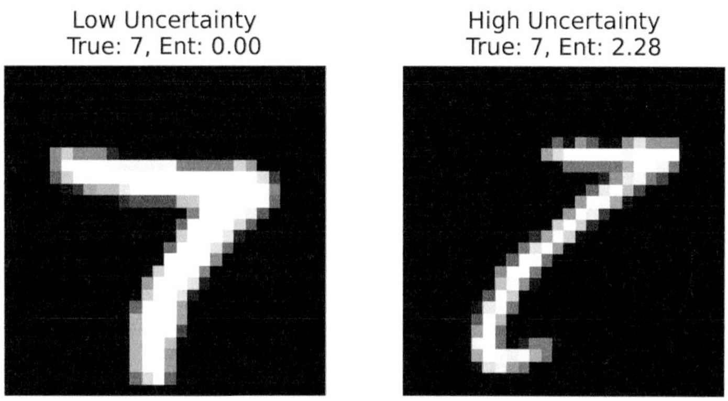

Figure 3.10. MNIST test images selected by predictive entropy under a stochastic dropout model. The left panel shows the correctly classified image with the lowest predictive entropy (high confidence), while the right panel shows the correctly classified image with the highest predictive entropy (low confidence).

3.2.3.3.2 Deep Ensembles

Deep ensembles (Lakshminarayanan et al., 2017) provide a simple yet powerful way to capture both aleatoric and epistemic uncertainty. Rather than relying on a single model, one trains M independent networks with different random initializations (and, optionally, different bootstrap samples of the data). At inference time, each model produces a predictive distribution, and these M predictions are averaged to form a more robust estimate of both the mean prediction and the model's uncertainty.

Practical Implementation:

(1) **Train M independent models:** Initialize and train $f^{(m)}(x; \theta^{(m)})$ for $m = 1, \ldots, M$ on the same dataset (optionally using different data subsets or data augmentation seeds).
(2) **Collect ensemble predictions:** At test time, pass the input x through each model to obtain SoftMax probabilities $\{p^{(m)}(y \mid x)\}_{m=1}^{M}$.
(3) **Compute predictive mean and variance:**

$$\hat{p}(y \mid x) = \frac{1}{M} \sum_{m=1}^{M} p^{(m)}(y \mid x)$$

$$\widehat{\mathrm{Var}}\,[p(y \mid x)] = \frac{1}{M} \sum_{m=1}^{M} \left(p^{(m)}(y \mid x) - \hat{p}(y \mid x) \right)^2$$

The mean $\hat{p}$ serves as the ensemble's final output, while the variance captures epistemic spread among models.

(4) Derive uncertainty metrics:

- *Total uncertainty (entropy of p):* $H[\hat{p}] = -\sum_k \widehat{p_k} \log \widehat{p_k}$.
- *Epistemic uncertainty (variance or mutual information):* With Var as above

$$MI = H[\hat{p}] - \frac{1}{M} \sum_m H[p^{(m)}]$$

Pseudocode for Deep Ensembles.

Algorithm 3.8. Deep Ensembles for Uncertainty

```
Require: input x, ensemble of models {f^(m)(·; θ^(m))}_{m=1}^M
Ensure: predictive mean p̂, total entropy H[p̂], epistemic variance or MI
Initialize P ← []
for m = 1 to M do
    Compute p^(m) = softmax(f^(m)(x; θ^(m)))
    Append p^(m) to P
end for
p̂ ← (1/M) Σ_{p∈P} p                              ▷ ensemble predictive mean
H_total ← − Σ_k p̂_k log p̂_k
Var[p(y | x)] ← (1/M) Σ_{p∈P} (p − p̂)^2
MI ← H_total − (1/M) Σ_{p∈P} (− Σ_k p_k log p_k)
return p̂, H_total, Var or MI
```

When to use Deep Ensembles:

- *High-stakes applications:* Where the highest possible predictive performance and reliable uncertainty estimates outweigh the cost of training multiple models.
- *Model misspecification detection:* When ensemble variance reveals disagreements that single models cannot.
- *Calibration improvement:* When ensembles are empirically among the best-calibrated methods without extra post-hoc steps.

3.2.4 Complementarity and Tensions Between Robustness and Uncertainty

Though both adversarial resilience and uncertainty quantification aim at enhancing system safety they interact in nuanced ways. On one hand, robust models often exhibit reduced overconfidence, since smoothing the decision boundary tends to improve calibration and produce more meaningful uncertainty estimates. This synergy means that measures such as predictive entropy or ensemble variance can more reliably distinguish out-of-distribution or adversarial inputs, creating a virtuous cycle: robustness strengthens uncertainty signals, and clear uncertainty signals guide further robustness testing.

On the other hand, conflict can arise when defensive mechanisms obscure the very indicators used for uncertainty estimation. For example, certain certified defenses enforce worst-case guarantees by projecting inputs into constrained regions, which may artificially reduce variance in ensemble outputs or compress the distribution of stochastic dropout samples. In these cases, conventional uncertainty metrics risk underestimating true epistemic risk, potentially masking novel attack types or domain shifts. Recognizing this tension, practitioners should validate uncertainty pipelines on both clean and adversarially perturbed data and consider hybrid approaches to balance the trade-offs between robustness and introspective clarity.

3.2.5 Operationalizing Uncertainty Quantification: Implementation and Limitations

To operationalize uncertainty quantification in safety-critical workflows, practitioners can translate any chosen uncertainty metric into concrete decision rules. For example, a prediction whose uncertainty exceeds a calibrated threshold (e.g. entropy above 0.5 bits or ensemble standard deviation beyond historical norms) can be automatically diverted to a human operator or a conservative fallback mechanism. In an automated inspection system for industrial controls, this means that any sample with uncertainty above the agreed limit triggers a manual override, ensuring that only high-confidence outputs proceed unattended. These thresholds are set via validation on held-out data, then encoded in service-level policies or real-time monitoring dashboards to guarantee consistent risk management.

Furthermore, embedding uncertainty scores in operational logs creates an auditable trail for both internal review and regulatory compliance. By recording each prediction alongside its uncertainty value, organizations can generate post-hoc analyses to refine risk-tolerance parameters and retraining cadences. Over time, this closed-loop approach not only mitigates individual risks but also informs governance processes and fostering transparent, data-driven improvements in safety-critical AI deployments.

However, both adversarial training and uncertainty quantification rest on assumptions that may not hold in real-time or rapidly evolving settings. Adversarial training typically requires prior knowledge of attack norms and budgets and incurs significant computational overhead, making it challenging to update models on-the-fly as data distributions shift. In fast-moving environments, the fixed perturbation budgets used in training may under or overestimate real threats, and retraining or fine-tuning at production environment can be prohibitively slow. Moreover, adversarial defenses often assume a stationary data distribution, whereas in dynamic deployments models may encounter novel modalities, temporal drift, or concept shift that fall outside the precomputed robustness bounds.

Uncertainty metrics depend on calibration data and model architectures that can degrade over time. Techniques like deep ensembles or Monte Carlo Dropout introduce non-negligible inference latency, conflicting with required real-time constraints in safety-critical loops. Thresholds set on historical validation sets may become misaligned through data shift, leading to both false alarms and missed detections of high-risk inputs. Finally, uncertainty estimates often assume independence of successive predictions, yet in sequential decision processes errors can compound, and unmodeled temporal correlations may erode the reliability of the uncertainty flags. Recognizing these limitations is essential for designing hybrid human–AI workflows and fallback protocols that maintain trust under real-world operational requirements.

3.2.6 Implications for Digital Sovereignty and AI Governance

The adversarial defenses and uncertainty quantification techniques presented above play a direct role in advancing digital sovereignty and strengthening AI governance (Misra et al., 2025). By hardening models against malicious perturbations, system operators retain control over the integrity of their data pipelines and decision boundaries, preventing unauthorized actors from covertly manipulating outcomes. This in turn supports the sovereign right and rights of a nation or organization to define and enforce its own security policies without relying on external black-box services.

Similarly, uncertainty quantification methods provide transparent insights into a model's confidence in its predictions. When deployed in regulated sectors such as healthcare, critical communications, or energy, these uncertainty measures become auditable evidence to ensure compliance with AI governance frameworks. Regulators and certification bodies can mandate minimum coverage thresholds (e.g., 90% prediction intervals) or maximum allowable calibration error, tying model release to demonstrable metrics of epistemic transparency. In practice, this approach,

- Ensures that decision makers can exercise sovereignty by specifying and enforcing their own risk-tolerance parameters (e.g. acceptable uncertainty bounds).
- Enables regulatory auditing of model behavior under both nominal and adversarial conditions.
- Integrates neatly with existing standards (ISO/IEC 27001 for information security, ISO/IEC 42001 for AI management) by providing quantifiable evidence of robustness and calibrated confidence.

Building on these governance connections, the robustness and uncertainty workflows dovetail with leading international standards and legislative initiatives for trustworthy AI. For example, ISO/IEC 42001[1] ("Governance of Artificial Intelligence") calls for demonstrable risk-management processes and resilience testing; the adversarial accuracy certificates and uncertainty calibration reports we propose directly satisfy clauses on robustness validation and transparency. Similarly, under the EU AI Act's Article 14[2] risk-management framework for high-risk systems, continuous monitoring and post deployment reviews are mandated—our logging of uncertainty metrics and periodic adversarial stress tests supply the required evidentiary trail.

Beyond Europe, global guidance such as the OECD AI Principles[3] and the U.S. NIST AI Risk Management Framework[4] emphasize accountability, human oversight,

---

1 https://www.iso.org/obp/ui/en/#iso:std:iso-iec:42001:ed-1:v1:en

2 https://artificialintelligenceact.eu/article/14/

3 https://www.oecd.org/going-digital/ai/principles/

4 https://www.nist.gov/itl/ai-risk-management-framework

and performance documentation. Our threshold-based uncertainty routing embodies the "human in-the-loop" principle, while our audit-ready logs of adversarial and uncertainty metrics align with calls for explainability and traceability in IEEE P7001[5] ("Transparency of Autonomous Systems").

3.3 Case Studies

3.3.1 Case Study 1: Robust Spectrum Sensing in 6G

3.3.1.1 Dataset Description

The spectrum-sensing dataset used in this case study is exactly the synthetic spectrogram collection introduced by Catak et al. (2025). It comprises N RGB images of size 256×256, each generated via a 4096-point FFT from complex baseband recordings of mixed signals (Radar – ASR, 5G NR, LTE, and AWGN noise). The data are split into training and testing sets in a 90%/10% ratio. Key parameters for signal generation are summarized in Table 3.1.

Data samples are constructed by superimposing one or more of the four signal types (e.g. ASR + NR + LTE + Noise). Each resulting spectrogram is saved in

Table 3.1. Signal generation parameters for the 6G spectrum-sensing dataset

Signal	Parameter	Value(s)
ASR (Radar)	Center frequency f_c	2.8 GHz
	Sampling rate f_s	61.44 MHz
	Pulse width	1 µs
	Transmit power	25 kW
	Antenna gain	32.8 dB
5G NR	Subcarrier spacing	15, 30 kHz
	Bandwidth	10, 15, 20, 25, 30, 40, 50 MHz
	Frame period	20 ms
	Transmit power	100, 250, 500 W
	Antenna gain	0, 4, 8, 12.2 dB
LTE	Reference channels	R.2, R.6, R.8, R.9
	Bandwidth	5, 10, 15, 20 MHz
	Duplex mode	FDD
	Transmit power	100, 250, 500 W
Noise	SNR	40, 50, 100 dB
Deployment & Imaging	Receiver placement	Random in 2 × 2 km^2
	Spectrogram size	256 × 256 pixels
	FFT length	4096 points
	Train/Test split	90%/10%

5 https://standards.ieee.org/ieee/7001/6929/

Table 3.2. Dataset and training hyperparameters

Parameter	**Value**	**Description**
Input shape	(256,256,3)	Spectrogram image dimensions
Number of classes	4	{Noise, LTE, NR, Radar}
Train/Validation split	90%/10%	Random stratified split
Batch size	20	Samples per mini batch
Epochs	Up to 10,000	Early stopping at patience
Early stopping patience	50	Monitored on val_accuracy
Optimizer	Adam (lr=default)	Learning rate = Keras default
Loss function	Categorical cross-entropy	$L = - P_k y_k \log^{yk}$

the folder structure according to its class label(s). This richly parameterized and heterogeneous dataset allows rigorous testing of decentralized federated learning algorithms under non-IID and interference-laden spectrums.

3.3.1.2 Experimental Setup

In this section we describe the experimental protocol used to evaluate both baseline and adversarially trained U-Net models on the 6G spectrum-sensing dataset. Pseudocode and parameter tables follow.

Data Preparation: We begin by downloading and extracting the spectrogram dataset, which yields N labelled samples $\{(X_i, Y_i)\}_{i=1}^{N}$, each $X_i \in R^{256\times256\times3}$ and $Y_i \in \{0,3\}^{256\times256}$. We split them into training and validation sets:

$$(X_{\text{train}}, Y_{\text{train}}), (X_{\text{val}}, Y_{\text{val}}) = \text{TrainTestSplit}\,(X, Y;\ \text{test\_size} = 0.1)$$

Each label map Y is one-hot encoded to $Y^{\text{onehot}} \in \{0,1\}^{256\times256\times4}$.

Model Architecture: We employ a standard U-Net (Ronneberger et al., 2015) for semantic segmentation:

$$f_\theta : R^{256\times256\times3} \longrightarrow [0,1]^{256\times256\times4}$$

with encoder–decoder blocks as detailed in the code. The final activation is SoftMax over classes.

Adversarial Attacks: To assess model robustness, we generate adversarial examples on a random set of $S = 5$ validation samples using four gradient-based attacks under an ℓ_2 norm constraint:

$$x_{\text{adv}} = \arg \max_{|\delta|_2 \le \epsilon} \mathcal{L}(f_\theta (x + \delta), y)$$

We vary ϵ over $E = 10$ values linearly spaced in $[0, 1/2 \max|X_{\text{train}}|]$. The attacks are:

- FGSM (single-step, Eq. (1))
- BIM/I-FGSM (40 steps, step size ϵ/40)
- MIM (momentum iterative with decay 0.9)
- PGD (40 steps, random restarts omitted)

Table 3.3. Adversarial attack parameters

Attack	Iterations	Step size
FGSM	1	ϵ
BIM (I-FGSM)	40	$\alpha = \epsilon/40$
Momentum Iterative (MIM)	40	$\alpha = \epsilon/40$, $\mu = 0.9$
PGD	40	$\alpha = \epsilon/40$

Evaluation Metrics: For each test or adversarial prediction Y, we compute per-class Intersection-over-Union (IoU) and Dice coefficient from the confusion matrix $C \in N^{4\times 4}$:

$$\text{IoU}_c = \frac{C_{c,c}}{C_{c,c} + \sum_{i\neq c} C_{i,c} + \sum_{j\neq c} C_{c,j}}$$

$$\text{Dice}_c = \frac{2C_{c,c}}{2C_{c,c} + \sum_{i\neq c} C_{i,c} + \sum_{j\neq c} C_{c,j}}$$

Experimental Loop: We perform $R = 10$ independent repeats with different random seeds. In each repeat:

(1) Load or train the U-Net model.
(2) Select a validation sample containing all four classes.
(3) Evaluate baseline IoU and Dice (no attack).
(4) For each ϵ and each attack, generate S adversarial examples and compute average IoU/Dice.
(5) Retrain the model on the union of original and strongest adversarial samples ($\epsilon_{\max}$) and repeat evaluation.

Algorithm 3.9. Experimental Protocol

for $r = 1, \dots, R$ **do**
    $\theta \leftarrow$ `load_or_train_model()`
    $i, x, y \leftarrow$ `select_valid_sample()`
    $\{\text{IoU}, \text{Dice}\}_{\text{base}} \leftarrow \text{evaluate}(\theta, x, y)$
    for $\epsilon \in \{\epsilon_k\}_{k=1}^{E}$ **do**
        for attack $\in$ {FGSM, BIM, MIM, PGD} **do**
            $x_{\text{adv}} \leftarrow \text{attack}(\theta, x, \epsilon)$
            $\{\text{IoU}, \text{Dice}\} \leftarrow \text{evaluate}(\theta, x_{\text{adv}}, y)$
        end for
    end for
    $\theta_{\text{adv}} \leftarrow \text{retrain}(\theta, \epsilon_{\max})$
    repeat evaluation for θ_{adv}
end for

All numerical results are aggregated into CSV files for subsequent statistical analysis. This setup allows a controlled comparison of robustness gains from adversarial retraining across multiple attack strengths and methods.

3.3.1.3 Experimental Results

Table 3.4 summarizes how baseline and adversarially trained U-Net models perform under an increasing adversarial budget ϵ. We report mean IoU and Dice scores averaged over the four classes {Noise, LTE, NR, Radar}.

Table 3.4 breaks down IoU and Dice for each class and each ϵ. At $\epsilon = 127.5$, for instance, *Noise* IoU increases from 0.355 to 0.529 (+48.8%), and Dice from 0.452 to 0.647 (+43.0%). The *LTE* class sees the largest relative IoU gain (+85.5%) and Dice gain (+60.5%). Even the most robust class, *Radar*, benefits by +13.5% IoU and +9.0% Dice. These results confirm that adversarial training not only smooths the worst-case performance curve, but also substantially improves per-class segmentation quality under strong attacks.

To distill the detailed class-wise results into an overall picture of robustness gains, we summarize in Table 3.5 the average IoU and Dice scores across all four classes for each perturbation strength ϵ, comparing the baseline and adversarially trained models. We also report the relative improvement in percentage points, which highlights how adversarial training progressively enhances model resilience as attacks become stronger.

3.3.2 Case Study 2: Uncertainty Quantification for MATH-500 Reasoning

Following our earlier study on large language model uncertainty (LLM) (Catak and Kuzlu, 2024; Catak et al., 2024), we adopt a *geometric* proxy for epistemic risk: the total area of the convex hulls that surround DBSCAN clusters in the 2D response embedding space. Concretely, for each question $q_{i.}$ w_e (i) embed the $T = 30$ generated solutions $\{r_{i,t}\}_{t=1}^{T}$ with all-MiniLM-L6-v2, (ii) project the 384-D vectors to two principal components, and (iii) cluster them with an adaptive-ε DBSCAN. For every cluster containing at least three points, we construct its planar convex hull and sum the enclosed areas,

$$A(q_i) = \sum_{c \in C(q_i), |c| \geq 3} \text{Area}(\text{Hull}(c))$$

which grows monotonically with the spread (and thus disagreement) of the model's responses.

The MATH-500 dataset (H4, 2023) comprises 500 mathematical reasoning problems covering algebra, calculus, geometry, and number theory, sourced from the MATH dataset's test split. Each problem includes a question, a solution, and a difficulty level (easy, medium, hard). 35 random problems are selected to evaluate uncertainty quantification in large language models (LLMs), ensuring diverse problem types. The dataset is ideal for testing reasoning under uncertainty, as problems vary in complexity and require precise, interpretable outputs.

We employ the Mathstral model, a transformer-based LLM optimized for mathematical reasoning, accessed via the Ollama API. For each of the 35 selected questions, we generate 30 response iterations with a temperature of 0.6 and a maximum of 10,000 tokens, ensuring varied outputs. Responses are expected to include a final answer wrapped in \boxed {} for consistency. The experimental pipeline is as follows:

Table 3.4. Class-wise IoU and dice under attack across all ϵ values

ϵ	Class	Base IoU	Adv. IoU	Δ IoU (%)	Base dice	Adv. dice	Δ dice (%)
14.167	Noise	0.835	0.811	−2.8	0.894	0.880	−1.5
	LTE	0.386	0.391	1.3	0.400	0.416	4.0
	NR	0.644	0.686	6.5	0.692	0.743	7.5
	Radar	0.682	0.697	2.3	0.799	0.811	1.5
28.333	Noise	0.734	0.753	2.5	0.826	0.838	1.4
	LTE	0.303	0.365	20.5	0.342	0.398	16.1
	NR	0.612	0.646	5.5	0.671	0.717	6.9
	Radar	0.646	0.670	3.7	0.774	0.790	2.1
42.500	Noise	0.638	0.710	11.2	0.749	0.805	7.5
	LTE	0.238	0.346	45.4	0.289	0.383	32.5
	NR	0.568	0.614	8.1	0.640	0.694	8.4
	Radar	0.621	0.646	4.2	0.756	0.773	2.3
56.667	Noise	0.561	0.674	20.2	0.680	0.778	14.3
	LTE	0.207	0.329	58.7	0.261	0.369	41.1
	NR	0.525	0.592	12.7	0.606	0.676	11.5
	Radar	0.599	0.629	5.0	0.738	0.759	2.8
70.833	Noise	0.504	0.639	26.7	0.624	0.749	20.0
	LTE	0.189	0.312	65.1	0.242	0.353	45.9
	NR	0.477	0.570	19.4	0.559	0.659	17.8
	Radar	0.581	0.615	5.8	0.722	0.748	3.6
85.000	Noise	0.458	0.606	32.2	0.575	0.721	25.3
	LTE	0.173	0.297	71.5	0.226	0.340	50.9
	NR	0.438	0.550	25.5	0.517	0.641	24.0
	Radar	0.550	0.604	7.9	0.703	0.740	5.2

(Contd.)

(*Contd.*)

ϵ	Class	Base IoU	Adv. IoU	Δ IoU (%)	Base dice	Adv. dice	Δ dice (%)
99.167	Noise	0.416	0.577	38.8	0.527	0.694	31.8
	LTE	0.160	0.283	76.8	0.212	0.327	54.0
	NR	0.402	0.532	32.2	0.480	0.626	30.4
	Radar	0.542	0.594	9.5	0.688	0.731	6.2
113.333	Noise	0.385	0.552	43.3	0.491	0.670	36.4
	LTE	0.152	0.274	80.4	0.204	0.318	56.1
	NR	0.375	0.517	37.9	0.450	0.614	36.4
	Radar	0.526	0.584	11.0	0.674	0.723	7.2
127.500	Noise	0.355	0.529	48.8	0.452	0.647	43.0
	LTE NR	0.144	0.266	85.5	0.194	0.311	60.5
		0.370	0.504	36.4	0.442	0.603	36.5
	Radar	0.506	0.574	13.5	0.655	0.715	9.0

Table 3.5. Mean IoU and dice scores across all classes for baseline vs. adversarial training, with color-coded improvements

ϵ	Base IoU	Adv. IoU	Δ IoU (%)	Base dice	Adv. dice	Δ dice (%)
14.167	0.637	0.646	↑1.5	0.696	0.713	↑2.3
28.333	0.574	0.608	↑6.0	0.653	0.686	↑5.0
42.500	0.516	0.579	↑12.1	0.609	0.664	↑9.1
56.667	0.473	0.556	↑17.6	0.571	0.646	↑13.0
70.833	0.438	0.534	↑22.1	0.537	0.627	↑16.9
85.000	0.407	0.514	↑26.3	0.505	0.610	↑20.8
99.167	0.380	0.497	↑30.7	0.477	0.595	↑24.7
113.333	0.360	0.482	↑34.1	0.455	0.581	↑27.8
127.500	0.344	0.468	↑36.2	0.436	0.569	↑30.6

(1) Response Generation: Query Mathstral for 30 iterations per question, saving each response as a text file. Empty or malformed responses (e.g., missing \boxed {}) are filtered out.
(2) Answer Extraction: Parse \boxed {} content from each response, counting the frequency of unique answers to assess consistency.
(3) Embedding Generation: Encode responses into 384-dimensional vectors using the all-MiniLM-L6-v2 SentenceTransformer model. Apply PCA to reduce embeddings to 2D, followed by normalization to [0,1] using MinMaxScaler.
(4) Clustering and Uncertainty Quantification: Use DBSCAN clustering with an adaptively estimated eps parameter (via KneeLocator on k-distance plots) to group similar responses. For each cluster with at least three points, compute the convex hull area in a 2D embedding space as a proxy for epistemic uncertainty. Larger areas indicate greater response variability, reflecting model uncertainty.
(5) Evaluation Metrics: Compute:
- *Answer Accuracy:* Proportion of iterations where the \boxed {} answer matches the dataset's ground-truth solution.
- *Total Hull Area:* Sum of convex hull areas across clusters, indicating overall uncertainty.
- *Number of Clusters:* Reflects the diversity of response groups.
- *Noise Points:* Outliers identified with DBSCAN, indicating inconsistent responses.

(6) Visualization: Generate scatter plots of 2D embeddings with density contours and convex hull boundaries, saved as clusters_question_{id}.pdf.

The pseudocode for this pipeline is summarized in Algorithm 3.10.

Algorithm 3.10. MATH-500 Uncertainty Quantification Pipeline

Require: MATH-500 dataset $\{(q_i, s_i)\}_{i=1}^{35}$, Mathstral model f, iterations $T = 30$
Ensure: Answer accuracy, total hull area, cluster statistics
for each question q_i **do**
  $\{r_{i,t}\}_{t=1}^{T} \leftarrow$ Query $f(q_i)$ for T iterations
  $\{a_{i,t}\} \leftarrow$ Parse `\boxed{}` from $\{r_{i,t}\}$
  Compute answer frequencies and accuracy against s_i
  $E \leftarrow$ Encode $\{r_{i,t}\}$ to 384D via SentenceTransformer
  $E_{2D} \leftarrow$ PCA(E, n_components=2), normalize to $[0, 1]$
  Estimate `eps` via `KneeLocator` on k-distance plot
  $C \leftarrow$ DBSCAN(E_{2D}, eps, min_samples=2)
  Compute convex hull areas for clusters with ≥ 3 points
  Save scatter plot with density contours and hulls
end for
return Accuracy, total hull area, number of clusters, noise points

Table 3.6 presents uncertainty metrics for six representative questions, with three high-uncertainty (hull area $\geq$3.0) and three low uncertainty (hull area $<$ 2.0) instances. Accuracy reflects the frequency of the most common generated answer matching the actual answer. Figure 3.11 shows scatter plots for these questions, grouped by uncertainty level, with density contours and convex hulls. The

Table 3.6. Detailed uncertainty metrics for selected MATH-500 questions

ID	Type	Acc.	Hull area	Clusters (noise)	Actual	Generated answers (Freq)
2 (High)	Algebra	0.23	3.495	3 (0)	49	49 (5)
5 (High)	Calculus	0.60	3.152	3 (1)	–1	–1 (18)
28 (High)	Word Problem	0.10	3.640	3 (1)	37	0 (7)
12 (Low)	Probability	0.23	1.772	3 (1)	1 over 22	1 over 1 (7)
23 (Low)	Algebra	0.97	1.801	4 (0)	10	10 (29)
26 (Low)	Word Problem	0.00	1.360	5 (2)	1023	1034 (4)

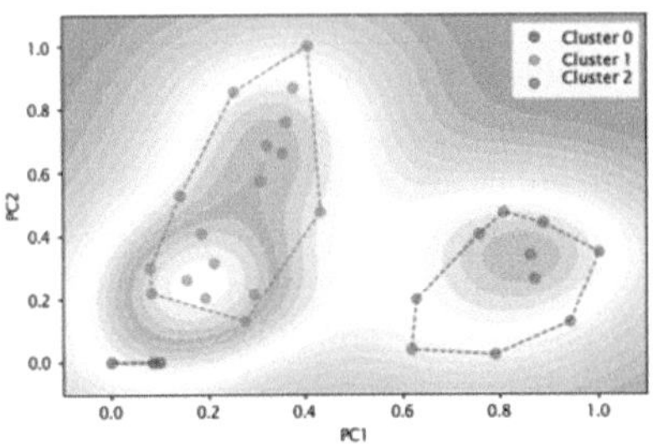

(a) Question 2 (High, Hull Area: 3.495)

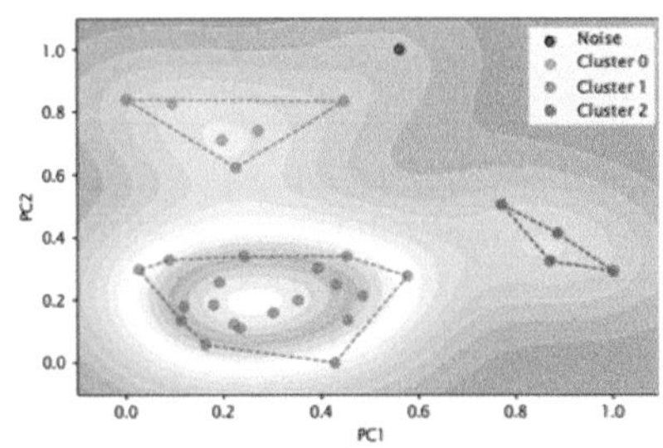

(b) Question 5 (High, Hull Area: 3.152)

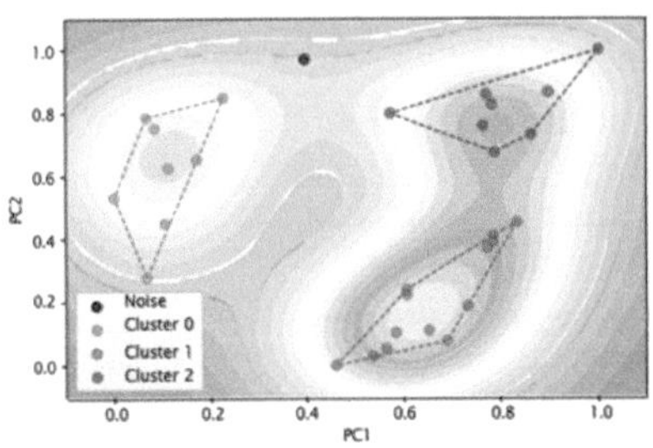

(c) Question 28 (High, Hull Area: 3.640)

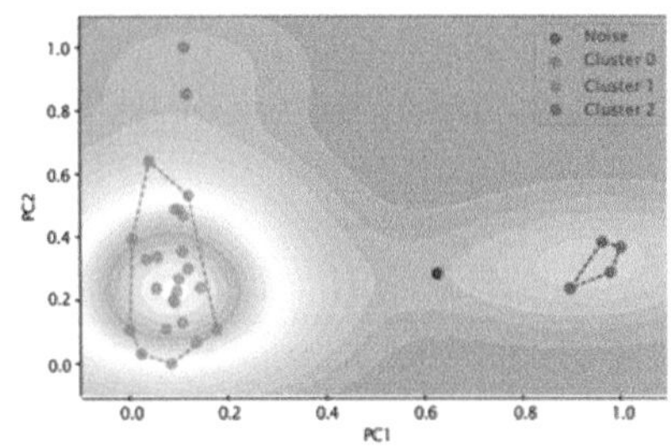

(d) Question 12 (Low, Hull Area: 1.772)

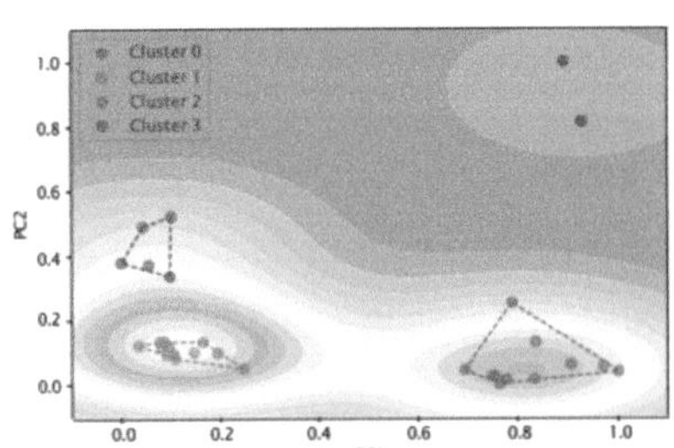

(e) Question 23 (Low, Hull Area: 1.801)

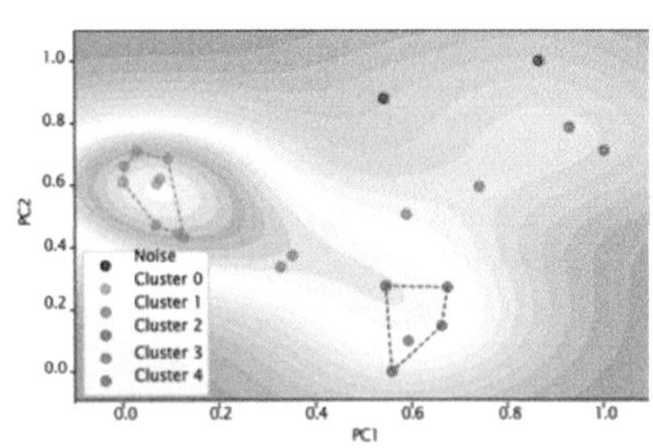

(f) Question 26 (Low, Hull Area: 1.360)

Figure 3.11. 2D embedding scatter plots for selected MATH-500 questions, showing DBSCAN clusters, convex hulls, and density contours.

histogram in Figure 3.12 (showing a single bar of height 5) requires refinement for a complete distribution.

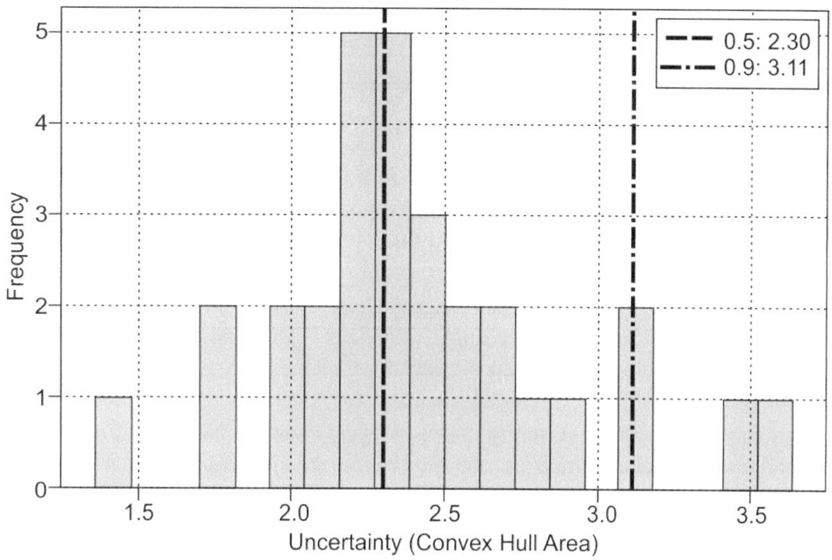

Figure 3.12. Histogram of uncertainty metrics across 35 questions (limited data visible).

The convex hull-based method effectively highlights uncertainty, with high uncertainty cases (e.g., question 28, hull area 3.640) showing low accuracy (0.10) and dominant incorrect answers (e.g., 0 with 7/30 frequency vs. 37). Low-uncertainty cases (e.g., question 23, hull area 1.801) achieve high accuracy (0.97) with consistent answers (10 with 29/30). The geometric insight of the approach helps interpretability, but the 2D PCA can lose detail, and the truncation of the histogram indicates a need for better distribution visualization. Future work could explore HDBSCAN or entropy metrics for enhanced robustness.

To reinforce the connection between our technical evaluations and the overarching goal of trustworthy AI, we reflect on each case study through a governance lens. In the first case study, the deployment of adversarial training yielded appreciable enhancements in model resilience under attack conditions, providing robustness certificates that can be seamlessly integrated into audit reports and regulatory submissions. These certificates offer stakeholders a clear assurance that the model meets predefined resilience standards without exposing proprietary algorithmic details.

Similarly, the second case study's uncertainty analysis revealed a pronounced distinction between high- and low-confidence predictions, enabling straightforward rules for escalating uncertain cases to human oversight. By translating uncertainty metrics into operational confidence bands, organizations acquire a transparent mechanism for triaging outputs, documenting deviations, and continuously refining risk policies.

3.4 Conclusion and Future Work

This chapter has explored the critical dimensions of trustworthy AI in safety-critical systems, emphasizing adversarial robustness, uncertainty quantification, and their practical implications. The chapter presents a comprehensive analysis of adversarial attack strategies (FGSM, BIM, MIM, PGD) and defense mechanisms (adversarial training, defensive distillation), highlighting their role in enhancing model reliability against malicious perturbations. Techniques for uncertainty quantification, including MC-Dropout and deep ensembles, were introduced to address the need for transparent and reliable decision-making in high-stakes domains. Two case studies demonstrated the real-world challenges and solutions. In the 6G case, adversarial training improved IoU and Dice scores by up to 48.8% and 60.5%, respectively, under strong attacks. For MATH-500, the convex hull-based uncertainty metric effectively identified high-uncertainty scenarios, with hull areas ranging from 1.360 to 3.640, guiding improved model interpretability. These findings underscore the necessity of integrating robustness and uncertainty awareness into AI systems to ensure safety, reliability, and ethical deployment in critical applications.

Our robustness and uncertainty results suggest concrete pathways for regulators to operationalize technical metrics into enforceable standards. In healthcare, agencies like the FDA or EMA may require AI vendors to submit robustness certificates as part of pre-market approval. Likewise, uncertainty calibration reports could be mandated in post-market surveillance, with any prediction exceeding a regulator-defined uncertainty threshold automatically routed for human oversight or patient notification. Embedding these criteria into guidance documents transforms abstract robustness and calibration gains into clear compliance checkpoints.

In telecommunications, bodies can similarly require annual reporting of robustness metrics under simulated attack scenarios and uncertainty summaries for automated network management tools. Service-level agreements could tie automated handoffs or spectrum allocations to minimum confidence levels, ensuring that only high certainty decisions proceed without operator intervention. By standardizing audit procedures—combining adversarial testing protocols with uncertainty logging—regulators both empower network operators to self-certify and provide end users transparent comparisons across AI offerings. Together, these measures align technical advances in trustworthy AI with policy levers that safeguard safety-critical infrastructures.

Despite the advancements presented, several challenges remain for trustworthy AI in safety-critical systems. First, scaling uncertainty quantification methods like convex hull computation to high-dimensional spaces is computationally intensive; future research should explore efficient approximations or alternative metrics such as HDBSCAN or entropy-based approaches. Second, adversarial training, while effective, incurs significant computational overhead—faster methods like randomized inner maximization or lightweight defenses warrant investigation. Third, the trade-off between robustness and accuracy needs further exploration, particularly in resource-constrained environments like edge devices in 6G networks. Additionally, standardizing governance frameworks for adversarial resilience and uncertainty reporting is crucial for widespread adoption, especially in regulated sectors like healthcare and autonomous driving. Finally, integrating these techniques with emerging paradigms, such as federated learning for privacy-preserving AI, could enhance digital sovereignty while maintaining trustworthiness. Addressing these challenges will pave the way for more reliable, ethical, and scalable AI systems in safety-critical applications.

While our adversarial robustness and uncertainty quantification methods show promising results in controlled experiments, real-world deployment introduces additional hurdles. First, latency constraints in safety-critical loops can preclude expensive defenses such as large ensembles or multi-step adversarial training; models must balance robustness gains against the necessity for millisecond-level inference in domains like autonomous navigation or industrial automation. Second, evolving attack types—ranging from novel perturbation strategies to adaptive, context-aware exploits—require that defenses be continuously updated; static certificates risk obsolescence unless paired with monitoring systems that detect changes in input distributions and automatically flag potential new threat vectors. Finally, integrating these techniques with existing safety protocols and regulatory workflows demands careful engineering: uncertainty triggers or robustness alarms must hook into established fail-safe mechanisms, human-in-the-loop decision points, and logging infrastructures without disrupting certified system behavior or invalidating prior safety certifications.

Declaration of Generative AI and AI-Assisted Technologies

During the preparation of this work, the authors utilized AI-assisted tools such as ChatGPT and Grok to improve English language clarity (spelling, grammar, punctuation and table formatting). All content generated by these tools was reviewed and edited by the authors, who take full responsibility for the originality and accuracy of the final manuscript.

References

Abdar, M., Pourpanah, F., Hussain, S., Rezazadegan, D., Liu, L., Ghavamzadeh, M., & Nahavandi, S. (2021). A review of uncertainty quantification in deep learning: Techniques, applications and challenges. *Information Fusion*, 76, 243–297.

Abdel Hakeem, S.A., Hussein, H.H., & Kim, H. (2022). Security requirements and challenges of 6G technologies and applications. *Sensors*, 22(5), 1969.

Akhtar, N., & Mian, A. (2018). Threat of adversarial attacks on deep learning in computer vision: A survey. *IEEE Access*, 6, 14410–14430.

Begoli, E., Bhattacharya, T., & Kusnezov, D. (2019). The need for uncertainty quantification in machine-assisted medical decision making. *Nature Machine Intelligence*, 1(1), 20–23.

Biggio, B., & Roli, F. (2018). Wild patterns: Ten years after the rise of adversarial machine learning. *Pattern Recognition*, 84, 317–331.

Carlini, N., & Wagner, D. (2017). Towards evaluating the robustness of neural networks. In: *IEEE Symposium on Security and Privacy*, pp. 39–57.

Catak, F.O., & Kuzlu, M. (2024). Uncertainty quantification in large language models through convex hull analysis. *Discover Artificial Intelligence*, 4(1), 1–14.

Catak, F.O., Kuzlu, M., & Patrick, T. (2024). Improving Medical Diagnostics with Vision-Language Models: Convex Hull-Based Uncertainty Analysis. arXiv e-prints, arXiv:2412.00056.

Cohen, J.M., Rosenfeld, E., & Kolter, J.Z. (2020). Certified adversarial robustness via randomized smoothing. *Journal of Machine Learning Research*, 21(1), 6485–6545.

Dong, Y., Liao, F., Pang, T., Su, H., Zhu, J., Hu, X., & Li, J. (2018). Boosting adversarial attacks with momentum. In: *Proceedings of the IEEE Conference on Computer Vision and Pattern Recognition*, pp. 9185–9193.

Eykholt, K., Evtimov, I., Fernandes, E., Li, B., Rahmati, A., Xiao, C. et al. (2018). Robust physical-world attacks on deep learning visual classification. In: *Proceedings of the IEEE Conference on Computer Vision and Pattern Recognition*, pp. 1625–1634.

Gal, Y., & Ghahramani, Z. (2016). Dropout as a bayesian approximation: Representing model uncertainty in deep learning. In: Balcan, M.F. and Weinberger, K.Q. (eds), *Proceedings of The 33rd International Conference on Machine Learning*, volume 48 of *Proceedings of Machine Learning Research*, pp. 1050–1059, New York, New York, USA. PMLR.

Gao, C., Wang, G., Shi, W., Wang, Z., & Chen, Y.. (2021). Autonomous driving security: State of the art and challenges. *IEEE Internet of Things Journal*, 9(10): 7572–7595.

Goodfellow, I., Shlens, J., and Szegedy, C. (2015). Explaining and harnessing adversarial examples. *International Conference on Learning Representations*. http://arxiv.org/abs/1412.6572.

Guembe, B., Azeta, A., Misra, S., Osamor, V.C., Fernandez-Sanz, L., & Pospelova, V. (2022). The emerging threat of ai-driven cyber attacks: A review. *Applied Artificial Intelligence*, 36(1), 2037254.

H4, H. (2023). MATH-500: A subset of the math benchmark. https://huggingface.co/ datasets/HuggingFaceH4/MATH-500. Accessed 30 May 2025.

Jones, N. (2024). AI now beats humans at basic tasks—New benchmarks are needed, says major report. *Nature*, 628(8009), 700–701.

Kumar, S., Singh, S.K., Kumar, R., Subba, C.K., Chui, K.T., & Gupta, B.B. (2025). Neoteric threat intelligence ensuring digital sovereignty and trust through ML-infused proactive defense analytics for NEXT-G and beyond ecosystems. In: International Conference on Digital Sovereignty (ICDS 2024), *Procedia Computer Science*, 254, 39–47.

Kurakin, A., Goodfellow, I.J., & Bengio, S. (2018). Adversarial examples in the physical world. In: *Artificial Intelligence Safety and Security*, pp. 99–112. Chapman and Hall/CRC.

Lakshminarayanan, B., Pritzel, A., & Blundell, C. (2017). Simple and scalable predictive uncertainty estimation using deep ensembles. *Advances in Neural Information Processing Systems*, 30.

Li, B., Qi, P., Liu, B., Di, S., Liu, J., Pei, J. et al. (2023). Trustworthy AI: From principles to practices. *ACM Computing Surveys*, 55(9), 1–46.

Madry, A., Makelov, A., Schmidt, L., Tsipras, D., & Vladu, A.(2017). Towards deep learning models resistant to adversarial attacks. arXiv preprint arXiv:1706.06083.

Misra, S., Barik, K., & Kvalvik, P. (2025). Digital sovereignty in the era of Industry 5.0: Challenges and opportunities. *Procedia Computer Science*, 254, 108–117.

Papernot, N., & McDaniel, P. (2016). On the effectiveness of defensive distillation. arXiv preprint arXiv:1607.05113.

Pelekis, S., Koutroubas, T., Blika, A., Berdelis, A., Karakolis, E., Ntanos, C. et al. (2025). Adversarial machine learning: A review of methods, tools, and critical industry sectors. *Artificial Intelligence Review*, 58(8), 226.

Ronneberger, O., Fischer, P., & Brox, T. (2015). U-net: Convolutional networks for biomedical image segmentation. In: *Medical Image Computing and Computer-Assisted Intervention*

(MICCAI) 2015: 18th International Conference. Munich, Germany, October 5–9, 2015, Proceedings, Part III 18, pp. 234–241. Springer.

Saad, W., Bennis, M., & Chen, M. (2020). A vision of 6G wireless systems: Applications, trends, technologies, and open research problems. *IEEE Network*, 34(3), 134–142.

Thudumu, S., Branch, P., Jin, J., & Singh, J.J. (2020). A comprehensive survey of anomaly detection techniques for high dimensional big data. *Journal of Big Data*, 7(1), 1–30.

Yuan, X., He, P., Zhu, Q., & Li, X. (2019). Adversarial examples: Attacks and defenses for deep learning. *IEEE Transactions on Neural Networks and Learning Systems*, 30(9), 2805–2824.

CHAPTER

4

Generative Artificial Intelligence and AI-Enabled Archiving to Promote Digital Sovereignty in the Context of Core International Crimes

Tetiana Lutchyn[1(0000-0001-9504-664X)] **Benjamin Ricaud**[1*(0000-0002-7611-4448)], **Artem Galushko**[2*(0000-0002-6029-3517)] **and Megumi Ochi**[3(0000-0001-6633-1564)]

[1] Faculty of Science, The Arctic University of Norway, Tromsø, Norway
[2] Faculty of Law, The Arctic University of Norway, Tromsø, Norway
[3] Graduate School of International Relations, Ritsumeikan University, Kyoto, Japan

4.1 Introduction

There is an urgent need to archive digital materials related to core international crimes, including genocide, war crimes and crimes against humanity that increasingly affect the global community amid the ongoing proliferation of armed conflicts.[1] Systematic archiving of such information is essential to support future efforts toward justice and accountability for victims, and to help prevent the recurrence of these crimes for generations to come. However, digital archiving of evidence and information related to core crimes faces various challenges. Among them is to conduct it independently and autonomously. Creation of a collective memory is a fundamental aspect of a community of people. In this sense, it is essential to exclude arbitrary political interference and ensure efficient management of sensitive data which could enable digital sovereignty. Use of open-source Generative artificial intelligence (AI) has significant potential to solve these political and technical problems. It is a significant novel technology that can provide continuous access to large volumes of data,

[1] See Peace Research Institute Oslo (PRIO) 'New data shows record number of armed conflicts, https://www.prio.org/news/3532 (accessed 12 May 2025).

*Corresponding authors: benjamin.ricaud@uit.no, artem.galushko@uit.no

DOI: 10.1201/9781003581581-4

ensure easy navigation, interconnect different data types, and support interactive user experiences.

Despite the ongoing public debate about the potential application of AI technology, limited attention has been paid to AI use in core crime archiving so far. Our work addresses this research gap by examining how AI open-source technologies can be used to enhance digital sovereignty through the creation of sovereign, intelligent archival systems. In this chapter, we present the results of our initial archiving experiments with AI tools implemented by a small interdisciplinary team of researchers in machine learning and law. As we seek to explain how AI tools can promote digital sovereignty in the field of core crimes archiving, our hypothesis is that generative AI is one of the key novel technologies that provides significant opportunities to retain efficient control over the exponentially growing volumes of core crimes-related data. This interdisciplinary research on AI-enabled core crimes archiving provides implications on how a more effective process of conflict-related AI-enabled archiving can contribute to stronger digital sovereignty. By increasing control over critical data flows and reducing reliance on external actors, AI tools can empower even less technologically developed countries or countries affected by war to manage their sensitive and crucial data, while contributing to national digital heritage and strategic autonomy in the cyber domain.

The experiments described in the following sections showcase the potential and diverse applications of AI models. In particular, the preliminary findings indicate a promising ability to extract and textualize relevant information, reduce the harmful effects of violent content, enhance multimedia data, as well as facilitate multilingual access to various types of conflict-related digital materials such as video, audio and images. It can offer customized data access, which meets the individual needs of a great variety of users from civil society, public institutions and academia. Many AI solutions are cost-efficient and can be employed even in war-affected countries. Most of the tested AI model scan have a strong impact on core crime archiving and sovereignty. Therefore their rapid adoption is recommended. This work presents evidence demonstrating that the proposed AI tools align with the latest regulatory frameworks and can be further developed in full compliance with them.

Simultaneously, the practical work and conducted experiments revealed key technical challenges and limitations that include the need for AI models to achieve higher accuracy across languages while retaining the crucial context and preserving relevant details in the processed data. Furthermore, this research outlines and identifies a broad range of legal challenges related to universal guidelines for core crimes archives, ethics and AI bias, privacy, and compliance with relevant regulations such as the EU AI Act.

In the first part, we introduce the context of core crime archiving, AI in archiving and relating them to digital sovereignty. In the second part, we present the methodology and results of our experiments with AI on different promising use cases for core crime archiving. In the third part, we discuss the technical and legal implications of these AI tools and show their potential impact on digital sovereignty.

4.2 Archival Challenges and AI Potential Solutions

4.2.1 Archiving Core Crimes

Core crimes are grave offenses of international concern (Greenawalt, 2020; Stahn, 2018). They include genocide, crimes against humanity, war crimes and crimes of aggression, each falling within the jurisdiction of the International Criminal Court (ICC). The evidence required for such crimes is distinct, shaped by their specific context.

First, core crimes often occur during armed conflict. This poses serious difficulties for investigators to access evidence. The digital evidence provided by military satellites, drones, CCTV cameras or individual smart phones becomes critical and is sometimes the only available evidence. Second, core crimes are committed by groups or organizations of people including armed groups or even a state. The evidence that connects the on-site criminals and the masterminds who directed the crimes are the key to prove the that people in high ranks are responsible. Such linkage evidence is often found in communication records, such as military orders, documents attached to emails or text messages sent via private chat. Third, media or online video platform appearances provide evidence for dissemination of propaganda and hatred, and thus become critical evidence of genocide or persecution.

The archives that collect such evidential data are called core/war crimes archives (Ochi & Dagenborg, 2025). They are not created only for the purpose of prosecution, but also for researching and remembering. Based on their purpose, they are divided into archives of evidence, legal materials and memories. Judicial authorities and investigators use archives of evidence to collect evidence for litigation purposes, lawyers and researchers cite archives of legal materials for legal research, and historians, museums and educators visit archives of memories for collective memory and peace education.

For the purpose of core crimes archiving, it is desirable to extract only the crime-related information from the evidence/archival data. Data often includes video, audio, image, text and log data. Information about a crime includes proof of certain speech, location, time, movement and tools used that will support eyewitnesses.

Extracted information should be basically recorded in text form. Textualization will enable users to search, access and store the data effectively. Having descriptive text in addition to extracted metadata will be beneficial. Textualizing the main topic of communication, location and time, description of visual images will be useful for the purpose of efficient indexing and tagging. New technologies based on AI offer solutions fulfilling these needs and can even go further. This is what we will see in the next section.

4.3 AI and Achiving

4.3.1 AI in Archival Science, State of the Art

Previous research discussed various possibilities for the use of AI in core crimes-archiving. Freeman identified what opportunities and challenges the emerging military applications of AI might offer international criminal investigators (Freeman, 2021). Kuczyńska analyzed the legal character of the ICC's usage of AI, which is known as "Project Harmony" and posits doubt that this is a real "AI Revolution" (Kuczyńska, 2024). Limited attention has been paid to AI use in core crime archiving, with remarkable exceptions including the research on the use of AI in preservation of holocaust heritage (Zucker et al., 2023), and one on the ethical problems surrounding the use of AI in curation of genocide-related information (Makhortykh, 2023). However, there is little research on the possibilities based on technical AI experiments conducted by computer scientists.

Over the past five years, archival science has witnessed a growing integration of AI, encompassing machine learning, deep learning, and natural language processing (NLP), as a strategic response to the increasing complexities of managing and providing access to ever-expanding digital collections (Colavizza et al., 2021; Shinde et al., 2024; Teel, 2024). This adoption of AI reflects a broader trend within memory institutions that recognize the significant potential of computational methods to augment traditional archival functions and effectively address the unique challenges presented by digital materials. The escalating volume and intricate nature of digital archives necessitate the application of computational techniques for efficient processing, organization, and retrieval, positioning AI as a natural and increasingly vital evolution in archival practice.

Traditional archival processes, including appraisal (the critical determination of which records merit permanent preservation), arrangement (the systematic organization of records into manageable units), description (the creation of metadata and finding aids to provide context and facilitate discovery), access (the provision of records to users), and preservation (the implementation of strategies to ensure long-term usability), are increasingly intersecting with AI technologies (Colavizza et al., 2021). This integration signals a significant shift toward augmenting the expertise of human archivists with automated tools, potentially transforming methodologies across the archival lifecycle, from initial selection to long-term care and accessibility. By automating routine, time-intensive tasks and enabling advanced analytical capabilities, AI allows archivists to focus on the more complex intellectual and ethical dimensions of their profession.

While AI applications in archiving are evolving, to the best of our knowledge, no existing study specifically addresses the topic or distinct requirements of archiving core international crimes.

4.4 Generative AI and RAG for Archiving

Deep learning models, which are a type of AI, are designed to learn patterns and key features from data, like text or images, in a step-by-step process. Through this process, these models generate "embeddings," which are numerical representations that encapsulate the most significant and informative aspects of the input data. They serve as a compressed summary of the original data, preserving its essential characteristics while reducing its complexity. Conceptually, they can be understood as coordinates that position the input data within a multi-dimensional space, often referred to as the "latent space."

The structure of these embeddings is such that data with similar meanings or characteristics is mapped to nearby points within this latent space. For instance, in the context of natural language processing, sentences or documents that convey related ideas or themes will have embeddings that are numerically similar, reflecting their conceptual proximity. Foundational research, such as Word2Vec (Mikolov et al., 2013) and subsequent advancements like BERT (Devlin et al., 2019), has established the ability of these models to represent not just the literal content of text but also its underlying meaning. This principle extends beyond text to other data types, including images (Radford et al., 2023; Rombach et al., 2022), audio (Kreuk et al., 2023), and video (Bar-Tal et al., 2024), where embeddings similarly capture the core attributes of the input.

Retrieval-Augmented Generation (RAG) (Lewis et al., 2020) is an advanced AI technique that leverages embeddings to enhance the accuracy and relevance of generated responses. When a query is made, the AI uses embeddings to search through a large database or corpus, identifying documents or passages with similar semantic meaning to the query. These embeddings allow the AI to efficiently locate and retrieve the most relevant information by comparing the "positions" of the query and the stored data in a multi-dimensional space. Once the relevant information is retrieved, the AI integrates it into its response, generating a detailed and contextually accurate answer. By combining the precision of retrieval with the flexibility of generation, RAG enables AI systems to provide informed and reliable outputs, particularly in tasks requiring synthesis of knowledge from extensive data sets, such as legal research or document summarization. The effectiveness of RAG is supported by empirical studies (Gienapp et al., 2024; X. Li et al., 2025) showing enhanced performance in scientific summarization, literature review, and knowledge extraction.

4.5 Importance of AI-enabled Core Crimes Archiving for Digital Sovereignty

Technological or digital sovereignty plays a key role in the cyber documentation of core crimes. The concept, which is linked to the strategic control over personal data and autonomy in the digital domain, is the basis of the theoretical framework we propose. There is ongoing interdisciplinary cooperation to ensure that countries, institutions and individuals have control over their own data related to international crimes. For instance, judicial institutions like the ICC,[2] legal and IT experts cooperate to develop basic rules and standards of digital documentation and archiving them would help provide easy and uninterrupted access to the archived data.[3] These

[2] See the Policy on Complementarity and Cooperation (PCC) published by the Office of the Prosecutor (OTP ICC) in April 2024, at https://www.icc-cpi.int/news/policy-complementarity-and-cooperation-2024 (accessed 23.04.2025).

[3] Eurojust and the ICC, 'Documenting International Crimes and Human Rights Violations for Accountability Purposes: Guidelines for Civil Society Organisations' (hereinafter: 'Guidelines for Civil Society Organisations'), https://www.eurojust.europa.eu/publication/documenting-international-crimes-and-human-rights-violations (accessed 13.05.2025).

interdisciplinary initiatives are closely linked to the concept of cyber sovereignty (Jensen, 2014). Most recently, the corona virus pandemic combined with foreign manipulation and disinformation activities motivated the European Parliament to draft a strategy on the 'Digital sovereignty for Europe' in 2020, which advocates for strategic digital autonomy and "ethically designed artificial intelligence (AI)."[4]

In the transnational context, current transatlantic tensions with the new US administration and diverse approaches to digital sovereignty have increased the 'geopolitical competition between the US, China and the EU.'[5] In this context, our research seeks to propose a more universal approach to digital sovereignty and archiving. In particular, this chapter will show that AI-based technologies can play a key role in the harmonization of diverse open-source based core crimes archiving platforms that have a potential to advance sovereignty in the cyber domain. This could further contribute to a concept of more open and grass-roots oriented digital sovereignty, which will be instrumental for enhancing the quality of archived data through global inter connectivity and interdisciplinary cooperation.

Achieving robust data sovereignty necessitates direct control over data storage and processing infrastructure. This can be realized by housing data and executing computational tasks on privately owned or state-controlled systems. The advent of sophisticated Artificial Intelligence (AI) technologies, particularly those available as open-source software, significantly reduces the reliance on external, often large-scale private entities or cloud-based services for data processing, even when dealing with substantial volumes and diverse data types.

A significant proportion of contemporary AI tools and models are distributed under permissive open-source licenses, such as MIT[6] or Apache 2.0[7]. This licensing framework grants users the freedom to access, utilize, modify, and build upon the source code without proprietary restrictions. A key advantage of the open-source paradigm is the inherent transparency it provides. The open nature of the source code allows for thorough inspection and verification, ensuring that no concealed processes are operating that could potentially compromise, alter, or exfiltrate data without explicit authorization or user awareness. This transparency is crucial for building trust and ensuring the integrity of data processing pipelines.

Effective data governance also relies on implementing particular access control mechanisms. Data access can be stratified into multiple levels to align with security requirements and user roles. These levels can range from restricted access, permitting interaction only with metadata, to progressively broader access with summaries, anonymized datasets, transcriptions, and ultimately, full access to the original source documents. Generative AI enables the automatic production of content at

4 See EPRS Ideas Paper Towards a more resilient EU, 'Digital sovereignty for Europe', at https://www.europarl.europa.eu/RegData/etudes/BRIE/2020/651992/EPRS_BRI(2020)651992_EN.pdf (accessed 23.04.2025).

5 See the World Economic Forum, 'What is digital sovereignty and how are countries approaching it?', 10.01.2025, https://www.weforum.org/stories/2025/01/europe-digital-sovereignty/ (accessed 23.04.2025).

6 https://mit-license.org/

7 https://www.apache.org/licenses/LICENSE-2.0

different layers of security, by, for instance, creating a description of an image as meta data, summarizing a long document or anonymizing videos by detecting and blurring faces.

It is important to note that in processing work flows involving AI, the original data typically remains unaltered (unmodified). AI models primarily function to extract, analyze, and transform information contained within the documents. This includes tasks such as generating translations, creating transcriptions, producing summaries, or providing automated recommendations. These processes enhance data accessibility and utility for human users without modifying the foundational data assets.

By integrating on-premise infrastructure, open-source AI, and structured access controls, organizations and states can significantly strengthen their data sovereignty and ensure accountable and transparent data stewardship.

4.6 Challenges and Potential Solutions

First, due to their open-source format, AI models have the potential to address the risk of over dependence on foreign actors and become an 'equalizer' among countries with significant disparities in technological development (Lehuedé, 2024). The proposed approach to archiving could advance digital autonomy of technologically under developed countries by providing them with more effective control over their own data and supporting their capacity to innovate. This is especially relevant in the context of armed conflicts when countries affected by military hostilities often cannot afford significant digital infrastructure and energy-intensive computations (Mamediieva & Moynihan, 2023). Thus, we argue that even during ongoing conflicts aggravated by unstable electricity supplies and failing digital infrastructure, war-affected countries can maintain and secure their digital sovereignty in the field of core crimes archiving by using the RAG-based solutions proposed in this chapter.

Second, AI-enabled tools discussed in the chapter address the ethical challenges of archiving war-related data (Makhortykh et al., 2023) by providing more efficient control over explicit materials on core crimes such as genocide, core crimes, crimes against humanity and the crime of aggression. The sensitive nature of digital content on crimes, which includes extreme examples of violence, necessitates a careful and balanced approach during an ongoing war (Koenig, 2022). While ensuring data privacy, state institutions are also responsible for the digital chain of custody and preventing unauthorized leaks or dissemination of violent war-related content. On the one hand, the RAG and Generative AI technologies ensure that digital evidence remains unaltered. On the other hand, it can decrease the level of psychological exposure to violent content among the public, investigators and archivists by making it less harmful and more emotionally acceptable. A lack of control over sensitive data can, on the contrary, potentially undermine the digital sovereignty of a state, which would be exposed to possible misuse. This information could be, for example, weaponized in disinformation campaigns (Zecchinon & and Standaert, 2025) launched by malicious external actors.

Finally, the key advantage of the proposed AI-based models is related to the possibility of offering instantaneous customized access to a large variety and quantity of digital materials in multiple languages and formats that could cater to the needs and preferences of interested individual users. AI-enabled systems can be used to inform and educate the public (Saltman, 2020) through summaries of conflict-related materials, translations or transcriptions. At the same time, investigative journalists and legal practitioners could employ the same systems when they look for linkage evidence (Porter, 2016), which connects alleged perpetrators to specific crimes. Therefore, the multimodal and multilingual capacities of the suggested AI-enabled tools address the challenge of the occupational, cultural and linguistic diversity of users who access digital core crimes archives. The performed experiments demonstrate the (future) potential of AI to either reduce or remove the barriers that prevent users from accessing and understanding conflict-related materials in connection with the local linguistic and cultural context. Developing national sovereign digital archiving capacity could ensure that this local context will be taken into consideration. The AI models can be biased toward a particular culture (Liu, 2024) and need to be adapted or fine-tuned within the local context.

In this context, the proposed Generative AI solutions in the field of core crimes archiving align with the relevant EU regulations and policies on human-centric and trustworthy AI within the EU. The interplay between the EU legal framework and research will be further explained in the section on legal and technological challenges.

RAG has the potential to become a central tool in the future of war crime archiving and for strengthening digital sovereignty. Its advanced capabilities bring solutions to the challenges identified previously in Table 4.1. Unlike traditional keyword-based search, RAG enables semantic search, allowing it to "understand" and retrieve information based on meaning rather than exact terms. It is also versatile, capable of working with multimedia data such as images and videos, making it ideal for handling diverse types of evidence. With many open-source implementations available, RAG can be deployed as free and secure software, and it can even be run on a local server to ensure data privacy and control. Additionally, its chatbot interface can adapt to the needs of users, providing an intuitive and user-friendly way to access and analyze critical information.

In the following section, we include the RAG system in a broader set of AI tools for core crime archiving. Table 4.1 lists challenges in the preservation of digital materials on core crimes and its impact in the context of digital sovereignty. In the last column, we propose possible AI methods addressing each challenge. More details about these AI solutions will be given in the section where the experiments referring to some of the solutions are mentioned. RAG is Retrieval Augmented Generation, an emerging Generative AI technique described in a previous section

4.7 Experiments

4.7.1 General Experimental Design

To evaluate the potential of AI-enabled archiving and its impact on sovereignty several experiments have been conducted. Each experiment relates to an aspect of digital sovereignty stated previously in Table 4.1 and to the challenges in core crimes archiving we have been described earlier. An overview of the experiments is given

Table 4.1. Advantages of AI-enabled archiving for challenges in war crimes digital preservation and sovereignty

Challenges in war crimes digital preservation and sovereignty	Description	Foreseen advantages of AI-enabled archiving
Control over sensitive data	**A. Data Authenticity and Integrity:** Ensuring that digital evidence remains unaltered. **B. Access Control and Privacy Protection:** Archival systems must balance open access for authorized legal experts with strong protection against unauthorized leaks or breaches. **C. Investigator Mental Health:** Investigators and archive curators' needs to look at sensitive data, containing violence, torture and death (Tsai et al., 2009).	**A. Data Authenticity and Integrity**: RAG models facilitate transparent linking between generated data and source documents or multimedia. **B. Access Control and Privacy Protection:** RAG integrated in databases, RAG running locally on servers, chatbots running locally. AI tools to anonymize documents. **C. Investigator protection:** AI can automatically flag sensitive content, generate text description and summaries, which are less harmful. AI can modify images or videos by changing the style. A cartoon-style version of a video could reduce the exposure of investigators to sensitive content. (Experiment 6 on style transfer)
Customized access for many audiences	**D. Multimodal and Multilingual Complexity:** Evidence often includes heterogeneous data types: video, audio, handwritten and printed text, images (Fig. 4.2) – with content in multiple languages. Handling such diversity requires sophisticated processing pipelines capable of unifying disparate formats and linguistic varieties.	**D. Multi modal Data, Automated Transcription and Translation:** The combination of AI models dedicated to different data sources can be used to enrich the sources with metadata and text. Audio transcription (Experiment 2), optical character recognition (OCR) (Experiment 3), automatic image description (Experiment 5) and automatic translation (Experiment 4) empower comprehensive archiving of diverse evidence types.
Own hosting of data thanks to cost efficiency	**E. Scalability and Longevity:** With increasing volumes of digital materials, solutions need to support scalable ingestion, processing, and retrieval, while ensuring long-term maintainability despite evolving technologies.	**E. Scalability and Longevity:** By indexing multimodal content semantically, RAG enables precise querying and retrieval of relevant information, facilitating faster legal research and case-building. Adaptive knowledge integration: constant updating and fine-tuning of the AI models ensure metadata and generated

		content improve in accuracy and reflect evolving legal standards and evidentiary criteria.
	F. Technical Expertise and Resource Limitations: Effective digital archiving demands domain expertise combining legal knowledge, digital forensics, and technological knowledge, which may be limited in some organizations or jurisdictions.	**F. Technical Expertise and Resource Limitations:** AI tools are making user interface simpler by interacting with chatbots in a question-answer style. However, the maintenance of AI requires technicians and engineers. But these positions could be made less technical with the assistance of AI. (Our experiments were made with limited computer and human resources)

Table 4.2. Table of experiments

Pipeline stage	Description	Relevant technologies	Archiving task category
1. Meta Preprocessing	Audio/video preprocessing for AI segments and frame extraction for video content sampling.	moviepy, OpenCV	(C)
2. Audio Extraction & Transcription	Extraction of audio segments from videos and conversion into text using Whisper or Speech Recognition APIs, with language-specific customization.	Whisper, Speech Recognition, pydub	(A) and (D)
3. Text Recognition	Recognition of printed text in images and handwritten text from scanned documents.	Tesseract OCR, OpenCV, pytesseract	(A) and (D)
4. Multilingual Translation & Subtitle Synthesis	Translation of transcribed text into multiple languages, followed by subtitle generation and embedding into video files.	Hugging Face MarianMT, FFmpeg	(A) and (B)
5. Semantic Indexing and Retrieval of Images	Creation of dense embeddings of textual and visual data enabling semantic search and contextual document retrieval.	LangChain, BLIP, FAISS, CLIP, Transformers	(B)
6. Style Transfer	Style transfer of images. Changing the style or turning images into cartoons while keeping the same content or information. Reduce the potential harm caused by sensitive content.	InstructPix2Pix, CartoonGAN	(B) and (D)

in Table 4.2. AI models can be used at different stages of the archiving process with distinct tasks. These have been related to each other in the table. Each experiment is independent, however, they can also be parts of a larger AI-enabled archiving framework for war crime archiving, where they are combined. This is illustrated in Fig. 4.1. The archiving system (RAG) is the central piece which receives input from different AI systems, each one specialized in a type of data (text, audio, image and video). This architecture shows how AI technologies can be combined to enable the secure, efficient, and intelligent archiving of audiovisual and textual materials supporting digital sovereignty.

AI has the ability to automate time-intensive tasks such as transcription, translation, document digitization, and content classification. Different AI models and tools have been designed for each of these tasks by the open-source community. Some examples used in the experiments shown in Fig. 4.1 are Whisper (Radford et al., 2023) for converting speech to text and CLIP (Radford et al., 2021) for generating images descriptions.

Before we present the experiments, it is notable that these experiments were performed in a research lab with limited human and equipment resources. It

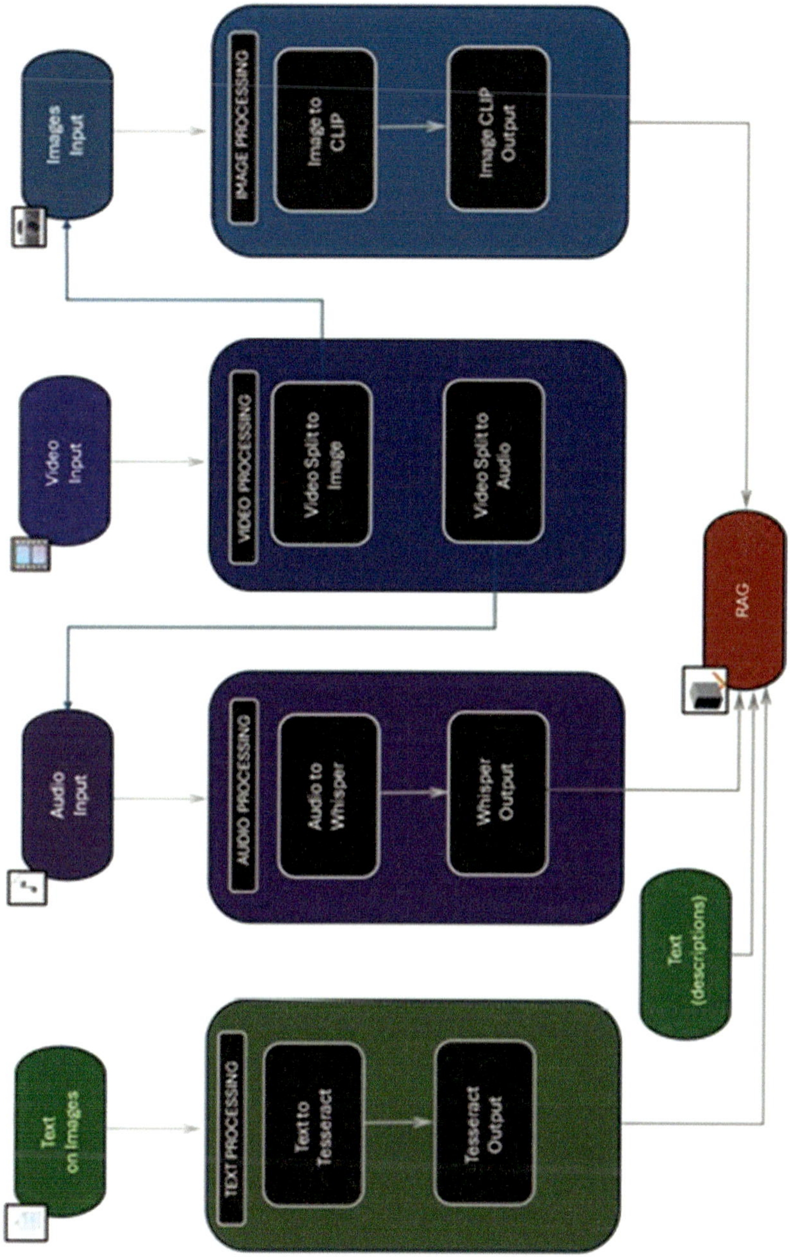

Figure 4.1. Proposed structure for archiving war crimes. The central part is a RAG system (in red). Data from different modalities (text audio, image, videos) are processed by different specialized AI models which enrich the original document before being stored in the RAG system.

demonstrates the possibility of setting up these systems even in difficult conditions with reduced resources.

To be representative of war crime archiving, the experiments have been conducted using open data available at Eyesonrussia.[8] This website collects data about Russia's aggression during the war in Ukraine. The data comprises texts, sounds, videos, images from social networks and are typically relevant to war crime archiving. A subset of approximately 20,000 documents was extracted from the available data. Figure 4.2 shows the type of files collected.

A combination of all image-related categories—still images, satellite images, and the image component of the combined image+video, constitute a significant portion of the overall dataset. It highlights the importance of these types of documents in the context of war crime archiving. Audio and video files are central to crime investigations and digital forensics (Pedapudi & Vadlamani, 2023) and even more for core crimes.

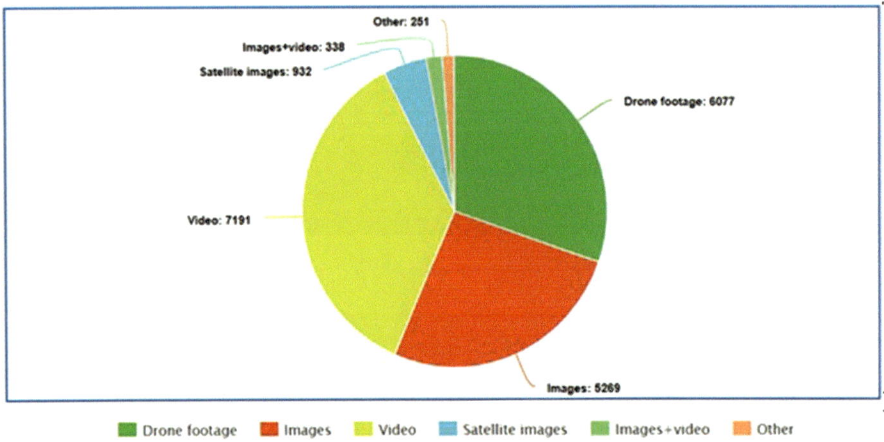

Figure 4.2. Structure of open-source data, from the sample extracted from the website Eyesonrussia.

4.8 The Six AI Experiments

In practice, there are multiple potential Contributions of Generative AI in Digital Archiving in general and war crime archiving in particular. We identify several key directions where AI can have an impact on archiving and core crimes archiving: (A) Enhanced Metadata Creation and Enrichment, (B) Improved Accessibility and Search Functionality, (C) Data Cleansing and Normalization, (D) Content Generation for Access and Engagement. For each direction, a list of use cases of AI is proposed for archiving core crimes, with concrete examples. This list is not exhaustive but it highlights the major impact AI can have on core crimes archiving. For each example, a prototype has been created and evaluated exposing benefits and limitations.

[8] https://eyesonrussia.org/

Experiment 1: Media Preprocessing

The video documents collected by Eyesonrussia typically last only a few minutes but important information can appear during durations of a few seconds. To extract such information effectively, and to avoid losing important details, the videos are split into short segments. Each segment is then processed independently. This can be done with open source tools such as Open CV,[9] or Python libraries such as pydub[10] and moviepy[11]. They do not involve AI, i.e. large neural network models, per se. They are simpler tools used to pre-process the data before its ingestion by AI models. However, they are an essential part of the processing chain and can greatly impact the results further down the line. Large language models have difficulties finding particular information in large documents. This fact is known and called the "needle-in-a-haystack" problem in Large Language Models (Kuratov et al., 2024; Yu et al., 2025). The natural solution is to cut documents into small pieces so that AI models have less information to handle, which is then implemented in RAG systems. However, each small piece may lack the general context of the document, which poses new problems, because the AI system is processing information with missing context.

As in the RAG approach for text, it is an open question on how to choose the best size for the segments and when to split the data (videos and text for standard RAG). There is a trade off between having a useful context background and reducing irrelevant information to identify a particular piece of context related information. This can be overcome in the future by having trained or fine-tuned AI models for specific war crime contexts, where they are already present (memorized) within the model when analyzing small document pieces.

Experiment 2: Audio Transcription

Here we explore the automated transcription of audio segments from video files. This is a central process in order to enrich audio-visual documents with transcripted speech. It opens the door to generating speech translations or document summaries and enhanced indexing in archives. OpenAI's Whisper model (Radford et al., 2023) and an open-source software suite are used for speech recognition (Zhang, 2014/2025). Thirty-second short videos are isolated and transcribed with high accuracy. Multiple languages were tested, leveraging Whisper's multilingual support.

Despite achieving high transcription accuracy, several limitations emerged in the given context. War-related speech is particularly challenging to process due to short and incomplete sentences, frequent use of abbreviations, language mixing, partial word ommisions, background noise, and low-quality audio recordings. Additionally, current tools are unable to capture voice intonation and emotion, both of which convey critical information. Transcription under these conditions remains

---

9 OpenCV – Open Computer Vision Library.

10 Robert, J. *pydub: Manipulate Audio with a Simple and Easy High-level Interface* [Computer software, MIT license]. https://github.com/jiaaro/pydub

11 Zulfikri, A. (2013–2023). *moviepy: Video editing with Python* [Computer software]. https://zulko.github.io/moviepy/

a significant challenge for existing AI models and constitutes an open research problem. Moreover, Whisper exhibited reduced performance in both speed and translation quality across several non-English languages, notably Ukrainian. In comparison, MarianTM (Junczys-Dowmunt et al., 2018), which is specifically trained on a range of non-English languages delivered superior results, highlighting the need for custom models for core crime archiving and, in particular, specific models for each war zone.

Experiment 3: Text Recognition

Optical character recognition (OCR) is another critical component of the digitization pipeline. The open-source software pytesseract (Hoffstaetter, 2018/2025) uses Tesseract OCR (Smith, 2007; *Tesseract-Ocr/Tesseract*, 2014/2025) and enables the extraction of text from scanned and handwritten documents. This is a computationally light solution which can produce high-quality texts. It works on a standard stand-alone computer. Recently, chatbots have developed the ability to analyze images and pdf documents and extract text within them. Hence, research and development on larger AI models proposes AI-powered OCR solutions.

The data from Eyesonrussia include handwritten documents, images of machines or weapons with identification numbers or text on them, images with city and street names, and satellite images with exactly mentioned coordinates. This can be useful information that can't be found by searching a standard archive but can be extracted automatically with OCR and becomes accessible metadata. This experiment,successfully extracted text appearing in war zone images. The results were excellent for English text, slightly lower for Ukrainian but acceptable. No real limitations were observed. OCR is very efficient and should be incurrent use for archiving.

Experiment 4: Speech Translation

To address access to audiovisual archives an AI pipeline was designed to automatically provide subtitles in multilingual videos. This is based on Whisper for transcription (see Experiment 2), open-source AI models for translation (the "medium" version of OpenAI's Whisper and the Marian MT model from Helsinki-NLP) available in the Hugging Face Transformers (Wolf et al., 2020; *Models - Hugging Face*, n.d.), and the open-source software FFmpeg (*FFmpeg/FFmpeg*, 2011/2025) extracting audio and subtitling. Our prototype produced a fully translated, dubbed and subtitled video, in different languages.

The ability to merge videos and overlay translated subtitles in different languages provides potential for a broader use of disseminating national or regional media. Reliance on audio transcription for performing speech translation, makes it suffer from the limitations, stated in Experiment 2. In particular, the lack of emotions and intonation (non-transcribed) in the dubbing is striking and damages the quality of the generated document. Better AI solutions should be used which do not rely on transcripted text but directly work on a speech-to-speech level such as mentioned by Le et al, 2024 and Lee et al, 2022. However, these solutions are not yet available for a wide range of languages.

Another notable limitation concerns translation accuracy. Precision in translation requires contextual understanding—something current AI tools do not yet possess. For instance, the English phrase "the Red Square," referring to the iconic location in Moscow, may be literally translated in other languages as a square that is red, failing to convey the intended reference. This stems from the translator's lack of contextual awareness. Short videos and testimonies related to core crimes often contain substantial implicit knowledge. Emotional intensity may further hinder verbal expression. To improve performance, both speech-to-text and translation models must be trained or fine-tuned to the specific linguistic and emotional context of core crime documentation.

Experiment 5: Semantic Indexing and Retrieval of Images

To improve visual data management, the use of OpenAI's CLIP (Cellular Logic Image Processor) model (Radford et al., 2021) shows promising results. This model is at the heart of many AI-based image-to-text and text-to-image applications and generative AI for images. For example it is a key component of Stable Diffusion (Rombach et al., 2022) which generates images from text prompts or of language models for their understanding of images (J. Li et al., 2022). CLIP enables image-to-image similarity matching archival image classification, allowing semantic grouping (similar context) of visual records. It can also link user-provided text to the most relevant image, allowing efficient searching of images in archives using text or keywords.

As a part of the developed RAG system, we apply CLIP to images either taken directly or extracted from videos. We then perform an image search by similarity matching. For example, a keyword search was performed on images using "water and flooding". As a result, a set of images were obtained where water was visible. A large number of images related to flooding caused by the destruction of the Kakhovka dam[12] by the Russian army were observed. Comparing the geolocation of all the images related to the keyword search, aggregation around large rivers in Ukraine was observed, which makes sense. Having the ability to search images is a highly valuable asset for users of war crime archives. It also enables the retrieval of data with missing or incorrect description, or wrongly classified when recorded in the archive. This strengthens control on the data and, as a consequence, digital sovereignty.

Experiment 6: Style Transfer

The direction of research called Neural Style Transfer (Jing et al., 2020) develops neural network models with the purpose of changing the style of images. It turns an input image into a new, modified, image that keeps the main image information while being artistically different. A typical example is changing an image into a famous artist style or changing an image into a cartoon. We applied style transfer to a selection

---

[12] 'New Report Claims That the Destruction of Kakhovka Dam is an Environmental War Crime – Truth Hounds'. https://truth-hounds.org/en/cases/new-report-claims-that-the-destruction-of-kakhovka-dam-is-an-environmental-war-crime/ (accessed 12 May 2025).

of images from our dataset depicting humans, landscapes and buildings. Recent AI style transfer models openly available on Hugging Face are Instruct Pix2Pix (Brooks et al., 2023) and CartoonGAN (Chen et al., 2018).

The results were convincing when humans appeared on the images. We noted difficulties for images with complex backgrounds such as destroyed buildings with poor lighting, where the style transfer lost important details. This approach is a promising solution for reducing harmful impact of sensitive images and videos, where the important information is not in small details contained in the images. It can also be used for anonymizing them as human faces turned into cartoons cannot be identified with certainty.

4.9 Summary of Result

A short description of the different AI experiments conducted for war crime archiving. We classify them in different categories for 6 experiments as listed in subsection 4.8.

4.10 Technical and Legal Challenges

4.10.1 For Effective Core Crimes Archiving

We have seen that limitations for AI-enabled core crimes archiving include (i) an "understanding" of the context by AI models and (ii) preservation of implicit subjective elements such as emotions, intonation and facial expressions in the processed data.

First, one of the challenges revealed in Experiment 1 and 4 was the lack of knowledge of premised context. The political context of war explains the purpose of certain statements or behavior and thus may indicate an intent to commit a crime. However, the contextual information is sometimes missing in the limited duration of the provided video, or the model misses the context even when it already exists (memorized) within the model when analyzing small pieces of documents. In experiments for an optimal transcription or translation, the models need to understand the exact historical, political and cultural context for accurate translation, as illustrated in the example of "the red square." It was suggested to adapt or train models on core crimes archival data.

Second, AI processing often misses the indications of human emotions. Core crimes cases are often the ultimate expression of dehumanization with extreme hatred or discriminatory ideology. Without recording such emotions, most core crimes-related information loses its value. Victim testimonies require recording the grief and pain that are expressed through cries, moaning and sighs. Especially in audio and video processing, the lack of emotions and intonation (non-transcribed) in the dubbing is striking and significantly damages the quality of the document and its perception of authenticity. Moreover, sensitive events may be difficult to express in words due to emotion. However, as the data is supposed to be used for core crimes investigation, litigation or memory creation, elements of emotions are critical and must be preserved in an accessible way. Voice tones or facial expressions are such indications, and preserving such emotional elements will be one of the main challenges for AI use for core crimes archiving.

4.11 Compliance with AI Regulations

The issues and concerns around AI addressed in this chapter go beyond core crimes archiving and touch upon topical questions related to the scope of AI regulation. The technological challenges of extensive volumes and diversity of collected digital materials also encompass legal issues such as the security of core crimes data, the protection of privacy-sensitive evidence, ethical implications of possible AI malperformance, information integrity and local control over data in compliance with national and international regulations. In this context, the European Union remains a champion in the field of AI regulation with its AI Act,[13] which is the first comprehensive international regulation on AI. EU institutions have also developed various legal instruments such as the General Data Protection Regulation (GDPR),[14] Directive on the Security of Network and Information Systems (NIS 1 and its successor NIS 2),[15] the Law Enforcement Directive (LED)[16] and other regulatory frameworks that can address risks associated with the collection of cyber evidence using novel technologies like AI.

While our research relies upon the EU legislation and strategic documents on digital sovereignty and AI, we believe that solutions envisaged in relevant norms of European Law can have the 'Brussels effect' (Bradford, 2020) and inspire a uniform transnational approach to AI-enabled core crimes archiving across multiple jurisdictions and disciplines.

In terms of developing a uniform approach to archiving across multiple jurisdictions, previous research in the field called for universal guidelines for core/war crimes archives to standardize the security management and user interface. The proposed fundamental principles are twofold: do-no-harm and prove effective. The

---

[13] Regulation (EU) 2024/1689 of the European Parliament and of the Council of 13 June 2024 laying down harmonised rules on artificial intelligence and amending Regulations (EC) No 300/2008, (EU) No 167/2013, (EU) No 168/2013, (EU) 2018/858, (EU) 2018/1139 and (EU) 2019/2144 and Directives 2014/90/EU, (EU) 2016/797 and (EU) 2020/1828 (Artificial Intelligence Act) (Text with EEA relevance), at https://eur-lex.europa.eu/legal-content/EN/TXT/?uri=CELEX:32024R1689 (accessed 14.04.2025).

[14] Regulation (EU) 2016/679 of the European Parliament and of the Council of 27 April 2016 on the protection of natural persons with regard to the processing of personal data and on the free movement of such data, and repealing Directive 95/46/EC (General Data Protection Regulation) OJ L 119/1. https://eur-lex.europa.eu/eli/reg/2016/679/oj/eng (accessed 23.04.2025).

[15] European Commission, 'Directive on measures for a high common level of cybersecurity across the Union (NIS 2 Directive) – FAQs' (2024). https://digital-strategy.ec.europa.eu/en/faqs/directive-measures-high-common-level-cybersecurity-across-union-nis2-directive-faqs (accessed 23.04.2025).

[16] Directive (EU) 2016/680 of the European Parliament and of the Council of 27 April 2016 on the protection of natural persons with regard to the processing of personal data by competent authorities for the purposes of the prevention, investigation, detection or prosecution of criminal offences or the execution of criminal penalties, and on the free movement of such data, and repealing Council Framework Decision 2008/977/JHA OJ L 119/89..https://eur-lex.europa.eu/eli/dir/2016/680/oj/eng (accessed 23.04.2025).

other three principles include: legality, data integrity, and transparency/accountability (Ochi & Dagenborg, 2025). The usage of AI technologies to create and manage storage is also required to adhere to these basic requirements. Meanwhile, the research result of this paper indicates that the universal guidelines for the use of AI in core crimes archiving should be developed especially in relation to the challenges pointed out above. Compliance with AI regulations will be incorporated into the principle of legality. However, the question of how to incorporate the issues of missing context and emotion will be addressed in our future research.

In terms of the cost-efficiency of suggested AI models, their transparent open-source format addresses the EU's primary concerns over the increasing dominance of non-European companies and potential loss of control over personal data. Developing open-source Generative AI models that do not require significant infrastructure and energy-intensive computations complies with the European Union's strategy of supporting innovation and a transparent European AI ecosystem outlined in the EU AI Act.[17] In practical terms, the EU's priority of supporting small and medium-sized enterprises (SMEs) and startups[18] could also advance European AI initiatives on developing new and cost-efficient open-access platforms that could be instrumental in securing the digital sovereignty of countries affected by armed conflicts around the world. Since scientific research and development are excluded from the scope of the EU AI Act, this could further promote academic innovation and experimentation with cost-effective AI-enabled models that will eventually become available for the work of journalists, civil society and non-profit organizations traditionally involved (Kohli, 2018) in international accountability efforts.

Our goal of integrating clear standards into the process of archiving explicit materials on core crimes complies with the EU AI Act and Ethics Guidelines for Trustworthy AI by the AI HLEG (High-level group on Artificial Intelligence).[19] These guidelines also emphasize the importance of human oversight, technical robustness and safety, privacy and data governance. The sensitive and harmful nature of archived core crimes data necessitates even broader interdisciplinary collaboration at the intersection of archival science, ethics, legal theory and practice in Europe and internationally. Furthermore, privacy-related provisions of the GDPR[20] and the

---

[17] Regulation (EU) 2024/1689 of the European Parliament and of the Council of 13 June 2024 laying down harmonised rules on artificial intelligence and amending Regulations (EC) No 300/2008, (EU) No 167/2013, (EU) No 168/2013, (EU) 2018/858, (EU) 2018/1139 and (EU) 2019/2144 and Directives 2014/90/EU, (EU) 2016/797 and (EU) 2020/1828 (Artificial Intelligence Act) (Text with EEA relevance), at https://eur-lex.europa.eu/legal-content/EN/TXT/?uri=CELEX:32024R1689 (accessed 14.04.2025).

[18] Articles 57-58 (AI Regulatory Sandboxes). EU Artificial Intelligence Act. (Text with EEA relevance), at https://eur-lex.europa.eu/legal-content/EN/TXT/?uri=CELEX:32024R1689 (accessed 14.04.2025).

[19] High-level group on Artificial Intelligence, https://digital-strategy.ec.europa.eu/en/policies/expert-group-ai (accessed 23.04.2025).

[20] Regulation (EU) 2016/679 of the European Parliament and of the Council of 27 April 2016 on the protection of natural persons with regard to the processing of personal data and on the free movement of such data, and repealing Directive 95/46/EC (General Data Protection Regulation) OJ L 119/1. https://eur-lex.europa.eu/eli/reg/2016/679/oj/eng (accessed 23.04.2025).

ePrivacy Directive[21] could serve as an example for the development of international guidelines on AI-enabled archiving of sensitive personal data with clear limits in relation to biometric identification and facial recognition, racial or ethnic data.[22] Furthermore, the EU has provisions and requirements on fundamental rights impact assessments[23] about AI-enabled archiving of sensitive private data. It further justifies the broad interdisciplinary cooperation among legal and machine learning experts adopted within this research.

The scientific mission of our research is to promote trustworthy, human-centric, transparent and versatile AI solutions that could meet the diverse needs of various groups seeking to access digital archives on armed conflicts. Following the previous research (Jaiswal & Schaathun, 2025), this chapter advocates for human-centric digital sovereignty in AI-enabled core crimes archiving, which empowers citizens to collect data as evidence of international law violations, rather than relying exclusively on regulations that often lag behind technological change. The empowerment and education of citizens can further legitimize the process of core crimes archiving, which is based on the 'grass-roots' evidence collection by affected communities, such as victims and witnesses.

The concept of human-centric digital sovereignty also corresponds to the EU core values and principles that support peace and security, and respect to fundamental rights and freedoms. On the one hand, providing the public with an opportunity to use AI-enabled digital archives for educational purposes could assist the EU in achieving its goal of promoting AI literacy (Audenhove et al., 2024). On the other hand, archiving raw data on core crimes and making it easily available for law-enforcement purposes will be entirely in line with the recent efforts of the EU justice initiatives, such as the launch of the Core Crimes Evidence Database and the establishment of the new International Centre for Prosecution of the Crime of Aggression at the EU Agency for Criminal Justice Cooperation.[24] Besides the importance of AI-enabled digital archiving for experimentation and innovation in the field of AI, our research is fundamentally aligned with the current EU strategies and policy aimed at promoting European digital sovereignty and autonomy in the cyber domain.

---

21 Directive 2002/58/EC of the European Parliament and of the Council of 12 July 2002 concerning the processing of personal data and the protection of privacy in the electronic communications sector (Directive on privacy and electronic communications) OJ L 201, 31.7.2002, pp. 37–47, at https://eur-lex.europa.eu/eli/dir/2002/58/oj/eng (accessed 14.04.2025).

22 Article 5 (Prohibited AI Practices). EU Artificial Intelligence Act. (Text with EEA relevance), at https://eur-lex.europa.eu/legal-content/EN/TXT/?uri=CELEX:32024R1689 (accessed 14.04.2025).

23 Article 27: Fundamental Rights Impact Assessment for High-Risk AI Systems. EU Artificial Intelligence Act (Text with EEA relevance), at https://eur-lex.europa.eu/legal-content/EN/TXT/?uri=CELEX:32024R1689 (accessed 14.04.2025).

24 'Start of Operations of Core International Crimes Evidence Database and New International Centre for Prosecution of the Crime of Aggression to be Based at Agency | Eurojust | European Union Agency for Criminal Justice Cooperation' https://www.eurojust.europa.eu/news/start-operations-core-international-crimes-evidence-database-and-new-international-centre (accessed 12 May 2025).

4.12 Conclusion

This research underscores the transformative potential of AI-enabled tools in the domain of core crimes archiving, with a particular focus on promoting digital sovereignty. By leveraging open-source technologies, we demonstrate how sovereign, intelligent archival systems can be developed to process, manage, and preserve vast amounts of multimedia data related to core crimes. These systems not only enhance accessibility and usability for diverse stakeholders but also reduce reliance on external actors, thereby strengthening the autonomy of nations, particularly those affected by armed conflicts.

The experiments conducted reveal the multifaceted contributions of AI in core crimes archiving, including transcription, translation, metadata enrichment, semantic search, and content generation. These tools enable efficient processing of complex and sensitive data, ensuring that critical information is preserved, searchable, and accessible in a secure and ethical manner. The integration of AI into archiving workflows also addresses key challenges such as multilingual access, data standardization, and the mitigation of harmful content, while maintaining the integrity of original documents.

However, the findings also highlight significant challenges, such as the need for AI models to better understand contextual nuances and preserve emotional elements in processed data. These limitations point to the necessity of developing tailored AI solutions, fine-tuned to the specific requirements of core crimes archiving and the cultural and linguistic contexts of affected regions. Furthermore, compliance with legal and ethical standards, such as the EU AI Act and GDPR, remains critical to ensuring the responsible use of AI in this sensitive domain.

Ultimately, this research demonstrates that AI-enabled core crimes archiving can serve as a cornerstone for digital sovereignty, empowering nations to retain control over their critical data flows and fostering innovation in the digital domain. By aligning with international regulations and ethical principles, these systems can contribute to justice, accountability, and the preservation of collective memory, while promoting a more equitable and transparent approach to digital documentation. The proposed framework and findings pave the way for future interdisciplinary collaboration and innovation, ensuring that AI continues to serve as a force for good in the pursuit of justice and human rights.

Acknowledgements

The authors wish to thank Daniel Kaiser for insightful discussions about the topic. B.R. acknowledges the support of the Research Council of Norway, project number 332645 (SFF Integreat). A.G. is supported by the Horizon Europe Research and Innovation Programme CYBERCOMM Grant agreement ID: 101107026.

Use of AI-Assisted Tools

During the preparation of this work, the authors utilized AI-assisted tools (Large Language Models) to enhance English language accuracy, including spelling, grammar, and punctuation. The content generated or corrected by these tools was thoroughly reviewed, revised, and edited by the authors to ensure accuracy and originality. The authors accept full responsibility for the originality of the final content of this publication.

References

Audenhove, L.V., Vermeire, L., Broeck, W.V. den, & Demeulenaere, A.(2024). Data literacy in the new EU DigComp 2.2 framework how DigComp defines competences on artificial intelligence, internet of things and data. *Information and Learning Sciences*, 125(5/6), 406–436. https://doi.org/10.1108/ILS-06-2023-0072

Bar-Tal, O., Chefer, H., Tov, O., Herrmann, C., Paiss, R., Zada, S. et al.(2024). Lumiere: A space-time diffusion model for video generation. *SIGGRAPH Asia 2024 Conference Papers*, 1–11. https://doi.org/10.1145/3680528.3687614

Bradford, A. (2020). *The Brussels Effect: How the European Union Rules the World*. Oxford University Press.

Brooks, T., Holynski, A., & Efros, A.A. (2023). *InstructPix2Pix: Learning to Follow Image Editing Instructions*. 18392–18402. https://openaccess.thecvf.com/content/CVPR2023/html/Brooks_InstructPix2Pix_Learning_To_Follow_Image_Editing_Instructions_CVPR_2023_paper.html

Chen, Y., Lai, Y.-K., & Liu, Y.-J. (2018). *CartoonGAN: Generative Adversarial Networks for Photo Cartoonization*. 9465–9474. https://openaccess.thecvf.com/content_cvpr_2018/html/Chen_CartoonGAN_Generative_Adversarial_CVPR_2018_paper.html

Colavizza, G., Blanke, T., Jeurgens, C., & Noordegraaf, J. (2021). Archives and AI: An overview of current debates and future perspectives. *J. Comput. Cult. Herit.*, 15(1), 4:1-4:15. https://doi.org/10.1145/3479010

Devlin, J., Chang, M.-W., Lee, K., & Toutanova, K. (2019). BERT: Pre-training of deep bidirectional transformers for language understanding. In: J. Burstein, C. Doran, & T. Solorio (eds.), *Proceedings of the 2019 Conference of the North American Chapter of the Association for Computational Linguistics: Human Language Technologies, Volume 1 (Long and Short Papers)* (pp. 4171–4186). Association for Computational Linguistics. https://doi.org/10.18653/v1/N19-1423

FFmpeg/FFmpeg. (2025). [C]. FFmpeg. https://github.com/FFmpeg/FFmpeg (Original work published 2011)

Freeman, L. (2021). Weapons of war, tools of justice. *Journal of International Criminal Justice*, 19(1), 35–53. https://doi.org/10.1093/jicj/mqab013

Gienapp, L., Scells, H., Deckers, N., Bevendorff, J., Wang, S., Kiesel, J. et al. (2024). Evaluating generative ad hoc information retrieval. *Proceedings of the 47th International ACM SIGIR Conference on Research and Development in Information Retrieval*. 1916–1929. https://doi.org/10.1145/3626772.3657849

Greenawalt, A.K.A. (2020). What is an international crime? In: K.J. Heller, F. Mégret, S.M.H. Nouwen, J.D. Ohlin, & D. Robinson (eds), *The Oxford Handbook of International Criminal Law* (1st ed.), pp. 293–316. Oxford University Press. https://doi.org/10.1093/law/9780198825203.003.0013

Hoffstaetter, S. (2025). *H/pytesseract* [Python]. https://github.com/h/pytesseract (Original work published 2018)

Jaiswal, R., & Schaathun, H.G. (2025). On human sovereignty in a digital age. *Procedia Comput. Sci.*, 254(C), 157–163. https://doi.org/10.1016/j.procs.2025.02.074

Jensen, E. (2014). Cyber sovereignty: The way ahead. *Texas International Law Journal*, 50, 275–304.

Jing, Y., Yang, Y., Feng, Z., Ye, J., Yu, Y., & Song, M. (2020). Neural style transfer: A review. *IEEE Transactions on Visualization and Computer Graphics*, 26(11), 3365–3385. https://doi.org/10.1109/TVCG.2019.2921336

Junczys-Dowmunt, M., Grundkiewicz, R., Dwojak, T., Hoang, H., Heafield, K., Neckermann, T. et al. (2018). *Marian: Fast Neural Machine Translation in C++* (No. arXiv:1804.00344). arXiv. https://doi.org/10.48550/arXiv.1804.00344

Koenig, A. (2022). From 'Capture to Courtroom': Collaboration and the digital documentation of international crimes in Ukraine. *Journal of International Criminal Justice*, 20(4), 829–842. https://doi.org/10.1093/jicj/mqac046

Kohli, A. (2018). Data-driven human rights investigations. In: O. Hahn & F. Stalph (eds), *Digital Investigative Journalism: Data, Visual Analytics and Innovative Methodologies in International Reporting*, pp. 67–77. Springer International Publishing. https://doi.org/10.1007/978-3-319-97283-1_7

Kreuk, F., Synnaeve, G., Polyak, A., Singer, U., Défossez, A., Copet, J. et al. (2023). *AudioGen: Textually Guided Audio Generation* (No. arXiv:2209.15352). arXiv. https://doi.org/10.48550/arXiv.2209.15352

Kuczyńska, H. (2024). The ICC enters into the future: The digital-evidence revolution or evolution? *Revista Brasileira de Direito Processual Penal*, 10(3). https://doi.org/10.22197/rbdpp.v10i3.1073

Kuratov, Y., Bulatov, A., Anokhin, P., Rodkin, I., Sorokin, D., Sorokin, A. et al. (2024). BABILong: Testing the limits of LLMs with long context reasoning-in-a-haystack. *Advances in Neural Information Processing Systems*, 37, 106519–106554.

Le, C., Qian, Y., Wang, D., Zhou, L., Liu, S., Wang, X. et al. (2024). TransVIP: Speech to speech translation system with voice and isochrony preservation. *Advances in Neural Information Processing Systems*, 37, 89682–89705.

Lee, A., Chen, P.-J., Wang, C., Gu, J., Popuri, S., Ma, X. et al. (2022). *Direct speech-to-speech Translation with Discrete Units* (No. arXiv:2107.05604). arXiv. https://doi.org/10.48550/arXiv.2107.05604

Lehuedé, S. (2024). An alternative planetary future? Digital sovereignty frameworks and the decolonial option. *Big Data & Society*, 11(1), 20539517231221778. https://doi.org/10.1177/20539517231221778

Lewis, P., Perez, E., Piktus, A., Petroni, F., Karpukhin, V., Goyal, N. et al. (2020). Retrieval-augmented generation for knowledge-intensive NLP tasks. *Advances in Neural Information Processing Systems*, 33, 9459–9474. https://proceedings.neurips.cc/paper/2020/hash/6b493230205f780e1bc26945df7481e5-Abstract.html

Li, J., Li, D., Xiong, C., & Hoi, S. (2022). *BLIP: Bootstrapping Language-Image Pre-training for Unified Vision-Language Understanding and Generation* (No. arXiv:2201.12086). arXiv. https://doi.org/10.48550/arXiv.2201.12086

Li, X., Jin, J., Zhou, Y., Zhang, Y., Zhang, P., Zhu, Y., & Dou, Z. (2025). From Matching to generation: A survey on generative information retrieval. *ACM Trans. Inf. Syst.*, 43(3), 83:1-83:62. https://doi.org/10.1145/3722552

Liu, Z. (2024). Cultural bias in large language models: A comprehensive analysis and mitigation strategies. *Journal of Transcultural Communication*. https://doi.org/10.1515/jtc-2023-0019

Makhortykh, M. (2023). No AI after Auschwitz? Bridging AI and memory ethics in the context of information retrieval of genocide-related information. In: A. Mukherjee, J. Kulshrestha, A. Chakraborty, & S. Kumar (eds.), *Ethics in Artificial Intelligence: Bias,*

Fairness and Beyond, pp. 71–83. Springer Nature. https://doi.org/10.1007/978-981-99-7184-8_4

Makhortykh, M., Zucker, E.M., Simon, D.J., Bultmann, D., & Ulloa, R. (2023). Shall androids dream of genocides? How generative AI can change the future of memorialization of mass atrocities. *Discover Artificial Intelligence*, 3(1), 28. https://doi.org/10.1007/s44163-023-00072-6

Mamediieva, G., & Moynihan, D. (2023). Digital resilience in wartime: The case of Ukraine. *Public Administration Review*, 83(6), 1512–1516. https://doi.org/10.1111/puar.13742

Mikolov, T., Chen, K., Corrado, G., & Dean, J. (2013). *Efficient Estimation of Word Representations in Vector Space* (No. arXiv:1301.3781). arXiv. https://doi.org/10.48550/arXiv.1301.3781

Models—Hugging Face. (n.d.). Retrieved January 20, 2023, from https://huggingface.co/models

Ochi, M., & Dagenborg, H. (2025). *Online War-crime Archives: A Call for a Universal Guideline* (SSRN Scholarly Paper No. 5128953). https://doi.org/10.2139/ssrn.5128953

Pedapudi, S.M., & Vadlamani, N. (2023). Digital forensics approach for handling audio and video files. *Measurement: Sensors*, 29, 100860. https://doi.org/10.1016/j.measen.2023.100860

Porter, M.D. (2016). A statistical approach to crime linkage. *The American Statistician*, 70(2), 152–165. https://doi.org/10.1080/00031305.2015.1123185

Radford, A., Kim, J.W., Hallacy, C., Ramesh, A., Goh, G., Agarwal, S. et al. (2021). Learning Transferable visual models from natural language supervision. *Proceedings of the 38th International Conference on Machine Learning*. 8748–8763. https://proceedings.mlr.press/v139/radford21a.html

Radford, A., Kim, J.W., Xu, T., Brockman, G., Mcleavey, C., & Sutskever, I. (2023). Robust speech recognition via large-scale weak supervision. *Proceedings of the 40th International Conference on Machine Learning*. 28492–28518. https://proceedings.mlr.press/v202/radford23a.html

Rombach, R., Blattmann, A., Lorenz, D., Esser, P., & Ommer, B. (2022). *High-Resolution Image Synthesis with Latent Diffusion Models*. 10684–10695. https://openaccess.thecvf.com/content/CVPR2022/html/Rombach_High-Resolution_Image_Synthesis_With_Latent_Diffusion_Models_CVPR_2022_paper

Saltman, K. (2020). Artificial intelligence and the technological turn of public education privatization: In defence of democratic education. *London Review of Education*, 18(2), 196–208.

Shinde, G., Kirstein, T., Ghosh, S., & Franks, P.C. (2024). *AI in Archival Science—A Systematic Review* (No. arXiv:2410.09086). arXiv. https://doi.org/10.48550/arXiv.2410.09086

Smith, R. (2007). An overview of the Tesseract OCR engine. *Ninth International Conference on Document Analysis and Recognition (ICDAR 2007)*, 2, 629–633. https://doi.org/10.1109/ICDAR.2007.4376991

Stahn, C. (2018, December 6). *A Critical Introduction to International Criminal Law*. Higher Education from Cambridge University Press. https://doi.org/10.1017/9781108399906

Teel, Z. (Abbie). (2024). Artificial Intelligence's role in digitally preserving historic archives. *Preservation, Digital Technology & Culture*, 53(1), 29–33. https://doi.org/10.1515/pdtc-2023-0050

Tesseract-ocr/tesseract. (2025). [C++]. tesseract-ocr. https://github.com/tesseract-ocr/tesseract (Original work published 2014)

Tsai, F.-J., Huang, W.-L., & Chan, C.-C. (2009). Occupational stress and burnout of lawyers. *Journal of Occupational Health*, 51(5), 443–450. https://doi.org/10.1539/joh.L8179

Wolf, T., Debut, L., Sanh, V., Chaumond, J., Delangue, C., Moi, A. et al. (2020). Transformers: State-of-the-art natural language processing. In: Q. Liu, & D. Schlangen (eds), *Proceedings of the 2020 Conference on Empirical Methods in Natural Language Processing: System Demonstrations*, pp. 38–45. Association for Computational Linguistics. https://doi.org/10.18653/v1/2020.emnlp-demos.6

Yu, Y., Zhang, Q.-W., Qiao, L., Yin, D., Li, F., Wang, J. et al. (2025). *Sequential-NIAH: A Needle-in-a-Haystack Benchmark for Extracting Sequential Needles from Long Contexts* (No. arXiv:2504.04713). arXiv. https://doi.org/10.48550/arXiv.2504.04713

Zecchinon, P., & Standaert, O. (2025). The war in Ukraine through the prism of visual disinformation and the limits of specialized fact-checking. A case-study at Le Monde. *Digital Journalism*, 13(1), 61–79. https://doi.org/10.1080/21670811.2024.2332609

Zhang, A. (2025). *Uberi/speech_recognition* [Python]. https://github.com/Uberi/speech_recognition (Original work published 2014).

Zucker, E.M., Makhortykh, M., Ulloa, R., Bultmann, D., & Simon, D.J. (2023). AI and archives: How can technology help preserve holocaust heritage under the risk of disappearance? *Eastern European Holocaust Studies*, 1(2), 357–363. https://doi.org/10.1515/eehs-2023-0052

CHAPTER

5

Secure and Collaborative Crop Disease Prediction with Federated Deep Learning: Safeguarding Data Sovereignty in Agriculture

Sadananda Behera[1(0009-0007-9785-4254)] **Neelamadhab Padhy**[1*(0000-0001-7997-2336)], **Rasmita Panigrahi**[1*(0000-0003-3980-7306)], **Pradeep Kumar Mahapatro**[2(0009-0009-0029-6167)] **and Dasaradha Arangi**[2(0000-0002-5329-4837)]

[1] School of Engineering and Technology, Department of Computer Science and Engineering, GIET University, Gunupur, India
[2] Aditya Institute of Technology and Management, Tekkali, India

5.1 Introduction

With the rapid rise in digital penetration, nearly everyone now maintains a digital presence within the social media ecosystem. Social media posts, online searches, cloud-stored photos, and e-commerce interactions reflect our real-life behaviours, choices, and emotions. However, the data generated is personal and valuable. The control and effective management of data are fundamental to shaping future outcomes across industries and society, as big data analytics enhances forecasting and decision-making capabilities (Roßmann et al., 2018; Chatterjee et al., 2023), while data governance reforms and controls rights critically influencing innovation, privacy, and market dynamics (UK Government, 2021; Corren E, 2024; Banerjee et al., 2020). In many ways broadly we can say, to control data is to control the future. Hence, it's safety, ownership, and use are more critical. Just like personal data can shape individual identity, a nation's digital data is equally vital, and it can reflect the country's economic strength, cultural heritage, governance systems, and national security (MeitY, 2025; PIB, 2025). At a national level, it extends to critical sectors like agriculture, where data on soil health, crop yields, weather patterns, and farming practices play a vital role in ensuring food security, guiding policymaking, and

*Corresponding authors: dr.neelamadhab@giet.edu; rasmita@giet.edu

DOI: 10.1201/9781003581581-5

empowering rural communities. In the current geopolitical situation, where tensions between global powers are escalating over technology, trade, and influence, data has become the new domain. Just like physical borders, nations must protect their digital assets.

As artificial intelligence (AI) technology is evolving, its role in agriculture is also expanding. From predictive analytics to precision farming, AI-powered tools offer benefits like real-time crop health monitoring, optimizing crop yields, monitoring climate impacts, and making data-driven decisions that enhance sustainability. Example: Irrigation pump control and scheduling using classification AI model (Behera et al., 2025b). Machine learning (ML) models can analyze huge amounts of agricultural data in real-time, identifying patterns and providing insights that might not be humanly possible and time-consuming unless they possess a specialized skillset. Maintaining the right balance in building a collaborative ecosystem with mutual support, uncompromised trust, and ethics, while taking advantage of technology, is important so that farmers are fairly compensated while protecting their privacy and digital assets.

Traditional ML models: Agriculture has become more sophisticated with devices like IoT sensors, drones, and cameras. The efficiency of the AI/ML model depends on the amount of training data. Greater diversity and volume of data typically enhance predictive performance. However, an individual farmer cannot encompass the full range of environmental conditions, setups, and historical records required to train a robust machine learning model. Consequently, training data from multiple farmers must be aggregated on a centralized server—typically a cloud-based platform. This architecture presents several drawbacks: potential model bias due to insufficiently diverse data sources; limited scalability; lack of farmer control over their data and its possible misuse; high bandwidth requirements for transferring large datasets; and, critically, a threat to digital data sovereignty.

Motivation: Multiple studies indicate that traditional ML models continue to be used for crop disease prediction. These models inherit several limitations, including vulnerability to data breaches and the risk of single point failure. In contrast, Federated Learning (FL) offers a distributed processing environment in which raw data remains local. This approach is lightweight in terms of data transfer, less prone to bias, and more aligned with ethical standards, transparency, personal data privacy, and digital sovereignty. The Federated Learning model inherently retains the raw data collected from various sources, like IoT sensors and cameras where one central server aggregates local client values and has control over client models till they converge to the optimal.

Objective: Day by day, data privacy, and digital data sovereignty awareness are increasing. With the changing demands, in this chapter, our major objectives are:

- To demonstrate a Federated Learning (FL) based distributed, collaborative environment for crop disease prediction with various Deep Learning (DL) models that protect farmer data privacy, safeguard digital data sovereignty and compare the performance and efficacy against standalone traditional DL models.

- To measure and compare traditional and FL models to assess which is better suited for a resource-constrained environment.
- To find which FL algorithm is better in terms of communication rounds (Lesser is better).

This chapter is structured as follows to systematically present our proposed work. It begins with a comprehensive literature review in section 5.2, which discusses existing studies relevant to the research problem, critically analyses methods, and associated challenges. In section 5.3, our proposed model, flowchart and step-by-step algorithm is presented. Section 5.4 presents the experimental results supported with figures and tables for clear visualization. Finally, the section 5.5 outlines the key findings and concluding remarks.

5.2 Literature Review

Machine Learning and Deep Learning are evolving, and so are their applications in crop disease prediction and management. Over the last two decades, it has increased significanrly. The application of Convolutional Neural Networks (CNNs) and Fully Connected Neural Networks (FCNNs) has shown better results than manual, cumbersome methods. Islam et al. (2025) in their research titled "Aggrotech: Leveraging Deep Learning for Sustainable Tomato Disease Management" to detect diseases in the tomato crop, have proposed a deep learning-based approach using Convolutional Neural Networks (CNNs), VGG19 and Inception v3. Their model achieved an accuracy of 93.93% whereas the model is a standalone conventional machine learning approach where their dataset from Tomato Villages stayed at the server where the actual model is being trained. Judith et al. (2025), in their research using remote sensing to classify crop health have proposed a fully connected Neural Network which replaces manual visual inspection or simple NDVI measurements. Their model achieved an accuracy of 97.80%. Their model uses satellite imagery from various agricultural regions, and pre-processed and then fed to the system for training and classification in one place. Ale et al. (2019) proposed deep learning approaches for plant disease detection, including a transfer learning method based on Densely Connected Convolutional Networks (DenseNet) and a lightweight Deep Neural Network (DNN). These methods require all crop images to be aggregated on a central server for processing and model training.

The review paper by Shoaib et al. (2023) considered research papers from 2015 to 2022 in the field of crop disease detection. Findings from the reviewed research papers indicate that all employed standalone centralized DL and ML models for the classification of crop image classification. Standalone systems inherently collect all the datasets on a single server. Similarly, Chaudhary et al. (2023), in their research have used an integration of CNN for image classification and LSTM for disease progression analysis for crop disease detection. They have used basic pre-trained models, and the model is a centralized training model requiring the presence of the entire dataset in one place, which is a primary concern in data privacy. Additionally, Lee et al. (2023), in their research, proposed a different model that predicts diseases through previous growth environment information of crops, including air temperature, relative humidity, dew point, and CO_2 concentration, using deep learning techniques. All these models lack the mechanism of digital data privacy, and there is no mention specifically of digital data security and sovereignty.

Other than freely available datasets, in 2024, there were some research studies focused on IoT and drone-based image collection. To improve the efficiency and accuracy of disease detection in mango trees, Husnain et al. (2024), used CNN models such as YOLOv5, Detectron2, and Faster R-CNN to process multispectral images of mango trees from a DJI Air 2s drone. Though there is no specific accuracy achieved and architecture used, there is no mention of distributed architecture or privacy-preserving models as well. Similarly, Specific to cucumber disease detection using augmented images collected from drones using traditional Deep Learning technologies such as VGG16, achieved 87.5% accuracy (Rahman et al., 2024). Drones also collect GPS locations, which is very sensitive digital data. Data privacy, security, and sovereignty are essential when we are dealing with such critical sensitive data. To predict grapevine diseases using climate variables derived from from multi-IoT sensor remote sensing imagery, Zhao et al. (2024) employed multiple classification models, including the TabPFN framework. This remote sensing technology is useful and effective and has been experimented with on balanced and imbalanced datasets. Accuracy varies from 69.17% to 79.72%. Apart from this, Ngugi et al. (2024) in their review paper have consulted research papers from 2021 to 2024, along with a few papers from 2019, focused on crop disease diagnosis, classification and detection using ML and DL algorithms. Their findings suggest that the models mentioned in these research papers are standalone, where images are transferred to the host machine.

Recent works in 2025 on crop disease prediction have explored convolutional neural networks (CNNs), mobile-centric architectures, and Inception models. Research has also advanced in ensemble deep learning and multi-crop disease detection. Slimani et al. (2025) proposed a deep transfer learning technique based on Neural Architecture Search (NAS) for identifying the degree of rust disease infection in Vicia faba L. production systems. Tonmoy et al. (2025) focused on handheld devices and proposed MobilePlantViT, a model designed specifically for mobile-friendly environments to classify crop diseases from images. Optimized for resource efficiency while maintaining high performance, MobilePlantViT achieved test accuracies ranging from 80% to over 99%, outperforming MobileViTv1 and MobileViTv2—both of which were developed specifically for mobile platforms. Vijayan et al. (2025) intended to address concerns of high computational and segmentation challenges in leaf images to predict rice crop diseases. They have proposed a hybrid bio-inspired algorithm, Hybrid WOA_APSO, which merges Adaptive Particle Swarm Optimization (APSO) with the Whale Optimization Algorithm (WOA). Disease classification is done by a Convolutional Neural Network (CNN). An accuracy of 97.5% is achieved by their model. Bouacida et al. (2025) proposed a deep learning system based on the Inception model architecture, capable of distinguishing between diseased and healthy leaves across various crops—including previously unseen ones. Although the model achieved a peak accuracy of 97.13%, it relies on a centralized architecture. In contrast, ensemble-based models can sometimes outperform individual deep learning models in terms of robustness and generalization. Aboneh et al. (2025) used different pre-trained models like Inceptionv3, Resnet50, and VGG19 as base models to conduct experiments and achieved 96.85% accuracy. Instead of focusing on single crop disease detection, Khandagale et al. (2025) proposed a standalone CNN-Based model for Multi-Crop Disease Detection and Management for crops including Cotton Leaf, Grape, Soybean, and Corn; which achieved a high accuracy of 99.7% for Grape, followed by 99.5% for Corn, and 95.3% for the combined dataset. In a recent review, by Jensen et al. (2025), 104 total publications were examined reporting on the development of 146 disease predictive models. The modelling approaches were categorized into 4 groups: Non-Statistical, Statistical, Traditional Machine Learning, and Deep Learning. Traditional Machine Learning models included support vector machines (SVM), decision trees, k-nearest neighbors (KNN), artificial neural networks (ANN), and Random Forests (RF). The findings indicate a growing trend in the application of machine learning techniques, such as SVM and RF, for predictive model development over the past two decades. The authors emphasized the need for further research into multi-model machine learning approaches that ensure model designs capture input variables related to environmental conditions, host characteristics, and pathogen dynamics. They have also pointed out that there might be a need for collaboration between researchers from different areas of expertise (agricultural and data analytics), farmers or agronomists, and crop protection. Federated learning can help in this regard. Antico et al. (2022) have used Convolutional Neural Networks (CNN) such as AlexNet, SqueezeNet, ResNet-18, VGG-11, and ShuffleNet with Federated Learning (FL) for Maize Leaf disease prediction to address the privacy concerns in central training. The results show that they have achieved 97.29% accuracy with VGG-11.

The reviewed literature surveys indicates a growing trend in the application of Artificial Intelligence (AI), Machine Learning (ML) for crop disease prediction. However, research addressing digital data security, privacy, and sovereignty remains limited. Rising awareness of data privacy and evolving geopolitical conditions underscore the need to safeguard agricultural practices while harnessing the capabilities of AI and ML. Federated Learning (FL) as a distributed privacy preserving framework, has demonstrated applicability across domains such as health care, finance, smart phones, smart city and transportation (Kolasa, 2025).

Akter et al (2022), in their study titled, "Edge intelligence: Federated Learning-Based Privacy Protection Framework for Smart Healthcare Systems" utilized Federated Learning (FL) and convolutional neural networks (CNNs) in healthcare, achieving 90% accuracy. ResNet-50 remains widely adopted due to its superior generalization and high accuracy. In the domain of plant disease detection, Khan et al. (2024) reported an accuracy of 98.67% of accuracy using ResNet-50, outperforming other models such as CNN, VGG-16, and DenseNet. This work aims to develop a Federated Learning (FL) framework integrated with Deep Learning to predict crop diseases while ensuring privacy preservation, protection against unauthorized data use, and reinforcement of digital data sovereignty in agricultural disease management.

5.3 Proposed Model

Governments protect digital data sovereignty by enacting rules, regulations and guidelines governing the collection, use and disposal of digital data. However, citizens should not rely solely on governmental protections; they must remain informed about the risks associated with sharing or transferring digital data beyond their control. Jaiswal et al. (2025) discuss both digital and human sovereignty emphasizing the importance of educating citizens in prudent usage and critical thinking to mitigate risks, especially when government mechanisms fail. They highlight the technological risks posed by centralized service providers, who can access and correlate user data across multiple, application soften gaining deeper insights into individuals than the users themselves possess. Data perceived as safe today may become hazardous in the future, much like, how personal identity sharing was once considered benign until misuse prompted regulatory intervention.

Currently, there are no specific laws in place to protect agricultural digital data, including the General Data Protection Regulation (GDPR) in Europe, American Data Privacy Protection Act (ADPPA) in USA, Personal Information Protection Law (PIPL) in China or Digital Personal Data Protection Act (DPDP Act) in India.

Federated Learning inherently is a distributed model that encourages and aligns with digital data sovereignty. The Federated learning system principally protects actual datasets collected by all the local clients which are retained by them. However, clients only share essential information like weights with the central server for aggregation in model optimization. Federated Learning is proposed for use as the central foundation of our model. The FL environment is combined with various DL models on the client side and secure data transfer algorithms to establish a future-ready, robust platform in the agricultural domain. Crop disease prediction models have been utilized alongside federated learning as a base reference (Behera et al., 2025a).

5.3.1 Model Flow Chart

This section outlines the different stages and steps involved in secure and collaborative crop disease prediction using a Federated Deep Learning model, as illustrated in Figure 5.1. The figure demonstrates how farmers benefit from a collaborative environment while maintaining control over their data, ensuring both data security and digital sovereignty. The framework also enables AI-driven smart agriculture for accurate crop disease prediction.

Stage 1: Client-side Data Collection and Pre-processing

Each client collects crop data using IoT sensors and performs local pre-processing. The remains securely stored data on the client's device and is never transmitted beyond local storage.

Stage 2: Client Model Training and Update

The pre-processed data from step 1 are used to train local models on each client device. Upon completion of training, the clients transmit their respective model weights or gradients to a central server for aggregation.

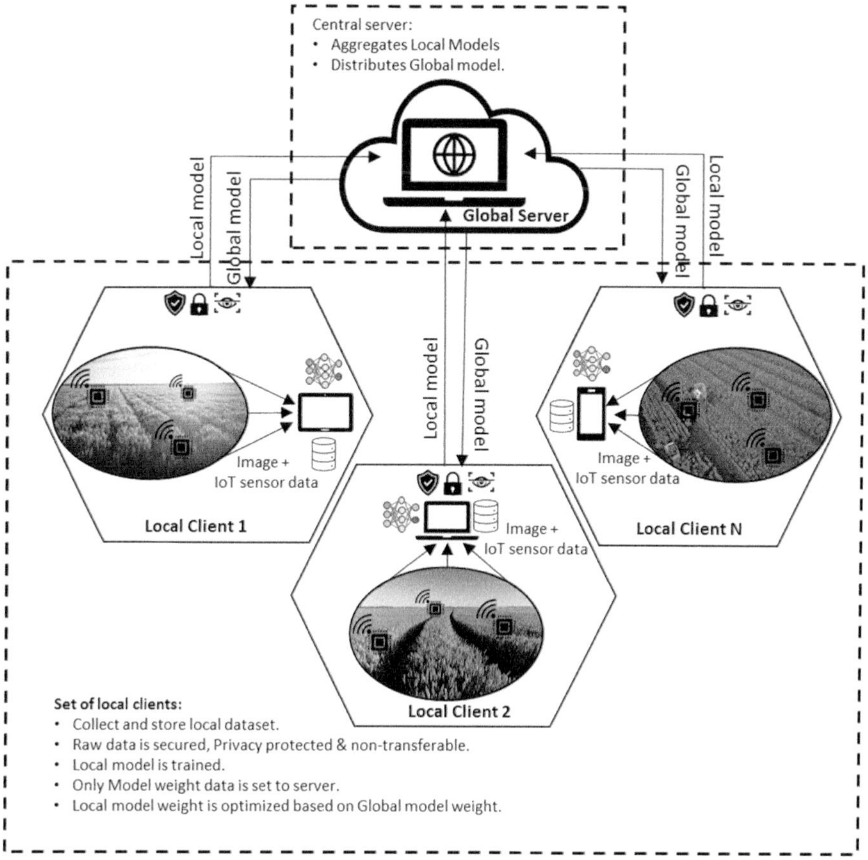

Figure 5.1. Proposed Model for secure and collaborative crop disease prediction with federated deep learning.

Stage 3: Central Server Aggregation and Update

Individual client weights or gradients are aggregated at the central server, where the global model parameters are updated and optimized. The newly computed global weights are then transmitted back to all clients for the next training cycle.

Stage 4: Client Alignment with Central Server

Upon receiving the global weights or gradients from the central server, each client updates and aligns its local parameters accordingly, ensuring synchronization with the global model state.

Stage 5: Model Evaluation and Deployment

The client model is re-executed using the updated weights or gradients and evaluated to determine whether optimal performance has been achieved. If the model meets the desired threshold, the training process is terminated, and the client model is prepared for deployment. Otherwise, the cycle resumes from step 2.

Figure 5.1 illustrates a distributed environment in which farmers retain control over their agricultural digital data sovereignty while collaborating with peers to mutually benefit from crop disease prediction. The digital data collected by each client remains entirely local and is never transmitted externally. Instead, only the trained model weights are shared for aggregation. This architecture significantly reduces data transmission requirements, enhances speed, and operates efficiently with minimal network bandwidth.

5.3.2 Algorithm

Input parameter: Data has been collected from different sources to create distributed datasets 1 D1, D2, …, DN across N clients (farms). The initial global model weights (W_0), and T (number of communication rounds) have been provided.

Output: The model generates the trained global model W_t for crop disease prediction.

Steps involved:

Step 1: Initialization

- Initially, the central server is created, and the global model weights W_0 are randomly initialized.
- The number of communication rounds T as well as the set learning rate η have been provided.

Step 2: Repeat for the communication round from 1 to *T*

- Client selection: Choose a random subset (C_t) of clients from the set of N clients.
- Client-Side Local Training: Repeat for each client $i \in C$.
- The central server provides the current global model (W_t) to the client.
- The model is trained locally on each client's dataset using stochastic gradient descent (SGD) or any other optimizer:

$$W_i^{t+1} = W_t - \eta \nabla F_i\,(W_t, D_i) \tag{1}$$

The gradient of the loss function DF_i, which was computed on the client's dataset D_i, is represented by the expression $\nabla F_i\,(W_t, D_i)$.

Model Update: With the exception of raw data, the updated model weights W_i^{t+1} are sent back to the central server by each client $i \in C_t$.

Step 3: Server-Side Aggregation: Federated Averaging (FedAvg) is employed by the central server to combine the model changes from clients:

$$W_{t+1} = \frac{1}{|C_t|} \sum\nolimits_{i \in C_t} W_i^{t+1} \tag{2}$$

Step 4: Global Model Update: The aggregated weights W_{t+1} are updated in the global model by the central server.

For a total of T rounds, repeat steps 2 through 4 until the global model converges to optimal performance. On completion of training, each client (farm) receives a copy of the global model W_T, which may be used to forecast crop diseases using unseen local data.

5.4 Experimental Results

This section presents the experimental results obtained using Federated Learning (FL) integrated with various convolutional neural network (CNN) models and compares them against centralized server-based methods. Centralized models pose significant risks to digital sovereignty and, data privacy, as they require aggregation of raw data at a single server. Without stringent safeguards, digital data security may also can be compromised. In contrast the FL framework enables a decentralized architecture that preserves data locality and enhances privacy. We evaluate whether the performance of FL-based models is comparable to centralized learning, ensuring that accuracy is not sacrificed in pursuit of privacy and sovereignty.

As shown in Table 5.1, Federated Learning (FL) approaches are compared with traditional centralized learning methods for crop disease prediction. In this study, the Plant Village dataset has been utilized. Table 5.2 summarizes the models used, their respective types, highest accuracy achieved, and key attributes such as privacy preservation and digital data sovereignty—based on the literature reviewed in the preceding survey section.

Our objective was to evaluate whether Federated Learning (FL) can deliver competitive performance while preserving data privacy. We assessed each algorithm's compatibility with privacy-preserving frameworks. Notably, the centralized ResNet-50 model does not support data privacy, whereas other algorithms do. Despite this limitation, ResNet-50 achieved the highest accuracy—approximately 98.7%. These findings demonstrate that FL can attain near-centralized accuracy without requiring the exchange of raw data, thereby upholding privacy and digital sovereignty.

Table 5.3 presents how the FedBN (Federated Batch Normalization) model performs across specific crop diseases in the PlantVillage dataset. From the PlantVillage dataset, we have analyzed the class-wise performance and focused on five common crop diseases – Tomato Early Blight, Potato Late Blight, Apple Scab, Corn Common Rust, and Grape Black Rot.

Figure 5.2 presents federated deep learning models for secure and collaborative crop disease prediction. The proposed system utilizes it to facilitate the secure and

Table 5.1. Performance comparison between FL and centralized learning (CL) on PlantVillage Dataset

Model	Accuracy (%)	Precision (%)	Recall (%)	F1-score (%)	Communication rounds	Data privacy
Centralized (ResNet-50)	98.7	98.5	98.6	98.5	–	☒ No
FedAvg (CNN)	96.2	95.8	96.0	95.9	50	☑ Yes
FedProx (CNN)	96.5	96.1	96.3	96.2	45	☑ Yes
FedBN (CNN)	97.1	96.8	97.0	96.9	40	☑ Yes

Table 5.2. Summary of literatures and their results, privacy preservation and data sovereignty

SL#	Author(s)	Model used	Model type	Accuracy (%)	Privacy preserve	Data sovereignty
1	Md. Mehraz Hosen et al.	VGG19 & Inception v3	Centralized	93.93%	⊗	⊗
2	J. Judith et al.	NDVI measurement	Centralized	97.80%	⊗	⊗
3	L. Ale et al.	DenseNet & DNN	Centralized	90%	⊗	⊗
4	M. Shoaib et al.	Various DL & ML models	Centralized	NA (Review)	⊗	⊗
5	Aryan Chaudhary et al.	CNN & LSTM	Centralized	98.40%	⊗	⊗
6	S. Lee et al.	–	Centralized	NA	⊗	⊗
7	Ali Husnain et al.	YOLOv5, Detectron2 & FRCNN	Centralized	NA	⊗	⊗
8	S.T. Rahman et al.	VGG16	Centralized	87.50%	⊗	⊗
9	W. Zhao and N. Efremova	TabPFN	Centralized	79.72%	⊗	⊗
10	H.N. Ngugi et al.	Various DL & ML models	Centralized	NA (Review)	⊗	⊗
11	H. Slimani et al.	NAS	Centralized	94.10%	⊗	⊗
12	M.R. Tonmoy et al.	MobilePlantViT	Centralized	99%	⊗	⊗
13	S. Vijayan et al.	Hybrid WOA_APSO	Centralized	97.50%	⊗	⊗
14	I. Bouacida et al.	Inception	Centralized	97.13%	⊗	⊗
15	T. Aboneh et al.	Inceptionv3, Resnet50 & VGG19	Centralized	96.85%	⊗	⊗
16	H.P. Khandagale et al.	CNN & LSTM	Centralized	95.30%	⊗	⊗
17	A. Jensen et al.	Various DL & ML models	Centralized	NA (Review)	⊗	⊗
18	T.M. Antico et al.	VGG11+ FL	Distributed	97.29%	☑	☑
19.	Our model	ResNet50 + FedBN	Distributed	97.10%	☑	☑

Table 5.3. Class-wise performance of FedBN on PlantVillage

Disease	Precision (%)	Recall (%)	F1-Score (%)
Tomato Early Blight	97.3	96.8	97.0
Potato Late Blight	96.5	97.1	96.8
Apple Scab	97.0	96.5	96.7
Corn Common Rust	96.8	97.2	97.0
Grape Black Rot	96.2	96.0	96.1

collaborative prediction of crop diseases while maintaining data sovereignty. Images of common crop diseases, including Tomato Early Blight, Potato Late Blight, Apple Scab, Corn Common Rust, and Grape Black Rot, are collected and stored locally by multiple peripheral devices that are deployed at various farms.

In this work, we train an individual CNN model independently and ensure that sensitive agricultural information is protected by retaining unprocessed image data on the local premises. Once the local model is trained, edge devices transition to transmitting encrypted model updates. Crucially, raw data is never sent to the central server. Instead, the server employs advanced federated algorithms—such as FedAvg, FedProx, or FedBN—to securely aggregate these updates. This privacy-preserving aggregation process constructs a global model that encapsulates the collective

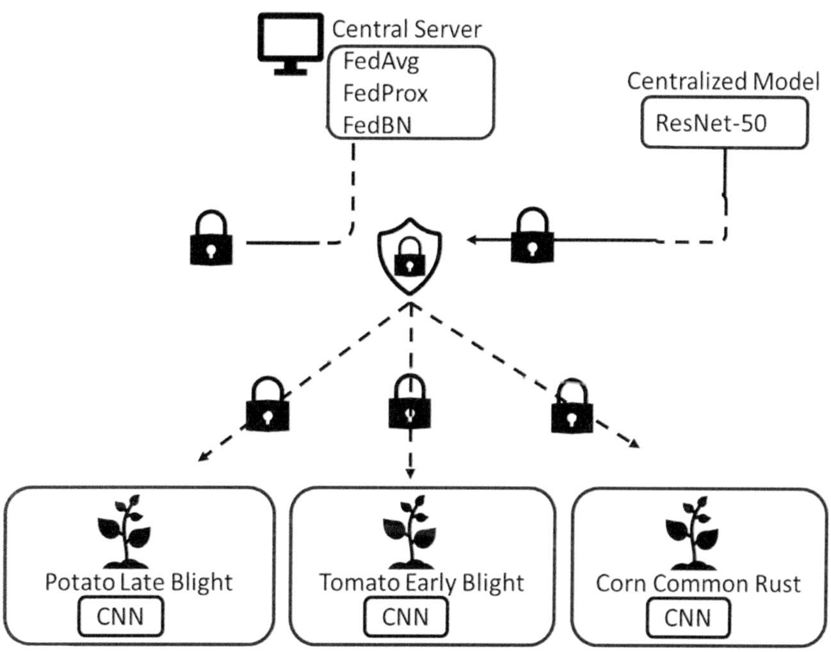

Figure 5.2. Federated deep learning models for secure and collaborative crop disease prediction.

expertise of all participating farms. Our experiments demonstrate that the proposed framework effectively balances the trade-off between accuracy and data privacy. Notably, FedBN achieved an accuracy of 97.1%.

Figures 5.3a and 5.3b illustrate the multi-phase process of crop disease using federated deep learning. In Phase 1, local model training is conducted by deploying nodes to collect real-time crop images for five specific diseases: Potato Late Blight,

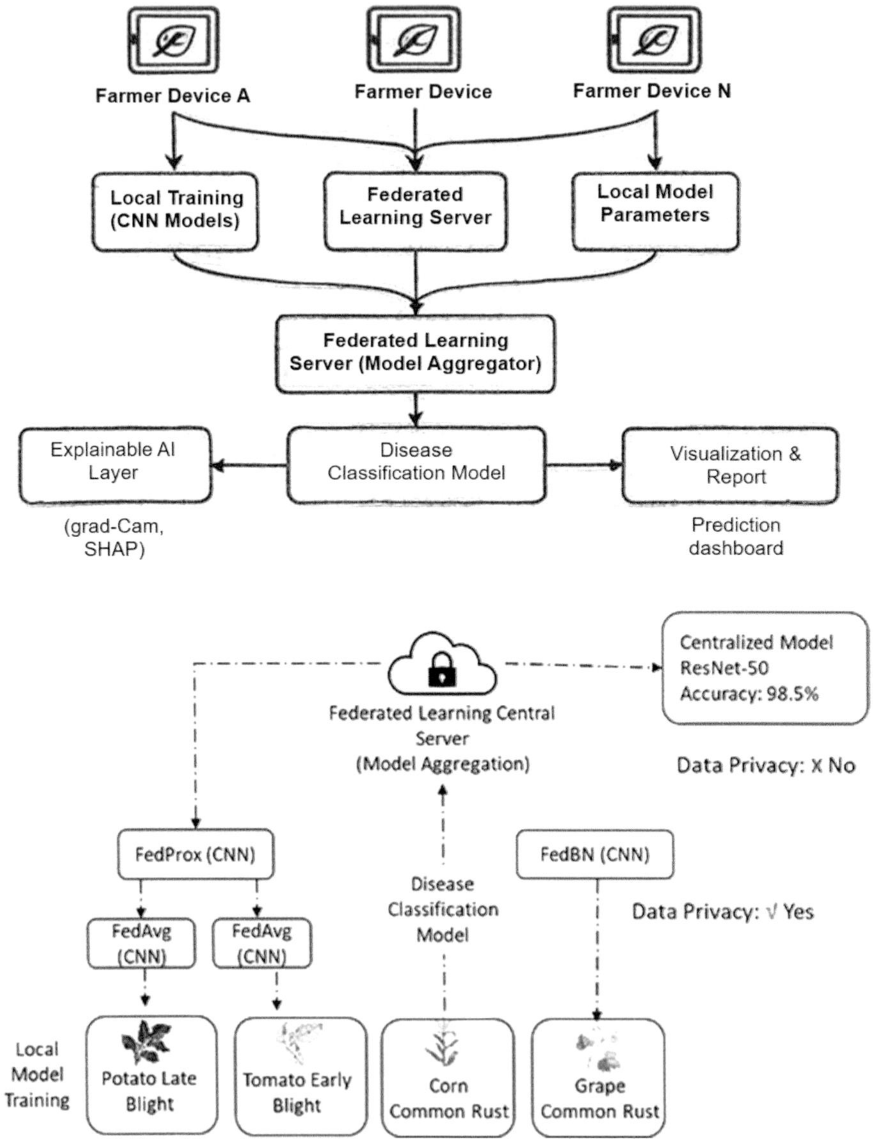

Figure 5.3(a, b). Secure and collaborative crop disease prediction with federated deep learning.

Tomato Early Blight, Corn Common Rust, Apple Scab, and Grape Black Rot. Each node trains a local CNN model—using algorithms such as FedAvg, FedProx, or FedBN—on its own data, without sharing raw images. This phase ensures data privacy and independent model training.

Phase 2 involves model aggregation at the central server. Only model updates, in the form of weights and biases, are transmitted. The server aggregates these updates using standard federated techniques like FedAvg or FedProx to construct a global model. The goal is to enhance disease prediction accuracy while preserving data sovereignty. In Phase 3, the trained global model is deployed for disease classification. Real-time images are collected to test the model's predictive capability in a privacy-preserving manner. Phase 4 addresses the performance and privacy trade-off. Experimental results show that the centralized ResNet-50 model achieves the highest accuracy (98.7%) but lacks privacy safeguards, as raw data must be centralized. In contrast, FL models yield slightly lower accuracy (~96–97%) while ensuring full data privacy. Among them, FedBN offers the best balance between privacy and performance, achieving approximately 97.1% accuracy.

RQ1: How does the accuracy of federated learning models compare to centralized deep learning models in crop disease prediction

To address this research question, we compared two approaches: centralized deep learning and Federated Learning (FL). For the centralized model, ResNet-50 was employed, while the FL models—FedAvg, FedProx, and FedBN—were trained on distributed data across multiple clients. Our objective was to assess whether FL could match the performance of the centralized model while preserving data privacy. Experimental results revealed that the centralized ResNet-50 model achieved an accuracy of 98.7%.

Figure 5.4 presents a comparative analysis of model accuracies. The centralized ResNet-50 model achieved an accuracy of 98.7%, while the Federated Learning models yielded slightly lower results: FedAvg (CNN) reached 96.2%, with a 2.5% difference from the centralized baseline; FedProx (CNN) achieved 96.5%, reflecting a 2.2% difference; and FedBN (CNN) attained 97.1%, with a 1.6% deviation. To statistically evaluate these differences, a paired t-test was conducted to compare the centralized and federated models.

Additionally, a per-disease accuracy analysis was performed for both approaches, and the results are summarized in Table 5.4.

It was observed that the centralized model achieved an accuracy of 98.00%, indicating that 98% of crop disease labels were correctly predicted. In comparison,the federated model attained an accuracy of 95%. To statistically assess the difference, a paired t-test was conducted, yielding a t-statistic of 1.1355 and a p-value of 0.2589. Since the p-value exceeds the conventional threshold of 0.05, we fail to reject the null hypothesis. This implies that, at the 95% confidence level, there is no statistically significant difference in accuracy between the centralized and federated models. Given that federated learning (FL) preserves data privacy by maintaining decentralized data ownership, this marginal reduction in accuracy represents trade-off in many real-world agricultural scenarios where data sovereignty and privacy are paramount. FL enables distributed model training across multiple clients, such

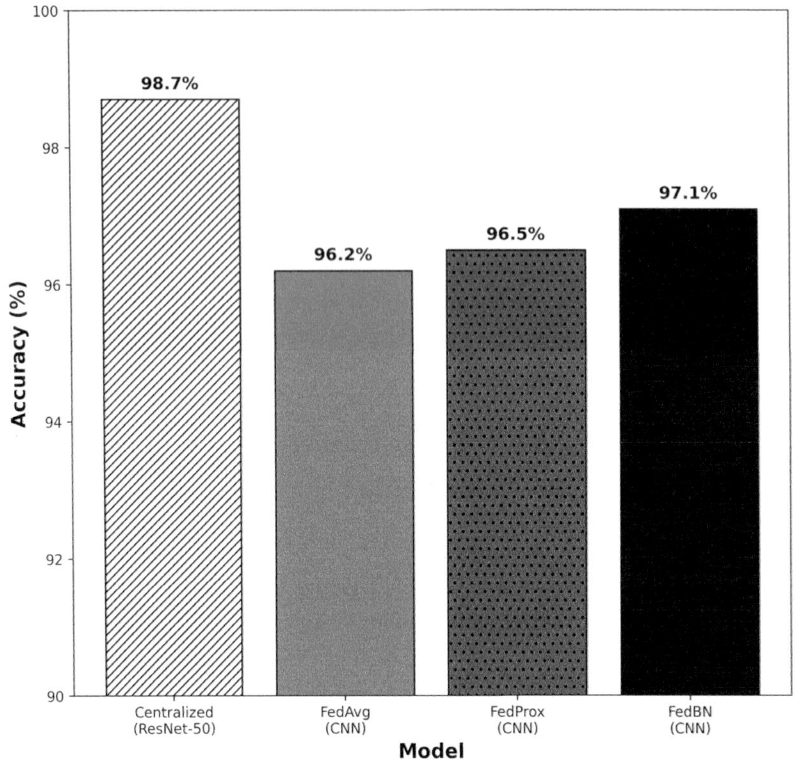

Figure 5.4. Comparison of accuracy between centralized and federated.

Table 5.4. Per-disease accuracy analysis of centralized and federated models

Disease	Centralized (ResNet-50)	FedAvg	FedProx	FedBN
Tomato Early Blight	99.20%	95.10%	96.30%	97.80%
Potato Late Blight	98.50%	94.70%	95.90%	97.20%
Apple Scab	97.80%	93.20%	94.10%	96.50%
Corn Common Rust	99.00%	96.50%	97.00%	98.10%
Grape Black Rot	96.30%	90.80%	92.40%	94.70%

as individual farms or edge devices, without sharing raw data, thereby safeguarding sensitive agricultural information. Despite the centralized model's slightly higher accuracy, FL demonstrates comparable performance while upholding privacy standards, as confirmed by the statistical analysis. This reinforces the viability of FL as a secure and collaborative framework for agricultural AI. Figure 5.5 illustrates the per-disease accuracy comparison between centralized and federated models. Despite the centralized model's slightly higher accuracy, FL demonstrates comparable performance while upholding privacy standards, as confirmed by the statistical analysis. This reinforces the viability of FL as a secure and collaborative framework for agricultural AI. Figure 5.5 illustrates the per-disease accuracy comparison between centralized and federated models.

RQ2: Which federated learning algorithm provides the best balance between model performance and data privacy preservation? (e.g., FedBN_CNN)

To address this research question, we conducted experiments using various Federated Learning algorithms—namely FedAvg, FedProx, and FedBN—combined with convolutional neural networks (CNNs). For each model, we recorded accuracy, F1-score, and a corresponding privacy preservation score to facilitate comparative analysis.

Table 5.5 summarizes these metrics across the different algorithms. Maintaining an appropriate balance between predictive accuracy and privacy preservation remains a critical consideration in the deployment of federated systems.

We evaluated the federated learning algorithms FedAvg, FedProx, and FedBN, and found that the FedBN_CNN model gives the best trade-off between predictive performance and communication efficiency while simultaneously maintaining data privacy. In particular, FedBN needed just 40 communication rounds, the fewest of the three, and demonstrated the best accuracy of 97.1% among all FL models along with a significant F1-score of 96.9% and a higher privacy preservation accuracy of 97%.

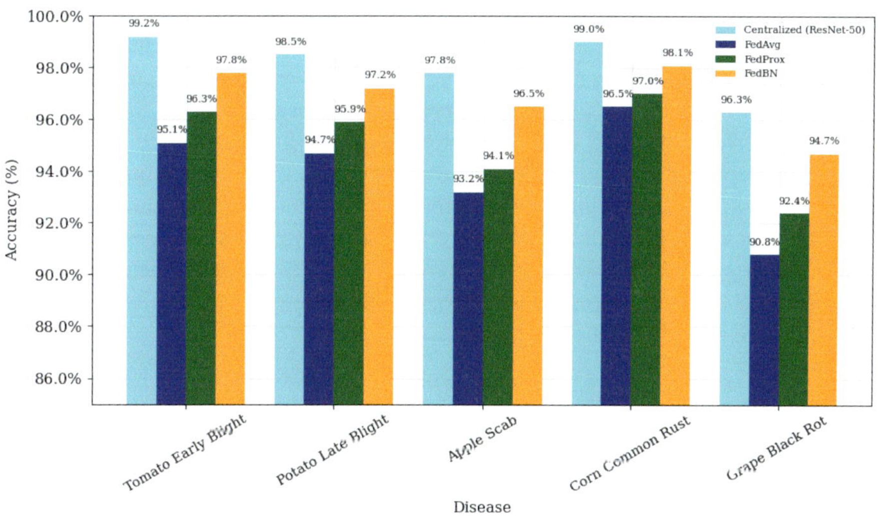

Figure 5.5. Per-disease accuracy comparison between centralized and federated models.

Table 5.5. Privacy protection vs various algorithms

Model	Accuracy	F1_ Score	Privacy protection
FedBN	97.1	96.9	97%
FedProx	96.5	96.2	95%
FedAvg	96.2	95.9	95%

RQ3: Which federated learning algorithm offers the best trade-off between data privacy protection and model performance?

FedAvg, FedProx, and FedBN are compared for their composite score to answer this research question.

Table 5.6 presents the performance of various Federated Learning approaches across different communication rounds. FedBN achieved the highest accuracy of 97.1% with the fewest communication rounds (40). FedProx followed with an accuracy of 96.5%, requiring 45 rounds. In contrast, FedAvg yielded the lowest accuracy of 96.2% and required the highest number of communication rounds (50).

Table 5.6. Federated learning communication round

Model	Accuracy	F1-score	Communication rounds	Composite score
FedBN	97.1	96.9	40	1.00
FedProx	96.5	96.2	45	0.37
FedAvg	96.2	95.9	50	0.00

Table 5.5 also presents the composite score of various Federated Learning (FL) algorithms. FedBN demonstrated the highest accuracy and achieved a composite score of 1.0, indicating an optimal balance between model performance and data preservation efficiency. This makes FedBN particularly well-suited for smart farming applications. While all FL models preserve data privacy by design, they differ in predictive performance and communication overhead. To identify the optimal FL model, we employed a straightforward multi-objective scoring system that integrates accuracy, F1-score, and the number of communication rounds—an indirect measure of processing efficiency. All metrics were normalized to a scale between 0 and 1, where higher F1 and accuracy scores combined with fewer communication rounds yield better composite scores. This approach enables a principled selection of the most effective privacy-preserving model.

RQ 4: What is the impact of communication overhead (number of communication rounds) on federated learning models' performance and rate of convergence?

Communication overhead is a critical challenge in Federated Learning (FL), particularly in distributed environments such as smart agriculture, where bandwidth and energy resources are constrained. Each communication round involves transmitting model updates between clients and a central server. While reducing the number of rounds can conserve energy and bandwidth, it may also impact model performance. This research question investigates the relationship between communication overhead and model convergence—specifically, how quickly a model reaches optimal accuracy. It further explores whether models with fewer communication rounds can still deliver strong performance in terms of accuracy and F1-score. To address this, we analyze the performance and communication round data of three FL algorithms: FedAvg, FedProx, and FedBN.

Our experimental results reveal a strong negative correlation between the number of communication rounds and model performance (accuracy: r = –0.9934; F1-score: r = –0.9930). This suggests that reducing communication rounds can lead to improved model accuracy. Notably, FedBN achieved the highest accuracy (97.1%) and F1-score (96.9%) with only 40 communication rounds. Compared to FedAvg and FedProx, FedBN demonstrated superior performance with fewer updates, indicating faster and more efficient convergence.

Figure 5.6 illustrares the relationship between the number of communication rounds and model performance specifically accuracy and F1-score. This research question investigates how communication overhead influences model convergence —that is, how efficiently a model reaches optimal accuracy—and whether models with fewer communication rounds can still deliver strong performance. To explore this, we analyzed the performance and communication round data of three Federated Learning algorithms: FedAvg, FedProx, and FedBN. The results are summarized below.

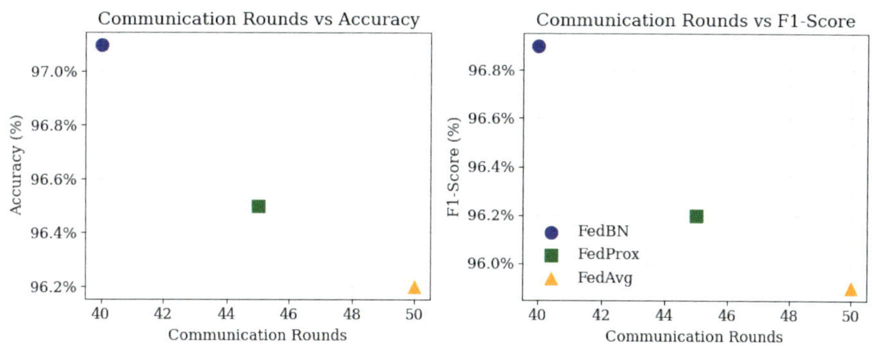

Figure 5.6. Relationship between communication rounds vs accuracy vs F1-score for crop disease prediction.

Table 5.7 presents the metrics related to communication rounds and their corresponding correlation analysis. The correlation between communication rounds and accuracy is –0.9820, indicating a strong negative association: as the number of communication rounds decreases, model accuracy improves. Similarly, the correlation with F1-score is –0.9744, further confirming a strong negative relationship—suggesting that fewer communication rounds are linked to enhanced F1-Score performance.

Table 5.7. Metrics with correlation value

Metric	Correlation value
Communication Rounds vs Accuracy	–0.9820
Communication Rounds vs F1-Score	–0.9744

5.5 Conclusion and Future Work

This study investigated the use of federated learning (FL) combined with Deep Learning algorithms for crop disease prediction, aiming to balance model performance with data privacy. The findings indicate that FL, particularly the FedBN approach, can achieve competitive accuracy and generalization compared to centralized models while preserving the privacy of client data. This indicates the growing potential of decentralized learning frameworks in domains where data sharing is restricted due to privacy concerns or resource-constrained environments. Importantly, the implications of this research not only focused on model performance; it aligns with the principles of digital sovereignty, empowering local data holders to retain control over their data without compromising the benefits of collective model learning. This paradigm is especially significant in agriculture, where data sensitivity, regional variability, and policy constraints can play a crucial role while adopting AI. The study thus supports the broader shift toward ethical and privacy-preserving AI practices in critical real-world applications.

In future work, we plan to integrate multimodal data sources such as weather patterns and soil composition into the FL framework which may further enhance model robustness and diagnostic accuracy. Another important direction is the development of adaptive communication strategies that optimize the training process based on network availability or device capacity. Finally, federated transfer learning approaches that enable knowledge sharing across different crops, geographies, or disease classes may enhance scalability and widen the applicability of our method across diverse agricultural contexts.

Declaration of Generative AI and AI-Assisted Technologies in the Writing Process

During the preparation of this work, the author utilized AI-assisted tools such as Grammarly to enhance English language accuracy, including spelling, grammar, and punctuation. The content generated or corrected by these tools was thoroughly reviewed, revised, and edited by the author to ensure accuracy and originality. The author accepts full responsibility for the originality of the final content of this publication.

References

Aboneh, T., Rorissa, A., & Srinivasagan, R. (2025). Revolutionizing crop disease detection: Harnessing ensemble learning and computer vision for enhanced accuracy. *Iris Journal of Educational Research*, 4(4). https://doi.org/10.33552/IJER.2025.04.000595.

Akter, M., Moustafa, N., Lynar, T., & Razzak, I. (2022). Edge intelligence: Federated learning-based privacy protection framework for smart healthcare systems. *IEEE Journal of Biomedical and Health Informatics*, 26(12), 5805-5816.

Ale, L., Sheta, A., Li, L., Wang, Y., & Zhang, N. (2019, December). Deep learning based plant disease detection for smart agriculture. In: *2019 IEEE Globecom Workshops (GC Wkshps)* (pp. 1-6). IEEE.

Antico, T.M., Moreira, L.F.R., & Moreira, R. (2024). Evaluating the potential of federated learning for maize leaf disease prediction. arXiv preprint arXiv:2412.07872.

Banerjee, S., Chen, Y., Nissim, K., Parkes, D., Siek, K., & Wilcox, L. (2020). Modernizing data control: Making personal digital data mutually beneficial for citizens and industry. arXiv preprint arXiv:2012.08571.

Behera, S., & Padhy, N. (2025, February). Classification algorithms for pump control as well as multi-objective optimization for pump scheduling. In: *2025 International Conference on Emerging Systems and Intelligent Computing (ESIC)* (pp. 578-583). IEEE.

Behera, S., Padhy, N., Panigrahi, R., & Kuanar, S.K. (2025). Crop disease prediction using deep learning in a federated learning environment: Ensuring data privacy and agricultural sustainability. *Procedia Computer Science*, 254, 137-146.

Bouacida, I., Farou, B., Djakhdjakha, L., Seridi, H., & Kurulay, M.(2025). Innovative deep learning approach for cross-crop plant disease detection: A generalized method for identifying unhealthy leaves. *Information Processing in Agriculture*, 12(1), 54-67.

Chatterjee, S., Chaudhuri, R., Gupta, S., Sivarajah, U., & Bag, S.(2023). Assessing the impact of big data analytics on decision-making processes, forecasting, and performance of a firm. *Technological Forecasting and Social Change*, 196, 122824.

Chaudhary, A., Gupta, M., & Tiwari, U. (2023). Crop disease detection using deep learning models. *International Journal of Innovative Science and Research Technology*, 8(12), 9. https://doi.org/10.5281/zenodo.10432632.

Corren, E (2024). Gaining or Losing Control? An Empirical Study on the Real Use of Data Control Rights and Policy Implications. SSRN preprint, 2024.

Department for Digital, Culture, Media and Sport. (2021). Data: A new direction-analysis of expected impact. https://assets.publishing.service.gov.uk/media/613a362ed3bf7f05afde0413/Data_Reform_Impact_Analysis_Paper.pdf

Hosen, M.D., & Islam, M.H. (2025). Aggrotech: Leveraging deep learning for sustainable tomato disease management. arXiv preprint arXiv:2501.12052.

Husnain, A., Ahmad, A., & Saeed, A. (2024). Enhancing agricultural health with AI: Drone-based machine learning for mango tree disease detection. *World Journal of Advanced Research and Reviews*, 23(02), 1267–1276.

Jaiswal, R., & Schaathun, H.G. (2025). On human sovereignty in a digital age. *Procedia Computer Science*, 254, 157-163.

Jensen, A., Brown, P., Groves, K., & Morshed, A. (2025). Next generation crop protection: A systematic review of trends in modelling approaches for disease prediction. *Computers and Electronics in Agriculture*, 234, 110245.

Judith, J., Tamilselvi, R., Beham, M.P., Lakshmi, S., Panthakkan, A., Mansoori, S.A., & Ahmad, H.A. (2025). Remote sensing based crop health classification using NDVI and fully connected neural networks. arXiv preprint arXiv:2504.10522.

Khan, S., Yadav, A.K., Shukla, S.S.P., & Shende, V. (2024). ResNet-50: A breakthrough in plant disease detection accuracy for agricultural empowerment. In: *Computational Methods in Science and Technology* (pp. 364-371). CRC Press.

Khandagale, H.P., Patil, S., Gavali, V.S., Chavan, S.V., Halkarnikar, P.P., & Meshram, P.A. (2025). Design and implementation of FourCropNet: A CNN-based system for efficient multi-crop disease detection and management. arXiv preprint arXiv:2503.08348.

Kolasa, I. (2025, January). Privacy-first AI: Exploring federated learning. *Edge AI and Vision Alliance*. https://www.edge-ai-vision.com/2025/01/privacy-first-ai-exploring-federated-learning/

Lee, S., & Yun, C.M. (2023). A deep learning model for predicting risks of crop pests and diseases from sequential environmental data. *Plant Methods*, 19(1), 145.

Ministry of Electronics and Information Technology. (2025). Estimation and measurement of India's digital economy. https://www.meity.gov.in/static/uploads/2025/01/5ff397f9e8152d5562ed4cef1a6b767b.pdf

Ngugi, H.N., Akinyelu, A.A., & Ezugwu, A.E. (2024). Machine learning and deep learning for crop disease diagnosis: Performance analysis and review. *Agronomy*, 14(12), 3001.

Press Information Bureau. (2025, January). India's Digital Economy to Contribute One-Fifth of National Income by 2029-30. https://www.pib.gov.in/PressReleaseIframePage.aspx?PRID=2097125

Rahman, S.T., Vasker, N., Ahammed, A.K., & Hasan, M. (2023, December). Advancing cucumber disease detection in agriculture through machine vision and drone technology. In: *International Conference on Cyber Intelligence and Information Retrieval* (pp. 477-486). Singapore: Springer Nature Singapore.

Roßmann, B., Canzaniello, A., von der Gracht, H., & Hartmann, E. (2018). The future and social impact of big data analytics in supply chain management: Results from a Delphi study. *Technological Forecasting and Social Change*, 130, 135-149.

Shoaib, M., Shah, B., Ei-Sappagh, S., Ali, A., Ullah, A., Alenezi, F., ... & Ali, F. (2023). An advanced deep learning models-based plant disease detection: A review of recent research. *Frontiers in Plant Science*, 14, 1158933.

Slimani, H., El Mhamdi, J., & Jilbab, A. (2025). Advanced algorithmic model for real-time multi-level crop disease detection using neural architecture search. In: *E3S Web of Conferences* (Vol. 601, p. 00032). EDP Sciences.

Tonmoy, M.R., Hossain, M.M., Dey, N., & Mridha, M.F. (2025). MobilePlantViT: A mobile-friendly hybrid ViT for generalized plant disease image classification. arXiv preprint arXiv:2503.16628.

Vijayan, S., & Chowdhary, C.L. (2025). Hybrid feature optimized CNN for rice crop disease prediction. *Scientific Reports*, 15(1), 7904.

Zhao, W., & Efremova, N. (2024). Grapevine disease prediction using climate variables from multi-sensor remote sensing imagery via a transformer model. arXiv preprint arXiv:2406.07094.

CHAPTER

6

Rent-Seeking in AI Infrastructure: A Structural Threat to Digital Sovereignty and Cybersecurity

Mazaher Kianpour[1*(0000-0003-2804-4630)] **and Iwona Maria Windekilde**[2(0000-0001-8084-6695)]

[1] Kristiania University of Applied Sciences

[2] Norwegian University of Science and Technology

6.1 Introduction

Artificial Intelligence (AI) is rapidly becoming a foundational layer of modern governance, embedded across domains such as critical infrastructure management and national defense (Adewusi et al., 2024; Dafoe, 2024). As states increasingly turn to AI to realize its potential benefits, they are confronting a new category of risk which is not rooted in the algorithms themselves, but in the economic and infrastructural imbalances that shape how AI is adopted and used. These risks extend beyond technical concerns. They raise important questions about national sovereignty and the resilience of broader systems. In other words, the challenges posed by AI are not just about technology, but about the underlying structures that determine who can use it, how, and to what effect.

This chapter investigates the rent-seeking behavior of dominant AI infrastructure providers as a central factor shaping current challenges in digital sovereignty. These providers, typically large, transnational firms, control access to AI models, cloud computing resources, and the systems used to train and deploy advanced technologies. By monetizing model usage, restricting interoperability, and enclosing data and inference processes within proprietary platforms, these firms create conditions where governments become dependent on external providers. This asymmetric dependency makes it more difficult for states to maintain independent control over their digital infrastructure. As a result, national cybersecurity can be directly affected, as such

*Corresponding author: mazaher.kianpour@ntnu.no

DOI: 10.1201/9781003581581-6

dependencies can limit a state's ability to protect its critical digital assets and respond effectively to cyber threats.

To address these issues, the chapter introduces the RESIST Framework, a new model for governing AI infrastructure that prioritizes digital sovereignty and cybersecurity. The RESIST Framework is built around six key principles: Reclaim, Ensure, Secure, Institutionalize, Standardize, and Target. These principles are designed to help governments create AI infrastructures that are resilient, transparent, and under their own control. To support the application of this framework, the chapter offers practical guidance for national cybersecurity agencies, AI regulators, and public technology leaders responsible for critical infrastructure and procurement.

This chapter adds to the growing debate about secure and sovereign AI by focusing on how AI infrastructure, cybersecurity, and digital sovereignty are deeply connected. It argues that the threat posed by concentrated control over AI systems is not just technical problems. They reflect deeper structural and economic imbalances. By framing rent-seeking as a key driver of these dependencies, the chapter shifts the focus from abstract principles to the actual conditions that shape how states govern and secure their digital systems. The RESIST framework offers a way to think about these challenges more concretely, and to act on them through regulation, procurement, and investment. In doing so, the chapter makes the case that digital sovereignty is not only about having the right tools. It is about building the right structures, policies, and capabilities to control and adapt them over time.

This chapter is structured as follows. Section 2 discusses the concept of rent-seeking and analyzes how it manifests in AI infrastructure through a set of distinct but interrelated mechanisms. Section 3 presents the RESIST framework as a conceptual governance model designed to counteract these mechanisms. Section 4 operationalizes the framework through policy tools, procurement standards, and investment strategies, and also identifies indicators for monitoring the implementation of the RESIST framework. Section 5 concludes the chapter by reflecting on the broader implications of AI infrastructure governance and outlining future directions.

6.2 Rent-Seeking in AI Infrastructure

The rise of large-scale AI systems has brought infrastructure,[1] especially compute capacity, model access, and data pipelines, to the center of geopolitical, economic, and technological power (Westgarth et al., 2024; OECD, 2023). As states and private actors increasingly compete for control over these infrastructures, a dangerous pattern emerges: instead of channeling resources into innovation or system resilience, many actors redirect investment into contests for control over key AI assets. This dynamic,

---

[1] In this chapter, we distinguish between AI systems (i.e., the applications or services that perform tasks using machine learning) and AI infrastructure (i.e., the underlying technical and institutional foundation that enables those systems (Marcus & Davis, 2019)). This includes compute hardware, orchestration environments, data pipelines, foundational models, and regulatory architectures. While AI systems are the visible layer of deployment, infrastructure determines who can build, govern, or adapt them, making it the locus of structural control and rent extraction (Sadowski, 2020).

recognized in economics as rent-seeking, becomes particularly dangerous when applied to foundational digital systems, where sovereignty and security are tightly coupled to infrastructural independence.

6.2.1 Conceptualizing Rent-Seeking and Its Relevance to AI Infrastructure

In its classical formulation, rent-seeking describes how individuals or firms expend real resources in order to secure access to economic rents[2] (Tullock, 1967; Krueger, 1974). In other words, rent-seeking refers to the pursuit of economic gain through control, restriction, or manipulation of access to resources, rather than through value creation or productive investment. Unlike profit-seeking, which rewards innovation, efficiency, or entrepreneurship, rent-seeking involves extracting value from artificially maintained scarcity or privileged market positions. Building on Gordon Tullock's original insight (Tullock, 1967), Richard Posner (Posner, 1975) formalized the phenomenon as a game in which each actor's probability of winning the rent is proportional to their investment. In equilibrium, the total resources spent by all competitors often equal or exceed the value of the rent itself. This means that the contest produces no net social benefit, and all gains are dissipated in the competition, leaving society no better off. In the case of AI infrastructure, such rent-seeking behavior can manifest as lobbying for favorable compute allocations (OD'onnel, 2025; Wiggers, 2025), regulatory barriers to open-source alternatives (Castro, 2024), or vertical integration strategies that enclose access to foundational models and training data (Trivedi, 2025).

Yet, this is only the economic surface of a much deeper political and strategic problem. In AI systems, control over infrastructure is not merely a source of profit, it is a lever of power (Sparrentak & de Heer, 2024; Robbins & Van Wynsberghe, 2022; Muldoon & Wu, 2023). Access to compute and model determines who can develop, deploy, and govern advanced capabilities. When rent-seeking drives the privatization and centralization of these infrastructures, the result is not just economic inefficiency but a direct threat to digital sovereignty (i.e., the capacity of states and institutions to exercise independent control over critical systems (Pohle & Thiel, 2020)). Unlike traditional public utilities, AI infrastructure is often globally scaled but driven by a small set of technology giants (Van Der Vlist et al., 2024), creating dependency structures where access can be monitored, restricted, or weaponized.

Some scholars may argue that infrastructure-focused investment, even when driven by private incentives, is still beneficial because it grows the technological base (i.e., technological spillovers) (Bennett, 2019; Diodato et al., 2018). In fact, many rent-seeking activities result in larger clusters, better models, and expanded capabilities. But this line of defense misses the core issue. The problem is not the technical improvement of infrastructure, but the political economy of its control. Innovation under enclosure conditions creates strategic asymmetries. As Henry Farrell and Abraham Newman argue in their theory of weaponized

---

2 In economics, economic rent refers to income derived from controlling scarce resources beyond the minimum required to incentivize their provision (Ricardo, 2005)

interdependence,[3] actors that control central digital infrastructure can leverage that position to exert political or strategic pressure on dependent states or institutions (Farrell & Newman, 2019). The actors who control core infrastructures can monitor data flows, enforce exclusions, and extract compliance from weaker nodes. In this context, even technical progress can undermine sovereignty if it comes with increased dependency on external actors.

From the perspective of state capacity, this pattern leads to a weakening of infrastructural power, in the sense argued by Michael Mann (1984). In today's world, a state's sovereignty is not just about controlling its land and borders. It also means having the power to run and manage the digital technologies that support its economy, security, and daily life. When access to AI models, data services, or compute clusters is governed by opaque commercial actors, especially those operating under foreign jurisdiction, states lose their ability to set autonomous policy, enforce cybersecurity norms, or respond decisively to strategic disruptions.

This dependency tends to intensify over time due to path dependence, as institutions increasingly structure their operations around proprietary platforms (Liebowitz & Margolis, 1995). As a result, internal expertise in alternative systems diminishes, and viable options for change become limited. The economic and political costs of transitioning to sovereign infrastructure subsequently rise, making such a shift increasingly difficult to justify or achieve (Helmrich et al., 2023; Simeonov, 2020). This phenomenon reflects the dynamics of infrastructure lock-in, where initial convenience and efficiency give way to long-term strategic vulnerability. These dynamics turn digital infrastructure into a soft-power dependency where states may be forced to align with the policies, threat perceptions, and even export controls of the vendor's host country.

6.2.2 Mechanisms of Rent-Seeking in AI Infrastructure

In the following, we examine how rent-seeking in AI infrastructure manifests itself through four structurally distinct but strategically interrelated mechanisms. Each is designed not to advance technical innovation[4] or reduce cost, but to extract economic

---

[3] Henry Farrell and Abraham Newman's theory of weaponized interdependence argues that the structure of global economic networks does not simply distribute economic benefits, but also enables certain actors, typically those occupying central positions within these networks, to exercise significant coercive power over others (Farrell & Newman, 2019). Rather than viewing globalization as a force that disperses power and encourages cooperation, the centralization of key nodes creates opportunities for these hub states to leverage their position strategically. This means that states at the center of crucial networks can monitor, influence, or even restrict the activities of others (Drezner et al., 2021). Their research highlights two primary mechanisms through which this coercive capacity is exercised: panopticon effects, where central actors gain informational advantages by monitoring network flows, and *chokepoint effects* where they can disrupt or block access to essential resources or connections for others in the network.

[4] Shapiro and Varian, in Information Rules, discuss how control over general-purpose infrastructure-such as platforms-enables firms to extract economic rents, not primarily through ongoing technical innovation, but by leveraging their position as gatekeepers. In their analysis, access to the platform itself becomes a key source of monetization, as firms can charge for entry, participation, or continued use, rather than relying solely on improvements in the underlying technology (Shapiro & Varian, 1999).

rents by controlling critical access points, reducing substitutability, and creating governance asymmetries. These mechanisms are not passive market outcomes. They are active institutional strategies that transform AI infrastructures into recurring revenue streams, with profound implications for digital sovereignty and national cybersecurity resilience.

6.2.2.1 Control of Essential Inputs with Access-Based Monetization

AI vendors have increasingly restricted access to essential productive inputs, such as foundational models, optimized inference pipelines, and compute environments. These are typically offered only through proprietary APIs with usage-based pricing models (e.g., charged per token, per inference, or on tiered subscription bases) rather than through deployable packages or local hosting rights. This approach is not primarily due to technical infeasibility but reflects a deliberate economic model that aims at the access to AI becoming a long-term service relationship, rather than a transferable capability.

For example, OpenAI's GPT-4,[5] Google's PaLM 2,[6] and Amazon's Titan models[7] are accessible only through hosted endpoints with no visibility into internal states or system-level telemetry. Organizations, public and private alike, interact with these systems on externally defined terms, without rights to modify, self-host,[8] or audit the models. Even models trained on publicly sourced or user contributed data are commercialized under closed-access regimes, converting public value into private rent.

This control is similar to classical licensing monopolies (Stigler, 2021), but at a deeper infrastructural level. It grants vendors monopoly rent over intangible assets while withholding productive rights from users. Such black-box MLaaS (machine learning-as-a-service) models not only impose ongoing costs but displace users' ability to independently manage or secure critical capabilities, replacing operational control with economic dependency.

---

[5] OpenAI's API provides no access to model weights, training data, or internal computations. The GPT-4 system card explicitly states that technical details (e.g., model size) are withheld (OpenAI, 2025c).

[6] PaLM 2's technical report withholds architecture specifics from external publication (Google, 2025)

[7] Titan models are exclusively available through Amazon Bedrock, with no self-hosting or internal visibility (Amazon, 2025).

[8] OpenAI's ChatGPT Gov, for example, is marketed to U.S. government agencies as a self-hosted solution deployed within Microsoft Azure's FedRAMP High-authorized cloud (OpenAI, 2025b). However, this self-hosting occurs within a logically isolated environment still maintained by the vendor. The model weights, update cycles, and operational control remain proprietary to OpenAI, and agencies cannot audit, modify, or relocate the model outside this environment. As such, even under enhanced compliance and data residency conditions, governments remain structurally dependent on the vendor for model access and functionality. This illustrates how self-hosting can serve as a nominal assurance of control while maintaining underlying vendor lock-in. The result is a form of platform rent-seeking that undermines full digital sovereignty and limits forensic and security oversight.

6.2.2.2 Structural Lock-In via Cross-Layer Integration

Another form of rent-seeking emerges from the vertical integration of AI services with broader cloud infrastructure. Rather than offering standalone, modular tools, dominant vendors bundle AI capabilities with proprietary identity management, orchestration, monitoring, and analytics platforms. Examples include the integration of Azure AI with Active Directory and GitHub Copilot, or the connection of Google Gemini with BigQuery and Vertex AI (Van Der Vlist et al., 2024). This layered integration increases exit costs, and migrating from one AI service requires replacing multiple dependent services, each with its own reconfiguration overhead, security implications, and compliance risks.

One notable example is Palantir's deployment of its Artificial Intelligence Platform (AIP) on Microsoft's Azure Government Cloud (Palantir, 2024). While Palantir supplies the AI application layer, it is integrated into Microsoft platform stack, creating an ecosystem where data handling, authentication, and monitoring are all tied to the same vendor's infrastructure (HASH, 2025). This bundling undermines substitutability and compounds dependency. A vulnerability or outage in any layer of the stack can cascade across the full system, while migrating away becomes technically and contractually constrained.

Economically, this is a case of rent via infrastructural entanglement. As Bessen has argued in the context of digital platforms, firms extract surplus not from direct innovation, but from controlling complementary services that lock users into their ecosystems (Bessen, 2022). In AI infrastructure, this control is compounded. This means that not only the model is non-substitutable, but the surrounding stack also reinforces that non-substitutability.

6.2.2.3 Artificial Scarcity of Compliance and Security Capabilities

While compute providers, who are also in most cases the dominant actors in AI infrastructure, are recognized for supporting regulatory compliance frameworks (Heim et al., 2024), many have adopted a business model that monetizes access to basic governance functions. Rather than embedding auditability, encryption, data residency, and telemetry access as defaults, these features are segmented across pricing tiers. As a result, security has become a service tier, not an architectural baseline.

OpenAI's ChatGPT Enterprise and API offerings provide key controls such as encrypted data handling, SAML SSO,[9] model usage logs, and configurable retention policies, only for high-paying clients (OpenAI, 2025a). These capabilities are fundamental for any institution operating in a regulated or security sensitive domain. Similarly, Microsoft Azure OpenAI provides network isolation and regional deployment controls only within bespoke enterprises or government specific agreements.

Google Cloud's Audit Manager exemplifies this segmentation model. While it offers a free level with minimal governance features (including some AI controls),

[9] Security Assertion Markup Language Single Sign-On (SSO).

access to essential compliance frameworks such as NIST 800-53, ISO 27001:2022, and PCI DSS 4.0 requires an annual $7,500 premium subscription (Cloud, 2025). Features like custom policy frameworks and integration with the Security Command Center Enterprise are also paywalled. The point is that these are not premium benefits. They are prerequisites for institutional accountability in sectors like finance, health, and public administration.

This segmentation creates what economists term artificial scarcity[10]. Rent is extracted not from functional capability, but from the right to observe and govern systems already in use. The result is a compliance asymmetry, which means well-funded institutions may purchase visibility, while others, including smaller agencies and less wealthy states, operate in strategic opacity.

6.2.2.4 Controlled Interoperability

As AI regulation and public procurement increasingly emphasize interoperability, vendors have adapted by supporting surface-level compatibility by adopting standard model formats (e.g., ONNX), open telemetry protocols, or frameworks like MLflow. However, these formal standards often mask deeper dependencies. Version-locking, proprietary execution environments, and managed-only deployment options ensure that systems built using open tools remain tied to a single vendor's infrastructure.

For example, several leading vendors now support exporting models to ONNX or accepting Hugging Face-compatible architectures, but still require inference to be run on proprietary backends or licensed runtimes. Model checkpoints may be exportable only under restrictive conditions or perform poorly outside of the vendor's own optimized infrastructure. These restrictions create the illusion of openness while preserving economic exclusivity.

This approach follows the broader patterns of platform dependency discussed in the political economy of digital infrastructure, where formally there is interoperability, but practical substitutability is obstructed by architectural coupling, performance constraints, or policy friction (Plantin et al., 2018). Rent is extracted not from functionality, but from restricting the conditions under which substitution is feasible. The ability to switch providers becomes theoretical rather than operational.

Together, these mechanisms do not represent flaws in an otherwise efficient market. They are deliberate and economically rational strategies to extract value through control, constraint, and asymmetry. Each converts what could be a transferable, inspectable, or interoperable asset into a gated service—generating recurring revenue while eroding user agency. Their cumulative effect is a deeply layered dependency architecture. States, agencies, and public institutions are increasingly unable to inspect, modify, audit, or replace the AI systems they depend on. This has direct implications for cybersecurity. Organizations cannot trace incidents, enforce access

---

[10] Artificial scarcity refers to the strategic limitation of access to a resource or capability that is technically reproducible or deliverable at scale, in order to extract economic rent or exert control (Daoud, 2015). In AI infrastructure, this often takes the form of segmenting access to audit logs, security features, or compliance tools across pricing tiers, not due to inherent cost or technical barriers, but to preserve asymmetric market power.

boundaries, or respond to evolving threats when core capabilities are externalized. It also undermines digital sovereignty. Public policy becomes reactive to vendor decisions, and national infrastructure is shaped by contractual dependencies rather than strategic design.

In response, the next section introduces the RESIST framework, a sovereignty-centered conceptual model for the governance of AI infrastructure. Each pillar of the framework corresponds to one or more of the mechanisms outlined above and aims to reverse these dependencies by embedding auditability, substitutability, and control into the foundations of AI systems.

6.3 The RESIST Framework

As the preceding section demonstrated, rent-seeking in AI infrastructure is not merely a byproduct of market concentration or regulatory delay. It is the result of deliberate strategies that restrict access, fragment oversight, and institutionalize dependency across technical and governance layers. These mechanisms are economically rational for the firms that deploy them, but their cumulative effect undermines cybersecurity preparedness and weakens national control over critical digital infrastructure.

To address these structural dependencies, this chapter proposes the RESIST framework. The framework does not aim to optimize the performance of AI systems per se, nor to propose abstract ethical principles. Rather, it is designed to directly counter the institutional and economic conditions that enable rent extraction from states and public institutions. It does so by offering a set of actionable governance principles, each grounded in a specific failure mode of the current infrastructure landscape.

The RESIST framework is composed of six pillars: Reclaim control, Ensure auditability, Secure diversity, Institutionalize interoperability, Standardize certification, and Target investment. These pillars are not mutually exclusive. Rather, they correspond to overlapping but analytically distinct modes of intervention, each of which aligns with one or more of the rent-seeking mechanisms detailed earlier. This framework was developed through an iterative synthesis of economic theories and comparative policy analysis. Each pillar is rooted in operational principles observed in adjacent domains, such as cloud security, platform governance, and critical infrastructure protection, but adapted to the context of AI infrastructures. The goal is not to offer a universal template, but to identify levers that states can pragmatically deploy to reduce their exposure to rent-extractive dependencies, and to rebuild the infrastructural conditions of sovereignty. In the remainder of this section, each pillar of the framework is presented.

6.3.1 Reclaim Control over Strategic AI Inputs

The first pillar of the RESIST framework addresses the most fundamental form of rent-seeking in AI infrastructure: the extraction of ongoing economic value from exclusive control over essential computational assets. This includes foundational models, inference environments, data flows, and even the underlying hardware layers (e.g., access to GPU-intensive compute). In classical economic terms, this represents a form of monopoly rent derived from withholding productive inputs and reselling limited access under usage-based conditions. The structural asymmetry is clear: the vendor retains operational sovereignty, while the client, whether a state, agency, or institution, remains a tenant in the vendor's cognitive infrastructure.[11]

From a digital sovereignty perspective, this arrangement is untenable. When a public body cannot host, inspect, or modify the AI systems that support its operations, such as language models embedded in citizen services or security screening systems, it loses the ability to govern its own digital territory. Decisions made by opaque, foreign-controlled systems can no longer be independently verified, contested, or recalibrated. This undermines national policy autonomy, erodes transparency, and introduces foreign veto points into core administrative processes.

In terms of cybersecurity, the implications are equally important. Standard security principles, such as trust boundaries, zero-trust design, and incident response readiness, are based on having technical control over runtime environments. When an incident occurs within a vendor-maintained black box, defenders are deprived of visibility into model behavior, telemetry, or failure modes. Incident reconstruction becomes dependent on vendor cooperation, and lack of access to model weights and deployment context disables meaningful threat modeling or patching. In this case, the client is not just exposed, it is powerless.

Reclaiming control is not to reject market participation or cloud-scale deployment. It is to reassert the baseline conditions for operational independence. This may take the form of requiring on-premise or sovereign-cloud deployment for high-risk workloads, contractual access to model artifacts, documentation, and inference logs, or enforcing jurisdictional alignment in procurement policies. In any case, the control must be architectural and allow national actors to secure, audit, and adapt AI systems on their own terms.

6.3.2 Ensure Auditability and Forensic Access

The second pillar responds to a rent-seeking pattern that we consider corrosive: the monetization of auditability and compliance as enterprise-only features. This practice places basic governance tools such as inference logs, model usage tracking, and telemetry control behind premium paywalls. The result is a two-tier system of observability: large, well-funded institutions can afford visibility, while others, including many public-sector agencies, operate without the means to perform even basic forensic oversight.

In economic terms, this constitutes a form of regulatory rent-seeking. Vendors extract value not by improving AI functionality, but by controlling the means through which users meet their legal and security obligations. Features such as encrypted logs, jurisdiction-specific data retention, or explainable outputs are not innovations. They are conditions for institutional accountability. When these are packaged

[11] Cognitive infrastructure refers to systems and frameworks where AI is deeply integrated into societal and technological infrastructures, enabling adaptive, networked decision-making that transcends traditional human or digital processes. It combines AI models, data ecosystems, and governance mechanisms to create intelligent, responsive environments that shape human cognition, governance, and urban systems (Sellar & Gulson, 2021).

as optional add-ons, the vendor profits by controlling access to the means of regulatory compliance.

The cybersecurity consequences are immediate and severe. Without guaranteed access to structured logs or inference traces, it becomes impossible to conduct post-incident analysis, determine liability, or even detect abnormal behavior in real time. Threat intelligence cannot be applied retroactively. Security monitoring must be performed under partial visibility conditions or outsourced to the same vendor whose infrastructure is under scrutiny. This undermines attribution, response coordination, and long-term defense planning. Furthermore, monetizing these features can undermine an organization's ability to meet regulatory obligations, increasing the likelihood of non-compliance and associated legal or financial penalties. A fragmented landscape where only select organizations can afford compliance tools also undermines collective cybersecurity. Attackers may target less-protected entities as entry points for broader campaigns, increasing risks for interconnected systems and supply chains.

From a sovereignty point of view, the issue goes beyond the technical domain and also includes legal aspects. States must be able to guarantee that AI systems used in public functions can be investigated, reviewed, and governed under national law. When logs are unavailable, redacted, or stored in extraterritorial jurisdictions, states forfeit their regulatory capacity. Auditability, in this sense, is not a service. It is an instrument of public power.

This framework positions auditability as a non-negotiable architectural requirement. Model providers must offer standardized, exportable logs, supported by schema documentation and time-stamped signatures. Compliance with regulations and acts (e.g., NIS2, GDPR, Executive Order 14028) must be enforced at the infrastructure level and via system design, not via user promises. Moreover, auditability should be integrated into the model interfaces by default, not as an upgrade. Only then can AI infrastructure support institutions in fulfilling their legal and security mandates.

6.3.3 Secure Diversity and Technical Redundancy

The third pillar targets the structural risks associated with monoculture dependency and the concentration of critical AI services within a handful of transnational vendors. When states rely on a single provider for foundational models, inference APIs, or orchestration layers, they become exposed to both commercial rent extraction and systemic fragility. The economic mechanism here is that when credible alternatives are absent or impractical, vendors can charge rents not for innovation, but for continuity (Isckia et al., 2020).

From a cybersecurity perspective, monoculture infrastructure amplifies the risk of correlated failure. A vulnerability in a widely used model, framework, or API can propagate across multiple institutions, sectors, or even national systems simultaneously. Without diversity in model behavior, deployment pipelines, and operational tooling, adversarial attacks can scale predictably. The lack of redundancy eliminates the capacity to return in times of compromise, outage, or geopolitical escalation.

In terms of digital sovereignty, concentration introduces structural dependence. States lose the ability to negotiate terms, enforce jurisdictional conditions, or exit vendor relationships without jeopardizing operational continuity. Moreover, the absence of domestic or aligned alternatives weakens strategic positioning. In this case, even when risks are acknowledged, the cost of transition may be prohibitively high.

Thus, securing diversity requires more than encouraging competition. It means deliberately cultivating alternative AI providers, whether through regional partnerships, open-source ecosystems, or national model initiatives, and embedding substitution pathways into procurement and architecture. Redundancy must be treated as a strategic asset. Systems should be designed to allow parallel deployment of multiple models, orchestration tools, or compliance frameworks.

6.3.4 Institutionalize Interoperability and Substitution

Interoperability has become a central theme in AI policy discourse, but its meaning is often diluted in practice. Superficial compliance with open formats or API compatibility is frequently treated as a sufficient condition for substitutability. However, from an economic and infrastructural perspective, interoperability without practical substitutability is largely performative. Vendors may advertise support for standard formats (e.g., ONNX, MLflow), but still maintain deep dependency through undocumented runtime constraints, version-locks, and tightly coupled orchestration tools. This controlled openness creates what economists call quasi-competition. This means even though formal alternatives exist, switching costs remain high, preserving vendor rents.

Interoperability must go beyond marketing language and become a structural guarantee, one that ensures that institutions can exit vendor ecosystems and maintain platform neutrality in practice. From the standpoint of digital sovereignty, if a government cannot move its models, data, or orchestration processes to a different provider without incurring prohibitive costs or compliance risk, it does not possess operational control. Similarly, in cybersecurity terms, the inability to migrate workloads in response to vendor failures, policy non-compliance, or national threats creates an unacceptable exposure. Lock-in is not merely a business inconvenience—it is a vector of systemic vulnerability.

Economically, rent-seeking thrives in ecosystems where technical lock-in persists under the illusion of openness. Interoperability in name allows vendors to meet procurement requirements, while preserving dependency beneath the surface. This framework suggests countering this by demanding interoperability with enforced substitutability. Through legal and technical mandates, model formats should be portable, telemetry and logs must conform to shared standards, and orchestration layers should be replaceable without compromising auditability or performance.

Procurement contracts should have exit clauses and built-in migration support as standard conditions, rather than issues to be negotiated when dependencies are already in place. Simultaneously, national institutions need to invest in shared interface standards and maintain open model registries that make it easier to switch between providers. True interoperability must work not only across different products, but also across jurisdictions and legal frameworks. This is essential to preserve operational continuity and sovereign control, especially in times of geopolitical disruption or infrastructure failure.

6.3.5 Standardize Certification for Sovereignty and Security

In current practice, certification regimes for AI services often emphasize broad ethical principles, performance metrics, or data protection requirements. These are important, but they rarely cover the operational details that actually define control, auditability, or security readiness. This gap has created space for a newer form of rent-seeking. Vendors can charge for access to oversight tools or claim compliance through self-declared assurances, while avoiding thorough and enforceable technical scrutiny.

This reflects a classic case of informational asymmetry, a foundational concept in institutional economics. When vendors have more knowledge and control over how their systems work than the clients dependent on them, they can shape the conditions of trust to their advantage. Certification in this kind of environment becomes more of a branding practice than a real safeguard. It often serves as a costly signal of alignment, but one thats difficult to verify. This puts smaller states and under-resourced agencies at a disadvantage, since they may lack the means to evaluate claims, negotiate custom terms, or build their own capacity to assess AI systems.

Our framework proposes a more grounded approach. Certification should be designed to address these structural imbalances directly. This begins with clear, independently verified standards, assessed by third parties, that evaluate not only system performance but also governance parameters: who holds control, who can access internal data, and who is authorized to observe or intervene when necessary. AI systems need to meet specific benchmarks related to sovereign governance. These include the ability to export and retain logs, apply patches without external approval, and enforce data residency requirements through architecture, not just contracts.

We are beginning to see progress in this direction. The European Union Cloud Services (EUCS) Scheme[12] proposes requirements for forensic audit and

[12] The initial drafts of the scheme included strong sovereignty conditions, such as requiring cloud providers to be headquartered in the EU for the highest assurance tier (Philpot, 2024). However, this requirement was removed in early 2024 after lobbying from major industry groups, who argued that such rules would limit market participation and impose regulatory complexity on global providers. Although the proposal remains under review, with Member States divided over how to balance digital sovereignty against commercial openness (Salmon et al., 2024), this case illustrates how certification regimes themselves can become targets of strategic lobbying, especially when certification controls access to high-value procurement markets. When sovereignty benchmarks threaten to disrupt existing rent flows, such as exclusive access to public sector infrastructure, dominant vendors often mobilize to weaken or redefine the terms of compliance. In this sense, regulatory capture becomes a meta-layer of rent-seeking. Not only do vendors monetize access and governance, they also shape the rules that determine who is considered trustworthy.

jurisdictional alignment (Commission, 2021). In Singapore, the Model AI Governance Framework includes provisions for explainability and system traceability, signaling an acknowledgment that trust must be built into the infrastructure itself. These initiatives exemplify how certification can evolve from principle to enforcement, and from promotional rhetoric to substantive governance.

In the cybersecurity domain, certification must reflect the needs of threat environments. If a system cannot provide transparent logs, local control, or secure ways to isolate faults, it should not be considered acceptable for deployment in critical sectors. Just as frameworks like ISO/IEC 27001 and Common Criteria have long served as baselines for information systems, a comparable model is needed for AI infrastructure to recognize both technical risk and the strategic value of jurisdictional control.

6.3.6 Targeted Strategic Investment in Public AI Capacity

Many of the vulnerabilities outlined above, such as limited access to logs, lack of auditability, and dependence on proprietary deployment environments, stem from a more fundamental issue: the absence of sovereign infrastructure and foundational AI capabilities within the public sector. Most governments do not operate their own large-scale compute facilities, train foundational models, or maintain national AI development teams. As a result, they are compelled to procure services from external vendors, many of whom operate under foreign jurisdictions and design their systems for rent extraction rather than public accountability.

This dynamic reflects more than an infrastructure gap—it represents a strategic vulnerability rooted in market structure. From a public economics perspective, foundational AI models exhibit characteristics of club goods (non-rivalrous but excludable via technical or legal barriers), while compute infrastructure operates as private goods (rivalrous and excludable). High capital costs for development and low marginal access costs incentivize market consolidation, as seen in the dominance of cloud providers like Microsoft Azure and AWS (Narechania & Sitaraman, 2024). This creates a dependency cycle where public institutions, lacking sovereign compute capacity or competitive alternatives, rely on proprietary systems they cannot independently audit or control.

Several governments have begun to address this issue through targeted investment. Norway, for instance, has funded the Norwegian Open AI Lab,[13] supporting domestic research on language models and sector-specific AI applications for both public and private stakeholders. This initiative helps reduce dependency while developing domestic expertise. On a broader scale, the European Union's EuroHPC Joint Undertaking[14] is investing in large-scale compute infrastructure across member states. Although not exclusive to AI, this investment provides the technical foundation for sovereign model training and high-performance simulation that would otherwise be inaccessible to most national institutions.

---

[13] https://www.ntnu.edu/ailab

[14] https://eurohpc-ju.europa.eu/index_en

These efforts reflect a growing recognition that foundational AI infrastructure is a strategic public asset. Investment in sovereign AI capacity is not about rejecting commercial innovation but about ensuring that governments retain the ability to govern. The other pillars of the RESIST framework, such as auditability, certification, and interoperability, depend on this foundation. Without sovereign control over the hardware and software stack, such mechanisms become aspirational rather than enforceable. Strategic investment is therefore not a final step, but a precondition for meaningful cybersecurity and digital sovereignty.

6.4 Operationalizing RESIST

The RESIST framework sets out a structural approach to countering rent-seeking in AI infrastructure by embedding the principles of cybersecurity and digital sovereignty into the way AI infrastructures are deployed and governed. But for this framework to have practical impact, its principles must be applied across different layers of governance, from procurement policy to regulatory oversight, from national investment strategies to agency-level decision-making. This section outlines concrete pathways through which the RESIST pillars can be translated into institutional practice.

6.4.1 Aligning Policy Instruments

At the national and regional level, governments should align existing digital regulation and cybersecurity mandates with the structural goals of the RESIST frame-work. For example, many countries have established data protection and privacy laws, critical infrastructure protections, or public sector procurement standards (UNCTAD, 2025; Karathanasis, 2025) that can be adapted to include requirements for model auditability, local inference control, or open model interfaces.

In the EU context, emerging legislation such as the AI Act, the NIS2 Directive, and potential future expansions to the EUCS certification scheme offer platforms to embed RESIST principles into binding requirements. These include defining model exportability, forensic logging, or runtime inspection as part of what constitutes a "trustworthy AI service" for public sector use.

At the national level, national cybersecurity strategies can treat AI infrastructure as a distinct risk category, requiring independent certification or inclusion in critical infrastructure regulation. At the international level, organizations such as the OECD, ITU, or ISO can also support the creation of benchmark frameworks that reflect these principles, especially for sovereign control over AI deployed in cross-border applications or infrastructure.

6.4.2 Public Procurement as a Strategic Tool

One of the most direct and powerful tools for operationalizing the RESIST framework lies in public procurement. Many systems deployed across education, healthcare, police, and welfare operate under long-term contracts with AI and cloud service providers (OECD, 2024; WHO, 2021). These contracts often shape the digital architecture of government services for years. Embedding RESIST into procurement standards gives states immediate influence over market behavior. This involves requiring vendors to:

- Demonstrate local control over inference and data flows;
- Provide access to standardized logs and exportable telemetry;
- Comply with open format and interface requirements;
- Offer clear, contractual guarantees for migration, substitution, and forensic audit.

To support this shift, governments can develop standardized procurement templates and compliance checklists based on the RESIST pillars. They can issue guidelines that encourage or require adoption across all government agencies.

6.4.3 Institutional Roles and Capacity

Operationalizing RESIST is not only about writing policies. It also depends on assigning clear roles to institutions that can monitor, enforce, and adapt to these requirements. In most national settings, several key actors are essential:

- Cybersecurity agencies (e.g. national CERTs) are best positioned to define the technical baselines for auditability, runtime control, and incident response standards. They should be involved in reviewing infrastructure proposals and certifying AI deployments used in critical sectors.
- Public procurement authorities can translate the RESIST pillars into legally binding contractual terms and pre-qualification requirements for service providers .
- National research institutes and AI labs can support technical implementation by developing reference models, secure infrastructure blueprints, and open-source toolkits aligned with RESIST.
- Data protection authorities can help enforce transparency and log access requirements, especially for systems handling personal or biometric data.

6.4.4 Managing Constraints and Trade-Offs

Implementing RESIST will entail short-term costs, constraints, and resistance . For example, vendors may delay or oppose provisions such as forensic access or mandatory exportability, citing concerns over intellectual property or competitive advantage. Additionally, requirements for on-premise control or sovereign hosting may increase deployment costs and hinder seamless integration with global toolchains.

To manage these trade-offs, governments should prioritize application in high risk and high-impact sectors (e.g. justice, defense, health) and provide transitional support for agencies adopting open-source or multi-vendor alternatives. Additionally, they should coordinate procurement at the national or regional level to create demand-side leverage. In this context, public communication plays a critical role in fostering cross-sectoral consensus and shared understanding.

Beyond technical and financial trade-offs, governments must also anticipate significant political resistance from incumbent providers. Efforts to impose stricter

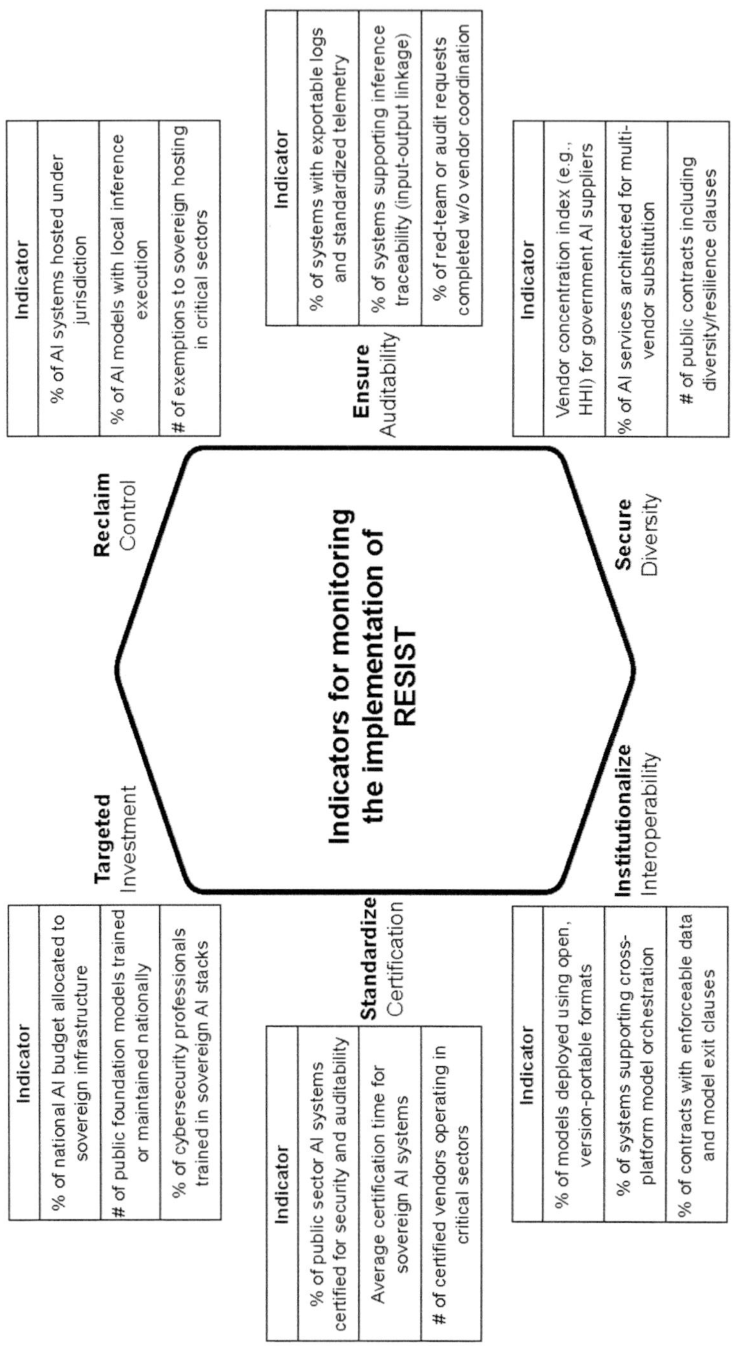

Figure 6.1. A set of suggested indicators for monitoring the implementation of RESIST across cybersecurity and digital sovereignty dimensions.

certification requirements, require forensic access, or restrict foreign control over critical infrastructure frequently encounter coordinated lobbying from major vendors and affiliated industry groups. This dynamic exemplifies a broader form of political capture, in which private actors actively shape the regulatory environment to maintain their structural advantage. For example, in the debate over sovereignty provisions in the EUCS (see Footnote 6), rent-seeking firms have opposed public-interest reforms by invoking arguments related to trade liberalization or administrative burden. Such pressures can stall or weaken policy implementation unless counterbalanced by strong political mandates, effective cross agency coordination, and sustained investment in public infrastructure. Recognizing lobbying as a strategic defense of rent extraction is therefore essential to achieving effective institutional change.

6.4.5 Indicators of Progress

Finally, to ensure that RESIST is adopted effectively, governments need indicators that track implementation. These indicators should be aligned with both cybersecurity readiness and sovereignty benchmarks, and should be publicly reported by designated entities or accountability bodies. Figure 6.1 illustrates a set of indicators aligned with the RESIST pillars, proposed in this study to support monitoring and evaluation of the framework's implementation. Although not exhaustive, these indicators provide a structured foundation for policy monitoring, strategic procurement, and compliance benchmarking across AI infrastructure.

6.5 Conclusion

Rent-seeking in AI infrastructure is not merely an economic inefficiency; it constitutes a structural threat to institutional control, cybersecurity resilience, and democratic governance. As AI systems become embedded in the daily operations of public services, ranging from administrative decision-making to national security functions, states are increasingly reliant on systems they do not control, cannot fully audit, and struggle to govern according to domestic legal and policy standards. These dependencies are not incidental; they are reinforced through platform strategies that monetize access, restrict substitution, and limit the visibility necessary for oversight. Understanding these practices through the lens of rent-seeking reveals the economic logic underlying technical dependency.

In response to these challenges, the RESIST framework has been introduced as a conceptual and operational model for integrating the principles of digital sovereignty and cybersecurity into AI governance. By delineating six pillars, Reclaim Control, Ensure Auditability, Secure Diversity, Institutionalize Interoperability, Standardize Certification, and Target Investment, the framework aims to bridge economic critique and actionable governance. Each pillar is grounded in an identifiable mechanism of rent extraction and maps onto specific institutional levers, such as procurement design, certification standards, and infrastructure investment strategies.

However, implementing the RESIST framework in practice poses substantial institutional and political challenges. Established vendors may resist constraints that threaten high-margin service models, while public institutions may lack the technical or legal capacity to enforce new standards. There is also a risk of fragmented implementation across jurisdictions, or of sovereignty-oriented reforms being co-opted by protectionist or exclusionary agendas. Addressing these barriers requires long-term investment in public sector capabilities, multilateral coordination around open standards, and independent oversight mechanisms capable of validating compliance.

This chapter has taken a conceptual and policy-driven approach, drawing on economic theory, empirical cases, and institutional analysis. However, it remains exploratory in scope. Future work could build on this foundation by conducting empirical assessments of vendor concentration, auditing the enforceability of interoperability claims, or evaluating the real-world implementation of procurement clauses aligned with RESIST. Comparative case studies across jurisdictions, such as the EU, the US, and emerging economies, would further illuminate the geopolitical dynamics of AI sovereignty and help validate the framework across different legal and infrastructural contexts.

Ultimately, the governance of AI infrastructure cannot be separated from the political economy into which it is embedded. Without confronting the economic structures that incentivize rent extraction and institutional opacity, efforts to secure AI systems will remain partial and reactive. The RESIST framework is intended as a step toward more proactive, accountable, and resilient governance, one that treats infrastructure not only as a technological concern, but as a foundational component of democratic capacity.

Declaration of Generative AI and AI-Assisted Technologies

During the preparation of this work, the authors utilized OpenAI's ChatGPT to enhance English language accuracy, including spelling, grammar, and punctuation. The content generated or corrected by these tools was thoroughly reviewed, revised, and edited by the authors to ensure accuracy and originality. The authors accept full responsibility for the originality of the final content of this publication.

References

Adewusi, Adebunmi Okechukwu, Ugochukwu Ikechukwu Okoli, Temidayo Olorunsogo, Ejuma Adaga, Donald Obinna Daraojimba, & Ogugua Chimezie Obi. (2024). Artificial intelligence in cybersecurity: Protecting national infrastructure. *World Journal of Advanced Research and Reviews*, 21(1), 2263–2275.

Amazon. (2025). *Overview of Amazon Titan models – Amazon Bedrock*. https://docs. aws. amazon.com/bedrock/latest/userguide/titan-models.html. [Accessed 13-05-2025].

Bennett, Daniel L. (2019). Infrastructure investments and entrepreneurial dynamism in the US. *Journal of Business Venturing*, 34(5), 105907.

Bessen, James. (2022). *The New Goliaths: How Corporations Use Software to Dominate Industries, Kill Innovation, and Undermine Regulation*. Yale University Press.

Castro, Daniel. (2024). *The EU's AI Act Creates Regulatory Complexity for OpenSource AI*. https://datainnovation .org /2024/ 03/ the-eus-ai-act-createsregulatory-complexity-for-open-source-ai/. [Accessed 19-02-2025].

Cloud, Goolge. (2025). *Audit Manager Pricing.* https://cloud.google.com/products/ audit-manager/pricing. [Accessed 02-05-2025].

Commission, European. (2021). *Critical Infrastructure Protection & Resilience – Eu Cloud Certification Scheme.* https://ec.europa.eu/ newsroom/cipr/items/713799/en. [Accessed 24-02-2025].

Dafoe, Allan. (2024). 21AI governance: Overview and theoretical lenses. In: *The Oxford Handbook of AI Governance.* Oxford University Press. DOI: 10.1093/ oxfordhb/9780197579329.013.2.

Daoud, Adel. (2015). Scarcity and artificial scarcity. *The Wiley Blackwell Encyclopedia of Consumption and Consumer Studies*, 1–3.

Diodato, Dario, Frank Neffke, & Neave O'Clery. (2018). Why do industries coagglomerate? how Marshallian externalities differ by industry and have evolved over time. *Journal of Urban Economics*, 106, 1–26.

Drezner, Daniel W., Henry Farrell, & Abraham L. Newman. (2021). *The Uses and Abuses of Weaponized Interdependence.* Brookings Institution Press.

Farrell, Henry, & Abraham L. Newman. (2019). Weaponized interdependence: How global economic networks shape state coercion. *International Security*, 44(1), 42–79.

Google. (2025). *PaLM2 Technical Report.* https://ai.google/static/documents/palm2techreport.pdf. [Accessed 13-05-2025].

HASH. (2025). *The Problem with Palantir.* https://hash.ai/blog/the-problem-withpalantir. [Accessed 13-05-2025].

Heim, Lennart, Tim Fist, Janet Egan, Sihao Huang, Stephen Zekany, Robert Trager et al. 2024. Governing through the cloud: The intermediary role of compute providers in AI regulation. arXiv preprint arXiv:2403.08501.

Helmrich, Alysha, Mikhail Chester, Thaddeus R. Miller, & Braden Allenby. (2023). Lock-in: Origination and significance within infrastructure systems. *Environmental Research: Infrastructure and Sustainability*, 3(3), 032001.

Isckia, Thierry, Mark De Reuver, & Denis Lescop. (2020). Orchestrating platform ecosystems: The interplay of innovation and business development subsystems. *Journal of Innovation Economics & Management*, 32(2), 197–223.

Karathanasis, Theodoros. (2025). *Challenges in AI Public Procurement – MIAI.* https://ai-regulation.com/ai-public-procurement-challenges/. [Accessed 25-042025].

Krueger, Anne O. (1974). The political economy of the rent-seeking society. *American Economic Review*, 64(3), 291–303. https://ideas.repec.org/a/aea/aecrev/ v64y1974i3p291-303.html.

Liebowitz, Stan J., & Stephen E. Margolis. (1995). Path dependence, lock-in, and history. *The Journal of Law, Economics, and Organization*, 11(1), 205–226.

Mann, Michael. (1984). The autonomous power of the state: Its origins, mechanisms and results. *European Journal of Sociology/Archives Européennes de Sociologie*, 25(2), 185–213.

Marcus, Gary, & Ernest Davis. (2019). *Rebooting AI: Building Artificial Intelligence We Can Trust.* Vintage.

Muldoon, James, & Boxi A, Wu. (2023). Artificial intelligence in the colonial matrix of power. *Philosophy & Technology*, 36(4), 80.

Narechania, Tejas N., & Ganesh Sitaraman. (2024). An antimonopoly approach to governing artificial intelligence. *Yale L. & Pol'y Rev.*, 43, 95.

OD'onnel, James. (2025). *OpenAI has Upped Its Lobbying Efforts Nearly Sevenfold.* https://www.technologyreview.com/2025/01/21/1110260/openai-ups-itslobbying-efforts-nearly-seven-fold/. [Accessed 29-04-2025].

OECD. (2023). *A Blueprint for Building National Compute Capacity for Artificial Intelligence.* Tech. rep. Organisation for Economic Co-operation & Development.

OECD. (2024). *Public Procurement for Public Sector Innovation*. https://www.oecd.org/en/publications/public-procurement-for-public-sector-innovation_9aad76b7-en.html. [Accessed 12-02-2025].

OpenAI. (2025a). *Enterprise Privacy at OpenAI*. https://openai.com/enterpriseprivacy/. [Accessed 02-05-2025].

OpenAI. (2025b). *Introducing ChatGPT Gov*. https://openai.com/global-affairs/ introducing-chatgpt-gov/. [Accessed 30-04-2025].

OpenAI. (2025c). *OpenAI Developer Platform*. https://platform.openai.com/docs/overview. [Accessed 13-05-2025].

Palantir. (2024). *Palantir and Microsoft Partner to Deliver Enhanced Analytics and AI Services to Classified Networks for Critical National Security Operations*. https://investors.palantir.com/news-details/2024/Palantir-and-Microsoft-Partnerto-Deliver-Enhanced-Analytics-and-AI-Services-to-Classified-Networksfor-Critical-National-Security-Operations/. [Accessed 13-04-2025].

Philpot, James. (2024). *Changes to the EU Cloud Services Cybersecurity Certification Scheme put EU Citizens' Data at Risk: A Call for Digital Sovereignty*. https://www. digitalsme.eu/changes-to-the-eu-cloud-services-cybersecurity-certificationscheme-put-eu-citizens-data-at-risk-a-call-for-digital-sovereignty/. [Accessed 11-03-2025].

Plantin, Jean-Christophe, Carl Lagoze, Paul N. Edwards, & Christian Sandvig. (2018). Infrastructure studies meet platform studies in the age of google and facebook. *New Media & Society*, 20(1), 293–310.

Pohle, Julia, & Thorsten Thiel. (2020). *Digital Sovereignty*. Pohle, J. & Thiel.

Posner, Richard A. (1975). The social costs of monopoly and regulation. *Journal of Political Economy*, 83(4), 807–827. http://www.jstor.org/stable/1830401 (29 April, 2025).

Rhoades, Stephen A. (1993). The herfindahl-hirschman index. *Fed. Res. Bull.*, 79, 188.

Ricardo, David. (2005). From the principles of political economy and taxation. In: *Readings in the Economics of the Division of Labor: The Classical Tradition*, 127–130. World Scientific.

Robbins, Scott, & Aimee Van Wynsberghe. (2022). Our new artificial intelligence infrastructure: Becoming locked into an unsustainable future. *Sustainability*, 14(8), 4829.

Sadowski, Jathan. (2020). The internet of landlords: Digital platforms and new mechanisms of Rentier capitalism. *Antipode*, 52(2), 562–580.

Salmon, John, Louise Crawford, Lavan Thasarathakumar, Daniel Lee, Alex Nicol, & Joyce Hoi Wun Leung. (2024). *EUCS: Controversial Sovereignty Issues Continue to Drive Debate for Cloud Services*. https://www.hoganlovells.com/en/publications/eucs-controversial-data-sovereignty-issues-continue-to-drivedebate-around-the-eu-certification-scheme-for-cloud-services. [Accessed 14-03-2025].

Sellar, Sam, & Kalervo N. Gulson. (2021). Becoming information centric: The emergence of new cognitive infrastructures in education policy. *Journal of Education Policy*, 36(3), 309–326.

Shapiro, Carl, & Hal R. Varian. (1999). *Information Rules: A Strategic Guide to the Network Economy*. Harvard Business Press.

Simeonov, Simeon. (2020). Path dependence: Determinants and impacts of technology adoption. *Economic Alternatives*, 2, 300–310.

Sparrentak, Kim Van, & Simona de Heer. (2024). *VII. Public Procurement as a Lever for Change*. https://ainowinstitute.org/publications/vii-public-procurementas-a-lever-for-change. [Accessed 29-04-2025].

Stigler, George J. (2021). The theory of economic regulation. In: *The Political Economy: Readings in the Politics and Economics of American Public Policy*, 67–81. Routledge.

Trivedi, Upmanyu. (2025). *Microsoft's $13 Billion OpenAI Investment Cleared by UK*

Watchdog. https://www.bloomberg.com/news/articles/2025-03-05/microsofts-13-billion-openai-investment-cleared-by-uk-watchdog. [Accessed 29-042025].

Tullock, Gordon. (1967). The welfare costs of tariffs, monopolies, and theft. *Economic Inquiry*, 5(3), 224–232. DOI: https://doi.org/10.1111/j.1465-7295.1967. tb01923.x.

UNCTAD. (2025). *Data Protection and Privacy Legislation Worldwide*. https:// unctad.org/page/data-protection-and-privacy-legislation-worldwide. [Accessed 15-05-2025].

Van Der Vlist, Fernando, Anne Helmond, & Fabian Ferrari. (2024). Big AI: Cloud infrastructure dependence and the industrialisation of artificial intelligence. *Big Data & Society*, 11(1), 20539517241232630.

Westgarth, Tom, Melanie Garson, Kayla Crowleycarbery, Alex Ot-Way, Joseph Bradley, & Jakob Mökander. (2024). *State of Compute Access 2024: How to Navigate the New Power Paradox*. Tech. Rep. Tony Blair Institute for Global Change.

WHO. (2021). *Ethics and Governance of Artificial Intelligence for Health*. https://www. who.int/publications/i/item/9789240029200. [Accessed 17-02-2025].

Wiggers, Kyle. (2025). *AI Companies Upped Their Federal Lobbying Spend in 2024 Amid Regulatory Uncertainty*. https://techcrunch.com/2025/01/24/ai-companiesupped-their-federal-lobbying-spend-in-2024-amid-regulatory-uncertainty/. [Accessed 19-02-2025].

CHAPTER

7

Enhancing Design Science Research Methodology with a Focus on Security (S-DSRM) and Data Sovereignty: A Proof-of-Concept

Ayan Chatterjee*(0000-0003-0407-7702)

Department of Digital Technology, NILU

7.1 Introduction

This study proposes an enhanced version of the DSRM (Peffers et al., 2007), termed as the Security-focused Design Science Research Method (S-DSRM), which integrates security (e.g., threat modeling, secure architecture design, data protection and privacy, principle of least privilege) at every stage of artifact development and validation lifecycle. The S-DSRM conceptual framework has been validated through a proof-of-concept (PoC) implementation of an automated coaching system (eCoaching) ensuring the secure transmission, storage, and processing of personal and person-generated health data. The increasing reliance on emerging healthcare technologies for personal health monitoring, presents significant challenges regarding data security, privacy, and regulatory compliance (Chatterjee et al., 2021; Chatterjee & Prinz, 2022; Chatterjee et al., 2021; Chatterjee et al., 2019; Chatterjee, 2023; Chatterjee, 2021; Chatterjee et al., 2022; Chatterjee & Prinz, 2022; Chatterjee et al., 2020). eCoaching systems typically collect sensitive personal and user-generated health data from users through wearable devices, questionnaires, and feedback to provide real-time guidance aimed at optimizing behaviors for a healthy lifestyle and/or goal management (Chatterjee et al., 2021; Chatterjee & Prinz, 2022; Chatterjee et al., 2021; Chatterjee et al., 2019; Chatterjee, 2023; Chatterjee, 2021; Chatterjee et al., 2022; Chatterjee & Prinz, 2022; Chatterjee et al., 2020). However, due to the highly sensitive nature of this data, any breach or misuse could lead to severe consequences, including identity theft and violations of patient confidentiality. In

*Email: ayan@nilu.no

DOI: 10.1201/9781003581581-7

the context of modern health technologies, this research is driven by the growing risk of cyberattacks on sensitive personal and user-generated health data (Chatterjee & Prinz, 2022; Luna et al., 2016; Argaw et al., 2019; Ahmed et al., 2021; Ibarra et al., 2019). Healthcare systems are prime targets for cyberattacks due to the high value of personal health data in illegal markets (Chatterjee & Prinz, 2022; Chatterjee et al., 2022). While traditional DSRM is effective for building functional artifacts, it often neglects security in the early-design stages, leaving systems vulnerable to compromise. Such vulnerabilities can be catastrophic in sensitive domains like healthcare. Health eCoaching systems, which continuously collect data, face growing security risks due to data flowing through multiple unsecured points (Chatterjee & Prinz, 2022; Chatterjee et al., 2022). Hence, embedding security into the system design from the beginning is essential to mitigate risks while ensuring a seamless user experience. This is especially critical to addressing privacy concerns and ensuring compliance with global privacy regulations such as the General Data Protection Regulation (GDPR) (Voigt & Bussche, 2017), NORMEN (Pedersen & Gaupseth, 2019), and the Health Insurance Portability and Accountability Act (HIPAA) (Gostin et al., 2009) This chapter aims to fill the gap in DSRM's approach to security by proposing a framework that integrates security throughout the development process, ensuring that systems remain secure and compliant without compromising availability or performance.

The novelty of this research lies in the S-DSRM conceptual framework, which marks a paradigm shift from traditional approaches to designing, developing, and validating scientific artifacts, where security is often treated as an afterthought. Instead, S-DSRM incorporates security as a primary design goal, embedding it in the problem identification, design, development, and evaluation phases, rather than applying it later. This enhanced methodology is applied to a proof of concept (PoC) for the design, development, and evaluation of a health eCoach system, focusing on securing system APIs, processed information, and both personal and user-generated health data across distributed infrastructures. The results from the PoC can be further generalized to broader research domains. In addition to addressing security and privacy, the proposed framework incorporates principles of data sovereignty (Hummel et al., 2021), ensuring compliance with jurisdictional regulations and safeguarding user trust. This study addresses the research problem that traditional software design, development, and evaluation methods, including conventional DSRM, have failed to effectively integrate security during the early stages of artifact development. In traditional DSRM, security is often addressed only after functional aspects have been prioritized, leaving significant system vulnerabilities. This reactive approach can lead to data breaches, leaks, and non-compliance with data protection regulations, particularly in healthcare, where sensitive data is continuously collected and transmitted across networks. Wearable medical devices in eCoaching systems introduce additional vulnerabilities, making secure data transmission, storage, and analysis essential. Accordingly, the research problem, centers on the need for a new approach to secure software design, development, and evaluation that integrates security throughout the lifecycle of healthcare systems to ensure both functionality and security without compromise. To address this problem, the following research questions are framed:

- How does S-DSRM address security challenges in early system design and development compared to traditional DSRM?
- How can S-DSRM balance usability, security, and regulatory compliance in systems?
- How does S-DSRM represent a paradigm shift in secure software design, development, and evaluation, and improve the creation of secure, adaptable, and compliant artifacts?

The research hypothesis tested through a proof-of-concept (PoC) study posits that integrating security considerations from the earliest design stages, through the S-DSRM frame-work, will result in a health eCoach system with enhanced security compared to systems developed using traditional DSRM, without compromising usability or regulatory compliance. This hypothesis was validated by evaluating the system's security performance, user feedback, and regulatory compliance in a PoC focused on optimizing physical activity behaviors. The main contributions are summarized as follows:

- It introduces the S-DSRM framework as an enhancement to the traditional Design Science Research Methodology.
- The conceptual framework is operationalized and validated through a proof-of-concept (PoC) implementation of a secure eCoaching system.
- By integrating security from the problem identification phase through to evaluation, the research advocates for a fundamental transformation in how secure software systems are designed and implemented.

Next section reviews key related literature to establish the foundation of this study and highlight its novelty.

7.2 Existing Literature

This section provides an overview of existing literature on DSRM, highlighting its focus, defining characteristics, role in developing innovative solutions, and the identified gaps in early-stage security integration. It also examines the need for robust security in healthcare technologies and emphasizes the importance of embedding security measures into artifact creation. Furthermore, it underscores the necessity of a more unified and secure approach within the DSRM framework, rather than treating DSRM and security modelling as separate domains. Although the acronym DSRM has yielded contradictory interpretations in the literature (e.g., Dynamic Security Risk Management, Directory Services Restore Mode), these have been filtered out for clarity.

7.2.1 Traditional Design Science Research Method (DSRM)

Design Science Research Methodology (DSRM) is widely used in disciplines such as information systems, computer science, and engineering to develop and validate innovative artifacts or solutions (Peffers et al., 2007; Geerts, 2011; Peffers et al., 2012; Offermann et al., 2009). It is a problem-solving approach that integrates the creation of new knowledge with practical solution development. The DSR process typically follows a series of iterative steps (Peffers et al., 2007; Offermann et al., 2009). It begins with problem identification, where the issue or opportunity requiring a solution is clearly defined and understood. Specific objectives and requirements are then established to guide the design process. During the design and development phase, novel artifacts, systems, or solutions are conceptualized and created to address the problem. This is followed by the demonstration phase, which showcases the functionality of the artifact and illustrates how it meets the defined requirements. The evaluation phase assesses the effectiveness and efficiency of the solution through data collection and analysis to determine its problem-solving capability. Finally the research findings are communicated to the academic and practitioner communities through publications, presentations or reports. DSR emphasizes the development and validation of innovative solutions that advance both academic knowledge and practical applications. Its iterative nature enables continuous refinement and improvement, making it especially valuable in domains that demand real-world problem solving and the creation of novel artifacts.

7.2.2 Identified Gaps in Traditional DSRM

While DSRM is highly effective for creating functional and innovative artifacts, it exhibits significant gaps in addressing security during the early stages of artifact development (Eteläaho et al., 2015; Gledson et al., 2024; Conboy et al., 2015; Hulshof, 2021; Maček et al., 2020) as outlined below:

- **Lack of Emphasis on Security in Initial Phases:** In traditional DSRM, the problem identification and goal definition phases focus primarily on the functional and performance aspects of the artifact being developed. While this ensures that the artifact meets the immediate needs of the stakeholders, security is not typically considered a critical element during this phase.
- **Security as a Reactive Measure:** In the DSRM process, security is often viewed as a reactive measure that is addressed only after the functional aspects of an artifact have been developed. Security mechanisms are often added late in the development process or even after deployment, which can expose vulnerabilities early in use.
- **Limited Security-specific Evaluation Criteria:** The evaluation phase of DSRM focuses on functional validation and user-centric testing. While performance and usability are thoroughly evaluated, security-specific evaluation criteria such as encryption strength, data protection, and attack resilience are often missed or underestimated.
- **Minimal Consideration of Regulatory Compliance:** DSRM does not prioritize compliance with privacy and security regulations (e.g., GDPR, HIPAA) during the early design phases. Although artifacts developed using DSRM may eventually comply with these regulations, such compliance is often not addressed until after key design decisions have been made, which can complicate or restrict system design.
- **Stakeholder Involvement Primarily Focused on Functionality:** DSRM emphasizes the importance of stakeholder involvement in the design and assessment phases. However, in traditional DSRM practices, stakeholders

typically focus on the functionality, performance, and usability aspects of the system. Although security aspects can be considered, they are usually secondary compared to the primary functional requirements.

- **No Iterative Security Testing:** In DSRM, the design and development of artifacts are usually done iteratively. However, security tests are not always integrated into each iteration; they are usually performed at the end of the process, after primary development is completed.
- **Lack of a Formalized Security Methodology:** DSRM lacks a formal framework to incorporate security-specific design practices, such as secure coding guidelines, data encryption policies, or secure communication protocols. This makes it difficult for developers using DSRM to systematically integrate security into their artifacts, especially in highly sensitive domains such as healthcare or finance.

7.2.3 Emerging Need for Security in Health Tech. and eCoaching

With the growing use of wearable devices and IoT-based health monitoring systems, the threat landscape for personal health data has expanded significantly (MacIntyre, 2018; Kerr et al., 2019; Takyi, 2019; Chaudhary et al., 2022). Devices such as fitness trackers and smartwatches continuously collect sensitive information, including heart rate, sleep patterns, physical activity, and geolocation (MacIntyre, 2018, Kerr et al., 2019; Takyi, 2019; Chaudhary et al., 2022; Terry, 2012). These devices often transmit data to remote platforms for analysis over unsecured or poorly secured networks. Research indicates that patients are especially concerned about data breaches, which could lead to identity theft or the misuse of sensitive health information. Such breaches may result in serious personal and financial consequences and erode trust between patients and healthcare providers (Terry, 2012, Price & Cohen, 2019). As health data becomes increasingly central to personalized medicine, behavioral interventions, and insurance decisions, safeguarding it from external threats is more critical than ever (Terry, 2012, Price & Cohen, 2019). Health eCoach systems, a growing area in digital health, continuously track users' behaviors to optimize lifestyles and reduce health risks (Terry, 2012, Price & Cohen, 2019). However, these systems raise heightened security and privacy concerns.

Health eCoach systems rely on real-time data to provide feedback and recommendations to users, which heightens their vulnerability to man-in-the-middle attacks, data interception, and unauthorized access during transmission (Chaudhary et al., 2022; Adams & Niezen, 2018; Toch et al., 2018; Ajayi et al., 2023; Bu et al., 2020). Since these systems handle data that reflects individuals' daily life patterns, breaches pose significant risks by exposing not only health conditions but also behavioural habits, routines, and personal information. To address these concerns, Privacy by Design (PbD) (Semantha et al., 2020; Garbagnati & Wu, 2022) has emerged as a foundational concept in healthcare technology security. PbD ensures that privacy and security are embedded into the design and development of healthcare systems from the outset, rather than retrofitted later. It emphasizes principles such as data minimization, strong encryption, user consent management, and transparent data processing. These principles are especially critical for health eCoach systems, where data protection must be upheld throughout the entire lifecycle, from collection to analysis. Beyond regulatory compliance, consumer expectations around security have evolved. Patients and users now demand robust safeguards and expect the technologies they use to manage their health to incorporate strong encryption, multi-factor authentication, and end-to-end privacy controls (Khatiwada et al., 2024; Nowrozy, 2024; Khatiwada et al., 2020; Toch et al., 2018). Failure to secure these systems can result in legal liabilities for healthcare providers, loss of patient trust, and reputational damage for technology vendors.

7.2.4 Novelty in Security-Focused Development Methodology

The transition from traditional artifact development to secure artifact development marks a significant paradigm shift in software engineering and information science research. Historically, artifact development has prioritized functionality, performance, and usability, often relegating security to an afterthought or a separate phase in the development cycle. However, as cyber threats become more sophisticated and privacy regulations become increasingly stringent, security can no longer be treated as an optional add-on (Andrade et al., 2022); it must be a foundational component integrated into every phase of the artifact development process. S-DSRM embodies this shift by embedding security at the core of artifact development. It not only enhances the traditional development life-cycle but also reshapes the way developers, researchers, and organizations approach software development. When compared to modern Information System frameworks such as Agile (Simos & Kumar, 2023), PbD (Semantha et al., 2020), and Zero Trust Architecture (Øvrelid et al., 2021), S-DSRM offers a comprehensive and forward-thinking methodology for developing secure systems, especially in sensitive sectors like healthcare. Table 7.1 highlights key differences between S-DSRM and traditional security frameworks in terms of research methods and artefact development, while Table 7.2 provides a broader comparative summary. Traditional security frameworks typically address known threats post-development. In contrasr S-DSRM represents a paradigm shift by incorporating security as a fundamental design element from the outset. Through continuous risk assessment and adaptation to emerging threats, S-DSRM ensures that security remains proactive rather than reactive.

The paradigm shift introduced by S-DSRM is critical for healthcare technology, as any delay in considering security can have serious consequences. By embedding security and privacy into the core of system design, S-DSRM not only protects users' health data, but also ensures regulatory compliance, enhances user trust, and improves the overall resilience of the system against future threats. Existing artifact development frameworks often over-look data sovereignty, despite its critical importance in ensuring that data remains under the jurisdiction of the country where it was collected, particularly in healthcare systems.

7.3 Proposed Work

This section defines the objectives, constraints, and structure of a problem, guiding systematic, efficient, and optimal solutions for the verification of study case using S-DSRM. Let:

Table 7.1. Comparison of S-DSRM vs. traditional security frameworks

Aspect	Traditional security frameworks	S-DSRM
Security Focus	Security is applied as an external layer after the artifact is developed.	Security is integrated throughout the entire development process as a core element.
Research Approach	Security considerations are often reactive, based on existing threats or incidents.	Proactive research, with security risks identified during the initial design phase via threat modeling and risk assessment.
Artifact Development	Artifacts are typically developed without considering security from the start.	Artifacts are developed with security embedded, addressing both functional and security goals simultaneously.
Evaluation Phase	Security evaluations are often limited to post-development (e.g., vulnerability scans, testing).	Continuous security evaluation and iteration at every stage of development, with multiple feedback loops.
Stakeholder Involvement	Stakeholder involvement is minimal or occurs only during testing or post-deployment phases.	Stakeholders, including developers, users, and security experts, are involved continuously throughout the process.
Adaptability	Frameworks are less adaptive to emerging security threats, resulting in reactive updates or patches.	Highly adaptive to new threats through continuous security assessments, proactive updates, and iterations.
Compliance Integration	Compliance with regulations is typically addressed after the artifact is built.	Compliance and privacy regulations are integral to the design phase, ensuring artifacts meet these requirements from inception.
Artifact Outcome	Focused on functionality and usability, with security features added afterward.	Balances security, functionality, usability, and compliance from the start, ensuring a more holistic artifact.
Iterative Process	Security adjustments are made after deployment, requiring retroactivities.	Iterative process with security built into each cycle, enabling preventive adjustments before deployment.
Innovation and Research	Incremental research focused on known vulnerabilities and solutions.	Innovation driven by continuous feedback, threat modeling, and proactive research, enabling novel solutions to emerging threats.

Table 7.2. Broader comparative summary of S-DSRM vs. related Methodologies

Aspect	S-DSRM	Traditional DSRM	PbD (Privacy by Design)	Zero Trust Architecture (ZTA)
Core Focus	Secure, sovereign, and usable artifact development	Functional artifact creation & Privacy-centric system design	Privacy-centric system design	Access control and trust elimination
Security Integration	Integrated across all lifecycle stages	Often post-development	Early-stage privacy; security implied	Security enforced at each access point
Data Sovereignty	Explicitly modelled (e.g., storage jurisdiction, access boundaries)	Not addressed	Implicit through consent	Not a core focus
Regulatory Compliance	Integrated in objectives and evaluation (e.g., GDPR, NORMEN)	Often post hoc	Compliance-driven	Aligned with security policies
Evaluation Approach	Mixed-methods: quantitative, qualitative, risk-based	Functional or usability-focused	Policy and risk impact driven	Threat-centric, technical audits
Methodological Rigor	Formalized through research design	Research-driven but security-agnostic	Design principles, less structured	Policy and security architecture centric
Adaptability to AI Systems	Yes (supports trust, explainability, personalization)	Limited	Emerging area	Limited applicability to AI logic
User Involvement	UCD-driven iterative co-design	Stakeholder-focused, less user depth	Focuses on user consent	System admin-centric, minimal end-user role
Proactive vs. Reactive	Proactive (threat modeling, iteration, compliance)	Reactive (security added late)	Proactive for privacy	Reactive to breaches, proactive in enforcement

- S represent the set of all **security requirements** to be integrated.
- F represent the set of all **functional requirements** for the system.
- U represent the **usability requirements** that define ease of use and user experience.
- C represent the set of **compliance requirements** for regulatory standards (e.g., GDPR).

Define

- **System artifact** A, which consists of a series of development phases (design, development, demonstration, and evaluation).
- Each phase P_i has outputs that include **security level** SL_i, **functionality level** FL_i, and **usability level** UL_i, all of which must satisfy the requirements for an optimal outcome.

Objective: The primary objective of S-DSRM is to maximize security, functionality, and usability while maintaining compliance within each phase P_i of artifact A. This objective can be expressed as a multi-objective optimization problem:

$$\text{Maximize} \sum_{i=1}^{n} (w_s SL_i + w_f FL_i + w_u\ UL_i), \text{ for all phases } P_i \text{ in } A,$$

Here, w_s, w_f and w_u are weights for security, functionality, and usability, respectively, that can be adjusted according to the importance of each factor in a specific application domain. SL_i, FL_i, UL_i are security, functionality, and usability levels at phase P_i.

Constraints

- **Security constraint:** Each phase must meet a minimum-security requirement $SL_i \geq SL_{\min}$, where $SL_{\min}$ is a threshold based on baseline security standards for the system. $SL_i \geq SL_{\min}\ \forall i$
- **Functionality constraint:** Each phase must meet or exceed a baseline functionality level $FL_{\min}$. $FL_i \geq FL_{\min}\ \forall i$
- **Usability constraint:** Each phase must satisfy usability requirements such that $UL_i \geq UL_{\min}$, ensuring the system remains accessible to users. $UL_i \geq UL_{\min}\ \forall i$
- **Compliance constraint:** Compliance requirements are binary constraints, where each requirement $C_j \in C$ must be fulfilled in the system artifact A: $C_j = 1$ $\forall_j \in \{1,..., |C|\}$
- **Iterative security and compliance update constraint:** To address new security threats and evolving regulations, the system must be periodically updated. Let T be the time period after which a new iteration of security compliance updates is applied: $SL(t) \rightarrow SL(t + T)$

7.3.1 Threat Minimization and Risk Assessment

In each phase P_i, the total risk R_i should be minimized by applying security protocols that reduce threat exposure. If T_i is the identified threat level in phase P_i, and M_i is the applied security measure, then to minimize the difference between threat level and security measure effectiveness has been focused on:

$$\min\,(T_i - M_i)\ \forall i$$

Subject to:

- $T_i \geq 0$ (non-negative threat levels),
- $M_i \geq 0$ (non-negative security measures).

Optimization Problem Summary
In summary, the S-DSRM problem can be formulated as follows:

$$\text{Maximize} \sum_{i=1}^{n} (w_s SL_i + w_f FL_i + w_u UL_i)$$

Subject to:

- $SL_i \geq SL_{\min}$ for all i,
- $FL_i \geq FL_{\min}$ for all i,
- $UL_i \geq UL_{\min}$ for all i,
- $C_j = 1$ for all j,
- $R_i = T_i - M_i \rightarrow$ minimized for all i,
- $SL(t) \rightarrow SL(t + T)$.

This empirical formulation ensures that security, functionality and usability of the eCoach prototype system are optimized at every stage of S-DSRM framework development under the laboratory settings, while maintaining compliance and adaptability to changing threats and user needs.

7.4 Methodology

This section details specific methods, study design, and approaches to prove the concept of enhancing security in the context of design science research.

7.4.1 S-DSRM Framework Overview

S-DSRM extends traditional DSRM by embedding security into every stage of the artifact development process. The goal is to ensure that security and privacy are priorities from the beginning, in line with PbD principles and legal requirements (e.g. GDPR, HIPAA):

- **Problem Identification:** Identify security risks unique to the health eCoach system, such as secure data transfer and privacy compliance for wearable devices.
- **Objectives Definition:** Define security goals as well as system availability and performance goals, ensuring all data transfers are encrypted and user authentication is robust.
- **Design & Development:** Develop artifacts (Secure DSR Framework) following the iterative user-centric design approach (with dialogue-lab method) with security as a core design element, focusing on secure communication protocols, encryption, authentication and authorization mechanisms.
- **Demonstration:** Implement the Health eCoach system in a controlled environment to demonstrate secure data collection and transfer while optimizing user behaviors such as physical activity.
- **Evaluation:** Evaluate system performance and security using quantitative and qualitative measures.

- **Communication:** Share findings with stakeholders, including healthcare providers, users, and regulatory bodies, to facilitate feedback and future enhancements.

7.4.2 Selection of Study Case

For the proof of concept, we implemented the S-DSRM framework to design, develop, and validate a secure health eCoach system aimed at improving physical activity behaviors in the adult population. The system collects real-time personal and self-generated health data from questionnaires and wearable devices (in JavaScript Object Notation (JSON) format), securely transmitting it to a remote Services for Sensitive Data (TSD) data storage platform (Toch et al., 2018; Robertson & Robertson, 2000) using a secure protocol. In TSD, data are stored in PostgreSQL relational database system for persistence (Robertson & Robertson, 2000). Users receive personalized feedback to help optimize their lifestyle goals. Key security features include data encryption, ensuring secure transmission of health data from wearable devices to remote storage, as well as authentication measures to restrict data access to authorized users only, and compliance with strict data protection regulations.

7.4.3 Study Scoping

This study focuses on enhancing DSRM by integrating a security-centric approach, referred to as S-DSRM. The framework is applied in developing a secure activity eCoach prototype system, ensuring that security, privacy, and regulatory compliance (e.g., GDPR, NORMEN) are incorporated throughout the design and development phases. As a result, system evaluations related to machine learning, semantic structuring, infrastructure, usability, and smartphone app prototyping are excluded from this scope.

7.4.4 Mapping S-DSRM Phases for Proof-of-Concept

To implement S-DSRM in the identified PoC study (i.e., the activity eCoach prototype system), each phase of the methodology has been divided. For each phase, specific research measures have been developed, along with corresponding methods and expected outcomes. The structured Table 7.3 illustrates how each phase of S-DSRM contributed to the PoC and the overall research objective.

7.4.5 Documenting Software Requirements

The Volere template (Gross & Doerr, 2012), a widely used requirements specification framework, has been chosen for its focus on capturing stakeholder needs and expectations. It organizes project drivers, functional and non-functional requirements, and project issues. This template aids in structuring requirements and aligning design with user-centric goals. User requirements have been gathered through UCD workshops, targeting specific user needs. ReqView software (Chatterjee et al., 2022) has been used to categorize and trace these requirements, ensuring alignment with project objectives. By emphasizing security, usability, and adaptability, the Volere template ensures that the activity eCoach system meets functional and security standards while incorporating user feedback.

Table 7.3. Mapping research actions, approaches, and expected outcomes in S-DSRM for activity eCoaching prototype system

Phase of S-DSRM	Research actions	Approaches	Expected outcomes
Problem Identification	Identify security challenges in real-time health data transmission and privacy requirements	Literature review, Interviews with health-care providers, Analysis of regulatory requirements	Clear definition of security vulnerabilities, Requirements for secure data transmission and privacy
Objectives Definition	Define security objectives such as encryption, authentication, and regulatory compliance	Stakeholder meetings, Threat modeling, Data Security, Security goal setting based on healthcare standards	List of security objectives (e.g., encryption strength, low latency, authorization, GDPR and NORMEN compliance)
Design & Development	Develop the secure DSR framework with security measures embedded (e.g., encryption, authentication)	Iterative UCD workshop, Secure software development lifecycle (DevSeqOps), Coding and prototyping	Prototype of health eCoach system with embedded encryption, authentication, and authorization mechanisms
Demonstration	Deploy the system in a controlled healthcare environment to test functionality and security	Simulated real-time health data transmission, Deployment in a PoC environment, Test scenarios, Proof of secure data transmission	Demonstration of system scalability and integration with healthcare devices
Evaluation	Assess security performance, usability, and compliance with privacy regulations	Penetration testing, User feedback surveys, Quantitative evaluation (e.g., latency, packet delivery ratio)	Detailed security performance metrics (e.g., encryption effectiveness, latency), Usability feedback
Communication	Present findings to stakeholders, regulators, and academic communities	Publication in journals, Presentations at conferences, Reports to healthcare providers/regulators	Knowledge dissemination, Feedback from the healthcare and security community

7.4.6 Iterative User-Centric Design Approach

The activity eCoach prototype is developed through an iterative UCD approach (Ajayi et al., 2023), utilizing the dialogue-lab method to engage users at every stage. This method facilitates user participation in shaping the prototype by encouraging creative input through structured design activities. The focus remains on meeting end-users' needs, security, privacy, and ethical criteria with continuous feedback loops ensuring the design aligns with their expectations. Wearable technology, a mobile app, and web content are integrated early on for self-monitoring and lifestyle recommendations. This iterative process refines the prototype, improving the fit between technology, users, and researchers, while considering cultural diversity and individual values, and the detailed elaborations can be found in (Ajayi et al., 2023).

7.4.7 Planning Phase

In the planning phase, the recruitment of participants for the UCD workshops is conducted with a focus on voluntary participation. Recruitment notices are disseminated via various channels, including the University of Agder (UiA) notice board, web portals, internal emails, and in-house health providers in Grimstad Kommune (Ajayi et al., 2023). The advertisements are kept concise, clearly stating the inclusion criteria to avoid confusion. Participants who meet the specified criteria are invited to provide signed consent. Basic training is provided to ensure they understand the guidelines for participation, including the use of the eCoach prototype, activity devices, and the process for submitting self-report questionnaires online. Criteria for recruitment include adults registered with a general practitioner, aged 18-64, and within a targeted body mass index (BMI) range, including normal weight (18.5–25 kg/m^2) and overweight/obese (25–35 kg/m^2) individuals. Participants are required to have Wi-Fi access at home and motivation for self-monitoring and data collection. Individuals with major chronic conditions or disease episodes are excluded. Workshops are conducted with selected participants to avoid gender bias, ensuring a diverse representation of end-users from different professional backgrounds. Two virtual workshops with four groups headed by individual experts are held, each lasting two hours, to gather feedback and refine the design through an iterative process as elaborated in (Ajayi et al., 2023).

- **Workshop 1:** The first UCD workshop focuses on gathering user needs and preferences, laying the foundation for the initial development of the eCoach prototype (Ajayi et al., 2023). Participants engage in discussions about their expectations and preferences regarding health coaching systems with the aim of understanding the cultural, personal, and contextual factors that influence their health goals. These insights are translated into design requirements by the research and engineering teams, who collaborate to develop the first version of the eCoach prototype. This prototype integrates threat models, wearable technology, mobile apps, and web content to support self-monitoring, goal setting, and the delivery of lifestyle recommendations in an engaging manner. The iterative nature of this process allows continuous interaction between participants and the development team, ensuring that the evolving prototype reflects the user's needs at each stage.

Following feedback collection, the prototype undergoes further refinement, focusing on features like system security, data privacy, data encryption, recommendation visualization, usability, and interaction between users and the system. The primary outcome of Workshop 1 is the creation of a functional eCoach prototype that addresses the core needs of the end users while meeting the requirements for personalized health data collection and recommendation generation. This prototype serves as a preliminary solution further refined in subsequent workshops based on ongoing user input and feedback.

- **Workshop 2:** The second workshop builds on insights from Workshop 1, focusing on refining the initial eCoach prototype and addressing any gaps between user expectations and the technical solution (Ajayi et al., 2023). Participants provide targeted feedback on aspects such as goal setting, motivational feedback, and recommendation visualization. In response the engineering and research teams collaborate closely to enhance system functionality. Special attention is given to strengthening data security and improving the contextual and cultural relevance of recommendation visualizations. This iteration also emphasizes the integration of artificial intelligence (AI) to personalize feedback and recommendations (Kamphorst, 2021; Chatterjee et al., 2022; Chatterjee et al., 2022; Greenhalgh et al., 2018). Feedback from participants helps refine the AI-based recommendation system, making it more intuitive and responsive to individual user needs. The workshop fosters a creative dialogue between participants and developers, facilitating a deeper understanding of the user's motivational triggers and preferences, which are crucial for the success of the eCoach system. Participant input helps refine the AI-based recommendation system, making it more intuitive and responsive to individual needs.

7.4.8 Study Evaluation

This study uses both performance metrics and user-centered feedback to assess the effectiveness of security integration.

Qualitative: The qualitative evaluation follows these methods to assess the health eCoach system designed and developed using S-DSRM:

- NASSS (Non Adoption, Abandonment, Scale-Up, Diffusion, and Sustainability) framework: This framework evaluates complex healthcare technologies by focusing on socio-technical aspects such as complexity, scalability, and sustainability (Williams et al., 2015). This study examines how S-DSRM aligns with the NASSS framework in a health eCoaching case.
- Information system theories, such as Unified Theory of Acceptance and Use of Technology (UTAUT) (Almaiah et al., 2022) and the Information Systems Success Model (ISSM) (Bergen et al., 2023) provide foundational insights. UTAUT explains user acceptance based on factors like performance expectations and social influence, while ISSM evaluates system success, user satisfaction, and overall impact.
- Usability, adaptability and flexibility, assessing the system's ability to meet the needs of the health eCoach plarform, interoperate with other technologies (e.g., IoT devices), and scale to accommodate increasing data volumes and user demands.

Quantitative: The quantitative evaluation employs the following metrics to assess the performance of the health eCoach system designed and developed using the S-DSRM framework:

- **Performance metrics:** Measure latency, throughput, and resource utilization (CPU, memory, bandwidth) to evaluate the system's efficiency in data handling.
- **Security metrics:** Assess encryption strength, potential attack vectors through penetration testing, and response time to security incidents.
- **Scalability testing:** Test system performance under increasing user load and large data volumes from multiple devices.
- **Reliability metrics:** Evaluate Mean Time Between Failures (MTBF), system availability, and Packet Delivery Ratio (PDR).
- **User satisfaction and system health outcomes:** Measure user adoption rates and system response time to health alerts (e.g., abnormal walking cycle detection).

7.4.9 Ethical Approval

The eCoach solution's design ensures secure, ethical, and authorized data handling. Ethical approval has been granted by the Norwegian Agency for Shared Services in Education (SIKT) (Froud et al., 2019) (approval number: 797208) and the Regional Committees for Medical and Health Research Ethics (REK) (Deacon, 2009) (approval number: 53224). Written informed consent has been obtained, and all data is stored securely as per privacy guidelines.

7.5 System Design and Development as a Study Case

This section describes the mapping between project objectives and requirements to design and develop an activity eCoach system focusing on ethical and security guidelines.

7.5.1 Objectives and Requirements

The aim of this case study is to design, develop, and technically evaluate an intelligent eCoach system based on the S-DSRM framework, focused on monitoring, assessing, and managing health and well-being. The system collects personal and contextual data and delivers automated, personalized recommendations to encourage positive lifestyle changes. While it serves as a technical proof-of-concept (PoC,) to evaluate its effectiveness in promoting behaviour change, it is not intended for clinical treatment or medical interventions. A key aspect of the system is data collection, which involves gathering personal, behavioral, and contextual information, such as physical activity levels and weather conditions. Ensuring data privacy and ethical handling, the system complies with GDPR guidelines, implementing secure data-sharing protocols with authorized access. Personalized recommendations are automatically generated based on this data and are presented intuitively through a mobile app. The system's core features include data visualization, continuous monitoring, and real-time feedback, which help users track progress and receive meaningful recommendations.

The system's requirements are divided into functional and non-functional categories. Functional requirements involve data collection, user interactions, and activity goal management. Non-functional requirements address usability, security, scalability, and interoperability, ensuring a user-friendly, adaptable, and secure system. These requirements have been collected through UCD workshops and refined using the SMART (Specific, Measurable, Achievable, Relevant, and Time-bound) framework to align with the project's goals. Excluded elements include voice recognition and medical parameters, focusing on the scope of lifestyle management and self-motivation. Personal data and user preferences are collected using wearable sensors and questionnaires. The collected data is processed to generate personalized recommendations based on physical activity levels and contextual data such as weather. Privacy is maintained through anonymization techniques, secure data transmission, and strict access control. Data storage complies with Norwegian privacy regulations, allowing only authorized users access to the information. Recommendations are generated using a hybrid approach that combines data-driven and rule-based algorithms. The system also employs deep learning and ontologies to create context-specific recommendations and addresses the cold-start problem for new users. Recommendations are delivered in various formats, such as text, audio, or graphs, depending on user references, ensuring timely and motivational content delivery. The mapping between objectives and requirements is presented in Table 7.4.

Table 7.4. Mapping between objectives and requirements

Objective(s)	**Requirement(s) following GDPR guidelines**
What data to collect?	How to collect and manage required data?
What data to share?	How to share data and processed information?
What feedback to generate?	How to generate tailored recommendations?
What information to present?	How to present tailored recommendations?

7.5.2 Activity eCoach Prototype System Design

The design phase has been pivotal in establishing the foundation of the eCoach system, which is developed to support users with personalized physical activity coaching. User requirements, gathered through UCD workshops, have been carefully analyzed and translated into detailed system specifications to ensure that it aligns with end-user expectations. The eCoach solution focuses on a modular approach, leveraging modern tools such as Figma and Google Material Design to ensure user-friendly interfaces and consistency across the platform (Ajayi et al., 2023). Figma has been selected for its real-time collaboration capabilities, allowing the design team to efficiently work together and prototype solutions (Ajayi et al., 2023). It also provides offline functionality, making it versatile for cross-platform design (Ajayi et al., 2023). Google Material Design brings further structure with its consistent themes, system icons, and color palettes that improve accessibility and usability (Ajayi et al., 2023).

In terms of architecture, the eCoach system has been divided into two primary components (Ajayi et al.,2023)]: the eCoach mobile app and the back-end server. The mobile app handles user interactions and data collection, while the back end processes the data and generates personalized recommendations. The Model-View-Controller (MVC) architectural pattern has been adopted to separate data logic, business processes, and user interface functionalities (Singi et al., 2020). This pattern has been chosen to promote modularity and maintainability, allowing each component of the system to be developed and updated independently. A significant aspect of the design is the focus on semantic data integration. To ensure consistency in data interpretation, the team incorporated HL7 FHIR standards and SNOMED-CT ontologies (Adams & Niezen, 2018), which facilitate semantic annotation of health and wellness data. By utilizing these well-established standards, the system ensures interoperability across various platforms, enhancing the system's scalability and flexibility for future expansions.

The design also emphasizes security (e.g., threat modeling, secure architecture, data protection and privacy, access control), with the implementation of OAuth 2.0 for user authentication and a secure VPN channel for communication between the mobile app and the back-end (Toch et al., 2018). The decision to use a Restful Microservice Architecture enables flexible communication, allowing the mobile app to request resources securely via HTTP methods (Toch et al., 2018). Regarding personalized recommendations, the eCoach system integrates external data such as weather conditions and contextual information to generate tailored suggestions. By adopting a hybrid approach, leveraging both system-defined goals (based on WHO guidelines) and user-defined goals; the system provides highly individualized coaching experiences (Kamphorst, 2017; Chatterjee et al., 2022; Greenhalgh et al., 2018). Semantic ontologies further enrich the system by organizing data on personal preferences, ensuring that recommendations are not only goal-oriented but also contextually relevant to each user (Kamphorst, 2017; Chatterjee et al., 2022; Greenhalgh et al., 2018).

7.5.3 Activity eCoach Prototype System Development

The development phase translates the detailed design into a fully functional system, implementing the key features outlined during the design phase. The primary goal has been to ensure that the system supports data collection, personalized recommendation generation, and user interaction in a secure and scalable manner. The eCoach mobile app has been developed to facilitate several essential functions: managing user preferences, submitting daily questionnaires, uploading activity data from sensors, and displaying notifications and rewards. The app has been built on the Android platform and designed to ensure smooth user interaction, allowing users to monitor their activity, receive personalized recommendations, and adjust their preferences based on real-time feedback. Data collected from the app, including both quantitative sensor data and qualitative self-reported data has been transferred to the back-end system, where it has been semantically annotated and stored for further analysis. The back-end infrastructure has been deployed using Docker on an Infrastructure-as-a-Service (IaaS) platform, ensuring scalability and ease deployment. The modular back-end architecture includes components for data sharing, preference management, recommendation generation, and secure data handling. This approach allows for real-time processing of large volumes of data from multiple users, ensuring that personalized recommendations are generated efficiently and delivered.

Security has been a critical consideration throughout the development (e.g., secure coding practice, code review and static analysis, authentication and authorization, use of secure libraries and dependencies), underpinned by a hybrid framework that combines the Spring Framework (SF), TSD, and HTTP security protocols (Toch et al., 2018). Key security features include identity brokering, OAuth 2.0, multifactor authentication, and stringent access controls to secure the Microservices APIs. The system also ensures compliance with GDPR regulations to protect sensitive personal data. AES-256 and Bcrypt encryptions have been used for securing data in transit and password management, while SSL/TLS protocols protect HTTP communications. The TSD platform ensures that data at rest has been encrypted and accessed only by authorized personnel, with comprehensive logging for auditing purposes.

One of the key features of the development phase has been the implementation of a recommendation engine. The engine utilizes both rule-based and machine learning-based approaches to generate personalized recommendations. Time-series analysis and forecasting models have been developed to analyze user activity data, predict future activity levels, and provide real-time feedback. To ensure that the recommendation engine remain effective over time, an incremental learning approach has been adopted, allowing the system to continuously update its models as more user data has been collected. During development, significant effort has been made on data integration. The team used the SSN (Semantic Sensor Network Ontology) and SNOMED-CT to annotate data from activity sensors, questionnaires, and external data sources (e.g., open weather APIs). This semantic annotation allowed the system to process and reason about data in a meaningful way, ensuring that recommendations have been both personalized and contextually appropriate. The software architecture of the activity eCoaching solution with potential functional components is depicted in (Kamphorst, 2017).

7.5.4 Incorporating Data Sovereignty in S-DSRM Framework

Data sovereignty(Aydın & Bensghir, 2019; Halili, 2008), which refers to the concept that data is subject to the laws and governance of the country where it is collected and stored, was central to the development of the Activity eCoach system. Given the sensitivity of health data, ensuring compliance with data sovereignty principles aligns with the ethical, legal, and social expectations of the stakeholders involved. The following measures were implemented to address data sovereignty concerns within the S-DSRM framework:

- **Localized Data Storage:** The system leverages geographically bounded data storage solutions compliant with Norwegian and EU regulations, such as TSD (Services for Sensitive Data).
- **Regulatory Compliance:** Full compliance with GDPR and NORMEN guidelines ensures the lawful processing and storage of personal health data.
- **Access Control Policies:** Strict access policies limit data handling to authorized users within the jurisdiction of collection.
- **Data Minimization and Anonymization:** Ensuring only necessary data is collected and that personal identifiers are removed wherever possible.
- **Transparent Data Governance**: Users are informed about where their data is stored, how it is processed, and who has access, fostering trust and transparency.

7.6 Results

The activity eCoach system demonstrated compliance with security, usability, and data sovereignty requirements by ensuring localized data storage, jurisdictional governance, and transparency in data handling. The overall activity eCoach prototype system evaluation consists of the following approaches.

7.6.1 Qualitative Evaluation

The final eCoach prototype system designed and developed using S-DSRM paradigm complies with the NASSS framework. This evaluation ensures that the system addresses the complexity of secure health monitoring technologies in healthcare settings. It ensures the security of data transmission through encryption and threat modeling and meets the scope of conditions by securely monitoring the user's physical activities. The technology space covers secure routing and iterative improvements to maintain usability without compromising security. The value proposition is enhanced by emphasizing security as a differentiator, ensuring trust and acceptance from patients and healthcare providers. By emphasizing security as a core feature, the system improves its value proposition and builds trust between users and healthcare providers. Involving stakeholders throughout the process ensures that Adopter's needs for security and usability are met. GDPR compliance ensures that the system meets the needs of the organization and the overall system. Regular updates and security assessments ensure sustainability so that the system can adapt to evolving threats and maintain long-term functionality. By aligning with the NASSS framework, the eCoach prototype integrates security, scalability, and usability, making it adaptable, safe, and effective for widespread adoption in healthcare settings. Through this evaluation, S-DSRM proves effective in creating a robust, adaptable, and secure eCoach system.

The technical evaluation of the activity eCoach system designed and developed using S-DSRM, has been evaluated from the perspectives of UTAUT and ISSM theories. These theories helped measure user adoption and system effectiveness while ensuring security, usability, and scalability (see Table 7.5). UTAUT analyzed performance expectations by examining how users expect the system to improve their health and fitness. UCD workshops found that users believe that personalized recommendations will have a positive impact on their health. In addition, social influence has been shown to be an important factor in adoption, as recommendations from peers and professionals encouraged users to participate in the eCoach system. Social support from colleagues and professionals promoted greater acceptance and continued use. Through ISSM, the evaluation focused on information quality and system quality. The system delivered highly relevant and accurate health recommendations based on real-time data, with users expressing strong trust in the quality of the information provided. Personalized coaching and health tips have been perceived as both reliable and actionable. System Quality has been also positively evaluated, with users highlighting satisfaction with the system's performance, reliability, and seamless integration with wearable devices. The eCoach system efficiently handled data processing, even with varying loads, and provided a smooth user experience.

Table 7.5. Evaluation of activity eCoach system using UTAUT and ISSM frameworks of information systems

Phase of S-DSRM	Evaluation focus	Outcome	Evaluation process
Performance Expectancy (UTAUT)	Users' expectation of system impact	Positive expectations regarding improvement in fitness and health	User surveys and feedback from UCD workshops
Social Influence (UTAUT)	Impact of goal based, automatic, and tailored recommendations	Increased adoption due to social support and professional influence	Qualitative assessments through focus groups and interviews in UCD workshops
Information Quality (ISSM)	Accuracy and relevance of recommendations	Users reported high trust in personalized health advice	Surveys measuring user trust and perceived relevance of recommendations
System Quality (ISSM)	Reliability and performance	High user satisfaction with system reliability and smooth data handling	System testing for performance metrics and user feedback on prototype functional testing

The activity eCoach prototype emphasizes usability by integrating Google Material Design for an intuitive UI to enhance user experience in android smartphone mobile app navigation. Despite incorporating advanced security features, the system remains easy to navigate, as highlighted in user feedback. Adaptability and flexibility have been evaluated through its seamless integration with IoT devices and scalability to accommodate growing data volumes and users. The system also employs HL7 FHIR standards to ensure interoperability and uses semantic knowledge engineering with ontology to address data heterogeneity. The results of the UCD workshops provided valuable insights into the design and development of the activity eCoach prototype. The low-fidelity prototype presented in Workshop 1 has been improved based on user feedback from Workshop 2, addressing areas such as data security, login methods, data uploading, secure data exchange, data governance, processed data and feedback presentation. The functional design has been evaluated through hands-on testing, receiving an average rating of 4.1 out of 5 for its layout and functionality (Ajayi et al., 2023).

7.6.2 Quantitative Evaluation

The performance of the activity eCoach system has been tested using various technical tools, including Apache JMeter for load testing (Sanders, 2017), Wireshark for monitoring network utilization (Nagpure & Kurkure 2017), and OWSP ZAP for penetration testing to evaluate the security of the system. Performance metrics, including latency, throughput, security, scalability, and reliability, have been recorded during testing with a user load ranging from 100 to 1000 users (or concurrent loads), simulating real-world scenarios under laboratory settings in Ubuntu 20.4 environment with 80GB RAM and 1TB HDD. The overall system performance has been stable under heavy loads, with strong security resilience. Users expressed satisfaction with the intuitive user interface and the accuracy of health recommendations, showing the system remained responsive despite security features. POSTMAN, Swagger, and CURL have been used for API testing with necessary security headers. Key security features include identity brokering, OAuth2 for authentication, multifactor authentication, and strict access control for the eCoach system's APIs, protecting against various threats (Ajayi et al., 2023), such as cross-site scripting, brute-force attacks, and clickjacking. All experimental results are captured in Tables 7.6, 7.7, and 7.8.

The activity eCoach system performed well across all metrics. Latency and throughput stayed within acceptable limits, even with high user loads. Security has been robust with strong encryption and authorization, and the system quickly responded to threats. Scalability and reliability have been proven, handling increased data volumes with 99.95% availability. High user satisfaction and adoption further demonstrated the system's effectiveness. Overall, S-DSRM played a major role in the design and development of the eCoach event system by embedding security throughout the process. S-DSRM ensures that risks are identified early, leading to the integration of strong security protocols such as encryption, authorization, and continuous penetration testing. The iterative nature of the approach facilitates continuous security assessments while maintaining availability and scalability.

Table 7.6. Performance metrics, scalability, and reliability testing evaluation of the activity eCoach system

Metric	Evaluation focus	Measured value
Latency	Time taken to transmit data	≈ 250 ms
Throughput	Amount of data handled per second	≈ 500 requests/sec
CPU Utilization	Percentage of CPU used during operation	≈ 60
Memory Usage	Amount of memory consumed	≈ 3.0 GB
Bandwidth Utilization	Network bandwidth used during data handling	≈ 50 Mbps
User Load Stability	Performance under increasing load	1000 users with stable performance
Data Volume	Ability to handle large volumes from multiple devices	≈ 50 GB/day
MTBF	Time between system failures	500 hours
System Availability	Uptime percentage (e.g., 99.9%)	≈ 99.95%
PDR	Ratio of successfully delivered packets	≈ 98.7%
Data Loss in Exchange	A ratio between the number of bytes not received and the total number of bytes	0.0%
Probability of Unreliable Performances	Ratio between the number of failing cases and the total number of cases under consideration	0.0%

Table 7.7. Security metrics evaluation

Security step	Evaluation focus	Adopted (Yes/No)	Measured value
Encryption Strength	Assess encryption strength for user access and security log	[x] Yes [ ] No	Hashing Strength (AES-256, BCrypt)
Penetration Testing	Number of potential attack vectors assessed	[x] Yes [ ] No	3 attack vectors identified
Data Transmission Security	SSL/TLS encryption for secure transmission	[x] Yes [ ] No	Fully integrated
Incident Response Time	Time taken to detect and respond to breaches	[x] Yes [ ] No	5 seconds
Scalability Test	System performance under heavy load	[x] Yes [ ] No	1000 concurrent users
Data Storage Security	Secure storage in the TSD platform	[x] Yes [ ] No	Fully implemented

Table 7.8. User satisfaction and system health outcomes evaluation

Metric	Evaluation focus	Measured value
User Adoption Rate	Percentage of users adopting the system over time under laboratory settings	85%
Generation Time to Recommendations	Time taken to generate health alerts (e.g., low physical activity detected)	<5 seconds

S-DSRM enables the system to handle large user loads and evolve threats without sacrificing performance, resulting in a secure, scalable, and easy-to-use eCoach system that can adapt to future needs. Moreover, this study achieves a Technological Readiness Level (TRL) of 4 as elaborated inChatterjee et al., 2022.

7.6.3 Deduction of Problem Satisfaction in Activity eCoaching System Using S-DSRM

To solve the S-DSRM mathematical problem formulated for the adopted study case, it is demonstrated that each component of the objective function and constraints is met through the design, development, and deployment of the eCoaching solution.

7.6.3.1 Objective Function Satisfaction

The objective function aimed to maximize the weighted sum of security, functionality, and usability across all development phases of the system, expressed as:

$$\text{Maximize} \sum_{i=1}^{n} (w_s SL_i + w_f FL_i + w_u UL_i)$$

where w_s, w_f, and w_u are weights corresponding to security, functionality, and usability levels, respectively. For the activity eCoach system, the following have been achieved:

- **Security Level (**SL_i**)**: Each phase P_i incorporates robust security measures, including threat modeling, secure data transmission, and compliance with regulatory standards such as GDPR. These measures contribute significantly to high SL_i values at each phase.
- **Functionality Level (**FL_i**)**: Functional requirements are met through features like real-time health monitoring, data storage, and personalized feedback. Each phase enhances these functional elements, resulting in FL_i levels that align with stakeholder requirements.
- **Usability Level (**UL_i**)**: Iterative UCD workshops provided continuous feedback, allowing the refinement of the user interface and interaction design. This ensures that the system is both accessible and intuitive, thereby achieving high UL_i values. Thus, by achieving high values for SL_i, FL_i, and UL_i across all phases, the objective function for maximizing security, functionality, and usability has been satisfied.

7.6.3.2 Security Constraint Satisfaction

Each phase must satisfy the minimum-security requirement $SL_i \geq SL_{\min}$. In the activity eCoach system, this is achieved through:

$$SL_i \geq SL_{\min} \ \forall i$$

Key security measures like AES-256 and Bcrypt encryption, multi-factor authentication, and compliance with GDPR ensure that the security level SL_i at each phase meets or exceeds $SL_{\min}$, thus satisfying this constraint.

7.6.3.3 Functionality Constraint Satisfaction

The functionality constraint requires each phase to meet a baseline functionality level $FL_{\min}$:

$$FL_i \geq FL_{\min} \ \forall i$$

Functional requirements such as real-time data collection, personalized feedback, and interoperability with wearable devices were met throughout the system's development. This ensures that each FL_i meets $FL_{\min}$, satisfying the functionality constraint.

7.6.3.4 Usability Constraint Satisfaction

Each phase must achieve a usability level $UL_i \geq UL_{\min}$, as defined by user experience requirements:

$$UL_i \geq UL_{\min} \ \forall i$$

Through iterative UCD processes, the system achieved high usability levels, with user feedback consistently affirming the ease of interaction and intuitive design. This fulfills the usability constraint.

7.6.3.5 Compliance Constraint Satisfaction

The compliance constraint ensures that all regulatory requirements are fulfilled:

$$C_j = 1 \ \forall j \in \{1,..., |C|\}$$

By integrating GDPR and NORMEN guidelines into the system design, the activity eCoach solution ensures compliance throughout the data collection, storage, and transmission processes, thus satisfying the compliance constraint.

7.6.3.6 Iterative Security and Compliance Update Constraint

To address evolving security threats and regulatory updates, the system is designed for regular updates in compliance measures:

$$SL(t) \rightarrow SL(t + T)$$

Periodic security updates, continuous monitoring, and adaptive threat assessments ensure that *SL* is updated iteratively, maintaining a robust defence against new threats.

7.6.3.7 Threat Minimization and Risk Assessment

In each phase P_i, the total risk R_i is minimized by aligning threat level T_i with appropriate security measures M_i:

$$\min (T_i - M_i) \ \forall_i$$

Through proactive risk assessments, penetration testing, and secure data handling, the system reduces T_i effectively, minimizing the residual risk $T_i - M_i$ in each phase.

7.6.3.8 Problem Classification and Transformation

This problem belongs to the NP-hard class, as it involves multi-objective optimization with combinatorial and iterative constraints that make polynomial-time solutions and verifications improbable. The problem can be converted to an established NP-hard problem by drawing a parallel to the *Multi-dimensional Knapsack Problem* (MDKP). In MDKP, the objective is to maximize the total value of selected items subject to multiple resource constraints, where each item has a value and occupies specific resources, and all constraints must be satisfied while maximizing total value. This problem similarly involves maximizing a weighted sum of objectives for security, functionality, and usability across multiple phases, which can be mapped directly to the MDKP framework as follows. The objective function for this problem is expressed as:

$$\text{Maximize} \sum_{i=1}^{n} (w_s SL_i + w_f FL_i + w_u UL_i)$$

It resembles the goal of maximizing total value in MDKP. Here, each development phase P_i in S-DSRM can be viewed as an "item" with values for security (SL_i), functionality (FL_i), and usability (UL_i), and the weighted sum represents the "value" of each item. In MDKP, each item is limited by resource constraints, whereas in S-DSRM, each phase must satisfy minimum threshold requirements for security, functionality, and usability, specified by $SL_i \geq SL_{\min}$, $FL_i \geq FL_{\min}$, and $UL_i \geq UL_{\min}$. These constraints can be treated as the multi-dimensional resource constraints of MDKP, where each "item" or phase must satisfy these limits to be considered valid.

The binary compliance constraints in this problem, such as regulatory requirements $C_j = 1$, correspond to item selection constraints in MDKP, where certain items may be selected or omitted based on binary conditions. Additionally, the iterative nature, which involves selecting configurations of security, functionality, and usability across multiple phases, aligns with selecting an optimal subset of items across multiple knapsack dimensions to maximize total weighted value under the imposed constraints. Thus, by mapping each development phase in S-DSRM to an "item" in MDKP, where values and constraints are represented by security, functionality, and usability requirements, the problem is converted into a form of the Multi-dimensional Knapsack Problem. Given that MDKP is NP-hard, this conversion demonstrates that this problem is also NP-hard due to its need for combinatorial exploration of configurations across multiple phases under complex constraints.

7.6.4 Addressing Data Sovereignty in S-DSRM

Table 7.9 highlights specific steps taken to integrate data sovereignty principles into the system design and development.

Table 7.9. Addressing data sovereignty in S-DSRM

Aspect	Measures implemented	Outcome
Data Localization	Data stored within Norwegian data centres using TSD, adhering to GDPR and NORMEN guidelines	Ensures data is subject to local laws and regulations, preventing unauthorized cross-border transfers
Legal Compliance	Compliance with GDPR articles on data protection and subject rights, including access, rectification, and erasure	Protects user rights and meets international privacy and data governance standards
Access Restrictions	Role-based access controls enforce jurisdictional limitations on who can access the data	Limits data access to authorized personnel within Norway and the EU
Data Minimization	Collection limited to essential personal and activity data, with anonymization applied post-processing	Reduces risk of over-collection and misuse of sensitive data
User Transparency	Clear consent forms and accessible data policies inform users about data processing and storage locations	Builds trust and ensures user awareness of data handling practices

7.7 Discussion

This section provides substantial support for the study's hypothesis and research objectives while demonstrating the effectiveness of the S-DSRM methodology for the adopted case study. The activity eCoaching system designed using the S-DSRM framework satisfies each component of the mathematical problem formulation. By maximizing security, functionality, and usability, and satisfying the constraints of security, functionality, usability, compliance, and risk minimization, the S-DSRM framework ensures that the system is robust, adaptable, and safe in the healthcare environment. Empirical deduction confirms that the S-DSRM methodology has been successfully implemented in the Activity eCoaching system, providing a proactive and safe design approach that is compliant with regulatory and user requirements. By embedding data sovereignty principles such as localized storage, jurisdictional compliance, and access control into the S-DSRM framework, this study addresses a critical gap in the design of secure, adaptable, and ethically governed systems.

7.7.1 Security as a Core Design Principle

Incorporating security as a core design element into the S-DSRM framework represents a paradigm shifts from traditional software design, development, and evaluation research practices, where security is often considered as an afterthought (see Table 7.10). By embedding security into all phases, the eCoach healthcare system ensures regulatory compliance, strong data protection, and consistent availability.

Table 7.10. Addressing gaps in DSRM with S-DSRM for health (or activity) eCoach system

Gaps in DSRM	S-DSRM method in activity eCoach prototype system	Outcome
Security as an Afterthought	Security identified during problem definition through threat modeling and privacy concerns	Clearly identified security risks in health data transmission and wearable device communication
Secondary Security Objectives	Define security as a primary goal alongside functionality and usability	Specific security objectives such as encryption, authentication, and compliance
Reactive Security Design	Integrate security mechanisms (e.g., encryption, secure communication) during design	Secure system architecture with built-in encryption and data protection mechanisms
Limited Security Testing	Conduct continuous security tests (penetration, vulnerability, code audits) in each iteration	Early detection of vulnerabilities, ensuring the system remains secure through all development stages
Minimal Stakeholder Involvement	Involve stakeholders early to discuss security concerns and privacy expectations	Security features that meet stakeholder needs and foster user trust
Post-development Regulatory Compliance	Embed compliance with GDPR and HIPAA from the start	System that is fully compliant with legal requirements, avoiding late-stage adjustments
Non-adaptive Security Framework	Implement adaptive threat models and risk assessments that evolve with new security threats	Continuously resilient system capable of addressing new security threats

7.7.2 S-DSRM vs. Traditional DSRM

The comparison has been made as follows:

- **S-DSRM's Proactive Security Integration:** S-DSRM ensures that security is embedded from the outset of the project, resulting in a system that undergoes continuous threat assessments throughout the development phase. In contrast to traditional DSRM, which often addresses security reactively after functional designs are implemented, S-DSRM employs early-stage threat modeling and regular penetration testing to identify and mitigate vulnerabilities. This proactive approach enables the allowed the health (or activity) eCoach system to avoid common pitfalls such as late-stage security patches and post-deployment vulnerability fixes. It also ensures compliance with regulations like GDPR by supporting iterative improvements in both system security and functionality.
- **Balancing Usability and Security:** By embedding security protocols such as OAuth2 and hashing algorithms without compromising usability, the system maintained a high user satisfaction rate. Feedback from UCD workshops showed that users found the system intuitive despite the robust security measures. The adoption of Google Material Design principles facilitated smooth interaction with the app, while security protocols, such as multi-factor authentication and secure data transmission, remained largely invisible to the end-user. This balance has been critical in ensuring compliance with GDPR and NORMEN without sacrificing usability.

7.7.3 Balancing the Usage of Terms

Although the terms "security by design", "privacy by design", and "sovereignty by design" are often used interchangeably, they represent distinct yet complementary principles. "Security by design" refers to embedding security mechanisms (such as encryption, authentication, and threat modeling) throughout the system development life cycle to prevent vulnerabilities. "Privacy by design" emphasizes protecting personal data through privacy-friendly defaults and incorporating principles such as data minimization, purpose limitation, and user consent into system architecture. "Sovereignty by design" on the other hand, extends this focus to controls over data locality, jurisdiction, and governance. This ensures that data is always subject to local laws and cannot be arbitrarily transferred across borders. In the S-DSRM framework, these principles are not used interchangeably but integrated as multi-layered priorities: security forms the foundation of the architecture, data protection governs the processing of data, and sovereignty ensures compliance with regulations and case law.

7.7.4 Addressing Research Questions

- **RQ-1:** The S-DSRM approach has been particularly successful in addressing early security challenges. The use of threat modeling through UCD workshops and continuous security evaluations ensured that security risks were identified and mitigated early in the process. For instance, the introduction of identity breaking and multi-factor authentication during the design phase meant that security had been integral to the system's architecture rather than a post-development addition. Compared to traditional DSRM, which often leaves security as a post-design concern, S-DSRM embedded security into the very fabric of the system, preventing late-stage vulnerabilities.

- **RQ-2:** The experiment demonstrated that S-DSRM can successfully balance usability, security, and compliance in a health eCoach system. While the system employed robust security measures (AES-256, BCrypt, SSL/TLS, OAuth2), these had been seamlessly integrated, ensuring that users did not face complexity or reduced performance. The system's compliance with GDPR regulations was ensured without compromising its usability, as confirmed by the high user adoption rate and positive feedback on the system's responsiveness and ease of use.
- **RQ-3:** S-DSRM marked a significant shift from traditional research artifact development practices by embedding security into each stage of the development lifecycle. This shift has been evident in how security considerations have been introduced during the problem identification phase, influencing the overall design, development, and evaluation of the activity eCoach system. Continuous penetration testing, iterative threat assessments, and early-stage encryption integration helped prevent vulnerabilities rather than reacting to them post-deployment. This proactive approach represents a fundamental shift in system design research, particularly in the healthcare sector, where data sensitivity is paramount.

7.7.5 Relevance to Digital Sovereignty

The proposed S-DSRM framework introduces a structured approach for embedding sovereignty-aware practices into software systems from the earliest design stages. In particular, the proof-of-concept eCoach healthcare system demonstrates how cyber-physical software systems can be developed based on sovereignty-by-design principles, thereby ensuring local data governance, lawful processing, and legal oversight. As governments and institutions grapple with enforcing data residency, algorithmic accountability, and ethical AI practices, the S-DSRM provides a replicable approach for tightly integrating security, privacy, and compliance with AI system development. The proposed framework helps to implement digital sovereignty in sensitive areas by considering regulatory obligations (e.g. GDPR, standards), implementing secure and transparent AI workflows, and promoting user trust through sovereign infrastructure (e.g. TSD). Therefore, S-DSRM helps to bridge the methodological gap between digital innovation and sovereign control of digital ecosystems and is therefore of great significance to the scientific and policy discussions on sovereign AI systems.

7.7.6 Sustainability, Ethics, Economy, and Society

The iterative nature of S-DSRM enhances the sustainability of activity eCoach prototype systems by continually evaluating and updating security measures, ensuring adaptation to emerging threats, maintaining long-term system integrity and performance, and ensuring compliance with new regulations. It embeds privacy and security from the outset, securing user consent and adhering to ethical principles, ensuring proper data usage and protection in line with healthcare standards. Economically, S-DSRM reduces the risk of costly security breaches and downtime, offering long-term savings through proactive security measures and cost-effective deployment through iterative design. Socially, it promotes trust and user satisfaction by prioritizing user feedback, focusing on user-centric security, and fostering trust among patients and providers, creating a secure, user-friendly system that encourages stakeholder acceptance. The secure design and development of the activity eCoach system also promotes digital sovereignty, allowing users and organizations to maintain control of their data. This approach increases trust in the system by ensuring that sensitive health data is handled securely and is compliant with data protection regulations.

7.7.7 Paradigm Shift in Software Development

Overall, S-DSRM not only improves security, but it also shifts the focus of software design, development, and evaluation from reactive to proactive security practices. Traditional security frameworks typically apply fixes only after vulnerabilities are discovered. In contrast, S-DSRM integrates threat modeling and continuous security testing through-out the development life cycle, providing more adaptable and secure artifacts. To illustrate the methodological improvement of S-DSRM over traditional DSRM, Table 7.11 provides a structured comparison of the lifecycle phases. It shows how S-DSRM extends the original framework by embedding security, privacy, and sovereignty principles directly into the design, development, and evaluation processes. In addition, the table shows how the supporting frameworks—UTAUT, ISSM, and NASSS—are explicitly integrated into specific phases of S-DSRM. This highlights that their application is not random but strategically coordinated to enhance stakeholder trust, system quality, and socio-technical resilience in sensitive areas such as healthcare.

7.7.8 Limitations

Although the S-DSRM framework demonstrates high applicability in the design of security artifacts, this study is limited by its focus on a single healthcare use case in the Norwegian context. As a result, regulatory assumptions (e.g., GDPR, NORMEN) and infrastructure availability (e.g., TSD) may not be transferable to regions with different legal or technical ecosystems. Furthermore, the integration of AI with the system is preliminary and domain-specific, requiring further investigation in various AI-driven scenarios. The proof of concept has been validated under laboratory conditions; real-world deployments may present unforeseen challenges in terms of availability, performance, or compliance.

7.8 Conclusion

This study proposes the Security-Centric Design Science Research Method (S-DSRM) as a structured, proactive framework for incorporating security, privacy, and sovereignty considerations into every stage of product development. Using a

Table 7.11. Comparison of DSRM vs. S-DSRM across lifecycle stages with supporting frameworks

DSRM stage	Traditional DSRM activities	S-DSRM enhancements	Supporting frameworks in S-DSRM
Problem Identification	Define functional gap or research challenge	Include threat modeling, risk analysis, and legal/ data sovereignty concerns	NASSS: Identifies socio-technical risks; legal complexity
Objectives Definition	Functional, usability, or performance goals	Add security, privacy, compliance, sovereignty objectives (e.g., GDPR, NORMEN)	NASSS: Value proposition alignment; UTAUT: Performance expectations
Design & Development	Build artifact iteratively based on design goals	Use secure coding, encryption, authentication, data minimization, local storage	ISSM: System quality; UTAUT: Facilitating conditions
Demonstration	Validate functional proof-of-concept	Evaluate secure functionality in realistic, compliant environments	NASSS: Demonstrability in complex settings
Evaluation	Functional, usability, and performance testing	Include penetration testing, compliance audit, system resilience, and user trust	UTAUT: User acceptance; ISSM: Info/system quality
Communication	Academic dissemination of results	Include policy recommendations, open-source sharing, legal considerations	All: Drives cross-disciplinary knowledge transfer

proof-of-concept system, "Secure Healthcare eCoach", the study demonstrates that integrating security measures from the outset (rather than retroactively) ensures compliance, trust, and performance without compromising usability. Qualitative results show that despite enhanced security features, users remain confident in the system's recommendations, are influenced by social and professional networks, demonstrate active receptivity, and perceive the system as easy to use. The user-centric, iterative design process resulted in high usability ratings (average 4.1/5), seamless integration with wearables and IoT devices, and full alignment with stakeholder expectations. The system also achieves interoperability through HL7 FHIR and semantic ontologies, enhancing adaptability and scalability.

Quantitative results confirmed the technical effectiveness of the framework: average latency was approximately 250 milliseconds, throughput reached 500 requests per second, and system availability reached 99.95%. A packet delivery rate of 98.7% was achieved, with no packet loss recorded, and a mean time between failures of 500 hours. User adoption reached 85%, with a recommendation generation time of less than 5 seconds. Strong security was ensured by AES-256 and Bcrypt encryption, OAuth2 multi-factor authentication, TLS/SSL protocols, GDPR-compliant storage, and legal controls via TSD. The system remained stable with up to 1,000 concurrent users, achieved rapid incident response in approximately 5 seconds, and passed penetration tests with minimal vulnerabilities.

By addressing all established requirements for security, functionality, usability, compliance, and risk mitigation, S-DSRM is not only theoretically sound but also highly effective in practice. This work highlights a paradigm shift in design science research, from reactive patching to preventative security integration and provides a replicable approach for developing secure systems in healthcare, the Internet of Things, artificial intelligence, and other sensitive sectors. Future research will extend this framework to blockchain-based applications, broader healthcare environments, and large-scale IoT implementations to validate its adaptability and generalizability.

References

Adams, S., & Niezen, M. (2018). Digital 'solutions' to unhealthy lifestyle 'problems': The construction of social and personal risks in the development of eCoaches. In: *Digitised Health, Medicine and Risk* (pp. 68–84). Routledge.

Ahmed, M., Byreddy, S., Nutakki, A., Sikos, L.F., & Haskell-Dowland, P. (2021). ECU-IoHT: A dataset for analyzing cyberattacks in Internet of Health Things. *Ad Hoc Networks*, 122, 102621.

Ajayi, J., Di Maio, A., Braun, T., & Xenakis, D. (2023). An online multi-dimensional knapsack approach for slice admission control. In: *2023 IEEE 20th Consumer Communications & Networking Conference (CCNC)* (pp. 152–157). IEEE.

Almaiah, M.A., Al-Rahmi, A.M., Alturise, F., Alrawad, M., Alkhalaf, S., Lutfi, A. et al. (2022). Factors influencing the adoption of Internet banking: An integration of ISSM and UTAUT with price value and perceived risk. *Frontiers in Psychology*, 13, 919198.

Andrade, V.C., Gomes, R.D., Reinehr, S., Freitas, C.O.D.A., & Malucelli, A.(2022). Privacy by design and software engineering: A systematic literature review. In: *Proceedings of the XXI Brazilian Symposium on Software Quality* (pp. 1–10).

Argaw, S.T., Bempong, N.-E., Eshaya-Chauvin, B., & Flahault, A. (2019). The state of research on cyberattacks against hospitals and available best practice recommendations: A scoping review. *BMC Medical Informatics and Decision Making*, 19, 1–11.

Aydın, A., & Bensghir, T.K. (2019). Digital data sovereignty: Towards a conceptual framework. In: *2019 1st International Informatics and Software Engineering Conference (UBMYK)* (pp. 1–6). IEEE.

Bergen, B.N., Vangen, G.M., & Haugen, A.K. (2023). Building a national education registry in Norway. *Proceedings of European University*, 95, 161–169.

Bu, F., Wang, N., Jiang, B., & Liang, H. (2020). "Privacy by design" implementation: Information system engineers' perspective. *International Journal of Information Management*, 53, 102124.

Chatterjee, A. (2023). Automatic Generation of Personalized Recommendations in eCoaching. https://uia.brage.unit.no/uia-xmlui/handle/11250/3084549

Chatterjee, A., Gerdes, M.W., & Martinez, S. (2019). eHealth initiatives for the promotion of healthy lifestyle and allied implementation difficulties. In: *2019 International Conference on Wireless and Mobile Computing, Networking and Communications (WiMob)* (pp. 1–8). IEEE.

Chatterjee, A., Gerdes, M., Prinz, A., Martinez, S., & Medin, A.(2020). Reference design model for a smart e-Coach recommendation system for lifestyle support based on ICT technologies. In: *Proceedings of the Twelfth International Conference on eHealth, Telemedicine, and Social Medicine (eTELEMED)* (pp. 52–58).

Chatterjee, A., Gerdes, M., Prinz, A., & Martinez, S. (2021). Human coaching methodologies for automatic electronic coaching (eCoaching) as behavioral interventions with information and communication technology: Systematic review. *Journal of Medical Internet Research*, 23(3), 23533.

Chatterjee, A., Prinz, A., Gerdes, M., & Martinez, S. (2021). An automatic ontology-based approach to support logical representation of observable and measurable data for healthy lifestyle management: Proof-of-concept study. *Journal of Medical Internet Research*, 23(4), 24656.

Chatterjee, A., Prinz, A., Gerdes, M., & Martinez, S. (2021). Digital interventions on healthy lifestyle management: Systematic review. *Journal of Medical Internet Research*, 23(11), 26931.

Chatterjee, A., & Prinz, A. (2022). Applying spring security framework with keycloak-based OAuth2 to protect microservice architecture APIs: A case study. *Sensors*, 22(5), 1703.

Chatterjee, A., & Prinz, A. (2022). Personalized recommendations for physical activity e-Coaching (OntoRecoModel): Ontological modeling. *JMIR Medical Informatics*, 10(6), 33847.

Chatterjee, A., Gerdes, M.W., Khatiwada, P., & Prinz, A. (2022). SFTSDH: Applying spring security framework with TSD-based OAuth2 to protect microservice architecture APIs. *IEEE Access*, 10, 41914–41934.

Chatterjee, A., Pahari, N., & Prinz, A. (2022). HL7 FHIR with SNOMED-CT to achieve semantic and structural interoperability in personal health data: A proof-of-concept study. *Sensors*, 22(10), 3756.

Chatterjee, A., Pahari, N., & Riegler, M. (2022). LSTM step prediction and ontology-based recommendation generation in activity e-coaching. In: *2022 18th International Conference on Wireless and Mobile Computing, Networking and Communications (WiMob)* (pp. 13–18). IEEE.

Chatterjee, A., Pahari, N., Prinz, A., & Riegler, M. (2022). Machine learning and ontology in ecoaching for personalized activity level monitoring and recommendation generation. *Scientific Reports*, 12(1), 19825.

Chatterjee, A., Prinz, A., & Riegler, M. (2022). Prediction modeling in activity e-coaching for tailored recommendation generation: A conceptualization. In: *2022 IEEE International Symposium on Medical Measurements and Applications (MeMeA)* (pp. 1–6). IEEE.

Chatterjee, A., Prinz, A., Gerdes, M., Martinez, S., Pahari, N.,& Meena, Y.K. (2022). ProHealth eCoach: User-centered design and development of an eCoach app to promote healthy lifestyle with personalized activity recommendations. *BMC Health Services Research*, 22(1), 1120.

Chaudhary, S., Kakkar, R., Jadav, N.K., Nair, A., Gupta, R., Tanwar, S. et al. (2022). A taxonomy on smart healthcare technologies: Security framework, case study, and future directions. *Journal of Sensors*, 2022(1), 1863838.

Conboy, K., Gleasure, R., & Cullina, E. (2015). Agile design science research. In: *New Horizons in Design Science: Broadening the Research Agenda.* 10th International Conference, DESRIST 2015, Dublin, Ireland, May 20–22, 2015. Proceedings (Vol. 10, pp. 168–180). Springer.

Deacon, J. (2009). Model-View-Controller (MVC) architecture. Retrieved from http://www.jdl.co.uk/briefings/MVC.pdf.

Eteläaho, E., Pirinen, R., & Tuomi, P. (2015). Improvement suggestions for the DSRM model. AIS. https://api.semanticscholar.org/CorpusID:30276018

Froud, R., Meza, T., Ernes, K., & Slowther, A. (2019). Research ethics oversight in Norway: Structure, function, and challenges. *BMC Health Services Research*, 19, 1–6.

Garbagnati, A., & Wu, L. (2022). Creating competitive advantage: Privacy and security by design in mHealth and digital health products. *The Health Lawyer*, 34(4), 9–34.

Geerts, G.L. (2011). A design science research methodology and its application to accounting information systems research. *International Journal of Accounting Information Systems*, 12(2), 142–151.

Gledson, B., Rogage, K., Thompson, A., & Ponton, H. (2024). Reporting on the development of a web-based prototype dashboard for construction design managers, achieved through design science research methodology (DSRM). *Buildings*, 14(2), 335.

Gostin, L.O., Levit, L.A., & Nass, S.J. (2009). Beyond the HIPAA Privacy Rule: Enhancing Privacy, Improving Health Through Research.

Greenhalgh, T., Wherton, J., Papoutsi, C., Lynch, J., Hughes, G., A'Court, C. et al. (2018). Analysing the role of complexity in explaining the fortunes of technology programmes: Empirical application of the NASSS framework. *BMC Medicine*, 16, 1–15.

Gross, A., & Doerr, J. (2012). What you need is what you get!: The vision of view-based requirements specifications. In: *2012 20th IEEE International Requirements Engineering Conference (RE)* (pp. 171–180). IEEE.

Halili, E.H. (2008). Apache JMeter. https://jmeter.apache.org

Hulshof, M. (2021). Information security certification in context: A strategy selection maturity model. Master's thesis, University of Twente.

Hummel, P., Braun, M., Tretter, M., & Dabrock, P. (2021). Data sovereignty: A review. *Big Data & Society*, 8(1), 2053951720982012.

Ibarra, J., Jahankhani, H., & Kendzierskyj, S. (2019). Cyber-physical attacks and the value of healthcare data: Facing an era of cyber extortion and organised crime. In: *Blockchain and Clinical Trial: Securing Patient Data* (pp. 115–137).

Kamphorst, B.A. (2017). E-coaching systems: What they are, and what they aren't. *Personal and Ubiquitous Computing*, 21(4), 625–632.

Kerr, D., Butler-Henderson, K., & Sahama, T. (2019). Security, privacy, and ownership issues with the use of wearable health technologies. In: *Cyber Law, Privacy, and Security: Concepts, Methodologies, Tools, and Applications* (pp. 1629–1644). IGI Global.

Khatiwada, P., Bhusal, H., Chatterjee, A., & Gerdes, M.W. (2020). A proposed access control-based privacy preservation model to share healthcare data in cloud. In: *2020 16th International Conference on Wireless and Mobile Computing, Networking and Communications (WiMob)* (pp. 40–47). IEEE.

Khatiwada, P., Yang, B., Lin, J.-C., & Blobel, B. (2024). Patient-generated health data (PGHD): Understanding, requirements, challenges, and existing techniques for data security and privacy. *Journal of Personalized Medicine*, 14(3), 282.

Luna, R., Rhine, E., Myhra, M., Sullivan, R., & Kruse, C.S. (2016). Cyber threats to health information systems: A systematic review. *Technology and Health Care*, 24(1), 1–9.

Maček, D., Magdalenie, I., & Redep, N. B. (2020). Towards a hybrid model for the evaluation of critical IT systems. In: *Central European Conference on Information and Intelligent Systems* (pp. 249–255). Faculty of Organization and Informatics Varazdin.

MacIntyre, R., Engells, T.E., Scotch, M., Heslop, D.J., Gumel, A.B., Poste, G. et al. (2018). Converging and emerging threats to health security. *Environment Systems and Decisions*, 38, 198–207.

Nagpure, S., & Kurkure, S. (2017). Vulnerability assessment and penetration testing of web application. In: *2017 International Conference on Computing, Communication, Control and Automation (ICCUBEA)* (pp. 1–6). IEEE.

Nowrozy, R. (2024). A security and privacy compliant data sharing solution for healthcare data ecosystems. PhD thesis, Victoria University.

Offermann, P., Levina, O., Schönherr, M., & Bub, U. (2009). Outline of a design science research process. In: *Proceedings of the 4th International Conference on Design Science Research in Information Systems and Technology* (pp. 1–11).

Øvrelid, E., Bygstad, B., & Thomassen, G. (2021). TSD: A research platform for sensitive data. *Procedia Computer Science*, 181, 127–134.

Pedersen, K.S., & Gaupseth, M.O. (2019). Digital sikkerhetskultur i Norge – En studie av dokumenter utarbeidet av nasjonale aktører. Master's thesis, University of Stavanger, Norway.

Peffers, K., Rothenberger, M., Tuunanen, T., & Vaezi, R. (2012). Design science research evaluation. In: *Design Science Research in Information Systems. Advances in Theory and Practice*. 7th International Conference, DESRIST 2012, Las Vegas, NV, USA, May 14–15, 2012. Proceedings (Vol. 7, pp. 398–410). Springer.

Peffers, K., Tuunanen, T., Rothenberger, M.A., & Chatterjee, S. (2007). A design science research methodology for information systems research. *Journal of Management Information Systems*, 24(3), 45–77.

Price, W.N., & Cohen, I.G. (2019). Privacy in the age of medical big data. *Nature Medicine*, 25(1), 37–43.

Robertson, J., & Robertson, S. (2000). Volere requirements specification templates. Atlantic System Guild. www.systemguild.com

Sanders, C. (2017). *Practical Packet Analysis: Using Wireshark to Solve Real-World Network Problems.* No Starch Press.

Semantha, F.H., Azam, S., Yeo, K.C., & Shanmugam, B. (2020). A systematic literature review on privacy by design in the healthcare sector. *Electronics*, 9(3), 452.

Simos, M., & Kumar, N. (2023). *Zero Trust Overview and Playbook Introduction: Guidance for Business, Security, And Technology Leaders and Practitioners*. Packt Publishing Ltd.

Singi, K., Choudhury, S.G., Kaulgud, V., Bose, R.J.C., Podder, S., & Burden, A.P. (2020). Data sovereignty governance framework. In: *Proceedings of the IEEE/ACM 42nd International Conference on Software Engineering Workshops* (pp. 303–306). IEEE.

Takyi, H.K. (2019). Security, privacy, confidentiality and integrity of emerging healthcare technologies: A framework for quality of life technologies to be HIPAA/HITECH compliant, with emphasis on health kiosk design. PhD thesis, University of Pittsburgh.

Terry, N.P. (2012). Protecting patient privacy in the age of big data. *UMKC Law Review*, 81, 385.

Toch, E., Bettini, C., Shmueli, E., Radaelli, L., Lanzi, A.Riboni, D., & Lepri, B. (2018). The privacy implications of cyber security systems: A technological survey. *ACM Computing Surveys (CSUR)*, 51(2), 1–27.

Voigt, P., & Bussche, A. (2017). *The EU General Data Protection Regulation (GDPR): A Practical Guide* (1st ed.). Cham: Springer International Publishing.

Williams, M.D., Rana, N.P., & Dwivedi, Y.K. (2015). The unified theory of acceptance and use of technology (UTAUT): A literature review. *Journal of Enterprise Information Management*, 28(3), 443–488.

CHAPTER

8

Safeguarding Digital Sovereignty with Privacy-Preserving Edge Computing: A Hybrid Deep Learning Framework

Ikwuazom Callistus Tochukwu[1]*, Ogwueleka Francisca Nonyelum[1], Sabarathinam Chockalingam[2] and Sanjay Misra[3]

[1] Department of Computer Science, University of Abuja, Nigeria
[2] Department of Risk and Security, Institute for Energy Technology, 1777 Halden, Norway
[3] Department of Applied Data Science, Institute for Energy Technology, Norway

8.1 Introduction

In an era where data governance is critical to national resilience, both countries and individuals require digital sovereignty (DS) to maintain control over their digital environments, governmental systems, and electronic data flows. This control is essential for ensuring security, supporting ethical Artificial Intelligence (AI) initiatives, and preserving independence (Hummel et al., 2021; Ikwuazom et al., 2025; Misra et al., 2025). A core principle of digital sovereignty is minimizing dependence on foreign technology while remaining aligned with local cultures, legal frameworks and national priorities. However, achieving this balance is increasingly challenging, particularly as AI systems rely on growing volumes of sensitive and high-value data (Iqbal & Ismail, 2025).

Because Mobile Edge Computing (MEC) operates closer to the data source, it offers faster speed, enhanced privacy and greater localized control. Decentralized MEC inherently supports digital sovereignty (DS), however, it also introduces significant security and policy challenges. These include cross-border leakage of data, AI driven hostile actions, and vulnerabilities in distributed networks that threaten the integrity of digital assets across nations (Nencioni et al., 2023). General Data Protection Regulation (GDPR) and California Consumer Privacy Act (CCPA) demonstrate that data protection standards must evolve alongside technological innovation. Yet, most

*Corresponding author: callistus.ikwuazom2002@uniabuja.edu.ng

DOI: 10.1201/9781003581581-8

MEC security fall short of meeting these regulatory expectations (Chukwurah, 2024; Ranaweera et al., 2022).

AI-based security architectures, while dependable in centralized cloud environments, often falter when data is processed at the edge. Their reliance on centralized datasets leads to scalability limitations and persistent vulnerabilities such as data poisoning and model inversion (Ansarı et al., 2020; Chatterjee et al., 2025; Zhong et al., 2023). Federated Learning (FL) offers a promising alternative by enabling local data storage,but its real-world deployment faces significant hurdles—including computational overhead, susceptibility to model poisoning and communication inefficiencies (Ferrag et al., 2021; Sánchez Sánchez et al., 2024). Hybrid frameworks like Autoencoder-MLP contribute positively to anomaly detection; however, they lack the speed and scalability required for high-stakes domains such as healthcare, transportation and defense (Adeniyi et al., 2024).

Taken together, these insights underscore the urgent need for AI security strategies that integrate emerging technologies with regulatory compliance, enable efficient large-scale deployment at the edge and protect digital autonomy. In response to these challenges, this chapter introduces SECuRE-4, a unified hybrid framework comprising Convolutional Neural Networks (CNNs), Transformers and Graph Neural Networks (GNNs). SECuRE-4 is designed to detect cyber threats in real time while preserving individual privacy. Its core objectives include ensuring compliance with the General Data Protection Regulation (GDPR) and the California Consumer Privacy Act (CCPA), training AI models within secure jurisdiction-specific environments, and enhancing resilience against adversarial attacks. By leveraging AI and a federated architecture that respects national sovereignty, this chapter offers a secure and scalable approach to fortifying Mobile Edge Computing (MEC) infrastructure for mission-critical applications.

This section continues to highlight the intersection between Mobile Edge Computing, AI and digital sovereignty. After outlining the main contributions in Section 8.1.2, the rest of this chapter is split into different sections: Section 8.2 reviews known solutions and their limitations. Section 8.3 presents the SECuRE-4 architecture. Section 8.4 shows how measures of performance were established. Section 8.5 looks at digital sovereignty implications and Section 8.6 lays out the planned research topics of quantum-resistant AI and guiding cross-border MEC operations.

8.1.1 Study Background

Mobile Edge Computing enables the deployment of processing power close to the data it operates on. This proximity supports the goals of digital sovereignty (DS) by facilitating faster analytics, localized storage and enhanced privacy protections (Ikwuazom et al., 2025). Unlike traditional cloud architectures that store data remotely, MEC allows nations and institutions to retain data locally and comply with privacy regulations such as the General Data Protection Regulation (GDPR) and the California Consumer Privacy Act (CCPA) (Nencioni et al., 2023). However, this potential remains underutilized due to fragmented MEC infrastructure and inconsistent enforcement of security and privacy policies. These gaps create opportunities for adversaries to exploit system vulnerabilities, threatening operational integrity, data governance, and legal authority. As AI becomes increasingly integrated into national networks, the imperative to manage and secure localized data grows, reinforcing the importance of sovereign control over digital assets (Rao & Bertino, 2019).

The challenges confronting Mobile Edge Computing (MEC) ecosystems and digital sovereignty are no longer theoretical, they are unfolding in the here and now. As nations strive to advance MEC for speed, efficiency and alignment with global standards, the lack of unified frameworks for security, sovereignty and scalability leaves their digital infrastructures exposed. These vulnerabilities permeate every layer of MEC and can be broadly categorized as communication failures,data safety and access issues, and hardware-level attacks. The central dilemma has shifted from whether to decentralize to how best to implement decentralization without compromising innovation, system availability, autonomous control or overall security.

A. Network-based Threats

Fully secured communication across Mobile Edge Computing (MEC) layers is essential to ensure digital sovereignty and prevent unauthorized access through intercepted or tampered data. Cybercriminals employ various tactics—including Distributed Denial of Service (DDoS) attacks, Man-in-the-Middle (MitM) exploits (as shown in Figure 8.1), packet sniffing and Domain Name System (DNS) spoofing, to disrupt key government services, steal sensitive data, or compromise decision-making infrastructures (Moghaddasi et al., 2024; Yan et al., 2022).

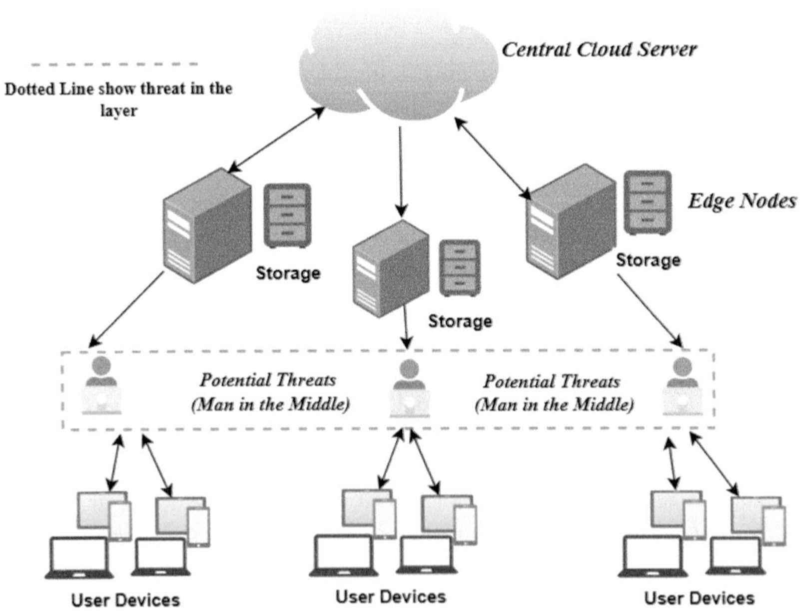

Figure 8.1. Network-based threats (MitM scenario) in MEC.

Frequently, MEC nodes do not have centralised intrusion protection, so often these attacks cannot be spotted early (Alsubhi, 2024). Because of this, a nation struggles to properly control its online assets and communication tools. With AI and specifically CNNs, it is possible to find potential threats quickly while ensuring privacy by running packet checks on the network (Liu & Wang, 2023).

B. Data-centric Threats

The protection of valuable data and understanding of where it takes place is made more difficult by attacks that take aim at data in MEC. These are data poisoning, model inversion and inference attacks, where hackers use methods to influence AI behavior, find sensitive data in model outputs and discover hidden details based on what the AI uses (Adeniyi et al., 2024; Ansari et al., 2020; Zhong et al., 2023). As shown in Figure 8.2, a data threat might occur in Multi-Access Edge Computing (MEC), as tampering, injection and exfiltration are possible risks within a distributed system.

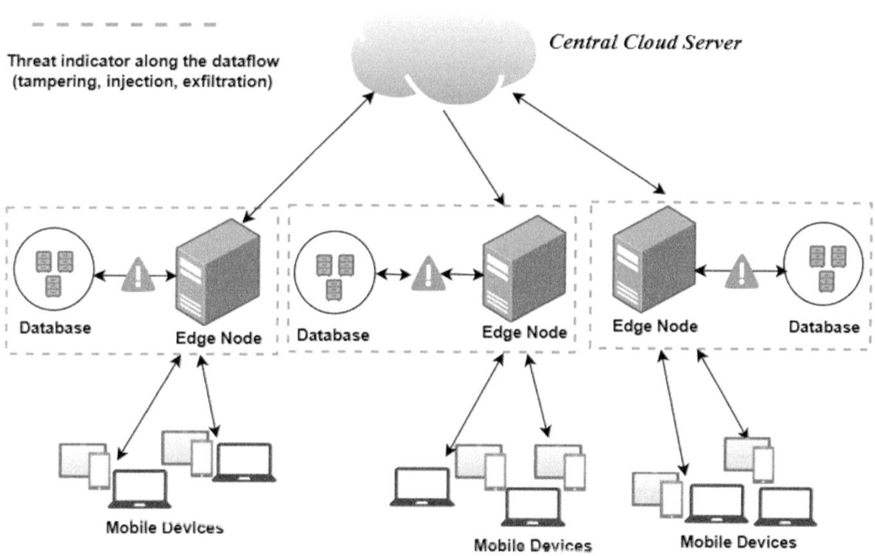

Figure 8.2. Data-based threat scenario in MEC.

The framework in this study uses federated learning (FL) to address this concern by holding data locally and making it possible for models to be trained collaboratively. In computing, transformer-based models improve the ability to detect minor anomalies in data streams and help ensure the system remains both technically strong and lawful.

C. MEC's Device-Based Threats

Sovereign control may be endangered by threats to edge nodes, specifically their sensors, smart routers and embedded systems, since they can be attacked via firmware weaknesses, snooping access or merging into botnets (Figure 8.3). By detecting weak points in both hardware and software such threats enable attackers to enter the national digital infrastructure (Hussain et al., 2019; Nguyen et al., 2020).

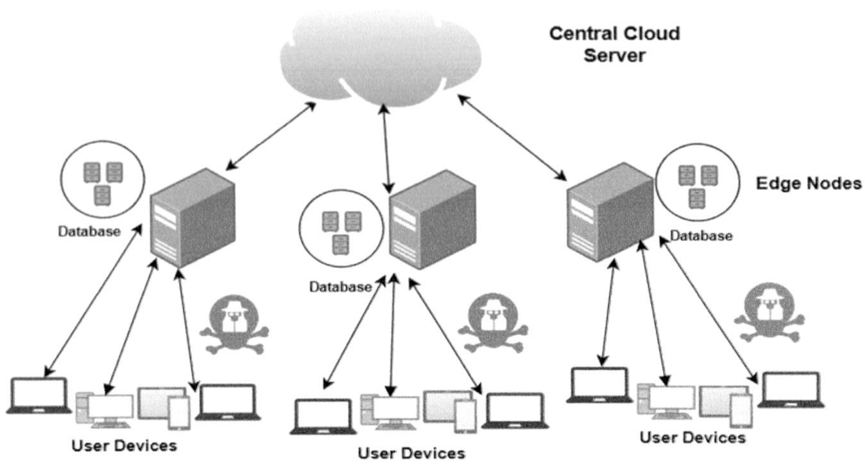

Figure 8.3. Device-based threats scenario in MEC.

Unlike regular computer systems, attacks on devices at the edge frequently escape notice. After being breached such devices can remove private information, insert troublesome signals into systems or encourage larger problems with computers or networks. Since edge nodes infected by botnets (as seen in Figure 8.3) are prone to attacks, cyberattacks such as ransomware and espionage can now be carried out easily (Nguyen et al., 2020). This study applies Graph Neural Networks (GNNs) to model how devices are linked and their information flows. Because of this, coordinated threats on the network are detected, ensuring unified decentralized responses without relying on central control.

8.1.2 Contributions

This chapter describes SECuRE-4, a new framework designed to defend mobile edge computing (MEC) environments and strengthen digital independence using architectural improvements and threat prevention policies. The main contributions of this study are:

(a) The system uses federated learning with Convolutional Neural Networks (CNNs), Transformers and Graph Neural Networks (GNNs) to recognize spatial, sequential and relational threats. Thanks to this architecture, data is kept close to its source and remains compliant with important data sovereignty regulations.

(b) A lightweight multi-layer perceptron (MLP) meta-learner blends different models' outputs using soft voting and achieves excellent results which allows it to work fast in edge devices.

(c) The model is stable enough to keep its performance high, reaching more than 99% accuracy for training-time poisoning and FGSM-based evasion, suggesting it is secure against both known and unknown attacks.
(d) To make the system scalable and respect privacy, an autoencoder is added to lower training costs by 62%. As a result, detection can be performed uniformly even on diverse hardware and data is not compromised.

8.2 A Review of Current Research Related to Security in MEC

8.2.1 Machine Learning's Role in Reinforcing Digital Sovereignty

Machine Learning (ML) and Deep Learning (DL) are key tools in this effort. They allow nations to protect essential infrastructure without the use of foreign technologies aiming to support public digital sovereignty goals. For example, (Joseph et al., 2025) proved that the ML-based anomaly detection systems can secure IoT networks in smart cities, while following GDPR, while remaining within the jurisdiction of the data. Nonetheless, (Nguyen et al., 2020) stressed that conventional ML approaches lack requisite finesse to identify complex threats such as adversarial attacks and therefore require DL techniques integration. Deep Learning, marked with its capability to identify the hidden attack patterns autonomously, has become indispensable in adaptive MEC security considering (Subramaniam & Kaur, 2019) who demonstrated the DL's capability of maintaining decentralized, scalable, and resilient networks.

Federated Learning (FL) increases sovereignty more by decentralizing model training as well as keeping sensitive data on local machines. (Ferrag et al., 2021) demonstrated how FL-based frameworks enhance privacy and malware detection in Industrial IoT applications and deliver better results than centralized models. Similarly, (Gopalakrishnan et al., 2020) and (Osia et al., 2020) argued that DL-powered MEC systems with reduced dependency on foreign AI solutions eliminate risks posed by hidden vulnerabilities. Transformers and Graph Neural Networks (GNNs) as suggested by (El Houda et al., 2023) and (Moghaddasi et al., 2024), have enhanced measures needed to defend against adversarial attacks made by artificial intelligence which are becoming more complex in cross border deployment of MEC.

Deep learning (DL) and federated learning (FL) techniques have driven tremendous research efforts into the security challenges in Mobile Edge Computing (MEC). This chapter summarizes the progress made on intrusion detection, adversarial robustness, privacy preservation, and federated frameworks, and points out gaps the proposed SECuRE-4 framework fills.

8.2.2 Related Works

Adeniyi et al. (2024) reported a hybrid Intrusion Detection System whereby an Autoencoder (AE) and Multi-Layer Perceptron (MLP) are integrated for use in a Mobile Edge Computing (MEC) environment. Our model has an unprecedented detection accuracy of 99.98% for NF-UQ-NIDS-V2 dataset, which requires 4.96s of training time and 0.74s per inference. Yet, there is a huge computational overhead associated with real-time deployment in MEC environments, and therefore, further optimization for such practical use is necessary.

Gopalakrishnan et al. (2020) presented the DLTPDO-CD system for MEC, using BiLSTM-based traffic prediction with lower NMSE than LSTM predictions, ASCE-based data offloading for better task completion and throughput and DBN with BMO for successful cyberattack detection (97.65% accuracy, 99.04% sensitivity and 97.77% F1). Security in MEC is provided by deep learning which could also benefit from alternative ways to estimate traffic. In the same way, Hnamte & Hussain (2023) introduced DCNNBiLSTM which merges DCNN for discovering spatial features with BiLSTM for sequential recognition. Modeling the traffic data from CICIDS2018 and Edge_IIoT, we observed that both datasets have robust and efficient multiclass intrusion detection at 100% and 99.64% accuracy respectively.

Akif et al. (2024) presented a hybrid approach, using mutual information, data balancing methods and PCA to manage feature selection and reduce the data dimension. According to the results on CICIDS-Collection, the model reached 99.24% accuracy while coping with both variety in data amount and confusion from different data points. In Rani & Reddy (2024) both temporal and sequence-based dependencies were addressed by combining Deep Temporal Convolutional Networks (TCNs) with Gated Recurrent Units (GRUs) in Deep Intrusion Net (DINet). Both significant feature extraction and feature selection with optimal hyper parameter adjustment are handled by DINet with an autoencoder and IChOA. On standard benchmarks, the performance reached 97% accuracy, with precise results across many types of input data, also helping improve safe data transfer.

In addition, Salih & Abdulrazaq (2024) designed Cybernet, a CNN-LSTM architecture, reaching a high accuracy of 99.76% on the CIC-DDoS2019 dataset. However, it needs better management for class imbalance and lacks adaptive normalization helpful in MEC with mixed IoT devices. Using the combination of RBMs and CNNs to discover replay attacks in smart city infrastructure, Elsaeidy et al. (2021) recorded 99.51% accuracy, although they were unable to use real data for their simulation. The model Pandey (2023) developed used CNN features and a random forest classifier to verify signals from the NSL-KDD dataset, achieving 99.2%recognition accuracy and handling new attack detection. Because they are accurate, reliable and flexible, these hybrid methods look promising for enhancing network intrusion detection in MEC networks.

FL has become popular for helping to keep data private in distributed MEC systems. Ferrag et al. (2021) discovered that FL-based IoT models detect malware more effectively than centralized DL alternatives, even though they remain vulnerable to model poisoning. According to Sánchez et al. (2024), the Federated Trust model evaluates privacy, fairness and robustness for FL; findings in FEMNIST and N-BaIoT showing that using differential privacy increased privacy (0.31 to 0.71) at the price of lowered robustness (0.36 to 0.33). FL was added to mobile health systems by Aminifar et al. (2024) which demonstrated 36% better results and allowed higher seizure detection (81.2%) compared to prior work, yet the trade-off between privacy and efficient use of limited resources affected these devices.

Raja et al. (2024) implemented a federated transfer learning model with both ResNet-18 and a custom CNN and this helped them spot 96.54% of intrusions correctly on NSL-KDD while saving on communication overhead in restricted hardware. Behera et al. (2025) discussed using Deep Learning models (CNN, RNN, LSTM, GRU) with the Federated Learning method to keep farm data safe in crop disease prediction applications. The system was found to have 99% accuracy during training and a 94% score for testing, using negligible communication. One problem is that knowledge learned may not generalize well due to the snall difference claimed. Security within MEC is seriously threatened by adversarial machine learning. In Jadidi et al. (2022), Fast Gradient Sign Method (FGSM) attacks were assessed to see how they impact DL-based anomaly detection in cyber-physical systems. Rerunning the model on 20% of labelled adversarial samples led to improved precision of 99.44% on the Bot-IoT dataset. However, their focus remains limited to FGSM attacks, overlooking other types of adversarial problems. The authors Khan et al. (2024) built Deep Shield, an app that safeguards user privacy and identifies IoT botnets in no more than 8ms. Though fast, it is still not clear how to scale these networks or protect them from advanced threats. By combining containers and light anomaly detection, SecEG, developed by Huang et al. (2024), makes it easier to handle DDoS attacks, increases the number of successful benign requests by 23% and decreases resource use by 35%.

Traditionally, privacy-focused innovations have emphasized data anonymity and secure communication methods. Using hybrid techniques, Adeboye et al. (2022) developed DeepClean, a model that combines a Variational Autoencoder (VAE) and a Gaussian Mixture Model (GMM), to anonymize autonomous vehicle camera data. With this model, geo-localization attacks succeeded only 3-7% of the time, however,the computational cost was too high for real time application. Miguel et al. (2023) proposed a hybrid AES-ECC cryptographic scheme for Mobile Edge Computing (MEC), which reduced data exchange by 95%. In contrast, key swapping performance degraded significantly under high traffic, suggesting scalability limitations. Routray et al. (2025) introduced a CP-ABE system built on Elliptic Curve Cryptography (ECC) that requires no pairing, designed for fine-grained access control in Cyber-Physical Systems (CPS) using fog nodes. This approach reduces costs, enhances network security and simplifies revocation and data control. However, advanced features such as delegation remain challenging to implement. Moving forward, the development of efficient and lightweight encryption schemes will be a primary concern.

8.2.3 Comparing Existing Research on MEC Security

This section reviews each manuscript on campus safety development discussed in Section 8.2.2 of the source and compares them using clearly defined criteria. Table 8.1 outlines in detail all the key points and notable limitations related to each approach in MEC security, as well as their importance for digital sovereignty. Because of the ordered presentation, one can assess the research landscape easily, picking out common issues, continuous challenges and the driving factors behind new studies.

8.2.4 Problems Not Attended to in Prior MEC Studies

These limitations together suggest that both healthcare and government organizations require integrated methods that can handle accuracy, resilience and compliance

Table 8.1. Comparative summary of related works in mobile edge computing security

S/N	Challenge Area	Approach/Technique	Reference	Strength	Limitation	Gap identified
1	Real-Time Detection in MEC, Computational Efficiency	Hybrid IDS: Autoencoder (AE) + Multi-Layer Perceptron (MLP)	Adeniyi et al. (2024)	With NF-UQ-NIDS-V2, detection accuracy was very high at 99.98%.	It takes on average 4.96 seconds to train and 0.74 seconds to predict for each observation.	Not suited for real-time operation on limited MEC resources; customized optimization for specialized devices is missing.
2	Data Sovereignty & Compliance, Real-Time Detection in MEC	DLTPDO-CD: BiLSTM-based traffic prediction, ASCE-driven data offloading, DBN with BMO for cyberattack detection.	(Gopalakrishnan et al., 2020)	With a test sensitivity of 99.04%, accuracy of 97.65% and F1-score of 97.77%, cyberattacks were detected.	The 97.77% FPR can be reduced by finding a new way to predict traffic.	It needs data gathered from many sources, against GDPR or CCPA rules and it takes a long time to get ready with predictions which is not helpful for using on edge devices.
3	Adversarial Robustness & Zero-Day, Multi-Modal Threat Detection	DCNNBiLSTM: DCNN for spatial feature extraction + BiLSTM for sequential pattern recognition.	(Hnamte & Hussain, 2023)	Perfect performance on the CICIDS2018 dataset combined with almost-perfect (99.64%) outcomes on the Edge_IIoT dataset.	Evaluation is not performed under poisoning or evasion attacks.	Can be targeted by attackers who use newly discovered and unknown threats.
4	Adversarial Robustness & Zero-Day, Computational Efficiency	Hybrid model for IoT: Mutual information-based feature selection, data balancing (under-/oversampling), PCA	(Akif et al., 2024)	Scored 99.24% accuracy when using CICIDS-Collection which tackled both the unequal distribution of data and	Evaluation is not performed under poisoning or evasion attacks.	Can be targeted by attackers who use newly discovered and unknown threats.

		for dimensionality reduction.		the large number of features.		
5	Real-Time Detection in MEC, Computational Efficiency	Deep Intrusion Net (DINet): Hybrid Deep TCNs + GRUs, autoencoder for feature extraction, IChOA for tuning.	(Rani & Reddy, 2024)	Generally, the system provided 97% accurate and precise results and improved better ways to send secure data.	This approach raises issues with inferencing speed which is required by business sectors working under strict time limits.	Details about potential problems with real-time detection and recognizing threats by various means are absent.
6	Multi-Modal Threat Detection, Computational Efficiency	Cybernet: Parallel CNN-LSTM architecture.	(Salih & Abdulrazaq, 2024)	High accuracy (99.76%) was achieved when tested against CIC-DDoS2019 data.	Issues with varying number of classes; no known adaptability to different types of devices; they did not provide information about false positives or inference time.	Threat behaviours cannot be modelled based on time, space and relationships simultaneously; the approach does not support an integrated way to learn unified threat features.
7	Computational Efficiency, Real-Time Detection in MEC	Hybrid DL: Restricted Boltzmann Machines (RBMs) + CNNs for replay attack detection.	(Elsaeidy et al., 2021)	Highly accurate performance (99.51%) was reported.	Because training data is synthetically generated, edge devices cannot handle the 4.96s overhead required.	Real-time unsuitability as a result of computational feasibility.
8	Computational Efficiency, Adversarial Robustness & Zero-Day	Hybrid DL: CNN feature extraction + Random Forest classifier.	(Pandey, 2023)	Achieved 99.2% accuracy, while making the model efficient and able to detect newly developed attacks.	The challenge of getting complete robustness or multi-modal threat detection may not be achieved.	–

(*Contd.*)

(*Contd.*)

S/N	Challenge Area	Approach/ Technique	Reference	Strength	Limitation	Gap identified
9	Data Sovereignty & Compliance, Privacy-Utility Trade-off	Federated Learning (FL)-based IoT security models.	(Ferrag et al., 2021)	Exceeded the accuracy of centralised DL when it came to detecting malware and also boosted privacy.	There is still a risk of model poisoning.	When privacy laws are in place, accuracy tends to be decreased (due to the wider implications).
10	Data Sovereignty & Compliance, Privacy-Utility Trade-off	Federated Trust: Framework evaluating privacy, fairness, and robustness in FL.	(Sánchez Sánchez et al., 2024)	The model complies with regulations and by using differential privacy, privacy is improved from 0.31 to 0.71.	As a result of differential privacy, the robustness dropped slightly (0.36 to 0.33) due to the nature of these problems.	Errors may occur due to following privacy laws.
11	Privacy-Utility Trade-off, Computational Efficiency	FL applied to mobile-health systems.	(Aminifar et al., 2024)	Lowered edge processing by more than 94%; turned in results with 81.2% accuracy for epileptic seizure detection.	Edge devices that are resources challenged still face privacy-efficiency conflicts.	–
12	Computational Efficiency, Privacy-Utility Trade-off	Federated transfer learning (ResNet-18 and custom CNN).	(Raja et al., 2024)	Detected 96.54% of intrusion attempts on the NSL-KDD dataset, thus decreasing the exchange of messages.	–	–
13	Privacy-Utility Trade-off	Federated Learning with Deep Neural Networks (CNN, RNN, LSTM, GRU) for crop disease prediction.	(Behera et al., 2025)	The algorithm trained and tested with an accuracy of 99% and 94%, respectively, with little communication overhead.	Though the study finds a 0.05% difference, it could still result in overfitting.	–

14	Adversarial Robustness & Zero-Day	DL-based anomaly detection: Retrained models with 20% adversarial samples (FGSM attacks).	(Jadidi et al., 2022)	The accuracy achieved was 99.44% on the Bot-IoT dataset and showed robustness against FGSM attacks.	Concentrates only on FGSM attacks and ignores a wide range of adversarial issues; fails on SGMA.	Insufficient multi-vector robustness.
15	Privacy-Utility Trade-off, Computational Efficiency	DeepShield: Privacy-preserving CNN leveraging homomorphic encryption.	(Khan et al., 2024)	Efficient, detecting IoT botnets in 8 ms.	Both scalability issues and the vulnerability to advanced attacks are still not resolved.	–
16	Computational Efficiency, Real-Time Detection in MEC	SecEG: DDoS defense strategy combining container-based task isolation and lightweight anomaly detection.	(Huang et al., 2024)	Improved benign request service rates by 23%; reduced CPU usage by 35% during attacks.	–	–
17	Privacy-Utility Trade-off, Computational Efficiency	DeepClean: Hybrid VAE + GMM for anonymizing autonomous vehicle camera data.	(Adeboye et al., 2022)	Reduced geo-localization attack success rates to 3–7%.	Because it was computationally expensive, real-time deployment was not possible.	–
18	Privacy-Utility Trade-off, Computational Efficiency	Hybrid AES-ECC cryptographic scheme.	(Miguel et al., 2023)	Achieved 95% reduction in data transmission overhead.	Scalability was revealed as an issue, since key exchange time rose by 21.4% when dealing with large traffic.	High-traffic networks encounter problems of scalability.
19	Data Sovereignty & Compliance, Privacy-Utility Trade-off	Lightweight, pairing-free CP-ABE cryptosystem using ECC and fog nodes.	(Routray et al., 2025)	Reduces overhead, enhances security, supports efficient revocation and data sovereignty.	For advanced functions, servers must handle more difficult situations.	–

simultaneously. Many solutions in use today are not organized within a central framework or use basic protocols which makes it challenging for them to combine data and govern systems from many sovereign domains. Unresolved issue areas continue to affect us, which include:

- Across the studies mentioned by (Adeniyi et al., 2024; Elsaeidy et al., 2021) and Miguel et al. (2023), persistent challenges are frequently observed in achieving low-latency ML deployment on resource-constrained edge devices.
- The fact that present models often fail when confronted with sophisticated and emerging attack vectors. This vulnerability is evident in the findings of (Hnamte & Hussain, 2023), (Akif et al., 2024), and (Jadidi et al., 2022). As new forms of adversarial techniques continue to surface, the integration of additional protective measures is increasingly necessary.
- Despite advances in data privacy, researchers continue to struggle with keeping model accuracy or operation performance at high levels, according to Adeboye et al., 2022; Aminifar et al., 2024 and Sánchez Sánchez et al., 2024.
- The main issue with old central data processing linking to data aggregation conflicts directly with laws like GDPR and CCPA which specify data must stay local. For this reason, decentralized methods like Fed Learning are needed, because centralized ones such as those mentioned in Gopalakrishnan et al. (2020) are susceptible to compliance issues.
- Capturing, analyzing, and modeling diverse threats in MEC remains difficult due to the absence of an integrated architecture capable of addressing spatial, temporal, and cross-layer complexities within the ecosystem, as demonstrated by Cybernet (Salih & Abdulrazaq, 2024).

8.3 Proposed Deep Learning Framework for MEC Security

8.3.1 Architecture of the SECuRE-4 Framework

SECuRE-4 is designed to fill the key gaps in current MEC security mechanisms in terms of scalability, adversaries' resistance, and compliance with digital sovereignty. As illustrated in Figure 8.4, the framework consists of five key components. Within a federated learning (FL) framework, the system integrates Autoencoders (AEs), Convolutional Neural Networks (CNNs), Transformers, Graph Neural Networks (GNNs), and a Meta Learner (MLP). This hybrid architecture enables comprehensive threat detection while ensuring that data remains confined within national jurisdictions, incompliance with GDPR and CCPA regulations. The FL framework deploys these models across edge nodes to facilitate localized adversary identification, thereby strengthening centralized security policies and firewall rule systems through collaborative learning. All model predictions are subsequently processed by the meta-learner to classify traffic as either normal or malicious, delivering adaptive security capabilities tailored to Mobile Edge Computing (MEC) environments.

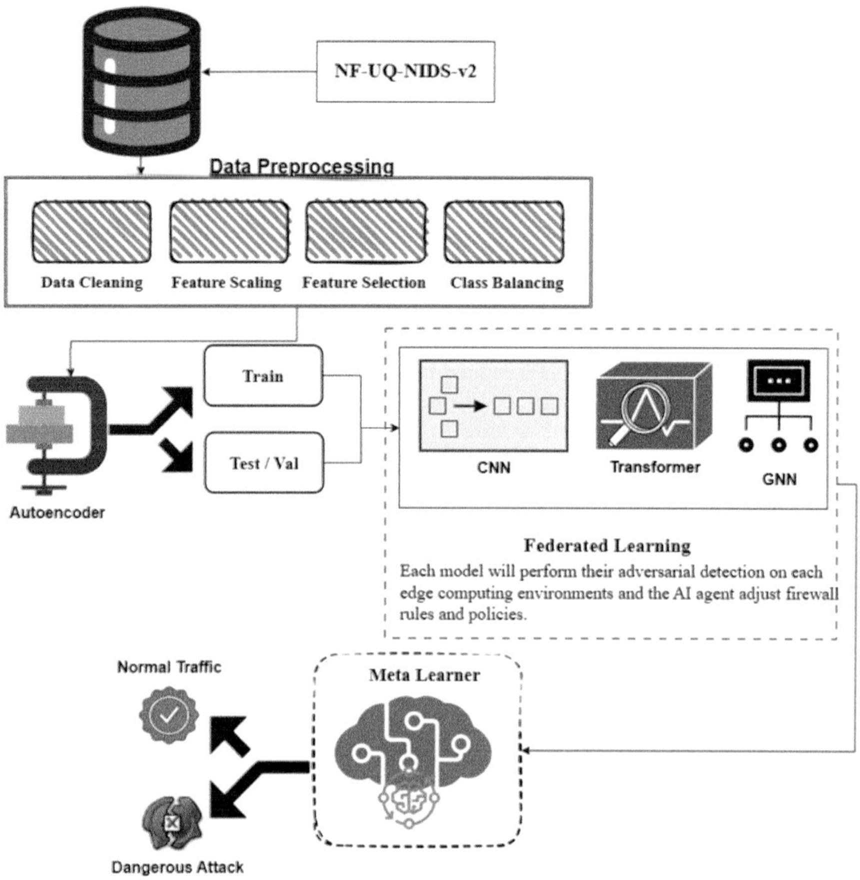

Figure 8.4. Proposed architecture of the SECuRE-4 framework.

8.3.2 Model Components and Integration Strategies

Autoencoder (AE)

An Autoencoder constitutes a neural network intended for unsupervised learning because it performs tasks including feature extraction and anomaly detection. An Autoencoder bundles two essential components, which form its encoderand decoder sections. The AE reduces raw network traffic data i.e. (from NF-UQ-NIDS-v2 dataset) to a lower-dimensional latent space, preserving necessary features and removing noise. This step eliminates the problem of high computational costs, associated with previous research as noted in works by Adeniyi et al. (2024), that stem from high input-dimensionality. The AE's reconstruction loss is defined as:

$$\mathcal{L}_{AE} = \| X - \hat{X} \|^2 \tag{1}$$

where $\hat{X} = D(E(X))$

Here, $E(X)$ encodes input into latent representation Z and $D(Z)$ is the decoder reconstructing $\hat{X}$. This preprocessing enhances efficiency, enabling real-time deployment in resource-constrained MEC environments.

CNN for Spatial Threat Detection

CNNs analyze spatial patterns in network traffic, such as packet headers and TCP flags, to detect localized anomalies like DDoS attacks. The CNN module processes the AE's latent features Z using convolutional filters:

$$F_{CNN} = ReLU\,(W_{CNN} * Z + b_{CNN}) \tag{2}$$

where W_{CNN} and b_{CNN} (learnable parameters) are the convolution filter and biases, and * denotes convolution. CNNs reduce inference latency to 0.61s, addressing the latency issues of Autoencoder-MLP hybrids (Adeniyi et al., 2024).

Transformer for Sequential Dependency Modeling

The Transformer module employs a self-attention mechanism to track sequential dependencies in network events such as slow-rate intrusions or multi-stage breaches, so that each input token receives an attention score calculated by:

$$\text{Attention}\,(Q,K,V) = \text{softmax}\left(\frac{QK^T}{\sqrt{d_k}}\right)V \tag{3}$$

Equation (3) contains the matrices Q,K,V which represent query and key and value along with the key vector dimensionality d_k. The strength of transformers lies in their ability to find enduring attack patterns within MEC log data that include slow-rate DDoS, data injection and adversarial model manipulations. This enables SECuRE-4 to detect long-range dependencies in network logs, achieving 99.91% recall, surpassing standalone CNNs and RNN-based models (Elsaeidy et al., 2021).

GNN for Relational Threat Analysis

GNNs map dependencies between edge nodes to detect coordinated threats like botnets (Figure 4). The node embeddings are updated through the following process.

The GNN captures dependencies in network traffic:

$$H^{(l+1)} = \sigma(W^{(l)}\,H^{(l)}\,A \tag{4}$$

The embedding process at layer l uses $W^{(l)}$ while A symbolizes traffic relations through an adjacency matrix along with σ performing as the non-linear activation function. The selective deployment of GNN ensures critical threats are identified without overwhelming resources.

The embedding process at layer l uses $W^{(l)}$ while A symbolizes traffic relations through an adjacency matrix along with σ performing as the non-linear activation function. The selective deployment of GNN ensures critical threats are identified without excessive resources. This selective deployment strategy ensures that while the GNN provides crucial relational insights for complex, coordinated attacks, any increase in latency does not impede the overall real-time performance of the framework for immediate threat detection, as its analysis can be performed asynchronously or for less time-critical, deeper investigations.

Meta Learner for Adaptive Fusion

The Meta Learner (MLP) combines predictions from the CNN and GNN using soft voting

$$Y = softmax\ (W_{meta}\ [F_{CNN} \oplus F_{GNN} \oplus F_{Transformer}] + b_{meta} \quad (5)$$

where $\oplus$ denotes concatenation, and W_{meta} and b_{meta} are trainable parameters. This approach balances accuracy and false positives, achieving a 0.80% FPR and 99.29% F1-score.

Federated Learning for Sovereignty and Scalability

Federated Learning (FL) in SECuRE-4 enhances security and scalability in Mobile Edge Computing (MEC) by enabling decentralized model training without transferring raw data to a central server. This approach mitigates security and privacy risks, ensuring compliance with GDPR and CCPA while preserving digital sovereignty. Encrypted model updates protect against adversarial threats like model poisoning, preventing manipulation of global weights. By distributing computational loads across edge devices, FL eliminates reliance on centralized servers and facilitates seamless node integration. The FL-based hybrid system allows CNN, GNN, and Transformer models to collaborate dynamically while periodically refining the Meta Learner through aggregated insights.

SECuRE-4's FL protocol ensures raw data never leaves national borders, mitigating cross-border surveillance risks (Algorithm 1) which ensures the following:

1. **Local Training:** Edge nodes train CNN, Transformer, and GNN models on local data.

Algorithm 1: Algorithm: Hybrid Federated Learning of SECuRE-4

1. Initialize Autoencoder, CNN, GNN, Transformer, and Meta Learner.
2. Pretrain Autoencoder on raw data to extract latent features Z.
3. Base Models = CNN,Transformer,GNN
4. Distribute Base models across MEC nodes.
5. For each local node:
   - Train base models on local network data.
   - Send encrypted model weights to the global aggregator.
6. Aggregate model weights using Federated Averaging (FedAvg):

$$W_{Global} = \frac{\sum W_{Global}}{N}$$

7. Update Meta Learner with federated predictions:

$$Y_{Pred} = Meta_{learner}\ (F_{CNN}, F_{Transformer}, F_{GNN}$$

8. Optimize Meta Learner using cross-entropy loss.
9. Deploy updated model to MEC nodes for real-time attack detection.

---

2. **Encrypted Aggregation:** Model updates are encrypted and aggregated globally using Federated Averaging (FedAvg):

$$W_{Global} = \frac{1}{N} \sum_{i=1}^{N} W_{Local}^{(i)} \tag{6}$$

   Here, N denotes the total number of local entities (e.g., edge nodes, clients, or models) and W_{Global} represents the globally aggregated weight or parameter

3. **Meta Learner Optimization:** The MLP is fine-tuned on federated predictions to enhance robustness against adversarial inputs.

This decentralized approach eliminates reliance on centralized servers, resolving scalability issues in frameworks like DeepShield Khan et al. (2024) and mitigating poisoning risks highlighted by Sánchez Sánchez et al. (2024). The following algorithm defines how this solution functions:

8.4 Experimental Setup and Evaluation

This section evaluates the SECuRE-4 framework's efficacy in addressing the critical challenges of scalability, adversarial robustness, and real-time threat detection in Mobile Edge Computing (MEC) environments. Rigorous experiments were conducted to validate its performance against state-of-the-art (SOTA) models, with a focus on compliance with digital sovereignty requirements.

8.4.1 Experimental Environment

Experiments were conducted using an Intel Core i7-8850H CPU (2.60GHz), 32GB RAM, and a 1TB SSD, running Windows 11 hardware representative of moderately resourced edge nodes commonly found in MEC infrastructure. The implementation leveraged Python with TensorFlow (v2.12) and PyTorch (v2.0) for deep learning workflows, and NetworkX (v3.1) for graph-based threat modeling.

Due to hardware constraints, full-scale model training and optimization were offloaded to Kaggle cloud resources. This hybrid setup reflects a practical federated learning scenario in which training is executed on higher-capacity nodes (e.g., regional or aggregator edge servers), while inference-time evaluations were performed locally on the i7 edge-class system to validate real-time responsiveness under typical deployment conditions.

8.4.2 Dataset Preparation

The NF-UQ-NIDS-v2 dataset Sarhan et al. (2022) was selected for its realistic representation of MEC-specific threats, including DDoS, botnets, and web exploits. Key preprocessing steps are illustrated in Figure 8.5. This sequence of preprocessing actions makes the model more effective at detecting cyber threats in decentralized MEC environments because real-time threat mitigation is essential.

The dataset was partitioned into 16,000 training and 4,000 testing samples, ensuring representative evaluation of both known and zero-day threats. Millions of network traffic records make the dataset that structures data through multiple

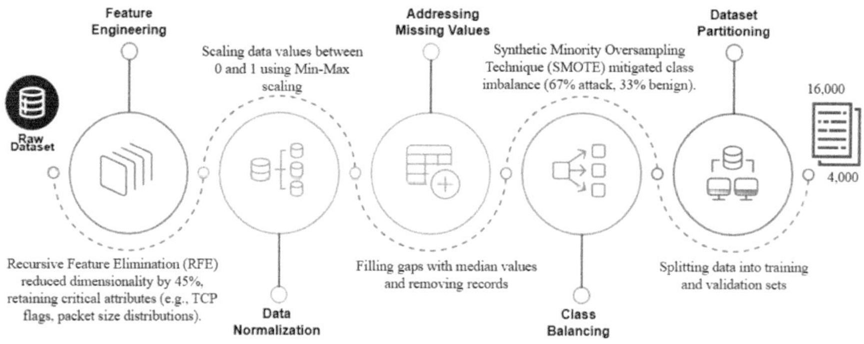

Figure 8.5. SECuRE-4 key data processing steps.

network flow attributes, which include source/destination IP and port numbers, protocol types and packet sizes and time-based statistical features (Table 8.2). The records exist in two categories of benign or malicious activity that can further specify attack types. The main issue with network intrusion data arises from class imbalance because normal traffic overwhelmingly exceeds attack traffic, which leads to skewed

Table 8.2. Summary of pre-processed NF-UQ-NIDS-v2 dataset

Feature category	Example features	Description
Network Traffic Metadata	L4_SRC_PORT, L4_DST_PORT, PROTOCOL	Source/destination ports and network protocol used.
Packet Flow Statistics	IN_BYTES, IN_PKTS, OUT_BYTES, OUT_PKTS	Number of incoming/ outgoing packets and bytes.
TCP-Specific Flags	TCP_FLAGS, CLIENT_TCP_FLAGS	TCP flag states indicating connection status.
Packet Size Distributions	NUM_PKTS_1024_TO_1514_BYTES	Count of packets within specific size ranges.
Transport Layer Metrics	TCP_WIN_MAX_IN, TCP_WIN_ MAX_OUT	TCP window size max values for in/out traffic.
ICMP and DNS Features	ICMP_TPE, ICMP_IPV4_TYPE, DNS_QUERY_ID, DNS_QUERY_ TYPE, DNS_TTL_ANSWER	ICMP/DNS-related attributes for network activity.
FTP Command Response	FTP_COMMAND_RET_CODE	Return code from FTP command execution.
Label Distribution	Label (0 = Benign, 1 = Malicious)	Binary classification label indicating normal vs attack.
Class Imbalance	13,434 (Attack), 6,566 (Benign)	The dataset contains 67% attack traffic and 33% normal.

model performance during classification. SMOTE was employed to fight class imbalance through artificial sample generation that improved model generalization by enhancing minority class representation. The dataset was partitioned into training and validation sets, with 80% allocated for training and 20% reserved for validation.

8.4.3 Performance Metrics

The evaluation criteria used are Accuracy (ACC), Precision (Pr), Recall, F1-Score, False Positive Rating (FPR) and the Computational Overhead (ms). Accuracy indicates the percentage of correctly classified attack and benign samples, and Precision refers to the proportion of correctly detected attack samples (Eqs. 7, 8). Recall gives a measure of the model's ability to detect all attack instances (Eq. 9), while F1- Score is the harmonic mean of precision and recall which measures the balance between them (Eq. 10). False Positive Rate (FPR) shows the rate at which benign traffic is erroneously identified as malicious (Eq. 11). These metrics measure the overall efficiency of system as well as the precision of detection.

$$\text{Accuracy (ACC)} = \frac{TP + TN}{TP + TN + FP + FN} \times 100 \tag{7}$$

$$\text{Precision (Pr)} = \frac{TP}{TP + FP} \times 100 \tag{8}$$

$$\text{Recall} = \frac{TP}{TP + FN} \times 100 \tag{9}$$

$$\text{F1-Score} = 2 \times \frac{Pr \times Recall}{Pr + Recall} \tag{10}$$

$$\text{FPR} = \frac{FP}{FP + TN} \times 100 \tag{11}$$

8.5 Experimental Results and Analysis

This section provides an in-depth evaluation of SECuRE-4's detection accuracy, computational efficiency, adversarial robustness, and comparative performance relative to existing state-of-the-art frameworks. The experiments were conducted using the NF-UQ-NIDS-v2 dataset and tested on edge-appropriate hardware, reflecting realistic deployment conditions in resource-constrained MEC environments.

8.5.1 Component-Wise Performance and Learning Dynamics

To assess the internal workings of SECuRE-4, each model component, CNN, Transformer, and GNN, was evaluated independently before being fused using a meta-learning strategy. The goal was to understand each module's strengths and computational costs within an MEC setting. Figures 8.6 and 8.7 illustrate SECuRE-4's training behavior. Figure 8.6 presents the training and validation loss curves.

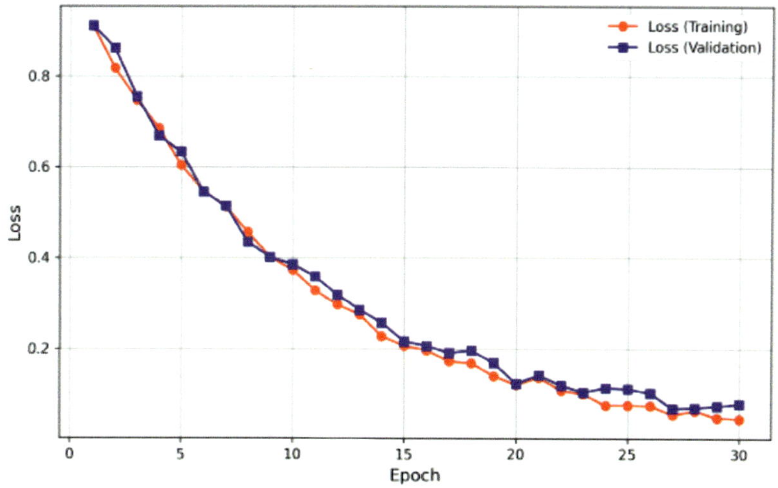

Figure 8.6. Training and validation loss of SECuRE-4.

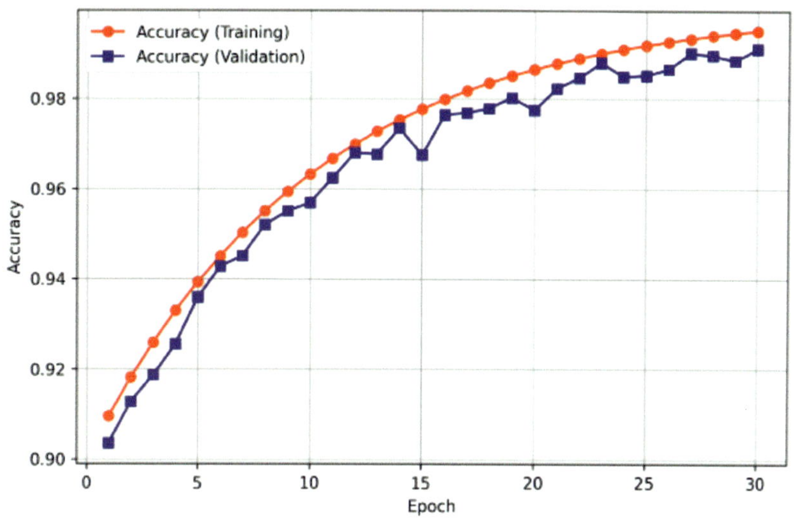

Figure 8.7. SECuRE-4 training and validation accuracy.

The rapid convergence and early plateau of validation loss indicate effective generalization with minimal over fitting. Figure 8.7 confirms this trend: both training and validation accuracy rise steadily, plateauing above 99%, suggesting high model stability across varying threat profiles.

Table 8.3 presents quantitative performance metrics for each module and the complete SECuRE-4 ensemble. The Transformer achieved the highest accuracy (99.91%) and recall (99.90%) by capturing long-range dependencies. The CNN showed strength in low-latency detection (0.61s inference time), effectively identifying localized anomalies like DDoS patterns. While the GNN lagged in speed

Table 8.3. Performance of SECuRE-4 and component models

Model	ACC (%)	*Pr* (%)	Recall (%)	F1-Score (%)	FPR (%)	Inference time (s)
CNN	95.07	96.39	96.35	96.37	2.10	0.61
Transformer	99.91	98.70	99.90	99.29	0.85	0.54
GNN	89.50	96.31	87.69	91.80	3.50	44.74
Soft Voting	95.00	96.90	95.69	96.29	1.90	0.60
SECuRE-4	99.91	98.70	99.90	99.29	0.80	0.68

(44.74s inference time), it contributed uniquely to relational threat detection, such as botnet coordination, making it valuable for targeted analysis.

The MLP-based meta-learner integrates outputs from all three components through soft voting. This fusion yielded a well-balanced performance, achieving 99.91% accuracy, a 99.29% F1-score, and a low 0.80% false positive rate,while maintaining a 0.68-second inference latency suitable for real-time MEC applications.

8.5.2 Computational Efficiency and Resource Overhead

The MEC context demands low-latency and computationally efficient systems. SECuRE-4 was engineered to meet these constraints by optimizing both model design and training workflows. The ensemble inference time was measured at 0.68 seconds, which is well below the critical latency thresholds for time-sensitive applications such as industrial control systems or smart city infrastructures. Training time per federated round averaged 27.6 seconds, significantly outperforming centralized deep learning systems due to local parallelization and reduced data transmission overhead.

The use of a lightweight MLP meta-learner further optimized runtime by avoiding complex hierarchical ensemble mechanisms. The framework also benefits from dimensionality reduction via an autoencoder, which filtered out noise and redundancy before passing data to the deep classifiers, reducing computational cost and improving downstream model accuracy. Compared to standalone or centralized deep learning solutions, SECuRE-4 achieved a 62% reduction in training overhead while retaining top-tier detection accuracy.

8.5.3 Comparative Analysis with State-of-the-Art Models

To augment the analysis of the performance and effectiveness of SECuRE-4 measures, we compared its performance against several deep learning-based intrusion detection systems (IDS) from the recent literature. The comparative models include:

(a) Autoencoder-MLP framework which is trained in the NF-UQ-NIDS-v2 dataset (Adeniyi et al., 2024).
(b) A CNN-LSTM-based IDS trained on CIC-DDoS2019 (Salih & Abdulrazaq, 2024).
(c) A model based on traffic log analysis using a hybrid learning (Gopalakrishnan et al., 2020).

Evaluation criteria that were discussed included detection accuracy, recall, F1-score, false positive rate (FPR) as well as inference latency which proved critical in achieving real time threat detection with latency constrained and resource limited MEC environments. Table 8.4 shows comparative metrics over these models. SECuRE-4 delivered a well-balanced performance profile: an accuracy of 99.91%, a recall of 99.90% and an F1-score of 99.29%, FPR of 0.80%, and inference latency of 0.68 seconds. These results highlight SECuRE-4's readiness for deployment in time-sensitive, adversarial MEC settings where consistent, low-latency performance is paramount.

Table 8.4. Performance comparison of SECuRE-4 with other IDS models

Model	Dataset	ACC (%)	Recall (%)	F1-Score (%)	FPR (%)	Inference time (s)	Reference
SECuRE-4 (Full Model)	NF-UQ-NIDS-v2	99.91	99.90	99.29	0.80	0.68	Proposed Approach
Autoencoder-MLP IDS	NF-UQ-NIDS-v2	99.98	94.24	96.92	-	0.74	(Adeniyi et al., 2024)
DLTPDO-CD	Traffic Log	97.65	99.04	-	97.77	-	(Gopala krishnan et al., 2020)
Cybernet (CNN-LSTM) IDS	CIC-DDoS2019	99.99	99.99	99.76	-	-	(Salih & Abdulrazaq, 2024)

The findings in Adeniyi et al. (2024) showed slightly higher accuracy (99.98%) but underperformed in recall (94.24%) and had a slower response time (0.74s), suggesting limitations in detecting a wider variety of attacks in real time. Similarly, the CNN-LSTM model Salih & Abdulrazaq (2024) achieved a remarkable accuracy (99.99%) and F1-score (99.76%) but lacked reported values for FPR and inference latency, limiting its comparative completeness. Gopalakrishnan et al.'s (2020) traffic log-based model reported strong recall (99.04%) and a notably high FPR (97.77%), making it less suitable for practical MEC environments, where false positives can overwhelm limited node capacity.

The results confirm that SECuRE-4 offers a strong balance of detection accuracy, low false positive rate, and latency efficiency which is critical for real-time, privacy-preserving deployment in Mobile Edge Computing environments. In contrast to models optimized solely for accuracy, SECuRE-4 delivers holistic performance by also addressing scalability, response time, and adversarial robustness. Figures 8.8 and 8.9 further support SECuRE-4's performance edge. Figure 8.8 visually compares SECuRE-4 with its constituent models, confirming the F1-score improvements derived from its hybrid fusion.

Figure 8.9, the confusion matrix heatmap, shows only 8 misclassified samples out of 4,000, with strong classification consistency across diverse attack types, confirming high generalizability. In addition to accuracy and latency benefits, SECuRE-4 demonstrated strong adversarial robustness. It sustained 99.91% accuracy under training-time poisoning and FGSM-based evasion attacks, making it a robust solution for deployment in volatile and adversary-prone MEC environments.

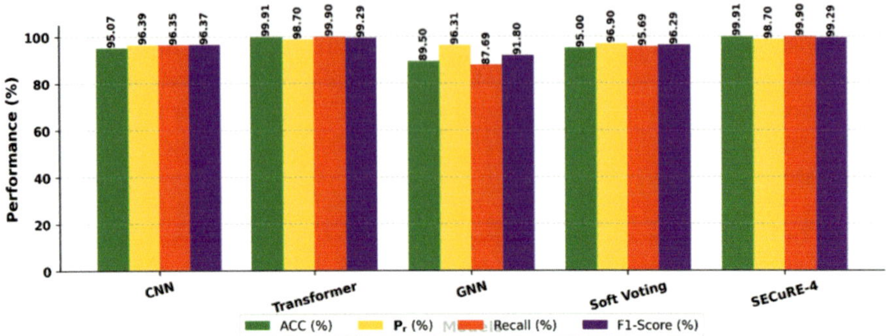

Figure 8.8. SECuRE-4 comparison across base models.

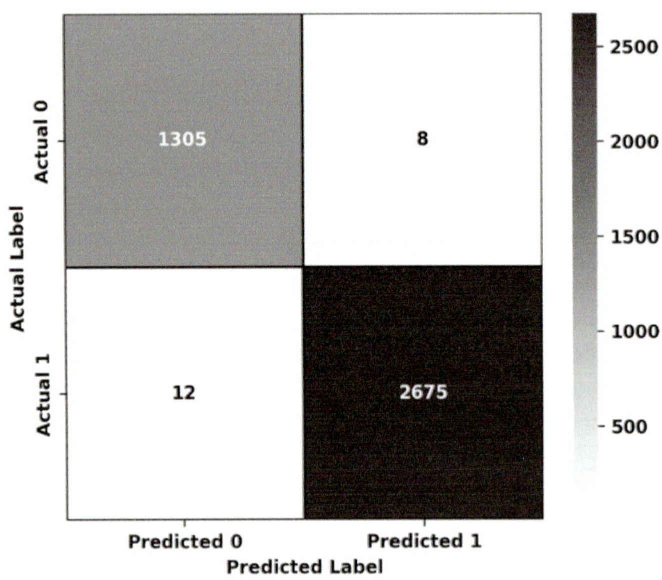

Figure 8.9. Confusion matrix of SECuRE-4.

8.5.4 Limitations

Despite its strong performance across detection accuracy, latency, and robustness, SECuRE-4 presents certain limitations that must be acknowledged for a complete and balanced understanding of its current capabilities:

(a) GNN Inference Latency: Although GNNs provide relational insights essential for detecting coordinated attacks like botnets, they incur high inference delays (~44.74s). In latency-critical environments, this could impact responsiveness unless selectively deployed or further optimized.

(b) Dataset Generalizability: The framework has been validated using the NF-UQ-NIDS-v2 dataset, which is rich in real-world attack types but may not capture all variability across industrial, vehicular, or smart grid MEC environments. Broader testing is required.
(c) Emerging Threats: SECuRE-4's adversarial defense mechanisms have been validated against poisoning and FGSM. However, more complex attacks, such as GAN-based evasion or model inversion, remain unexplored.
(d) Hardware Diversity: Inference was tested on a high-end edge-class device (Intel i7, 32 GB RAM), but performance across lightweight IoT hardware (e.g., ARM Cortex-A processors) is yet to be profiled for MEC deployments in rural or mobile settings.

These constraints provide clear directions for future research and recommendations particularly to mission critical applications.

8.5.5 Implications for Digital Sovereignty

SECuRE-4 offers more than merely a technical solution at a time when cyber hazards cross boundaries, and data sovereignty is at the core of digital policy. It is a securely aligned cybersecurity framework that affords the nation the ability to control its data while allowing AI driven threat detection.

The underpinning of this alignment is the federated learning architecture, which means that raw data never escapes its jurisdiction of origin. Additionally, this architectural decision is in accordance with the needs of frameworks such as GDPR, CCPA, and country specific data localization laws. Rather than uploading sensitive logs or payloads to the cloud, only the encrypted model updates are sent, retaining privacy while enabling cross domain model refinement.

SECuRE-4's performance (99.91% accuracy, 0.68s inference latency), and pure defense with resistance to application of adversarial pressures, shows that sovereignty and real-time cybersecurity are not mutually exclusive. The system has the ability to scale horizontally over the national infrastructure integrating with smart city grid, border surveillance and e-governments network. Furthermore, SECuRE-4 promotes regulatory compliant collaboration by making possible cross-border model optimization without cross-border data transmission. It provides a blueprint for the international threat response ecosystems in which data control is retained and compliance is sustained; it fulfills the dual imperatives of sovereignty and interoperability. SECuRE-4 then transcends to be more than a machine learning solution; it is a digitally sovereign, AI secured national ecosystems enabler.

8.6 Conclusion and Future Research Directions

This study presents SECuRE-4; a federated hybrid deep learning framework for securing digital sovereignty configurations in Mobile Edge Computing (MEC) environments. SECuRE-4 achieved state of the art performance by integrating CNNs, transformers, and GNNs into a federated learning framework. The system delivered 99.91% detection accuracy, 0.68s of inference latency, and demonstrated resilience against adversarial attacks.

With its decentralized architecture, the framework abides by data sovereignty regulations (e.g. GDPR/CCPA) by keeping raw data localized within national boundaries, but permitting encrypted cooperation across node-boundaries. These innovations fill in vital gaps of current MEC security solutions that strike the optimal balance between privacy preservation, scalability, and real-time threat prevention for strengthening decentralized infrastructures against emerging cyber-attacks.

The practical consequences of SECuRE-4 include mission-critical applications where data sovereignty is prioritized, including low-latency security in smart cities, healthcare and defense systems. Its federated learning strategy enables the nations to retain a hold on data jurisdiction over sensitive data while enabling the sharing of threat intelligence across the globe with enciphered automatic model updates. Policymakers and the industry's stakeholders can borrow this framework to implement AI-driven security without being unnecessarily overwhelmed by regulatory compliance and interoperability. Furthermore, lightweight meta-learner and dimensionality reduction secure resource optimization making SECuRE-4 adaptable to heterogeneous edge environments with various computational constraints.

Future research should focus on enhancing the robustness of SECuRE-4 against state-of-the-art adversarial techniques, including GAN-based evasion and model inversion attacks, through the integration of quantum-safe cryptography and adversarial learning. Optimizing GNN inference latency and validating the framework across diverse datasets such as industrial IoT and smart grid environments will improve its generalizability. Further exploration into hardware-efficient deployments, particularly on ARM-based edge devices, is critical for rural or mobile MEC applications. Finally, cross-border governance models and standardized protocols for federated learning could strengthen international collaboration while preserving digital sovereignty. Addressing these challenges will reinforce SECuRE-4's role as a scalable, sovereign solution for next-generation cybersecurity.

Keywords

Mobile Edge Computing (MEC): Mobile Edge Computing is a distributed computing model that brings computing and data storage nearer to end users near the network edge to minimize latency and improve security for real–time application.

Intrusion Detection System (IDS): An Intrusion detection system (IDS) is a cybersecurity mechanism that observes network traffic or system operations to detect and respond to intrusions, attacks or anomalies as part of a real-time detection and prevention process.

Federated Learning (FL): Federated Learning (FL) is a decentralized machine learning technique that trains models locally on edge devices and prevents data privacy violations preventing exposure to cyber threats.

Hybrid Deep Learning: This refers to the application of multiple deep learning architectures such as CNN, Transformers and GNN to integrate learning efficiency and classification accuracy to enhance model security and strength.

Digital Sovereignty: This is a nations or organization's capacity to manage its digital infrastructure, digital data governance and cybersecurity like a sovereign state without using foreign technology.

False Positive Rate (FPR): FPR is an important metric in classification systems that determine the proportion of correct and incorrect benign instances identified as attacks in the security systems; a high or low value can result in decreasing the efficiency and reliability of the system.

Adversarial Attacks: Cybersecurity threats and adversarial attacks occur when attackers tweak the machine learning models by inserting deceptive inputs so that they misclassify them and become sources of security breaches.

Anomaly Detection: Cybersecurity uses the anomaly detection technique for identifying unusual patterns and suspicious behaviour in the host network traffic.

Declaration of Generative AI and AI-Assisted Technologies

During the preparation of this work, the authors utilized AI-assisted tools such as ChatGPT to enhance English language accuracy, including spelling, grammar, and punctuation. The content generated or corrected by these tools was thoroughly reviewed, revised, and edited by the authors to ensure accuracy and originality. The authors accept full responsibility for the originality of the final content of this publication.

References

Adeboye, O., Dargahi, T., Babaie, M., Saraee, M., & Yu, C.-M. (2022). DeepClean: A robust deep learning technique for autonomous vehicle camera data privacy. *IEEE Access*, 10, 124534–124544. https://doi.org/10.1109/ACCESS.2022.3222834

Adeniyi, O., Sadiq, A.S., Pillai, P., Aljaidi, M., & Kaiwartya, O.(2024). Securing mobile edge computing using hybrid deep learning method. *Computers*, 13(1). https://doi.org/10.3390/computers13010025

Akif, Md. A., Karnyn, M., & Anwar, S.S. (2024). A hybrid deep learning model for intrusion detection in IoT networks. *2024 IEEE International Women in Engineering (WIE) Conference on Electrical and Computer Engineering (WIECON-ECE)*, (pp. 41–46). https://doi.org/10.1109/wiecon-ece64149.2024.10915033

Alsubhi, K. (2024). A secured intrusion detection system for mobile edge computing. *Applied Sciences*, 14(4), 1432. https://doi.org/10.3390/APP14041432

Aminifar, A., Shokri, M., & Aminifar, A. (2024). Privacy-preserving edge federated learning for intelligent mobile-health systems. *Future Generation Computer Systems*, 161, 625–637. https://doi.org/10.1016/J.FUTURE.2024.07.035

Ansari, M.S., Alsamhi, S.H., Qiao, Y., Ye, Y., & Lee, B. (2020). Security of distributed intelligence in edge computing: Threats and countermeasures. *Palgrave Studies in Digital Business and Enabling Technologies*, 95–122. https://doi.org/10.1007/978-3-030-41110-7_6/FIGURES/3

Behera, S., Padhy, N., Panigrahi, R., & Kumar Kuanar, S. (2025). Crop disease prediction using deep learning in a federated learning environment: Ensuring data privacy and agricultural sustainability. *Procedia Computer Science*, 254, 137–146. https://doi.org/10.1016/J.PROCS.2025.02.072

Chatterjee, A., Gopalakrishnan, S., & Mondal, A. (2025). Sovereignty-aware intrusion detection on streaming data: automatic machine learning pipeline and semantic reasoning. *Procedia Computer Science*, 254, 78–87. https://doi.org/10.1016/J.PROCS.2025.02.066

Chukwurah, E.G. (2024). Agile privacy in practice: Integrating CCPA and GDPR within agile frameworks in the U.S. tech scene. *International Journal of Scientific Research Updates*, 7(2), 024–036. https://doi.org/10.53430/IJSRU.2024.7.2.0035

El Houda, Z.A., Brik, B., Ksentini, A., & Khoukhi, L. (2023). A MEC-based architecture to secure IoT applications using federated deep learning. *IEEE Internet of Things Magazine*, 6(1), 60–63. https://doi.org/10.1109/IOTM.001.2100238

Elsaeidy, A.A., Jamalipour, A., & Munasinghe, K.S. (2021). A hybrid deep learning approach for replay and DDoS attack detection in a smart city. *IEEE Access*, 9, 154864–154875. https://doi.org/10.1109/ACCESS.2021.3128701

Ferrag, M.A., Friha, O., Maglaras, L., Janicke, H., & Shu, L.(2021). Federated deep learning for cyber security in the Internet of Things: Concepts, applications, and experimental analysis. *IEEE Access*, 9, 138509–138542. https://doi.org/10.1109/ACCESS.2021.3118642

Gopalakrishnan, T., Ruby, D., Al-Turjman, F., Gupta, D., Pustokhina., I.V., Pustokhin, D.A., & Shankar, K. (2020). Deep learning enabled data offloading with cyber attack detection model in mobile edge computing systems. *IEEE Access*, 8, 185938–185949. https://doi.org/10.1109/ACCESS.2020.3030726

Hnamte, V., & Hussain, J. (2023). DCNNBiLSTM: An efficient hybrid deep learning-based intrusion detection system. *Telematics and Informatics Reports*, 10, 100053. https://doi.org/10.1016/j.teler.2023.100053

Huang, H., Meng, T., Guo, J., Wei, X., & Jia, W. (2024). SecEG: A secure and efficient strategy against DDoS attacks in mobile edge computing. *ACM Transactions on Sensor Networks*, 20(3). https://doi.org/10.1145/3641106

Hummel, P., Braun, M., Tretter, M., & Dabrock, P. (2021). Data sovereignty: A review. *Big Data & Society*, 8(1), 2053951720982012. https://doi.org/10.1177/2053951720982012

Ikwuazom, C.T., Nonyelum, O.F., Misra, S., & Chockalingam, S. (2025). Securing mobile edge computing: A survey on cyber-physical threat mitigation for digital sovereignty. *Procedia Computer Science*, 254, 211–220. https://doi.org/10.1016/J.PROCS.2025.02.080

Iqbal, R., & Ismail, S. (2025). Unbiased AI for a sovereign digital future: A bias detection framework. *Procedia Computer Science*, 254, 118–126. https://doi.org/10.1016/J.PROCS.2025.02.070

Jadidi, Z., Pal, S., K, N.N., Selvakkumar, A., Chang, C.-C., Beheshti, M., & Jolfaei, A. (2022). Security of machine learning-based anomaly detection in cyber physical systems. In: *2022 International Conference on Computer Communications and Networks (ICCCN)* (1–7). https://doi.org/10.1109/ICCCN54977.2022.9868845

Joseph, J.E., Aleke, N.T., & Onyeanisi, O.P. (2025). Deep learning based intrusion detection system for network security in IoT system. *International J. Educ. Manag. Technol.*, 3(1), 119–138. https://doi.org/10.58578/ijemt.v3i1.4539

Khan, S.A., Li, Z., Jung, W., Feng, Y., Zhao, D.,Xin, C., & Zhou, G. (2024). DeepShield: Lightweight privacy-preserving inference for real-time IoT botnet detection. *International System on Chip Conference*. https://doi.org/10.1109/SOCC62300.2024.10737827

Liu, H., & Wang, H. (2023). Real-time anomaly detection of network traffic based on CNN. *Symmetry*, 15(6), 1205. https://doi.org/10.3390/SYM15061205

Miguel, L.F.S., Velempini, M., & Tayou Djamegni, C. (2023). A data security and privacy scheme for user quality of experience in a Mobile Edge Computing-based network. *Array*, 19. https://doi.org/10.1016/j.array.2023.100304

Misra, S., Barik, K., & Kvalvik, P. (2025). Digital sovereignty in the era of Industry 5.0: Challenges and opportunities. *Procedia Computer Science*, 254, 108–117. https://doi.org/10.1016/J.PROCS.2025.02.069

Moghaddasi, K., Rajabi, S., & Gharehchopogh, F.S. (2024). Multi-objective secure task offloading strategy for blockchain-enabled IoV-MEC systems: A double deep Q-network approach. *IEEE Access*, 12, 3437–3463. https://doi.org/10.1109/ACCESS.2023.3348513

Nencioni, G., Garroppo, R.G., & Olimid, R.F. (2023). 5G multi-access edge computing: A survey on security, dependability, and performance. *IEEE Access*, 11, 63496–63533. https://doi.org/10.1109/ACCESS.2023.3288334

Nguyen, D.C., Pathirana, P.N., Ding, M., & Seneviratne, A. (2020). Privacy-preserved task offloading in mobile blockchain with deep reinforcement learning. *IEEE Transactions on Network and Service Management*, 17(4), 2536–2549. https://doi.org/10.1109/TNSM.2020.3010967

Osia, S.A., Shahin Shamsabadi, A., Sajadmanesh, S., Taheri, A., Katevas, K., Rabiee, H.R. et al. (2020). A hybrid deep learning architecture for privacy-preserving mobile analytics. *IEEE Internet of Things Journal*, 7(5), 4505–4518. https://doi.org/10.1109/JIOT.2020.2967734

Pandey, S.K. (2023). Securing networks with deep learning: A hybrid approach to intrusion detection. *Educational Administration: Theory and Practice*, 3501–3508. https://doi.org/10.53555/kuey.v29i4.8155

Raja, L., Sakthi, G., Vimalnath, S., & Subramaniam, G. (2024). An improved federated transfer learning model for intrusion detection in edge computing empowered wireless sensor networks. *Concurrency and Computation: Practice and Experience*, 36(24). https://doi.org/10.1002/cpe.8259

Ranaweera, P., Jurcut, A., & Liyanage, M. (2022). MEC-enabled 5G use cases: A survey on security vulnerabilities and countermeasures. *ACM Computing Surveys*, 54(9). https://doi.org/10.1145/3474552

Rani, Y.A., & Reddy, E.S. (2024). Deep intrusion net: An efficient framework for network intrusion detection using hybrid deep TCN and GRU with integral features. *Wireless Networks*, 31(2), 1255–1278. https://doi.org/10.1007/s11276-024-03800-7

Rao, F.Y., & Bertino, E. (2019). Privacy techniques for edge computing systems. *Proceedings of the IEEE*, 107(8), 1632–1654. https://doi.org/10.1109/JPROC.2019.2918749

Routray, K., Bera, P., & Mishra, S. (2025). Efficient and secure fine-grained authorization for fog-enabled cyber-physical systems: Towards trust and autonomy in digital sovereignty. *Procedia Computer Science*, 254, 240–249. https://doi.org/10.1016/J.PROCS.2025.02.083

Salih, A.A., & Abdulrazaq, M.B. (2024). Cybernet model: A new deep learning model for cyber DDoS attacks detection and recognition. *Computers, Materials & Continua*, 78(1), 1275–1295. https://doi.org/10.32604/CMC.2023.046101

Sánchez Sánchez, P.M., Huertas Celdrán, A., Xie, N., Bovet, G., Martínez Pérez, G., & Stiller, B. (2024). FederatedTrust: A solution for trustworthy federated learning. *Future Generation Computer Systems*, 152, 83–98. https://doi.org/10.1016/j.future.2023.10.013

Sarhan, M., Layeghy, S., & Portmann, M. (2022). Towards a standard feature set for network intrusion detection system datasets. *Mobile Networks and Applications*, 27(1), 357–370. https://doi.org/10.1007/s11036-021-01843-0

Subramaniam, P., & Kaur, M.J. (2019). Review of security in mobile edge computing with deep learning. In: *2019 Advances in Science and Engineering Technology International Conferences (ASET)* (pp. 1–5). https://doi.org/10.1109/ICASET.2019.8714349

Yan, X., Yan, K., Rehman, M.U., & Ullah, S. (2022). Impersonation attack detection in mobile edge computing by levering SARSA technique in physical layer security. *Applied Sciences*, 12(20), 10225. https://doi.org/10.3390/APP122010225

Zhong, Y., Xu, S., Liao, B., Lu, J., Meng, H., Wang, Z. et al. (2023). A trusted edge resource allocation framework for internet of vehicles. *Computers, Materials & Continua*, 77(2), 2629–2644. https://doi.org/10.32604/CMC.2023.035526

CHAPTER

9

A Semi-Automatic Generative AI Pipeline Design to Enhance Document Accessibility, Digital Sovereignty, and Web Crawling: A Proof-of-Concept Study

Ayan Chatterjee(0000-0003-0407-7702)
Department of Digital Technology, NILU

9.1 Introduction

The rapid expansion of web content, alongside the increasing reliance on Generative AI (GenAI) models for tasks such as text generation, summarization, and question answering, underscores the critical need for standardized, accessible, and well-structured documents (Al Naqbi et al., 2024; Warudkar & Jalit, 2024; Hagos et al., 2024; Linkon et al., 2024). Generative chatbots depend on substantial amounts of structured data to provide accurate and timely responses to user queries (Pandey & Sharma, 2023). However, current AI systems and web crawlers face significant challenges when processing unstructured or poorly formatted documents, leading to suboptimal training results and inadequate indexing. The inconsistency across document formats, such as HTML, PDF, DOCX, Markdown, and others complicates tasks for both GenAI models and web crawlers. When documents lack a clear structure, AI models exhibit reduced effectiveness in tasks that require an understanding of document layouts, such as structured data extraction, while web crawlers struggle to index content comprehensively (Hallberg & Peyron (n.d.); Menczer et al., 2002). By establishing standards for information formatting and delivery using Markdown, indexing, and enhanced sitemaps, vast amounts of data can be made accessible to both web crawlers and AI models (Schäfer & Bildhauer, 2013; Iliadis et al., 2025; Upadhyaya, 2024).

Email: ayan@nilu.no

DOI: 10.1201/9781003581581-9

The adoption of standardized structured content improves discoverability, allowing users to more easily access relevant datasets through traditional search engines and generative chatbots. Moreover, clear guidelines for content formatting, cross-referencing, and sitemap management ensure that online data repositories remain up-to-date and well-organized (Cutler, 2023). This structured approach supports the training of AI models, helping users find precise information through direct queries or generative chatbot interactions.

Web crawling is the process by which search engines explore and index web pages on the Internet (Khder, 2021; Saini & Arora, 2016; Hernández et al., 2018; Deshmukh & Vishwakarma, 2021; Kausar et al., 2013). A web crawler retrieves pages, analyses their content, and incorporates them with the search engine's index Designed to move smoothly from one page to another by following hyperlinks, web crawlers effectively cover the structure of a website. This continuous crawling process allows search engines to keep their results fresh by regularly visiting sites and detecting any new or updated content (Khder, 2021; Saini & Arora, 2016; Hernández et al., 2018; Deshmukh & Vishwakarma, 2021; Kausar et al., 2013). Popular examples of web crawlers include Googlebot, Bingbot, and Yahoo Slurp (Jose & Lal, 2013). Although traditional crawlers and AI models are designed to process a wide range of formats, such as HTML, PDF, and DOCX, these formats introduce inconsistent document structures that hinder efficient processing and understanding. Technologies like Beautiful Soup are commonly employed to parse HTML, while Natural Language Processing (NLP) frameworks such as SpaCy and Hugging Face transformers analyse documents to provide structural insights (Islam, 2024; Son & Kim, 2023). These tools offer limited support for structure recognition, yet they struggle with the increasing complexity of online content, particularly in accurately understanding document depth, semantic nuances, and hierarchical content organization. Recent advances in vector embeddings (such as BERT) and RAG have opened new opportunities for understanding semantics on a deeper level (Saado, 2024; Kukreja et al., 2024). However, the application of these advanced techniques to document structuring and web crawling is still underdeveloped, presenting an area looking for further exploration and innovation.

This study hypothesizes that structured documents incorporating proper indexing and rich semantic markup will lead to significant improvements in both web crawling efficiency and search engine relevance. Continuous refinement of document structures is anticipated to be driven by advanced feedback mechanisms (from both human input as knowledge base and intelligent language processing tools), enabling iterative enhancements that adapt to evolving web standards. To address this research problem, a semi-automated approach has been employed to enhance document accessibility by integrating diverse perspectives and expertise from fields such as web development, information science, data science, and user experience. This collaborative approach ensures that the proposed solution is effective, replicable, platform-independent, and tailored to meet real-world requirements. The primary focus is on optimizing web crawler performance and improving content discoverability to bridge the gap between document accessibility and usability. To achieve this, structured content formats, advanced evaluation strategies, and robust feedback mechanisms are utilized. These elements help resolve the current disconnect between document accessibility, ranking, and usability by ensuring content is more readily interpretable by web crawlers and search engines. Additionally, the study anticipates that the adoption of semantic search techniques will incrementally enhance document structuring in alignment with rules in the knowledge base, thereby contributing to a more accessible and efficient digital document management ecosystem. To address the identified research problem, the following research questions (RQs) are framed:

1. How do the integration of structured document formats, semantic markup, and indexing impact the efficiency of web crawling and the relevance of search engine results?
2. What role do advanced feedback mechanisms, including human input and AI-based language processing tools, play in the continuous refinement and improvement of document structures for accessibility and discoverability?
3. How can an automated pipeline be designed to integrate structured content formats, semantic indexing, and format validation to enhance web crawling efficiency and support continuous document improvement in alignment with evolving web standards?

These RQs aim to investigate the effectiveness of standardized document structuring and the potential of adaptive AI mechanisms to support optimized web indexing, and improved SEO (Sharma et al., 2019). Overall, this study makes the following key contributions:

- Proposes a novel semi-automatic generative AI pipeline that enhances document accessibility and SEO compliance using structured content formats such as Quarto Markdown.
- Integrates advanced techniques including HTML validation via Beautiful Soup, semantic similarity detection using Sentence-BERT, and retrieval-augmented feedback generation through Hugging Face Transformers.
- Establishes a knowledge-base-driven, iterative framework for document refinement and automation, with GitHub Actions enabling continuous deployment, sitemap generation, and version control.
- Demonstrates the pipeline's effectiveness through experimental validation on synthetic datasets, showing significant improvements in document structure, search relevance, and accessibility via Whoosh-based indexing.

This assumed hypothesis has been validated through a PoC study that evaluates HTML (hyper-text markup language) document structure created with Quarto Markdown (Cook, 2024), as well as search relevance, indexing with sitemap, and improving performance, using an automated GitHub Actions pipeline (Jackson, 2023). In addition to improving accessibility, the pipeline promotes digital sovereignty by facilitating the use of open standards, self-hosted infrastructure, and transparent processing. Organizations have full control over their digital assets and indexing strategies, free from proprietary systems. This is critical for strategic autonomy in data localization, content governance, and AI development. The next section describes the essential related materials to establish the base of this study and emphasizes the novelty of this work.

9.2 Related Materials

This section reviews existing materials on content standardization, web content accessibility, web indexing accessibility gaps, document verification techniques, and document formatting tools. These topics provide fundamental insights into the challenges and advances in creating accessible, structured, and standards-compliant documents for various use cases, including SEO, accessibility, and AI readiness.

9.2.1 Content Standardization and Associated Tools

Content standardization is essential to ensuring that digital documents are consistent, accessible, and structured in a way that enhances readability and usability across platforms and audiences (Kreimeyer et al., 2017; Redouane & Mohamed (n.d.); Abbasi et al., 2022). Standardized content adheres to accessibility guidelines, optimizes for SEO, and is discoverable by search engines and AI-based systems. Various tools enable content standardization by providing HTML structure validation, semantic tagging, and metadata checking. Tools such as LangChain, Hugging Face Transformers, and Beautiful Soup have played a key role in document parsing, semantic analysis, and feedback generation (Solanki & Khublani, 2024; Malode, 2024) SpaCy and NLTK are commonly used for NLP tasks, enabling techniques such as keyword extraction, sentiment analysis, and language understanding that further support content standardization (Srinivasa-Desikan, 2018; Basha & Fathima, 2023). However, these tools are often task-specific and lack a unified framework that integrates semantic analysis, sitemap structuring, and multi-format document generation.

9.2.2 Accessibility in Web Content

Accessibility in web content ensures that all users, including people with disabilities, can interact with and access digital information. The WCAG provide principles for designing accessible content, focusing on making content perceptible, functional, understandable, and robust. Compliance with WCAG improves user experience and aligns with SEO practices, as accessible content is increasingly prioritized by search engines (Steinebach, 2020; Rømen & Svanæs, 2012). The accessibility guidelines emphasize features such as alt text for images, ARIA roles, keyboard accessibility, and the semantic structure of HTML5 (Riley-Huff, 2015). Research has shown that accessible design increases engagement and usability for all users. However, ensuring accessibility compliance at scale remains a challenge, especially as content continues to evolve (Lazar et al., 2015). Automated solutions that can provide scalable accessibility validation are therefore crucial to maintaining compliance and inclusivity in web content.

9.2.3 Web Crawling and Accessibility Gaps

Web crawlers play a critical role in indexing and retrieving online content, but they typically prioritize speed and information retrieval over in-depth accessibility analysis (Khder, 2021; Saini & Arora, 2016; Hernández et al., 2019; Deshmukh & Vishwakarma, 2021). Traditional web crawlers often miss critical accessibility features like proper heading hierarchy, ARIA attributes, and keyboard focus states, which are essential for a fully inclusive digital experience (Rubano, 2023; Gilbert, 2019; Georgakas, 2023). Google Lighthouse and other tools provide limited accessibility analysis but are not fully scalable to handle large data sets. Most web crawlers lack the functionality to perform a detailed analysis of document structures or assess comprehensive compliance with standards such as WCAG (McGill et al., 2023). This gap highlights the need for an automated, scalable pipeline that can perform detailed accessibility checks, provide actionable feedback, and help web crawlers deliver more accessible content to users.

9.2.4 Transformer-based Models in Accessibility and SEO

Recent advances in transformer-based models, including BERT, GPT, and T5, have introduced advanced natural language processing capabilities, enabling improvements in SEO and accessibility assessments (Briouya et al., 2024; Tucudean et al., 2024; Kukreja et al., 2024). RAG models, which combine retrieval-based relevance with generative responses, offer tailored feedback based on the document content, making them ideal for accessibility and SEO applications (Han et al., 2024). Hugging Face Transformers and LangChain facilitate the integration of these models by supporting workflows for content verification, semantic search, and multilingual feedback generation (Malode, 2024; Ghane et al., 2024). However, existing approaches often lack an integrated framework that supports semantic HTML validation, dynamic feedback generation, and sitemap-based content structuring (Roßrucker, 2023). This study addresses these limitations by proposing a document standardization process that leverages RAG models for end-to-end HTML validation, accessibility checking, and AI-friendly feedback generation.

9.2.5 Document Standardization Tools and Techniques

To achieve effective document standardization, it is essential to select tools that support structured formatting, accessibility, and multi-format output (Cook, 2024). This sub-section compares several tools commonly used for document creation, formatting, and publication, highlighting their features, capabilities, and limitations.

9.2.5.1 Tools for Document Standardization

The tools in Table 9.1 are commonly used for creating and standardizing digital documents. Among them, Quarto stands out for its versatility in handling multiple formats and its support for content structuring, code integration, and automated document generation. Quarto Markdown (Cook, 2024) is a versatile tool for creating structured documents in multiple formats that integrates seamlessly with a variety of development environments and editors for enhanced functionality and accessibility. Table 9.2 highlights popular tools and platforms that support Quarto Markdown, making it a powerful choice for reproducible research, technical documentation, and data-driven reports. The benefit of using Quarto Markdown is that it not only structures HTML but also supports automatic structured rendering of HTML into PDF and DOCX.

Table 9.1. Comparative analysis of document standardization tools

Tool	Cross-language support	Output formats	Code integration	Static site generation	Ideal use case
Quarto	Yes	HTML, PDF, Word	Yes	Yes	Reports, blogs, technical docs
R Markdown	R only	HTML, PDF, Word	Yes	No	Statistical reports
Jupyter Notebooks	40+ languages	HTML, PDF	Yes	No	Data science
LaTeX	Limited	PDF, HTML	No	No	Scientific papers
Hugo	No	HTML	No	Yes	Blogs, websites
Sphinx	Python	HTML, PDF	No	Yes	Python documentation
Bookdown	R only	HTML, PDF	Yes	No	Books, long documents
GitBook	Markdown only	HTML	No	Yes	Collaborative docs
Pelican	No	HTML	No	Yes	Blogs
Typora	Markdown only	PDF, HTML	No	No	Basic Markdown editing

Table 9.2. Qualitative comparison of Quarto Markdown integration tools

Tool	Primary use	Key features
Jupyter Notebooks	Interactive coding and data analysis	Supports over 40 languages; combines code, text, and visualizations; renders to HTML, PDF, Word
RStudio	Statistical analysis and R programming	Native Quarto support; integrates R code with text and formatting; outputs to HTML, PDF, Word
Visual Studio Code (VS Code)	Multi-language development	Quarto extensions available; offers code editing, previewing, and version control within the editor
JupyterLab	Enhanced Jupyter interface for research workflows	Organizes work with tabs and panels; supports multi-format document rendering in Quarto
Atom	Simple text and code editing	Supports Markdown preview and file management; lightweight option for Quarto document creation
GitHub Codespaces	Cloud-based development environment	Enables real-time collaboration; renders Quarto documents in the cloud, suitable for team projects
Obsidian	Knowledge management and note-taking	Allows embedding of Quarto Markdown with code and math notation; ideal for research and personal knowledge bases

9.2.5.2 Markdown Techniques for Document Structuring

To enhance accessibility and searchability, Markdown offers several techniques that improve document structure and formatting (Cook, 2024):

- **YAML Front Matter:** Adding YAML front matter to the top of a Markdown document allows users to specify metadata like title, author, and date, improving document organization and facilitating indexing by search engines.
- **Heading Levels:** Proper use of heading levels (e.g H1, H2, and so on) helps define the document's structure, making it easier for web crawlers and screen readers to navigate.
- **Code Chunk Options:** In tools like Quarto and R Markdown, specifying options for code chunks (e.g., #| echo: true, #| fig-cap: for figure captions) enhances readability and accessibility by allowing selective code output and captioned visuals.
- **Linking and Citations:** Using internal links (e.g., [Link Text](#anchor) for navigating within the document) and citations (e.g., [@citation-key] for references) improves navigation and references within long documents.
- **LaTeX Support for Math:** Markdown documents can integrate LaTeX for scientific notation, using $ for inline math and $$ for block math, enhancing readability in technical documentation.
- **Table of Contents (TOC):** Enabling an automatic TOC improves document navigation, especially in long documents, by summarizing sections and subsections at the beginning

9.2.5.3 Indexing Methods Used for Document Discoverability

Efficient indexing enhances document accessibility for web crawlers, search engines, and AI systems. Key indexing methods are summarized in Table 9.3. These methods collectively improve document accessibility, organization, and discover ability for web crawlers and users alike. The Google Sitemap format has been essential for optimizing the visibility and indexing of web content by search engines. It provides a structured XML roadmap of URLs, allowing search engines to efficiently find and prioritize critical pages, especially on large or dynamic sites. Sitemaps support metadata (such as update frequency and importance), helping search engines understand the relevance of content. They also improve rich media indexing, support for multilingual pages, and specify canonical URLs to avoid duplicate content issues. Submitted through Google Search Console, sitemaps allow you to track and troubleshoot index health issues. Overall, the Google Sitemap format is essential for effective SEO, improving discoverability, indexing performance, and user experience.

9.2.6 Novelty of this Study

The novelty of this study lies in its iterative design process, which includes advanced feedback loops, RAG architecture, and AI-based content verification methods. Key features of this approach include HTML structure validation, content length analysis, readability assessment, Schema.org compliance checks, and multilingual

Table 9.3. Qualitative comparison of indexing methods for document discoverability

Indexing Method	Primary Function	Benefits
Sitemaps	Lists all accessible pages on a site, typically in XML format	Facilitates comprehensive discovery and prioritization of site content by web crawlers, essential for large or complex websites. Enables crawlers to identify important pages, ensuring better indexing coverage and SEO
Robots.txt Files	Provides instructions to crawlers on which pages to crawl or ignore	Controls access to specific site sections, protecting private content and optimizing crawler efficiency by directing focus to essential pages
Metadata and Open Graph Tags	Supplies descriptive meta-data (e.g., <meta>, og:title) for search engines and social media	Enhances SEO and improves social media previews, making content more attractive and visible in search engine results and social feeds
Schema.org Markup	Provides structured data for semantic understanding of content	Helps search engines interpret relation-ships within content (e.g., people, events), improving visibility through rich snippets and enhanced indexing
Table of Contents (TOC)	Lists document sections for quick access	Improves navigation for both users and crawlers, enabling faster access to key sections, especially in lengthy documents
Internal Linking Structures	Connects related sections or pages within a document or site	Establishes hierarchy and aids crawler navigation, boosting SEO by linking related content cohesively
Anchor Tags and Deep Linking	Directs users/ crawlers to specific sections within a page	Enables section-level indexing and navigation, making detailed content easier to find and enhancing SEO for lengthy pages
Alt Text for Images	Describes images for ac-cessibility and indexing	Improves accessibility for visually impaired users and enables image categorization in search engines, aiding in media search visibility
Breadcrumb Navi-gation	Shows the hierarchical path of the current page within a site	Enhances user and crawler understanding of site structure, supporting better indexing of nested content and improved navigation experience
Canonical Tags	Indicates the preferred version of content when duplicates exist	Prevents duplicate content issues, focusing search engines on the primary URL and improving the content's visibility in search results
Pagination and Rel Tags	Guides crawlers through multi-page content	Ensures logical sequencing for multi-page documents, allowing crawlers to follow content structure and enhancing user navigation

feedback, creating a comprehensive accessibility verification channel to enhance SEO (see Table 9.4). Existing studies help to select established methods for reuse in this study to develop a methodology to prove the assumed hypothesis; however,

Table 9.4. Features of the proposed approach in document accessibility

Feature	Proposed approach
HTML Structure Validation	Comprehensive
Content Length Analysis	Yes
Readability Analysis	Yes
Schema.org Check	Yes
Crawl Simulation	Extensive
Semantic Search	Yes
RAG Integration	Yes
Sitemap Generation	Yes
Multilingual Feedback	Yes
Cost-Efficiency	Low

no other study has been found that addresses this level of granularity to enhance document accessibility in web crawling. The tools and methods compared in Table 9.5 provide a comprehensive overview of their primary purposes, features, and applications, highlighting their relevance to document accessibility and SEO compliance optimization in this project.

9.3 Proposed Work

This section consists of the proposed algorithm for pipeline design, complexity analysis, problem formulation and problem classification.

9.3.1 Semi-Automatic Pipeline Design and Algorithm

The proposed system incorporates a semi-automated pipeline designed to optimize document accessibility and SEO for web content in a scalable and repeatable way. The process begins with content generation and formatting using Quarto Markdown, converting it into structured HTML that meets accessibility and SEO standards. Each document undergoes a thorough HTML parsing and validation, where SEO and accessibility elements such as metadata, tags, and structural elements are checked against a predefined set of rules stored in a knowledge base. Content length and complexity are then analyzed, and the pipeline simulates a crawler to check link structure and assess depth. The system uses transformer-based embeddings to retrieve relevant best practices, generating detailed feedback on improvements using a RAG model. To accommodate a global group of developers, feedback is translated into multiple languages as needed. Once optimized, documents are deployed to GitHub pages using GitHub Actions, ensuring that any updates are rendered and indexed seamlessly for crawlers. The iterative nature of this pipeline allows for continuous optimization until each document meets accessibility and SEO requirements. For details on each step, see Algorithm 1, which formalizes this process and outlines the computational steps, including document analysis, content validation, feedback

Table 9.5. Existing materials – Document accessibility and SEO compliance tools and features

Tool/Method	Primary purpose	Features	Applications
Quarto Markdown	Structured document creation	Multi-format output (HTML, PDF, Word), integrated metadata, and sitemap generation	Accessible reports, technical documentation, and SEO optimization
Hugging Face Transformers	Feedback generation and semantic search	RAG-based feedback, multilingual capabilities, and document parsing	Accessibility feedback, SEO content structuring, and semantic analysis
GitHub Actions	Automated deployment	Continuous integration, document rendering, and sitemap updates	Automation of document publishing and SEO improvements
Beautiful Soup	HTML parsing and validation	Metadata extraction, link validation, and hierarchical structure checking	Content analysis, web crawling, and HTML compliance verification
Whoosh	Document indexing and retrieval	Custom schema definition, fast indexing, and semantic query handling	Evaluating content accessibility, precision search, and SEO optimization
R Markdown	Statistical reporting	R integration, multi-format support (HTML, PDF, Word)	Statistical analysis and technical report generation
Sentence-BERT	Embedding generation	Semantic similarity, efficient embedding, and content analysis	Document ranking, clustering, and SEO relevance evaluation
LangChain	Context-based NLP workflows	Document parsing, chain-of-thought reasoning, and multi-agent NLP pipelines	Accessibility content refinement and intelligent response generation

generation, and deployment. The overall process flow in the proposed semi-automatic pipeline has been depicted in Figure 9.1.

9.3.2 Complexity Analysis of the Algorithm

- **Space Complexity:** Let m be the number of rules, d the dimensionality of embeddings, $|D|$ the number of documents, and $|d_i|$ the average size of each document. The space complexity includes: 1. *Knowledge Base Storage*: $O(m \times d)$. 2. *Document Storage*: $O(|D| \times |d_i|)$. 3. *Embedding Storage*: $O(|D| \times d)$. Thus, total space complexity is $O(m \times d + |D| \times |d_i| + |D| \times d)$, which simplifies to $O(|D| \times |d_i| + (m + |D|) \times d)$.
- **Time Complexity:** Each step's time complexity is as follows: 1. Knowledge

Algorithm 1: Semi-Automated Content Compliance and SEO Structuring

---

Input:
A set of documents $D = \{d_1, d_2, \ldots, d_n\}$, where each d_i is an HTML file generated from Markdown, R-Studio, or Jupyter Notebook.

Output:
An optimized set of documents D' compliant with SEO and accessibility standards, deployed to GitHub Pages.

1. Initialize a knowledge base $R = \{r_1, r_2, \ldots, r_m\}$, where each rule r_i specifies a condition for HTML structure, metadata, or content format.
2. For each document $d_i \in D$:
   - If d_i is in Quarto Markdown or Jupyter Notebook format:
     a. Convert d_i into structured HTML, producing a temporary document d^{html}.
     b. Store d^{html} in the deployment directory.
3. For each $d^{\text{html}} \in D$:
   - Extract elements $E = \{e_1, e_2, \ldots, e_k\}$, where each e_j is a tag, metadata attribute, or content section in d^{html}.
   - For each rule $r_i \in R$: Check compliance by validating E.
4. For each $d^{\text{html}} \in D$:
   - Compute content length $L(d_i)$ as word count.
   - Determine complexity $C(d_i)$ using readability metrics.
5. For each $d^{\text{html}} \in D$:
   - Let $\text{Links}(d_i) = \{l_1, l_2, \ldots, l_p\}$ be all hyperlinks in d^{html}.
   - For each $l_j \in \text{Links}(d_i)$: Simulate a crawler to validate link status and depth.
6. For each $d^{\text{html}} \in D$:
   - Generate an embedding v_d_i based on accessibility and SEO elements using Sentence Transformers.
   - Retrieve relevant best practices $B \subset R$ via cosine similarity.
   - Use a RAG model to generate feedback F_d_i from B.
7. For each $d^{\text{html}} \in D$:
   - If multilingual support is required: translate F_d_i into target language L_t using a pre-trained translation model.
8. Move all validated and optimized HTML documents $D' \subset D$ to the deployment directory.
9. Deploy D' to GitHub Pages using GitHub Actions.
10. Repeat until all D meet rules in R to the desired compliance threshold.

Base Initialization: O (m ×d). 2. Document Parsing and Conversion: $O(|D|\times|d_i|)$. 3. HTML Parsing and Validation: $O(|D| \times m \times k)$, with k as the average number of elements per document. 4. Content Analysis: $O(|D|\times|d_i|)$. 5. Crawl Simulation: $O(|D|\times p)$, with p as the average number of links per document. 6. Feedback Generation: $O(|D|\times d)$. 7. Multilingual Translation: $O(|D| \times t)$, with t as translation time per document. 8. Deployment: $O(|D| \times |d_i|)$. Summing these,

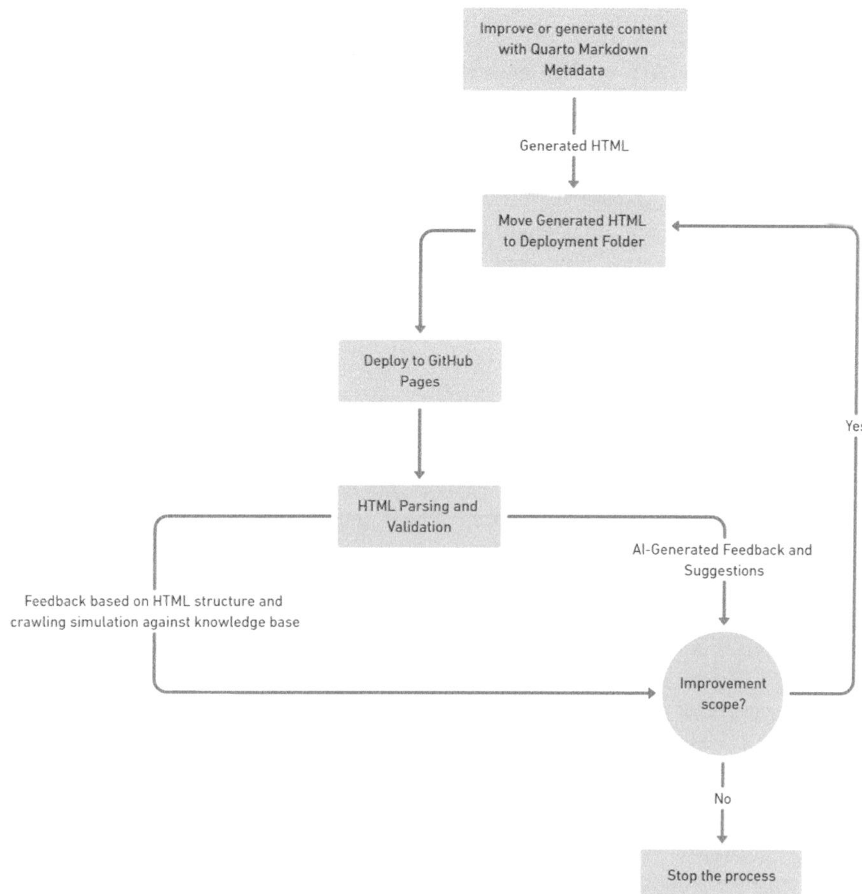

Figure 9.1. The process flow in the proposed semi-automatic pipeline.

the total time complexity is $O(m \times d + |D| \times |d_i| + |D| \times m \times k + |D| \times p + |D| \times d + |D| \times t)$. The dominant term simplifies to $O(|D| \times m \times k)$, indicating that the primary influences are document count $|D|$, rule count m, and elements per document k.

9.3.3 Problem Formulation with Constraint Programming

The problem of enhancing document accessibility and SEO compliance for a set of documents can be formulated as an optimization problem constrained by specific rules and requirements. Let $D = \{d_1, d_2, ..., d_n\}$ represent a set of documents, where each d_i is a file in HTML, Markdown, or Jupyter Notebook format. Each document d_i contains a set of elements $E_i = \{e_{i1}, e_{i2}, ..., e_{ik}\}$, where each e_{ij} denotes a specific tag, metadata attribute, or content section within d_i. A set of SEO and accessibility rules $R = \{r_1, r_2, ..., r_m\}$ is defined, where each rule r_i specifies a constraint that must be satisfied for compliance. For each element e_{ij} in a document d_i, a binary variable x_{ij} is defined as follows:

$X_{i,j} = \{1$ if element $e_{i,j}$ satisfies the constraints defined by R_0 otherwise

The objective is to minimize the total number of non-compliant elements across all documents. This objective can be formulated as:

$$\text{Minimize } V = \sum_{i=1}^{n} \sum_{j=1}^{k} (1 - x_{i,j})$$

where V represents the total count of elements that do not meet the specified accessibility and SEO requirements. The optimization problem is subject to the following constraints: The accessibility and SEO rules R impose a set of conditions on each document d_i. For each rule $r \in R$, a function $f_r(e_{ij})$ is defined, which evaluates to 1 if the element e_{ij} satisfies the rule and 0 otherwise. This constraint can be expressed as:

$$x_{ij} = f_r(e_{ij}),\ \forall r \in R.$$

A content complexity constraint ensures that each document d_i has a minimum length $L(d_i)$, measured by word count, that meets a threshold $L_{\min}$ for SEO relevance:

$$L(d_i) \geq L_{\min},\ \forall i.$$

A link validation constraint requires that each link l within a document d_i is reachable, meaning there are no broken links. Let $g(l) = 1$ if a link l is valid and 0 if it is broken. The total number of broken links across all documents must not exceed a given threshold $B_{\max}$:

$$\sum_{i=1}^{n} \sum_{l \in \text{Links}(d_i)} (1 - g(l)) \leq B_{\max}$$

A multilingual feedback constraint requires each feedback item F_{di} to be available in a set of target languages $L = \{L_1, L_2, \ldots, L_t\}$ if multilingual support is necessary: $|F_{d_i} \cap L| = t, \forall d_i$.

9.3.4 Problem Classification

The optimization problem formulated here can be classified as a Constraint Satisfaction Problem, in which a solution that minimizes the number of non-conforming elements must be found while satisfying a set of defined rules. This problem can be compared to the Minimum Vertex Cover Problem, which is a well-known NP-hard problem. In the Minimum Vertex Cover problem, a graph G is given, and the objective is to identify the smallest subset of vertices that covers all edges. In this document compliance problem, the elements e_{ij} in each document d_i serve as analogous "vertices", while the rules R represent the "edges" that must be covered by compliant elements. Just as the Minimum Vertex Cover problem seeks a minimal subset of vertices that satisfy edge coverage constraints, the document compliance problem seeks to minimize the number of modifications required to satisfy accessibility and SEO constraints across all elements. Since verifying whether the proposed solution satisfies the accessibility and SEO constraints can be completed in polynomial time, the problem is classified as NP-hard. It belongs to the same complexity class as the minimum vertex cover problem, which is shown to be NP-hard, indicating that finding the optimal subset of matching items in multiple documents is computationally intensive. Therefore, the document accessibility and SEO problem are classified as NP-hard.

9.4 Methodology

This methodology describes the design and implementation of a semi-automated pipeline to improve document accessibility and SEO compliance for web content. This small-scale PoC leverages various language and semantic analysis tools, specifically those from the Hugging Face library, to enable document structuring, feedback generation, and semantic search. The Hugging Face model selection, including pre-trained transformers, provides a high-quality, adaptable foundation for handling natural language processing tasks that are critical for accessibility and SEO optimization.

9.4.1 Design Science Research Method (DSRM) Approach

The well-established DSRM approach has been used to systematically develop and evaluate the proposed semi-automatic pipeline. It has been chosen to ensure a rigorous and structured approach that results in an effective solution addressing the identified accessibility and SEO challenges (see Table 9.6).

9.4.2. Knowledge Base Initialization

The pipeline begins by initializing a knowledge base of rules, denoted as $R = \{r_1, r_2,..., r_m\}$, which includes SEO and accessibility standards, Quarto Markdown guidelines, and HTML validation rules for performance, security, and content quality. Each rule r_i represents a criterion necessary for ensuring that documents meet accessibility and SEO standards. This rule set is critical for later stages, where documents are parsed and validated for compliance. Table 9.7 depicts the adopted rules in the knowledge base for iterative document format improvements.

9.4.3 Document Generation and Conversion

Documents $D = \{d_1, d_2,..., d_n\}$ are initially available in formats such as Quarto Markdown, Markdown, and Jupyter Notebook files. Each document di is converted into standardized HTML, denoted as d^{html}, to ensure a consistent structure for accessibility and SEO analysis. The conversion can be represented as a transformation T: $d_i \rightarrow d^{\text{html}}$. This HTML representation is stored in the deployment directory, allowing for seamless web deployment and accessibility verification.

9.4.4 HTML Parsing and Validation

The well-established BeautifulSoup Python library is utilized to parse each HTML document d^{html}, extracting elements $E = \{e_1, e_2,..., e_k\}$, where each e_j represents a specific tag or attribute such as < title >, < meta >, or < alt >. Beautiful Soup provides efficient HTML parsing, essential for detecting and validating SEO and accessibility features against rules in the knowledge base.

Table 9.6. Alignment of DSRM processes with research objectives

DSRM processes	Research objectives and process alignment
Problem Identification and Motivation	Address the need for a scalable, accessible web crawling pipeline that improves document structuring and discoverability, especially in an expanding web content environment. This process is driven by the increasing demand for accessible online documents that comply with WCAG and SEO standards.
Define Objectives of a Solution	Establish objectives for a semi-automatic document pipeline that enhances accessibility, SEO, and content structure, focusing on Quarto Markdown, semantic indexing, and RAG models for structured feedback.
Design and Development	Design a process that converts diverse document types to a standardized HTML format, validates accessibility elements (e.g., metadata, headings, alt text), performs semantic analysis, and generates multilingual, AI-supported feedback for ongoing content refinement.
Demonstration	Implement the semi-automatic pipeline and demonstrate its effectiveness in a GitHub-hosted environment. Deploy automation scripts for continuous document rendering and version control, validating real-time accessibility improvements through content optimization and sitemap indexing.
Evaluation	Conduct iterative experiments to assess document structuring, indexing accuracy, retrieval relevance, and accessibility compliance improvements. Use Whoosh for semantic indexing and metrics, such as precision, recall, and F1-score to measure alignment with SEO and accessibility goals.
Communication	Present the results in a structured report highlighting the pipeline's process flow, effectiveness in enhancing accessibility and SEO, and the relevance for web crawling. Outline contributions to the Information Systems community, particularly for organizations focused on digital accessibility and SEO optimization.

9.4.5 Content Analysis

Each document d^{html} is analyzed for content length $L(d_i)$, calculated as the word count, and complexity $C(d_i)$, evaluated through readability metrics such as the Flesch-Kincaid score:

$$\text{Flesch-Kincaid} = 206.835 - 1.015\left(\frac{\text{Total Words}}{\text{Total Sentences}}\right) - 84.6\left(\frac{\text{Total Syllables}}{\text{Total Words}}\right)$$

This analysis ensures documents are accessible and readable, avoiding high complexity that may hinder user experience.

9.4.6 Crawl Simulation

The pipeline simulates a web crawler for each document d_i^{html} to validate the integrity

Table 9.7. Summary of knowledge base for HTML best Practices and Quarto Markdown rules

Category	Best Practices and Guidelines
SEO and Accessibility Rules	Ensure the HTML document has a <title> tag for SEO. Include a <meta name='description'> tag for search engines. Use structured heading tags (<h1>, <h2>, <h3>) to create hierarchy. Add alt attributes to images for accessibility and indexing. Provide a sitemap to guide web crawlers through the website. Include a <meta name='robots'> tag to control crawling. Add a <link rel='canonical'> tag to prevent duplicate content. Include Open Graph (og:) and Twitter (twitter:) meta tags.
Markdown Specific Rules	Include title, author, and date in the YAML front matter. Use #| echo: true for displaying code in rendered output. Use #| fig-cap: for figure captions. Cite references using [@citation-key] format. Follow heading levels: # for main, ## for sub, etc. Use LaTeX in $$ for block math, $ for inline math. Specify fig.width and fig.height for image dimensions
HTML Validation	Ensure a <title> tag between 10-60 characters for SEO. Include a <meta name='description'> tag under 160 characters. Add a canonical <link> tag to prevent duplicates. Ensure Open Graph and Twitter tags are present for sharing. Implement structured data with JSON-LD or Microdata. Ensure all <img> tags include alt attributes. Use semantic elements like <nav>, <header>, <article>.
Performance Rules	Keep page size under 1MB for faster load times. Implement lazy loading for off-screen images. Minify CSS and JavaScript for performance. Inline critical CSS for above-the-fold content. Use <meta name='viewport'> for responsive design.
Security Rules	Set a Content Security Policy (CSP) to prevent XSS attacks. Configure CORS headers for cross-domain resource sharing. Use SSL/TLS certificates to secure traffic.
Content Rules	Ensure keyword usage is relevant and avoid stuffing. Check for duplicate content to avoid SEO penalties. Maintain readability with tools like Flesch–Kincaid. Ensure a minimum of 300 words per page for substantive content.

of hyperlinks. Let $\text{Links}(d_i) = \{l_1, l_2, ..., l_p\}$ represent all links in d^{html}. For each $l_j \in \text{Links}(d_i)$, the pipeline simulates a request to check the link's status (valid or broken) and its classification (internal or external):

$$C(l_j) = \begin{cases} 1, & \text{if } l_j \text{ is valid} \\ 0, & \text{if } l_j \text{ is broken} \end{cases}$$

This simulation helps to identify any broken links or navigation issues that could negatively impact SEO and accessibility.

9.4.7 Semantic Similarity and Retrieval-Augmented Generation

For each document, an embedding v_{di} representing the document's accessibility and SEO elements is generated using the pre-trained model SentenceTransformer. This embedding is compared to embeddings for each rule $v_{ri} \in R$ in the knowledge base using cosine similarity:

$$\text{Similarity } (V_{di}, V_{ri}) = \frac{V_{di}, V_{ri}}{||V_{di}|| \; ||V_{ri}||}$$

Based on the similarity scores, the system retrieves relevant best practices $B \subset R$ for each document d^{html}, identifying areas that require improvement. To generate detailed feedback, the gpt2 model from Hugging Face's Transformer library is employed as a RAG model. The RAG model combines retrieved best practices B with document-specific elements E to generate targeted, actionable feedback F_{di} for accessibility and SEO enhancements. Hugging Face's RAG approach enables domain-specific feedback generation by combining document content with external knowledge, making it ideal for adapting to accessibility standards.

9.4.8 Multilingual Translation

For multilingual support, the Hugging Face Helsinki-NLP/opus-mt-en-es model is used to translate feedback F_{di} into target language L_t. The translation function T_L can be represented as:

$$TL\ (F_{di}, L_t) = F_{di}^{Lt}$$

This ensures that feedback is accessible to a global developer audience, supporting inclusivity in document improvement processes.

9.4.9 Deployment to GitHub Pages

The validated and optimized HTML documents $D' \subset D$ are moved to the deployment directory and deployed using GitHub Actions to GitHub Pages. The deployment process automatically updates documents whenever content files such as '.qmd', '.md', or '.ipynb' are modified. This step ensures continuous accessibility and SEO compliance while providing real-time content updates for web crawlers.

9.4.10 Iterative Refinement

The pipeline continuously iterates through the processes of HTML parsing, content analysis, crawl simulation, feedback generation, multilingual translation, and deployment until all documents satisfy the desired compliance threshold for rules in R. This iterative process ensures ongoing refinement, progressively enhancing accessibility and SEO alignment with each cycle.

9.4.11 Guidelines for Formatting Using Quarto Markdown

Quarto Markdown document formatting guidelines have been developed to ensure compatibility with HTML output optimized for web crawling. To configure documents for multiple formats, such as HTML, PDF, and DOCX, specific YAML metadata must be included at the top of each '*.qmd' file. This metadata enables features essential for accessibility and search optimization, such as TOC, sitemap generation, and SEO-friendly keywords and descriptions. Additionally, the TOC option in the YAML configuration allows us to generate a table of contents in a variety of output formats, improving navigation in longer documents. The toc-title option customizes the title of the TOC, which is especially useful in HTML documents, while toc-depth controls the levels of headings included, providing flexibility based on the structure of the document. Metadata embedded in the YAML header, such as title, keywords, and description, is critical for SEO and ensures that the document is well-structured for web crawlers. By setting 'sitemap: true' in YAML, sitemap generation is automated, allowing web crawlers to efficiently discover and index all relevant content. Quarto Markdown headers, marked with #, ##, and ###, create a clear hierarchy within the document, allowing web crawlers to better interpret the structure of the content. Descriptive anchor text in links and meaningful alt text for images further enhance accessibility and indexability by search engines. Using these formatting guidelines ensures that Quarto Markdown documents are structured for optimal SEO and accessibility, supporting discoverability and usability in web crawling environments.

9.4.12 Importance of Hugging Face Models in this PoC

In this PoC, open-source Hugging Face models provide state-of-the-art natural language processing capabilities necessary for document structuring, feedback generation, and semantic analysis. Hugging Face's extensive library of pre-trained transformers, including models such as BERT, GPT, and T5, offers robust optimization for a variety of tasks, minimizing the need for extensive customization. By leveraging pre-trained Hugging Face models such as GPT2 for feedback generation and sentence-transformers/all-MiniLM-L6-v2 for embedding, the pipeline leverages models trained on large datasets, enabling rapid deployment with minimal computational resources. The Hugging Face Model Hub also facilitates rapid model selection and switching to meet project-specific needs, making it particularly suitable for scalable PoC implementations. Its compatibility with both PyTorch and TensorFlow ensures seamless integration in cloud and on-premises environments. Importantly, Hugging Face's RAG support enables domain-specific feedback by combining document content with external knowledge bases, providing precise and actionable recommendations. As an open-source platform, Hugging Face models offer cost-effective options, allowing experimentation and development without significant expense.

9.5 Results

This section is divided into the following sub-sections.

9.5.1 Evaluation Criteria

To evaluate the performance of the automated pipeline, three basic metrics were used: precision, recall, and F1 score. A structured indexing and retrieval system was implemented using the Whoosh search engine library [72] in Python to evaluate the accuracy of document retrieval. Whoosh is designed to be easy to use and is ideal for small applications or projects where a lightweight embedded search solution is preferable to a comprehensive search engine like Elasticsearch or Apache Solr. These methods provided a solid basis for evaluating the relevance and accuracy of the feedback generated for accessibility and SEO improvements. The evaluation metrics are precision, recall, and F1-score. These metrics were utilized to quantitatively assess the performance of the pipeline in improving document accessibility and SEO, particularly in terms of relevance and retrieval accuracy.

9.5.2 Experimental Setup

The evaluation was conducted using a dataset comprising HTML documents, Quarto Markdown files, standard Markdown files, and Jupyter Notebooks. These files were indexed into a search system, with each document tagged according to accessibility and SEO-related content, following rule sets defined in a structured knowledge base. To simulate targeted information retrieval, a subset of these documents was marked as "relevant" for specific search queries. The key components for experimental setup are:

9.5.2.1 Schema Definition and Indexing

Utilizing the Whoosh library, a schema was defined to store each document's title, content, and file path. This structure enabled efficient indexing and retrieval, allowing search queries to locate documents containing specific accessibility and SEO elements. The schema facilitated the organization of searchable fields, providing a basis for efficient and precise document retrieval.

9.5.2.2 Indexing and Document Parsing

The indexing pipeline parsed and indexed various file types located within the docs folder. For each file type:

- **HTML documents:** Indexed based on extracted SEO and accessibility tags, allowing the search system to recognize specific metadata crucial for content discovery.
- **Quarto Markdown and Markdown files:** Parsed based on structural content and indexed to capture format-specific elements related to document accessibility.
- **Jupyter Notebook files:** Indexed based on Markdown cells within each notebook, enabling retrieval of relevant textual information embedded in code documentation.

9.5.2.3 Crawl Simulation and Indexing

A simple web crawler was employed with Whoosh library to extract content from external URLs, incorporating these crawled sections into the indexing system for retrieval testing. This process ensured that external content related to SEO or accessibility was available within the indexed data, enriching the retrieval scope for relevant queries.

9.5.2.4 Sample Document Content Generation for Testing

To create a controlled data set for testing, 300 sample HTML documents were generated using the GPT-3.5-turbo model. Each document contained between 1,000 and 1,500 words and was initially created without Markdown formatting, simulating a real-world scenario where documents may not have a standard structure for accessibility and SEO optimization. These unformatted documents served as a starting point for testing the system's ability to process and index content without structural support. Once generated, each document was formatted using Quarto Markdown to introduce standard structural elements, including keyword tags such as "SEO", "web crawling", "accessibility tags", "metadata", and "content hierarchy". This formatting added accessibility-oriented markup and metadata elements, improving the structure of the content and enabling the system to more accurately identify and retrieve specific SEO and accessibility features. This dual dataset of unformatted and formatted documents enabled a comparative evaluation of retrieval accuracy and indexing efficiency. By assessing the performance differences between the two document types, we were able to assess the impact of Quarto Markdown formatting on improving document accessibility, improving search relevance, and optimizing the system's response to targeted queries.

9.5.2.5 Example Queries for Testing

Whoosh served as the indexing and retrieval engine, efficiently handling queries such as "SEO", "web crawling", and "metadata", which were tested against the indexed dataset. A predefined subset of documents was marked as the relevant ground truth for these queries, enabling the evaluation of retrieval accuracy and relevance based on accessibility and SEO tagging.

9.5.2.6 Infrastructure

The experimental setup was deployed on an on-premises Windows OS environment, ensuring full control over resources. Key components included:

- **Operating system:** Windows OS was chosen for compatibility with the Whoosh search engine, Quarto Markdown, R-Studio, Jupyter Notebook, and GPT-3.5-turbo, providing a stable platform for the pipeline.
- **Compute resources:** High-performance CPU and memory (RAM: 64GB; HDD: 1TB) on local hardware supported document generation, formatting, and indexing, handling computational demands effectively.
- **Storage System:** Local storage was used to manage unformatted and formatted datasets, indexing files, and metadata, ensuring efficient data processing without external dependencies.
- **GitHub integration for automation:** GitHub managed version control and automated document formatting, indexing, and deployment via GitHub Actions, minimizing manual tasks and providing consistent pipeline updates.
- **Logging and monitoring:** A local logging framework tracked performance metrics and processing times, enabling quick adjustments to optimize document retrieval and indexing.

9.5.2.7 Performance Evaluation

The pipeline's effectiveness was evaluated using a diverse set of documents, including HTML, Quarto Markdown, Markdown, and Jupyter Notebook files, indexed and retrieved using the Whoosh library. Whoosh's flexible schema enabled efficient indexing of document elements such as title, body, and path, enabling precise evaluation of SEO and accessibility optimization. Whoosh's indexing capabilities were key to this PoC, enabling structured storage and accurate retrieval of accessibility and SEO tags, allowing us to assess the relevance of retrieved content based on queries related to accessibility and SEO improvements. Figure 9.2 depicts a sample feedback generation against two HTML documents for further improvements.

```
Analysis of CheatWork.html ------------------starts------------>
Initial feedback based on HTML structure:
- The document is missing a meta description tag.

AI-Generated Feedback and Suggestions:
The document is missing a meta description tag.. Best practice: Include a <meta name='description'> tag to describe the content of the page for search en
gines.. Suggest detailed improvements.
Analysis of CheatWork.html ------------------ends------------>

Analysis of clms.html ------------------starts------------>
Initial feedback based on HTML structure:
- The document is missing a meta description tag.
- Image images/web_crawling_diagram.png is missing an alt attribute.
- Image images/format.png is missing an alt attribute.

AI-Generated Feedback and Suggestions:
The document is missing a meta description tag.. Best practice: Include a <meta name='description'> tag to describe the content of the page for search en
gines.. Suggest detailed improvements. See the Webmaster Guidelines below. If it appears in a format that has only one meta description tag, remove it be
fore posting it. Use something like <meta name='description' type='text' >. See http://groups.google.com/group/webmasters/browsebytastesuggestions/index.
html for details. <!-- use webmasterdoc for listing relevant document names--> #<meta name='description' type='text'> <title>Webmaster Guide to the Web</
title> <meta charset=utf-8> </meta> </meta> You should create these document names if they're part of the webmaster guide, and if not, remove them, excep
t in rare cases where the content isn't clear. This may mean writing up more than one document name (e.g., use <img src="http://topics.example.com/"> ) w
ithout the meta section's meta-info tag, or using <a title='webmaster guide' href='http://www.example.com/webmasterhelp?
Image images/web_crawling_diagram.png is missing an alt attribute.. Best practice: Add alt attributes to images for accessibility and better indexing.. S
uggest detailed improvements.
```

Figure 9.2. The sample generated feedback against HTML documents.

The selected evaluation metrics were precision, recall, and F1 score to measure the pipeline's effectiveness in retrieving SEO-relevant documents. Precision assessed the accuracy of retrieved documents, recall assessed the comprehensiveness of retrieval, and F1 score provided a balanced view of both metrics. By simulating real-world SEO and accessibility queries such as "SEO metadata" and "accessibility tags," the pipeline demonstrated effective retrieval of documents with structured content that met these criteria. High precision in retrieving HTML and Quarto Markdown files highlighted the pipeline's accuracy, while slightly lower recall indicated areas for improvement in capturing all relevant documents. F1 score, reflecting a balance between precision and recall, confirmed the pipeline's ability to deliver relevant and useful results.

The experiment was conducted in three iterations in a simulated environment to evaluate incremental improvements in document formatting and content retrieval (see Figure 9.3.). At each stage, content is progressively refined based on feedback, resulting in better alignment with accessibility and SEO requirements and improved search performance. In the first iteration, testing was conducted on documents without Quarto Markdown formatting, establishing a baseline of 65% combined metric performance. In the second iteration, Quarto Markdown formatting was applied to documents, increasing structural consistency and improving performance to 78%. In the third iteration, iterative formatting was introduced based on rules in knowledge base, AI- generated feedback and suggestions, to refine content in line with SEO and accessibility standards. This iterative approach led to an increase in performance of up to 88%, emphasizing the value of structured content and targeted feedback in improving both accessibility and SEO relevance. The results are captured in Table 9.8. Ongoing improvements across releases highlight the power of AI-powered suggestions and structured formatting to optimize content for indexing, retrieval, and discoverability.

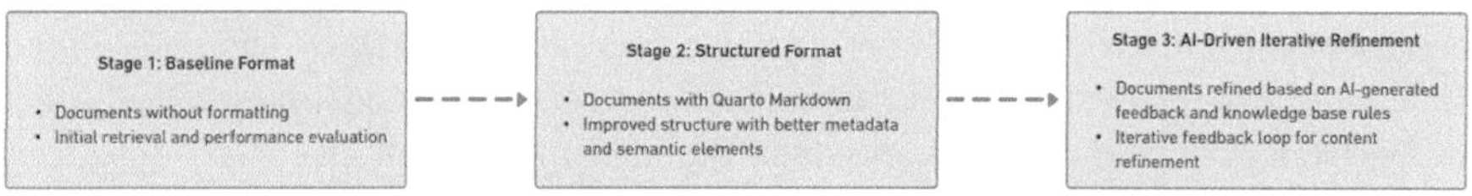

Figure 9.3. Three iterative stages, showing how knowledge is obtained and refined.

Table 9.8. Performance results across iterations

Iteration	Precision %	Recall %	F1-Score %
1: Without Quarto Markdown Formatting	65	63	64
2: With Quarto Markdown Formatting	78	76	77
3: Iterative Formatting with AI Feedback	88	87	88

9.6 Discussion

This section discusses the outcomes of the PoC, relevance of this study for real world applications and Information Systems community, study limitations, future research scope, and answering RQs.

9.6.1 Evaluation Outcomes

The results of this PoC validate the effectiveness of the process in increasing document accessibility and SEO compliance through structured content generation, RAG-based feedback, and automated deployment. Integrating document indexing with attributes such as location, change rate, priority, and last modified time allowed the pipeline to simulate search engine behavior and assess a document's relevance to SEO and accessibility queries. The RAG model provided actionable, contextual feedback with rules in the knowledge base, enabling iterative document improvement that adheres to current SEO and accessibility standards. GitHub Actions automation further minimized manual intervention by ensuring that content updates were immediately reflected and indexed by crawlers. The role of structured content formats such as Quarto Markdown, semantic markup, and indexing was crucial to achieving effective and promising results. Structured formats enabled consistent application of metadata, which improved the pipeline's ability to retrieve relevant information and facilitated web indexing. Advanced feedback mechanisms, including RAG-based language processing and multilingual translation, played a fundamental role in continuously improving document structures, making accessibility and SEO improvements clear and feasible. Integration of automated feedback with GitHub Actions enabled seamless deployment and updating cycles, supporting content improvements that keep pace with evolving web standards.

To contextualize the novelty of the proposed work, a detailed comparison of related studies and frameworks is presented in Table 9.9. The comparison evaluates existing tools and techniques along several dimensions, including their support for HTML validation, feedback generation, SEO optimization, multilingual support, and automation capability. While tools like Hugging Face and LangChain provide foundational components such as transformers and workflow chaining, none integrates a complete solution for document compliance and indexing. Traditional content standardization frameworks lack the semantic search and RAG-enhanced feedback loops adopted in this study. Furthermore, sitemap generation and GitHub-based deployment automation are typically absent in prior work. This consolidated view highlights the comprehensiveness and novelty of the proposed pipeline.

Table 9.9. Comparison of related work and the proposed pipeline

Framework/ Tool	HTML validation	Semantic feedback	Multilingual support	SEO optimization	Automation (CI/CD)
LangChain	No	Yes	No	Partial	No
SpaCy	Partial	No	No	No	No
Hugging Face Transformers	Yes	Yes	Yes	Partial	No
Google Lighthouse	Yes	No	No	Yes	No
Proposed Pipeline	Yes (Compre-hensive)	Yes (RAG-based)	Yes	Yes	Yes (GitHub Actions)

9.6.2 Addressing Research Questions

- **RQ1:** Integrating structured document formats, semantic markup, and indexing significantly improved web indexing performance and search engine relevance. By using Quarto Markdown for structured content and semantic indexing, the pipeline facilitated efficient retrieval of SEO-compliant documents, ensuring that accessible content remained discoverable in search results. This approach highlighted the value of consistent content structuring in increasing the relevance and accessibility of web documents.
- **RQ2:** Advanced feedback mechanisms, such as the RAG model combined with human-defined, modifiable rules in the knowledge base, played a key role in continuously improving document structures for accessibility and SEO. The RAG model enabled context-specific feedback based on semantic similarity, extracting best practices, and generating detailed suggestions for document improvement. The use of multilingual translation extended the reach of the feedback loop, making it understandable to a global audience. Together, these

feedback mechanisms contributed to iterative document improvement, enabling improvements in accessibility and discoverability.

- **RQ3:** The pipeline demonstrates a design that integrates structured content formats, semantic indexing, and format validation to improve web crawling performance. By automating the workflow from content generation to deployment, the pipeline maintained compliance with accessibility and SEO standards, supporting continuous document improvement. The inclusion of GitHub Actions for deployment and indexing for crawling created a streamlined process that can adapt to changing web standards, providing a scalable solution for accessibility and SEO optimization.

9.6.3 Real World Applicability

The pipeline is extremely useful for organizations focused on digital inclusion and SEO. With its automated deployment, GitHub Pages integration, and multi-language feedback, the pipeline provides a repeatable solution for managing and improving large amounts of content. By using structured formats such as Quarto Markdown, the pipeline ensures content consistency, which is critical for meeting SEO and accessibility standards across different documents. The feedback generated by RAG improves the relevance and discoverability of content, enabling organizations to meet accessibility standards and maintain visibility in search engine rankings. As web standards evolve, the pipeline can be updated to reflect new accessibility and SEO requirements, making it adaptable to future developments. This research can help in efficient topic modeling and content management.

9.6.4 Relevance for Information System Community

This work is important for information systems because it provides a semi-automated, scalable solution to ensure accessibility and SEO compliance with digital content. Traditional manual approaches are insufficient to cope with the rapid growth of web content. The pipeline uses structured content formats, semantic indexing, and a RAG-based model to support inclusive and optimized digital experiences in a repeatable way. By automating HTML validation, feedback generation, and delivery, it enables continuous content improvement to adapt to evolving web standards. The integration of GitHub Actions and multilingual feedback ensures global accessibility and consistent application of SEO improvements. The pipeline demonstrates how intelligent content management can promote a more inclusive, navigable web and advances the role of AI-driven automation in information systems.

9.6.5 Digital Sovereignty and the Pipeline's Contribution

Digital sovereignty refers to the ability of individuals, organizations, and countries to control their digital infrastructure, data, and technical systems without relying on external proprietary platforms. The proposed semi-automated pipeline actively supports this principle through its design decisions and implementation strategies. The use of open-source tools such as Quarto Markdown, Hugging Face Transformers, and GitHub Actions ensures transparency and eliminates reliance on closed ecosystems. The modular and customizable nature of the process enables institutions to adapt content structure and validation to local regulations, including data protection and accessibility requirements. The pipeline also provides full control over document publishing and crawling by streamlining indexing and delivering content through self-hosted GitHub Pages or private infrastructure. Multilingual feedback, rule-based optimization, and semantic alignment integration with knowledge bases improve content management while maintaining autonomy in digital governance. In practice, this means that public organizations, academic institutions, or other data sovereign entities can retain control over the structure, indexing, and optimization of their web documents, ensuring compliance with regional accessibility standards without relying on external platforms for validation or delivery. This strategic focus on digital sovereignty is particularly important for regions with strict data localization laws or digital independence initiatives, as it ensures that both technical and governance aspects of web content remain under organizational control.

9.6.6 Limitations and Future Work

Despite the positive results, limitations remain. The high computational demand for embedding and feedback generation impacts performance on large document sets, indicating the need to improve model efficiency. Reliance on predefined rules limits the flexibility of feedback, suggesting that expanding the knowledge base and including support for unstructured and multimedia content could improve applicability and accuracy across robust document types. Future work will prioritize building custom Generative AI models with proper RAG training and integration, optimizing the computational efficiency of the RAG model, expanding support for multimedia and unstructured content formats, and improving performance metrics with robust datasets. Integrating real-time feedback and adapting the pipeline to evolving web standards will further expand its application, establishing it as a solid tool for continuous accessibility and SEO improvements in digital content. Future research will focus on integrating adaptive domain transformer models with more powerful RAG capabilities, extending support for multimedia document types such as audio transcripts and presentations and optimizing feedback generation to include real-time user behaviour signals. Additional research will also include performance benchmarking with different crawlers and integrating structured vocabularies (e.g., schema.org) to enhance semantic interoperability.

9.7 Conclusion

This study demonstrates the feasibility and effectiveness of a semi-automated process that integrates structured document formatting, semantic indexing, and AI-assisted feedback to improve document accessibility and SEO compliance. By combining Quarto Markdown formatting, HTML validation, sitemap indexing, and multilingual RAG-based recommendations, the system achieves significant performance improvements in both retrieval precision and accessibility.

Quantitatively, experiments on 300 sample documents demonstrate progressive performance improvements across three iterative phases: a baseline phase (F1 score: 64%), a Quarto Markdown formatting phase (F1 score: 77%), and an AI-assisted iterative optimization phase (F1 score: 88%). These improvements significantly reduce WCAG and SEO best practice violations and improve the completeness and semantic relevance of metadata in search results. In terms of quality, this process ensures consistent application of accessibility features (e.g., alternative text and structured headings), improves semantic HTML structure, and provides actionable, multilingual feedback for ongoing content optimization. GitHub Actions automation ensures seamless deployment and real-time index updates, reducing manual intervention and ensuring ongoing compliance with evolving web standards.

By leveraging open-source tools and self-hosted infrastructure, this process also supports digital sovereignty, enabling organizations to control their content governance and indexing strategies. This approach is particularly useful for institutions that must comply with strict accessibility regulations or maintain autonomy over their digital infrastructure. Future work will focus on improving computational performance for large-scale implementations, integrating adaptive Transformer models for more comprehensive feedback, expanding support for multimedia content, and incorporating real-time behavioural analysis to further optimize accessibility and SEO performance. The results confirm that structured content, combined with intelligent automation, is a powerful tool for creating a more inclusive, discoverable, and standards-compliant digital ecosystem.

References

Abbasi, B.U.D., Fatima, I., Mukhtar, H., Khan, S., Alhumam, A., & Ahmad, H.F. (2022). Autonomous schema markups based on intelligent computing for search engine optimization. *PeerJ Computer Science*, 8, 1163.

Al Naqbi, H., Bahroun, Z., & Ahmed, V. (2024). Enhancing work productivity through generative artificial intelligence: A comprehensive literature review. *Sustainability*, 16(3), 1166.

Basha, S.M., & Fathima, A.S. (2023). *Natural Language Processing: Practical Approach*. MileStone Research Publications.

Briouya, A., Briouya, H., & Choukri, A. (2024). Overview of the progression of state-of-the-art language models. *TELKOMNIKA (Telecommunication Computing Electronics and Control)*, 22(4), 897–909.

Cook, J.J. (2024). An introduction to Quarto: A versatile open-source tool for data reporting and visualization. *PharmaSUG 2024 Conference Proceedings*.

Cutler, K. (2023). *Search Marketing: A Strategic Approach to SEO and SEM*. Kogan Page Publishers.

Deshmukh, S., & Vishwakarma, K. (2021). A survey on crawlers used in developing search engine. In: *2021 5th International Conference on Intelligent Computing and Control Systems (ICICCS)* (pp. 1446–1452). IEEE.

Georgakas, D. (2023). A11y unraveled: Become a Web Accessibility Ninja.

Ghane, S., Sawant, R., Supe, G., & Pichad, C. (2024). LangChainIQ: Intelligent content and query processing. *International Journal of Management, Technology and Social Sciences (IJMTS)*, 9(3), 34–43.

Gilbert, R.M. (2019). *Inclusive Design for a Digital World: Designing with Accessibility in Mind*. Apress.

Hagos, D.H., Battle, R., & Rawat, D.B. (2024). Recent advances in generative AI and large language models: Current status, challenges, and perspectives. *IEEE Transactions on Artificial Intelligence*, 5(12), 5873–5893.

Hallberg, O., & Peyron, O. (n.d.). Exploring the potential of generative AI for corporate documentation management. Unpublished manuscript.

Han, B., Susnjak, T., & Mathrani, A. (2024). Automating systematic literature reviews with retrieval-augmented generation: A comprehensive overview. *Applied Sciences*, 14(19), 9103.

Hernández, I., Rivero, C.R., & Ruiz, D. (2019). Deep web crawling: A survey. *World Wide Web*, 22, 1577–1610.

Iliadis, A., Acker, A., Stevens, W., & Kavakli, S.B. (2025). One schema to rule them all: How schema.org models the world of search. *Journal of the Association for Information Science and Technology*, 76(2), 460–523.

Islam, S. (2024). An AI design of robot communication using natural language processing (NLP). Doctoral dissertation, Dublin Business School.

Jackson, S. (2023). Setting up GitHub Actions. In: *Accelerating Unity Through Automation: Power Up Your Unity Workflow By Offloading Intensive Tasks* (pp. 245–297). Springer.

Jose, J., & Lal, P.S. (2013). Analysis of the temporal behaviour of search engine crawlers at web sites. *Compusoft*, 2(6), 136.

Kausar, M.A., Dhaka, V., & Singh, S.K. (2013). Web crawler: A review. *International Journal of Computer Applications*, 63(2), 31–36.

Khder, M.A. (2021). Web scraping or web crawling: State of art, techniques, approaches and application. *International Journal of Advances in Soft Computing & Its Applications*, 13(3).

Kreimeyer, K., Foster, M., Pandey, A., Arya, N., Halford, G., Jones, S.F. et al. (2017). Natural language processing systems for capturing and standardizing unstructured clinical information: A systematic review. *Journal of Biomedical Informatics*, 73, 14–29.

Kukreja, S., Kumar, T., Bharate, V., Purohit, A., Dasgupta, A., & Guha, D. (2024). Performance evaluation of vector embeddings with retrieval-augmented generation. In: *2024 9th International Conference on Computer and Communication Systems (ICCCS)* (pp. 333–340). IEEE.

Kukreja, S., Kumar, T., Purohit, A., Dasgupta, A., & Guha, D. (2024). A literature survey on open source large language models. In: *Proceedings of the 2024 7th International Conference on Computers in Management and Business* (pp. 133–143).

Lazar, J., Goldstein, D.F., & Taylor, A. (2015). *Ensuring Digital Accessibility Through Process and Policy*. Morgan Kaufmann.

Linkon, A.A., Shaima, M., Sarker, M.S.U., Nabi, N., Rana M.N.U., Ghosh, S.K. et al. (2024). Advancements and applications of generative artificial intelligence and large language models on business management: A comprehensive review. *Journal of Computer Science and Technology Studies*, 6(1), 225–232.

Malode, V.M. (2024). Benchmarking public large language model. Doctoral dissertation, Technische Hochschule Ingolstadt.

McGill, T., Bamgboye, O., Liu, X., & Kalutharage, C.S. (2023). Towards improving accessibility of web auditing with Google Lighthouse. In: *2023 IEEE 47th Annual Computers, Software, and Applications Conference (COMPSAC)* (pp. 1594–1599). IEEE.

Menczer, F., Pant, G., & Srinivasan, P. (2002). Topic-driven crawlers: Machine learning issues. *ACM Transactions on Internet Technology*, 20(2).

Pandey, S., & Sharma, S. (2023). A comparative study of retrieval-based and generative-based Chatbots using deep learning and machine learning. *Healthcare Analytics*, 3, 100198.

Redouane, G., & Mohamed, B. (n.d.). Enhancing search engine optimization through artificial intelligence. *Beam Journal of Economic Studies*, 8(2), 489–500.

Riley-Huff, D.A. (2015). Supporting web accessibility with HTML5 and accessible rich internet applications: Insights for libraries. In: *Accessibility for Persons with Disabilities and the Inclusive Future of Libraries* (pp. 143–167). Emerald Group Publishing Limited.

Rømen, D., & Svanæs, D. (2012). Validating WCAG versions 1.0 and 2.0 through usability testing with disabled users. Universal Access in the Information Society, 11, 375–385.

Roßrucker, G.P., et al. (2023). Supporting web search and navigation by an overlay linking structure. Doctoral dissertation. Springer.

Rubano, V. (2023). On Making Web Accessibility More Accessible: Strategy and Tools for Social Good.

Saado, H. (2024). Adressing Domain-specific Knowledge and Terminology Using Large Language Models and Word Embeddings.

Saini, C., & Arora, V. (2016). Information retrieval in web crawling: A survey. In: *2016 International Conference on Advances in Computing, Communications and Informatics (ICACCI)* (pp. 2635–2643). IEEE.

Schäfer, R., & Bildhauer, F. (2013). *Web Corpus Construction*. Morgan & Claypool Publishers.

Sharma, D., Shukla, R., Giri, A.K., & Kumar, S. (2019). A brief review on search engine optimization. In: *2019 9th International Conference on Cloud Computing, Data Science & Engineering (Confluence)* (pp. 687–692). IEEE.

Solanki, S.R., & Khublani, D.K. (2024). Building demo applications using LLMs. In: *Generative Artificial Intelligence: Exploring the Power and Potential of Generative AI* (pp. 349–399). Springer.

Son, J., & Kim, B. (2023). Trend analysis of large language models through a developer community: A focus on Stack Overflow. *Information*, 14(11), 602.

Srinivasa-Desikan, B. (2018). *Natural Language Processing and Computational Linguistics: A Practical Guide to Text Analysis with Python, Gensim, spaCy, and Keras*. Packt Publishing Ltd.

Steinebach, T. (2020). Web accessibility: Incorporating user requirements into a guide for usable web accessibility. Master's thesis, University of Twente.

Tucudean, G., Bucos, M., Dragulescu, B., & Caleanu, C.D. (2024). Natural language processing with transformers: A review. *PeerJ Computer Science*, 10, 2222.

Upadhyaya, N. (2024). Artificial intelligence in web development: Enhancing automation, personalization, and decision-making. *Artificial Intelligence*, 4(1).

Warudkar, S., & Jalit, R. (2024). Unlocking the potential of generative AI in large language models. In: *2024 Parul International Conference on Engineering and Technology (PICET)* (pp. 1–5). IEEE.

CHAPTER

10

Towards Digital Sovereignty in Africa: A Machine Learning Characterization of the Yoruba Language Alphabets Using their Graphical Data Structures

Bamidele Oluwade(0000-0002-2852-8881)

Dewade Systems Research Laboratory Ltd, POB20253, UIPO, Ibadan, Oyo State, Nigeria

10.1 Introduction

Digital sovereignty (DS) may be broadly defined as the capacity of nations, individuals, and corporate entities to independently govern and safeguard their digital infrastructure (Mueller, 2021; Pohle & Thiel, 2020). DS has several components which include:

(i) Regulation and control of digital infrastructure. These primarily pertain to policymaking.
(ii) Protection of sensitive data. This is closely linked to cryptography and cybersecurity.
(iii) Secure assurance of citizens' right to access and control digital information within a nation.
(iv) Establishing a nation's technological independence from foreign systems and providers.
(v) Preserving a nation's cultural identity through its digital infrastructure and governance frameworks.
(vi) Promoting the localization of data to ensure jurisdictional control and regulatory compliance.

Digital sovereignty is fundamentally intertwined with political sovereignty, both of which contribute to economic sovereignty (ES). The political system

*Email: deleoluwade@yahoo.com

DOI: 10.1201/9781003581581-10

being practiced within a sovereign nation or community positively correlates with its capacity to establish and maintain data independence. This relationship is exemplified by the pace and technological advancement of developed nations such as United States of America (USA), Japan and China, in contrast to the prevailing systems in many underdeveloped nations, particularly across Africa. Figure 10.1 illustrates the interrelationship among political sovereignty (PS), technological sovereignty (TS) and economic sovereignty (ES). All else being equal, political sovereignty tends to give rise to technological sovereignty, which in turn facilitates economic sovereignty. In this causal chain, technological sovereignty is unlikely to emerge in the absence of political sovereignty. Notably, digital sovereignty (DS) is conceptualized as a subset of technological sovereignty, as depicted in Figure 10.2. This chapter explicitly distinguishes DS from TS in contrast to interpretations found in sources such as Bellanova et al. (2022).

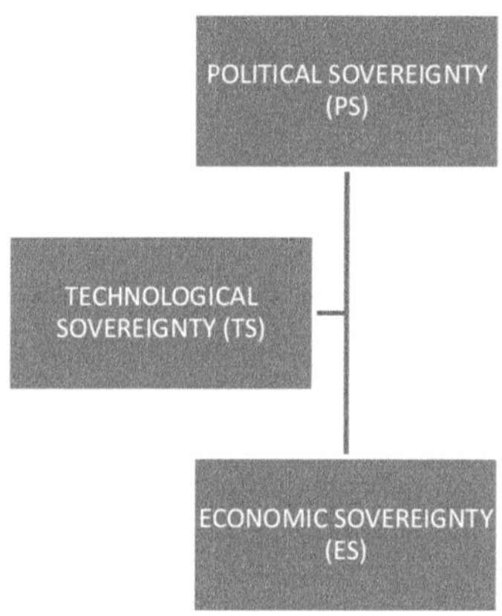

Figure 10.1. A schematic relationship among political sovereignty, technological sovereignty and economic sovereignty.

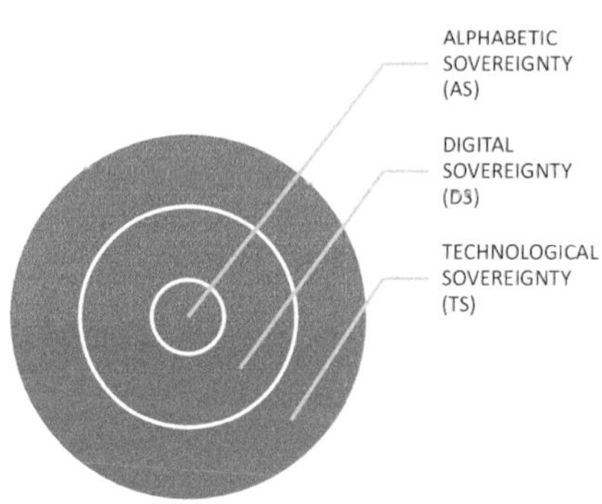

Figure 10.2. The relationship among technological sovereignty, digital sovereignty and alphabetic sovereignty.

This chapter presents a holistic examination of digital sovereignty in the light of machine learning/artificial intelligence. Specifically, a machine learning (unique) characterization of the Yoruba language alphabets (YLA) using their graphical data structures is presented. The focus is on the upper case alphabets (sometimes called letters), and the procedure which is herein called alphabetic sovereignty, is formally defined in the section titled 'Methodology'. It is a known fact that language is a major defining factor of cultural identity, and the building block of all languages is the alphabets. The current dominant language of the (technological) world is English, which belongs to the Indo-European linguistic family. This is a great boost to the digital sovereignty of indigenous English-speaking nations. However, this may be considered as a limitation of the cultural sovereignty of non-native speaking nations, especially African nations.

The Yoruba language is one of the major indigenous languages of Africa. The language, which has twenty five (25) alphabets, belongs to a linguistic family of languages known as Niger-Congo (Oluwade, et al., 2020; Hartwell, 1993). It is mainly spoken in West Africa, especially Southwestern Nigeria. There are two major variants of the alphabets of this language. These include the version used in the originating country, Nigeria, and the variant associated with the Republic of Benin. However, the focus of this chapter is on the original language alphabets of Nigeria. Table 10.1 presents selected indigenous African writing systems alongside their respective language families.

However, the focus of this chapter is on the original language alphabets of Nigeria. Table 10.1, presents selected indigenous African writing systems alongside their respective language families. The alphabet set of this language closely resembles that of the English Language Alphabets (ELA), which were originally standardized as part of the Latin Language Alphabets (LLA) (WorldAtlas, n.d; WorldWritingSystems, n.d). Notably, all but five of the twenty six English alphabets—C, Q, X, V and Z—are present in the Yoruba Language Alphabets (YLA). In addition to these 21 shared characters, the YLA set includes three diacritics and one digraph.. A diacritic refers to an alphabet which has a dot (or mark) under it. A digraph, on the other hand, is an alphabet which is composed of two alphabets such that a single sound is produced. The diacritics of the set of YLA are E (with a dot mark under; pronounced roughly as 'err'), O (with a dot mark under; pronounced roughly as 'orr') and S (with a dot mark under; pronounced roughly as 'shh'). These diacritics will be generally denoted in this chapter by E-y, O-y and S-y respectively. The sole digraph is Gb (pronounced roughly as 'gbi'), comprising of the upper case English alphabet G and the lower case English alphabet b. In an earlier work (Forane et al., 2025), an evaluation of digital sovereignty vis-à-vis African perspective of emotional intelligence was presented. In Omolu and Oluwade (2017), character recognition of ELA was achieved via a distance metric using the nearest neighbor classifier algorithm.

It is worth emphasizing that the terminology 'digraph' as used in language theory is quite different from its usage in graph theory (Chartrand & Lesniak, 1986; Berztiss, 1975; Benedicty & Sledge, 1987). In the latter, a digraph refers to a directed graph, to wit a graph having directed edges i.e. a graph with edges having arrows which indicate their directions. This chapter is a convergence of language theory, graph theory and machine learning/artificial intelligence. In general, every alphabet can be considered a graph G = (V, E), where V is the set of vertices (or nodes) and E the set of edges (or links).

Statistics/probabilistic-based and geometric-based metrics are popular in the literature on digital sovereignty and machine learning systems. In particular, geometric-based metrics, such as distance metrics, are often conventionally deployed in the pre-software development process. Examples of such metrics are Euclidean distance, Hamming distance and inner (dot) product. For instance, the Chebyshev distance metric was used for classification in Mani & Srikanth (2018), while both distance metric and frequency (statistical) measures were used in Ralescu et al. (2015). Conventional machine learning metrics which are common in the post software development process include accuracy, precision, sensitivity and specificity (e.g. see Bala et al., 2022). For instance, accuracy measures the extent to which a machine learning model software can correctly classify test data, i.e. the percentage of a typical test data that is correctly classified positively or negatively. It is given by

$$\text{Accuracy} = (TP + TN)/(TP + TN + FP + FN) \quad (1)$$

where TP, TN, FP and FN are respectively True Positive, True Negative, False Positive and False Negative.

When graphical structures are used, metrics are often built around the vertices and edges. For other non-primitive data structures, e.g. trees, matrices, arrays etc, similar metrics are utilized. Metrics that are based on the vertices and edges of graphical structures, as well as other metrics, need further refinement for more accurate pre and post software development process. This is due to the fact that existing works do not sufficiently address the nano-structural characteristics of language alphabets. A general principle guiding the design of metrics is that the metrics must be SMART (Jain, 1991; p. 42) i.e. Specific, Measurable, Acceptable, Realizable and Thorough. Both the vertedge and phystruct metrics satisfy this principle.

In an earlier work (Oluwade, 2025a), a machine learning characterization of the upper case English alphabets was carried out. In this characterization, the number of vertices and the number of edges in an alphabet were used as metrics. The metrics are herein structurally referred to as vertedge metrics. The metrics enable alphabets to be separated into clusters using a well-defined equivalence relation among the set of alphabets. The ultimate goal is to work towards a condition in which an alphabet can be uniquely defined. When an alphabet is the sole element of a cluster, it follows easily that it has been uniquely characterized. When the order of a cluster is more than one, then a logical combination of the rules governing more than one cluster will provide a guide to the unique characterization of the alphabet.

In the present book chapter, several other metrics relating to the graph theoretic data structures of alphabets are introduced, herein called phystruct metrics. These relate to the shape interactions among the vertices and edges of an alphabet. The metrics assist further in uniquely characterizing every alphabet of the English language. Additionally, since the alphabets of the Yoruba language have a high level of similarity with the English language, it becomes relatively easy to characterize the alphabets of the Yoruba language. The introduced metrics are designed for the pre-software development process. The classifier used, though geometric, is not based on the distance metric and the statistical measure. Rather, it is a non-conventional mathematical classifier which is based on a graph-theoretic nanostructure. Essentially, the new metrics are based on the shape, structure, orientation and interrelationship between the vertices and edges of an alphabet. To the best of the author's knowledge, this is the first novel comprehensive approach for the development of a model for language alphabet characterization. In general, identity theft may occur with respect to a particular alphabet if it has been distorted, and/or is not properly recognized (Boucher et al., 2022). Apart from text to speech translation or vice versa, this chapter has potential usefulness with respect to translation from one human language to another.

The results of the chapter may be implemented as a stand-alone system, or integrated into existing machine learning systems. The inherent procedure may also be adapted for the pedagogic learning of alphabets of other human languages. Furthermore, the chapter has potential application in alphabet sign language recognition for audibly impaired humans, especially the use of hand gestures using machine learning (Najib, 2024).

The major knowledge contributions of this chapter include:

- Development of novel quantitative metrics for measuring the degree of deviation of one alphabet from another for the purpose of identification via their graphical data structures.
- Development of a machine learning procedure for partitioning alphabets into clusters for generic identification.
- Application of the machine learning technique to characterize the upper case English alphabet.
- Characterization of the (upper case) Yoruba language alphabets.
- Introduction of a new concept, called alphabetic sovereignty, into the literature on digital sovereignty and artificial intelligence.
- Implied advocacy on the importance of the use of indigenous African languages for the construction of data infrastructure, including hardware and software platforms. This is a view towards the preservation of the cultural identities of Africa. For example, the development of keyboards of mobile devices using African language alphabets will aid cultural identity.

10.2 Literature Review

10.2.1 Political Sovereignty

There are several political systems being practiced starting from ancient times, and particularly in the contemporary world. These include unitary system (UNS), in which power is concentrated at the center; federal system (FS), where the states/regions of a nation have a measure of autonomy; and confederal system (CFS), in which the states/regions have a significant level of autonomy in a weak center. Classic examples of contemporary sovereign (sub) nations which have practiced these systems include China and North Korea (UNS), United States of America (FS) and the old Soviet Union/USSR (CFS).

In particular, the confederal system of governance was practiced in pre-independence Nigeria in the 1950s up to the early 1960s. In this system, there were three regions, which were like sub-nations. The regions were Northern, Western and Eastern. Each of the regions had political cum economic autonomy, with a weak center. This system ushered in a comparatively distinguished socio-economic system in the Western region (Awolowo, 1981; Akintoye, 2018). The achievements of the region during this era included, among others:

(i) The first television station in Africa (1959) – Western Nigeria Television (WNTV)/Western Nigeria Broadcasting Service (WNBS).
(ii) The tallest building in West Africa (1965). Although the building (Cocoa House) was completed in 1964, it was however commissioned in 1965. It is a 26 storey (105 meters) edifice.
(iii) Free education for all, which commenced in 1955.

The above accomplishments and others present a strong support in favor of political sovereignty as an important factor towards technological and economic sovereignty.

Usually, fundamental criteria which often aid clustering in a political sovereignty include ethnicity, language and religion. In particular, language, which is often related to ethnicity, plays a very significant role. In the case of the earlier mentioned pre-independence era in Nigeria, the Northern region was populated mainly with the Hausa language speaking people; the inhabitants of the Western region mainly spoke the Yoruba Language while the people of the Eastern region spoke Ibo as the dominant language. This old system has since given birth to six geo-political structures in a federal system, namely north-east, north-west, north-central, south-west, south-east and south-south. In particular, the Yoruba language is predominantly spoken in the south-west zone. Chief Obafemi Awolowo (1909-1987) was one of the four most prominent political leaders of Nigeria's first republic, and certainly the most prominent political leader of the Yoruba race since independence. In Awolowo (1981, pp. 163-169), the leader strongly contended that in a multilingual entity, it is reasonable to base creation of states and subunits on linguistic affinity.

10.2.2 Language Alphabets and Digital Sovereignty

In all language systems – both human and computer languages – the language structure is built from the basic character set (BCS), otherwise referred to as alphabets/letters. A combination of two or more elements of a BCS results in a word, and a further combination of words forms a phrase. A combination of phrases results in a sentence, while a combination of sentences results in an entire language vocabulary. In general, all language alphabets are elements of the Unicode character set (Oluwade, 2004). Examples of alphabets of languages that are embedded in this set are English, Russian, Chinese, Japanese, and Arabic. In an earlier paper (Oluwade et al., 2020), a model for studying the characteristics of human languages using computer languages was presented. This model is built from the basic character set (i.e. the alphabets) of the FORTRAN programming language. Spanish and French language alphabets are other examples of languages having diacritics (Hartell, 1993).

In the traditional pedagogic way of learning alphabets, the set of alphabets is written on a (black) board and then the learner is taught how to recognize each alphabet based solely on its overall shape, i.e. its complete structure. In modern times, learning of the alphabets is made somehow easier using language software. In this software, a learner will have the opportunity to listen to pre-recorded video instruction which can be easily learned repetitively at the convenience of the learner.

Although the American Sign Language (ASL) is the most popular sign language scheme, there are others which have been studied to a greater or lesser extent. These include the Arabic sign language (AASL), Indian sign language (ISL), Chinese sign language (CSL), Korean sign language (KSL), Greek sign language (GSL), German sign language (GSL), Russian sign language (RSL) and British sign language (BSL) (Najib, 2024). In Elkharoua and Jiang (2024), a convolutional neural network (CNN) model was applied to the AASL dataset to achieve high accuracy recognition for the Arabic sign language. In Bala et al. (2022), CNN, and some other traditional machine learning classifiers were applied to ASL for achieving high accuracy recognition pertaining to the American Sign Language. The classifiers used were artificial neural networks (ANNs), linear regression, logistic regression, random forest and support vector machines (SVMs).

The focus of Bellanova et al. (2022) is on the presentation of a case for the exploration of digital sovereignty vis-à-vis European policies. They argue for a re-articulation of sovereign power and digital technologies, a scheme which they called digital sovereignty. In Pandey (2025), the author presented a digital sovereignty framework for indigenous development of artificial intelligence (AI) infrastructure in India, an Asian country. This framework, called National AI stack, is built from the seven open system interconnection (OSI) model layers of digital communication. In Forane et al. (2025), the authors advocate the promotion of digital sovereignty in the regional mental health sphere, according to the cultural identities of the constituent communities. The emphasis is on South Africa. A policy of the European parliament on digital sovereignty was stated in one of their position papers (European Parliament, 2020). The paper was designed for the following: minimize or prevent the loss of control over data, enhance capacity for innovation, as well as ability to shape and enforce legislation in the digital environment of citizens and member states of the European Union (EU). The paper provides an overview of measures being considered or utilized towards enhancing the autonomy of European nations in the digital world.

10.2.3 Machine Learning, Graph Theory and Data Structures

In more recent contemporary times, machine learning and artificial intelligence have simplified alphabet (and language) learning. Using a text to speech converter, for instance, a learner need not literally master an alphabet or language in its textual form. The effectiveness of the converter in itself depends on the robustness of the algorithm used. Several deep learning algorithms exist for image recognition based on neural networks (e.g. Zhang et al., 2024). There are typical challenges affecting the efficiencies of many contemporary algorithms. These relate to the large memory space required for storage and processing, high processing time, large amount of processing power, and ultimately the processing cost.

A method for overcoming these challenges is the representation of (alphabetic) images using graphs. In this approach, an alphabet is represented based strictly on its internal structure which is independent of the image size and image orientation. Essentially, an alphabet is represented in form of nodes, lines and curves. This method was used in the image recognition system with the United States Patent Number 5267332 (Walch & Pawlicki, 1993). This is also the approach used in Oluwade (2025a) in which a machine learning model for resource sharing in humanitarian camps was reported. Additionally, however, the latter work includes the integration of the qualitative equivalence of differential equations for the classification of the alphabets. Elastic bunch graph matching is also based on graph theory.

In graph theory (Benedicty & Sledge, 1987; Chartrand & Lesniak, 1986), the number of edges incident on a vertex is called the degree of a vertex, while an isolated vertex is a vertex which has zero degree. A dynamical system approach to machine learning has been developed and applied to obtain novel results (Oluwade, 2024; Oluwade, 2025b). Data structures, in conjunction with graph theory, provide a good synergy for the study of alphabets. There are two basic categories of data structures. These are primitive and non-primitive data structures (Tremblay & Sorenson, 1984). Examples of the former are the sets of natural numbers, integers, rational numbers, real numbers and complex numbers. Examples of non-primitive data structures are graphs, trees, queues, dequeues, trees and stacks.

There are approximately 300 writing systems in the world, which can be traced from antiquity (world writing systems (n.d); Oluwade et al., 2020). Some of the writing systems of African origin are shown in Table 10.1. Throughout this chapter, the emphasis will be on the set of alphabets of the Yoruba language used in Nigeria, and not on the one used in the Republic of Benin which has slight variations (Hartell, 1993).

Table 10.1. Examples of African writing systems

S/N	African indigenous writing system	Region of Africa where the system primarily originated from	Language family
1	Egyptian Hieroglyphs2	North Africa	Afro-Asiatic
2	Ethiopic	East Africa	Afro-Asiatic
3	Hausa 1 (Salifou Hausa)	West Africa	Afro-Asiatic
4	Hausa 2 (Raina kama)	West Africa	Afro-Asiatic
5	Hausa 3 (Tafi)	West Africa	Afro-Asiatic
6	Nwagu Aneke Igbo	West Africa	Niger-Congo
7	Bassa Vah	West Africa	Niger-Congo
8	Yoruba – Nigeria	West Africa	Niger-Congo
9	Yoruba – Republic of Benin	West Africa	Niger-Congo
10	Afrikaans	South Africa	Indo-European
11	Siwu – Ghana	West Africa	Niger-Congo

10.3 Methodology

In this section, some basic terminologies are introduced and defined within the realms of graph theory, data structure and measurement theory. Some machine learning theorems are then stated and proved.

Definition 10.1: Horizontal Edge – A horizontal edge is an edge which can be considered to be parallel to the horizontal axis.

Definition 10.2: Vertical Edge – A vertical edge is an edge which is perpendicular to the horizontal axis.

Definition 10.3: Slanted Edge – A slanted edge is an edge which is straight but is neither horizontal nor vertical.

Definition 10.4: Curved Edge – A curved edge is an edge which has a curved structure, i.e. it is not horizontal, vertical or slanted.

Definition 10.5: Open Space – An open space/surface exists within the configuration of an alphabet such that none of its vertices are connected to another vertex.

Definition 10.6: Closed Space – A closed space/surface is one that is enclosed by two or more edges joined together.

Definition 10.7: Vertex Invisible and Vertex Visible Alphabet – An alphabet is said to be vertex invisible if none of its vertices can be visually seen. Otherwise, the alphabet is said to be vertex visible.

Remark 10.1: The alphabet 'O' is the only vertex invisible English alphabet. The alphabet 'Q' is vertex visible even though its vertex on the 'O' component of its structure is vertex invisible.

Definition 10.8: Alphabetic Sovereignty – An alphabet is said to be sovereign if it can be uniquely identified solely by one or more of the vertedge and phystruct metrics, i.e. alphabetic sovereignty refers to the act of unique characterization of an alphabet.

Definition 10.9: Normal Alphabetic Metric – A metric for the characterization of an alphabet is said to be a normal metric if the alphabet being characterized is not a special alphabet, i.e. it is neither a diacritic nor a digraph .

Definition 10.10: Special Alphabetic Metric – A metric for the characterization of an alphabet is said to be a special metric if the alphabet being characterized is a special alphabet which is a diacritic or digraph.

Definition 10.11: Vertedge Metric – A vertedge metric is a metric which is based on the order of the set of an alphabet's vertices or edges.

Definition 10.12: Phystruct Metric – A phystruct metric is based on the physical structure of an alphabet, as determined by the vertices and/or edges.

Three vertedge metrics were applied in Oluwade (2025a). They have been generalized in this chapter. These are respectively represented here by VE_1, VE_2 and VE_3, with definitions depicted in Table 10.2.

Additional thirteen metrics, generically called phystruct metrics, are introduced here and described in Table 10.3.

Table 10.2. Definitions of vertedge metrics

S/N	Metric symbol	Meaning of metric
1	VE_1	Number of vertices in an alphabet
2	VE_2	Number of edges in an alphabet
3	VE_3	Total number of vertices and edges in an alphabet

Table 10.3. Definitions of phystruct metrics

S/N	Metric symbol	Meaning of metric	Remark
1	PS_1	Number of non-curvy closed spaces/ surfaces which the edges of an alphabet enclose within	The focus is on the structure of the edges. A consideration of a continuous edge as a distinct edge or not is not applicable in this metric
2	PS_2	Number of vertices in which two or more edges intersect, such that a continuous edge containing some other edges on it is not considered as a distinct edge	The focus is on the interaction between the vertices and the edges. Normally, the value of this metric will be less than or equal to the value of PS_{11}
3	PS_3	Number of edges which are completely (100%) horizontal, such that a continuous edge which contains some other edges is treated as a distinct edge	The focus is on the structure of the edges
4	PS_4	Number of edges which are perpendicular to the horizontal, such that a continuous edge which contains some other edges is treated as a distinct edge	The focus is on the structure of the edges
5	PS_5	Number of edges which are vertically slanted in a non-curvy manner, such that a continuous edge which contains some other edges is treated as a distinct edge	The focus is on the structure of the edges
6	PS_6	Number of non-curvy horizontal edges in an alphabet, such that a continuous edge which contains some other edges is treated as a distinct edge	The focus is on the structure of the edges
7	PS_7	Number of curved edges in an alphabet, such that a continuous edge which contains some other edges is treated as a distinct edge	The focus is on the structure of the edges
8	PS_8	Total number of edges which are completely horizontal or perpendicular to the horizontal and are vertically slanted in a non-curvy manner	This is the sum of PS_3, PS_4 and PS_5

(*Contd.*)

(*Contd.*)

S/N	Metric symbol	Meaning of metric	Remark
9	PS_9	Number of open spaces/surfaces which are bounded by the edges within the alphabet	The focus is on the structure of the edges
10	PS_{10}	Number of curved edges of an alphabet which encompass another edge (curved or non-curved) of the alphabet, such that a continuous edge which contains some other edges is treated as a distinct edge	The focus is on the structure of the edges. Normally, the value of this metric will be greater than or equal to the value of PS_{12}
11	PS_{11}	Number of vertices in which two or more edges intersect, such that a continuous edge which contains some other edges is treated as a distinct edge	The focus is on the interaction between the vertices and edges. Normally, the value of this metric will be greater than or equal to the value of PS_2
12	PS_{12}	Number of curved closed surfaces which the edges of an alphabet enclose within the alphabet, such that a continuous edge which contains some other edges is NOT treated as a distinct edge	The focus is on the structure of the edge. Normally, the value of this metric will be less than or equal to the value of PS_{10}
13	PS_{13}	Number of curved edges which are connected to just one vertex/mode of another curved or non-curved edge, such that a continuous edge which contains some other edges is treated as a distinct edge	The focus is on the structure of the edges

These metrics are deployed towards finding a unique pattern for the behavior of an alphabet. This uniqueness assists in formulating equivalence classes for alphabets and also for developing a distinct algorithm for the recognition of each alphabet. Theorem 10.1 is a generalization of the procedure used in Oluwade (2025a) to partition the set of uppercase English language alphabets into clusters via the vertedge metrics.

Theorem 10.1

Let $\Theta = \{\Theta_i: i = 1, 2, \ldots, 26\}$ be the set of uppercase English alphabets where the number of vertices, number of edges and total number of vertices and edges of Θ_i are respectively denoted by $n_i(v)$, $n_i(e)$ and $n_i(tve)$. Define a relation ~ on Θ such that $\Theta_i \sim \Theta_j$ iff

(a) $n_i(v) = n_j(v)$;
(b) $n_i(e) = n_j(e)$;
(c) $n_i(tve) = n_j(tve)$;

for all $i, j \in \{1, 2, \ldots, 26\}$. Then ~ is an equivalence relation.

Proof

It is sufficient to show that ~ satisfies the reflexivity, symmetry and transitivity properties in (a), as a similar statement of proof applies to each of (b) and (c). Obviously, $n_i(v) = n_i(v)$ and so the reflexivity property is satisfied. $n_i(v) = n_j(v)$ implies that $n_j(v) = n_i(v)$ i.e. ~ is symmetric. Finally, $n_i(v) = n_j(v)$ and $n_j(v) = n_k(v)$ implies that $n_i(v) = n_k(v)$. Thus ~ it is transitive. Hence ~ is an equivalence relation.

Remark 10.2

It was shown in Oluwade (2025a) that Θ has ten clusters, arising from the distinct equivalent classes of the relation. Further improvement and generalization on clustering can be made via Theorem 10.2.

Theorem 10.2

Let $\Theta = \{\Theta_i: i = 1, 2, \ldots, 26\}$ be the set of uppercase English alphabets. Suppose λ is a vertedge metric (or a phystruct metric) of Θ_i with value $n(ve_i)$ (or $n(ps_i)$, as appropriate). Define a relation ~ on Θ such that $\Theta_i \sim \Theta_j$ iff $n(ve_i) = n(ve_j)$ (or $n(ps_i) = n(ps_j)$, as appropriate) for all i, j. Then ~ is an equivalence relation.

Proof

Obviously $n(ve_i) = n(ve_i)$, hence the relation is reflexive. Also, $n(ve_i) = n(ve_j)$ implies that $n(ve_j) = n(ve_i)$, therefore, the relation is symmetric. Finally, if $n(ve_i) = n(ve_j)$ and $n(ve_j) = n(ve_k)$, then $n(ve_i) = n(ve_k)$. Thus, the relation is transitive, and hence it is an equivalence relation.

Remark 10.3

The distinct equivalent classes are clusters such that the order of a particular metric for each member of a cluster is the same. These clusters are described in Section 4.

10.4 Results

This section presents the results on the characterization of the Yoruba language alphabets using the methodology introduced in the preceding section.

Definition 10.13 (Yoruba Language Alphabet Order Equation)

Suppose o(ELA) is the order of the (set of) English Language Alphabet and o(ELA\YLA) the order of the set of English alphabets that are not in the Yoruba language. Also, suppose $o(YLA_d)$ is the order of the diacritics of the Yoruba language, and $o(YLA_g)$ the number of digraphs in the Yoruba language. Then the order of the (set of) Yoruba Language Alphabet, denoted by o(YLA) is given by

$$o(YLA) = o(ELA) - o(ELA \backslash YLA) + o(YLA_d) + o(YLA_g) \quad (2)$$

Table 10.4 highlights elements of the results in Oluwade (2025a) in terms of the general terminology called vertedge metrics. Table 10.5 shows the new results on phystruct metrics.

The clusters arising from the phystruct metrics are presented in Tables 10.6 to 10.18.

In view of Tables 10.6 to 10.18, unique characterization of the Yoruba language alphabets can be presented. This is done in Table 10.19.

Table 10.4. Characteristics of the uppercase English alphabets with respect to Vertedge metrics

S/N	Alphabet	VE_1	VE_2	VE_3
1	A	5	10	15
2	B	3	4	7
3	C	2	2	4
4	D	4	4	8
5	E	6	10	16
6	F	5	8	13
7	G	3	4	7
8	H	6	10	16
9	I	6	10	16
10	J	4	6	10
11	K	5	8	13
12	L	3	4	7
13	M	5	7	12
14	N	4	6	10
15	O	1	0	1
16	P	3	4	7
17	Q	3	4	7
18	R	5	10	15
19	S	2	2	4
20	T	4	5	9
21	U	2	2	4
22	V	3	4	7
23	W	5	8	13
24	X	5	8	13
25	Y	4	6	10
26	Z	4	6	10

Table 10.5. Characteristics of the uppercase English alphabets with respect to phystruct metrics

S/N	Alphabet	PS_1	PS_2	PS_3	PS_4	PS_5	PS_6	PS_7	PS_8	PS_9	PS_{10}	PS_{11}	PS_{12}	PS_{13}
1	A	1	6	1	0	6	1	0	7	1	0	9	0	0
2	B	0	6	0	3	0	0	2	3	1	2	8	2	0
3	C	0	0	0	0	0	0	1	0	1	0	0	0	0
4	D	0	6	0	1	0	0	4	1	1	2	8	1	2
5	E	0	5	3	3	0	3	0	6	2	0	7	0	0
6	F	0	4	2	3	0	2	0	5	2	0	5	0	0
7	G	0	1	1	0	0	1	1	1	1	0	1	0	1
8	H	0	4	1	6	0	1	0	7	2	0	6	0	0
9	I	0	6	6	1	0	6	0	7	2	0	8	0	0
10	J	0	3	3	0	0	3	1	3	2	0	4	0	3
11	K	0	4	0	3	2	0	0	5	3	0	6	0	0
12	L	0	1	1	1	0	1	0	2	1	0	1	0	0
13	M	0	3	0	2	2	0	0	4	2	0	3	0	0
14	N	0	2	0	2	1	0	0	3	2	0	2	0	0
15	O	0	0	0	0	0	0	0	0	0	0	0	0	0
16	P	0	3	0	3	0	0	1	3	1	1	4	1	1
17	Q	0	3	0	0	0	0	3	0	2	0	4	0	2
18	R	0	5	0	3	0	0	5	3	2	1	7	1	2
19	S	0	0	0	0	0	0	1	0	2	0	0	0	0
20	T	0	3	3	1	0	3	0	4	2	0	4	0	0

(Contd.)

(Contd.)

S/N	Alphabet	PS_1	PS_2	PS_3	PS_4	PS_5	PS_6	PS_7	PS_8	PS_9	PS_{10}	PS_{11}	PS_{12}	PS_{13}
21	U	0	0	0	0	0	0	1	0	1	0	0	0	0
22	V	0	1	0	0	2	0	0	2	1	0	1	0	0
23	W	0	3	0	0	4	0	0	4	2	0	3	0	0
24	X	0	2	0	0	6	0	0	6	4	0	6	0	0
25	Y	0	3	0	1	2	0	0	3	3	0	3	0	0
26	Z	0	2	2	0	1	2	0	3	2	0	2	0	0

Table 10.6. Clusters of phystruct metric PS_1

S/N	Cluster	Order of cluster
1	A	1
2	B,C,D,E,F,G,H,I,J,K,L,M,N,O,P,Q,R,S,T,U,V, W,X,Y,Z	25
	Total	26

Table 10.7. Clusters of phystruct metric PS_2

S/N	Cluster	Order of cluster
1	C,O,S,U	4
2	G,L,V	3
3	N,X,Z	3
4	J,M,P,Q,T,W,Y	7
5	F,H,K	3
6	E,R	2
7	A,B,D,I	4
	Total	26

Table 10.8. Clusters of phystruct metric PS_3

S/N	Cluster	Order of cluster
1	I	1
2	A,G,H,L	4
3	F,Z	2
4	E,J,T	3
5	B,C,D,K,M,N,O,P,Q,R,S,U,V,W,X,Y	16
	Total	26

Table 10.9. Clusters of phystruct metric PS_4

S/N	Cluster	Order of cluster
1	H	1
2	D,I,L,T,Y	5
3	M,N	2
4	B,E,F,K,P,R	6
5	A,C,G,J,O,Q,S,U,V,W,X,Z	12
	Total	26

Table 10.10. Clusters of phystruct metric PS_5

S/N	Cluster	Order of cluster
1	W	1
2	A,X	2
3	N,Z	2
4	K,M,V,Y	4
5	B,C,D,E,F,G,H,I,J,L,O,P,Q,R,S,T,U	17
	Total	26

Table 10.11. Clusters of phystruct metric PS_6

S/N	Cluster	Order of cluster
1	I	1
2	F,Z	2
3	E,J,T	3
4	A,G,H,L	4
5	B,C,D,K,M,N,O,P,Q,R,S,U,V,W,X,Y	16
	Total	26

Table 10.12. Clusters of phystruct metric PS_7

S/N	Cluster	Order of cluster
1	Q	1
2	R	1
3	D	1
4	B	1
5	C,G,J,P,S,U	6
6	A,E,F,H,I,K,L,M,N,O,T,V,W,X,Y,Z	16
	Total	26

Table 10.13. Clusters of phystruct metric PS_8

S/N	Cluster	Order of cluster
1	C,O,Q,S,U	5
2	D,G	2
3	L,V	2
4	B,J,N,P,R,Y,Z	7
5	M,T,W	3
6	F,K	2
7	E,X	2
8	A,H,I	3
	Total	26

Table 10.14. Clusters of phystruct metric PS_9

S/N	Cluster	Order of cluster
1	X	1
2	K,Y	2
3	O	1
4	A,B,C,D,G,L,P,U,V	9
5	E,F,H,I,J,M,N,Q,R,S,T,W,Z	13
	Total	26

Table 10.15. Clusters of phystruct metric PS_{10}

S/N	Cluster	Order of cluster
1	D	1
2	B	1
3	P,R	2
4	A,C,E,F,G,H,I,J,K,L,M,N,O,Q,S,T,U,V,W,X, Y,Z	22
	Total	26

Table 10.16. Clusters of phystruct metric PS_{11}

S/N	Cluster	Order of cluster
1	A	1
2	B,D,I	3
3	E,R	2
4	H,K,X	3
5	F	1
6	J,P,Q,T	4
7	M,W,Y	3
8	N,Z	2
9	G,L,V	3
10	C,O,S,U	4
	Total	26

Table 10.17. Clusters of phystruct metric PS_{12}

S/N	Cluster	Order of cluster
1	B	1
2	D,P,R	3
3	A,C,E,F,G,H,I,J,K,L,M,N,O,Q,S,T,U,V,W,X,Y,Z	22
	Total	26

Table 10.18. Clusters of phystruct metric PS_{13}

S/N	Cluster	Order of cluster
1	J	1
2	D,Q,R	3
3	G,P	2
4	A,B,C,E,F,H,I,K,L,M,N,O,S,T,U,V,W,X,Y,Z	20
	Total	26

Table 10.19. Unique identity characterization of the Yoruba language alphabets

S/N	Alphabet	Remark on unique identification with respect to a single independent metric
1	A	Unique, in view of Table 10.6 and Table 10.16
2	B	Unique, in view of Table 10.12, Table 10.15 and Table 10.17
3	D	Unique, in view of Table 10.12 and Table 10.15
4	E	Not unique
5	F	Unique, in view of Table 10.16
6	G	Not unique
7	H	Unique, in view of Table 10.9
8	I	Unique, in view of Table 10.8 and Table 10.11
9	J	Unique, in view of Table 10.18
10	K	Not unique
11	L	Not unique
12	M	Not unique
13	N	Not unique
14	O	Unique, in view of Table 10.14
15	P	Not unique
16	R	Unique, in view of Table 10.12
17	S	Not unique
18	T	Not unique
19	U	Not unique
20	W	Unique, in view of Table 10.10
21	Y	Not unique
22	E-y	This diacritic is unique in view of its distinct structure with a tonal mark
23	O-y	This diacritic is unique in view of its distinct structure with a tonal mark
24	S-y	This diacritic is unique in view of its distinct structure with a tonal mark
25	Gb	This digraph is unique in view of its distinct structure with a tonal mark

10.5 Discussion

Phystruct metric PS_1 has two clusters, which is the lowest number among all the clusters. PS_{11} has the highest number of clusters, which is ten. PS_{12} has three clusters. Each of PS_3, PS_4, PS_5, PS_6 and PS_9 has five clusters. Each of PS_{10} and PS_{13} has four clusters; PS_7 has six clusters; PS_2 has seven clusters while PS_8 has eight clusters. Thirteen alphabets of the English language (ELA) are uniquely identified based on a single metric, as shown in Tables 10.6 to 10.18. This is 50% of all the alphabets. In these tables, the order of a cluster is one iff an alphabet is uniquely identified.

Based on Table 10.19, fourteen of the Yoruba language alphabets (YLA) are uniquely identified directly using solely phystruct metrics PS_1 to PS_{13} without combining two or more metrics. This gives a percentage of 56%. In particular, each of the three diacritics and one digraph of the YLA is uniquely identifiable vis-à-vis ELA. This shows, among others, that ELA has a close structural affinity with YLA. For instance, when two or more of the developed metrics are combined to improve the percentage accuracy of English alphabets, the accuracy of Yoruba alphabets will be similarly improved in almost the same proportion. Thus, it will be relatively easier to develop a natural language processing (NLP) system for the Yoruba language from the perspective of alphabetic sovereignty, via close imitation of existing works on the English language alphabets. This is unprejudiced towards other approaches used in ongoing research on African indigenous natural language processing system and related areas.

In Oluwade (2025a), a clear application of the vertedge metrics for fair resource scheduling was presented. This relates to the distribution of scarce resources to refugees in a humanitarian camp. In this procedure, the metrics are applied to the surnames of the refugees to determine the protocol to be used in serving them. For instance, the management may decide to attend to the refugees sequentially by totaling the values of the constituent alphabets representing surnames using a vertedge metric, and ranking the respective values. A refugee whose surname records the highest value may then be selected, followed by the person who has the next total value etc. The ultimate goal is to device a fair protocol which is not easily guessed or predictable, unlike a process based on well-known protocols such as Last Come First Served (LCFS), age, sex, or marital status. A similar process may be applied to the phystruct metrics.

Furthermore, the presented clustering analysis has potential application in cryptographic systems. In such a system, a piece of information, called the key, is necessary in decrypting encrypted (secret) information in a communication system (Oluwade & Osofisan, 2001). A group of alphabets in the same cluster in a specified metric (i.e. having the same order) can be used as the key. In particular, an alphabet which does not have another alphabet in its cluster may be more appropriately used as the key. Two basic characteristics of this key are: (i) It has to be sent in advance via a suitably safe procedure; (ii) The key is known ahead of the encryption-decryption process by both the potential sender and receiver of message. The above application is relevant to the two main cryptosystems, namely public key cryptosystem and public key distribution system.

In particular, in the public key cryptosystem such as the Merckle-Duffie-Hellman system, two keys are kept, namely the public key and the private key. Whereas the public key is widely available to the generality of the public, the private key is only known to the two parties involved in the process. In the public key distribution system, on the other hand, both the potential sender and receiver of a message will continue to exchange information until a common key is found the data structures of the alphabets considered in this chapter, as well as those arising from the interpretation/realization of the metrics, are non-primitive data structures which appear as graphs and trees. In general, if O is considered as vertex visible, then it may be reasonable to also consider Q as vertex visible. This means the value of VE_1 in Table 10.4 with respect to Q will be four (4) instead of three (3). This will automatically change the value of VE_3 for the alphabet to be eight (8).

The (mathematical) classifier used in this chapter has a tendency to achieve an accuracy which tends to 100% when applied to a dataset in the post software development phase. This peculiarity is due to the statements of logical facts, backed by valid proofs, which are inherent in the equivalence relations defined on the vertedge and phystruct metrics.

In general, the results in this chapter are independent of the qualitative equivalence (theory) of differential equations (QEDE). The results only depend on the fundamental theorem of equivalence relations, an essential component of OEDE which serves as a classifier.

10.6 Limitation

This chapter is limited to the alphabets of the English language and the Yoruba language, and by extension, to their sign language alphabets. The alphabets of these languages have minimal complexity with respect to the diacritics and digraphs.

10.7 Conclusion

This chapter has presented a procedure for characterizing the alphabets of the Yoruba language, with a focus on digital sovereignty. This language has a high level of similarity with the English language alphabets. The procedure involves the development of a machine learning process for sharing these alphabets in clusters. The metrics that were introduced are novel and unique, and are fundamentally different from popular metrics such as accuracy, precision, and recall among others. 50% and 56% of the English language alphabets (ELA) and Yoruba language alphabets (YLA) respectively were uniquely identified directly by the metrics. Other alphabets may be uniquely identified indirectly via a logical relationship among all the metrics. The procedure has the tendency to improve the unique identification and recognition of all language alphabets.

Further work can be done as follows:

- Development of additional metrics to increase the percentage of alphabets that can be directly identified and recognized uniquely.

- Application of the developed machine learning procedure to other language alphabets, as captured in the Unicode system. In particular, all known diacritics, digraphs and other peculiar alphabets of different languages would be taken care of. Particular emphasis would be on non-Yoruba African language alphabets. This will, among others, enable the identification of other language alphabets which have prima facie structural affinity with ELA.
- Logical combination of the interaction among all the clusters to improve the percentage of alphabets that can be uniquely characterized.
- Standardization of the procedure of labelling the vertices and edges of an alphabet sequentially to facilitate a uniform scientific description of the graphical data structures of the alphabet.
- Standardization of the nomenclature for writing all alphabets, especially those which have variations across various keyboards of computers, phones and other keyboard devices. These alphabets include B, D, J, K, Q, R and U.
- Development of a software for unique language alphabet identification using the vertedge and phystruct metrics.
- Discovery of the limitations in using YLA as a natural language processing system via alphabetic sovereignty.

Declaration of Generative AI and AI-Assisted Technologies

The author did not use AI-based tools in preparing the manuscript. He takes full responsibility for the final content of the manuscript.

References

Akintoye, Banji. (2018). *University Education in Nigeria: Revisiting the Ife Dream* (43rd Convocation Lecture). Obafemi Awolowo University.

Awolowo, Obafemi. (1981). *Voice of Courage*. Olaiya Fagbamigbe Publishers Ltd.

Bala, D., Hossain, M.A., Islam, M.A., Mynuddin, M., Hossain, M.I., & Abdullah, M.I. (2022). Effective recognition system of American sign language alphabets using machine learning classifiers, ANN and CNN. *2022 IEEE Conference on Interdisciplinary Approaches in Technology and Management for Social Innovation (IATMSI)*, pp. 1-6. https://doi.org/10.1109/IATMS156455.2022.10119336.

Bellanova, R., Carrapico, H., & Duez, D. (2022). Digital sovereignty and European security integration: An introduction. *European Security*, 31(3), 337-355. https://doi.org/10.1080/09662839.2022.2101887.

Benedicty, M., & Sledge, F.R. (1987). *Discrete Mathematical Structures*. Harcourt Brace Jovanovich Publishers.

Berztiss, A.T. (1975). *Data Structures: Theory and Practice*. Academic Press, Inc.

Boucher, N., Shumailov, I., Anderson, R., & Papernot, N. (2022). Bad characters: Imperceptible NLP attacks. *2022 IEEE Symposium on Security and Privacy (SP)*. IEEE. https://doi.org/10.1109/SP46214.2022.9833641.

Chartrand, G., & Lesniak, L. (1986). *Graphs and Digraphs*. Wadsworth Inc.

Elkharoua, R., & Jiang, X. (2024). Deep learning recognition for Arabic alphabet sign language RGB dataset. *Journal of Computer and Communications*, 12(03), 32-51. https://doi.org/10.4236/jcc.2024.123003.

European Parliament. (2020). *EPRS Ideas Paper: Towards a more Resilient EU*. https://www.europarl.europe.au/EPRS_BRI(2020)651992_EN.pdf.

Forane, S.G., Ezugwu, A.E., & Igwe, K. (2025). Digital sovereignty through Africa-centric emotional intelligence: A proof of concept for AI-enhanced mental health support. In: Misra, S., Damasevicius, R. & Kvalvik, P. (eds.), *Procedia Computer Science* (International Conference on Digital Sovereignty (ICDS)) (pp. 269-278). https://doi.org/10.1016/j.procs.2025.02.086.

Hartell, R.L. (1993). *Nigeria: Yoruba Alphabets of Africa*. UNESCO Regional Office, Dakar.

Jain, Raj (1991). *The Art of Computer Systems Performance Analysis: Techniques for Experimental Design, Measurement, Simulation, and Modeling*. John Wiley & Sons, Inc.

Mani, M.R., & Srikanth, T. (2018). Design of novel approach for conformal vortex induced flow based shape descriptor for object recognition. *Sens Imaging*, 19, 22. https://doi.org/10.1007/s11220-018-0206-y.

Mueller, M. (2021). Digital sovereignty: What does it mean? *Internet Governance Project*, Georgia Tech, https://www.internetgovernance.org/Digital-sovereignty-IGF2021(1).

Najib, F.M. (2024). Sign language interpretation using machine learning and artificial intelligence. *Neural Computing and Applications*, 37(2), 841-857. https://doi.org/10.1007/s00521-024-10395-9.

Oluwade, (Bami)dele, & Osofisan, A.O. (2001). Data encryption and decryption using the stacking public key cryptosystem, *Journal of Computer Science & Its Applications* (Journal of the Nigeria Computer Society), 8(1), 17-20. https://www.academia.edu/37544086.

Oluwade, B. (2004). *Design and Analysis of Computer-Coded Character Sets* (unpublished doctoral dissertation). University of Ibadan.

Oluwade, B., Osofisan, A., Ilori, S.A., Shola, P.B., & Akin-Ojo, R. (2020). A computational model for studying the characteristics of languages using coded character sets. *University of Ibadan Journal of Science and Logics in ICT Research*, 4(1), 85-95. https://journals.ui.edu.ng/index.php/uijslictr/article/view/83/65.

Oluwade, B. (2024). Qualitative classification of an autonomous differential equation and its application to image recognition system. *Journal of the Nigerian Mathematical Society*, 43(3), 273-286. https://ojs.ictp.it/jnms.

Oluwade, B. (2025a). A fair resource-sharing AI algorithm for humanitarian camps. In: A.A. Ajibesin & N.R. Vajjhala (eds.), *AI for Humanitarianism: Fostering Social Change through Emerging Technologies* (Artificial Intelligence and Robotics Series) (pp. 106-118). Chapman & Hall/CRC Press. https://doi.org/10.1201/9781003479109.

Oluwade, B. (2025b). Optimization of the output of a group of proportionate healthcare equipment manufacturing plants. In: A.A. Ajibesin, G.N. Sundar & T.S. Kumar (eds.), *Synergizing Data Envelopement Analysis and Machine Learning for Performance Optimization in Healthcare* (pp. 455-494). IGI Global Scientific Publishing. https://doi.org/10.4018/979-8-3373-0081-8.ch019.

Omolu, B. & Oluwade, B. (2017). On the application of the nearest neighbor classifier algorithm to character pattern recognition. *African Journal of Computing & ICT*, 10(1&2), 1-17. https://afrjcict.net/wp-content/uploads/2019/06/Vol1012Paper1journalFormat-with-numbers.pdf.

Pandey, P. (2025). Digital sovereignty and AI: Developing India's national AI stack for strategic autonomy. In: Misra, S., Damasevicius, R., & Kvalvik, P. (eds.), *Procedia Computer Science* (International Conference on Digital Sovereignty (ICDS)), (pp. 250-259). https://doi.org/10.1016/j.procs.2025.02.084.

Pohle, J., & Thiel, T. (2020). Digital sovereignty. *Internet Policy Review*, 9(4), https://doi.org/10.14763/2020.4.1532.

Ralescu, A., Diaz, I., & Rodriguez-Muniz, L.J. (2015). A classification algorithm based on geometric and statistical information. *Journal of Computational and Applied Mathematics*, 275, 335-344. https://doi.org/10.1016/j.cam.2014.07.012.

Tremblay, J., & Sorenson, P.G. (1984). *An Introduction to Data Structures with Applications*. McGraw-Hill Book Company.

Walch, Mark A., & Awlicki, John A. (1993). *Image Recognition System* (United States Patent 5267332). United States Patent and Trademark Office. https://patft.uspto.gov/netacgi/nph-Parser?patentnumber=5267332.

WorldWritingSystems (n.d). The World's Writing Systems, https://www.worldswritingsystems.org.

WorldAtlas (n.d). The World Atlas, https://www.worldatlas.com.

Zhang, L., Li, W., Sun, L., Yu, L., Ning, X., & Dong, X. (2024). Learning to represent 2D human face with mathematical model. *CAAI Transactions on Intelligence Technology*, 9(1), 54-68. https://doi.org/10.1049/cit2.12284.

CHAPTER

11

Rethinking Data Sovereignty through Convivial AI

Sabrina Sacco[1*(0009-0000-2008-9274)] **and Maria Cerreta**[2(0000-0002-7717-6210)]

[1] Department of Design, Polytechnic University of Milan

[2] Department of Architecture, University of Naples Federico II

11.1 Introduction

The concept of digital sovereignty (DS) has emerged as a multifaceted and evolving construct (Robert et al., 2021; Misra et al., 2025; Pohle & Thiel, 2020), with interpretations that vary significantly across political, institutional and geographical contexts. Initially, DS was conceived as the exercise of exclusive control over a nation-state's, digital domains, mirroring traditional notions of sovereignty over land and other resources (Hummel et al., 2021). This foundational interpretation adopts a defensive posture, emphasizing the state's authority over digital content, data, and infrastructure within its borders, with a focus on security, data protection and control over cyberspace. However, as digital systems have expanded in scale and complexity, this narrow, state-centric perspective has proven increasingly inadequate lens. The evolving nature of DS now necessitates broader engagement from a diverse array of actors, including private enterprises, civil society, and transnational institutions (Khan et al., 2023).

This openness becomes particularly evident in the expansive definition of artificial intelligence (AI) ecosystems, which encompass emerging actors, big data and large-scale infrastructures (Feijóo et al., 2020).

The growing capacity of artificial intelligence (AI), to shape everyday life in urban environments, from public services and urban governance to healthcare and education, raises a series of urgent questions (Cugurullo et al., 2023; Robbins & van Wynsberghe, 2022; Fontes et al., 2024). Who controls, understands, and produces these systems? These questions compel a critical reexamination of what digital sovereignty (DS) signifies within today's socio-technical landscape (Woods, 2023;

*Corresponding author: sabrina.sacco@polimi.it

DOI: 10.1201/9781003581581-11

Monsees & Lambach, 2022; Novelli et al., 2023; Robert et al., 2023). On one end of the spectrum China, exemplifies a model of total technological control, grounded in a state-centred, centralized vision of sovereignty over data and digital infrastructures (Creemers, 2020). In contrast, the European Union advances a rights-based model (Fratini et al., 2024; Farrand & Carrapico, 2022; Hacker, 2020) operationalized through regulatory frameworks such as the General Data Protection Regulation (GDPR)—emphasizing fundamental rights, data protection, and user empowerment (Herian, 2020). Yet, both models fall short of capturing the full complexity of contemporary digital ecosystems. They remain anchored in a conception of DS defined by fixed territorial borders and centralized authority—an increasingly outdated paradigm that fails to reflect the fluid, decentralized nature of today's digital infrastructures (Fratini et al., 2024). Indeed, models predicated on over-control, characterized by pervasive state surveillance and digital isolation, are misaligned with the interconnected architecture of global networks. Such approaches risk stifling innovation, restricting information flows, and impeding transnational cooperation, ultimately undermining the collective potential for social and technological advancement (Fratini, 2024; Walter et al., 2020; Musiani, 2022).

The growing concentration of technological and data-related power in the hands of a few global tech giants has become a pressing concern (Coeckelbergh, 2022; Tretter, 2023). These corporations possess vast technical, financial, and infrastructural resources, enabling them to circumvent territorial constraints and exert influence through proprietary algorithms and highly centralized platforms. Consequently, local institutions, and the citizens they serve, often find themselves disempowered, as private interests increasingly override the public good.

Addressing this complexity and asymmetry means adopting and defining new models and governance approaches that consider the speed of technological change and the interconnection of digital environments, going beyond extractive practices. In this direction, DS should involve multiple dimensions, including technological, political, economic and social factors, critically questioning how governance is exercised and what interests it ultimately serves (Fratini et al., 2024). From this perspective, digital sovereignty (DS) is shifting from a mechanism of control and strict regulation toward a framework that ensures digital infrastructures align with democratic values, promote awareness, uphold ethical standards and contribute to collective well-being (Couture & Toupin, 2019; Tretter, 2023).

This shift is particularly salient in the context of artificial intelligence. AI infrastructures introduce new forms of dependency, power asymmetry, and governance complexity. Simultaneously, they offer an opportunity to reconceptualize digital sovereignty (DS) as dynamic, distributed, and relational, emerging through the ongoing interaction among diverse actors and institutions. Viewed through this lens, DS may be understood as a process of negotiation within complex socio-technical systems (Floridi, 2020; Passey et al., 2018). This process enables what is increasingly referred to as digital agency (Aagaard & Lund, 2019; Etelepälto et al., 2013): the capacity of various actors to meaningfully participate in the creation of digital technologies and infrastructures. Crucially, this does not imply that those with greater power merit a stronger voice; rather, it affirms that all individuals and groups possess an equal right to shape the development and trajectory of AI systems.

From this perspective, DS can be understood as inherently participatory. It depends on the active involvement of a broad range of stakeholders such as governments, civil society, communities, and technical actors alike (Shaffer & Clinton, 2006; Schmitter, 2001; Cooper, 2019; Steward, 2017; Raymond & DeNardis, 2015). Participatory sovereignty, underlining the importance of grassroots involvement and collective governance, demands tools, policies, and infrastructures that facilitate shared decision-making and sustained dialogue (Taylor & Kukutai, 2016; Mauri et al., 2024; Birhane et al., 2022; Delgado et al., 2023; Jaiswal & Schaathun, 2025). This chapter explores digital agency as a key lens through which to reframe digital sovereignty in pluralistic, interdependent societies. At the heart of this reconfiguration lies the concept of conviviality, drawing on the work of Ivan Illich (1973). Illich imagined technologies serve individuals and communities without dominating them, promoting reciprocity, creativity and empowerment.

When applied to AI, a convivial approach entails designing systems that support exploration rather than dictate solutions; that render processes transparent rather than obscure; and that embrace pluralism rather than suppress diversity (Varon & Peña, 2021; Zhang et al., 2023; Arora, 2024). Convivial AI reframes the field as a constellation of democratic, participatory and ethical practices that, instead of reinforcing power aim to build local capacity foster public dialogue, and empower communities to shape technologies to reflect their needs and values. To examine how this approach functions in practice, the chapter draws on three pilot projects conducted across urban and rural contexts. These initiatives employed a hybrid methodology that integrated participatory design with situated knowledge production, grounded in the principles of convivial AI. The experiments served as provocations, intended to challenge the dominant logics of mainstream AI development and to open space for data practices that cultivate agency, dialogue, and shared understanding.

In doing so, they reposition individuals and communities not as passive users of technology, but as co-creators of socio-technical systems that have the power to shape, and potentially disrupt, their lives. This is particularly significant within the framework of DS, where control must be distributed, reflective, and continuously renegotiated (Yadav, 2025). These three pilot experiments aim to highlight the transformative potential of rethinking data from a convivial perspective, underlining challenges and structural limitations that must be addressed to scale such an approach.

This chapter is organized as follows: Section 2 examines the role of data in shaping digital sovereignty in the AI era, highlighting the transition toward data agency. Section 3 introduces the concept of Convivial AI and outlines its theoretical and methodological foundations. Then, Section 4 presents three real-world experiments where convivial methodologies have been applied. Section 5 reflects on the challenges and limitations encountered in these experiments. Lastly, Section 6 concludes with some final reflections and future research directions.

11.2 The Role of Data in Shaping Digital Sovereignty in the AI Era

The rapid evolution of AI is inseparable from the rise of data extractivism—the systemic collection, commodification, and monetization of personal and collective data (Prasad, 2022). Everyday interactions, from online searches to social media activity, are transformed into behavioral surplus (Zuboff, 2019), fuelling targeted advertising, predictive analytics, and platform economies (D'Ignazio & Klein, 2020; Whitehead, 2020; Zuboff, 2015). In this model, users are treated as "natural sources" of data (Srnicek, 2017; Celis & Schultz, 2021; Celis, 2017), their online behavior repurposed as unpaid labour (Terranova, 2000). The compulsive drive to accumulate data feeds not only economic and social asymmetries, but also environmental degradation. AI training and data storage demand vast energy, water, and land resources (Brevini, 2021; Brevini & Pasquale 2020; Crawford, 2021), often with little transparency or accountability. The logic of "capture everything" fosters anxiety with information, motivated less by necessity than by the fear of losing future revenues. In this paradigm, efficiency is valorised at the expense of sustainability, and algorithmic optimization becomes a rationale for ecological irresponsibility. This anxiety invites a crucial question: how can we break free from a data-centric worldview dominated by extraction and control? The answer begins by revisiting the definition of data. Rather than viewing data as neutral inputs for optimization, starting to reclaim and promote a relational and contextual understanding of data as situated, participatory, and embedded values. This perspective reframes data as a medium through which communities narrate their histories, express their values, and engage in collective meaning-making (Granata, 2021; Choo, 2002; Ricaurte, 2019; Fanon et al., 1968; Iaconesi, 2018). It also encourages more ecological and sustainable approaches to data connectivity and analysis (Barbierato & Gatti, 2024), recognizing that digital systems are inseparable from the material world. By making the environmental footprint of AI visible, this view calls for practices that embed care, both for social systems and for planetary health. Data is not merely a representation of reality; it performs and produces reality by shaping what is seen, what is ignored, and what is possible to imagine. In this light, datasets are not just containers of information; they are infrastructures of meaning that carry assumptions about gender, race, class, ability, and geography, shaping our idea of the world. Therefore, redefining data also means redefining whose knowledge counts and how plural perspectives can be made visible within AI systems. This redefinition of data challenges the epistemic authority traditionally held by institutional, corporate, or technical actors, asserting instead that knowledge is co-constructed and deeply political. Drawing on feminist epistemology (Haraway, 1988), this chapter recognizes that all knowledge production, including that enabled through AI, is partial, situated, and shaped by power. Increasing awareness around the topic of data leads to greater consciousness and control over it, fostering attentiveness to its impact, to the tools employed, and to the knowledge produced through data. This knowledge becomes instrumental in disseminating alternative visions of the world. Such a process implies ownership not only of data, but also of the knowledge produced, both individual and collective, thereby reinforcing community agency and sovereignty. Achieving a balance between society's vision and the informational environment (Floridi, 2013) means resisting techno-solutionism and reasserting the value of collective intelligence (Levy, 1997; 2004; Mazzucato, 2018; Latour, 2005). This recognizes the potential of individuals and communities to co-create knowledge and technology. By embracing collective intelligence and relational knowledge systems, this chapter aims to encourage communities to participate in how data is collected, interpreted and used. In the AI era, where data fuels algorithmic decisions and vast data sources such as personal, environmental behavioral, or historical, are continuously collected and repurposed with far-reaching consequences, the exercise of digital agency becomes critical. This agency challenges dominant narratives and compels us to interrogate how data is generated, collected, categorized, interpreted, and applied. This shift demands a redefinition of data: not as a static, extractable resource to be mined and monetized, but as a relational, co-constructed artifact that embodies values, intentions, and power dynamics. The adoption of this collective vision invites us to embrace the idea of slow data (Chiolero, 2022; 2023)—data that is generated through thoughtful, inclusive processes, and grounded in local knowledge, social bonds, and temporal depth. Slow data resists the logic of instant capture and rapid consumption. It requires time, reflection, and dialogue. It reflects community priorities that cannot be reduced to metrics or modelled through abstraction. This leads to a fundamental rethinking of AI's epistemological and political function, requiring policies and infrastructures that treat data not as a proprietary asset, but as a common—a shared resource governed by and for the public good (Ostrom, 1990). Governing data as common does not mean neutralizing power but redistributing it, creating processes of deliberation and repair that amplify underrepresented voices. This includes building mechanisms for collective redress, storytelling, and data reimagination, in which communities are not merely consulted, but lead in defining what counts as knowledge (Apostolou et al., 2000; Bhatt, 2002; Choo, 2002; Davis, 1993). It calls for moving beyond a protective or defensive posture, focused merely on limiting access or enforcing privacy, toward an active, participatory model in which communities reclaim the right to shape the meaning, boundaries, and uses of their own data. Such a reorientation elevates the concept of DS into a broader framework of political and epistemic agency: the capacity not only to consent or opt out, but to critically question what counts as valid data, who defines its categories, and to what ends it is mobilized. This requires us to move from a logic of compliance to the politics of co-production. Communities should not simply react to pre-existing systems but actively participate in their formation, determining not just how data is used, but what data is created in the first place, and whose voices are encoded in its structure. In this sense, data agency becomes central to the democratic governance of AI and digital infrastructures, inviting us to build systems that are accountable not only to legal regulations but to the communities whose lives they shape.

11.3 Convivial AI as a New Paradigm

Convivial AI emerges as a critical alternative to dominant, extractivist AI models, proposing a framework grounded in ethics, participation, and collective intelligence. Grounded in the theories of Ivan Illich (1973) and extended by contributions such as those proposed by the Manifesto Convivialista (2014) and the critique of productivism by André Gorz (2015), the conviviality approach calls for a fundamental reconsideration of how algorithmic systems are conceived, built, and governed. In the context of AI, adopting convivial approach is an act of reclaiming the technology from its foundational assumptions, intervening at the level of data

Table 11.1. Summary of related works informing the convivial AI paradigm

Author(s) & Year	Domain/ Perspective	Key concept(s)	Approach to data	Contribution to digital sovereignty	Relevance to convivial AI
Prasad (2022)	Digital political economy	Data extractivism	Data as commodity	Critiques commodification of citizen data, highlights state-level implications	Highlights need for alternative frameworks beyond extraction
Zuboff (2015, 2019)	Surveillance capitalism	Behavioral surplus, predictive economies	Data as behavioral by-product used for economic gain	Exposes asymmetries in data ownership and control	Implicitly supports calls for user agency and control
D'Ignazio & Klein (2020)	Feminist data studies	Data feminism	Data as power-laden and value-driven	Emphasizes inclusive, justice-oriented data practices	Strongly aligned with participatory and relational aspects
Whitehead (2020)	Critical data studies/ Political critique	Surveillance and liberation	Data as tool for governance and resistance	Challenges narrative of tech-enabled freedom	Supports critical reflection on AI design aims
Srnicek (2017)	Platform capitalism	Data extractivism	Users as sources of extractable data	Identifies structural exploitation in digital platforms	Foundational critique enabling alternative imaginaries
Celis (2017); Celis & Schultz (2021)	Critical media theory	Cognitive capitalism, machinic vision	Data as product of attention and perception	Links human behavior to machine training logics	Supports awareness of epistemic dimensions of data
Terranova (2000)	Digital labor theory	Free labor, unpaid data work	Data production as unpaid digital labor	Reframes users as laborers in data economies	Underscores the political economy behind data production
Brevini (2021); Brevini & Pasquale (2020)	AI & environmental ethics	Ecological costs of AI	Data infrastructures as extractive and unsustainable	Connects AI systems to resources degradation	Supports environmental accountability in AI design

(*Contd.*)

(Contd.)

Author(s) & Year	Domain/ Perspective	Key concept(s)	Approach to data	Contribution to digital sovereignty	Relevance to convivial AI
Crawford (2021)	AI materiality	Planetary AI, environmental footprint	Data as environmentally embedded	Demands recognition of AI's material and ecological costs	Reinforces need for sustainable data practices
Granata (2021); Choo (2002); Ricaurte (2019); Fanon et al. (1968); Iaconesi (2018)	Cultural theory / Epistemology	Relational data, situated knowledge	Data as medium for community meaning-making	Challenges universalist and extractive data models	Core to convivial AI: plural, community-rooted knowledge
Barbierato & Gatti (2024)	AI & sustainability	Green AI, ecological analysis	Data as materially and ethically consequential	Promotes sustainability in AI methods	Directly supports convivial approaches to AI
Haraway (1988)	Feminist epistemology	Situated knowledge, partial perspective	Data as socially and politically constructed	Challenges universal claims to objectivity in data systems	Foundational for participatory and relational data models
Floridi (2013)	Philosophy of information	Infosphere, digital ethics	Data as environment shaping human agency	Calls for ethical alignment between data systems and societal values	Supports normative frameworks for data as common good
Levy (1997, 2004)	Collective intelligence	Distributed knowledge production	Data as co-created through networked participation	Promotes decentralized, inclusive data creation	Central to convivial models of intelligence
Mazzucato (2018)	Political economy of innovation	Public value, mission-driven innovation	Data as a public good and collective asset	Reframes innovation toward collective benefit	Supports state and citizen co-responsibility in digital futures

Latour (2005)	Science and technology studies	Actor-network theory	Data as shaped by socio-technical networks	Highlights non-neutrality and relational character of systems	Affirms need for democratic governance of AI systems
Chiolero (2022, 2023)	Public health / Data ethics	Slow data	Data as deliberate, contextual, community-rooted	Opposes extractive, high-speed data regimes	Strongly aligned with care, temporality, and collective meaning-making
Ostrom (1990)	Commons governance	Data as a common resource	Data managed collectively for long-term sustainability	Provides institutional principles for shared governance	Offers a framework for cooperative data infrastructures
Apostolou et al. (2000)	Knowledge management	Knowledge processes	Knowledge as process involving human and system interaction	Supports participatory knowledge production	Offers a technical underpinning for co-designed data practices
Bhatt (2002)	Organizational theory	Individual and organizational knowledge	Knowledge as embedded and strategic	Connects knowledge ownership with agency	Reinforces sovereignty at both personal and collective levels
Choo (2002)	Organizational knowledge/ Sensemaking	Knowledge creation, interpretation	Data as shaped through meaning-making processes	Bridges information and decision-making	Relevant for interpretive, co-constructed AI systems
Davis (1993)	AI and cognitive science	Knowledge representation	Data as performative structure of understanding	Questions assumptions behind data schemas	Supports critical interrogation of algorithmic categories
Illich (1973)	Philosophy of technology	Conviviality	Technology as a tool for autonomy and mutual aid	Advocates human-centric, non-extractive tech use	Foundational source for convivial AI paradigm
Manifesto Convivialista (2014)	Political philosophy	Conviviality, ethics of interdependence	Data and tech governed by values of care and cooperation	Calls for collective responsibility in shaping the digital	Provides ethical and ideological grounding for conviviality

(*Contd.*)

(Contd.)

Author(s) & Year	Domain/ Perspective	Key concept(s)	Approach to data	Contribution to digital sovereignty	Relevance to convivial AI
Gorz (2015)	Post-growth critique	Anti-productivism	Critique of efficiency-driven technology use	Supports decommodified, value-based data practices	Aligns with slow data and localized governance
Culkin (1967)	Media theory	Medium as message	Technology shapes society and behavior	Warns against uncritical tech adoption	Reinforces need for active, community-based tech design
Haraway (1985, 1988)	Feminist theory/ STS	Situated knowledge, cyborg theory	Data as embedded in power and context	Challenges neutrality of AI systems	Core influence for inclusive, reflexive AI design

to initiate a fundamental rethinking of its design and purpose. The first step is to critically examine how data is collected, produced and analyzed, and to explore ways of constructing datasets that arise from local realities, lived experiences and shared values. Such datasets could form the basis for future AI tools that are more attentive to the communities they engage. This brings us back to the concept of digital agency.

This perspective underlines the importance of exercising the agency on both data and technology, allowing communities to participate actively in designing systems that reflect their needs, values and world views (Culkin, 1967).

Such an approach stands in sharp contrast to data extractivism. It calls for a series of paradigm shifts that reorient AI toward the collective good and transform it into a facilitator of collective knowledge and inclusive decision-making. Among these are a move from centralized, top-down governance toward more community-led, bottom-up processes; a reconceptualization of AI not as a finished product but as something adaptive and evolving, shaped by cultural and social diversity; and a rejection of the relentless pursuit of big data in favour of slow data, gathered intentionally, with care and consent.

A convivial approach underscores the importance of inclusivity, care ethics, and situated knowledge, recognizing that AI technologies are never neutral but always embedded in specific power relations, cultural dynamics, and ecological contexts (Haraway, 1985; 1988).

The following table presents key theoretical contributions that inform the Convivial AI paradigm in this research, outlining how each work conceptualizes data, contributes to the understanding of digital sovereignty, and supports the development of a convivial approach (Table 11.1).

11.4 A Convivial Methodology

This chapter proposes a convivial methodology as a civic practice that empowers communities to reclaim agency over data and digital infrastructures. Grounded in participatory design, ecofeminist ethics, and situated knowledge, the methodology unfolds in three interconnected phases: (1) Context awareness, (2) Tools co-design, and (3) Knowledge co-creation.

1. Context awareness marks the initial phase, where local stakeholders, including civic actors, institutions, and community members, collaboratively identify the issues, needs, and priorities to be addressed. This phase defines the purpose and focus of the methodology's application, establishing a shared agenda. Engagement with local institutions and partners plays a crucial role in facilitating access, trust, and participation, anchoring the process in territorial and cultural specificity. Here, the foundations of data agency are laid: the community begins to shift from being data subjects to active agents in shaping what data will be collected and why.
2. Tools co-design is the second phase, wherein communities engage in a variety of participatory activities such as exploratory walks, co-mapping exercises, thematic workshops, and feedback loops. These activities are structured to support the co-design of data collection and analysis tools that are meaningful

to the context and aligned with the priorities identified earlier. This phase draws attention to the need for grounding data practices in local knowledge and shared values. It's not just about what data is gathered, but about interrogating whose experiences it represents, how it was collected, and why it holds significance within a given context. It's not just about what data is gathered, but about interrogating whose experiences it represents, how it was collected, and why it holds significance within a given context. By taking these questions seriously, communities can begin to influence the structure and interpretation of data itself, embedding forms of collective agency and sovereignty into the very fabric of technical design.

3. The final phase focuses on knowledge co-creation. Here, insights developed earlier are synthesized and translated into outputs that communities can use and adapt, whether as policy proposals, shared vocabularies, visual tools, or frameworks for ongoing governance. It's a moment where abstract analysis becomes concrete, situated, and actionable.

The implementation of this methodology across diverse pilot experiments in urban neighbourhoods such as Castellammare di Stabia and Utrecht, and in rural settings like Atena Lucana, demonstrates its adaptability and relevance to a wide range of social and geographic contexts. Furthermore, for operationalizing this methodology, cultural heritage (Council of Europe, 2005)—what is considered meaningful for a community—serves as a gateway for community members to engage in self-representation, enabling them to structure their knowledge systems in a way that reflects local priorities rather than valuable external criteria. This serves as both an anchor and catalyst throughout this process, grounding the methodology in local memory, identity, and symbols, and providing a foundation for communities to reimagine their futures through technology. The presented methodology emphasizes the critical importance and transformative potential of reclaiming data as a collective act of agency. At its core lies the conviction that rethinking data is not merely a technical adjustment, but a foundational shift that redefines the very epistemological and political ground on which AI systems operate. Focusing on slow data, the convivial methodology proposed here encourages communities to reframe their view of data as part of a common knowledge infrastructure that reflects the values, priorities and experiences of those who produce it. At the heart of this perspective is the idea that people should be able to decide which data matter, how they are interpreted, and for what purpose. This means fostering collective forms of data sovereignty and providing a basis for long-term transformations. It creates opportunities for municipalities, grassroots organizations, civic groups, and even private actors to collaborate in shaping AI systems as the result of socially negotiated choices grounded in collective agency.

11.5 Lessons Learnt from Three Pilot Experiments

This section reflects on insights gained from three pilot projects where the convivial methodology was tested in the field. Castellammare di Stabia (Italy), Utrecht (Netherlands), and Atena Lucana (Italy) each present distinct territorial, social, and institutional dynamics. These differences made it possible to explore how various communities, in varied settings, can reclaim agency over data, technology, and the narratives that emerge from them.

11.5.1 Castellammare di Stabia: Emotional Mapping of Water Heritage

The first pilot experiment took place in Castellammare di Stabia, a small coastal town in southern Italy known for its hot springs and hydrogeological wealth. Unfortunately, despite this city's wealth of water resources, urban degradation and the abandonment of thermal infrastructures have caused a slow deterioration of this heritage, causing its inaccessibility to the community. This complex and frustrating condition has encouraged a certain interest to conduct the experiment here with the intention of underlining the strong link between the community and this heritage, using water as a symbolic and emotional means from which to generate situated data. The community engaged was diverse, ranging from students and local cultural activists to residents with long-standing ties to the city's heritage. The co-design tools phase began with participatory walks and co-mapping sessions that invited participants to recall and spatially annotate personal memories linked to water. The process emphasized affective and situated knowledge, positioning the community as both data producers and interpreters. Data was collected through hand-drawn maps, photographs, and annotated texts. These were digitized and processed using fuzzy logic tools (Zadeh, 1973; Cardone, 2024) and GIS-based tools (Cinderby, 1999) to visualize emotional geographies. The resulting visualizations, including emotional maps and relational diagrams, offered not only an alternative narrative of the city but also a platform for knowledge co-creation and future planning. This method helped participants become aware of their own memory as data, and of data as a form of civic power. The data generated was not a passive representation but a co-authored narrative that challenged official top-down representations of urban space. In this way, Castellammare's experiment contributed to the creation of slow data capable of informing future localized AI tools grounded in emotional relevance (Figure 11.1).

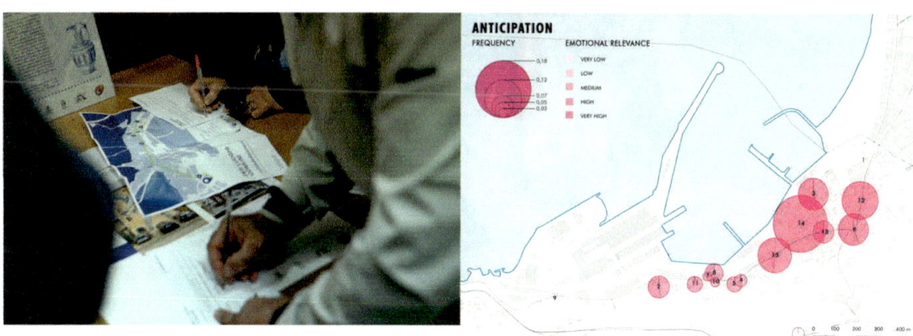

Figure 11.1. Results of first pilot experiment.

11.5.2 Utrecht: Co-Creation of Urban Vocabularies

Utrecht, a rapidly growing and multicultural city in the Netherlands, was selected as a pilot to explore how Convivial AI could function in a dense and policy-driven urban environment. The experiment was developed in collaboration with the NEB-STAR project and focused on the articulation of shared urban values like safety, vibrancy, beauty and belonging in the context of the "10-minute city" framework. The community involved included university researchers, civic organizations, and policy actors. Through a series of workshops, participants were invited to reflect on their personal and collective understandings of the main research themes, collaboratively building a relational vocabulary that more accurately captured how residents of Utrecht experience safety, beauty, vibrancy, and belonging across the city's neighbourhoods. The co-design tools phase employed included open-ended interviews, collaborative brainstorming sessions, semantic clustering, and GIS-based mapping. These enabled the participants to reframe key urban concepts using their own terms and categories. They discussed, selected, and annotated terms, which were then linked to places on the city map. The process allowed for the generation of a dataset built on shared values rather than statistical abstraction. It gave visibility to participants' priorities, highlighting how their perspectives could contribute to the creation of more robust and context-aware datasets, potentially informing the training of future AI systems adopted by institutions for urban planning. At the same time, the process fostered the construction of collective knowledge around key urban themes, offering valuable insights for shaping future planning strategies in ways that are more inclusive and grounded in lived experience (Figure 11.2).

Figure 11.2. Results of second pilot experiment.

11.5.3 Atena Lucana: Collective Clustering of Family Archives

Atena Lucana is a small rural town in Southern Italy, part of the country's so-called Inner Areas, which face chronic depopulation and cultural erosion. Despite its marginalization, the town retains a rich cultural heritage, particularly embedded in family archives and intergenerational memory. This rural pilot was selected to address critical issues of data sovereignty in fragile contexts where infrastructural and social capital are limited, but cultural and affective capital remain deeply rooted. The context awareness phase engaged residents and local associations, centring on a community archive of family photographs. The use of family photographs in this experiment offered a powerful entry point into the values, memories, and everyday life of the local community. Through participatory photo-tagging sessions, the local community was invited to collectively define how to categorize these photographs, not adopting a pre-existing algorithmic logic, but participating in iterative feedback loops to improve this categorization based on their collective values. The process began with a simple invitation: participants were encouraged to bring in personal photos, share the stories behind them, and collaboratively identify the themes that mattered most. To surface the contrast between machine-driven classification and community logic, the experiment initially employed algorithmic tools like FREDoC and semantic clustering to generate preliminary groupings. These results are a provocative starting point for collective discussions on photo-labels. From these incremental and dialogic processes emerged a community-led taxonomy, obtaining different categories that resonated with the local socio-cultural fabric avoiding generic archival standards. This participatory approach made visible how deeply knowledge is embedded in affective and lived relationships. The community became aware that their family archives were not inert traces of the past but living data sources, capable of shaping classification systems, informing future AI training datasets, and contributing to broader public narratives. In this experiment, data became both a mirror of identity and a tool for empowerment, demonstrating how communities can reclaim authorship over data and assert agency in shaping how their culture is represented and preserved (Figure 11.3).

Figure 11.3. Results of third pilot experiment.

11.5.4 Challenges and Limitations

These experiments reveal that data sovereignty is a dynamic process of negotiation, reflection, and co-creation, where communities actively define how their data is generated, interpreted, and used. In reclaiming their data, communities also reclaim their power to narrate their own stories, shape their own futures, and engage more meaningfully in public life. While the three pilot experiments showcased the transformative potential of the convivial methodology in fostering data agency, they also encountered a number of critical challenges and structural limitations that must be addressed to enable the broader adoption, sustainability, and institutionalization of such approaches. These challenges span across infrastructural, educational, financial, and cultural domains, highlighting the complex ecosystem required to support genuinely participatory data sovereign practices. First and foremost, the issue of funding emerged as a major constraint. All three experiments were resource-intensive, requiring time, facilitation, tools, and continuous engagement with diverse stakeholders. The success of these projects hinged on sustained, often volunteer-based efforts, with limited financial support. Implementing similar initiatives at scale or embedding them within institutional processes, requires dedicated funding streams. These should support not only initial design and data collection but also long-term community engagement, data stewardship, and integration into planning or policy frameworks. Without sustained financial resources, the opportunity to develop grassroots data infrastructures that foster community-driven AI risks remaining a one-off experiment rather than a replicable practice of digital sovereignty. Second, there is a pressing need to strengthen data literacy among citizens (Ala-Mutka, 2011). Across all sites, participants began with varying levels of understanding about data and its role in shaping digital systems and public decisions. While the participatory formats facilitated learning by doing, a more structured investment in data education is necessary. This includes developing accessible curricula and workshops that demystify data collection, AI mechanisms, and governance implications. Data literacy is foundational for cultivating data agency—the ability of individuals and communities to not only generate data but to critically interpret and strategically mobilize it. Third, cultural and institutional openness to alternative models remains uneven. In several instances, the insights and outputs generated through community processes struggled to connect with formal planning or governance mechanisms. This gap is partly due to the inertia of bureaucratic systems and the dominance of technocratic logics, which prioritize efficiency, standardization, and scalability over contextual nuance and relational knowledge. For convivial AI to move from experiment to implementation, institutional actors must embrace new epistemologies of data, rooted in care, plurality, and lived experience, and make space for non-standard formats of knowledge and evidence. Recognizing and legitimizing alternative data practices is a necessary condition for redistributing power and enabling community-led expressions of digital agency (Edwards, 2017). A fourth challenge relates to the technical limitations of scaling participatory approaches to AI. Datasets developed through community-led, slow data processes tend to be small in volume, even if they are rich in meaning. This mismatch can make it difficult to integrate them into conventional AI systems that depend on massive training corpora. But this doesn't make them less valuable. On the contrary, it points to the need for a shift in AI design itself: toward models that are modular, interpretable, and locally adaptable, capable of incorporating qualitative knowledge. A fifth difficulty lies in sustaining long-term community engagement. As seen in all three pilot sites, energy tends to peak when outcomes are visible and closely tied to local values. Yet that momentum can fade if results aren't reinforced or carried forward. This means that there is a need to ensure continuous facilitation, feedback cycles and visible results, making them more effective through the definition of long-term strategies and institutional commitment. Finally, even within inclusive frameworks, the risk of exclusion remains real. While the convivial approach is designed to center marginalized voices, the dynamics of power, language, and access can still shape who gets to participate and how. This makes ongoing reflection essential, along with open communication, iterative co-design and making all practices that ensure results remain open and accessible to all.

11.6 Conclusion

Who decides which data to collect? Whose knowledge and experiences are represented in the training datasets? How is data used to shape results? These questions lie at the heart of a digital sovereignty, understood as the power to imagine and build futures rooted in shared values, collective knowledge, and democratic control.

This need is underscored by recent controversies, such as Meta's decision to use European user data for AI training by default, unless users actively opt out. Despite the existence of robust legal frameworks like the GDPR, this episode reveals a profound gap between regulatory intention and actual public control over personal data. The Meta case is emblematic of a broader tension in contemporary digital governance: the contradiction between formal rights and real agency (Bradford, 2023). While individuals may technically possess the right to consent or refuse, these choices are often presented in ways that are opaque, manipulative, or cognitively overwhelming. True sovereignty cannot be reduced to ticking a box. It must be embedded in processes of education, deliberation, and collective sense-making that allow communities to understand the implications of data use and articulate their preferences in meaningful ways. The recent controversy surrounding Meta's use of user-generated content to train its generative AI models sparked widespread public backlash (and for good reason). In response, opt-out mechanisms were introduced to give individuals more control over their data. On the surface, this seems like a step forward: opting out offers a way to protect one's privacy and push back against exploitative data mining. But the situation is more complicated. When only certain groups opt out, often those more informed or digitally literate, it can skew the models being trained (Iqbal & Ismail, 2025). The result is a new form of exclusion, where absence from the dataset becomes another route to invisibility.

This raises a complex ethical question: how could communities simultaneously protect their data sovereignty and ensure they are adequately represented in the technologies shaping their futures? This paradox brings to the surface a deeper political issue: the right to be represented in data infrastructures cannot depend solely on individual literacy or choice but should be embedded in institutional frameworks of care, inclusion, and governance. Otherwise, DS risks becoming a privilege of those already having power. This underlines the urgency of redefining this concept beyond individuality to collective dimensions. This vision requires a cultural change that positions data as something pertaining to collective responsibility (Ansell et al., 2024).

Through the three pilot experiments explored in this contribution, involving communities in co-designing vocabularies, emotional mappings and interpretive frameworks, the chapter offers a possible path towards a redefinition of DS. The proposed conviviality methodology seeks not only to empower communities to opt-in or opt-out for data extraction, but to promote a new type of data literacy that allows them to act as custodians of their own digital identities and collective memories. In this way, this chapter aims to contribute to the wider debate on digital and data sovereignty by demonstrating that alternative practices on data might be possible.

A Convivial Agenda for Data Sovereignty

The idea of convivial AI suggests that the future of artificial intelligence cannot be understood solely in technical terms. Innovation, in this view, is not solely about more powerful algorithms or faster systems, it depends equally on the social and institutional infrastructures that support democratic deliberation about the kind of AI systems desired, who they serve, and under what conditions they should operate. This vision, in these terms, aims to propose a radical change, namely to view AI governance as an ecosystem of bottom-up practices, requiring cross-sectoral collaboration between politicians, technologists and cultural actors, by helping to create an ethical infrastructure that puts the common good at the centre of data innovation. Starting from this statement, several key opportunities emerge for defining a common agenda (Ansell & Trondal, 2018). One key priority is the development of hybrid infrastructures that combine participatory approaches with scalable technologies, allowing local data to be aggregated without excluding local specificity. This means building mechanisms through which communities can create and interpret their own datasets, shaping technologies that respond to their values and contexts. A second priority involves ensuring that institutional actors facilitate the integration of community-generated knowledge into policy making. This, of course, demands a willingness to redistribute power and reshape traditional decision-making structures. Third, explore new models of collective data governance which institutionalize the role of the community both as a donor and custodian of data. Finally, any meaningful shift will depend on prioritizing digital education and capacity building to ensure that communities have the tools, language and confidence to navigate, challenge and shape the AI systems that affect their lives. Taken together, these four pillars – hybrid infrastructures, institutional inclusion, community-led governance, and digital capacity-building – form a constellation of practices through which a convivial approach to AI and digital sovereignty might take root. Furthermore, promoting a common agenda for data and digital sovereignty requires a solid research base that supports both conceptual understanding and practical implementation. Research has the opportunity to play an important role in assessing how community-generated data practices affect AI systems over time, understanding the social dynamics of participatory governance and exploring how local and situated practices interact with or challenge global standards. Of course, interdisciplinary efforts through design, human studies, data studies and technology can help to define tools that incorporate convivial values into digital infrastructures. By promoting these research directions and addressing the structural gaps identified above, it is possible to give a new direction to AI as a civic infrastructure that reflects care, reciprocity, and collective intelligence, values often left out of dominant technological narratives.

Declaration of Generative AI and AI-Assisted Technologies

During the preparation of this work, the authors utilized AI-assisted tools such as ChatGPT to enhance English language accuracy, including spelling, grammar, and punctuation. The content generated or corrected by these tools was thoroughly reviewed, revised, and edited by the authors to ensure accuracy and originality. The authors accept full responsibility for the originality of the final content of this publication.

References

Aagaard, T., & Lund, A. (2019). *Digital Agency in Higher Education: Transforming Teaching and Learning*. Routledge Focus.

Ala-Mutka, K. (2011). Mapping Digital Competence: Towards a Conceptual Understanding. European Commission, Joint Research Centre, Institute for Prospective Technological Studies.

Ansell, C., & Trondal, J. (2018). Governing turbulence: An organizational-institutional agenda. *Perspectives on Public Management and Governance*, 1(1), 43–57. https://doi.org/10.1093/ppmgov/gvx013

Ansell, C., Sørensen, E., Torfing, J., & Trondal, J. (2024). Robust governance in turbulent times. *Elements in Public Policy*. https://www.cambridge.org/core/elements/robust-governance-in-turbulent-times/AB44DBE9AA636390EC114E8A428BF188

Apostolou, D., Mentzas, G., Young, R., & Abecker, A. (2000). Consolidating the product versus process approaches in knowledge management: The Know-net approach.

Arora, P. (2024). *From Pessimism to Promise: Lessons from the Global South on Designing Inclusive Tech*. MIT Press.

Barbierato, E., & Gatti, A. (2024). Toward Green AI: A methodological survey of the scientific literature. *IEEE Access*, 12, 23989–24013. https://doi.org/10.1109/ACCESS.2024.3360705

Bhatt, G.D. (2002). Management strategies for individual knowledge and organizational knowledge. *Journal of Knowledge Management*, 6(1), 31–39. https://doi.org/10.1108/13673270210417673

Birhane, A., Isaac, W., Prabhakaran, V., Diaz, M., Elish, M.C., Gabriel, I., & Mohamed, S. (2022). Power to the people? Opportunities and challenges for participatory AI. *Equity and Access in Algorithms, Mechanisms, and Optimization*, 1–8. https://doi.org/10.1145/3551624.3555290

Bradford, A. (2023). *Digital Empires: The Global Battle to Regulate Technology*. Oxford University Press.

Brevini, B. (2021). *Is AI Good for the Planet?* John Wiley & Sons.

Brevini, B., & Pasquale, F. (2020). Revisiting the Black Box Society by rethinking the political economy of big data. *Big Data & Society*, 7(2). https://doi.org/10.1177/2053951720935141

Cardone, B., Cerreta, M., Di Martino, F. et al. (2024). A fuzzy-based emotion detection method to classify the attractiveness of urban green spaces. *Evolutionary Intelligence*, 17, 3921–3933. https://doi.org/10.1007/s12065-024-00964-1

Celis Bueno, C. (2017). *The Attention Economy: Labour, Time and Power in Cognitive Capitalism.* Rowman & Littlefield.

Celis Bueno, C., & Schultz Abarca, M.J. (2021). Memo Akten's Learning to See: From machine vision to the machinic unconscious. *AI & Society*, 36(5), 1177–1187. https://doi.org/10.1007/s00146-020-01071-2

Chiolero, A. (2022). How infodemic intoxicates public health. Surveillance: From a big to a slow data culture. *Journal of Epidemiology and Community Health*, 76(7), 623–625. https://doi.org/10.1136/jech-2022-219051

Chiolero, A., Tancredi, S., & Ioannidis, J.P.A. (2023). Slow data public health. *European Journal of Epidemiology*, 38, 1219–1225. https://doi.org/10.1007/s10654-023-01049-6

Choo, C.W. (2002). Sensemaking, knowledge creation, and decision making: Organizational knowing as emergent strategy. In: C.W. Choo & N. Bontis (eds.), *The Strategic Management of Intellectual Capital and Organizational Knowledge* (pp. 79–88). Oxford University Press.

Cinderby, S. (1999). Geographic information systems (GIS) for participation: The future of environmental GIS? *International Journal of Environment and Pollution*, 11(3), 304. https://doi.org/10.1504/ijep.1999.002263

Coeckelbergh, M. (2022). *The Political Philosophy of AI: An Introduction.* John Wiley & Sons.

Cooper, L.R. (2019). A future perfect: Queer digital sovereignty in Joshua Whitehead's Jonny Appleseed and full-metal indigiqueer. *Contemporary Literature*, 60(4), 491–514.

Council of Europe. (2005). Council of Europe Framework Convention on the Value of Cultural Heritage for Society. In: *Faro Declaration of the Council of Europe's Strategy for Developing Intercultural Dialogue*.

Couture, S., & Toupin, S. (2019). What does the notion of "sovereignty" mean when referring to the digital? *New Media & Society*, 21(10), 2305–2322. https://doi.org/10.1177/1461444819865984

Crawford, K. (2021). *The Atlas of AI: Power, Politics, and the Planetary Costs of Artificial Intelligence.* Yale University Press.

Creemers, R. (2020). China's conception of cyber sovereignty: Rhetoric and realization. *SSRN Electronic Journal*. https://doi.org/10.2139/ssrn.3532421

Cugurullo, F., Caprotti, F., Cook, M., Karvonen, A., McGuirk, P., & Marvin, S. (2024). The rise of AI urbanism in post-smart cities: A critical commentary on urban artificial intelligence. *Urban Studies*, 61(6), 1168–1182. https://doi.org/10.1177/00420980231203386

Culkin, J. (1967, March). A schoolman's guide to Marshall McLuhan. *Saturday Review*, 51–53, 70–72.

D'Ignazio, C., & Klein, L.F. (2020). *Data Feminism*. MIT Press.

Davis, R., Shrobe, H., & Szolovits, P. (1993). What is a knowledge representation? *AI Magazine*, 14(1), 17–33.

Delgado, F., Yang, S., Madaio, M., & Yang, Q. (2023). The participatory turn in AI design: Theoretical foundations and the current state of practice. *Equity and Access in Algorithms, Mechanisms, and Optimization*, 1–23. https://doi.org/10.1145/3617694.3623261

Edwards, A. (Ed.). (2017). *Working Relationally in and Across Practices: A Cultural-Historical Approach to Collaboration.* Cambridge University Press.

Etelepälto, A., Vähäsantanen, K., Hökkä, P., & Paloniemi, S. (2013). What is agency? Conceptualizing professional agency at work. *Educational Research Review*, 10, 45–65. https://doi.org/10.1016/j.edurev.2013.05.001

Fanon, F., Sartre, J.P., & Farrington, C. (1968). *The Wretched of the Earth* (First Evergreen Black Cat Edition). Grove Press.

Farrand, B., & Carrapico, H. (2022). Digital sovereignty and taking back control: From regulatory capitalism to regulatory mercantilism in EU cybersecurity. *European Security*, 31(3), 435–453. https://doi.org/10.1080/09662839.2022.2102896

Feijóo, C., Gómez-Barroso, J.L., Lago, A., & Bohlin, E. (2020). Harnessing artificial intelligence (AI) to increase wellbeing for all: The case for a new technology diplomacy. *Telecommunications Policy*, 44(6), 101988. https://doi.org/10.1016/j.telpol.2020.101988

Floridi, L. (2013). *The Ethics of Information*. OUP Oxford.

Floridi, L. (2020). The fight for digital sovereignty: What it is, and why it matters, especially for the EU. *Philosophy & Technology*, 33, 369–378.

Fontes, C., Al Haddad, C., Antoniou, C., & Lütge, C. (2024). Assessing the collective challenges of AI: An applied framework focused on people centeredness and public participation. *Urban Governance*, 4(4), 245–254. https://doi.org/10.1016/j.ugj.2024.12.003

Fratini, S. (2024). Performing privacy culture. The platform Threema and the contestation of surveillance made in Switzerland. *Studi Culturali*, 1, 3–26. https://doi.org/10.1405/113065

Fratini, S., Hine, E., Novelli, C., et al. (2024). Digital sovereignty: A descriptive analysis and a critical evaluation of existing models. *DISO*, 3, 59. https://doi.org/10.1007/s44206-024-00146-7

Gorz, A. (2015). Ecologia e libertà. Edizioni Ambiente.

Granata, E. (2021). Placemaker. Gli inventori dei luoghi che abiteremo. Einaudi.

Hacker, P. (2020). *AI Regulation in Europe*. SSRN Scholarly Paper. Rochester, NY. https://doi.org/10.2139/ssrn.3556532

Haraway, D. (1988). Situated knowledges: The science question in feminism and the privilege of partial perspective. *Feminist Studies*, 14(3), 575–599. https://doi.org/10.2307/3178066

Haraway, D.J. (1985). A manifesto for cyborgs: Science, technology, and socialist-feminism in the 1980s. In: *Simians, Cyborgs, and Women: The Reinvention of Nature* (pp. 149–181). Routledge.

Herian, R. (2020). Blockchain, GDPR, and fantasies of data sovereignty. *Law, Innovation and Technology*, 12(1), 156–174. https://doi.org/10.1080/17579961.2020.1727094

Hummel, T., Braun, M., Dabrock, P., Heesen, J., & Hausstein, A. (2021). Various approaches to digital sovereignty. *European Journal of Risk Regulation*, 13(2), 270–294. https://doi.org/10.1017/err.2021.52

Iaconesi, S. (2018, September). The perception of the city. *Medium*. https://xdxd-vs-xdxd.medium.com/the-perception-of-the-city-6ac4644e3619

Illich, I. (1973). *Tools for Conviviality*. Glasgow: Fontana/Collins.

Iqbal, R., & Ismail, S. (2025). Unbiased AI for a sovereign digital future: A bias detection framework. *Procedia Computer Science*, 254, 118–126. https://doi.org/10.1016/j.procs.2025.02.070

Jaiswal, R., & Schaathun, H.G. (2025). On human sovereignty in a digital age. *Procedia Computer Science*, 254, 157–163. https://doi.org/10.1016/j.procs.2025.02.074

Khan, M., Haleem, A., & Javaid, M. (2023). Changes and improvements in Industry 5.0: A strategic approach to overcome the challenges of Industry 4.0. *Green Technologies and Sustainability*, 1(2), 100020. https://doi.org/10.1016/j.grets.2023.100020

Latour, B. (2005). *Reassembling the Social: An Introduction to Actor-Network-Theory*. Oxford University Press.

Lévy, P. (1997). *Collective Intelligence: Mankind's Emerging World in Cyberspace*. Perseus Books.

Lévy, P. (2004). Ciberdemocracia: Ensayo sobre filosofía política. Editorial UOC.

Manifesto Convivialista. (2014). Retrieved from https://manifestoconvivialista.org

Mauri, A., Hsu, Y.-C., Verma, H., Tocchetti, A., Brambilla, M., & Bozzon, A. (2024). Policy sandboxing: Empathy as an enabler towards inclusive policy-making. *Proceedings of the ACM on Human-Computer Interaction*, 8(CSCW2), Article 369, 1–42. https://doi.org/10.1145/3686908

Mazzucato, M. (2018). *The Value of Everything: Making and Taking in the Global Economy*. Penguin UK.

Misra, S., Barik, K., & Kvalvik, P. (2025). Digital sovereignty in the era of Industry 5.0: Challenges and opportunities. *Procedia Computer Science*, 254, 108–117. https://doi.org/10.1016/j.procs.2025.02.069

Monsees, L., & Lambach, D. (2022). Digital sovereignty, geopolitical imaginaries, and the reproduction of European identity. *European Security*, 31(3), 377–394. https://doi.org/10.1080/09662839.2022.2101883

Musiani, F. (2022). Infrastructuring digital sovereignty: A research agenda for an infrastructure-based sociology of digital self-determination practices. *Information, Communication & Society*, 25(6), 785–800. https://doi.org/10.1080/1369118X.2022.2049850

Novelli, C., Casolari, F., Rotolo, A., Taddeo, M., & Floridi, L. (2023). Taking AI risks seriously: A new assessment model for the AI Act. *AI & Society*. Advance online publication. https://doi.org/10.1007/s00146-023-01723-z

Ostrom, E. (1990). *Governing the Commons: The Evolution of Institutions for Collective Action.* Cambridge University Press.

Passey, D., Shonfeld, M., Appleby, L. et al. (2018). Digital agency: Empowering equity in and through education. *Tech Know Learn*, 23, 425–439. https://doi.org/10.1007/s10758-018-9384-x

Pohle, J., & Thiel, T. (2020). Digital sovereignty. *Internet Policy Review*, 9(4). https://doi.org/10.14763/2020.4.1532

Prasad, R. (2022). People as data, data as oil: The digital sovereignty of the Indian state. *Information, Communication & Society*, 25(6), 801–815. https://doi.org/10.1080/1369118X.2022.2056498

Raymond, M., & DeNardis, L. (2015). Multistakeholderism: Anatomy of an inchoate global institution. *International Theory*, 7(3), 572–616.

Ricaurte, P. (2019). Data epistemologies, the coloniality of power, and resistance. *Television & New Media*, 20(4), 350–365. https://doi.org/10.1177/1527476419831640

Robbins, S., & van Wynsberghe, A. (2022). Our new artificial intelligence infrastructure: Becoming locked into an unsustainable future. *Sustainability*, 14(8), 4829. https://doi.org/10.3390/su14084829

Roberts, H., Cowls, J., Casolari, F., Morley, J., Taddeo, M., & Floridi, L. (2021). Safeguarding European values with digital sovereignty: An analysis of statements and policies. *SSRN Electronic Journal*. https://doi.org/10.2139/ssrn.3937345

Roberts, H., Hine, E., & Floridi, L. (2023). Digital sovereignty, digital expansionism, and the prospects for global AI governance. In: M. Timoteo, B. Verri, & R. Nanni (eds.), *Quo vadis, sovereignty?* (Vol. 154, pp. 51–75). Philosophical Studies Series. Springer Nature Switzerland. https://doi.org/10.1007/978-3-031-41566-1_4

Schmitter, P.C. (2001). What is there to legitimize in the European Union...and how might this be accomplished? Working Paper, Institut für Höhere Studien, Political Science Series, 75. https://jeanmonnetprogram.org/archive/papers/01/011401-01.html

Shaffer, D.W., & Clinton, K.A. (2006). Toolforthoughts: Reexamining thinking in the digital age. *Mind, Culture, and Activity*, 13(4), 283–300. https://doi.org/10.1207/s15327884mca1304_2

Srnicek, N. (2017). *Platform Capitalism*. Polity Press.

Stewart, M. (2017). Of digital selves and digital sovereignty: Of the North. *Film Quarterly*, 70(4), 23–38. https://doi.org/10.1525/fq.2017.70.4.23

Taylor, J., & Kukutai, T. (2016). Indigenous data sovereignty: Toward an agenda. In: *Indigenous Data Sovereignty* (pp. 1–22). Australian National University Press.

Terranova, T. (2000). Free labor: Producing culture for the digital economy. *Social Text*, 18(2), 35–58.

Tretter, M. (2023). Sovereignty in the digital and contact tracing apps. *Digital Society*, 2(1), 2. https://doi.org/10.1007/s44206-022-00030-2

Varon, J., & Peña, P. (2021). Artificial intelligence and consent: A feminist anti-colonial critique. *Internet Policy Review*, 10(4). https://doi.org/10.14763/2021.4.1602
Walter, M., Kukutai, T., Russo Carroll, S., & Rodriguez-Lonebear, D. (2020). *Indigenous Data Sovereignty and Policy* (1st ed.). Routledge. https://doi.org/10.4324/9780429273957
Whitehead, M. (2020). Surveillance capitalism in the time of Covid-19. Independent Social Research Foundation. https://www.isrf.org/2020/05/11/surveillance-capitalism-in-the-time-of-covid 19-the-possible-costs-of-technological-liberation-from-lockdown/
Woods, A. (2023). Digital sovereignty + artificial intelligence. In: *The Rise of Digital Constitutionalism* (pp. 101–122). Oxford University Press. https://doi.org/10.1093/oso/9780197582794.003.0006
Yadav, Y.S. (2025). Agile organizing of national cyber defence capabilities: Decoupling external dependencies and catalysing digital sovereignty. *Procedia Computer Science*, 254, 260–268. https://doi.org/10.1016/j.procs.2025.02.085
Zadeh, L.A. (1973). Outline of a new approach to the analysis of complex systems and decision processes. *IEEE Transactions on Systems, Man, and Cybernetics*, SMC-3(1), 28–44. https://doi.org/10.1109/tsmc.1973.5408575
Zhang, A., Walker, O., Nguyen, K., Dai, J., Chen, A., & Lee, M. K. (2023). Deliberating with AI: Improving decision-making for the future through participatory AI design and stakeholder deliberation. *Proceedings of the ACM on Human-Computer Interaction*, 7(CSCW1), 1–32. https://doi.org/10.1145/3579601
Zuboff, S. (2015). Big other: Surveillance capitalism and the prospects of an information civilization. *Journal of Information Technology*, 30(1), 75–89. https://doi.org/10.1057/jit.2015.5
Zuboff, S. (2019). The age of surveillance capitalism: The fight for a human future at the new frontier of power. *PublicAffairs*.

CHAPTER
12

From Benefits to Ethics of Artificial Intelligence Application Towards the Industry 4.0 and Beyond

Le Nam Hai Pham(0000-0003-4578-2811)
University of South-Eastern Norway

12.1 Introduction

Artificial Intelligence (AI) technology has undergone nearly 70 years of development since the term was first introduced in 1956 (Crevier, 1994). As AI techniques continue to mature and become more integrated into human work, we can expect an increase in robots and intelligent programs that can assist humans in various tasks, such as replying to emails, cleaning, and driving cars.

The definition and understanding of AI are indeed crucial when discussing ethics in AI applications. The term "Artificial Intelligence" reflects a technology designed to replicate or even enhance the cognitive abilities of the human mind. This encapsulates a wide range of capabilities, from reasoning and learning to generalizing and problem-solving. Alan Turing's pioneering work laid the foundation for the idea that machines could simulate human thinking processes (Muggleton, 2014). Building on this, B.J. Copeland, a well-known scholar in the field of AI, described it as the capability of a digital computer or a computer-controlled robot to execute tasks typically requiring human intelligence (Copeland, 1999). These tasks include reasoning, understanding context, learning from experience, and adapting to new situations. Understanding AI like this highlights its potential and the ethical considerations it entails. Since AI systems are increasingly integrated into various aspects of human life, from healthcare to finance to everyday decision-making, their ability to emulate human thought raises questions about autonomy, responsibility, fairness, and the potential consequences of delegating critical decisions to machines.

Email: le.pham@usn.no

DOI: 10.1201/9781003581581-12

Ethics in AI thus involve ensuring that these systems are designed, deployed, and managed in ways that respect human values and prevent harm.

The advancement of digital transformation, driven by cutting-edge information and communication technology, has shaped Industry 4.0, also known as the Fourth Industrial Revolution as shown in Figure 12.1. This era is characterized using intelligent machines equipped with wireless networks and sensors that can visualize production processes and make autonomous decisions. It reflects the modern trend of integrating automation technologies into manufacturing and implementation sectors. AI plays a pivotal role in this revolution, spearheading progress through its capacity to collect, organize, and analyse vast datasets. However, the ethical implications of AI in Industry 4.0 continue to spark debate.

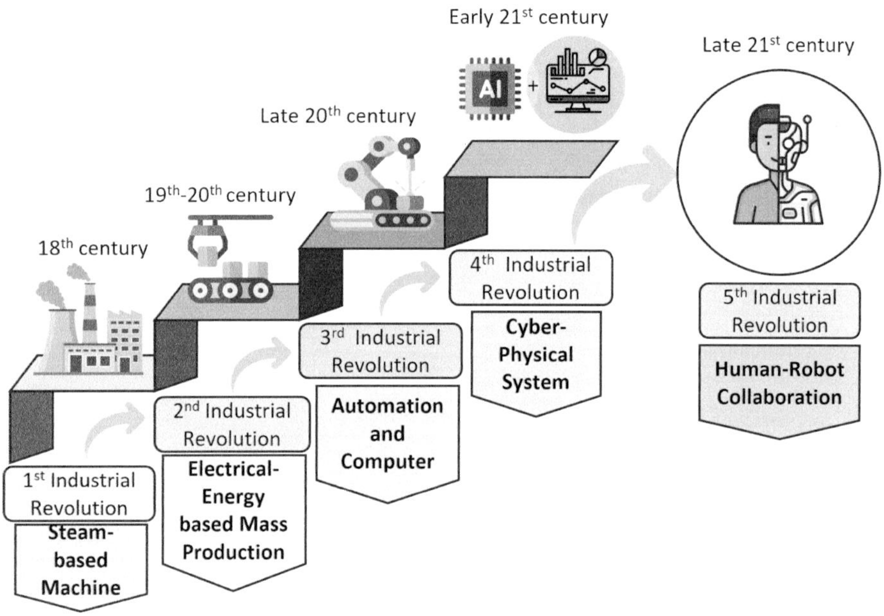

Figure 12.1. The fourth industrial revolution within the human interface.

In recent years, extensive research has examined the ethical implications of AI applications(Vollmer et al., 2018; Shaheen, 2021). While the influence and value of AI are widely acknowledged, contemporary discourse reveals a diversity of perspectives. For example, Toll et al. (2020) analyzed 522 statements on AI found in policy documents, categorizing them by value ideals and inductively derived themes. Notably, 46% of these statements (240 out of 522) focused on considerations and risks, underscoring the growing concerns surrounding AI deployment. Furthermore, in the open-access volume "Artificial Intelligence for a Better Future" (Stahl, 2021), Bernd Carsten Stahl and colleagues introduced a novel ethical framework for AI use, addressing problematic consequences such as bias, discrimination, violations of privacy and security. With the relevant concepts, the studies evaluating the ethical issues involving AI use are also cited by Li & Zhang,2017. However, this body of research focuses primarily on the ethical aspects of AI use, offering limited insight into future solutions and developmental pathways—particularly within industrial contexts.

This chapter, pursuing a similar objective, examines the ethical challenges surrounding AI deployment in the Industry 4.0 era and proposes strategic directions for addressing them.It aims to answer the following key questions: (1) What are the current ethical concerns surrounding AI use? (2) What are the future directions for AI development in addressing these ethical concerns?

Figure 12.2 represents visually the keywords extracted from the benefits and ethics of this chapter.

The main contributions of this chapter can be outlined as follows:

- Identifying the benefits and ethical challenges of AI applications in industrial contexts. This contribution offers a comprehensive overview of both the advantages and ethical concerns associated with AI integration, supported by relevant and up-to-date literature.
- Proposing strategic solutions for future AI deployment. The chapter outlines considerations to guide the responsible implementation of AI technologies in future industrial applications.

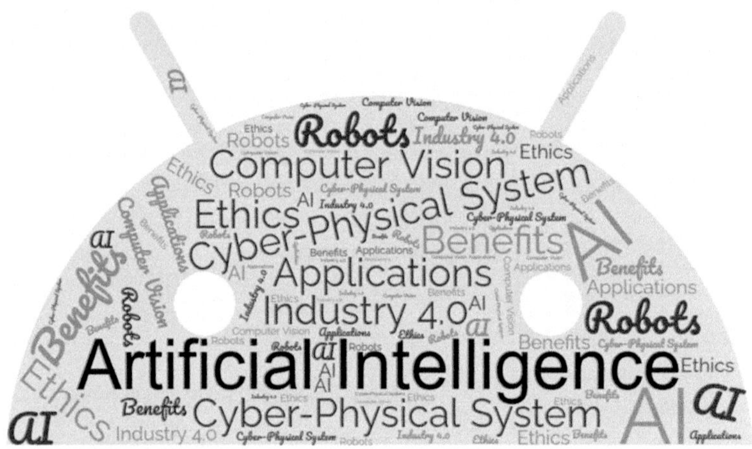

Figure 12.2. Keyword cloud based on the terms used in this project.

The structure of this chapter begins with an overview of the benefits of AI in industrial applications, followed by a discussion of instances where AI systems may breach ethical boundaries, and concludes with an exploration of the future prospects for Industry 4.0 in addressing these ethical challenges.

12.2 Benefits of AI in Industry 4.0

Previously confined to the realm of science fiction, AI has increasingly become a part of our daily lives and industries in recent years (Vollmer et al., 2018). With its broad range of applications, AI enables more natural and effective interactions between humans and machines, offering deeper insights into consumer relationships, behaviors, and motivations. By rapidly analysing data to make predictions and identify trends, AI is at the forefront of recent innovations in the ongoing industrial revolution, driven by digital transformation and big data.

Compared to traditional systems without AI integration, AI-enabled systems offer numerous benefits that significantly enhance operational performance (Pham et al., 2025a), decision-making (Pham et al., 2025b), and adaptability. In sectors like manufacturing, logistics, healthcare, and finance, AI integration leads to enhanced resource optimization, cost savings, better quality control, and improved customer satisfaction (Eckhart & Ekelhart, 2019). While traditional systems rely heavily on fixed rules and human oversight, AI introduces agility, scalability, and data-driven intelligence, key features for staying competitive in the fast-paced environment of Industry 4.0.

The benefits of AI integration into modern industries bring aspects of social and economic development. Table 12.1 provides social impacts and economic impacts corresponding to the main benefits of AI applications.

Table 12.1. Social and economic impacts with main benefits of AI applications

Aspect	Main benefits	Social impacts	Economic impacts
Productivity & Efficiency	• Automation of repetitive tasks • Increased speed and accuracy • Optimised operation	• Potential for job displacement • Creation of new job roles • Improved work-life balance	• Cost reduction • Increased output and revenue • Higher labour productivity
Decision-making & Insights	• Advanced data analysis • Enhanced decision-making • Predictive analytics	• Improved public services • More information policymaking • Ethical concerns	• Enhanced competitiveness • New product and service development • Better risk management
Innovation	• Accelerated research and development • Simulation and design	• Advancements in critical sectors • Addressing complex societal problems	• Creation of new industries • Increased investment and economic growth

As shown in Table 12.1, entering a new decade, it is unsurprising that AI technology is expected to deliver further innovations, offering distinct and measurable advantages through its applications.

The deployment of AI in Industry 4.0 can take the following forms according to Figure 12.3: (1) Smart factories (Soori et al., 2023), (2) Predictive maintenance (Aivaliotis et al., 2019), (3) Computer vision (Voulodimos et al., 2018), (4) Cyber-physical systems (Pham, 2023), and (5) Industrial robots (Grau et al., 2021).

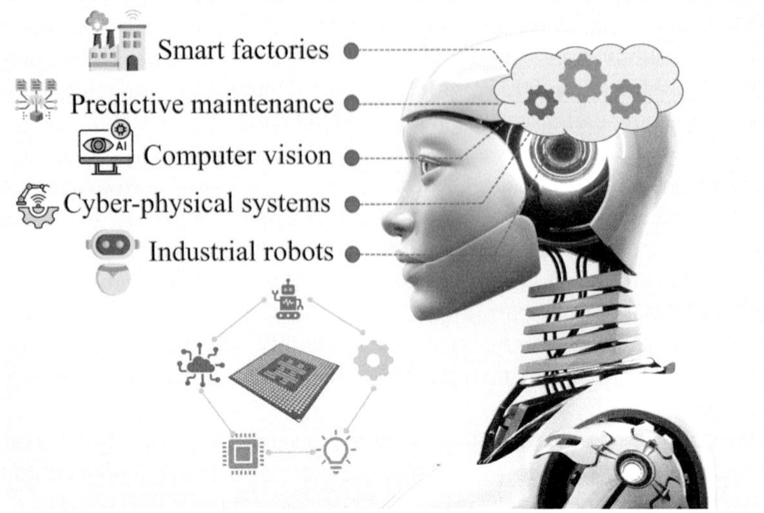

Figure 12.3. Benefits of AI in Industry 4.0.

Firstly, the concept of smart factories is derived from IoT, which envisages a production environment as a fully automatic and intelligent network of systems enabling facilities, machines, and logistics chains within the manufacturing process without human intervention (Evjemo et al., 2020). AI plays a transformative role in smart factories by driving digital innovation that enhances quality control, standardization, and maintenance. Through predictive analysis of equipment functionality and status, AI enables the thorough streamlining of factory lines. Wireless sensor networks, connecting machines, tools, materials, and production surfaces, like conveyor belts, allow all manufacturing assets to be tracked in real time, providing operators with full visibility across the entire production chain (Shrouf et al., 2014). Consequently, the integration of AI in smart factories contributes to reduced production downtime and improved overall operational efficiency (Abidi et al., 2022).

To enhance the reliability and safety of factories and industrial production chains, large volumes of collected f data are being leveraged to predict maintenance schedules and prevent equipment and process failures. Predictive maintenance can be automated, enabling plant operations to be strategically aligned with equipment condition and estimated maintenance duration (Falekas & Karlis, 2021). This approach offers significant benefits to industry, including cost saving, improved predictability and increased system availability.

Within the scope of computational capabilities, computer vision is a key industrial application focused on enabling machines to encode and identify objects for decision-making processes. The vast volumes of data generated daily can be harnessed to train, refine, and optimize computer vision systems (Li & Zhang, 2017). This AI application is critical in the automation driven industries, where machines can make independent decisions in real-time scenarios, such as self-driving car technology.

Cyber-physical systems represent a convergence of physical and computational processes applicable across a broad spectrum of domains including smart grids (Wagle et al., 2023), autonomous automotive systems (Brenner & Herrmann, 2018), robotics and smart manufacturing (Soori et al., 2023). The integration of internet-based systems further expands industrial possibilities, transforming how humans interact with the physical world via cyber workspaces. This AI driven application enables real-time problem solving facilitating global collaboration and supporting fully remote and efficiently distributed manufacturing environments (Pham, Rosero-Morillo, et al., 2024). For instance, in smart grid systems, cyber-physical technologies enable real-time monitoring and management of energy distribution, leading to more efficient and reliable power supply networks (Gonzalez-Longatt & Pham, 2024; Pham, Wagle, et al., 2024). A notable example of such systems in smart grids is the development of virtual protection relays (Pham et al., 2023; Pham & Gonzalez-Longatt, 2023).

Additionally, one of the significant programmable benefits derived from AI applications is the industrial robot (Boyer, 2021). These robots, equipped with multiple manipulators and the ability to be programmed across three or more axes, offer enhanced precision and operational accuracy. Their versatility allows them to be effectively utilized in various industries, particularly in tasks such as welding, painting, and other processes that require high levels of consistency and precision. Industrial robots, powered by AI, are transforming manufacturing and production, driving efficiency and improving the quality of outcomes across a range of applications.

12.3 Ethical Issues of AI

Though the remarkable benefits of AI in the industrial revolution 4.0, the potential issues in the ethics field are indisputable and debated on for many years recently. Amid global fluctuations and the pursuit of self-interest across public and private industries, ethical concerns surrounding AI applications are becoming increasingly frequent. It is essential to highlight the key ethical issues arising from the development, deployment and use of AI within the context of Industry 4.0.

12.3.1 Incorrect Decision-making

AI is increasingly integral to the ongoing industrial revolution. Technologies such as autonomous transportation, robotic security systems and companion robots are either already in use or expected to become widely available in the near future. However, these advancements are not without limitations and raise critical questions of accountability when AI systems fail or make errors.

AI in human society, including industrial workshops, are the black-box problem and algorithmic bias (Can We Open the Black Box of AI? : Nature News & Comment, n.d.). The term "Black-Box issue", refers to the opacity of AI decision-making processes, which cannot be evaluated either during or after the decision is made. AI systems operate autonomously based on pre-programmed parameters, often without human intervention. When harm or injury results from an AI-driven action, the opaque nature of its decision-making poses significant challenges for assigning liability. The absence of full human control over AI behavior leads to a lack of foreseeability and complicates the establishment of causal links between the victim and culprit, or between the damage and the liable party (Yu & Alì, 2019). The attribution of legal responsibility to a specific liable entity, therefore, is hindered.

The second major liability concern involves bias, which arises when AI systems behave in ways that reflect social intolerance or institutional discrimination. These systems learn from training data that may embed biased human decisions, reflect historical and social inequities, including sensitive variables such as gender, race, sexual orientation and culture (Ntoutsi et al., 2020). The resulting bias can have serious consequences for organizations and industries, ranging from legal liabilities to lost financial opportunities. Additionally, bias in AI can inflict direct harm on humans, for instance, by influencing admissions to schools or companies, authorizations for bank loans, or approvals for rental applications. Inaccurate decision-making can also affect critical areas such as scheduling medical appointments or responding to emergencies, thereby posing risks to human health and safety.

Data manipulation is a significant factor contributing to flawed decision-making by AI systems in Industry 4.0. When the input data is inaccurate, incomplete, or biased, even technically sound algorithms can produce erroneous outcomes. In industrial environments, this may result in misclassification of product defects, inaccurate demand forecasting, or inefficient logistical planning. For instance, if an AI system is trained on historical data that underrepresents certain operational conditions or anomalies, it may fail to detect critical machinery faults or respond effectively during emergencies. Moreover, intentional data manipulation, such as data poisoning attacks, can be used by malicious actors to compromise AI systems, leading to costly errors, safety risks, or competitive disadvantages.

12.3.2 Personal Privacy

In today's data-rich environment—where quintillions of bytes are generated daily, the velocity of data flow enables real time analysis and sharing, a capability increasingly accelerated by AI. As AI evolves, it amplifies the ability to use large amounts of private and sensitive data, such as personal information, in ways that can be analyzed at ultra-high speed and advanced computational power.

Regarding privacy issues of AI use, facial recognition technology is increasing significantly as organizations employ the technology for a variety of reasons, including verifying or identifying individuals to grant access to online accounts, authorizing payments, tracking and monitoring attendance without their consent. In addition, with the benefit of rich digital photograph databases available via social media, websites, surveillance cameras, and many other sources, machine recognition of faces has progressed rapidly through the recognition of individual humans. This emerging technology leads to capabilities of leveraging AI to reconstruct facial properties or identifying and tracking a person when they move from the perspective of attackers.

The spread of fake news also poses significant threats to personal privacy in Industry 4.0. AI-driven misinformation campaigns can involve the unauthorized use of personal data, often collected through connected industrial systems, social platforms, or IoT devices. Individuals' private information can be exploited to create deepfakes, impersonate identities, or target specific people with false or harmful narratives. Such misuse not only violates privacy rights but also damages reputations and undermines public trust in digital and industrial systems. Additionally, AI algorithms that analyze personal behaviours or preferences may be manipulated to spread customised fake news, increasing its persuasive power while breaching individual privacy boundaries (Markovsky et al., 2023). As AI becomes more embedded in both professional and personal spheres, safeguarding privacy from the misuse of data in fake news creation and distribution becomes a critical ethical responsibility.

Another factor relevant to personal privacy of AI use is health tracking or monitoring. The integration of modern health care checker apps has been regarded as a powerful tool to stay healthier, whether losing weight, managing stress, or just staying on top of overall wellness. The rise of AI-based apps has increased significantly during COVID-19 pandemic (Sepasgozar, 2021). However, the use of such applications allows AI devices to collect daily life data such as eating habits, health indicators of users, and diseases. The data retrieved from AI-based devices may be sent to third parties for the purposes of advertising medical equipment, gyms, or profiting from these parties. These actions are breaking the law according to HIPAA (Health Insurance Portability and Accountability Act) privacy rules of the United States Act of Congress in order to protect individual's medical records and other individually identifiable health information (*Privacy | HHS.Gov*, n.d.).

12.3.3 Social Impact

AI and automation technologies are transforming industries by enhancing efficiency and productivity, but this shift also presents a serious threat to employment, particularly for jobs involving repetitive tasks (Hagerty & Rubinov, 2019). As machines and AI systems increasingly take over these roles, many workers may face unemployment or be compelled to transition to new sectors. This situation raises ethical concerns about the economic impact on workers and the responsibility of corporations and governments to address these challenges. Additionally, the economic benefits of AI may not be evenly distributed, potentially exacerbating economic inequality. Those who own and control AI technologies could see substantial gains, while displaced workers might struggle to find new employment opportunities, deepening the divide between different economic groups.

12.4 The Way Forward of AI Development

Looking ahead to the next generation of AI development in Industry 4.0 and beyond, the focus is on paving the way toward Industry 5.0, where the collaboration between humans and machines is heightened. Therefore, the remaining ethical issues of AI applications should be addressed. Figure 12.4 shows the overview of ethical issues and the corresponding solutions in the forward direction for AI development.

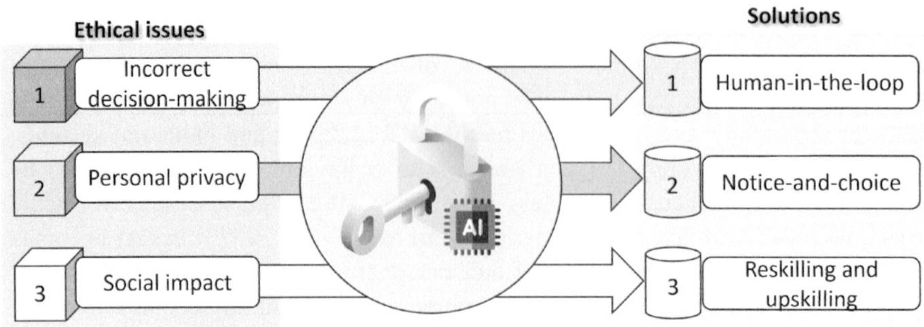

Figure 12.4. Ethical issues and corresponding solutions.

12.4.1 Responsibility on Incorrect Decision-making

It has become increasingly difficult to disregard the substantial contributions of AI systems to the fields of the industrial revolution in 21st century. Notwithstanding current ethical challenges with the widespread adoption of AI application, the use of AI in providing high efficiency, in-depth benefits in industries are likely to substantially increase in the near future. Furthermore, industries will continue to benefit from the expanding framework of AI applications to optimize the possibilities and address ethical issues.

The question of who is responsible for incorrect decisions from AI is complex requiring consideration of the entire relevant contexts such as the production of AI devices or products, distribution, original programming, and end users or consumers. This analysis usually takes time and has to judge multiple aspects. Therefore, avoiding or minimizing incorrect decisions made by AI is an urgent and necessary development direction to be undertaken for AI technology. Growing academic research into AI bias, has proposed several approaches. Considering how humans and machines can work together to mitigate bias, the "human-in-the-loop" systems make recommendations or provide options that humans double-check or can supervise for AI decision-making. Transparency in algorithmic confidence can help humans understand and recommend how much importance is to be given to attribute accountability easily in incident cases. Additionally, investing more, providing more data, and taking a multi-disciplinary approach in bias research must continue to advance enhanced AI decision-making (Ntoutsi et al., 2020).

12.4.2 Personal Privacy

Addressing privacy issues in the use of AI is of paramount importance and requires careful consideration. Enhancing data protection impacts privacy impact assessments with additional questions specific to responsible AI practices to help identify and mitigate the risks AI may pose to individual rights and freedoms. This approach ensures that potential harm resulting from bias or inaccuracies in algorithms and data sets are thoroughly assessed, and the proportion of AI use or machine learning algorithms is carefully documented.

Currently, the predominant privacy protection model employed by most organizations relies on a "notice-and-choice" approach. This method inundates consumers with notifications and banners linked to lengthy, often uninformative privacy consents, which are rarely read or fully understood. To address this, there is a growing need to enhance the fundamental understanding of privacy rights among consumers. By fostering a clearer comprehension of these rights, individuals can make more informed decisions before consenting to data collection by AI systems, thereby ensuring that their privacy is better protected in an increasingly automated world.

12.4.3 Social Impact

Reskilling and upskilling are ethical imperatives in the face of AI-driven job displacement, ensuring that workers can adapt to new roles in the evolving job market. A collaborative approach involving governments, businesses, educational institutions, and civil society is essential to address this challenge effectively. One typical strategy is to implement progressive tax policies that capture the financial gains of those who own and control AI technologies, using this revenue to fund social welfare programs, education, and retraining displaced workers.

Additionally, establishing partnerships between governments and the private sector can help develop accessible online courses, vocational training, and apprenticeships tailored to prepare workers for jobs less prone to AI automation. It is also crucial to promote the development of AI technologies that prioritize inclusivity and accessibility, aiming to enhance worker productivity rather than merely replacing human roles. Investments should be focused on sectors less vulnerable to automation, such as healthcare, education, and creative industries, while fostering entrepreneurship and innovation in these areas to create sustainable job opportunities.

12.4.4 Limitations

This chapter presents the ethical dimensions of AI applications. It offers a general overview of the benefits of AI, along with the key issues and challenges associated with its use. The goal is to help readers—whether to apply AI in their professional work or everyday life, recognize the potential pitfalls and understand the consequences that may arise when ethical concerns are overlooked.

However, like any work, this article has its limitations. Broad descriptions may not provide a detailed understanding of the complex ethical landscape. To deepen insight, future work should incorporate concrete case studies, real-world examples, and empirical surveys that capture the diverse perspectives of AI users across industries and demographics. In addition, exploring domain-specific ethical challenges, for instance, in healthcare, finance, or education—would enhance the practical relevance of the discussion. A more data-driven approach could also help identify patterns in public concern, regulatory gaps, and areas where ethical guidelines are most urgently needed.

12.5 Conclusions

Artificial Intelligence plays an indispensable role in the Fourth Industrial Revolution, bringing with it undeniable benefits. However, the widespread adoption of AI applications has significantly heightened concerns about ethical issues, including the responsibilities associated with flawed AI-based decision-making, the protection of personal privacy, and the broader social impact of these technologies. Ensuring the responsible development and deployment of AI in industry and other areas is crucial to harnessing its full potential without crossing legal or ethical boundaries. This chapter serves as a valuable resource for individuals working with AI, offering insights into navigating the complex ethical challenges that arise in this rapidly evolving field.

Future research should focus on developing robust frameworks for ethical AI governance that are adaptable across different sectors and jurisdictions. Studies could explore the implementation of explainable AI techniques to enhance transparency and trust in automated decision-making processes. Additionally, interdisciplinary research involving ethics, law, and computer science is essential to establish standardized guidelines for AI accountability and data protection. Investigating public perception and societal acceptance of AI, especially in high-stakes areas like healthcare, law enforcement, and finance, can offer valuable insights into the social readiness for AI deployment. Finally, longitudinal studies assessing the real-world impact of AI policies and regulations would contribute significantly to shaping a sustainable and ethically sound AI-driven future.

Acknowledgements

The author would like to express his thanks to University of South-Eastern Norway for providing the PhD course – Theory of Science and Research Ethics. This chapter is based on the report on this PhD course.

Disclaimer

During the preparation of this work, the author utilized AI-assisted tools such as ChatGPT, Grammarly, etc. to enhance English language accuracy, including spelling, grammar, and punctuation. The content generated or corrected by these tools was thoroughly reviewed, revised, and edited by the author to ensure accuracy and originality. The author accepts full responsibility for the originality of the final content of this publication.

References

Abidi, M.H., Alkhalefah, H., & Umer, U. (2022). Fuzzy harmony search based optimal control strategy for wireless cyber physical system with industry 4.0. *Journal of Intelligent Manufacturing*, 33(6), 1795–1812. https://doi.org/10.1007/S10845-021-01757-4/FIGURES/9

Aivaliotis, P., Georgoulias, K., & Chryssolouris, G. (2019). The use of Digital Twin for predictive maintenance in manufacturing. *International Journal of Computer Integrated Manufacturing*, 32(11), 1067–1080. https://doi.org/10.1080/0951192X.2019.1686173

Boyer, A. (2021). Towards an ethic of robotics. *Journal of Organizational Psychology*, 21(3), 83.

Brenner, W., & Herrmann, A. (2018). An overview of technology, benefits and impact of automated and autonomous driving on the automotive industry. *Digital Marketplaces Unleashed*, 427–442. https://doi.org/10.1007/978-3-662-49275-8_39

Copeland, J. (1999). *Artificial Intelligence: A Philosophical Introduction*. Wiely Blackwell available at: https://books.google.com/books?hl=en&lr=&id=CfJRCgAAQBAJ&oi=fnd&pg=PR10&dq=Copeland,+J.+(1999).+Artificial+Intelligence:+A+philosophical+introduction&ots=iF8wfvq8sr&sig=xPzo1kKBnuQPfEAxpy0gqXHLNfQ

Crevier, D. (1994). *The Tumultuous History of the Search for Artificial Intelligence* (pp. 432). Basic Books, New York, NY.

Eckhart, M., & Ekelhart, A. (2019). Digital Twins for cyber-physical systems security: State of the art and outlook. *Security and Quality in Cyber-Physical Systems Engineering*, 383–412. https://doi.org/10.1007/978-3-030-25312-7_14

Evjemo, L.D., Gjerstad, T., Grøtli, E.I., & Sziebig, G. (2020). Trends in smart manufacturing: Role of humans and industrial robots in smart factories. *Current Robotics Reports 2020*, 1(2), 35–41. https://doi.org/10.1007/S43154-020-00006-5

Falekas, G., & Karlis, A. (2021). Digital Twin in electrical machine control and predictive maintenance: State-of-the-art and future prospects. *Energies*, 14(18), 5933. https://doi.org/10.3390/EN14185933

Gonzalez-Longatt, F., & Pham, L.N.H. (2024). Intelligent electronic device-in-the-loop: A real-time simulation as modern educational aid. *IEEE Access*, https://doi.org/10.1109/ACCESS.2024.3512779

Grau, A., Indri, M., Lo Bello, L., & Sauter, T. (2021). Robots in industry: The past, present, and future of a growing collaboration with humans. *IEEE Industrial Electronics Magazine*, 15(1), 50–61. https://doi.org/10.1109/MIE.2020.3008136

Hagerty, A., & Rubinov, I. (2019). Global AI ethics: A Review of the Social Impacts and Ethical Implications of Artificial Intelligence. https://arxiv.org/abs/1907.07892v1

Li, X., & Zhang, T. (2017). An exploration on artificial intelligence application: From security, privacy and ethic perspective. *2nd IEEE International Conference on Cloud Computing and Big Data Analysis, ICCCBDA 2017*, 416–420. https://doi.org/10.1109/ICCCBDA.2017.7951949

Markovsky, I., Huang, L., & Dörfler, F. (2023). Data-driven control based on the behavioral approach: from theory to applications in power systems. *IEEE Control Systems Magazine*, 43(5), 28–68.

Muggleton, S. (2014). Alan Turing and the development of Artificial Intelligence. *AI Communications*, 27(1), 3–10. https://doi.org/10.3233/AIC-130579

Nature News & Comment. (n.d.). Can we open the black box of AI? Retrieved August 17, 2024, from https://www.nature.com/news/can-we-open-the-black-box-of-ai-1.20731

Ntoutsi, E., Fafalios, P., Gadiraju, U., Iosifidis, V., Nejdl, W. … Staab, S. (2020). Bias in data-driven artificial intelligence systems—An introductory survey. *Wiley Interdisciplinary Reviews: Data Mining and Knowledge Discovery*, 10(3), e1356. https://doi.org/10.1002/WIDM.1356

Pham, L.N.H. (2023). Exploring cyber-physical energy and power system: Concepts, applications, challenges, and simulation approaches. *Energies*, 16(1). https://doi.org/10.3390/EN16010042

Pham, L.N.H., & Gonzalez-Longatt, F. (2023). Distance protection relay testing using virtual hardware-in-the-loop device. In: Tripathi, S.M., Gonzalez-Longatt, F.M. (eds.), *Real-Time Simulation and Hardware-in-the-Loop Testing Using Typhoon HIL* (pp. 379–424). Transactions on Computer Systems and Networks. Springer, Singapore. https://doi.org/10.1007/978-981-99-0224-8_13

Pham, L.N.H., Wagle, R., Gonzalez-Longatt, F., & Acosta, M. (2023). Non-directional overcurrent protection relay testing using virtual hardware-in-the-loop device. In: Tripathi, S.M., Gonzalez-Longatt, F.M. (eds.), *Real-Time Simulation and Hardware-in-the-Loop Testing Using Typhoon HIL* (pp. 283–337). Transactions on Computer Systems and Networks. Springer, Singapore. https://doi.org/10.1007/978-981-99-0224-8_11

Pham, L.N.H., Rosero-Morillo, V., Shukla, A., Gonzalez-Longatt, F., & Meza-G, V. (2024). Real-time cyber–physical power system testbed for international electrotechnical commission 61850 generic object-oriented substation event transfer time measurements. *Engineering Proceedings 2024*, 77(1), 17. https://doi.org/10.3390/ENGPROC2024077017

Pham, L.N.H., Wagle, R., Tricarico, G., Melo, A.F.S., Rosero-Morillo, V., Shukla, A., & Gonzalez-Longatt, F. (2024). Real-time cyber-physical power system testbed for optimal power flow study using co-simulation framework. *IEEE Access*, 1–1. https://doi.org/10.1109/ACCESS.2024.3472748

Pham, L.N.H., Riquelme-Dominguez, J.M., & Gonzalez-Longatt, F. (2025a). Exploring multiple functionalities of CyberPhysical power system within digital substation-based laboratory environment. *IEEE Access*. https://doi.org/10.1109/ACCESS.2025.3563260

Pham, L.N.H., Riquelme-Dominguez, J.M., & Gonzalez-Longatt, F. (2025b). Exploring data-driven technique in optimal power flow study through real-time cyber-physical power system under uncertainties. *Energy*, 137091. https://doi.org/10.1016/J.ENERGY.2025.137091

Privacy | HHS.gov. (n.d.). Retrieved August 16, 2024, from https://www.hhs.gov/hipaa/for-professionals/privacy/index.html

Sepasgozar, S.M.E. (2021). Differentiating digital twin from digital shadow: Elucidating a paradigm shift to expedite a smart, sustainable built environment. *Buildings*, 11(4), 151. https://doi.org/10.3390/BUILDINGS11040151

Shaheen, M.Y. (2021). AI in healthcare: Medical and Socio-Economic Benefits and Challenges. https://doi.org/10.31219/OSF.IO/UM38T

Shrouf, F., Ordieres, J., & Miragliotta, G. (2014). Smart factories in Industry 4.0: A review of the concept and of energy management approached in production based on the Internet of Things paradigm. *IEEE International Conference on Industrial Engineering and Engineering Management* (pp. 697–701). 2015-Jan, https://doi.org/10.1109/IEEM.2014.7058728

Soori, M., Arezoo, B., & Dastres, R. (2023). Internet of things for smart factories in industry 4.0, a review. *Internet of Things and Cyber-Physical Systems*, 3, 192–204. https://doi.org/10.1016/J.IOTCPS.2023.04.006

Stahl, B.C. (2021). *Artificial Intelligence for a Better Future* (pp. 124). Springer Nature, https://doi.org/10.1007/978-3-030-69978-9

Toll, D., Lindgren, I., Melin, U., & Madsen, C. (2020). Values, benefits, considerations and risks of AI in government: A study of AI policies in Sweden. *JeDEM – EJournal of EDemocracy and Open Government*, 12(1), 40–60. https://doi.org/10.29379/jedem.v12i1.593

Vollmer, S., Mateen, B.A., Mbbs, P., Bohner, G., Franz, B.S., Király, J. et al. (2018). Machine Learning and AI Research for Patient Benefit: 20 Critical Questions on Transparency, Replicability, Ethics and Effectiveness. https://arxiv.org/abs/1812.10404v1

Voulodimos, A., Doulamis, N., Doulamis, A., & Protopapadakis, E. (2018). Deep learning for computer vision: A brief review. *Computational Intelligence and Neuroscience*, 2018(1), 7068349. https://doi.org/10.1155/2018/7068349

Wagle, R., Pham, L.N.H., Tricarico, G., Sharma, P., Rueda, J.L. & Gonzalez-Longatt, F.(2023). Experiences in a cyber-physical co-simulation testbed development for a smart-er distribution network. *2023 IEEE PES Conference on Innovative Smart Grid Technologies – Middle East (ISGT Middle East)* (pp. 1–5). https://doi.org/10.1109/ISGTMIDDLEEAST56437.2023.10078722

Yu, R., & Alì, G.S. (2019). What's inside the black box? AI challenges for lawyers and researchers. *Legal Information Management*, 19(1), 2–13. https://doi.org/10.1017/S1472669619000021

CHAPTER

13

Data Governance in the Digital Era: How BRICS Nations Balance Sovereignty and Global Data Transfers

Jitendra Singh Tomar(0000-0003-2880-5495)
Amity University, Noida, India

13.1 Introduction

In modern society, where almost everything is digitally interconnected, data has emerged as the primary source of power in political, economic, and social domains (Pohle & Thiel, 2020). The rise of digital services, cloud computing, and AI (artificial intelligence) technologies have provided never-before-seen opportunities for the processing of both personal and impersonal data (Misra et al., 2024a). While these advancements fuel innovations and transformations in the digital world, they also pose considerable challenges in terms of control, privacy, and national security, all of supreme significance to the digital sovereignty (DS) discourse (Mondschein & Monda, 2018, 2020; Jiang & Belli, 2021).

Digital sovereignty is defined as a nation's capability to govern its digital ecosystems, including data repositories, and support systems for decision making, that incorporate AI (Kelly & Satola, 2024). Within an AI governance framework, DS encompasses, data confidentiality, and the development of ethical policies (Saba & Ngepah, 2024). It supports self-directing technological evolution, and protects against dominant technological organizations in the IT world. This is beyond safeguarding citizens in its periphery by protecting their information (Jiang & Belli, 2025; Floridi & Cowls, 2022).

This chapter discusses how the BRICS countries: Brazil, Russia, India, China, and South Africa are restructuring their digital sovereignty by changing their data governance frameworks and AI policies. These countries account for more than 40%

*Corresponding author: jitendratomar@hotmail.com

DOI: 10.1201/9781003581581-13

of the world's population and are altering global digital standards from a non-Western perspective (Jiang & Belli, 2021). Regardless of their dissimilarities in economic status, political systems, and digital divides, the BRICS nations strategically focus on sovereignty goals that will result in control over the data flow, and ensure AI innovations (Saba & Ngepah, 2024; Jobin et al., 2019; Roberts et al., 2023).

This chapter intends to explore fundamentals of digital sovereignty and AI governance. In addition to analyzing the DS and AI governance intricacies in BRICS nations, it introduces a Multilayered Digital Sovereignty and AI Governance Framework (Multi-DiSIGN Framework) as a tool to evaluate the readiness of BRICS nations. Then, it provides a summative evaluation of the national data governance policies and legal instruments of the BRICS countries. The chapter proceeds with the intricacies on cross-border data flows and consequently discusses the role of AI in addressing sovereignty matters (Rodriguez et al., 2021). In doing so, using a Multi-DiSIGN Framework, the it offers a comparative evaluation of DS and AI governance among the BRICS nations.

The structure of the chapter is as follows: section 2 exhibits the theoretical foundations of digital sovereignty and AI governance followed by section 3 which presents a comparative analysis of the BRICS national strategies. Section 4 reveals challenges and risks experienced by each of the BRICS nations and section 5 discusses strategies adopted by them. Section 6 of the chapter proposes a Multi-DiSIGN Framework which can be used for policy evaluation of BRICS nations. Section 7 explains key findings and uses a DS & AI governance matrix, before moving into limitations and future research directions in sections 8 and 9.

This chapter suggests that the BRICS countries are attempting to achieve digital sovereignty as a counter reaction to digital colonialism, while simultaneously trying to form a more multipolar world (Belli & Magalhães, 2024). This will help in integrating digital order which allows nations to exercise control over their digital growth in a technologically connected world (Levchenko, 2024; DeNardis, 2020). Such advancements are not only of national importance, but also impact international debates on ethics, governance, and international collaboration in the digitally connected world (Couture & Toupin, 2019; Belli & Magalhães, 2024).

Key Contributions of the Chapter:

- The chapter presents a comparative study of BRICS nations' tactics to achieve digital sovereignty and AI governance.
- The chapter compares the challenges and contextual issues impacting each nation's readiness.
- The chapter proposes a Multi-DiSIGN Framework to measure maturity across seven relevant governance layers.
- The chapter uses a scoring matrix for policy comparisons among BRICS nations by mapping their strategies.
- The chapter delivers actionable suggestions for public policy makers on how to balance global digital rules and national sovereignty.

13.2 Theoretical Foundations of Digital Sovereignty and AI Governance

13.2.1 Defining Digital Sovereignty

Digital sovereignty (DS) can be broadly defined as the capacity of a state or region to independently govern the digital sphere (Iqbal & Zahra, 2024), encompassing infrastructure, data, technologies, and algorithms, in line with its own values, norms, and strategic priorities (Jiang & Belli, 2021; Couture & Toupin, 2019). Unlike traditional sovereignty focusing on the territories and borders, digital sovereignty expands across cyberspace, involving control over intangible assets such as data flows, cloud computing, and software ecosystems (Rodriguez et al., 2021). Three critical pillars underpin digital sovereignty:

- **Infrastructure Sovereignty:** Infrastructure sovereignty is understood as a state's possession of critical digital infrastructure, such as hardware systems, communication, networks, cloud storage, and data centers (Zinovieva & Shitkov, 2023). Put simply, this form of sovereignty is defined as the physical and legal location of digital infrastructure within the state, allowing the state to avoid relying on foreign technology providers (Belli et al., 2024). At a basic level, sovereign infrastructure is important for national security, as well as for ensuring data privacy and uninterrupted access to digital services (Awosusi et al., 2022). Without this, there would be the possibility of foreign manipulation of the state's digital environment and foreign surveillance of the same (Pohle & Thiel, 2020).
- **Data Sovereignty:** Data sovereignty is defined as a state's legal and regulatory jurisdiction over the collection, storage, processing, and transfer of data, specifically personal and sensitive data (Balaguer et al., 2023). Data sovereignty allows data created in a country to be governed by local laws. This occurs when the data is processed offshore by a firm based in another country (Belli & Magalhães, 2024). As much of the data flow is handled by global cloud providers and tech platforms, data sovereignty is becoming more significant (Belli et al., 2024). Good data sovereignty can protect citizens' privacy and enhance trust in the digital governance ecosystems (Mondschein & Monda, 2018; Greenleaf, 2023); and enable intelligent technologies to be used for socio-economic benefits (Barik et al., 2024).
- **Algorithmic Sovereignty:** Algorithmic Sovereignty is the ability of a state or organization to design, regulate, and audit AI systems freely, independent of foreign algorithms and platforms (Taylor, 2020). Algorithmic sovereignty entails transparency over decision processes, accountability mechanisms, and the ability to customize AI to local ethical cultural norms (Kelly & Satola, 2024). Once a state or organization achieves algorithmic sovereignty, the risk of exposure to algorithmic bias or malicious manipulation implicit in foreign technological environments is mitigated, and consequently country decision-makers can configure its AI systems in ways that support public values and democratic constructs (Floridi & Cowls, 2022).

DS is assuming importance as countries have become cautious of foreign surveillance, cyber-espionage, monopolistic practices by big global technological companies, handling global operations, leading to the uneven distribution of digital value creation (DeNardis, 2020; Belli & Magalhães, 2024).

13.2.2 AI Governance: A Subdomain of Digital Sovereignty

AI governance is defined as the comprehensive set of policies, laws, ethical norms, and technical standards that guide the ongoing regulation and operations of AI and its systems (Saba & Ngepah, 2024). AI governance is increasingly important for digital sovereignty as nations seek to establish proficient regulations to prevent the oversight of automated systems, and ensure they operate transparently, fairly, and safely (Zheng et al., 2023; Jiang & Belli, 2025).

AI systems fundamentally rely on access to data, the underlying computational infrastructure, and the algorithmic design, all of which are connected to and encompass sovereignty (Chatterjee & Chatterjee, 2025). In particular, there are several identified AI related challenges that overlap with digital sovereignty:

- **Ethical AI:** The ability of the AI systems to be aligned with national values, citizen charter, human rights, and privacy and confidentiality norms (Floridi & Cowls, 2022).
- **Regulatory Autonomy:** The ability of the states to establish their own legal and ethical standards around artificial intelligence without reliance on frameworks established by other foreign bodies such as EU's AI Act, U.S. (Jobin et al., 2019; Veale & Edwards 2018).
- **Technological Independence:** The ability to be less dependent on foreign AI technologies, and develop internal capabilities for innovation (Rodriguez et al., 2021; Jiang & Belli, 2021).

13.2.3 The Global Shift Toward Sovereign Tech Governance

Although early deliberations about digital governance focused primarily on the liberal democracies of the Global North, BRICS and other Global South countries are now pushing for "technological non-alignment" and resisting the digital hegemony of a handful of nation states (Hintz et al., 2019; Belli et al., 2024). There seems to be a desire for more equitable control of the digital infrastructure and the establishment of digital standards and data governance frameworks (Ignatov, 2023). The movement towards sovereign digital strategies involves:

- The establishment of national cloud policies (e.g. India – MeghRaj, Russia – Sovereign Internet) (Belli & Magalhães, 2024; Greenleaf, 2023).
- The investment in suitable open-source and indigenous technologies (Gurumurthy & Chami, 2022).
- The enactment of data localization laws to keep such data in the country concerned, within national jurisdiction (Kuner, 2020).
- The establishment of state-led AI research in order to encourage independent innovation (Jiang & Belli, 2025; Mondschein & Monda, 2018).

This theoretical foundation is valuable for the rest of this chapter. The author will investigate how BRICS countries enact and operationalize these thoughts on digital governance through various means including legislative action, infrastructure investment, and representative diplomacy (Jiang & Belli, 2021; DeNardis, 2020).

13.3 Comparative Overview of Data Governance Approaches in BRICS Nations

Digital sovereignty in the BRICS countries—Brazil, Russia, India, China, and South Africa—is expressed in diverse ways, conditioned by different political priorities, regulatory contexts, technology capabilities, and geopolitical strategies, (Srivastava & Bullock, 2024). Yet all share a basic desire: To have a national stake in their digital ecosystems and lessen their dependence on western technological infrastructures and norms (Jiang & Belli, 2021; DeNardis, 2020).

This section examines the policy approaches and strategies in the BRICS state that strive for digital sovereignty, focusing in particular on their data governance framework, AI regulatory approach, and environment for cross-border data flows.

13.3.1 Brazil: Balancing Open Internet Norms with Data Sovereignty

Brazil is a prominent actor on issues of digital governance in Latin America. It is known for its commitment to an open, global internet, while placing significant emphasis on user privacy, public interest, and accountability/regulation (Couture and Toupin 2019). The passage of the General Data Protection Law (LGPD) demonstrates Brazil's commitment to protecting private data as well as holding digital service providers accountable (Johansson et al., 2024). In addition to protecting citizens via the LGPD, Brazil actively promotes a multi-stakeholder governance model that balances innovation with social responsibility (Bonfacio et al., 2025).

Key Initiatives:

- General Data Protection Law (LGPD, 2018), which is modeled after the EU's General Data Protection Regulation (GDPR). The LGPD outlines the principles for lawful processing of data, user consent, and the rights of data subjects. The National Data Protection Authority is the enforcement body (Greenleaf, 2023).
- Artificial Intelligence Strategy, 2021, which prioritizes the ethical, inclusive, and rights-based development of artificial intelligence (Wagner, 2025). Brazil's AI Strategy also incorporates elements of digital inclusion, and the transparent governance of AI, which takes a holistic approach (OECD, 2021).
- Open Data, Sovereign Infrastructure is implemented in Brazil by promoting the reuse of data and transparency. However, it intends to also invest in building domestic cloud computing infrastructure to ensure non-interference of foreign entities in managing sensitive public sector data (Rodriguez et al., 2021).

In a practical sense, Brazil has advanced its aspirations toward digital sovereignty through plans including the Plano Nacional de Internet das Coisas (IoT) and working collaboratively to carry out indigenous tech development. The Brazilian government is establishing national data centers to lessen dependence on foreign cloud-based infrastructure with GovCloud Brasil as an example of hosting data for public administration in Brazil. Moreover, municipal-level plans regarding digital inclusion like the Smart City Plan of São Paulo, have established principles defining the authority over citizen data and digital infrastructure. It also suggests individuals to engage with their respective local governments to realize their rights and sovereignty over citizen data (Bonfacio et al., 2025; Filgueiras & Junquilho, 2023). One might view these as deliberate acts to prioritize the principles of sovereignty in infrastructure and governance.

Through different strategic frameworks engaging both the public and private sectors, Brazil has been pushing AI and data governance for a long-time. For example, Start-Up Brasil and Embrapii AI Hub are both spooling funds and capacity building for nascent early-stage AI centered firms, including MSMEs, for the improvement of innovation and inclusion (Johansson et al., 2024). To address the digital divide, the country is focusing on augmenting broadband coverage in less-developed areas through programs like the Internet para Todos. All this while, Brazil's 'Estratégia Brasileira para a Transformação Digital' has goals related to digital literacy, especially among SMEs, as well as digitizing 90% of micro-enterprises in Brazil by 2030, to help them engage in the digital economy (Pereira, 2024). These objectives are fundamentally geared towards constructing a more inclusive digital ecosystem aligned with digital sovereignty.

Brazil's model appears to be a hybrid one that recognizes the role of both openness and interoperability while also placing value on national regulation and governance of AI and data (Hoffmann et al., 2021). The LGPD, in fact, reflects a clear advancement in citizens' digital sovereignty, effectively giving them rights over their own personal data (Filgueiras & Junquilho, 2023).

13.3.2 Russia: Authoritarian Model of Digital Sovereignty

Russia's conception of digital sovereignty is quite state-centric, with an emphasis on control of information, autonomy over infrastructure, and cyber defense (Epifanova & Dietrich, 2022; Belli & Magalhães, 2024). Russia's approach includes a regulatory framework, data localization, and attempts to construct an independent future internet infrastructure (Martynova & Shcherbovich, 2024) – such as "Runet".

Key Examples:

- **Sovereign Internet Law (2019):** This law requires that all internet traffic passes through chokepoints controlled by the state, while allowing centralized monitoring and disconnection from the world internet, in emergencies (Gromova & Ferreira, 2024);
- **Personal Data Law (2006):** This law mandates that the data on Russian citizens must be both stored and processed in Russian territory (Greenleaf, 2023);
- **AI Roadmap (2020):** The Roadmap not only focuses on national security and military aspirations, but state-centric competitiveness. The state has a leading role in both developing and deploying AI solutions (Jiang & Belli, 2025).

Russia has put its DS strategy into action, primarily through projects aimed at technological independence, such as the domestic development of operating systems with Astra Linux, and the promotion of domestic alternatives to Western platforms (e.g., Yandex, VK, Mail.ru). The Digital Economy National Program introduced by the Kremlin provides funding and authorization to strengthen Russia's capacity to build a self-sufficient digital environment. Russia is also focusing on having an independent DNS (Domain Name System) that will help create a country specific internet system. This will assist in operating effectively and independently in case of geopolitical isolation and reduce risks (Martynova & Shcherbovich, 2024; Saveliev & Zhurenkov, 2021).

The Russian Government is providing incentives related to AI while focusing on reducing the Digital Divide. The government has taken a centralized approach to enable a broader adoption of AI to support the Digital Economy through the Russian Federation Program. The program provides funding to the organizations, and also supports subsidized adoption of AI, cloud computing, and weapons of cybersecurity by companies, including MSMEs (Martynova & Shcherbovich, 2024). The other project is the National Project for Education and AI Talent Development that has a target of training 120,000 professionals in AI by 2030. The Digital School program confronts rural-urban divergences by making AI-based learning systems accessible to more remote villages. The Technopark System also supports MSMEs across the country to digitize their operations and impact the national data economy through innovation clusters (Epifanova & Dietrich, 2022). These strategies show a state-initiated state-led approach to add DS to the grassroots and industry levels.

Russia views digital sovereignty to be inseparably linked to national security. Russia's digital sovereignty approach is deeply rooted in controlled infrastructure, and working to reduce its dependency on foreign systems (Epifanova & Dietrich, 2022). AI plays a role as a geopolitical good, and its governance is firmly, yet flexibly; configured alongside authoritarian governance (Jiang & Belli, 2021).

13.3.3 India: Data for Development, Data for Sovereignty

India blends developmental objectives into robust, sovereign data governance approaches. As one of the biggest data producing countries, India sees itself as both a custodian and beneficiary of sovereign data (Whittlestone et al., 2019).

Notable Initiatives:

- Digital Personal Data Protection Act (DPDP, 2023) – establishes the principles related to personal data protection, fiduciary obligations of data fiduciaries, and rights of data subjects (Greenleaf, 2023).
- India AI Mission – focuses on enabling ethical and inclusive AI development based on explainability, fairness, and trust (OECD, 2021).
- Data localization proposals – while local data retention was emphasized in the 2019 draft e-commerce policy and by the Reserve Bank, a clearer picture of appropriate cross-border and regulated cross-border data flow keeping pace with local data storage was evolving (Kuner, 2020; Gurumurthy & Chami, 2022).

India's operationalization of digital sovereignty is exemplified through the BharatNet initiative which aimed at establishing ongoing broadband and internet connectivity to over 250,000 gram panchayats. This way, it is advancing rural digital inclusion under India's national jurisdiction. Further examples of institutional frameworks that build on digitally sovereign pillars that India adopts can be seen in the National AI Portal and the INDIAai knowledge platform. These platforms provide clarity on AI initiatives by the government and support the AI research scenario under state control. India is also piloting public digital infrastructure projects such as DigiLocker and the Unified Health Interface (UHI) that in some cases stores sensitive personal information in government operated servers for data localization purposes (Chatterjee & Chatterjee, 2025; Saba, 2025). These platforms reflect India's initiatives and the proactive approach to embedding digital sovereignty into foundational public infrastructures.

The Indian Government is committed to AI Democratization, MSME empowerment, and closing the digital divide through initiatives such as the Responsible AI for Social Empowerment (RAISE) summit. The government is promoting inclusive AI usage in agriculture, health care, education, and various other primary domains. Initiatives like PM Gati Shakti and Digital India are supporting the MSME sector to adopt AI as they also provide funding, cloud infrastructure, and training, as per the mandate for the digital compliance (Bentalha & Boukare, 2024). MSMEs are supported by the Champions Portal that connect them to AI-based analytics, and support in providing real-time, data-driven decision-making. India plans to upskill over 1 million people in AI-related skills by 2025 and plans to include 75% of the organized -sector MSMEs to digital platforms as a way to consolidate their integration into the national knowledge economy (Rout et al., 2021). Such policies will connect grassroots entrepreneurship to sovereign digital aspirations.

India's "data for development" aspiration links DS with promoting inclusive growth across sectors of the economy. In this sense, governance for AI becomes a hybrid of ethics and technology innovation-driven policy responses (Chatterjee & Chatterjee, 2025). The DPDP is a first step towards data protection, a pivot toward data sovereignty, and a direction that is not rigidly locked into particulars but also remains open to interoperable global avenues (Rodriguez et al., 2021).

13.3.4 China: Full-Stack Digital Sovereignty

The digital sovereignty model in China is the most all-encompassing and centralized among BRICS nations (Ma, 2024). Its model mixes authoritarian power with government enabled technological innovation (Floridi & Cowls, 2022).

Key development initiatives:

- **Cybersecurity Law and Data Security Law (2017 and 2021):** Both enact localization laws for data and the regulation of cross-border data transfers (Mondschein & Monda, 2018).
- **Personal Information Protection Law (2021):** Similar to GDPR-style protections within a national security and Partly oversite (Greenleaf, 2023).

- **AI Governance Guidelines:** Created by the CAC and other agencies, suggest rules on ethics in AI applications, algorithmic and data transparency, and social order (Jobin et al., 2019; Veale & Edwards, 2018).

China happens to be the most prominent technologically reliant country among the BRICS nations. In creating its own Beidou Navigation Satellite System as a substitute for GPS, China reflects its capacity for self-sufficiency in spatial data infrastructure, as it strengthens its digital sovereignty. The Great Firewall and real time content moderation requirements are also very tangible markings of China's algorithmic sovereignty and infrastructure sovereignty. The emphasis on "indigenous innovation" backed by funding of AI chip development (e.g., Cambricon) and AI platforms (e.g., SenseTime) illustrates China's ambitions to create a self-sufficient AI ecosystem (Ma, 2024; Shi & Wei, 2025). These policies exemplify a vertically integrated sovereignty framework that combines policy and technological sovereignty.

China's focus is on holistic AI Governance and Rural Inclusion. It has established AI adoption across society through the New Generation Artificial Intelligence Development Plan (AIDP), which defines industry-specific targets for AI adoption and reform in traditional industries like manufacturing and services (Yina & Yangxu, 2024). The Digital Village Strategy closes the rural-urban gap through an e-learning platform and AI-enabled agritech tools. MSMEs have additional support through AI Innovation Zones which provide access to R&D funded by the government and tax incentives. The AI Talent Development Initiative in China has already trained over 500,000 entities. The plan allows for AI incubators to operate in the regions that are less developed and offer fair equitable access to innovation (Shi & Wei, 2025). These systemic approaches collectively substantiate China's desire to embed DS through widescale integration of AI.

China represents "technological nationalism" by promoting "home-grown" platforms (i.e. Bai-du, Alibaba, Tencent), developing and acquiring indigenous AI chips, and asserting data control as a sovereign strategic resource (Yina & Yangxu, 2024) and has a vertically integrated model, from regulating, infrastructure, to ideology (Jiang & Belli, 2025; DeNardis, 2020).

13.3.5 South Africa: A Rights-based and Developmental Approach

South African digital sovereignty is rooted in the idea of rights, constructed around constitutional values, local coordination, and developmental priorities (Couture & Toupin, 2019). This means that South African digital sovereignty is most concerned with individual rights in the realms of privacy, access to information, and freedom of expression offered by digital sustainability (Soulé, 2024). Its legal and policy frameworks are derived from the constitutional provisions that promote openness, inclusiveness, and accountability (Saba & Pretorius, 2024). South Africa attempts to engage in multi-regional forums when it aligns its digital policies to broader developmental and human rights goals across the Africa continent (Iqbal & Zahra, 2024). Some significant initiatives include the following:

- **Protection of Personal Information Act (POPIA, 20212):** Lawful processing, data subject consent, and accountability (Greenleaf, 2023).
- **AI Policy Development:** Currently implementing consultation led strategies to align the deployment of AI with ethical frameworks and inclusion strategies (OECD, 2021).
- **African Union Digital Strategy Alignment:** Aligns domestic data governance with Pan African initiatives such as the African Data Policy Framework, which supports sustainable development across the continent (Hintz et al., 2019).

A few observations related to Digital Sovereignty initiatives:

Digital sovereignty in South Africa is a priority, as exhibited by the national initiatives that have been undertaken. The initiatives include the Digital Economy Masterplan and the Presidential Commission on the Fourth Industrial Revolution (PC4IR). Both national initiatives prioritize data management, youth skilling, and public-led digital infrastructure projects. Public private opportunities, like the SA Digital Villages, aim to decentralize data and offer local digital asset ownership. Working with the African Union, South Africa is even allowing some degree of flexibility in its continental digital policy standards, grounding its sovereignty to a pan-African domain (Saba & Ngepah, 2024; Soulé, 2024). These principles reflect a localized and collaborative use of DS principles.

As a nation, South Africa is engaged in Improving Inclusive Digital Sovereignty and Industry Upliftment. It is establishing inclusive AI policies through the AI Institute of South Africa (AIISA). Engaging universities and technology hubs, the policies are being established to continue growth of AI awareness, education, training and research for the public good. The government's Broadband Access for all initiative aims to close the digital divide, to connect 80% of under-serviced community members by 2025. To uplift the industry, the Digital Economy Masterplan offers capacity-building grants and digital toolkits to small enterprises to enable them to integrate AI and analytics into their operations (Soulé, 2024). South Africa is committed to cultivating ethical AI practices aligned with existing rights embedded in its constitution to be part of creating a people-centered, sovereign digital economy and capabilities (Saba & Pretorius, 2024).

South Africa's DS journey is guided by democratic values and regional collaboration. It aims to develop Data Protection governance and ethical AI frameworks with an organized approach to digital inclusion. It has a high priority to develop local infrastructure needed for local and regional structure for DS governance (as a service) and data privacy (Jiang & Belli, 2021).

13.3.6 Cross-BRICS Analysis

Table 13.1 provides a comparative analysis of the digital sovereignty and AI governance models of BRICS nations across five dimensions: data protection law, AI strategy, data localization, AI governance focus, and digital sovereignty model.

13.3.7 Summary of Key Insights

- All BRICS nations acknowledge data as a strategic resource and are establishing governance mechanisms to manage it (Belli et al., 2024).

Table 13.1. Mapping digital policy landscapes: Data, AI, and sovereignty in BRICS

Country	Brazil	Russia	India	China	South Africa
Data Protection Law	LGPD (2018)	Personal Data Law	DPDP (2023)	PIPL (2021)	POPIA (2013)
AI Strategy	Yes	Yes	Yes	Yes	Drafting
Data Localization	Partial	Mandatory	Partial/ Proposed	Strict	Limited
AI Governance Focus	Rights-based, inclusive AI	National security, control	Ethical, innovation-driven	Social stability, control	Rights-based, inclusive AI
Model of Digital Sovereignty	Hybrid (open + sovereign)	Authoritarian, centralized	Developmental + strategic	Full-stack authoritarian	Rights-centric, cooperative

- AI governance in BRICS aligns with digital sovereignty, but have varying emphasis—from security and control (Russia, China) to ethics and development (India, Brazil, South Africa) (Floridi & Cowls, 2022; Hoffmann et al., 2021).
- Data localization policies are emerging as a priority for asserting sovereignty, but must also consider trade and innovation (Kuner, 2020).
- All of these approaches provide key knowledge opportunities for the developing nations across the globe who want to pursue sovereignty without technological decoupling (Gurumurthy & Chami, 2022; Rodriguez et al., 2021).

13.4 Challenges and Risks in Implementing Digital Sovereignty and AI Governance in BRICS

The implementation of digital sovereignty and AI governance within the BRICS nations presents a host of challenges and risks, ranging from technological and economic hurdles to ethical and political complexities (Beeson & Zeng, 2018). As these countries continue to develop their digital and AI policies, it is crucial to recognize the various obstacles that can impede the successful realization of a balanced, secure, and ethically sound framework for digital sovereignty (Cihon et al., 2020). This section explores some of the key challenges and risks that BRICS nations face in this domain.

13.4.1 Technological and Infrastructure Gaps

Although digital technology and AI are expanding rapidly, BRICS countries often deal with considerable digital infrastructure gaps that may pose challenges to achieving digital sovereignty and implementing AI governance (Ma, 2024). Historically, these countries have a lack of digital connectivity, data storage, and computer processing power to build sophisticated AI systems and retain data sovereignty (Belli & Magalhães, 2024).

In addition, inequities in access to advanced technologies between urban and rural areas remain in countries like Brazil and South Africa, compromising the fair distribution of AI outcomes (Pereira, 2024). The shortage of human capital in AI research, data science, cybersecurity, and other related fields also contributes to those gaps and prevents BRICS countries from leveraging and optimizing AI technologies while ensuring control retention of data and associated digital infrastructures (DeNardis & Musiani, 2016).

13.4.2 Legal and Regulatory Complexities

Creating an effective legal and regulatory framework for digital sovereignty and governance of AI is complicated (Vila Seoane, 2021). The lack of uniform, transparent, and enforceable statures across BRICS countries sometimes leads to clumsy approaches regarding the use and governance of digital data and AI technologies (Rossi, 2020).

Every BRICS state has its own legal and regulatory context that responds to its own socio-political and economic climate (Bentalha & Boukare, 2024). This diversity can lead to competing policies and rules, such as differing aspects of data privacy and allowing for cross-border data flows (Haryono, 2024; Monsees & Lambach, 2022). While India and China have made regulatory progress on data privacy, Brazil and South Africa are just beginning to develop a unified data protection legislative process (Kuner, 2020). International trade agreements, not to mention data-sharing agreements like the ones described under the WTO or in regional trade agreements, complicate the factors involved in establishing national data sovereignty (DeNardis, 2020).

13.4.3 Geopolitical Tensions and Global Power Dynamics

One of the primary challenges to digital sovereignty among the BRICS nations, however, is geopolitical tensions and global power dynamics that shape international digital governance (Jiang & Belli, 2025). The influence of global power players such as the United States/U.S., European Union/EU, multinational technology companies, regarding their jurisdiction and capacity to govern the digital economy, creates an obstacle to BRICS' efforts to assert their data sovereignty (DeNardis & Musiani, 2016).

Western nations have historically dominated the development, application, and governance of global digital standards and AI technology (McKinsey, 2021), which contributes to a substantial imbalance in data flow meaning that large volumes of data originating within BRICS nations are produced and dominated by foreign entities (Levchenko, 2024). Therefore, there is a recognized need for BRICS nations to exert their sovereignty by governing and protecting their data. This may also conflict with their aim for development and will create potential friction in diplomatic relations related to trade, technology partnership relationships, and security relations (Gill, 2024).

13.4.4 Ethical and Privacy Concerns

AI regulation in BRICS countries will also have to manage ethical issues related to data privacy, surveillance, and accountability for system-wide algorithmic systems (Saba, 2025). Integrating AI technologies can produce substantial evidence-based benefits especially in terms of improving public service and governance. However, they also have their own unintended consequences (Binns et al., 2018). The more challenging task will be to ensure AI is used to protect individual human rights and civil liberties tied to privacy, non-discrimination, and fairness (Misra et al., 2024b). For instance, AI has the potential to be misappropriated for surveillance, especially in countries with authoritarian tendencies, and to facilitate encroachments on individual citizen privacy and freedom (Belli et al., 2024). Secondly, there are ethical issues surrounding an AI's algorithmic use, since many BRICS countries lack the framework for auditing and regulating AI's decision-making. This can facilitate bias and discrimination as well as lack of transparency (Yeung, 2018).

13.4.5 Economic and Developmental Constraints

The diversified economic development status of BRICS nations also creates unique challenges for the realization of digital sovereignty and governance of AI. Countries like China and India are leading the AI race, but other BRICS countries, such as South Africa and Brazil, are experiencing severe economic pressures on their ability to develop and deploy AI and AI governance systems (Rossi, 2020).

For economically weak countries in the BRICS cohort, there is little to no funding for the development of the digital economy and AI governance (Furendal & Klamberg, 2023). Furthermore, foreign investment of any kind, often in partnership with global companies, potentially stands to erode the prospects of achieving digital sovereignty. Moreover, the reliance on international firms to provide technological solutions results in dependence on foreign companies. This is a counter to establishing the sovereignty of national ecosystems of data governance using AI (Kuner, 2020).

13.4.6 Balancing National Interests with Global Collaboration

A key challenge of implementing digital sovereignty within BRICS in the context of geo-political tensions, is balancing national interests and a need for international cooperation. Digital sovereignty requires tight control over data and AI systems. However, international cooperation is necessary to develop international standards, trade policies, or to collectively manage the digital economy (Gill, 2024). For example, China and India as two democratic nations may each develop their own data localization policies, but they will likely face barriers to implementing them due to competing international free trade rules and regulations on the free flow of information (Andrei, 2021). This discord can cause diplomatic challenges, especially when trying to unite BRICS into a larger global digital governance ecosystem (DeNardis & Musiani, 2016).

13.4.7 Challenges and Risks Faced by Individual BRICS Nation

Table 13.2 provides a systematic overview of how each of the BRICS nations fares individually on the key challenges of Digital Sovereignty and AI Governance. It highlights readiness and disparities among the nations in infrastructure, legality, geopolitical dynamics, ethics, economic constraints, and global cooperation. The

Table 13.2. Challenges in digital sovereignty and AI governance across BRICS nation

Challenge area	Brazil	Russia	India	China	South Africa
4.1 Technological and Infrastructure Gaps	Faces regional disparity in broadband and limited sovereign cloud capabilities; initiatives like GovCloud Brasil and Programa Norte Conectado are responses (Pereira, 2024; Johansson et al., 2024).	Strong cyber capabilities, but rural connectivity and chipset dependence are major gaps; mitigated through Technoparks and national 5G rollout (Martynova & Shcherbovich, 2024).	Large-scale gaps in rural access to broadband; addressed by Digital India, BharatNet, and PM-WANI schemes (Chatterjee & Chatterjee, 2025).	Closed urban gaps, but rural western regions still lag; addressed by New Infrastructure Strategy and state-backed AI infrastructure (Shi & Wei, 2025).	Deep rural-urban digital divide; only partially addressed by National Broadband Plan and Digital Villages (Saba & Pretorius, 2024).
4.2 Legal and Regulatory Complexities	LGPD provides a strong privacy base, but coordination between federal and state authorities is lacking; AI ethics framework under development (Greenleaf, 2023; (Bonfacio et al., 2025).	Sovereign Internet Law and Personal Data Law offer clarity but are rigid; creates compliance burdens for private sector (Saveliev & Zhurenkov, 2021).	DPDP Act 2023 introduced, but lacks specific AI legislation; overlapping jurisdiction among ministries slows enforcement (Bentalha & Boukare, 2024; Kuner, 2020).	Legal regime includes PIPL, Cybersecurity Law, Data Security Law—comprehensive but complex (Ma, 2024).	POPIA is still new, and AI law is under consultation; regulatory fragmentation slows implementation (Soulé, 2024).
4.3 Geopolitical Tensions and Global Power Dynamics	Struggles to balance EU-style digital rights and US-style platform economy; lacks leverage in global forums (Bonfacio et al., 2025).	Under Western sanctions; isolates digital systems and promotes digital decoupling through domestic internet architecture (Martynova & Shcherbovich, 2024; Saveliev & Zhurenkov, 2021).	Balances QUAD and non-alignment; hesitant to sign binding cross-border data agreements (Rout et al., 2021).	Faces tech decoupling from the West; exports digital norms via Digital Silk Road (Shi & Wei, 2025; Yina & Yangxu, 2024).	Remains neutral in global data geopolitics; engages regionally via AU but relies on Western platforms (Hintz et al., 2019).

4.4 Ethical and Privacy Concerns	Weak enforcement of AI ethics; data misuse in public services reported; LGPD not fully operationalized in rural areas (Johansson et al., 2024; Filgueiras & Junquilho, 2023).	AI ethics align with national security; widespread use of surveillance tech raises civil liberties concerns (Saveliev & Zhurenkov, 2021; Martynova & Shcherbovich, 2024).	Public AI systems (e.g., Aadhaar, digital credit) criticized for lack of transparency; ethics frameworks emerging but not yet enforced (Floridi & Cowls, 2022; Bentalha & Boukare, 2024).	Ethics tied to state values; mandatory algorithm filing and social scoring create transparency gaps (Shi & Wei, 2025).	AI systems lack robust auditing; risks of bias and exclusion, especially in healthcare and policing (Saba & Pretorius, 2024; Soulé, 2024).
4.5 Economic and Developmental Constraints	High operational costs and weak SME digital maturity; limited state funding for AI in rural regions (Pereira, 2024; Johansson et al., 2024).	Innovation hindered by state dominance; SMEs struggle under centralized AI investment models (Gromova & Ferreira, 2024).	MSMEs under-digitized; government support exists (e.g., MSME Champions Portal, SAMARTH), but adoption is slow (Saba, 2025).	Urban-focused AI boom; rural SME integration remains marginal (Yina & Yangxu, 2024; Shi & Wei, 2025).	Funding gaps limit AI ecosystem; innovation hubs centered in major cities only (Saba & Pretorius, 2024; Soulé, 2024).
4.6 Balancing National Interests with Global Cooperation	Participates in G20, IGF, and supports GDPR-aligned standards, but lacks unified digital sovereignty roadmap (Bonfacio et al., 2025).	Promotes cyber sovereignty in BRICS/SCO; avoids Western digital standards (Belli et al., 2024; Saveliev & Zhurenkov, 2021).	Balances local control and global engagement via GPAI, QUAD, and DEPA architecture (Kuner, 2020; Chatterjee & Chatterjee, 2025).	Leads global standard-setting through ITU and Belt & Road; prefers state-centric model over multistakeholderism (Shi & Wei, 2025; Yina & Yangxu, 2024).	Promotes regional cooperation through AU Digital Strategy; struggles with national implementation (Hintz et al., 2019; Saba & Pretorius, 2024).

table illustrates an evidence-based picture of the distinctive and shared challenges in each BRICS nation and provides an informed understanding of both opportunities and challenges in building sovereign digital futures.

13.5 Strategies for Enhancing Digital Sovereignty and AI Governance in BRICS Nations

As BRICS countries continue to build their digital economies and AI capacity, advancing creative strategies to develop digital sovereignty and AI governance will be paramount to managing their future digital ecosystems (Birkstedt et al., 2023). This section outlines a several strategies that could assist BRICS nations in dealing with the above mentioned challenges, to promote national control of their data and AI technologies, while also empowering them to develop sustainable and ethical futures (Monsees & Lambach, 2022; Sahoo & Bhujabal, 2024).

13.5.1 Strengthening Legal and Regulatory Frameworks

The first necessary avenue for advancing digital sovereignty is the establishment of strong, coherent, and viable legal jurisdictions that offer clear guidelines to regulate both data and AI technologies (Pechegin, 2022; Pierucci, 2025). Notably to address the fragmented regulatory approach across BRICS, it will be important to have national policies related to data protection, privacy rights and responsible AI development (Rossi, 2020; Kuner, 2020).

BRICS countries will need a commitment to establish legislation that clarifies data ownership, data flows across borders, and data localization (UNCTAD, 2021; Pigola et al., 2021). Countries such as India, with their Personal Data Protection Bill, and Brazil, with their General Data Protection Law (LGPD), have made advances in terms of significant laws and legal frameworks. Other countries in the region will similarly need robust or comprehensive laws that cover the same range of issues (Belli, 2024). Further, they must recognize and address the dynamic nature of AI and use efforts to monitor and audit AI systems to ensure adherence to ethical considerations and human rights protection to have digital sovereignty (Rossi, 2020; Yeung, 2018).

13.5.2 Investing in Digital Infrastructure and Innovation

Local manufacturers of digital technology should substantially enhance funding in their digital infrastructures and innovations in order to fill the technology gaps that prevent BRICS from fully implementing digital sovereignty (Shi & Wei, 2025). A strong digital infrastructure helps to improve the technological capabilities of the BRICS countries while simultaneously ensuring that data sovereignty is established (DeNardis & Musiani, 2016).

Investments into cloud computing, data storage, AI research, and high-performance computing infrastructure are imperative for BRICS countries to develop and maintain local ecosystems independent of foreign technologies (Andrade & Gonçalo, 2021). Public-private partnerships and collaborations with universities, research institutes, and industry leaders can encourage digital and AI technology innovation that are developed domestically to address the needs of BRICS countries (Werthner, 2022; Rossi, 2020).

Promoting startups and local technology companies to develop innovative AI solutions will ensure BRICS countries possess technologies that determine new directions for their economies and societies (Gill, 2024).

13.5.3 Promoting Multilateral Collaboration and Standards Development

Due to the interconnected digital economy, it is important for BRICS members to pursue a multilateral path in order to develop a common foundation for digital sovereignty and AI governance (Dokumacı, 2024). BRICS countries also need to collaborate and make their legal and regulatory frameworks interoperable or at least agree on shared principles regarding common issues like data privacy, data localization, and ethical AI development (Kuner, 2020; Gill, 2024).

They also need to be at the forefront of developing international standards for AI and data. This includes participating in global conversations about AI ethics, data privacy, data management, transparency and accountability (Dahiya & Sharma, 2025). Involvement of the BRICS members in establishing principles for global digital governance can ensure that BRICS values and concerns are being incorporated in the shaping of global digital commons (DeNardis & Musiani, 2016). These partnerships can also allow BRICS nations to partner with other nations or regions which share similar intricacies over digital sovereignty and change the perceptions of digital interventions to implement collective measures in order to address global problems (Belli, 2024).

13.5.4 Enhancing Public Awareness and Digital Literacy

Another important tactic for strengthening digital sovereignty is the advancement of digital literacy and public understanding of the legal and ethical implications of AI and data governance (Cihon, 2019). As AI technologies are increasingly getting embedded in everyday life, citizens need to understand their rights potential exposure to AI risks, and data protection measures (Yeung, 2018).

BRICS countries should develop and fund digital literacy schemes to ensure that wider populations are willing to interact with AI technologies in an informed and responsible manner (Saba, 2025). This will include familiarity with data privacy, cybersecurity, algorithmic transparency and access to systems that enable them to manage and control their personal data (Binns et al., 2018).

Moreover, governments can also encourage discussion between civil society organizations, academia, and the tech sector to develop more inclusive dialogue around digital sovereignty and AI governance (Folorunso et al., 2024). Such engagement could help ensure that AI policies meet the varying needs of stakeholder purposes, including those of underrepresented groups in the sector (Kuner, 2020).

13.5.5 Encouraging Ethical AI Development and Innovation

An ethical approach to AI development must be integral to plans promoting digital sovereignty. The BRICS countries should focus on producing ethical guidelines for AI development with a framework that promotes fairness, transparency, accountability, and non-discrimination (Saba & Ngepah, 2024). Such guidelines will help ensure that AI technologies are developed and deployed without violating human rights and supporting societal welfare (Yeung, 2018; Binns et al., 2018).

BRICS countries should create guidelines that contribute toward auditing and explainability of AI, as it is imperative that AI systems should provide explanations for how they arrive at decisions, and to enhance transparency in decision-making processes (Wagner, 2025). A focus on explainability builds trust in AI technologies and inhibits the emergence of algorithmic biases that threaten social equity (DeNardis, 2020).

Moreover, the establishment of ethical guidelines should be accompanied by interdisciplinary research promotion in AI ethics, social sciences, and law, with a view to establishing more comprehensive models of AI development that can consider metrics for technical work components and societal implications (Binns et al., 2018; Gill, 2024).

13.5.6 Building Capacity and Expertise in AI Governance

To implement digital sovereignty and AI governance, BRICS countries should invest in building AI capacity and expertise (Belli, 2021). Establishing institutions and developing academic programs around AI governance and data protection is a specific first step towards developing a skilled workforce with a grip on both data and AI governance (Rossi, 2020).

Also, training public sector agencies, regulatory bodies, and policymakers on modern developments in AI, and critical digital technology aspects is important for developing and enforcing AI regulations (Chatterjee & Pathak, 2021). A collaborative effort with government, universities, and the private sector can develop the talent pipeline in these nations to innovate AI, while maintaining and securing institutional governance structures (Ayodele & Petla, 2024; Belli, 2024).

13.5.7 Developing National and Regional AI Strategies

Finally, each BRICS country should develop a national AI strategy that reflects its own developmental objectives, goals and ethical values with respect to digital sovereignty (Ma, 2024). The strategies should contain clear milestones for AI development, data governance, and ethical considerations. They should incorporate a clear plan of action for implementing legal, political, and regulatory policies, with respect to AI technology, and absorb the idea of reasserting national control over data and AI (Gill, 2024).

The BRICS nations could also collaborate regionally to develop coordinated AI strategies to assert greater collective digital sovereignty with respect to analogous cross-border situations (Rout et al., 2021). Regional collaboration could facilitate particular knowledge and resource sharing and elevate best practices that would benefit all parties based on knowledge gained collectively in the areas of AI and data governance (DeNardis, 2020).

Table 13.3. Nation specific BRICS strategies for enhancing digital sovereignty and AI governance

Section	Brazil	Russia	India	China	South Africa
5.1. Strengthening Legal and Regulatory Frameworks	Enforced LGPD aligned with GDPR; EIA strategy supports AI ethics (Johansson et al., 2024).	Sovereign Internet Law, AI Ethics Code, and state-centered regulation (Martynova & Shcherbovich, 2024).	DPDP Act 2023; DEPA framework supports data empowerment (Kuner, 2020).	Multi-layered regulation via PIPL, Cybersecurity, and Data Security Laws (Shi & Wei, 2025).	POPIA enforced; PC4IR developing AI law based on rights and equity (Saba & Pretorius, 2024).
5.2. Investing in Digital Infrastructure and Innovation	Investments in GovCloud, Norte Conectado, Embrapii AI Units (Pereira, 2024).	Technoparks, national DNS, and domestic AI chips development (Gromova & Ferreira, 2024).	BharatNet, Digital India, IndiaAI portal, and public digital platforms (Chatterjee & Chatterjee, 2025).	Beidou satellite, AI Innovation Zones, 5G, and cloud via Alibaba, Huawei (Ma, 2024).	Broadband for All, township data hubs, regional AI pilots (Soulé, 2024).
5.3. Promoting Multilateral Collaboration and Standards Development	Active in IGF, G20, supports GDPR-compliant AI norms (Bonfacio et al., 2025).	Promotes digital sovereignty via BRICS, SCO; rejects Western AI models (Belli et al., 2024).	Participates in GPAI, QUAD, DPI; balances sovereignty with openness (Kuner, 2020).	Influences global AI standards via Digital Silk Road, ITU, UN bodies (Shi & Wei, 2025).	Supports AU Digital Strategy and Smart Africa standards (Hintz et al., 2019).
5.4. Enhancing Public Awareness and Digital Literacy	Educa Digital and public digital inclusion programs (Pereira, 2024).	Coding bootcamps and AI Olympiads for national AI awareness (Saveliev & Zhurenkov, 2021).	PMGDISHA, FutureSkills Prime, and rural digital training centers (Rout et al., 2021).	AI integrated into school and vocational curricula (Yina & Yangxu, 2024).	NGO-school collaboration for AI literacy in underserved regions (Soulé, 2024).
5.5. Encouraging Ethical AI Development and Innovation	AI Ethics Commission and bias prevention built into EIA (Filgueiras & Junquilho, 2023).	AI Ethics Code (2021) prioritizes military and security applications (Martynova & Shcherbovich, 2024).	RAISE Summit, ethical sandbox testing, and explainability mandates (Floridi & Cowls, 2022).	CAC mandates algorithmic fairness with state-centric values (Shi & Wei, 2025).	Draft AI Ethics Framework focused on justice and inclusion (Saba & Pretorius, 2024).

(Contd.)

(Contd.)

Section	Brazil	Russia	India	China	South Africa
5.6. Building Capacity and Expertise in AI Governance	University-government partnerships and Embrapii AI labs (Johansson et al., 2024).	State-led research centers and defense-based capacity building (Gromova & Ferreira, 2024).	CoEs in IITs, AI research clusters, and NITI Aayog support (Chatterjee & Chatterjee, 2025).	State-university AI labs (Tsinghua, Peking), regional tech clusters (Ma, 2024).	AIISA, CSIR, and public university partnerships (Soulé, 2024).
5.7. Developing National and Regional AI Strategies	EIA (2021) sets principles for responsible and inclusive AI (Johansson et al., 2024).	National Strategy (2019–2030) promotes AI for sovereignty and security (Martynova & Shcherbovich, 2024).	NSAI and IndiaAI initiatives focus on social impact and scalable governance (Bentalha & Boukare, 2024).	NG-AIDP aims for global AI leadership by 2030 (Shi & Wei, 2025).	PC4IR developing national AI strategy within AU framework (Saba & Pretorius, 2024).

13.5.8 Strategies by Individual BRICS Nation to Enhance Digital Sovereignty and AI Governance

Table 13.3 presents a summary of how BRICS countries address digital sovereignty and AI governance. Brazil and India advocate for an inclusive framework based on ethics; Russia favors a state-controlled model focusing on state security; China has already positioned itself in terms of infrastructure and global AI standards; and South Africa focuses on rights, though with limited resources. In all cases, countries are balancing innovation against sovereignty, but in very different ways.

13.6 Towards a Multilayered Framework for Digital Sovereignty and AI Governance

The previous sections of this chapter provided a comparative view of the approaches and challenges adopted by BRICS countries to achieve digital sovereignty and effective AI governance. Despite having substantial differences such as institutional maturity, legal frameworks, geographical context, and so on, the BRICS nations share a common outlook i.e. balancing sovereign authority with global interoperability, ethical considerations, and inclusive development for effective AI adoption. Keeping in view the common insights, this chapter proposes a unified, yet flexible framework – the Multilayered Digital Sovereignty and AI Governance Nitigrities Framework (Multi-DiSAIGN). The framework will assist and help future policymaking and cross-national benchmarking not only among the BRICS nations, but also to understand that DS and AI Governance are developing alongside developed economies.

13.6.1 Rationale for a Unified Framework

While global frameworks such as the OECD 2019, UNESCO 2021, GDPR are well-established, they t assume an effective presence in institutional capacities, digital architecture, and uniform legislation within a country. This assumption is not universally true, especially in the case of BRICS nations which differ in their governance structures, growth needs, and technical capabilities. The author believes there is a need for a framework that integrates the best models and permits flexibility as per the requirement of the BRICS countries (Floridi & Cowls, 2022; Gromova & Ferreira, 2024).

13.6.2 Global Alignment and Adaptability

Since the Multi-DiSIGN Framework incorporates intricacies of OECD AI Principles (2019), UNESCO AI Ethics Guidelines (2021), the EU AI Act, GPAI, and the G20 Digital Economy Task Force, it supports human centric design, ethics, justice, and data governance. At the same time, the proposed framework offers flexibility to the BRICS nations where they can tailor its layers to national contexts enabling state-driven AI governance in countries like Russia and China, while supporting rights-based and inclusive digital development in Brazil, South Africa, and India.

13.6.3 The Multilayered Digital Sovereignty and AI Governance Nitty-gritty Framework (Multi-DiSAIGN)

The new framework that is proposed in the current study comprises of seven interlinked layers, representing the indicators for a robust, ethical, and sovereign digital governance. It is depicted in Table 13.4.

Table 13.4. The proposed Multi-DiSIGN framework

Layer	Evaluation indicators	Sample measures/Questions
1. Normative Foundations	• Adoption of AI ethics principles • Cultural and constitutional alignment • Human rights protections	• Does the country have a published AI ethics policy? • Are AI uses reviewed for cultural appropriateness and human dignity?
2. Legal and Regulatory Alignment	• Existence of comprehensive AI/data laws • Cross-border data flow regulation • Alignment with global norms (GDPR, UNESCO)	• Is there a national AI law or policy? • Are international standards incorporated into national legislation?
3. Institutional Mechanisms	• Independent regulatory bodies • Inter-agency coordination • Public oversight mechanisms	• Is there a dedicated AI oversight body? • How independent is it? • Are citizens involved in AI policy feedback?
4. Infrastructure and Innovation Readiness	• Availability of sovereign cloud/ data centers • Investment in R&D • Domestic AI capabilities (compute, chips, language tools)	• Does the country host national supercomputing facilities? • Are funds allocated for AI innovation zones?
5. Ethical AI Innovation Ecosystems	• Existence of regulatory sandboxes • AI start-up support • Multi-stakeholder collaboration	• Are public-private AI innovation hubs operating? • Is there an ethics-by-design requirement for AI startups?
6. Capacity Building and Digital Literacy	• AI and digital literacy in education • Workforce upskilling programs • Inclusion of marginalized groups	• Are AI modules part of school curricula? • Are rural or underrepresented communities being trained in digital skills?
7. Monitoring, Evaluation, and Interoperability	• Performance monitoring of AI systems • Audit trails and transparency reports • Compliance with national/global standards	• Are AI systems subject to algorithmic audits? • Are indicators tracked at the national level (e.g., AI index)?

13.6.4 Implications for Research and Policy

The Multi-DiSAIGN provides a flexible and concrete framework for analyzing the digital governance status in specific countries, and may be used for tracking national progress on AI deployment and data sovereignty. The framework offers nations endorsement of their governance policies vis-à-vis global standards while not relinquishing any national autonomy. Moreover, the framework can contribute in capacity building in both civil society and institutions. Future research can engage this framework to assess national AI governance maturity in developing economies, evaluate various cross-border data strategies, and scrutinize ethical innovation through factors that are critical to the success of societies such as health, education, and finance.

13.7 Conclusion and Discussion

In the current digital economy, BRICS countries have the challenge of balancing multi-domain and across-nation governance of AI. The governments need to establish a comprehensive legal and ethical framework alongwith a sustainable infrastructure to support digital transformation. To overcome regulatory discrepancies they must establish a governance framework that can provide more coherent, inclusive, and ethical regulatory models to support digital sovereignty and its alignment with the global AI agenda.

For AI development and Digital Sovereignty, the BRICS states can develop a framework for human rights, equity, and social good. They should focus on developing citizens' action and awareness programs which will help them develop indigenous digital strategies that require educating citizens about the growing nuances of AI, data, and privacy rights. To build digital sovereignty, the BRICS nations must allow citizens to become more informed as digital citizens. Public awareness initiatives could also provide educational opportunities to help emphasize how AI can transform areas such as governance, healthcare, education, and the economy. In addition, a focus on privacy, data protection, and other considerations should be in place to ensure a sustainable and equitable digital future.

By using the proposed Multi-DiSIGN Framework in this chapter, the observations on the BRICS nation are consolidated herewith (Table 13.5). From legal to ethical foundations to DS readiness and monitoring, the matrix reflects the status of each BRICS nation based on the seven-core dimension of the framework. The discussed literature in the chapter offers the score based on the snapshot of maturity, strengths, and gaps in each country that helps them to achieve digital sovereignty and AI governance. It serves not only as a summary of the chapter's core findings but also as a practical tool for benchmarking and policy reflection across similar emerging economies.

The scores in the Digital Sovereignty and AI Governance Matrix are based on strong observations. Brazil is strong with ethical policies and legal restructuring having systems like LGPD and EIA, but holds moderate infrastructure and institutional capacity. The country also lacks robust evaluation tools. Russia on the other hand possesses centralized control over resources, and a decent legal

Table 13.5. Digital sovereignty & AI governance matrix

Multi-DiSIGN framework layers	Brazil	Russia	India	China	South Africa
1. Normative Foundations	4	2	4	3	3
2. Legal and Regulatory Alignment	4	4	4	5	3
3. Institutional Mechanisms	3	3	4	5	2
4. Infrastructure and Innovation Readiness	3	3	4	5	2
5. Ethical AI Innovation Ecosystems	3	2	4	4	2
6. Capacity Building and Digital Literacy	3	3	4	5	2
7. Monitoring, Evaluation, and Interoperability	3	2	3	4	2
Total Score (out of 35)	23	19	27	31	16
Maturity Level	Maturing	Developing	Maturing	Advanced	Nascent

framework. However, it is challenged with limited civil oversight and ethical openness. India is observed as having a balanced model and shows legal maturity with systems like DPDP in place, displaying healthy institutional innovation, and possesses good ecosystem support. China has the highest score among all BRICS nations, has the most advanced infrastructure, AI leadership, and institutional depth, but lacks participatory governance and limited transparency. South Africa has a limited infrastructure lacking institutional support. Thus it scores lowest among all BRICS nations, though they have certain positives like having clarity in their regional alignment and possessing appreciable ethical intentions.

The above is also depicted through the radar chart in Figure 13.1 which helps in visualizing the status of each BRICS nations across the seven layers of the Multi-DiSIGN Framework.

To conclude, the journey towards the attainment of total digital sovereignty and proper governance of artificial intelligence may be challenging. However, the BRICS nations' initiatives to circumvent these challenges are essential as the future of digital governance unfolds worldwide. The interdependence of technological, legal, ethical, and social factors will ultimately determine whether digital sovereignty and AI governance could be feasible outcomes for BRICS countries. If the BRICS countries endorse innovation, create regulatory frameworks, and focus on ethical AI development then they will be in a position to assure reliable, sustainable digital systems ensuring a sound and secure digital future aligned with their national aspirations. Furthermore, a collaborative, inclusive, and dynamic outlook will allow the BRICS nations to cultivate exciting new digital futures that not only secure the

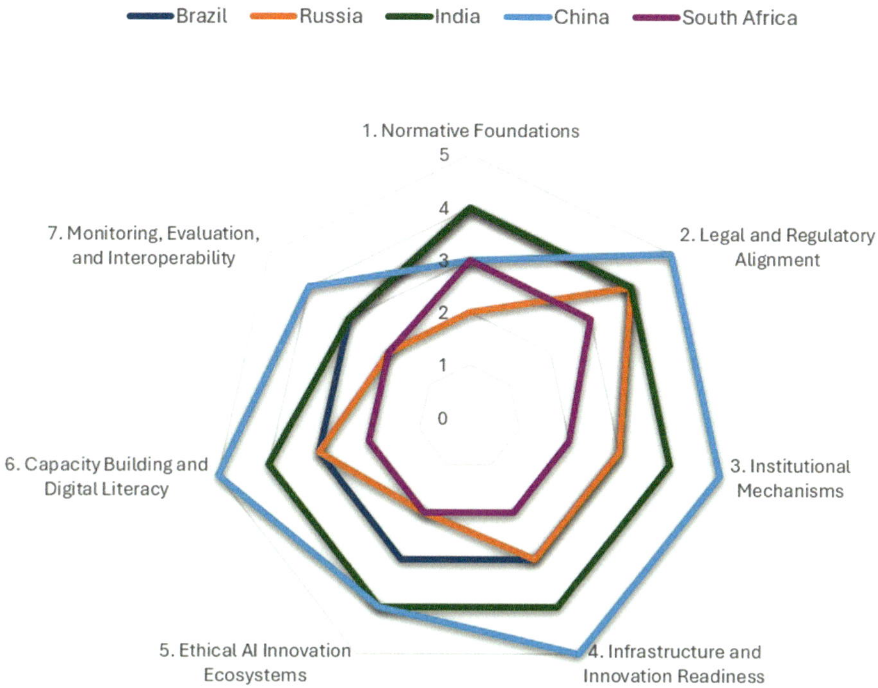

Figure 13.1. BRICS digital sovereignty and AI governance.

nation's sovereignty but also add positively to their global future. Quite simply, the success of BRICS in this area influences the future of digital governance worldwide and sets a new global benchmark for balancing the complexity of technology, governance, and sovereignty.

13.8 Limitations of Research

While this chapter provides an in-depth discussion of digital sovereignty and AI governance in BRICS context, there are some limitations that need to be acknowledged:

- **Limited Access to Up-to-Date Data and Policy Documents:** The digital governance landscape is constantly evolving, reflecting frequent updates in policy across BRICS member states. Due to the evolving nature of AI regulations and digital sovereignty initiatives, some of the legislative developments or bilateral agreements may have developed after this chapter was written, limiting the analysis.
- **Comparative Constraints Across BRICS Nations:** While the chapter endeavors to examine each BRICS country in a unified framework, the BRICS nations are quite heterogeneous in terms of technological readiness, political systems, legal traditions, and economic priorities. This heterogeneity may lead

to unevenness in depth of analysis for each country, with more established countries like China and Russia getting more attention given their larger and richer datasets with available policy documents.

- **Scope of Sources and Language Barriers:** The research for this chapter relied mainly on English-language academic sources, policy documents, or journalism from reputable sources. While it may be true some of the key primary sources in Mandarin, Portuguese, Russian, or Hindi may not have been adequately considered. Due to this, the presence of local or national perspectives or important debates about policy, may be missing important nuances.
- **Lack of Empirical Validation or Stakeholder Input:** This chapter is conceptual and geared towards policy. There are no empirical interviews or surveys data from policy makers, regulators, or industry actors in BRICS nations. Because of the lack of first-hand qualitative data, our insights into how digital sovereignty and AI governance is achieved in practice may be weak.
- **Generalizability of Findings:** The conclusions and policy recommendations are site-specific to the BRICS context therefore cannot be generalized to other regional blocs or developing knowledge economies that have different digital ecosystems, governance capacity or geopolitical factors.
- **Evolving Nature of AI and Geopolitical Dynamics:** As there are significant geopolitical sensitivities with data sovereignty and the developmental trajectories of AI, and as geopolitical tensions and trade disputes have spiked globally, a future change in international relations could shift BRICS's plans rapidly. In essence, the chapter provides a snapshot in time rather than a long term outlook.

13.9 Future Research Directions

While this chapter provides a basis for understanding BRICS' plans for digital sovereignty and AI governance, there are many possible areas for future research:

- **Comparative Policy Impact Studies:** Future research should investigate empirically the outcomes of different BRICS' countries' legal systems for digital sovereignty which might include local innovation, foreign investment trends from or local product adoption rates, or AI adoption processes and rates.
- **Stakeholder Perspectives and Case Studies:** Adding qualitative dimensions from interviews with policymakers, data protection authorities, civil society actors, and private sector actors may provide a nuanced understanding of implementation, obstacles, and notably possible discrepancies across the BRICS countries.
- **Cross-Regional Comparisons:** The differences between BRICS' approaches and other regional blocs such as the European Union, ASEAN, or the African Union may also promote a better understanding of the uniqueness and global relevance of BRICS digital approaches.
- **AI Ethics and Algorithmic Justice in the Global South:** Future studies could examine how the AI ethics frameworks in BRICS countries mirror or divert from Western frameworks, with specific consideration for data justice, algorithmic discrimination, and citizen's rights across different sociopolitical contexts.

- **Geopolitical Influence of BRICS in Global Norm-Setting:** As BRICS countries become increasin1gly vocal in multilateral settings such as the United Nations, World Trade Organization, and International Telecommunication Union, new research can examine BRICS' role in establishing international regimes around global digital governance, standardization, and cross-border data regulation.
- **Technological Dependence and Indigenous Innovation:** There is also the opportunity for deeper analysis of the national efforts undertaken by the BRICS countries to reduce dependence on foreign nations for digital infrastructure and the promotion of domestic AI ecosystems in public and private organizations.

By pursuing these avenues of research, scholars and policymakers alike can engage in the collective understanding of how digital sovereignty and AI governance can develop in a multipolar world with the BRICS countries as crucial references.

Declaration of Generative AI and AI-Assisted Technologies

During the preparation of this work, the author utilized AI-assisted tools such as ChatGPT, MIKI K1.5, and Grammarly to enhance English language accuracy, including spelling, grammar, and punctuation. The content generated or corrected by these tools was thoroughly reviewed, revised, and edited by the author to ensure accuracy and originality. The author accepts full responsibility for the originality of the final content of this publication.

References

Andrade, C.R.D., & Gonçalo, C.R. (2021). Digital transformation by enabling strategic capabilities in the context of "BRICS". *Revista de Gestão*, 28(4), 297–315. https://doi.org/10.1108/REGE-12-2020-0154

Awosusi, A., Adebayob, T.S., Kirikkaleli, D., & Altuntaş, M. (2022). Role of technological innovation and globalization in BRICS economies: Policy towards environmental sustainability. *International Journal of Sustainable Development & World Ecology*, 29(7), 593–610. https://doi.org/10.1080/13504509.2022.2059032

Ayodele, O., & Petla, V. (2024). Leveraging the BRICS digital partnership for collaborative digital governance. *Journal of BRICS Studies*, 3(1), 1–7. https://doi.org/10.36615/feg0h138.

Balaguer, A., van den Hoven, J., & Zeng, J. (2023). Digital sovereignty: Mapping norms, paradigm shifts, and future pathways. *Ethics and Information Technology*, 25(2), 421–439. https://doi.org/10.1007/s10676-023-09709-1

Barik, K., Misra, S., Mohan, R., & Mishra, B. (2024). AIoT and its trust models to enhance societal applications using intelligent technologies. In: S. Misra, K. Siakas, & G. Lampropoulos (eds.), *Artificial Intelligence of Things for Achieving Sustainable Development Goals* (Vol. 192). Springer. https://doi.org/10.1007/978-3-031-53433-1_16

Beeson, M., & Zeng, J. (2018). The BRICS and global governance: China's contradictory role. *Third World Quarterly*, 39(10), 1962–1978. https://doi.org/10.1080/01436597.2018.1438186

Belli, L. (2021). Cybersecurity policymaking in the BRICS countries: From addressing national priorities to seeking international cooperation. *African Journal of Information and Communication*, 28, 1–14. https://doi.org/10.23962/10539/32208

Belli, L. (2024). BRICS countries and AI sovereignty: Introduction to Thematic Section. *The African Journal of Information and Communication*, (34), 1–6. https://doi.org/10.23962/ajic.i34.20864

Belli, L., & Magalhães, L. (2024). Toward a BRICS stack? Leveraging digital transformation to construct digital sovereignty in the BRICS countries. *Computer Law & Security Review*, 106064. https://doi.org/10.1016/j.clsr.2024.106064

Belli, L., Gaspar, W.B., & Jaswant, S. (2024). Data sovereignty and data transfers as fundamental elements of digital transformation: Lessons from the BRICS countries. *Computer Law & Security Review*, 54, 106017. https://doi.org/10.1016/j.clsr.2024.106017

Bentalha, B., & Boukare, M. (2024). AI-Driven territorial intelligence: An integrated approach to enhancing digital sovereignty. In: *Generative AI and Implications for Ethics, Security, and Data Management* (pp. 231–261). https://doi.org/10.4018/979-8-3693-8557-9.ch008

Binns, R., Veale, M., Van Kleek, M., & Shadbolt, N. (2018). 'It's reducing a human being to a percentage': Perceptions of justice in algorithmic decisions. *Proceedings of the 2018 CHI Conference on Human Factors in Computing Systems*, 1–14. https://doi.org/10.1145/3173574.3173951

Birkstedt, T., Minkkinen, M., Tandon, A., & Mäntymäki, M. (2023). AI governance: Themes, knowledge gaps and future agendas. *Internet Research*, 33(7), 133–167. https://doi.org/10.1108/INTR-01-2022-0042

Bonfacio, C., Schapachnik, F., & Porto, F. (2025). Generative AI and the Transformation of Work in Latin America – Brazil. arXiv. https://doi.org/10.48550/arXiv.2505.13490

Chatterjee, D., & Pathak, B. (2021). Digital literacy initiatives in India: Evaluating PMGDISHA's impact on rural empowerment. *Government Information Quarterly*, 38(1), 101644. https://doi.org/10.1016/j.giq.2021.101644

Chatterjee, T., & Chatterjee, N. (2025). Digitalisation, skill development and sustainable economic growth: Theories and empirics in the context of BRICS. *Quality & Quantity*. https://doi.org/10.1007/s11135-025-02144-4

Cihon, P. (2019). Standards for AI governance: International standards to enable global coordination in AI research & development. *Future of Humanity Institute*. University of Oxford, 40(3), 340–342.

Cihon, P., Maas, M.M., & Kemp, L. (2020). Should Artificial Intelligence Governance be Centralised? Design Lessons from History. arXiv. https://doi.org/10.48550/arXiv.2001.03573

Couture, S., & Toupin, S. (2019). What does the notion of "sovereignty" mean when referring to the digital? *New Media & Society*, 21(10), 1553–1570. https://doi.org/10.1177/1461444819865984

Dahiya, K., & Sharma, U. (2025). Challenges and responses across BRICS. *Navigating the Deepfake Conundrum: A Manager's Roadmap*, 44, 239.

DeNardis, L. (2020). The Internet in Everything: Freedom and Security in a World with no off Switch. Yale University Press. https://doi.org/10.12987/yale/9780300233070.001.0001.

DeNardis, L., & Musiani, F. (2016). Governance by infrastructure. In: F. Musiani, D.L. Cogburn, L. DeNardis, & N.S. Levinson (eds.), *The Turn to Infrastructure in Internet Governance* (pp. 3–21). Palgrave Macmillan. https://doi.org/10.1057/9781137483591_1

Dokumacı, M. (2024). Legal frameworks for AI regulations. *Human–Computer Interaction*, 8(1), Article 133. https://doi.org/10.62802/ytst2927

Epifanova, A., & Dietrich, P. (2022). Russia's Quest for Digital Sovereignty: Ambitions, Realities, and Its Place in the World. https://nbn-resolving.org/urn:nbn:de:0168-ssoar-77994-6

Filgueiras, F., & Junquilho, T.A. (2023). The Brazilian (Non) perspective on national strategy for artificial intelligence. *Discover Artificial Intelligence*, 3(1), 7. https://doi.org/10.1007/s44163-023-00052-w

Floridi, L., & Cowls, J. (2022). A unified framework of five principles for AI in society. In: *Ethics, Governance, and Policies in Artificial Intelligence* (pp. 5–17). Springer. https://doi.org/10.1007/978-3-030-81907-1_2

Folorunso, A., Olanipekun, K., Adewumi, T., & Samuel, B. (2024). A policy framework on AI usage in developing countries and its impact. *Global Journal of Engineering and Technology Advances*, 21(01), 154–166.

Furendal, M., & Klamberg, M. (2023). International governance of artificial intelligence. *AI & Society*, 40, 3019–3044. https://doi.org/10.1007/s00146-024-02050-7

Gill, A.S. (2024). Building digital cooperation in a fragmented world. *Time*. https://time.com/7012779/amandeep-singh-gill/

Greenleaf, G. (2023). Global data privacy laws 2023: 162 national laws and 20 bills. *Privacy Laws & Business International Report*, 181, 1–4. https://doi.org/10.2139/ssrn.4426146

Gromova, E., & Ferreira, D.B. (2024). On the way to BRICS+Digital sovereignty: Opportunities and challenges of a new era. *BRICS Law Journal*, 11(3), 54–69. 10.21684/2412-2343-2024-11-3-54-69

Gurumurthy, A., & Chami, N. (2022). Beyond data bodies: New directions for a feminist theory of data sovereignty. *Data Governance Network Working Paper*, 24. http://dx.doi.org/10.2139/ssrn.4037321

Haryono, H. (2024). BRICS in the digital age: Investigating technological innovation and knowledge sharing as catalysts for economic transformation. *The Eastasouth Journal of Information System and Computer Science*, 2(02), 84–91. https://doi.org/10.58812/esiscs.v2i02.399

Hintz, A., Dencik, L., & Wahl-Jorgensen, K. (2019). *Digital Citizenship in a Datafied Society*. Polity Press. https://doi.org/10.1080/1369118X.2019.1635186

Hoffmann, R., Šedová, B., & Vinke, K. (2021). Improving the evidence base: A methodological review of the quantitative climate migration literature. *Global Environmental Change*, 71, 102367. https://doi.org/10.1016/j.gloenvcha.2021.102367

Ignatov, A. (2023). Global governance of cyberspace: The BRICS agenda. In: *Digital International Relations* (pp. 305–327).

Iqbal, S., & Zahra, S.T. (2024). Digital strategic autonomy in South Asia: Artificial intelligence and cyberspace. *Journal of Security & Strategic Analyses*, 10(1), 72–86. https://doi.org/10.57169/jssa.0010.01.0300

Jiang, M., & Belli, L. (Eds.). (2021). *Digital Sovereignty in the BRICS Countries*. Cambridge University Press. Accessed from: https://cyberbrics.info/wp-content/uploads/2024/05/DIGITAL-SOVEREINGTY-IN-BRICS-COUNTRIES_3_3_2023.pdf

Jiang, M., & Belli, L. (Eds.). (2025). *Digital Sovereignty in the BRICS Countries: How the Global South and Emerging Power Alliances are Reshaping Digital Governance*. Cambridge: Cambridge University Press. https://www.cambridge.org/core/books/digital-sovereignty-in-the-brics-countries/27E9FD7E4579C76C8D4BA52F7670B431

Jobin, A., Ienca, M., & Vayena, E. (2019). The global landscape of AI ethics guidelines. *Nature Machine Intelligence*, 1(9), 389–399. https://doi.org/10.1038/s42256-019-0088-2

Johansson Neto, G.P., Farias da Costa, V.C., & Gaspar, W.B. (2024). Brazil's Artificial Intelligence Plan (PBIA) of 2024: Enabler of AI sovereignty? *The African Journal of Information and Communication*, 34, 1–15. https://doi.org/10.23962/ajic.i34.20424.

Kelly, M. J. & Satola, D.E. (2024). Digital sovereignty and AI: New threats to corporate participation in internet governance? *Case Western Reserve Journal of International Law*, 57(1), 43–75. https://scholarlycommons.law.case.edu/jil/vol57/iss1/5

Kuner, C. (2020). Data Nationalism and its discontents. *Emory Law Journal Online*, 64, 2089–2105. Available at https://scholarlycommons.law.emory.edu/elj-online/25

Levchenko, D. (2024). Artificial Intelligence as an object of global digital governance. *Advanced Space Law*, 14, 45–52. https://doi.org/10.29202/asl/14/4.

Ma, A. (2024). Regulation in pursuit of artificial intelligence (AI) sovereignty: China's mix of restrictive and facilitative modalities. *African Journal of Information and Communication*, (34), 1–15. https://doi.org/10.23962/ajic.i34.20103

Martynova, E., & Shcherbovich, A. (2024). Digital transformation in Russia: Turning from a service model to ensuring technological sovereignty. *Computer Law & Security Review*, 55, 106075. https://doi.org/10.1016/j.clsr.2024.106075

Misra, S., Barik, K., & Kvalvik, P. (2024). Digital sovereignty in the era of Industry 5.0: Challenges and opportunities. *Procedia Computer Science*, 254, 108–117. https://doi.org/10.1016/j.procs.2025.02.069

Misra, S., Barik, K., Thunem, H.P.J., & Chockalingam, S. (2024). Human factors and security in digital twins: Challenges and future prospects. In: A. Moallem (ed.), *HCI for Cybersecurity, Privacy and Trust* (HCII 2024, Lecture Notes in Computer Science, vol. 14728, pp. 250–258). Springer. https://doi.org/10.1007/978-3-031-61379-1_18

Mondschein, C.F., & Monda, C. (2018). The EU's general data protection regulation (GDPR) in a research context. In: P. Kubben et al. (eds.), *Fundamentals of Clinical Data Science* (pp. 55–71). Springer.

Monsees, L., & Lambach, D. (2022). Digital sovereignty, geopolitical imaginaries, and the reproduction of European identity. *European Security*, 31(3), 377–394. https://doi.org/10.1080/09662839.2022.2101883

OECD. (2021). *OECD Economic Outlook*. Volume 2021 Issue 1. OECD Publishing. https://doi.org/10.1787/edfbca02-en

Pechegin, D.A. (2022). Legal mechanisms for the protection of state digital sovereignty: A comparative legal aspect. *Russian Journal of Legal Studies Moscow*, 9(2), 9–20. https://doi.org/10.17816/RJLS106912

Pereira, L.D.A. (2024). State-led or private innovation: Looking at the Brazilian Strategy on AI (so far). *Brazilian Journal of Law, Technology and Innovation*, 2(1), 50–70. https://doi.org/10.59224/bjlti.v2i1.50-70

Pierucci, F. (2025). Sovereignty in the digital era: Rethinking territoriality and governance in cyberspace. *Digital Society*, 4(27). https://doi.org/10.1007/s44206-025-00189-4

Pigola, A., da Costa, P.R., Carvalho, L.C., Silva, L.F.d., Kniess, C.T., & Maccari, E.A. (2021). Artificial Intelligence-driven digital technologies to the implementation of the sustainable development goals: A perspective from Brazil and Portugal. *Sustainability*, 13(24), 13669. https://doi.org/10.3390/su132413669

Pohle, J., & Thiel, T. (2020). Digital sovereignty. *Internet Policy Review*, 9(4). https://doi.org/10.14763/2020.4.1532

Roberts, M.H., Hine, E., & Floridi, L. (2023). Digital sovereignty, digital expansionism, and the prospects for global AI Governance. In: *Quo Vadis, Sovereignty? New Conceptual and Regulatory Boundaries in the Age of Digital China* (pp. 51–75). Cham: Springer Nature Switzerland. https://doi.org/10.1007/978-3-031-41566-1_4

Robles-Carrillo, A. (2023). Sovereignty vs digital sovereignty. *Journal of Digital Technologies and Law*, 1(3). https://www.lawjournal.digital/jour/article/view/236

Rodriguez, C., Belli, L., & De Filippi, P. (Eds.). (2024). *Digital Sovereignty in the BRICS Countries: How the Global South and Emerging Power Alliances are Reshaping Digital Governance*. Cambridge University Press.

Rossi, A. (2020). Data protection frameworks emerging in the BRICS countries. *CyberBRICS*. https://cyberbrics.info/data-protection-frameworks-emerging-in-the-brics-countries/

Rout, S.K., Gupta, M., & Sahoo, M. (2021). The role of technological innovation and diffusion, energy consumption and financial development in affecting ecological footprint in BRICS: An empirical analysis. *Environmental Science and Pollution Research*, 29, 25318–25335. https://doi.org/10.1007/s11356-021-17734-6

Saba, C.S. (2025). AI–poverty–economic growth nexus in selected BRICS-Plus countries: Does the moderating role of governance matter? *AI & Society*. https://doi.org/10.1007/s00146-025-02213-0

Saba, C.S., & Ngepah, N. (2024). The impact of artificial intelligence (AI) on employment and economic growth in BRICS: Does the moderating role of governance matter? *Research in Globalization*, 8, 100213. https://doi.org/10.1016/j.resglo.2024.100213

Saba, C.S., & Pretorius, M. (2024). The mediating role of governance in creating a nexus between investment in artificial intelligence and human well-being in the BRICS countries. *BRICS Journal of Economics*, 5(2), 5–44. https://doi.org/10.3897/brics-econ.5.e117358

Sahoo, M., & Bhujabal, P. (2024). Empowering BRICS economies: The crucial role of green finance, ICT and innovation in sustainable development. *Sustainable Development*, 32(6), 7292–7308. https://doi.org/10.1002/sd.3083

Saveliev, A., & Zhurenkov, D. (2021). Artificial intelligence and social responsibility: The case of the artificial intelligence strategies in the United States, Russia, and China. Kybernetes, 50(3), 656–675. https://doi.org/10.1108/K-01-2020-0060

Shi, Y., & Wei, F. (2025). Comparative analysis of digital economy-driven innovation development in China: An international perspective. *Journal of the Knowledge Economy*, 16, 4422–4464. https://doi.org/10.1007/s13132-024-02128-z

Shoker, A. (2022). Digital sovereignty strategies for every nation. *Applied Cybersecurity & Internet Governance*, 1(1), 01–17. https://doi.org/10.5604/01.3001.0016.0943

Soulé, F. (2024). *Digital Sovereignty in Africa: Moving beyond Local Data Ownership.* CIGI Policy Brief No. 185. https://www.cigionline.org/publications/digital-sovereignty-in-africa-moving-beyond-local-data-ownership/

Srivastava, S., & Bullock, J. (2024). *AI, Global Governance, and Digital Sovereignty* [Preprint]. arxiv. https://doi.org/10.48550/arXiv.2410.17481

Taylor, R. D. (2020). Data localization: The internet in the balance. *Telecommunications Policy*, 44(8), 102003. https://doi.org/10.1016/j.telpol.2020.102003

UNCTAD. (2021). *Digital Economy Report 2021: Cross-border Data Flows and Development – For Whom the Data Flow*. United Nations Conference on Trade and Development.

Veale, M., & Edwards, L. (2018). Enslaving the algorithm: From a 'right to an explanation' to 'right to better decisions'. *IEEE Security & Privacy*, 16(3), 46–54. https://doi.org/10.1109/MSP.2018.2701152

Vila Seoane, M.F. (2021). Data securitisation: The challenges of data sovereignty in India. *Third World Quarterly*, 42(8), 1733–1750. https://doi.org/10.1080/01436597.2021.1915122

Wagner, B. (2025). The sovereignty–internationalism paradox in AI governance: Digital federalism and global algorithmic control. *Discover Artificial Intelligence*, 5, 123. https://doi.org/10.1007/s44163-025-00374-x

Werthner, H. (2022). Geopolitics, digital sovereignty… What's in a word? *Perspectives on Digital Humanism*, https://doi.org/10.1007/978-3-030-86144-5.

Whittlestone, J., Nyrup, R., Alexandrova, A., Dihal, K., & Cave, S. (2019). Ethical and societal implications of algorithms, data, and artificial intelligence: A roadmap for research. *London: Nuffield Foundation*, 1–59.

Yeung, K. (2017). Algorithmic regulation: A critical interrogation. *Regulation & Governance*, 12(4), 505–523. https://doi.org/10.1111/rego.12158

Zheng, X., Zhou, G., & Zeng, D.D. (2023). Platform governance in the era of AI and the digital economy. *Frontiers of Engineering Management*, 10(1), 177–182. https://doi.org/10.1007/s42524-022-0241-1

Zinovieva, E., & Shitkov, S. (2023). Sovereignty as practice in digital age. In: Baykov, A., Zinovieva, E. (eds.), *Digital International Relations*. Palgrave Macmillan, Singapore. https://doi.org/10.1007/978-981-99-3467-6_5

CHAPTER
14

European Digital Sovereignty in the Age of AI: Regulation, Infrastructure, and Democratic Legitimacy

Hamza Aarab(0009-0006-0061-3888)
Sciences Po University

14.1 Introduction

Artificial intelligence (AI) in recent years has become a major focus of global competition, with governments recognizing AI as a space where sovereignty intersects economic power and social impact. The United States (US), with its extensive private sector innovation ecosystem is dominating AI models, computing capabilities and the cloud infrastructure, while China has opted for a contrasting state-led approach that combines rapid investment in national AI capabilities with strict political oversight. Meanwhile, the European Union (EU) has positioned itself as a moral guardian of AI by trying to regulate it to be aligned with human rights and democratic values (Floridi, 2020) ignoring the ground reality that it might become solely a rule-maker without any real control over the technologies it seeks to govern.

The EU's initiatives in this regard have gained international visibility and influence: the General Data Protection Regulation (GDPR), the Digital Services Act (DSA), and, most recently, the AI Act. These frameworks articulate a normative vision for AI governance grounded in rights and accountability, however, digital sovereignty cannot be secured through legal instruments alone (Floridi, 2020; OECD, 2023). The EU remains structurally dependent on foreign-owned cloud and AI infrastructure, particularly US-based technologies, causing a critical asymmetry between normative ambitions and technical autonomy (Gomes & Okano-Heijmans, 2024). In the same context, no matter how value-aligned they are, governance frameworks require corresponding technical and infrastructural capacities to be

Email: hamza.aarab@sciencespo-lille.eu

DOI: 10.1201/9781003581581-14

enforceable and effective. This chapter contends that the EU must move beyond a regulation-only process toward a more integrated model of digital sovereignty. It introduces a tripod model as a strategic framework for aligning law, infrastructure, and public legitimacy. This chapter offers a fresh perspective, one that moves beyond the conventional framing of digital sovereignty as solely a legal or technical issue. Instead, it integrates these dimensions while emphasizing the democratic agency necessary to legitimize them.

The EU's AI Act presents a robust normative framework on the regulatory front embedding principles of safety, transparency and accountability. However, its enforcement remains contingent on the technical capacities that Europe continues to lack (European Commission, 2025). While most efforts are still in their early stages, several initiatives have been launched to address this critical infrastructure gap, including efforts to build European compute capacity, cloud alternatives and open-source AI models. Despite tools like the Assessment List for Trustworthy Artificial Intelligence (ALTAI), public participation remains largely,symbolic with deliberative engagement still rare and non-binding (Cupać & Sienknecht, 2024).

This chapter builds on previous academic literature, EU project data and policy documents to propose a pragmatic path for the future. It offers a conceptual and empirical analysis of the European model of digital sovereignty in AI, focusing on how regulation, infrastructure and public legitimacy can be aligned. In this context, it evaluates key initiatives such as Gaia-X, OpenGPT-X, and the AI Alliance, highlights the limitations of current regulatory efforts, and proposes practical strategies to overcome infrastructure dependency and institutional fragmentation. Furthermore, it compares the EU's approach with those of the US and China to illuminate the EU's distinctive challenges and opportunities. Where the US relies on market-led innovation and China on centralized self-sufficiency, the EU seeks a third path grounded in democracy and ethics (Mayer & Nock, 2025). However, this ambition requires a coherent strategy to bind values, tools, and the public together.

The stakes are high. If Europe fails to protect its digital sovereignty, it will be unable to control how AI shapes its economies, societies, and democratic institutions. On the other side, if the EU succeeds, it will offer the world a new model that shows how high-tech futures can be both globally competitive and fundamentally humane.

This chapter aims to enrich the academic discourse on European digital sovereignty, by making five main contributions:

1. Introduces an original tripod model of European digital sovereignty, combining regulation, infrastructure, and public legitimacy.
2. Maps the EU's current efforts to build sovereign technical capabilities, including cloud infrastructure, supercomputing and foundation models.
3. Examines how the democratic participation from expert-stakeholder networks to citizen assemblies, contributes to strengthening democratic governance in AI.
4. Critically evaluates the limitations of regulation-only strategies for digital sovereignty, especially in the absence of computing sovereignty.
5. Offers policy and technical recommendations for a cohesive and democratic European sovereignty model.

14.2 Conceptualizing Digital Sovereignty in the Age of AI

Sovereignty before the 21st century was always defined through borders, flags, anthems and mainly on the visible apparatus of the state, shaped by the Westphalian model. The thing is that in the era of AI, sovereignty is no longer secured by territorial control alone; it is increasingly encrypted in code, embedded in algorithmic infrastructures, and mediated by entities beyond democratic oversight. What does it mean for a state, a union, or a citizen to be sovereign when the cloud is owned elsewhere, the chips are made abroad, and the models are trained beyond national oversight? Within the EU, the urgency of this question has grown in recent years. In strategic communications and legal frameworks, "digital sovereignty" has emerged as a buzzword, invoked to assert autonomy from US-based tech giants, reduce dependence on Chinese systems and build a distinct European path in technological governance. Nevertheless, a comprehensive, agreed-on definition of the term is still lacking, even though its use has grown in recent years; it doesn't seem like a coherent governance principle, as Roberts (2024) and Floridi (2020) argue, much of the digital sovereignty debate remains descriptive, focused on who controls the infrastructure or makes the laws rather than if such control is legitimate or accountable in a democratic sense.

This chapter proposes a conceptual reframing of European digital sovereignty in the age of AI, grounded in public legitimacy, by building on emerging scholarship that critiques simplistic framings of sovereignty as binary or static, focusing mainly on power and autonomy. Drawing on Roberts et al. (2023) and the typology introduced by Fratini et al. (2024), sovereignty is understood here as a sort of multidimensional framework integrating normative values, control over digital infrastructure and real mechanisms for democratic accountability. In this sense, digital sovereignty isn't only about where the data resides or who makes the chips. It also matters whether people and institutions can meaningfully shape the digital environments that increasingly impact their rights, economies, and social interactions.

This conceptual move make us think beyond regulation alone, and as the EU has earned justified recognition to be a global norm-setter via instruments like the GDPR, the AI Act, the Digital Services Act (DSA) and the Digital Markets Act (DMA), reflecting a commitment to ethics, privacy, transparency, and risk mitigation, still, as Mügge (2024) cautions, the EU's approach to digital sovereignty often prioritizes geopolitical competitiveness over democratic empowerment or global responsibility. Despite its advanced legal frameworks, the EU lacks the infrastructural and societal capacity required to realize real sovereignty, and these legal instruments address mainly downstream harms while neglecting upstream enablers such as computing power, data access and technical autonomy (Mügge, 2024). Regulations alone will never ensure digital sovereignty as they merely constrain or channel the use of others' AI and digital systems. Therefore, the EU may legislate for trustworthy AI, but without sovereign infrastructure, it remains like a conductor without an orchestra.

A comprehensive way to understand digital sovereignty in the age of AI should therefore consider three mutually reinforcing pillars: regulation, sovereign infrastructure, and public legitimacy. A framework where the regulation provides the legal architecture and ethical baseline, infrastructure delivers the material backbone on which AI capabilities depend (including data centers, chips, language models, and compute capacity) and where public legitimacy ensures that both pillars are tied to democratic processes, public trust, and participatory governance. The aim of this tripod model is to expand the field of vision for European policymakers. It urges them to see digital sovereignty not just as a legal or technical project but as a societal one. It invites them to ask whether European firms can build large language models and whether European citizens have a say in how these models are governed. It insists that regulation must be designed alongside investments in infrastructure and innovations in civic participation not sequentially but simultaneously as interdependent levers of sovereignty.

The implications of this multi pillar sovereignty model extend beyond European borders, and when expanding the lens of digital sovereignty to include infrastructure and legitimacy in addition to regulation, Europe distinguishes itself from American and Chinese trajectories. The US, as Roberts et al. outline in their 2023 comparative study, keeps maintaining a *laissez-faire* model of AI development based on the private sector's dynamics with limited federal regulation and almost an absence of public engagement in shaping technological trends. Here, sovereignty is *de facto* outsourced to Big Tech, whose models, data centers, and governance mechanisms serve global users but are answerable to neither international institutions nor citizen accountability. The US model in practice prioritizes innovation over any democratic alignment, often concealing the concentration of power behind open markets.

On the other hand, China frames its AI sovereignty through national strategies like the New Generation AI Development Plan, that promotes technological self-sufficiency, surveillance infrastructure and ideological control. Still, implementing China's AI agenda is not strictly top-down or centrally coordinated as Zeng (2020) argues, it is instead primarily driven by market forces and subnational actors, with fragmented bureaucratic oversight. Despite this decentralized approach, the state has strategically used AI to increase surveillance and to guide public opinion and consolidate its legitimacy. This model has accelerated infrastructure development at the expense of transparency and pluralism, asserting sovereignty through ideological alignment, far from any democratic contestation.

The EU faces a critical choice then: emulate one of these extremes or come up with a hybrid alternative that aligns its core values of human dignity, pluralism, and democracy with the material conditions of AI power. The tripod framework offers this third path. Its strength lies in its balance. Unlike the US approach, it does not treat infrastructure as a private-sector afterthought. However, in contrast to the Chinese model, it does not centralize control in opaque state mechanisms. Instead, it fuses normative legitimacy with strategic capacity, a model of sovereignty where democratic institutions co-design the infrastructures on which they rely. Table 14.1 illustrates how the EU's AI sovereignty strategy diverges from those of China and the US across all three core dimensions.

This vision is not as it may seem theoretical, but it is already beginning to materialize in EU initiatives like Gaia-X, which seeks to establish a federated, open, and interoperable cloud ecosystem governed by European stakeholders. Gaia-X

Table 14.1. Comparative models of ai sovereignty across the tripod pillars

Pillar	United States	China	European Union
Regulation	Minimal federal oversight; fragmented sectoral rules	Centralized, top-down regulation via party-state coordination	Robust legal frameworks (e.g., GDPR, AI Act, DSA)
Infrastructure	Dominated by private hyperscalers (AWS, Microsoft, Google)	State-led control over full AI stack (cloud, chips, models)	Federated sovereign infrastructure efforts (e.g., Gaia-X, EuroHPC, OpenGPT-X)
Public Legitimacy	Market-based legitimacy assumed via innovation success	Ideological legitimacy through state framing	Early-stage participatory mechanisms (e.g., AI Alliance, ALTAI, citizens' panels in Belgium and Finland)

Source: The table is an original creation by the author, drawing on information from Roberts et al. (2023), Floridi (2020), Zeng (2020), OECD (2023), and official EU policy documents (2023–2025)

aims to ensure that data generated locally (in Europe) can be stored, processed and analyzed within a sovereignty-respected infrastructure that complies with GDPR principles and offers alternatives to US-dominated hyperscalers. Therefore, and even with slow progress, the project's ambition still exemplifies the infrastructure pillar of the sovereignty tripod. Similarly, a German-led initiative like OpenGPT-X has developed Teuken-7B, a multilingual large language model, that is trained on all 24 official EU languages. This model is an open-source model that was designed in compliance with the GDPR and can be hosted within EU-based infrastructures, including certified data centers in Germany to ensure data sovereignty and alignment with European privacy standards. This makes OpenGPT-X an added value in this regard, which reinforces this pillar by providing a European alternative to non-EU AI models.

Without public legitimacy, even most ethically coded and technically sovereign systems will likely fall short. Procedural compliance under the EU AI Act risks masking ethical complexity behind standardized checklists as Laux et al. (2022) argue. They also caution that legitimacy must come from inclusive, context aware decision-making rooted in stakeholder participation instead of pre-defined formalism. Legitimacy, they argue, must be earned through transparency, accountability, and civic involvement. The public must be empowered to understand and shape AI systems, and the legitimacy pillar should be the anchor that holds the other two pillars in democratic alignment.

This principle underpins participatory initiatives like the European AI Alliance, which is a multi-stakeholder forum influencing the EU's AI policy through community consultations, working groups, and the ALTAI toolkit (Independent High-Level Expert Group on AI, 2020). It is also evident in emerging experiments like citizens' panels in Belgium and Finland, where randomly selected residents deliberate on AI-related risks and advise policymakers on how to design systems that reflect their values (Ministry of Foreign Affairs of Belgium, 2024; FCAI, 2022; Stanford Deliberative Democracy Lab, 2023). These models reinsert the citizen into the sovereignty equation.

Reframing sovereignty through this tripod model also has the advantage of resilience. Infrastructure and public oversight can fill the gap when regulation fails to anticipate a new risk. When infrastructure lags, regulation can set directional norms. When both falter, public legitimacy expressed through civic protest, litigation, or democratic deliberation can steer policy back toward accountability. A flexible, multidimensional sovereignty framework is essential in an era of rapid AI evolution. Moreover, the tripod model helps address a specific European pain point: fragmentation. With 27 member states with differing levels of digital maturity, national strategies often conflict or compete. A sovereignty model rooted in shared ethical standards (regulation), pooled investment in common infrastructure (e.g., EuroHPC, LEAM), and distributed civic participation offers a unifying blueprint.

14.3 The Regulation Pillar of Digital Sovereignty

For nearly two decades, the EU has been the world's foremost laboratory for digital regulation. From the groundbreaking GDPR to the more recent DSA, DMA, and AI Act, the EU has positioned itself as the global leader in governing emerging technologies through a value-driven, human-centric approach. This model, described by Bradford (2020) as the "Brussels Effect", has shaped internal markets and external actors, who often align with EU norms to retain market access. It enables the EU to externalize its regulatory preferences globally not through coercion or diplomacy but by leveraging its market size and regulatory strictness as de facto global standards. However, while the EU's AI regulation has been visionary and influential, cracks are beginning to show. As AI becomes more embedded in critical infrastructure, national security, and democratic life, questions arise about whether legal instruments alone can sustain Europe's digital sovereignty. Can rules preserve autonomy when the compute infrastructure runs on American chips, the cloud is hosted on Amazon Web Services (AWS), and the most powerful language models are fine-tuned in San Francisco?

Finalized in 2024, The AI Act adopts a multi level and risk-based regulatory model. Generally, it prohibits AI systems that pose "unacceptable risks", imposes transparency on systems that interact with people or generate synthetic content and imposes strict obligations on high-risk systems: from risk management to conformity assessments and post-market surveillance (European Parliament and Council of the European Union, 2024). In theory, this law upholds core EU principles such as dignity, fairness, and accountability, but critics argue that in practice, its approach is overly procedural. That's why Laux et al. (2022) for example, warn that by engineering trust through certification schemes rather than building it through real institutional legitimacy and accountability, the AI Act risks mixing "trustworthiness" with procedural compliance. They argue that legal conformity becomes a proxy for legitimacy, sidelining public engagement and masking deeper systemic harms.

Moreover, the AI Act places the burden of trust primarily on regulatory performance assuming that institutions can identify and mitigate harm in advance. This assumption becomes unreliable, especially since ethical risks often come in unpredictable contexts. These risks include bias in hiring algorithms, censorship in public sector deployments, or cognitive distortions caused by the regulation of personalized content. In such cases, the harms are not always seen in advance or can be prevented through design-stage assessments alone. However flexible or well-intentioned, regulation cannot act in isolation when safeguarding democratic values in real-world AI systems. When considering Europe's infrastructural dependencies, this regulatory fragility becomes clearer. GDPR may prohibit unlawful cross-border data transfers, but enforcing this becomes a mission impossible without sovereign data centers. The DSA may require transparency from the platforms, but the algorithmic logic behind content moderation still tends to sit within US-based corporate firewalls.

These challenges keep getting worse due to political and institutional division, because as Hulkó et al. (2025) noted, efforts to harmonize AI Act often encounter national sovereignty concerns, particularly in Central and Eastern Europe, where political leaders view EU-level regulatory mandates as a technocratic bypass that threatens to undermine national innovation strategies and regulatory autonomy. The resulting frictions slow enforcement and open different gaps in governance, that multinational tech companies can exploit.

Furthermore, Mügge (2024) says that the EU's regulatory vision increasingly risks becoming technocratic and judicial by prioritizing legal autonomy and global competitiveness rather than democratic empowerment. Mügge also sees, when regulation is treated as an end goal rather than an element of a broader sovereignty strategy, it risks enhancing some sort of legalism and disabling civic agency. Efforts like ALTAI, a voluntary self-assessment tool launched in 2020, reflected Europe's ethics-led vision, and without enforceability it has unfortunately ended up being more symbolic than structural (Independent High-Level Expert Group on AI, 2020). To address this, the EU has proposed institutions like the European AI Office to monitor high-risk systems and coordinate national supervisory bodies. However, its mandate remains narrow as it is focused on compliance rather than innovation, governance, or capacity-building (European Commission, 2024a). While useful, these tools still operate downstream· after models are built, data is collected, and architectures deployed, which are often outside Europe.

The EU's regulatory strategy has developed strong protections against rights-based harms, such as bans on facial recognition and manipulative profiling, but remains ill-equipped to mitigate systemic harms to democracy. Cupać and Sienknecht (2024) caution that "the widespread use of AI still has significant potential to inflict systemic harm to democracy in the EU", harms which are "inherently difficult, perhaps even impossible, to regulate effectively". Transparency, for instance, is essential, but when it reveals problems without triggering institutional response, it can lead to public disillusionment and weaken trust in democracy. In short, legality is not legitimacy, and compliance is not empowerment, especially when core harms are diffuse, accumulative, and structural.

This is why regulation must be reimagined not as an end state but as one leg of a broader sovereignty framework. As argued earlier, its effectiveness depends on institutional coherence with infrastructural and democratic ambitions. Some signs of the shift towards public participation in AI governance are emerging. The AI4Gov Horizon project explores how regulatory frameworks can be co-designed with public actors, embedding democratic values into the governance and deployment of AI systems in the public sector (AI4Gov, 2023; AI4Gov, 2024). The European AI Alliance, with over 6,000 stakeholders, provides a forum for participatory dialogue, although it is still advisory (European Commission, 2020). Emerging proposals for citizen assemblies and AI panels suggest a future where regulation is not just top-down but also bottom-up (Cupać & Sienknecht, 2024).

14.4 The Infrastructural Pillar of Digital Sovereignty

If regulation defines the why of European digital sovereignty, infrastructure defines the how; without control over the foundational layers of AI – data, compute, cloud, chips, and models – sovereignty remains aspirational. The challenge is stark and Europe cannot govern what it does not build or train. As of 2023, the three largest US cloud service providers (Amazon, Microsoft and Google) controlled approximately 72% of the European cloud market (Synergy Research Group, 2022), and the total US share has jumped to 90% when other major US service providers, such as IBM and Oracle are included, underscoring Europe's over reliance on foreign infrastructure providers (Gomes & Okano-Heijmans, 2024). Even with regard to advanced computing capabilities such as high-performance computing (HPC) essential for training sovereign models, Europe lags far behind the US and China, projecting an asymmetry that goes beyond the technical to influence geopolitical power.

Recognizing vulnerabilities in digital sovereignty, the EU has prompted a wave of initiatives to restore autonomy: Efforts like Gaia-X (cloud/data sovereignty), OpenGPT-X (sovereign models), and Large European AI Models (LEAM) (next-generation, value-aligned LLMs); each of these initiatives is addressing distinct layers of the AI infrastructure challenge. Designed as a federated, secure and interoperable European data infrastructure, Gaia-X which was launched in 2020, stands out as an ambitious project, facilitating cross-border, standards-based data sharing aligned with EU principles such as privacy, data sovereignty, and data minimization. By 2024, Gaia-X had developed foundational frameworks for sector-specific data spaces in health, mobility, and industry, setting the stage for value-aligned compute environments. As progress has been uneven, critics highlight that Gaia-X, despite its normative strength, faced challenges in scaling and was somehow blocked by a complex and standardized governance model involving many independent actors across jurisdictions. This complexity has added to perceptions of bureaucratic overhead and slowed operationalization. Some participants have withdrawn, citing unclear governance structures and overlapping layers. Nonetheless, key member states such as France and Germany have reaffirmed their commitment, integrating Gaia-X into broader industrial strategies and national cloud procurement policies (Gaia-X AISBL, 2024).

Another example relating to sovereign compute is The EuroHPC initiative that was launched in 2018. It was expanded under the Digital Europe Programme aiming to deploy pan-European supercomputers and scale systems to support AI research and innovation. These efforts include the LUMI supercomputer in Finland and the Leonardo system in Italy to compete with the world's most powerful machines. As of 2025, EuroHPC actively supports sovereign large language models (LLM) development, edge AI deployment, and energy-efficient compute architectures through its AI Factories, exascale infrastructure, and pan-European training programs. Still, coordination remains fragmented, and access remains unequal across member states (EuroHPC Joint Undertaking, 2025).

To complement compute, the EU is also investing in local production of chips. The EU Chips Act, adopted in 2023, mobilizes over €43 billion in public and private funding to strengthen Europe's semiconductor ecosystem. It aims to double Europe's global market share to 20% by 2030, focusing on advanced, energy-efficient, and AI-relevant chip design. Key mechanisms include pilot line investments, first-of-a-kind manufacturing support, and a pan-European design infrastructure platform to foster co-design between chip producers and AI developers (European Commission, 2022). While this represents a bold move toward strategic autonomy, the global gap remains daunting as TSMC, Intel, and Samsung continue to dominate. Europe's path will likely rely on targeted specialization, such as ultra-low-power processors for AI, rather than full-stack duplication. Meanwhile, on the software frontier, Europe is advancing sovereign models. OpenGPT-X, funded by the German Federal Ministry for Economic Affairs and Climate Action (BMWK), which aims to build open, multilingual large language models tailored to European values and languages (OpenGPT-X, n.d.). Unlike US models, OpenGPT-X emphasizes explainability, transparency, and federated deployment within Gaia-X-compliant data spaces. Early outputs include open-source models with legal compliance layers and tools for domain-specific tuning. While still in their infancy, these efforts signal a shift from dependency to design.

These initiatives represent more than industrial policy. By shaping who builds, owns, and governs AI systems, the EU can move from regulation as a reaction to infrastructure as preemption. Nevertheless, success depends on coordination between states, sectors, and civil society. That brings us to the final leg of the sovereignty tripod: public legitimacy. Infrastructure without public legitimacy is brittle. The EU's approach must, therefore, ensure that sovereign infrastructures not only align with legal and ethical norms but also reflect shared democratic values. This is where initiatives like the Gaia-X Trust Framework gain significance. Rather than relying solely on legal compliance, Gaia-X directly incorporates principles such as transparency, reversibility, and data sovereignty into its architecture, which we can describe as "embedded ethics" (Gaia-X AISBL, 2024).

The LEAM project, exemplifies the integration of advanced AI infrastructure with European values and regulatory standards. Coordinated by a consortium of research institutions and industry partners, LEAM aims to develop LLMs trained on European datasets, adhering to the anticipated requirements of the EU AI Act (German AI Association, 2023). Unlike foundation models developed primarily in the US or China, LEAM models emphasize trustworthiness, explainability, and regulatory compliance. The initiative also prioritizes open benchmarking and public oversight, with ongoing discussions to include civil society representatives in model evaluation panels. Although LEAM models are currently smaller in scale than American counterparts such as GPT-4, the project is a pioneering prototype for ethically grounded AI development based on European infrastructure and values. Yet even the most advanced projects face two recurring threats: institutional incoherence and underinvestment. Different member states back overlapping initiatives (Gaia-X in Germany and France, Mistral AI in France, Aleph Alpha in Germany) while others struggle to keep up. Without unified oversight, projects risk duplication, stagnation, or divergence in technical norms (Mayer & Nock, 2025).

Securing long-term investment remains a structural challenge. Sovereign AI infrastructure requires sustained investment in hardware and training energy systems, cybersecurity, and human capital. The EU's Digital Europe Programme allocated €1.3 billion for 2025–2027 to support AI, cybersecurity, cloud infrastructure, and digital skills (European Commission, 2025a). In its 2023–2024 work program, Horizon Europe invested over €112 million in AI and quantum technologies, including €50 million to develop large-scale multimodal AI models (European Commission, 2024b). Although the Horizon Europe Strategic Plan 2025–2027 reaffirms the EU's commitment to digital sovereignty, tangible financial commitments for the next phase remain pending (European Commission, 2023a). Academic and policy analyses warn that the scale of EU investments still lags behind geopolitical competitors (Mügge, 2024). For example, the US CHIPS and Science Act authorized around $280 billion in funding, including $52.7 billion for semiconductor manufacturing and research foundational to AI development (CHIPS and Science Act, 2022).

Looking forward, one promising direction is the bundling of digital sovereignty goals into broader public missions. For instance, the Green Deal and NextGenerationEU recovery funds could embed AI infrastructure into sustainable development and industrial policy (European Commission, 2024c). Sovereign AI could be framed as a defense strategy and as a foundation for health, climate, and education resilience. Institutional innovation must align with technical ambition. The proposal for a European AI Infrastructure Agency tasked with coordinating cloud resources, computational capacity, and model development has gained support among researchers and policymakers. Such an institution could reduce redundancy, streamline funding allocation, and ensure coherence with democratic oversight mechanisms (Stix, 2021).

14.5 The Public Participation Pillar of Digital Sovereignty

It was always regulatory and infrastructural measures that dominated the debate in Europe's pursuit of digital sovereignty, with public legitimacy as a third and equally important pillar remaining underdeveloped. The EU has championed for a long time a human-centered approach to AI, but its governance mechanisms are largely technocratic-designed by institutions, implemented through compliance frameworks, and shaped by expert discourse. This mismatch in discourse between citizen empowerment and the actual distribution of authority is creating what some observers have called a "democratic deficit" in digital governance (Burns, 2025).

Launched by the European Commission in 2018, the European AI Alliance is a multi-stakeholder platform with more than 6,000 members from academia, civil society and industry. The Alliance played an important role in the pilot phase of the Trustworthy AI Checklist, contributing practical feedback that informed the development of the Trustworthy AI Ethical Guidelines of the High-Level Expert Group on Artificial Intelligence (AI HLEG) (Independent High-Level Expert Group on Artificial Intelligence, 2019). However, studies assessing the impact of the coalition have revealed a range of limitations: The coalition had minimal impact on final legislative outcomes, despite its consultative design. It lacked transparency in feedback mechanisms, particularly regarding how input was incorporated, and failed to redistribute decision-making power. This aligns with critiques of symbolic participation, where institutional inclusion exists in form but lacks substantive function (Morley et al., 2020).

Academic assessment of the participatory governance in AI, highlights several important limitations. For example, Kuzemski and Misuraka (2020) argue that public sector AI projects across Europe often reinforce bureaucratic or expert-driven norms, so that non-experts find themselves automatically excluded from any process of design or oversight. Empirical research in public administration and digital governance, already highlighted the need for mechanisms that ensure transparency, interpretability, and public participation, to avoid furthering structural inequalities through automated decision-making systems (Koziemski and Misuraca, 2020). Without real civic input, AI applications risk conserving rather than correcting prevailing institutional biases, especially in sensitive areas like welfare eligibility, predictive policing, or housing allocation.

What is encouraging is that more recent initiatives have begun to experiment with democratic innovation. In 2024, Belgium conducted a pilot experiment to create a national citizens' assembly on artificial intelligence, formed by random ballot and composed of 60 citizens representing different segments of the population. The assembly's final recommendations on algorithmic fairness, data governance, and the use of AI in public services were formally presented to federal authorities and EU regulators, with binding requirements for policy review (Ministry of Foreign Affairs of Belgium, 2024). This model resonates with the literature on deliberative mini-publics, which shows that sortition-based panels can improve the legitimacy, diversity, and epistemic quality of policy outcomes (Grönlund et al., 2022). When institutionalized with legal guarantees and follow-through mechanisms, such assemblies offer more than ritualized consultation; they can help rebuild trust and reduce the tendencies of technocratic rule.

The AuroraAI program, developed by the Finnish Ministry of Finance to deliver AI-based public services tailored to life events, such as starting school or applying for social welfare, illustrates how principles of participation principles can be institutionalized at the state level. The program includes an ethics council (composed of technologists, ethicists, social scientists and civil society representatives), created to review societal risks and ensure alignment with values such as inclusivity and fairness. Leikas et al. (2022) argue that accountability and public trust can be enhanced by incorporating ethical deliberations into their design and management of AI systems from the outset, rather than relying solely on post-hoc audits or complaint mechanisms.

Alongside these state-led projects are civil society-led experiments in participatory AI. The Participatory AI project, conducted by Nesta and the Center for Participatory AI, launched by the Idiap Research Institute in Switzerland, was willing to incorporate public inputs into algorithmic systems throughout their lifecycle (Nesta, n.d.; Idiap Research Institute, n.d.). These projects have adopted a co-design process that defines participation as situations where stakeholders impacted by the created algorithm system collaborate with developers to identify risks, define the performance criteria, and to assess model outputs. Observed data from participatory design research suggests that such inclusion improves both fairness and robustness, particularly in contexts with high social stakes (Zhang et al., 2023). Instead of relying on the public as a passive recipient or an abstract beneficiary, these projects welcome them as holders of lived experience and knowledge that can inform and enrich technical development.

Participatory AI governance remains the exception rather than the norm, despite all encouraging signs, as many promising initiatives exist on the margins of policymaking are limited by institutional resistance with fragmented mandates and inadequate legal assurances. Furthermore, Kuziemski and Misuraca's (2020) cross-national analysis of European AI deployment found that even well-intentioned projects often default to technocratic logic, where citizens are only "invited to participate" after important design decisions have already been taken, in a clear contrast with co-decision or co-production models that can truly redistribute power and enhance structural accountability.

This limitation on public participation raises a broader concern in democratic theory, which is "tokenistic consultation". As Mushkani et al. (2025) warn, forms of participation in AI governance often prioritize symbolic inclusion at the expense of real power sharing, legitimizing predetermined outcomes while denying affected communities real agency, especially when the public is asked to participate but excluded from shaping decisions. This legitimacy trap becomes evident in AI governance, as technical transparency, unequal access to expertise and institutional complexity constrain democratic accountability. This gap between the democratic discourse and the bureaucratic practices, can lead to further weakening of trust in technologies and institutions as well.

A more substantive model of civic engagement that would institutionalize public oversight throughout the AI lifecycle, and one of the European Commission's initial tools in this area was the Assessment List for Trustworthy Artificial Intelligence (ALTAI). Developed by the High-Level Expert Group on AI, ALTAI it provides a voluntary checklist to support ethical self-assessment by developers. Though valuable as a starting point, ALTAI has been critiqued in academic literature for its conceptual and practical limitations, including its inability to support deep ethical reasoning and reliance on uncertain ex-ante assumptions. Stahl and Leach (2023) warn that ALTAI may create a false sense of ethical completeness while lacking the mechanisms to build accountability or reflexivity into real-world development processes. Radclyfe et al. (2023) also contend that as a self-assessment tool ALTAI deviates from standard audit theory and risks superficial compliance, unless it gets supplemented by third-party review, risk assessment and the integration of fundamental rights assessments.

Scholars and civil society organizations have proposed more binding, participatory models of AI oversight to overcome this. One proposal is the establishment of AI Citizenship Councils, randomly selected, legally empowered panels similar to climate assemblies that reflect on high-stakes AI deployments in different areas such as biometric surveillance, predictive policing, or algorithmic eligibility screening. Given that public authorities are obliged to respond to their recommendations, these councils would receive expert support and be integrated into formal governance structures. Demonstrable studies of mini-publics suggest that this format can improve policy robustness, foster civic learning and enhance institutional legitimacy, particularly when coupled with transparency and accountability mechanisms (Roberts et al., 2023).

A second proposal involves making Participatory AI Impact Assessments mandatory for all high-risk AI systems in the public sector. Similar to environmental impact assessments, these procedures require technical analysis and civic consultation before system deployment. As Mushkani et al. (2025) argue, AI governance must move beyond abstract rights-based frameworks toward "embedded accountability" as a model where affected communities are directly involved in designing, deploying and evaluating AI systems. Embedding accountability in practice, especially in large and multi-level bureaucracies such as the European Union, remains an operational challenge, but should never prevent meaningful civic participation. Unlike standard audits or "human in the loop" mechanisms that focus on expert supervision or ex-post compliance, built-in accountability focuses on continuous civic participation, feedback-driven development and transparent data processes that help uncover risks and biases before they become established. Participatory evaluations, besides revealing local risks and hidden biases, can provide early warnings that technical audits may overlook.

Trust in AI as Roberts et al. (2023) argue, cannot be achieved through technical design or legal compliance alone. Instead, they define digital sovereignty as "legitimate control over the digital", which includes not only jurisdiction over infrastructure but also the participatory and accountable processes through which such control is exercised. They emphasize, that this form of legitimacy stems from accepted authority and inclusive decision-making, such that democracy is more of a functional necessity for trustworthy AI and not only a procedural ideal. In short, if Europe wants to achieve its ambition of true digital sovereignty alongside its efforts for ethical and democratic AI, it must institutionalize public legitimacy as a fundamental pillar of digital sovereignty. This requires more than just consultations, checklists, or ethics councils. It requires a systemic shift toward participatory infrastructures that give citizens a voice and influence throughout the entire lifecycle of AI systems, from design and procurement to oversight and redress.

14.6 Comparing Digital Sovereignty Models: The EU, US and China

The EU seeks to achieve digital sovereignty through AI in a competitive and ideologically fragmented global environment. The EU's preferences for regulation, ethical alignment, and democratic values contrast with the prevailing approaches in the US and China, with each model embodying a specific strategy for asserting control over digital infrastructure and shaping the future of AI. Comparing these paths would help provide metrics for measuring Europe's progress and strategic lessons about the inherent trade-offs in different models of sovereignty.

Arguably, the US has conceded important elements of its digital sovereignty to private actors, as power no longer lies with the central government, but in the hands of giant companies such as OpenAI, Google, Meta, and Microsoft, which control the majority of global computing, basic models and data assets. The Organization for Economic Cooperation and Development (OECD) reports that there is a high concentration of AI computing among a small number of hardware, software, and cloud providers, particularly in the US, where private companies dominate the internal use and commercial provision of AI infrastructure (OECD, 2023). While recent federal initiatives such as the Artificial Intelligence Rights Act and the Executive Order on Safeą and Trustworthy Artificial Intelligence (2023) have begun to outline ethical controls, they remain mostly non-binding (White House Office of Science and Technology Policy, n.d.; Executive Office of the President, 2023). The US model assumes that innovation flourishes best under minimal state interference, with public authority intervening primarily to defend geopolitical or economic interests such as export controls on chips or subsidies for domestic manufacturing (Allen, 2022). In this model, legitimacy is derived from market success and industrial dominance, not democratic participation or legal frameworks.

By contrast, China has embedded AI development into a centralized state-capitalist paradigm. Since the New Generation Artificial Intelligence Development Plan (2017), China has treated AI as a core element of its national development strategy (Webster et al., 2017). China's AI strategy articulates digital sovereignty through techno-industrial autonomy organizing control over the full AI stack from semiconductors (e.g., SMIC) to national cloud infrastructure (e.g., Huawei Cloud, AliCloud) to domestic foundation models (e.g. Baidu's ERNIE). This state-led whole-of-nation approach reflects an infrastructural model of sovereignty designed to secure independence in strategic technologies amid geopolitical fragmentation (Arcesati, 2024). This infrastructure is tightly interwoven with state authority, allowing Beijing to pursue what Kwet and Prins have termed digital authoritarianism: using AI for surveillance, behavioral control, and ideological enforcement (Shahbaz, n.d.). While efficient and vertically integrated, China's model sacrifices pluralism, transparency, and civil liberties, earning global criticism for human rights violations in algorithmic policing and censorship (Human Rights Watch, 2019).

In comparative terms, the EU stands between these two poles in terms of both scale and ambition. It lacks the US's compute and industrial concentration, and China's top-down mobilization capacity. In contrast, Europe promotes a model grounded in regulatory coherence and democratic values, distinct from US deregulation or Chinese centralization. Nevertheless, it offers a third way: a model based on democratic accountability, regulatory coherence, and ethical pluralism. Europe's approach has been hailed for its normative leadership, which the GDPR, the AI Act, and the DSA have emphasized (European Parliament and Council of the

European Union, 2024; Fratini et al., 2024). However, it suffers from fragmentation, underinvestment in sovereign infrastructure, and slow policy execution (European Court of Auditors, 2024a). Unlike China, Europe does not control its chip or cloud stack. Unlike the US, it lacks globally dominant AI firms. This asymmetry risks turning the EU into what could be termed a "normative island": a polity that produces ethical standards that others do not follow while relying on technological systems it cannot shape.

The tension at the heart of Europe's model is whether regulation without infrastructure or participatory governance can deliver real sovereignty. Lessons from China and the US suggest that technical capacity and policy centralization are decisive. China's AI-driven public services (from city-level surveillance networks to credit scoring systems) are deployed quickly and scale due to central coordination and legal permissiveness (European Parliament and Council of the European Union, 2024; Chen, 2024). The US, though lacking centralized oversight, benefits from an industrial ecosystem that drives global adoption by sheer volume and technical leadership (OECD, 2023). The EU, by contrast, must coordinate 27 member states, each with distinct strategies, legal systems, and political cultures (European Court of Auditors, 2024a).

Despite these disadvantages, Europe has an asset neither the US nor China possesses: an emerging ecosystem of participatory governance and ethical standard-setting. Initiatives like the European AI Alliance, Belgium's citizens' panel on AI, and the AI4Gov Horizon project represent an evolving civic infrastructure to embed democratic values into AI policy (AI4Gov, 2024; Belgian citizens meet & reflect on AI, 2024; European Commission, 2020). While often dismissed as symbolic, these mechanisms demonstrate Europe's willingness to experiment with deliberative governance a necessary, if incomplete, response to global governance gaps in AI ethics and participation, as UNESCO underscores (UNESCO, 2022).

Moreover, Europe is not entirely without infrastructural ambition. As discussed above, the EuroHPC program, Gaia-X, OpenGPT-X, and LEAM represent early-stage efforts to build sovereign compute and model capacity (EuroHPC Joint Undertaking, 2025; Gaia-X AISBL, 2024; OpenGPT-X, n.d.; German AI Association, 2023). These projects are not yet comparable to GPT-4 or China's ERNIE, but they point to a strategic shift from regulating foreign systems to designing European alternatives.

However, time is not on Europe's side. The pace of model evolution, compute scaling, and platform consolidation favors early movers. Fragmentation will persist without bold coordination mechanisms such as a centralized EU AI Agency or a sovereignty-oriented funding instrument (European Court of Auditors, 2024b).

While this section has focused on the strategic models of the US, China, and the EU, it is important to note that emerging approaches in the Global South as well as multilateral frameworks such as UNESCO's Recommendation on the Ethics of Artificial Intelligence and the OECD AI Principles, offer complementary perspectives on AI governance, equity, and digital sovereignty (UNESCO, 2022; OECD, 2024a).

14.7 Pathways to Digital Sovereignty in Europe: Policy Recommendations

This section offers policy recommendations with relevance to the digital sovereignty tripod (regulation, infrastructure, and public legitimacy). As such, the recommendations were prioritized for their institutional endorsement, strategic importance, and alignment with the governance gaps previously analyzed. While not exhaustive, they offer representative strategies from the evolving European AI policy landscape.

1. **Establish a European AI Infrastructure and Governance Agency:** The need for a dedicated agency to coordinate infrastructure development and governance standards in AI is supported by recent EU-level discussions and expert analyses. The European AI Office, established under the AI Act, offers institutional oversight, but as discussed before, its narrow compliance mandate highlights the need for expanded governance structures. Policy research has called for an expanded role analogous to the European Data Protection Board, capable of aligning infrastructure investments, standardizing metrics, and coordinating compliance across Member States (Bria et al., 2025; Council of the European Union, 2024).
2. **Launch a European AI and Digital Sovereignty Facility:** The Coordinated Plan on AI and Strategic Foresight Reports emphasize the importance of pooling funding for AI infrastructure, particularly sovereign compute, multilingual LLMs, and trusted cloud environments. A European AI Sovereignty Facility, complementing Digital Europe and Horizon Europe, has been proposed to integrate conditional funding criteria: open licensing, privacy-by-design, and language inclusivity (European Commission, 2021; European Commission, 2023b).
3. **Operationalize Participatory AI Impact Assessments (PAIAs):** PAIAs build upon practices tested in the AI4Gov project and are supported by the m's recommendation for stronger civic engagement in algorithmic governance. These assessments would institutionalize structured citizen involvement in high-risk AI deployments, mirroring environmental assessment frameworks. Their relevance is underscored by critiques of the AI Act's proceduralism and limited enforceability regarding participatory mechanisms (AI4Gov, 2024; CAHAI, 2021; Cupać & Sienknecht, 2024).
4. **Create a Public Registry of Sovereign LLMs and Compute Resources:** The LEAM project and Digital Europe Programme underscore the importance of auditability and technical transparency in sovereign AI systems. A registry maintained by a European agency could include model architecture, training data sources, GDPR compliance indicators, and energy usage benchmarks. Such a registry addresses calls for stronger transparency infrastructure in the AI governance ecosystem (German AI Association, 2023; European Commission, 2025; OECD, 2024b).
5. **Institutionalize AI Citizenship Councils for High-Stake Systems:** Inspired by successful national pilots and supported by UNESCO and Council of Europe

recommendations, AI Citizenship Councils offer a mechanism for legally mandated citizen deliberation on algorithmic systems. Empirical studies show that sortition-based panels enhance policy robustness and legitimacy when paired with binding response mechanisms (UNESCO, 2022; Mushkani et al., 2025).

6. **Expand Public-Sector Access to Privately Held Data:** While the Data Act (Regulation EU 2023/2854) lays important groundwork by enabling public authorities to access non-personal data held by private entities, further action is needed to ensure operational effectiveness (European Parliament & Council of the European Union, 2023). The EU should establish clear implementation guidelines, create secure data-sharing platforms, and fund technical capacity-building within public institutions to make full use of these data rights. Strengthening enforcement mechanisms and extending access to select categories of anonymized personal data for legitimate public interest purposes, under strict safeguards, would further enhance infrastructural sovereignty and data-driven policymaking.

14.8 Limitations

While this chapter offers an integrated framework for protecting and developing European digital sovereignty in the age of AI, it is not without analytical, empirical, and structural limitations. First, the digital sovereignty tripod model (regulation, infrastructure, and public legitimacy) is necessarily a simplification. Each pillar contains internal tensions: infrastructure includes chips, data, models, and ownership rights; legitimacy spans trust, participation, and civic culture. While the model structures the argument, it does not capture the whole messiness of AI governance in practice. Second, many initiatives analyzed, such as Gaia-X, EuroHPC, OpenGPT-X, and citizen assemblies, are in the early or pilot stages, and their outcomes remain uncertain, as for instance, Gaia-X has faced governance issues and slow industry adoption, while OpenGPT-X is still developing. This chapter draws on policy documents, project reports and early-stage academic commentary, which limits the strength of claims regarding their effectiveness. Third, the chapter focuses primarily on EU-level efforts and flagship national programs, with limited attention to subnational actors (e.g., cities), sect oral variations (e.g., defense vs. health), or judicial mechanisms (e.g., digital rights litigation). Likewise, global alliances, such as Europe's partnerships with the Global South on AI standards, are mentioned only in passing. A fuller sovereignty picture would need to account for these dimensions. Fourth, while the US and China are analyzed as comparative models, the discussion does not cover internal heterogeneity within those states. The decentralized nature of US AI oversight and the provincial variance in China's tech policy suggest that national models are complex, and similarly, rising powers in the field of artificial intelligence, such as India and Brazil, were not considered in this study. Finally, sovereignty itself remains a controversial and evolving concept. This chapter should therefore be read as a normative and strategic intervention based on the best available evidence, rather than a blueprint. Digital sovereignty is a process, not a fixed end point, and must evolve in parallel with the technologies and societies it seeks to govern.

14.9 Conclusion

Europe has positioned itself as a normative leader in the digital and AI governance landscape by building pioneering regulatory frameworks, setting ethical standards and declaring its commitment to human-centered AI. However, regulation alone will not ensure digital sovereignty. This chapter has shown that the tripod model (regulation, sovereign infrastructure and public legitimacy) can offer Europe a framework for achieving digital sovereignty in practice, rather than just aspirations. Without infrastructure, regulation remains toothless. Without public participation, even well-meaning laws risk losing legitimacy. Without binding regulation, technical autonomy may slide into market capture or geopolitical dependence.

This chapter addresses the EU's evolving attempts to build and protect its digital sovereignty. With tools such as the General Data Protection Regulation (GDPR), the Digital Services Act (DSA) and the Artificial Intelligence Act (AI Act) the EU has helped shape global standards on data protection, transparency, and algorithmic fairness at the regulatory level. However, they are insufficient without the appropriate infrastructure. Despite strategic ambitions, data and model infrastructures in place Europe remain largely external, limiting its ability to control or shape AI systems within its borders. This has prompted initiatives such as Gaia-X, EuroHPC, LEAM, and OpenGPT-X to bridge this gap by providing the technical support necessary for Europe's independence.

Although recent civic experiments show its growing importance, public legitimacy remains the least institutionalized of the three pillars. Unlike the United States, which mainly outsources AI development to private actors, or China, which centralizes it through state control, Europe offers the possibility of a third model: A democratic digital sovereignty rooted in pluralism, ethics and shared governance. Realizing this vision would require structural reforms. First, investment must match ambition, and sovereign mechanisms and related digital infrastructure must be treated as strategic assets on the same level as energy, health or defense. Second, governance mechanisms must advance from consultation to deliberation, as binding requirements for citizen participation in AI development, impact assessments for high-risk deployments, and transparent review systems are necessary to maintain legitimacy as AI's societal impact is growing.

Further research is needed to better understand this evolving field. How can European LLMs scale in practice? How can we build participatory governance systems without losing local differences? What metrics can capture not only infrastructure capacity but also democratic quality and public trust? How might Europe's approach to digital sovereignty interact with those of the Global South, where data asymmetries and AI colonialism present real challenges? Such inquiries could be advanced through comparative case studies, participatory governance pilots or mixed-method evaluations of civic engagement tools and infrastructure deployment across EU regions.

Without timely action, Europe risks seeing its ethical frameworks sidelined by infrastructural realities shaped elsewhere, reducing sovereignty to a symbolic gesture rather than a lived capacity. No matter how well orchestrated, ethical vision alone will fail without implementation instruments. Ultimately, even the most refined regulatory scores need an orchestra of infrastructure and civic harmony to be heard. As digital sovereignty evolves, Europe must remain adaptive: committed to pluralism, subsidiarity, and procedural legitimacy, not as static ideals but as dynamic tasks to be continuously constructed.

Disclaimer

During the preparation of this work, the author utilized AI-assisted tools such as ChatGPT, DeepL and Grammarly to enhance English language accuracy, including spelling, grammar, and punctuation. All content generated or corrected with these tools was thoroughly reviewed, revised, and edited to ensure accuracy and originality. The author accepts full responsibility for the final content of this publication. All ideas, analysis, and interpretations remain the author's own.

References

AI4Gov: Trusted AI for Transparent Public Governance fostering Democratic Values. (2023). *Deliverable 2.1 AI4Gov Holistic Regulatory Framework V1.* Retrieved from https://ai4gov-project.eu/wp-content/uploads/2023/07/AI4Gov_D2.1_AI4Gov-Holistic-Regulatory-Framework.pdf

AI4Gov: Trusted AI for Transparent Public Governance fostering Democratic Values. (2024). *Deliverable 3.3: Policy Recommendation Toolkit V1.* Retrieved from https://ai4gov-project.eu/wp-content/uploads/2024/07/AI4Gov_D3.3_Policy-Recommendation-Toolkit-V1.pdf

Allen, G.C. (2022). *Choking off China's Access to the Future of AI: New U.S. Export Controls on AI and Semiconductors Mark a Transformation of U.S. Technology Competition with China.* Center for Strategic and International Studies. Retrieved from https://www.csis.org/analysis/choking-chinas-access-future-ai

Arcesati, R. (2024). *China's AI Development Model in an Era of Technological Deglobalization.* University of California Institute on Global Conflict and Cooperation (IGCC) and the Mercator Institute for China Studies (MERICS). Retrieved from: https://merics.org/en/report/chinas-ai-development-model-era-technological-deglobalization

Belgian Citizens Meet & Reflect on AI. (2024, May 29). *Kingdom of Belgium: Federal Public Service, Foreign Affairs, Foreign Trade and Development Cooperation.* Retrieved from https://diplomatie.belgium.be/en/policy/policy-areas/highlighted/belgian-citizens-meet-reflect-ai?utm_source=chatgpt.com

Bradford, A. (2020). *The Brussels Effect: How the European Union Rules the World.* Oxford University Press.

Bria, F., Timmers, P. & Gernone, F. (2025). *EuroStack – A European Alternative for Digital Sovereignty* (DOI 10.11586/2025006). Bertelsmann Stiftung. Retrieved from https://www.bertelsmann-stiftung.de/index.php?id=5772&tx_rsmbstpublications_pi2%5bdoi%5d=10.11586/2025006&no_cache=1

Burns, W. (2025, April 22). *A Democratic Deficit is Killing Europe's Digital Industrial Policy, but No One Talks About It.* Tech Policy Press. Retrieved from https://www.techpolicy.press/a-democratic-deficit-is-killing-europes-digital-industrial-policy-but-no-one-talks-about-it/

CAHAI [Council of Europe Ad hoc Committee on Artificial Intelligence]. (2021). *Possible Elements of a Legal Framework on Artificial Intelligence, based on the Council of Europe's Standards on Human Rights, Democracy and the Rule of Law.* Council of Europe. Retrieved from https://rm.coe.int/cahai-2021-09rev-elements/1680a6d90d

Chen, Q. (2024). *China's Emerging Approach to Regulating General-Purpose Artificial Intelligence: Balancing Innovation and Control.* Asia Society Policy Institute. Retrieved from https://asiasociety.org/policy-institute/chinas-emerging-approach-regulating-general-purpose-artificial-intelligence-balancing-innovation-and

CHIPS and Science Act of 2022. Pub. L. No. 117-167, 136 Stat. 1366 (2022). Retrieved from https://www.congress.gov/bill/117th-congress/house-bill/4346

Council of the European Union. (2024, December). *Council Conclusions on the use of Artificial Intelligence in the Field of Justice* (Document No. 16933/24). Retrieved from https://data.consilium.europa.eu/doc/document/ST-16933-2024-INIT/en/pdf

Cupać, J., & Sienknecht, M. (2024). Regulate against the machine: How the EU mitigates AI harm to democracy. *Democratization*, 31(5), 1067–1090. https://doi.org/10.1080/13510347.2024.2353706

EuroHPC Joint Undertaking [The European High Performance Computing Joint Undertaking]. (2024). *Decision of the Governing Board of the EuroHPC Joint Undertaking No. 11/2024: Amending the Joint Undertaking's Work Programme and Budget for the year 2024 (Amendment No. 1)*. Retrieved from https://eurohpc-ju.europa.eu/document/download/a7d83d79-b70e-4700-a401-8de4c65f9d94_en?filename=Decision%2011.2024.-%20WP%202024%20amendment_V2.pdf

EuroHPC Joint Undertaking [The European High Performance Computing Joint Undertaking]. (2025). *Decision of the Governing Board of the EuroHPC Joint Undertaking No. 08/2025: Amending the Joint Undertaking's Multi-Annual Strategic Plan 2021-2027 (Amendment No 3)*. Retrieved from https://eurohpc-ju.europa.eu/document/download/a4c7e874-845b-4ff8-9f78-ec0747d180ec_en?filename=Decision%2008.2025%20Revised%20MASP%20%28Amendment%20No%203%29.pdf

European Commission. (2020). *European AI Alliance*. Retrieved from https://digital-strategy.ec.europa.eu/en/policies/european-ai-alliance

European Commission. (2021). *Coordinated Plan on Artificial Intelligence 2021 Review*. Retrieved from https://digital-strategy.ec.europa.eu/en/library/coordinated-plan-artificial-intelligence-2021-review

European Commission. (2022). *A Chips Act for Europe* (COM(2022) 45 final). Retrieved from https://eur-lex.europa.eu/legal-content/EN/TXT/?uri=CELEX:52022DC0045

European Commission. (2023a). *Horizon Europe Strategic Plan 2025–2027 Analysis*. Publications Office of the European Union. Retrieved from https://op.europa.eu/en/publication-detail/-/publication/b3baec75-fdd0-11ed-a05c-01aa75ed71a1/language-en

European Commission. (2023b). *Strategic Foresight Report 2023: Sustainability and People's Wellbeing at the Heart of Europe's Open Strategic Autonomy* (Project Number: 2023.3503). Publications Office of the European Union. Retrieved from https://commission.europa.eu/system/files/2023-07/SFR-23-beautified-version_en_0.pdf

European Commission. (2024a, May 29). *Commission establishes AI Office to Strengthen EU Leadership in Safe and Trustworthy Artificial Intelligence* (Press release). Retrieved from https://ec.europa.eu/commission/presscorner/detail/en/ip_24_2982

European Commission. (2024b, April 23). *Commission invests €112 million in AI and Quantum Research and Innovation* (Press release). Retrieved from https://digital-strategy.

ec.europa.eu/en/news/commission-invests-eu112-million-ai-and-quantum-research-and-innovation

European Commission. (2024c). *Achievements of the von der Leyen Commission: The European Green Deal*. Retrieved from https://ec.europa.eu/commission/presscorner/api/files/attachment/879954/3%20European%20Green%20Deal.pdf

European Commission. (2025). *Work Programme 2025-2027 of the Digital Europe Programme (DIGITAL) (C(2025) 1839 final)*. Retrieved from https://digital-strategy.ec.europa.eu/en/library/work-programme-2025-2027-digital-europe-programme-digital

European Parliament and Council of the European Union. (2023). *Regulation (EU) 2023/2854 of the European Parliament and of the Council of 13 December 2023 on Harmonised Rules on Fair Access to and Use of Data and Amending Regulation (EU) 2017/2394 and Directive (EU) 2020/1828 (Data Act)*. Official Journal of the European Union. Retrieved from https://eur-lex.europa.eu/eli/reg/2023/2854/oj/eng

European Parliament and Council of the European Union. (2024). *Regulation (EU) 2024/1689 of the European Parliament and of the Council of 13 June 2024 Laying Down Harmonised Rules on Artificial Intelligence and Amending Regulations (EC) No 300/2008, (EU) No 167/2013, (EU) No 168/2013, (EU) 2018/858, (EU) 2018/1139 and (EU) 2019/2144 and Directives 2014/90/EU, (EU) 2016/797 and (EU) 2020/1828 (Artificial Intelligence Act) (Text with EEA relevance)*. Official Journal of the European Union. Retrieved from https://eur-lex.europa.eu/eli/reg/2024/1689/oj/eng

Executive Office of the President. (2023, November 1). *Safe, Secure, and Trustworthy Development and Use of Artificial Intelligence* (Exec. Order No. 14110, 88 FR 75191). Federal Register. Retrieved from https://www.federalregister.gov/documents/2023/11/01/2023-24283/safe-secure-and-trustworthy-development-and-use-of-artificial-intelligence

FCAI [Finnish Center for Artificial Intelligence]. (2022, February 8). *Participatory Research to Improve Artificial Intelligence-based Public Sector Services and Empower Citizens*. Retrieved from https://fcai.fi/news/2022/2/8/participatory-research-to-improve-artificial-intelligence-based-public-sector-services-and-empower-citizens

Floridi, L. (2020). The fight for digital sovereignty: What it is, and why it matters, especially for the EU. *Philosophy & Technology*, 33, 369–378 (2020). https://doi.org/10.1007/s13347-020-00423-6

Fratini, S., Hine, E., Novelli, C., Roberts, H., & Floridi, L. (2024). Digital sovereignty: A descriptive analysis and a critical evaluation of existing models. *Digital Society*, 3, Article number 59. https://doi.org/10.1007/s44206-024-00146-7

Gaia-X AISBL. (2024). *Gaia-X Architecture Document 24.04 Release*. Retrieved from https://docs.gaia-x.eu/technical-committee/architecture-document/24.04/pdf/document.pdf

German AI Association. (2023). *Large AI Models for Germany* (Feasibility study). Retrieved from https://leam.ai/wp-content/uploads/2023/05/LEAM-Feasibility-STudy.pdf

Gomes, A., & Okano-Heijmans, M. (2024). *Too Late to Act? Europe's Quest Policy Brief for Cloud Sovereignty* (Policy Brief). Clingendael: Netherlands Institute of International Relations. Retrieved from https://www.clingendael.org/sites/default/files/2024-02/Policy_brief_Cloud_sovereignty.pdf

Grönlund, K., Herne, K., Jäske, M., & Värttö, M. (2022). Can politicians and citizens deliberate together? Evidence from a local deliberative mini-public. *Scandinavian Political Studies*, 45(4), 383-575. DOI: 10.1111/1467-9477.12231

Hulkó, G., Kálmán, J., & Lapsánszky, A. (2025). The politics of digital sovereignty and the European Union's legislation: Navigating crises. *Frontiers in Political Science*, 7, 1548562. DOI: 10.3389/fpos.2025.1548562

Human Rights Watch. (2019, May 1). *China's Algorithms of Repression: Reverse Engineering a Xinjiang Police Mass Surveillance App*. Retrieved from https://www.hrw.org/

report/2019/05/01/chinas-algorithms-repression/reverse-engineering-xinjiang-police-mass

Idiap Research Institute. (n.d.). *Center for Participatory AI*. Retrieved from https://www.idiap.ch/en/scientific-research/center-for-participatory-ai

Independent High-Level Expert Group on Artificial Intelligence. (2019). *Ethics Guidelines for Trustworthy AI*. European Commission. Retrieved from https://digital-strategy.ec.europa.eu/en/library/ethics-guidelines-trustworthy-ai

Independent High-Level Expert Group on Artificial Intelligence. (2020). *The Assessment List for Trustworthy Artificial Intelligence (ALTAI) for Self-assessment*. European Commission. Retrieved from https://op.europa.eu/en/publication-detail/-/publication/73552fcd-f7c2-11ea-991b-01aa75ed71a1/language-en

Kuziemski, M., & Misuraca, G. (2020). AI governance in the public sector: Three tales from the frontiers of automated decision-making in democratic settings. *Telecommunications Policy*, 44(6), 101976. https://doi.org/10.1016/j.telpol.2020.101976

Laux, J., Wachter, S., & Mittelstadt, B. (2022). *Trustworthy Artificial Intelligence and the European Union AI Act: On the Conflation of Trustworthiness and the Acceptability of Risk*. SSRN (Social Science Research Network). Retrieved from http://dx.doi.org/10.2139/ssrn.4230294

Leikas, J., Johri, A., Latvanen, M., Wessberg, N., & Hahto, A. (2022). Governing ethical AI transformation: A case study of AuroraAI. *Frontiers in Artificial Intelligence*, 5, Article 836557. https://doi.org/10.3389/frai.2022.836557

Mayer, M., & Nock, P.J. (2025). Digital fragmentations, technological sovereignty, and new perspectives on the global digital political economy. *Global Political Economy*, 4(1), 2–13. https://doi.org/10.1332/26352257Y2024D000000029

Morley, J., Floridi, L., Kinsey, L., & Elhalal, A. (2020). From what to how: An initial review of publicly available AI ethics tools, methods and research to translate principles into practices. *Science and Engineering Ethics*, 26, 2141–2168. https://doi.org/10.1007/s11948-019-00165-5

Mügge, D. (2024). EU AI sovereignty: For whom, to what end, and to whose benefit? *Journal of European Public Policy*, 31(8), 2200–2225. https://doi.org/10.1080/13501763.2024.2318475

Mushkani, R., Berard, H., Cohen, A. & Koseki, S. (2025, July 13-19). Position: The right to AI. In: *Proceedings of the 42nd International Conference on Machine Learning*. ICML 2025: Vancouver, Canada. Retrieved from https://arxiv.org/abs/2501.17899

Nesta. (n.d.). *Participatory AI*. Retrieved from https://www.nesta.org.uk/project/participatory-ai/

OECD. (2023). *A Blueprint for Building National Compute Capacity for Artificial Intelligence* (OECD Digital Economy Papers No. 350). OECD Publishing. https://doi.org/10.1787/876367e3-en

OECD. (2024a). *Recommendation of the Council on Artificial Intelligence*. OECD Legal Instruments. Retrieved from https://legalinstruments.oecd.org/en/instruments/oecd-legal-0449

OECD. (2024b). *Shaping a Rights-oriented Digital Transformation* (OECD Digital Economy Papers No. 368). OECD Publishing. https://doi.org/10.1787/86ee84e2-en

OpenGPT-X. (n.d.). *Über das Projekt* [About the Project]. KI Bundesverband. Retrieved from https://opengpt-x.de/ueber/

Radclyfe, C., Ribeiro, M., & Wortham, R.H. (2023). The assessment list for trustworthy artificial intelligence: A review and recommendations. *Frontiers in Artificial Intelligence*, 6, Article 1020592. https://doi.org/10.3389/frai.2023.1020592

Roberts, H. (2024). Digital sovereignty and artificial intelligence: A normative approach. *Ethics and Information Technology*, 26, Article number 70. https://doi.org/10.1007/s10676-024-09810-5

Roberts, H., Hine, E., & Floridi, L. (2023). *Digital Sovereignty, Digital Expansionism, and the Prospects for Global AI Governance*. SSRN (Social Science Research Network). Retrieved from https://papers.ssrn.com/sol3/papers.cfm?abstract_id=4483271

Shahbaz, A. (n.d.). *Freedom on the Net 2018: The Rise of Digital Authoritarianism*. Retrieved from https://freedomhouse.org/report/freedom-net/2018/rise-digital-authoritarianism

Stahl, B.C. & Leach, T. (2023). Assessing the ethical and social concerns of artificial intelligence in neuroinformatics research: An empirical test of the European Union assessment list for trustworthy AI (ALTAI). *AI and Ethics*, 3, 745–767. https://doi.org/10.1007/s43681-022-00201-4

Stanford Deliberative Democracy Lab. (2023). *The Citizens' Parliament: Finland*. Retrieved from https://deliberation.stanford.edu/sites/g/files/sbiybj21211/files/media/file/citizens-parliament_stanford-webpage.pdf

Stix, C. (2022). Foundations for the future: Institution building for the purpose of artificial intelligence governance. *AI and Ethics*, 2, 463–476. https://doi.org/10.1007/s43681-021-00093-w

Synergy Research Group. (2022, September 27). *European Cloud Providers Continue to Grow But Still Lose Market Share*. Retrieved from https://www.srgresearch.com/articles/european-cloud-providers-continue-to-grow-but-still-lose-market-share

UNESCO. (2022). *Recommendation on the Ethics of Artificial Intelligence*. Retrieved from https://digitallibrary.un.org/record/4062376?v=pdf

Webster, G., Creemers, R., Kania, E., & Triolo, P. (2017). *Full Translation: China's 'New Generation Artificial Intelligence Development Plan' (2017)*. DigiChina: Stanford Cyber Policy Center. Retrieved from https://digichina.stanford.edu/work/full-translation-chinas-new-generation-artificial-intellige nce-development-plan-2017/

White House Office of Science and Technology Policy. (n.d.). *Blueprint for an AI Bill of Rights: Making Automated Systems Work for the American People*. Retrieved from https://bidenwhitehouse.archives.gov/ostp/ai-bill-of-rights/

Zeng, J. (2020). Artificial intelligence and China's authoritarian governance. *International Affairs*, 96(6), 1441–1459. https://doi.org/10.1093/ia/iiaa172

Zhang, A., Boltz, A., Lynn, J., Wang, C.W., & Lee, M.K. (2023). Stakeholder-centered AI design: Co-designing worker tools with gig workers through data probes. ArXiv preprint. Retrieved from https://doi.org/10.48550/arXiv.2303.03367

CHAPTER
15

AI Governance for Digital Sovereignty in Smart City Surveillance

Sanjay Misra[1(0000-0002-3556-9331)], **Kousik Barik**[2* (0000-0001-9296-9561)], **Petter Kvalvik**[1(0000-0002-4913-5374)] **and Per-Arne Jørgensen**[1]

[1] Department of Digital Sovereignty, Institute for Energy Technology, Halden, Norway
[2] Department of Computer Sciences, Universidad de Alcalá, Alcalá de Henares, Madrid,Spain

15.1 Introduction

As smart cities continue to grow, Artificial Intelligence (AI) has become a central force in how urban areas are governed. Across the globe, AI-driven surveillance systems are being deployed to oversee public spaces, manage infrastructure, and enhance the delivery of public services. However, this shift is more than just a technological touch on fundamental issues like democracy, human rights, politics, and ethics. These AI surveillance tools often operate through opaque algorithms, centralized data frameworks, and third-party providers. This combination raises serious questions about national sovereignty and personal autonomy. As Calzada (2021, 2024) notes, the rise of algorithmic governance and data-centric cities demands a revaluation of how democratic societies uphold sovereignty in the digital era.

Despite growing interest in AI ethics and urban digital policy, existing research tends to address AI governance and digital sovereignty as separate issues. Literature on smart cities often celebrates technological efficiency and innovation while underplaying the political consequences of AI-driven surveillance (Den Hartog et al., 2024). At the same time, work on digital sovereignty frequently focuses on national-level data governance without adequate consideration of how local implementations, particularly in smart city contexts, influence sovereignty from the ground up (Lawo, Neifer, Esau et al., 2023). This separation overlooks the critical intersection where municipal AI deployment affects not just policy efficiency but also power structures, civil liberties, and citizens' rights.

*Corresponding author: kousikbarik@gmail.com

DOI: 10.1201/9781003581581-15

This chapter is motivated by the growing recognition that smart surveillance systems, though often framed as neutral tools for efficiency, have deep implications for autonomy, trust, and democratic participation. Cities in both the Global North and South are increasingly adopting AI surveillance technologies sourced from multinational firms, reinforcing concerns about "digital colonialism" and technological dependency (Sadi, 2025; Wernick et al., 2024). Moreover, as Roberts et al. (2023) note, digital sovereignty itself has become a contested concept, caught between the geopolitical tug-of-war of digital expansionism and emerging calls for global AI governance. There is an urgent need to assess how digital sovereignty can be protected not only at the level of international diplomacy but also within local AI practices embedded in everyday urban life. To address these gaps, the study systematically reviews the intersection of smart city surveillance practices with AI governance and digital sovereignty, aiming to answer the following research questions.

RQ1: How do AI-enabled smart city surveillance systems impact digital sovereignty?

RQ2: Which governance models are currently employed to regulate these systems, and how effective are they in safeguarding democratic values and digital rights?

RQ3: What insights can be drawn from international comparisons to design more inclusive and sovereignty-preserving AI governance frameworks?

Drawing on recent literature from both domains, the chapter positions smart surveillance as a test case for the tensions between technological innovation and sovereign governance. Using a structured review methodology guided by PRISMA, the study synthesizes findings across peer-reviewed literature and policy reports to identify common risks, regulatory models, and governance strategies. In doing so, it provides a nuanced and contextualized understanding of how digital sovereignty is negotiated in AI-powered urban environments. This chapter offers three main contributions.

1. It synthesizes interdisciplinary research to reveal how AI surveillance technologies in smart cities directly influence the implementation of digital sovereignty at the municipal level.
2. It identifies ethical, legal, and political challenges associated with current governance approaches and highlights differences between Global North and South responses.
3. It contributes to a structured framework to inform future research and policymaking by aligning AI governance strategies with sovereignty-preserving practices in urban digital infrastructures.

The remaining chapter is structured as follows. Section 2 outlines the methodology, including the selection of the database and the application of the PRISMA framework. Section 3 defines key concepts, AI governance, digital sovereignty, and smart city surveillance, and explores their intersections. Section 4 presents the main findings from the literature, highlighting thematic insights and regional differences. Section 5 presents a discussion of policy and governance implications. Finally, the chapter concludes in Section 6 with key insights and directions for future research.

15.2 Methodology

This study employs a systematic literature review to examine the relationship between AI governance frameworks and digital sovereignty in the context of smart city surveillance. The review is conducted to synthesize current scholarly perspectives, identify knowledge gaps, and provide a foundation for developing governance models that prioritize sovereignty and citizen rights.

To ensure transparency and reproducibility, the review followed the PRISMA (Preferred Reporting Items for Systematic Reviews and Meta-Analyses) guidelines. The literature search is conducted across two major academic databases: Scopus and Google Scholar. The following query was used in both databases:

"AI Governance" AND "Digital Sovereignty" AND "Smart City".

Using this query, we found 20 papers from Scopus and 110 from Google Scholar. After removing duplicates and checking for relevance, we selected 30 papers for full-text analysis. The selection criteria centered on peer-reviewed journal articles, book chapters, and policy papers that explore AI governance, digital sovereignty, and their

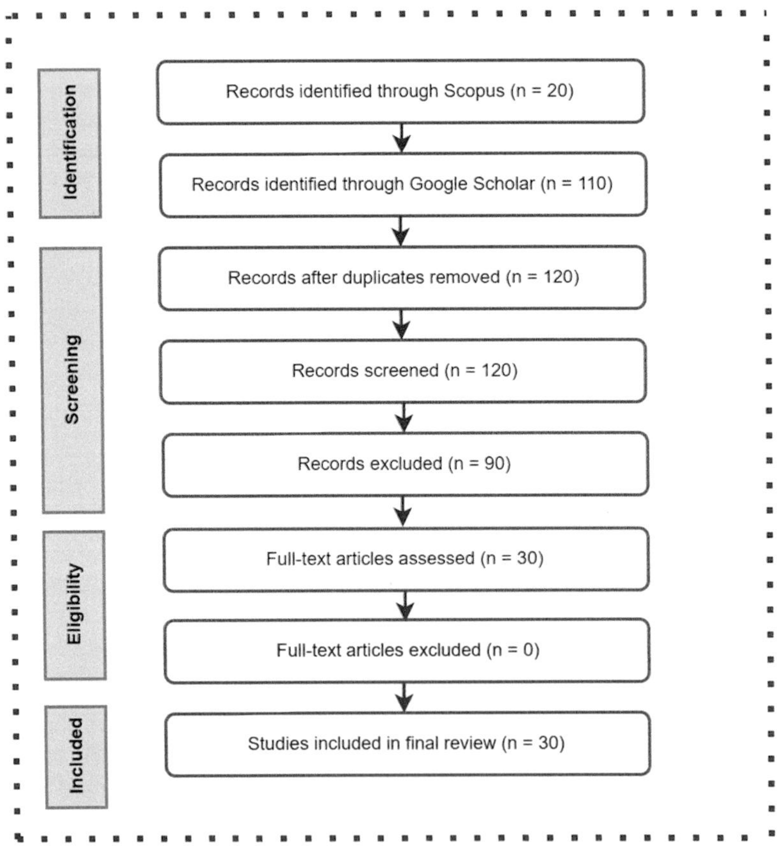

Figure 15.1. The PRISMA methods used for selecting identified studies.

implications or applications within smart city contexts. Technical documents lacking a focus on governance or ethical considerations were excluded from the final review. Figure 15.1 outlines the PRISMA methodology employed to filter and identify the relevant studies.

The reviewed papers were analyzed through thematic coding to identify recurring themes and conceptual frameworks within the literature (Ahmed et al., 2025). The findings were categorized into four key areas: (1) governance models and existing regulatory shortcomings, (2) issues surrounding data ownership and sovereignty, (3) the ethical and legal challenges posed by surveillance technologies, and (4) contrasting implementations between the Global North and Global South.

15.3 Conceptual Framework

This section introduces the core concepts that underpin this review: AI governance, digital sovereignty, and surveillance in smart cities. Together, these three pillars establish a framework for examining how urban technologies shape political authority, civil liberties, and autonomy in technological development.

15.3.1 Artificial Intelligence Governance

AI governance involves the structures, principles, and systems that guide and oversee the creation and use of artificial intelligence. It addresses concerns such as transparency, accountability, fairness in algorithms, and adherence to legal and ethical norms (Bosco et al., 2024). As AI becomes more integrated into city services and decision-making, robust governance is vital to protect democratic principles (Ghosh et al., 2025; Paul et al., 2024; Roberts et al., 2023). For instance, the European Union and the United States have taken different paths in regulating AI. The EU emphasizes ethics and human rights, while the US prioritizes innovation and market-driven approaches. These differing philosophies shape the governance tools cities utilize to implement AI technologies (Roberts et al., 2021).

AI governance is also highly political. It reflects underlying institutional structures, ideological commitments, and geopolitical priorities. Filgueiras (2022) shows how democratic and authoritarian regimes take different approaches to AI regulation. This influences not just the outcomes but also who decides the risks and opportunities related to AI.

15.3.2 Digital Sovereignty

Digital sovereignty is the ability of individuals, organizations, and governments to exert control on their digital infrastructure, data flows, and technology choices (Foth et al., 2021). Originally framed at the level of national cybersecurity and digital infrastructure, the concept has expanded to include civic and human-cantered dimensions. Lawo, Neifer, Esau-Held et al. (2023) emphasize that digital sovereignty should not be reduced to state control, but must also include the autonomy of users and communities to manage their digital presence and identity. Similarly, Calzada (2025) argues that the growing influence of "data-opolies" like Google and Meta has eroded democratic oversight, creating an urgent need for decentralized alternatives and citizen empowerment.

The use of digital sovereignty in smart cities is quite complicated. Cities often depend on proprietary platforms and foreign technologies. This dependency makes them vulnerable to outside control and restricts their ability to enforce local regulations (Anthony & Sarshar, 2025). In response, certain cities have adopted the concept of data sovereignty, leveraging decentralized Web3 technologies, data cooperatives, and municipal data trusts to reclaim authority over the flow of urban data (Calzada, 2024; Calzada et al., 2025). This shift reframes sovereignty as a collaborative and inclusive process rather than a state-controlled one.

15.3.3 Smart City Surveillance

Smart city surveillance refers to the deployment of digital tools, particularly AI-driven technologies, to oversee and control activities within urban environments (Raghav et al., 2025). These technologies encompass facial recognition, predictive policing, traffic oversight, and real-time crowd monitoring (Kaiser, 2024; Zhou & Kankanhalli, 2021). Although they enhance efficiency and security, they also present ethical dilemmas regarding surveillance, privacy, and algorithmic bias. According to Den Hartog et al. (2024), ethical frameworks in the Netherlands frequently overlook the needs of citizens, promoting a governance style that emphasizes data efficiency over public accountability.

Moreover, smart surveillance can perpetuate or intensify existing social disparities. Wernick et al. (2024) critique the export of smart city frameworks from the Global North to the Global South, warning that without proper localization, such technologies risk becoming instruments of digital colonialism. In cities such as Lagos, the adoption of externally developed surveillance tools has led to growing concerns about who gains from these systems and who bears the consequences, particularly when international firms control the underlying data infrastructure.

15.3.4 Intersections and Tensions

The convergence of AI governance, digital sovereignty, and smart city surveillance presents both potential benefits and significant risks. AI offers powerful capabilities to enhance city management and public safety. Yet, deploying these technologies without adequate safeguards can undermine democratic institutions and civil liberties. Tensions are mounting between international efforts to regulate AI and the desire of national or local governments to maintain control. Roberts et al. (2023) point out that the push for global oversight often clashes with the rise of digital expansionism. In this situation, powerful states and corporations extend their influence across borders, making it harder for smaller entities to maintain control.

At the city level, this dynamic is reflected in decisions regarding vendor selection, data storage, and algorithmic transparency. Municipalities increasingly serve as frontline actors in navigating these challenges, but they are often ill-equipped to manage the geopolitical and ethical complexities of AI-powered systems. As Calzada et al. (2023) note, the concept of "smart city citizenship" needs to evolve to encompass not only participation in digital services but also active involvement in shaping how data is collected, utilized, and governed. The proposed conceptual framework is presented in Figure 15.2.

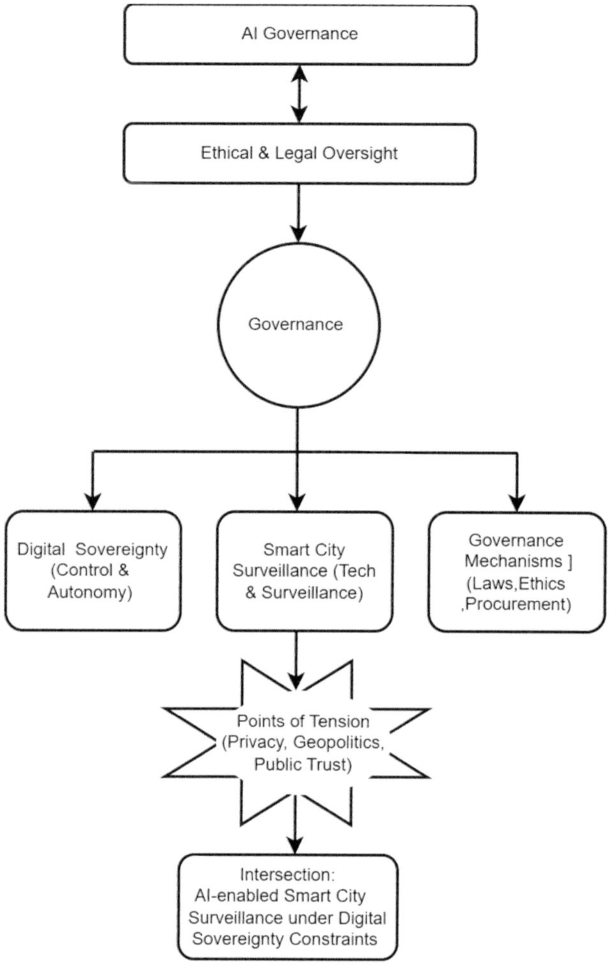

Figure 15.2. The proposed conceptual framework.

15.4 Results and Analysis

The findings of this review are presented across four key themes, derived through thematic coding of the selected literature. These themes relate directly to the research questions. They offer insights into how AI-enabled surveillance systems affect digital sovereignty, current governance mechanisms, and the differences between them in various global contexts.

15.4.1 Governance Structures and Regulatory Gaps

The use of AI in smart city surveillance often goes faster than the creation of governance structures. Many cities adopt surveillance technologies without clear rules, relying on vendors or higher government bodies to set standards. As noted by Roberts et al. (2021) and Sanchez-Graells (2024), the lack of proactive legal regulation usually leads to governance through procurement or soft law. This situation creates confusion and inconsistent protections. For example, European cities have tried ethical guidelines, but enforcement is weak and public accountability is limited (Bazoobandi et al., 2025; Den Hartog et al., 2024).

This regulatory delay is particularly worrisome because of the sensitive nature of AI surveillance systems. These technologies, such as facial recognition and predictive policing, often gather, process, and act on large amounts of personal data with little oversight (McKenna, 2025). Paul et al. (2024) point out that public sector AI projects face issues with democratic legitimacy, especially when they involve unclear partnerships with private companies. These gaps raise serious questions about who is ultimately responsible for algorithmic decision-making in city environments.

The review in Table 15.1 shows that governance frameworks for AI in smart city surveillance are often fragmented, reactive, or too dependent on soft mechanisms like ethical guidelines and procurement contracts. While regions like the EU advocate for regulatory ethics, actual enforcement is often inconsistent. Public sector deployments frequently lack transparency and often leave out meaningful citizen oversight. This highlights a significant gap between governance goals and operational realities.

Table 15.1. Governance structures and regulatory gaps in smart city AI deployment

Study	Focus area	Governance approach	Key insights	Identified gaps
Roberts et al., 2021	EU vs. US AI strategy	Regulatory ethics (EU) vs innovation-led (US)	Compared to global visions of "Good AI Society"	Lack of enforcement; diverging goals hinder cooperation
Paul et al., 2024)	AI & public policy	Critical inquiry into AI in policy	Identifies contradictions in policy practices	Limited accountability in public sector deployment
Sanchez-Graells, 2024)	Public procurement	Regulation by contract	Uses procurement as a regulatory workaround	Lacks oversight; false sense of legal coverage
Den Hartog et al., 2024	Smart city ethics in NL	Ethical guidelines review	Reveals vague guidelines; citizens' interests not central	Ethical norms are not legally binding or enforceable
Filgueiras, 2022	Developing countries	Institutional comparison	Authoritarian regimes implement AI faster	Oversight sacrificed for rapid deployment
Al Mokdad, 2025	AI governance models	Integrated "intelligent governance"	Combining tech foresight, democracy, and policy	Abstract model; lacks operational clarity

15.4.2 Data Sovereignty and Ownership

Smart city surveillance systems depend on gathering and centralizing urban data. This raises questions about who owns and controls that information. Calzada (2024, 2025) and Lawo et al. (2023) argue that sovereignty in digital systems should involve not just the state but also citizens and communities. These groups often have little say in how their data is used. Current models, particularly those involving cloud-based storage and proprietary AI platforms, often externalize data control to tech vendors, undermining local autonomy.

Emerging alternatives aim to address this imbalance through decentralized technologies, including data cooperatives, blockchain governance, and Web3 mechanisms (Calzada et al., 2025). These approaches aim to realign power by giving citizens a stake in how urban data is managed. However, their adoption remains limited and uneven, often restricted to experimental pilot projects. This

Table 15.2. Data sovereignty and ownership in smart city surveillance

Study	Focus area	Data control model	Key insights	Identified gaps
Calzada, 2025	Data-opolies & sovereignty	Centralized Big Tech platforms	Highlights how dominant tech firms undermine democratic sovereignty	Calls for decentralization via blockchain and DAOs
Calzada et al., 2025	Web3 trust ecosystems	Decentralized AI & data governance	Explores federated learning and DAOs for trust in GenAI	Limited adoption; policy integration remains weak
Lawo et al., 2023)	Human-centred sovereignty	Conceptual model	Advocates shifting from state-centric to citizen-centric data control	Still theoretical; lacks actionable strategies
Calzada, 2024	AI & social innovation	Data co-ops, community ownership	Demonstrates the use of blockchain & DAOs for rural inclusion	Lacks large-scale urban deployment examples
Tan et al., 2024	Self-sovereign identity (SSI)	Decentralized identity models	Details of technical challenges for citizen-controlled data	Issues with scalability, interoperability, and standardization
Calzada, 2023	Smart city citizenship	People-centered governance	Frames sovereignty through democratic urban data practices	Highlights the divide between policy rhetoric and actual control
Bentalha & Boukare, 2024	Territorial intelligence	Hybrid AI and data models	Shows how AI can support regional sovereignty	Needs better alignment with legal and ethical norms

indicates a growing awareness of the need for data sovereignty, despite institutional structures lagging.

From Table 15.2, it is observed that there is a clear shift in the literature toward advocating for decentralized and citizen-centered data governance models. Studies promote approaches like data cooperatives, blockchain, and self-sovereign identity systems. However, these alternatives remain largely conceptual or pilot-based. The barriers, including legal complexity, technical limitations, and institutional inertia, continue to impede the mainstreaming of sovereignty-preserving data systems.

15.4.3 Ethical and Legal Implications of Surveillance Technologies

Surveillance technologies used in smart cities raise numerous ethical and legal concerns, particularly around privacy, discrimination, and due process. While many jurisdictions have released high-level ethical principles, such as the EU's Ethics Guidelines for Trustworthy AI, actual implementation is inconsistent. Den Hartog et al. (2024) found that even in progressive urban contexts, ethical guidelines often fail to center citizen rights and do not address how AI reshapes governance itself.

Moreover, DeVrio et al. (2024) emphasize that the harms caused by algorithmic systems are not always visible to those in power. A growing body of research suggests that people affected by AI-driven decisions often develop "responses from below" to resist or adapt to these systems. These dynamics underscore the need for participatory governance models that go beyond compliance and actively involve the public in shaping surveillance practices.

The literature (Table 15.3) emphasizes growing ethical concerns in smart city surveillance, particularly regarding privacy, discrimination, and democratic accountability. Although ethical guidelines exist, they are often vague, lack enforceability, and are disconnected from practical governance. Several studies emphasize the importance of participatory, rights-based approaches; however, formal legal protections remain weak or inconsistently applied.

15.4.4 Regional Differences: Global North and Global South

Smart city surveillance is not implemented uniformly across the world. In the Global North, governance efforts often focus on aligning with human rights frameworks and ethical standards, as seen in the EU's regulatory agenda (Roberts et al., 2023). Nevertheless, genuine digital sovereignty remains constrained by technological dependencies and the sway of multinational corporations. In the Global South, many smart city projects are financed and constructed by external actors, heightening fears of digital colonialism (Wernick et al., 2024).

In African cities like Lagos, surveillance systems have been implemented without adequate local governance frameworks or mechanisms for public accountability. This situation poses significant risks to autonomy and the protection of human rights (Wernick et al., 2024). As Sadi (2025) notes, countries with weaker domestic capabilities may find themselves strategically dependent on geopolitical powers like China or the US, further complicating efforts to establish national or municipal digital sovereignty.

Table 15.3. Ethical and legal implications of surveillance technologies

Study	Focus area	Ethical/Legal dimension	Key insights	Identified gaps
Den Hartog et al., 2024	NL smart cities	Ethical guideline review	Ethical norms fail to prioritize citizen rights	Guidelines are vague, non-binding
DeVrio et al., 2024	Algorithmic harm	Taxonomy of public responses	Highlights power dynamics and resistance from below	Limited integration into governance structures
Timoteo et al., 2021	EU vs China ethics	Comparative AI ethics frameworks	Shows differing strategic approaches	Lack of global ethical consensus
Roberts et al., 2023	Global governance	Digital sovereignty vs global AI regulation	Conflicting goals between sovereignty and cooperation	Tension between ethical alignment and state power
Calzada, 2020	Pandemic surveillance	Techno-political democracy & civil liberties	Surveillance expands without democratic oversight	Democratic erosion through unchecked AI use

AI governance strategies and their impact on digital sovereignty vary significantly across different regions. In the Global South, surveillance technologies are often externally sourced, reinforcing dependency and digital inequality, as presented in Table 15.4. In contrast, Global North actors grapple with regulating AI while balancing innovation, ethics, and international competition. Across both contexts, cities and smaller states face challenges asserting sovereignty within broader geopolitical and corporate power dynamics.

We conducted a bibliographic analysis using the R tool, based on the selected studies, to explore deeper insights. Figure 15.3 presents the outcomes of a word cloud study conducted on the abstracts of the selected studies, with ‘digital sovereignty’ being the most common occurrence, followed by ‘digital rights’, ‘smart city’, and ‘data sovereignty’.

Figure 15.4 illustrates the word cloud analysis based on the keywords identified in the selected studies. It shows that ‘artificial intelligence’ is the most common occurrence, followed by ‘digital sovereignty’, ‘United States’, ‘smart city’, ‘democratic state’, and ‘urban policy’.

Factorial analysis assesses similarity by allowing users to formalize bibliographic coupling, co-occurrence, and cocitation criteria. It sketches a domain’s conceptual framework by analyzing word frequency within distinct bibliographic clusters, as depicted in Figure 15.5. The key factors identified include policy, artificial intelligence, potential, technological, role, challenges, and sovereignty.

Table 15.4. Regional differences in AI governance and digital sovereignty

Study	Region/Context	Governance style	Key insights	Identified gaps
Wernick et al., 2024	Global South (Lagos)	Post-colonial critique	Highlights digital colonialism and human rights risks	Imported models ignore local needs
Sadi, 2025	Pakistan	Strategic dependence	AI rivalry exposes vulnerabilities in sovereignty	Reliance on foreign tech threatens autonomy
Filgueiras, 2022	30 developing countries	Regime-based comparison	Authoritarian states advance AI faster	Raising ethical and democratic concerns
Calzada, 2024	Europe	Algorithmic nations	Frames digital sovereignty through technopolitics	Cities lack power against global tech firms
Roberts et al., 2023	EU, US, China	Geopolitical tension	Digital expansionism undermines global governance	Misalignment weakens cooperation frameworks
Valle et al., 2025	China	Soft power diplomacy	AI used to shape global narratives	Sovereignty used strategically, not ethically

Figure 15.3. Word cloud analysis based on the abstracts.

Figure 15.4. Word cloud analysis based on the keywords.

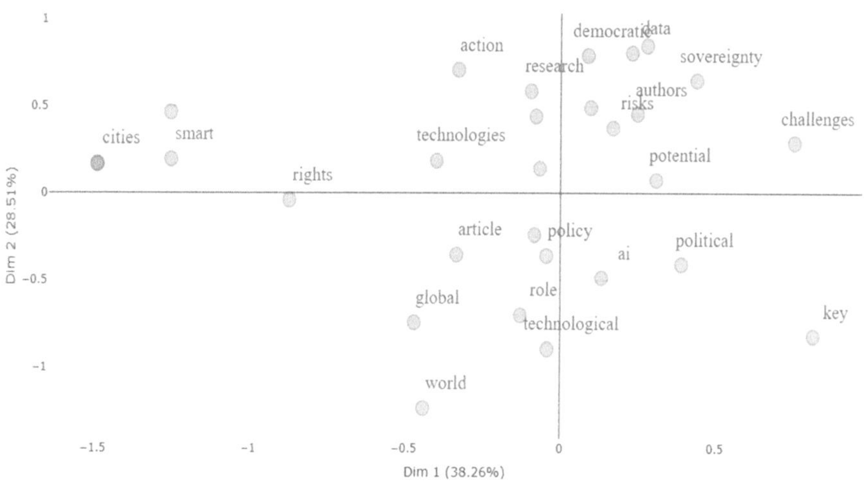

Figure 15.5. Factorial analysis based on the abstracts.

In bibliometric analysis, a treemap is a visualization tool used to depict hierarchical data, typically illustrating the associations between keywords or other elements within a body of literature. This enables easy identification of prevalent themes and practices in the research area. The treemap analysis, based on the abstracts of the selected studies, is presented in Figure 15.6, which shows that artificial intelligence is the dominant group, followed by digital sovereignty and algorithms.

Network analysis, in particular, enriches bibliometric analysis by indicating complex associations within study landscapes. We have identified three clusters and presented the relationship between them, as demonstrated in Figure 15.7.

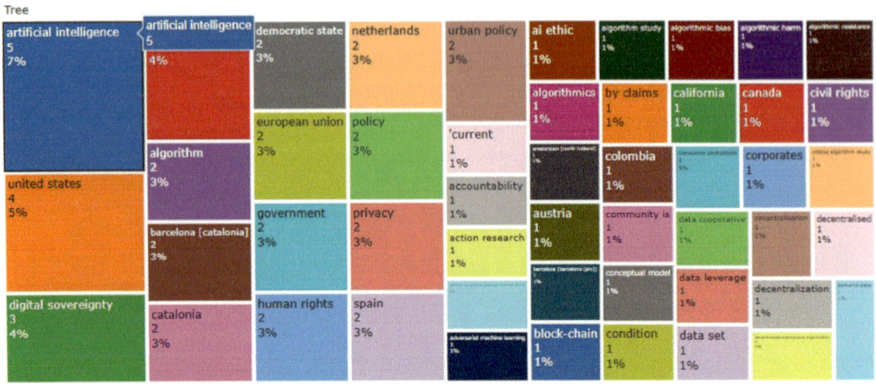

Figure 15.6. Treemap analysis based on the abstracts.

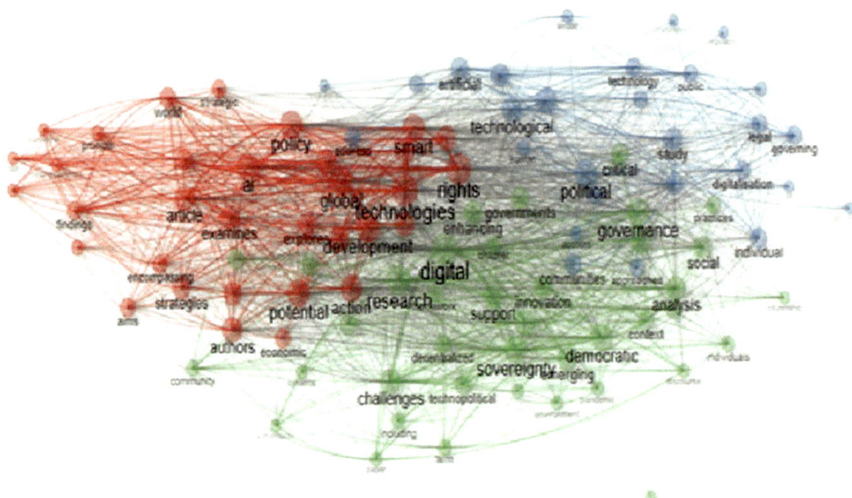

Figure 15.7. Network analysis based on the abstracts.

15.5 Discussion

This section discusses how the literature responds to the three core research questions posed in this review. Each question is addressed through the lens of the four major themes identified: governance structures and regulatory gaps, data sovereignty and ownership, ethical and legal implications of surveillance technologies, and regional differences in implementation across the Global North and South.

RQ1: How do AI-enabled smart city surveillance systems impact digital sovereignty?

Based on the reviewed literature, it is evident that AI-driven surveillance systems pose significant challenges to digital sovereignty. From a governance perspective, many cities lack the institutional capacity to regulate or oversee these systems, particularly when they are deployed through public-private partnerships. This results in a governance vacuum where tech vendors often control key infrastructure and data flows (Roberts et al., 2021; Sanchez-Graells, 2024).

In the theme of data sovereignty, smart city surveillance typically involves large-scale data extraction, storage, and analysis, often via proprietary or cloud-based platforms managed outside the jurisdiction of the implementing city or country (Calzada, 2025). This undermines both national and municipal autonomy, especially when data ownership is not clearly defined or protected by law. Although alternative models, such as decentralized Web3 ecosystems and data cooperatives, are emerging (Calzada et al., 2025; Lawo et al., 2023), their implementation remains limited.

Ethically, these surveillance systems also create power asymmetries. Citizens are frequently unaware of how their data is being used or have no means of recourse. Legal mechanisms for protecting digital rights are either underdeveloped or insufficiently enforced (Den Hartog et al., 2024). As a result, digital sovereignty is compromised not just at the institutional level, but also at the level of individual autonomy.

RQ2: What governance models are currently employed to regulate these systems, and how effective are they in safeguarding democratic values and digital rights?

The literature presents a range of governance models, from state-led regulatory frameworks (e.g., the EU's ethics-focused approach) to market-driven innovation regimes similar to those in the US. However, effectiveness is often limited by the absence of binding regulations and weak institutional enforcement mechanisms (Paul et al., 2024; Timoteo et al., 2021). Ethical guidelines, although symbolically important, often lack legal standing and fail to protect citizens in practice in a meaningful way.

In terms of data governance, newer models such as self-sovereign identity systems and blockchain-based data control frameworks are being proposed as solutions to reassert democratic data control (Tan et al., 2023; Calzada, 2024). However, these models face substantial implementation hurdles, including interoperability challenges, unclear regulatory support, and limited user accessibility.

Moreover, the current governance landscape rarely includes mechanisms for public participation or consent. As DeVrio et al. (2024) point out, affected individuals often develop ad hoc strategies to resist or circumvent algorithmic systems, reflecting a disconnect between formal governance frameworks and real-world experiences of digital harm.

RQ3: What insights can be drawn from international comparisons to design more inclusive and sovereignty-preserving AI governance frameworks?

International comparisons reveal stark contrasts in how AI and surveillance technologies are deployed and governed. In the Global South, cities often adopt imported surveillance systems without sufficient legal frameworks, technical capacity, or democratic oversight (Wernick et al., 2024; Sadi, 2025). This leads to forms of digital dependency that mirror historical patterns of economic and political subordination. The lack of localization in governance models—especially those transplanted from the Global North—limits their effectiveness and relevance.

By contrast, cities and states in the Global North face distinct challenges. While they often have advanced regulatory ecosystems, they are constrained by geopolitical pressures, commercial lobbying, and the influence of powerful transnational tech companies (Calzada, 2023; Roberts et al., 2023). Even in well-regulated regions, a clear tension exists between innovation policy and digital sovereignty goals.

One promising direction is the adoption of participatory governance models that include local communities in decisions about data use and technology deployment. While these approaches are still in infancy, they suggest that digital sovereignty must be both structurally and socially embedded. Adaptive regulation, civic engagement, and technical decentralization must work in tandem with AI governance to support inclusive, sovereignty-preserving outcomes.

15.6 Conclusion

This literature review reveals a growing yet fragmented landscape in the governance of AI-powered smart city surveillance, particularly concerning digital sovereignty. By synthesizing insights from 30 scholarly works, the study offers several novel observations. First, while ethical principles and governance frameworks exist across regions, they often remain detached from the realities of implementation, particularly at the municipal level, where smart surveillance is most prevalent. This misalignment between normative frameworks and ground-level practices is a critical and underexplored area highlighted by this review.

Second, although decentralization and data cooperatives are widely proposed as solutions for reclaiming digital sovereignty, this review reveals a lack of institutional readiness and regulatory scaffolding to operationalize such alternatives. Existing studies often treat decentralization as a technical fix; however, this review identifies the absence of social, legal, and political ecosystems necessary to embed these models sustainably. This disconnection between technical promise and governance capacity adds a critical layer to the conversation on digital autonomy.

Third, through the comparative lens between the Global North and South, this review underscores that sovereignty is not merely about control over infrastructure, but also about epistemic and procedural autonomy, as well as how cities conceptualize and implement governance based on local values, capacities, and risks. In the Global South, dependency on external technologies is not just a matter of procurement, but a structural barrier to civic agencies and human rights. This review highlights the urgent need for localized, context-sensitive frameworks that transcend the mere transposition of global ethical norms.

Limitations of this study include its reliance on publicly available, peer-reviewed English-language literature, which may potentially exclude region-specific grey literature or community-based insights. Additionally, the thematic synthesis was based on conceptual analysis rather than empirical case validation, which may limit the generalizability of some conclusions.

Future work should explore empirical case studies to assess how alternative governance frameworks, especially participatory, citizen-led, or decentralized models, perform in real urban settings. Further research should also examine how power asymmetries, both geopolitical and corporate, shape the feasibility of digital sovereignty across diverse city and state contexts.

Disclaimer

The Authors used Grammarly and Generative AI to improve their English and presentation. The content generated or corrected by these tools was thoroughly reviewed, revised, and edited by the author to ensure accuracy and originality.

References

Ahmed, S.K., Mohammed, R.A., Nashwan, A.J., Ibrahim, R.H., Abdalla, A.Q., Ameen, B.M.M., & Khdhir, R.M. (2025). Using thematic analysis in qualitative research. *Journal of Medicine, Surgery, and Public Health*, 6, 100198.

Al Mokdad, A. (2025). Inclusive and intelligent governance: Enabling sustainability through policy and technology. In: M. Mokdad (ed.), *Social System Reforms to Achieve Global Sustainability* (pp. 173–238). IGI Global. https://doi.org/10.4018/979-8-3373-1280-4.ch008

Anthony, B., & Sarshar, S. (2025). Enhancing data sovereignty to improve intelligent mobility services in smart cities. *Urban Governance*, 5(1), 20–31. https://doi.org/10.1016/j.ugj.2025.02.002

Bazoobandi, Sara, Mahapatra, S., Schipper, T., & Wieczorek, I. (2025). From global governance to nationalism: The future of AI. *GIGA Focus Global*, 2. https://doi.org/10.57671/GFGL-25022

Bentalha, B., & Boukare, M. (2024). AI-driven territorial intelligence: An integrated approach to enhancing digital sovereignty. In: J. Gomathi Sankar & A. David (eds.), *Advances in Computational Intelligence and Robotics* (pp. 231–261). IGI Global. https://doi.org/10.4018/979-8-3693-8557-9.ch008

Bosco, G., Riccardi, V., Sciarrone, A., D'Amore, R., & Visvizi, A. (2024). AI-driven innovation in smart city governance: Achieving human-centric and sustainable outcomes. *Transforming Government: People, Process and Policy*. https://doi.org/10.1108/TG-04-2024-0096

Calzada, I. (2021). *Smart City Citizenship* (pp. 1–254). Elsevier. DOI: 10.1016/B978-0-12-815300-0.09993-7

Calzada, I. (2024). Artificial intelligence for social innovation: Beyond the noise of algorithms and datafication. *Sustainability*, 16(19), 8638. https://doi.org/10.3390/su16198638

Calzada, I. (2025). *Decentralizing Power? Data Sovereignty in the Age of AI and Web3*. SSRN. https://doi.org/10.2139/ssrn.5081504

Calzada, I., Pérez-Batlle, M., & Batlle-Montserrat, J. (2023). People-centered smart cities: An exploratory action research on the Cities' coalition for digital rights. *Journal of Urban Affairs*, 45(9), 1537–1562. https://doi.org/10.1080/07352166.2021.1994861

Calzada, I., Németh, G., & Al-Radhi, M.S. (2025). Trustworthy AI for whom? GenAI detection techniques of trust through decentralized Web3 ecosystems. *Big Data and Cognitive Computing*, 9(3), 62. https://doi.org/10.3390/bdcc9030062

Den Hartog, F.B., Van Den Akker, R., & Van Houdt, F. (2024). To what extent are Dutch citizens' interests and rights protected by ethical guidelines for smart cities? *Cities*, 146, 104690. https://doi.org/10.1016/j.cities.2023.104690

DeVrio, A., Eslami, M., & Holstein, K. (2024). Building, shifting, & employing power: A taxonomy of responses from below to algorithmic harm. *The 2024 ACM Conference on Fairness, Accountability, and Transparency*, 1093–1106. https://doi.org/10.1145/3630106.3658958

Filgueiras, F. (2022). The politics of AI: Democracy and authoritarianism in developing countries. *Journal of Information Technology & Politics*, 19(4), 449–464. https://doi.org/10.1080/19331681.2021.2016543

Foth, M., Anastasiu, I., Mann, M., & Mitchell, P. (2021). From automation to autonomy: Technological sovereignty for better data care in smart cities. In: B.T. Wang & C.M. Wang (eds.), *Automating Cities* (pp. 319–343). Springer Singapore. https://doi.org/10.1007/978-981-15-8670-5_13

Ghosh, A., Saini, A., & Barad, H. (2025). Artificial intelligence in governance: Recent trends, risks, challenges, innovative frameworks and future directions. *AI & SOCIETY*. https://doi.org/10.1007/s00146-025-02312-y

Kaiser, Z.R.M.A. (2024). Smart governance for smart cities and nations. *Journal of Economy and Technology*, 2, 216–234. https://doi.org/10.1016/j.ject.2024.07.003

Lawo, D., Neifer, T., Esau, M., & Stevens, G. (2023). Human-centred digital sovereignty: Explorative conceptual model and ways forward. In: H.P. Da Silva & P. Cipresso (eds.), *Computer-Human Interaction Research and Applications* (Vol. 1997, pp. 84–103). Springer Nature Switzerland. https://doi.org/10.1007/978-3-031-49368-3_6

Lawo, D., Neifer, T., Esau-Held, M., & Stevens, G. (2023). Digital sovereignty: What it is and why it matters for HCI. Extended Abstracts of the *2023 CHI Conference on Human Factors in Computing Systems* (pp. 1–7). https://doi.org/10.1145/3544549.3585834

McKenna, H.P. (2025). *AI in Urban Life: Perspective, Challenges, and Opportunities*. Springer Nature Switzerland. https://doi.org/10.1007/978-3-031-88765-9

Paul, R., Carmel, E., & Cobbe, J. (2024). Introduction to the Handbook on Public Policy and Artificial Intelligence: Vantage points for critical inquiry. In: R. Paul, E. Carmel, & J. Cobbe (eds.), *Handbook on Public Policy and Artificial Intelligence* (pp. 1–25). Edward Elgar Publishing. https://doi.org/10.4337/9781803922171.00006

Raghav, A., Singh, B., Raghav, R., & Edina, K.D. (2025). AI and robotics in smart city governance: Ethical and legal pathways for sustainable urbanization. In: K. Ravesangar, C. Kaunert, B. Singh, S. Lal, & M.K. Arora (eds.), *Advances in Computational Intelligence and Robotics* (pp. 1–24). IGI Global. https://doi.org/10.4018/979-8-3693-9410-6.ch001

Roberts, H., Cowls, J., Hine, E., Mazzi, F., Tsamados, A., Taddeo, M., & Floridi, L. (2021). Achieving a 'Good AI Society': Comparing the aims and progress of the EU and the US. *Science and Engineering Ethics*, 27(6), 68. https://doi.org/10.1007/s11948-021-00340-7

Roberts, H., Hine, E., & Floridi, L. (2023). Digital sovereignty, digital expansionism, and the prospects for global AI governance. In: M. Timoteo, B. Verri, & R. Nanni (eds.), *Quo Vadis, Sovereignty*. (Vol. 154, pp. 51–75). Springer Nature Switzerland. https://doi.org/10.1007/978-3-031-41566-1_4

Sadi, A. (2025). U.S.-China AI rivalry and its implications on Pakistan's cybersecurity and digital sovereignty. *Journal of Regional Studies Review*, 4(1), 414–423. https://doi.org/10.62843/jrsr/2025.4a088

Sanchez-Graells, A. (2024). *Digital Technologies and Public Procurement: Gatekeeping and Experimentation in Digital Public Governance* (1st ed.). Oxford University Press, Oxford. https://doi.org/10.1093/oso/9780198866770.001.0001

Valle, S., Wang, Y., & Lian, D. (2025). A vision from China on Artificial Intelligence. Implications for soft power in global cultural exchange. *Revista UNISCI*, 67.

Tan, K.L., Chi, C.-H., & Lam, K.-Y. (2024). Survey on digital sovereignty and identity: From digitization to digitalization. *ACM Computing Surveys*, 56(3), 1–36. https://doi.org/10.1145/3616400

Timoteo, M., Verri, B., & Wang, Y. (2021). Ethics guidelines for artificial intelligence: Comparing the European and Chinese approaches. *China and WTO Review*, 7(2). DOI 10.14330/cwr.2021.7.2.03

Wernick, A., Udoh, G., & Banzuzi, E. (2024). Reimaging smart city transplants for the global south. In: A. Akbari & S. Masiero (eds.), *Critical ICT4D (Information and Communication Technologies for Development)* (1st ed., pp. 109–135). Routledge. https://doi.org/10.4324/9781003395966-10

Zhou, Y., & Kankanhalli, A. (2021). AI regulation for smart cities: Challenges and principles. In: E. Estevez, T.A. Pardo, & H.J. Scholl (eds.), *Smart Cities and Smart Governance* (Vol. 37, pp. 101–118). Springer International Publishing. https://doi.org/10.1007/978-3-030-61033-3_5

CHAPTER

16

Digital Linguistic Sovereignty: The Exclusion of African Languages in Natural Language Processing

Muhammad Aliyu Sulaiman(0000-0003-0465-8689)

Computer Science Department, Nile University of Nigeria

16.1 Introduction

Digital sovereignty refers to the capacity of a state, community, or individual to exercise control over digital infrastructure, data flows, technologies, and the rules that govern them. It encompasses political, economic, and cultural autonomy in a digitally networked world (Pohle & Thiel, 2020; Milan & Treré, 2019). At its core, digital sovereignty addresses who has the power to define, govern, and benefit from digital systems, including platforms, algorithms, and standards. Traditionally discussed at the level of states and firms, digital sovereignty includes:

1. Technological control (e.g., cloud, hardware, software)
2. Data governance (e.g., localization, privacy, surveillance)
3. Platform regulation
4. Cultural representation and access (Couldry & Mejias, 2019)

Digital linguistic sovereignty as a subdomain of digital sovereignty refers to the rights and capacity of linguistic communities, especially minoritized or Indigenous groups, to develop, use, and govern their languages within digital systems and technologies (Bird, 2020; Perley, 2012). This concept emphasizes language as a core vector of epistemic justice and cultural autonomy in digital contexts (de Sousa Santos, 2014). It argues that digital inclusion must go beyond access to infrastructure to include the sovereign use and control of language resources in digital formats and systems (Paris & Winn, 2014; Walter & Suina, 2019). Key dimensions of Digital Linguistic Sovereignty include:

Email: muhammad.suleiman@nileuniversity.edu.ng

DOI: 10.1201/9781003581581-16

1. Ensuring that digital tools (e.g., keyboards, OCR, ASR, NLP) support diverse languages, including tonal and agglutinative languages often excluded from mainstream NLP (Joshi et al., 2020).
2. Enabling communities to influence how their languages and cultural knowledge are represented and structured in digital systems (Mohamed et al., 2020).
3. Advocating for community control over linguistic data and its use in AI or large language models (LLMs) (Rainie et al., 2017).
4. Digitally sustaining and revitalizing languages at risk of extinction or marginalization (Perley, 2012; Bird, 2020).
5. Challenging the overrepresentation of English and select global languages in the digital ecosystem, and addressing their structural privileging in AI systems (Blodgett et al., 2020).

If one may ask, why does Digital Linguistic Sovereignty matter in the Digital Sovereignty Debate? Digital linguistic sovereignty has expanded the scope of digital sovereignty by:

1. Bringing non-state actors, particularly language communities and indigenous peoples, into focus.
2. Reframing sovereignty to include cultural and epistemic domains, not just infrastructures (Milan & Treré, 2019).
3. Linking language rights to broader conversations on AI ethics, data colonialism, and decolonial digital governance (Couldry & Mejias, 2019; Mohamed et al., 2020).
4. Highlighting the interdependence of language justice, technological inclusion, and cultural autonomy (Walter & Suina, 2019).

16.1.1 Problem Statement

The limited representation of African languages in Natural Language Processing (NLP) systems is not merely a technical oversight, it is a form of digital marginalization with socio-political, economic, and epistemological consequences. While modern NLP has seen rapid advancements in multilingualism, most African languages remain underrepresented or absent from major language models and platforms (Blodgett et al., 2020; Joshi et al., 2020). This exclusion cannot be seen as natural occurrences, as it reflects the general patterns of inequality in global technological development and it aligns very well with the historical antecedents of colonialism that placed colonizers' language above the indigenous languages of colonies (Mohamed et al., 2020; de Sousa Santos, 2014).

Language as a means of expressing knowledge, identity, and worldview is central to how people relate to technology and the digital public sphere. Looking at the low NLP research output or low-quality NLP research tools for sub-Saharan African languages, and their classification as low-resource languages, it is easy to see that it reflects data colonialism, which is a term that implies privileging certain linguistic and cultural data at the expense of others (Couldry & Mejias, 2019). When African languages are poorly represented in NLP tools (such as machine translation, speech recognition, and digital assistants) due to low-performance outcomes, speakers of these languages become digitally invisible. They are unable to fully participate in digital economies, governance, or public discourse (Bird, 2020). This exclusion further undermines linguistic justice. As linguistic inclusion becomes ever more central to meaningful digital participation, access to computational language tools is increasingly foundational to what scholars refer to as *full digital citizenship;* the ability to express oneself, be heard, and access services in one's language (Pimienta et al., 2009; Walter & Suina, 2019). Absent of such inclusion, resulted in denying African language speakers fair access to the advantages provided by AI and NLP technologies, hence deepening the existing digital divides along linguistic and cultural lines. Viewed through the lens of postcolonial theory, this marginalization emerges as part of a broader justification rooted in rank and status. It manifests in the classification of high resource languages of the global West, those readily identified and rendered intelligible to computational systems, and low resource languages of the Global South, particularly African languages, whose linguistic structures and communities remain obscured. This technological intelligibility dictates who is acknowledged, engaged, and ultimately represented within digital infrastructures (Spivak, 1988; Mignolo, 2009). In this sense, linguistic exclusion in AI not only reflects existing inequalities but actively reproduces them, contributing to a digital landscape in which only certain voices are empowered, and others are systematically silenced.

16.1.2 Hypothesis

We hypothesize that the marginalization of African languages in NLP systems is both a cause and an effect of broader social inequalities. It reinforces a digital ecosystem where language, identity, and power are tightly coupled, and where linguistic invisibility translates into socio-economic and epistemic disenfranchisement.

The key contributions of this Chapter include:

1. Framing Language as digital infrastructure in the context of sovereignty.
2. Exposing systemic exclusion in mainstream NLP.
3. Connecting linguistic marginalization to political and economic disempowerment.
4. Highlighting local innovation and grassroots resistance.
5. Providing actionable policy recommendations.

The rest of the study is structured as follows: Section 16.2 discusses digital sovereignty and the role of language. The African NLP landscape: Sub-Saharan and beyond is discussed in Section 16.3. Other sections include exclusion and its implications for sovereignty, linguistic colonialism in the age of AI, emerging efforts & local resistance, and finally pathways toward digital linguistic sovereignty.

16.2 Digital Sovereignty and the Role of Language

In this Section, we established the importance of linguistic infrastructure as a structural determinant of access, agency, and power in digital spaces. The Section also discusses how language sovereignty as a subdomain of digital sovereignty ensures cultural justice, geopolitical equity, and digital autonomy to African languages.

Lastly, a need for state, firms, and citizens to co-invest in local language technologies as a foundational pillar of a sovereign and inclusive digital future.

16.2.1 Conceptual Overview of Digital Sovereignty: State, Firms, and Citizens

Digital sovereignty is a multidimensional concept that encompasses *state control over data flows*, *corporate governance of digital infrastructures*, and *citizen autonomy in accessing and influencing digital services* (Floridi, 2020).

For states, digital sovereignty involves asserting authority over data localization, cybersecurity, and AI governance. The European Union, for instance, emphasizes "technological autonomy" as central to its digital sovereignty agenda, aimed at reducing dependency on non-European tech giants (European Commission, 2020). For private firms, particularly tech multinationals, digital sovereignty is entangled with *platform capitalism*, where firms host data and shape societal norms through algorithmic control and economic ecosystems (Zuboff, 2019). Meanwhile, for citizens, digital sovereignty concerns *rights to privacy, access, and agency* in digital environments, emphasizing the ability to engage meaningfully with platforms in their own languages and cultural contexts (Couldry & Mejias, 2019).

This triangulated model of sovereignty (i.e., state, firm, and citizen) reveals inherent tensions. While states push for regulatory control, firms seek economic dominance, and citizens demand inclusive and participatory digital infrastructures. However, one often overlooked yet foundational element across these domains is *language* frequently invisible in sovereignty debates, yet central to shaping access and control. Figure 16.1 illustrates a conceptual overview of digital sovereignty, comprising the three actors: State, firm, and citizen, and indicating language as a core layer mediating between them.

The triangle illustrates interdependence and tension among stakeholders. Language is central because it shapes access, representation, and rights. Exclusion from this infrastructure leads to *digital marginalization*, as in the case of low-resource language communities in Africa and the Global South.

16.2.2 Language as Infrastructure: A Hidden but Critical Layer in Digital Systems

Language underpins nearly every digital interaction, from search engines and virtual assistants to customer support and civic technology platforms. Yet, it remains *an under-recognized layer of digital infrastructure.* Natural Language Processing (NLP) tools, which power of AI applications such as machine translation, summarization, and voice assistant rely on large datasets for effective modeling. These datasets disproportionately represent high-resource languages such as English, Spanish, and Mandarin (Joshi et al., 2020). This imbalance creates structural barriers that exclude or marginalize speakers of low-resource languages, especially in Sub-Saharan Africa,, limiting their access to and benefits from AI technologies

The disparity in languages is not merely technical; it carries ideological and geopolitical connotations. It shapes perceptions of what is legible, intelligible, and computable in AI Applications, thereby influencing whose voices are amplified and

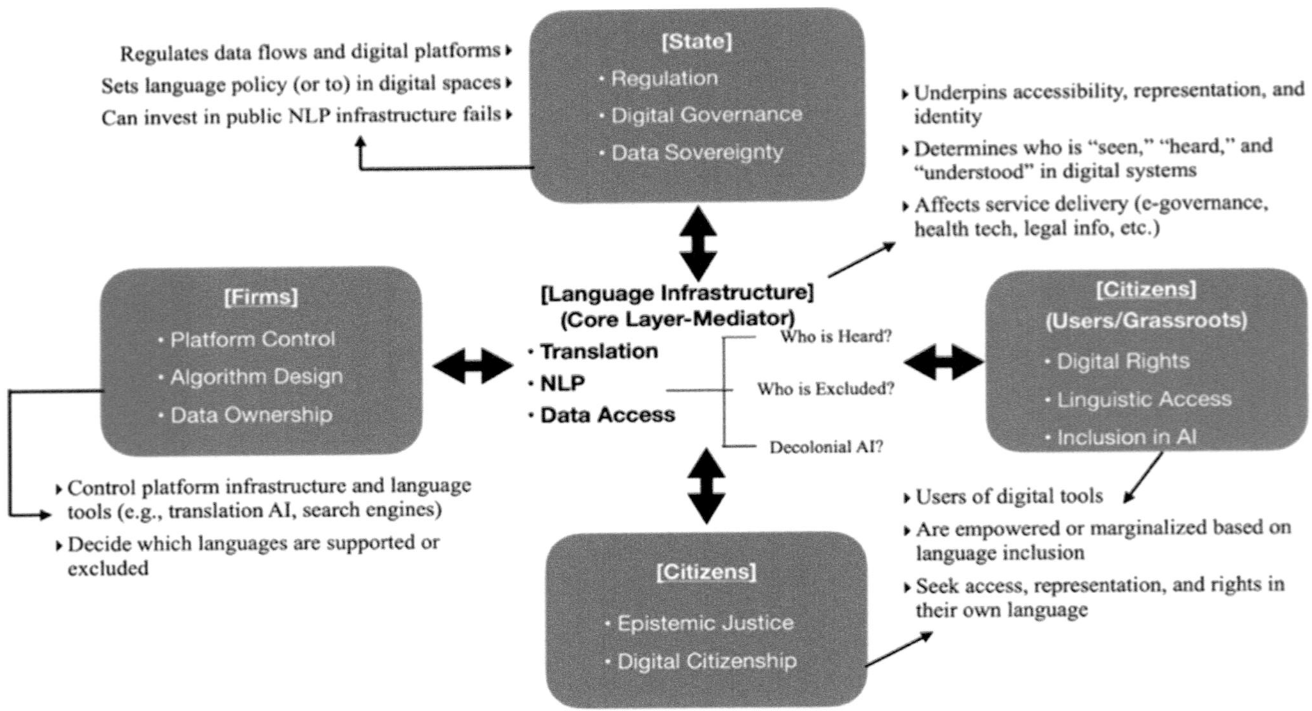

Figure 16.1. Illustrates a conceptual overview of digital sovereignty with language infrastructure.

whose are silenced (Birhane, 2021). For instance, the digital exclusion of sub-Saharan African languages comes in the form of indirect systemic denial of communities' access to digital services, representation in AI applications, and inclusion of knowledge production processes. Therefore, language plays a critical role in digital participation and its neglect reproduces historic patterns of colonial marginations in the digital age (Emezue, 2022).

Furthermore, language functions as an *ideological tool* in digital infrastructure. By privileging certain languages, systems reinforce power asymmetries and cultural hegemony, allowing dominant tech firms to define what constitutes knowledge, identity, and legitimacy online. The centrality of language underscores the need to treat linguistic diversity as a strategic priority in digital sovereignty frameworks.

16.2.3 The Connection Between Digital Rights and Services and Linguistic Representation

There is direct link between how language is represented in digital infrastructure and the right to access digital services. Governments and firms provide digital infrastructure such as chatbots, mobile apps, and automated systems as means of interaction with citizens for service delivery. These digital infrastructures rely on NLP models specifically trained to provide specific support or services to citizens. When such digital systems are trained using high resource languages, they definitely fail to understand or respond in local languages, hence, denied access to services (such as e-governance, healthcare, disaster alert, and financial tools) for monolingual citizens of entire populations. (Sambuli et al., 2021).

Additionally, the *algorithmic invisibility* of Natural Language Processing (NLP) systems stems from linguistic exclusion, a condition in which communities are either partially or entirely absent from training data, and consequently from AI system outputs. This absence can render such communities statistically irrelevant effectively denying *them digital rights* such as fair access, redress, and representation (Mohamed et al., 2020). The implications are especially concerning in critical applications ncluding biometric identity verification, predictive policing, and algorithmic decision-making in welfare distribution.

From the above discussion, one can clearly see the interdependency between the language and digital rights, and how it has a huge effect on justice and equity in the digital age. This calls for reframing digital human rights to explicitly include language inclusion, on par with algorithmic transparency and data protection. Strategically, digital linguistic sovereignty can be advanced through grassroots innovation, as exemplified by initiatives like Masakhane, which envisions the development of open Natural Language Processing (NLP) models for African languages (Orife et al., 2020).

16.3 The African NLP Landscape: Sub-Saharan and Beyond

Despite the presence of over 1000 languages and a highly diverse linguistic population across the continent, African languages continue to be classified as low resource in the field of Natural Language Processing (NLP). This classification results in limited access to information, reduced digital inclusion, and constrained development of AI applications that serve African populations in their native tongues. This section provides an extensive review of the current state of NLP resources for African languages.

Effective NLP systems are not only the result of algorithmic modeling but also depend heavily on the availability of large and clean text corpora. Such corpora remain extremely limited for African languages like Hausa, and many others. Although some digital text exists in Hausa, a West African language spoken by over 80 million people, the volume is insufficient to train reliable NLP models. For example, compared to high-resource languages, Hausa has fewer than 100,000 parallel sentences available for machine translation tasks (Korir, 2023).

Speech data is crucial for developing applications like speech recognition and synthesis. However, African languages suffer from a lack of extensive and annotated speech datasets. Initiatives like AfroDigits have begun to address this gap by creating community-driven spoken digit datasets for 38 African languages, including Yoruba and Somali. These datasets are essential for building foundational speech technologies (Emezue et al., 2023).

Pretrained language models have revolutionized NLP, but their benefits have not been evenly distributed. Most existing models are trained on data from high-resource languages, leading to poor performance on African languages. Projects like SERENGETI have made strides by developing massively multilingual language models covering 517 African languages, outperforming existing models on several tasks (Adebara et al., 2022). Additionally, tools like FastText have provided word embeddings for African languages, but their quality varies due to limited training data (Delani, 2021).

Evaluation benchmarks are essential for assessing the performance of NLP models. The MasakhaNER project has created the first large publicly available high-quality dataset for named entity recognition (NER) in ten African languages, including Hausa, Yoruba, and Zulu. The MasakhaNER resource enables researchers to evaluate and improve their NLP models for these languages (Adelani et al., 2021). AfriSenti (Muhammad et al., 2023) is a standard benchmark developed, specifically for sentiment analysis covering fourteen (14) African languages. However, most of these languages lack application-specific benchmarks, which limits their usability in real-world NLP tasks (Nekoto et al., 2020).

This section reviews the representation of African languages in prominent global NLP applications. For instance, Google Translate, a widely known language translator tool, currently supports translation to and from 133 languages, include 25 African Languages such as Hausa, Yoruba, Amharic, Zulu, and Somali. However, the quality of translation remains inconsistent due to limited training corpora. Users have frequently reported errors and inconsistencies in translations for several African Languages, underscoring the urgent need for more comprehensive datasets and improved models (Adeola, 2020). Meta's "No Language Left Behind" (NLLB) initiative is an ambitious effort to develop efficient machine translation models for 200 languages, with a focus on low resource languages. The project includes 55 African Languages. While this marks a significant step toward linguistic inclusion, the effectiveness of a unified machine translation model depends heavily on the availability of training data and the linguistic complexity of the target languages (Meta AI, 2023). GPT models from OpenAI have shown remarkable performance in a range of NLP tasks. However, the lack of training data limits their performance on African languages. Models trained specifically on African language data are necessary, as comparative studies have demonstrated that Africa-centric models, such as AfroXLMR, perform better than GPT-3.5 on tasks involving African languages (Lelapa AI, 2023). Also, a recent analytical study by Salihu-Lukman et al. (2025) examines the effectiveness of transformer-based AI models in learning and representing the nuanced socio-political context of Nigeria. The research findings demonstrate both the potential and limitations of applying mainstream pre-trained language models to underrepresented, culturally rich text. It further, suggests the need for domain-specific fine-tuning and bias mitigation to enhance AI's interpretability and applicability in a local context. Due to a lack of speech data and the commercial preference for high-resource languages, major voice assistants (such as Siri, Alexa, and Google Assistant) do not support African languages (Adelani et al., 2023). This exclusion reflects more general trends of AI linguistic marginalization. There are a few ASR models for Afrikaans and Swahili, but none for Hausa or Somali (Adelani et al., 2023).

Table 16.1 presents a Case Study: Hausa vs. Other Major Sub-Saharan Languages. The comparative analysis of NLP resources varies significantly among African languages:

1. Hausa has moderate availability of text corpora and some speech data; limited pretrained models and evaluation benchmarks.
2. Yoruba is similar to Hausa, with additional resources like the Yoruba Bible and some speech datasets.
3. Amharic is better resourced due to its status as Ethiopia's official language; more extensive corpora and some pretrained models.
4. Zulu has limited resources, though efforts like the South African government's language initiatives have provided some corpora.
5. Somali has scarce resources, with minimal text corpora and virtually no speech data.

Table 16.1. Case study: Hausa vs. other major Sub-Saharan languages

Language	Text corpora	Speech data	Pretrained models	In global NLP?
Hausa	Moderate (news, religious texts)	~50 hours (ALFFA)	mBERT, AfriBERTa	Google Translate, NLLB
Yoruba	Small (YorubaNLP)	<10 hours	NLLB, mBERT	Google Translate, NLLB
Amharic	Large (OSCAR, CC-100)	~200 hours	NLLB, mBERT	Google Translate, NLLB
Zulu	Very small	<5 hours	NLLB	Google Translate
Somali	Very small	~20 hours	NLLB	Google Translate

Hausa and Amharic are relatively better-resourced, but even they lag far behind European/Asian languages. Zulu and Somali remain critically underserved.

The African NLP landscape is marked by severe data scarcity, poor model performance, and systemic exclusion from global AI systems. While efforts like MasakhaNER, AfriBERTa, and NLLB have made strides, most Sub-Saharan languages remain digitally marginalized.

Key research gaps include:

1. More diverse, large-scale corpora (especially for speech).
2. Better tokenization strategies for African languages.
3. Stronger benchmarks to measure progress.
4. Decolonial AI approaches centre African linguistic sovereignty.

16.4 Exclusion and Its Implications for Sovereignty

The integration of artificial intelligence (AI) into various facets of society has revolutionized communication, governance, and commerce. However, the underrepresentation of African languages in AI ecosystems poses significant challenges to digital sovereignty across multiple levels: state, corporate, and citizen. This exclusion not only affects technological inclusivity but also exposes perpetual systemic inequalities rooted in historical and socio-political contexts.

AI technologies created primarily in high-resource languages are overused at the state level. National autonomy is weakened by this. Governments start to rely on outside platforms whose AI models and data pipelines are opaque and lack local accountability. Due to this dependence, the state is less equipped to effectively regulate digital communication infrastructures and ensure that AI applications align with cultural norms and national interests (Chatham House, 2024). In addition, because these AI systems are built on high resource languages and lack customization for African languages, governments face limitations in delivering inclusive e-governance services to non-dominant language speakers. This restricts access to essential public services for many communities (Brookings Institution, 2024).

For firms (particularly local ones) within the state, absence or insufficient local language-specific NLP tools limit innovation for businesses such as starups and small to medium-scaled enterprises (SMEs). For instance, such businesses because of the limited linguistic resources, will find it challenging to develop AI-driven products or services that appeal to local or regional markets. In reality, this restriction can potentially limit the development of a thriving tech ecosystem on the entire continent and limit entrepreneurship (Carnegie Endowment for International Peace, 2024). Furthermore, it can be argued that the presumed market monopoly created by dominant foreign AI technologies prolongs economic dependencies, making it exceedingly difficult for local businesses to compete successfully.

At the level of citizens, since a majority of them speak native languages, lack of AI applications in African languages, will surely limit their access to digital public goods. In other words they may not be able to accesss information, use government portals, and communicate through AI-driven services like chatbots, facial recognition and speech-to-text apps. This form of a digital marginalization will potentially restrict citizens ability to participate in the digital economy and may augment existing social inequalities within communities (Brookings Institution, 2024). Arguably, if these communities' identites and experiences are not included in digital narratives, it can result in cultural extinction.

The above discussion is best captured by the concept of **"digital divides within the digital divides"** a term that describes layered disparities within groups already affected by digital exclusion. It refers to gaps and inequalities in access, usage, or the impact of technology that persist even among those who are nominally connected. This framing reveals more complex forms of exclusion embedded within the digital ecosystem. Beyond technological access, linguistic discrimination plays a critical role. For instance even among individuals with internet access, limited availability of language resources and services that they hinder digital engagement, literacy, and meaningful online participation (Brookings Institution, 2024). This multifaceted exclusion highlights the urgent need for more inclusive policies that recognize linguistic diversity and promote technologies attuned to the full spectrum of human languages.

16.5 Linguistic Colonialism in the Age of AI

The colonization period in Africa witnessed the widespread use of European languages such as English, French, and Portuguese at the expense of native languages. The African languages faced erasure or at least severe cultural and social devaluation due to this linguistic control. Moreover, the education systems set up during the colonial period enforced learning of European languages, causing systematic damage to the local languages and dialects. The outcome of these policies was the social disruption of cultures and deeply rooting social inequalities or class structures based on the ability to speak certain languages (Data-Pop Alliance, 2022). Many African countries however, embraced the use of foreign colonial languages as their official languages of communication. The impact of these policies was the further relegation of local languages in official domains such as administration, education, and the media. The use of languages therefore becomes a tool or symbol of power representing the far reaching impact of colonialism (Data-Pop Alliance, 2022).

Colonial languages continue to dominate even in modern times, particularly with the advancement in AI and NLP. Due to limited resources, African languages, for instance, are neglected in multiple AI applications like voice and translation tools. This phenomenon is a 21st-century form of exclusion, akin to historical patterns of technological advancement that have favoured nations bearing English and other European Languages. The lack of multicultural AI models, besides lacking in infrastructure for non-English speakers, sows the seeds of digital colonialism where Western languages and culture dictate global digital engagement. This leads to the suppression of local culture, and creation of imbalance in the digital scene (Korir, 2025). This digital exclusion is reminiscent of past marginalization trends in which dominant language groups gain from technological advancements while others are marginalized. In addition to restricting accessibility for non-native English speakers, AI's lack of linguistic diversity feeds a kind of digital colonialism in which the boundaries of digital interaction are shaped by Western languages and epistemologies (Salami, 2024).

Through language, one can express culture, identity, and power. In the case of AI systems, the prevalence of specific languages exerts some influence geopolitically, meaning the languages integrated in the AI systems influence the standards of international interaction and the flow of information. By excluding African languages, these systems severely limit the ability of entire populations to truly participate in the global digital conversation and access the services available to others (Chatham House, 2024). Also, the use of AI technologies developed in the West by African countries can result in a kind of technological servitude, where the society's necessities and circumstances are poorly understood and therefore inadequately addressed. Such dependency mirrors colonial patterns, where there is largely control by foreign forces on how things are done, which undermines local development (Salami, 2024).

Soft power theory, which was formulated by Nye (2004), is the ability of a country to influence others on cultural or ideological bases rather than resorting to coercion. Online, the diffusion of AI systems that privilege Western languages and values can be seen as an exercise in soft power, subtly shaping global norms and practices. Data colonialism, as defined by Couldry and Mejias (2019), is the process of extracting data from people and communities without compensating or representing them appropriately. In Africa, evidences suggest that it is actualized through crowdsourcing of linguistic dataset to train AI models that are not useful to communities of origin, an indication of a perpetual cycle of exploitation and marginalization (Birhane, 2021).

To address linguistic colonialism in AI applications, efforts needs to be directed towards inclusion of low resources languages like "African" languages in the development of AI models. To this end, initiative such as Masakhane and Mozilla's common voice project are creating open-source datasets for African languages, intended to promotes inclusion and presentation (Korir, 2025). Futrue policy interventions that will address linguistic diversity in AI applications should look out for possible domination of Western languages and promote fair and transparent access to digital technologies. Encouraging diverse efforts that engage researchers, and communities from various localities in the development of the AI applications that incorporate linguistic and cultural specificities is essential. Such initiatives can help dismantle the lingering vestiges of linguistic colonialism and realizing a more inclusive digital future.

16.6 Emerging Efforts and Local Resistance

There are several efforts intended to address the limited presence of African language in AI driven applications. These include the springing up of open source communities, grassroot and academic initiatives with a common goal of changing the narratives of colonization of AI applications to decolonizing the development of AI applications and upholding linguistic sovereignty. This is seen as a paradigm shift language based AI application development, that departs from the top down extractive method to moves towards community oriented participatory approaches.

Maskhane is an open research project initiated in 2019, currently the leading source of African NLP resources and tools. Its future goal is to foster African research capabilities by developing machine translation models for African languages in a participatory and decentralized approach (Nekoto et al., 2020) through crowdsourcing data annotation and multilingual benchmarking (e.g., Masakhane MT Benchmark). The project has produced over 38 language models for African languages through participatory community led research. Its Ubuntu and respect principles are an ethics strategy which differentiate it from a dominant approach that is based on extractive data practices (Nekoto et al., 2020).

Another leading project for vital language infrastructure curation is Lanafrica. Its core mandate is to provide a bridge that enables accessibility of digital resources in Africa languages. It serves as a unified platform for the curation, cataloguing, and inerlinking of linguistic dataset, tools, and models created for African languages (Onose et al., 2021). The Lanafrica initiative uses inclusive metadata models that ensure language resources are categorized in culturally and linguistically appropriate words, which can perceive discrimination in global AI application development (Onose et al., 2021).

African NLP initiatives have placed a strong emphasis on ethical data practices, in contrast to mainstream NLP development, which frequently entails the collection of data without context or consent. Native speakers participate in data annotation, validation, and model evaluation through participatory research approaches, like those promoted by the Masakhane community. In keeping with the ideas of data justice, this guarantees linguistic correctness and community ownership (Paullada et al., 2021). Projects like Mozilla's Common Voice, which incorporates African languages like Kinyarwanda and Kiswahili, also prioritize volunteer-driven, open-source data collection that prioritizes local participation and consent (Mozilla Foundation, 2022).

African governments and regional organizations are starting to understand the significance of linguistic inclusion in digital development, going beyond grassroots and academic actors. Language diversity has been emphasized by the African Union (AU) as a crucial element of inclusive digital growth in its Digital Transformation Strategy for Africa (2020–2030) (African Union, 2020). Investment in digital public goods and language technologies that promote indigenous languages is encouraged by the strategy. Nigeria has implemented local content policies at the national level to promote the creation and acquisition of ICT tools that are suited to regional contexts, including those that promote indigenous languages (National Information Technology Development Agency [NITDA], 2021). An essential first step in establishing linguistic equity in digital governance is represented by these policy frameworks.

Taken together, these efforts signify a decentralization of AI development. By building local capacity, infrastructure, and knowledge systems, African researchers and communities are reclaiming voice, agency, and technological sovereignty. These initiatives disrupt the hegemony of global AI by asserting the value of African languages, epistemologies, and lived experiences in the digital age. The rise of collaborative research practices, ethical data standards, and inclusive policies marks a critical shift toward a more equitable and pluralistic AI future, one where linguistic diversity is seen not as a problem to be solved but as a resource to be nurtured and celebrated.

16.7 Pathways Toward Digital Linguistic Sovereignty

To attain digital linguistic sovereignty, Africa needs a comprehensive, coordinated effort that not only focuses on technical language solutions, but includes governance, rights-based frameworks, and cultural sustainability. This section presents a collection of interconnected strategies that include technical, collaborative, regulatory and infrastructural advancements.

16.7.1 State Investment in Linguistic Infrastructure

Many African languages currently face limited or complete absence of essential NLP tools like corpora, lexicons, part-of-speech taggers, and speech datasets. These foundational resources are critical for developing AI applications that account for linguistic nuances, enabling meaningful localization and sovereign AI solutions. Achieving this requires direct government involvement through sustained investment in the development of language basic resources.

Governments must prioritize the development of language resource banks as part of national digital infrastructure, akin to roads or electricity. This includes investing in the collection, digitization, and annotation of oral and written materials across dialects. In the case of South Africa, for instance, the PanSALB has initiated corpus-building projects for official languages (Prinsloo & de Schryver, 2005), but such efforts remain sparse continent-wide.

Investment should also extend to open-source language tools to encourage innovation. As Bird (2020) notes, "Openness in data and tools is essential for equitable language technology development, particularly in linguistically diverse regions."

16.7.2 Regulatory Oversight of Foreign NLP Systems

Currently, many African nations rely on black box NLP systems developed by large foreign firms such as Google, Meta, and OpenAI, whose training data, model biases, and error margins are opaque. This undermines digital sovereignty, as language users are subject to misrepresentation or exclusion. African states must therefore *establish regulatory frameworks* to evaluate and monitor the linguistic fairness of imported NLP technologies. Such oversight could include mandating *language inclusivity audits*, transparency on training data sources, and culturally sensitive error reporting protocols. This mirrors the emerging regulatory trends in the European Union's AI Act, which categorizes language bias as a risk that must be assessed and mitigated (European Commission, 2021). African digital governance bodies can adopt similar frameworks, tailored to regional linguistic realities.

16.7.3 Promotion of Linguistic Rights on Online Platforms

Digital linguistic sovereignty must be grounded in linguistic human rights. As Skutnabb-Kangas and Phillipson (2017) argue, "*denying access to one's language in critical domains is a form of structural discrimination."* Online platforms, especially those offering public services, civic information, or educational content, must be required to offer access to major national and regional languages.

This requires institutionalizing *multilingual digital standards*, such as ensuring translation tools are integrated into e-governance platforms or mandating multilingual support in AI-powered customer services. Crucially, language accessibility should not be an afterthought or corporate courtesy but a *legal mandate* tied to rights-based digital inclusion.

16.7.4 Public-Private-Academic Collaborations for Resource Creation

No single actor can address the complex task of building NLP systems for hundreds of African languages. Governments, tech startups, universities, and civil society need to co-invest in shared linguistic infrastructures through consortia models. One example is the *Masakhane project*, which has demonstrated how grassroots researchers, universities, and NGOs can collectively build high-quality translation models (Nekoto et al., 2020).

Policymakers should support similar consortia through *research grants, incubators, and innovation hubs*, focusing on low-resource languages. Universities offer linguistic expertise and data curation capabilities, while local startups can be crucial in creating language-specific AI applications (such as chatbots, voice assistants, or OCR systems).

16.7.5 AI for Language Revitalization and Cultural Sustainability

AI not only poses a threat to minoritized languages, but it can also potentially be an opportunity for their revitalization. TTS, ASR, and machine translation, along with other technologies, can be employed to save threatened languages, facilitate bilingual education, and create engaging digital material for the youth. For example, Mozilla's Common Voice project has successfully employed crowdsourcing to build open speech corpora for languages like Kinyarwanda and Kiswahili (Mozilla Foundation, 2022). Pedagogical materials, dictionaries, and pronunciation guides artificially created can activate interest in heritage languages and support intergenerational transmission.

Furthermore, African countries can build digital repositories, repositories of native knowledge, oral histories, and folk literatures, tagged and searchable with NLP technologies. These archives constitute linguistic preservation and epistemological sovereignty, a counter to the excellence of Western languages and narratives in digital realms (Oyedemi, 2020).

16.7.6 Embedding Local Governance in Digital Infrastructure

Language technologies must function within local governance frameworks that guarantee accountability, transparency, and cultural context responsiveness in order to be sustainable over the long run. This comprises:

1. Community review boards to check algorithms and datasets for cultural sensitivity.

2. Ethical guidelines for payment and consent in the gathering of language data.
3. Metrics for linguistic inclusion in national digital performance indices.

16.8 Limitations of the Study

This chapter provides a critical and interdisciplinary analysis of linguistic exclusion in AI systems, it is limited by the availability and granularity of publicly accessible data on the representation of African languages in commercial and open-source NLP models. Many proprietary models (such as those developed by OpenAI or Google) do not fully disclose the linguistic distribution of their training data, making it difficult to quantify the exact extent of underrepresentation for languages like Hausa, Yoruba, or Amharic.

Additionally, although the chapter draws on case studies, comparative resource mapping, and examples from prominent grassroots initiatives, it does not present a systematic empirical evaluation (e.g., model performance metrics or language usability studies), which would strengthen claims about practical implications. Furthermore, the fast-paced development of AI and NLP technologies means that the landscape is constantly evolving, and newer initiatives may emerge after the chapter's publication that either mitigate or exacerbate the issues discussed. Lastly, while the chapter highlights regional variation, it cannot fully account for the rich diversity of Africa's 2,000+ languages, and thus focuses mainly on Sub-Saharan African languages with relatively higher visibility in the existing NLP ecosystem.

16.9 Conclusion

One crucial element of this chapter is the call for language digital sovereignty and how African languages are currently at a disadvantage in NLP applications. As hypothesized in this chapter, language is a core infrastructure that influences access, identity, and services in the digital world. It goes well beyond being seen as a mere means of communication. As a result of poor governance, inadequate datasets, and poor or scanty Africa specific AI solutions in multilingual systems, African languages appear marginalized or underrepresented in global AI models. This type of linguistic invisibility denies citizens fair access to digital services and rights, restricts state autonomy over digital platforms, and inhibits innovation among local businesses.

This exclusion is not, however, uncontested. By creating inclusive language technologies and pushing for legislative changes, grassroots projects, open-source communities, and regional organizations are actively combating linguistic marginalization throughout the continent. These initiatives highlight how urgent it is to treat language as essential digital infrastructure rather than as a post-mortem. Achieving digital linguistic sovereignty requires stakeholders to make investments in African language resources, ensure that foreign AI systems are regulated, and promote cross-sector partnerships that prioritize cultural sustainability and linguistic diversity. The promise of AI will remain unequally distributed without such dedication, leaving Africa's linguistic majority unaccounted for and unheard in the development of digital systems.

Declaration of Generative AI and AI-Assisted Technologies

During the preparation of this work, the authors utilized AI-assisted tools such as Grammarly to enhance English language accuracy, including spelling, grammar, and punctuation. The content generated or corrected by these tools was thoroughly reviewed, revised, and edited by the authors to ensure accuracy and originality. The authors accept full responsibility for the originality of the final content of this publication.

References

Adebara, I., Elmadany, A., & Abdul-Mageed, M. (2022). SERENGETI: Massively Multilingual Language Models for Africa. arXiv preprint arXiv:2212.10785. https://arxiv.org/abs/2212.10785

Adelani, D.I., Abbott, J., Neubig, G., D'souza, D., & Kreutzer, J. (2021). MasakhaNER: Named Entity Recognition for African Languages. arXiv preprint arXiv:2103.11811. https://arxiv.org/abs/2103.11811

Adelani, D.I., Alabi, J., & Ruiter, D. (2022). AfroNLP: Advancing African NLP through shared tasks and multilingual datasets. *Proceedings of the ACL Workshop on AfricaNLP 2022*. https://aclanthology.org/2022.afronlp-1.1/

Adelani, D.I., Alabi, J.O., Fan, A., Kreutzer, J., Shen, X., & Reid, M. (2023). A few thousand translations go a long way! Leveraging pre-trained models for African news translation. *Proceedings of NAACL 2023*.

Adeola, A. (2020). Lost in translation: Why Google translate often gets Yoruba—and other languages—wrong. *Rising Voices*. https://rising.globalvoices.org/blog/2020/11/20/lost-in-translation-why-google-translate-often-gets-yoruba-and-other-languages-wrong/

African Union. (2020). *The Digital Transformation Strategy for Africa (2020–2030)*. https://au.int/en/documents/20200518/digital-transformation-strategy-africa-2020-2030

Bird, S. (2020). Decolonising speech and language technology. *Proceedings of the 28th International Conference on Computational Linguistics*.

Birhane, A. (2021). Algorithmic injustice: A relational ethics approach. *Patterns*, 2(2), 100205. https://doi.org/10.1016/j.patter.2021.100205.

Blodgett, S.L., Barocas, S., Daumé III, H., & Wallach, H. (2020). *Language (Technology) is Power: A Critical Survey of "Bias" in NLP*. ACL.

Brookings Institution. (2024). *Closing the Gap: A Call for more Inclusive Language Technologies*. Retrieved from https://www.brookings.edu/articles/closing-the-gap-a-call-for-more-inclusive-language-technologies/Brookings+1Brookings+1

Carnegie Endowment for International Peace. (2024). *How African NLP Experts are Navigating the Challenges of Copyright, Innovation, and Access*. Retrieved from https://carnegieendowment.org/research/2024/04/how-african-nlp-experts-are-navigating-the-challenges-of-copyright-innovation-and-accessCarnegie Endowment

Chatham House. (2024). *Artificial Intelligence and the Challenge for Global Governance*. Retrieved from https://www.chathamhouse.org/2024/06/artificial-intelligence-and-challenge-global-governance/06-resisting-colonialism-why-aiChatham House

Couldry, N., & Mejias, U.A. (2019). *The Costs of Connection: How Data is Colonizing Human Life and Appropriating It for Capitalism*. Stanford University Press.

Data-Pop Alliance. (2022). *The Return of East India Companies: AI, Africa and the New Digital Colonialism*. Retrieved from https://datapopalliance.org/the-return-of-east-india-companies-ai-africa-and-the-new-digital-colonialism/Data-Pop Alliance de Sousa Santos, B. (2014). *Epistemologies of the South: Justice Against Epistemicide*. Routledge.

Delani, D. (2021). African NLP Resources. *GitHub Repository*. https://github.com/dadelani/africanlp-resources

Emezue, C.C. (2022). The forgotten voices: A manifesto for equitable NLP in Africa. *Communications of the ACM*, 65(9), 30–33. https://doi.org/10.1145/3512955

European Commission. (2020). *Shaping Europe's Digital Future*. https://digital-strategy.ec.europa.eu/en

European Commission. (2021). *Proposal for a Regulation Laying Down Harmonised Rules on Artificial Intelligence (Artificial Intelligence Act)*. https://eur-lex.europa.eu/legal-content/EN/TXT/?uri=CELEX:52021PC0206

Floridi, L. (2020). The fight for digital sovereignty: What it is, and why it matters, especially for the EU. *Philosophy & Technology*, 33(3), 369–378. https://doi.org/10.1007/s13347-020-00423-6

Joshi, P., Santy, S., Budhakoti, R., Bali, K., & Choudhury, M. (2020). *The State and Fate of Linguistic Diversity and Inclusion in the NLP World*. ACL.

Korir, K. (2023). The linguistic diversity of Africa: A treasure at risk and the role of AI. *LinkedIn Article*. https://www.linkedin.com/pulse/linguistic-diversity-africa-treasure-risk-role-ai-kiplangat-korir-t4v2f

Lelapa AI. (2023). Comparing Africa-centric Models to OpenAI's GPT3.5. *Lelapa AI Blog*. https://lelapa.ai/comparing-africa-centric-models-to-openais-gpt3-5-2/

Meta AI. (2023). No language left behind. *Meta AI Research*. https://ai.meta.com/research/no-language-left-behind/

Mignolo, W.D. (2009). Epistemic disobedience, independent thought and decolonial freedom. *Theory, Culture & Society*, 26(7-8), 159–181.

Milan, S., & Treré, E. (2019). Big data from the South(s): Beyond data universalism. *Television & New Media*, 20(4), 319–335. https://doi.org/10.1177/1527476419837739

Mohamed, S., Png, M.-T., & Isaac, W. (2020). Decolonial AI: Decolonial theory as sociotechnical foresight in artificial intelligence. *Philosophy & Technology*, 33(4).

Mozilla Foundation. (2022). *Common Voice: Multilingual and Community-driven Speech Datasets*. https://commonvoice.mozilla.org

Muhammad, S.H., Abdulmumin, I., Ayele, A.A., Ousidhoum, N., Adelani, D.I., & Yimam, S.M. (2023). AfriSenti: A sentiment analysis benchmark for African languages. *Proceedings of AfriNLP 2023*.

Nekoto, W., Marivate, V., Matsila, T., Fasubaa, T., Fagbohungbe, T., & Akinola. (2020). Participatory research for low-resourced machine translation: A case study in African languages. *Findings of EMNLP 2020*.

NITDA. (2021). *Nigeria ICT Local Content Development and Promotion Policy*. National Information Technology Development Agency. https://nitda.gov.ng/nit/

Nye, J.S. (2004). *Soft Power: The Means to Success in World Politics*. Public Affairs.

Onose, C., Kreutzer, J., & Adewumi, T. (2021). Lanfrica: A language resource discovery platform for African languages. *Proceedings of EMNLP 2021: System Demonstrations*, 239–245. https://doi.org/10.18653/v1/2021.emnlp-demo.27

Orife, I., Dossou, B.F., Emezue, C., Sefara, T., & Nabende, P. (2020). Masakhane – Machine Translation for Africa by Africans. In: *Proceedings of the 2020 EMNLP Workshop on African NLP* (pp. 86–95). https://aclanthology.org/2020.africanlp-1.11

Oyedemi, T. (2020). African languages and digital sovereignty: Challenges and possibilities. *Critical African Studies*, 12(3), 295–314. https://doi.org/10.1080/21681392.2020.1787157

Paris, D., & Winn, M.T. (2014). *Humanizing Research: Decolonizing Qualitative Inquiry with Youth and Communities*. SAGE.

Paullada, A., Raji, I.D., Binns, R., Denton, E., & Hanna, A. (2021). Data and its (dis)contents: A survey of dataset development and use in machine learning research. *Patterns*, 2(11), 100336. https://doi.org/10.1016/j.patter.2021.100336

Perley, B.C. (2012). Zombie linguistics: Experts, endangered languages and the curse of undead voices. *Anthropological Forum*, 22(2).

Pimienta, D., Prado, D., & Blanco, Á. (2009). *TICs, Desarrollo y Lenguas Indígenas*. UNESCO.

Pohle, J., & Thiel, T. (2020). Digital Sovereignty. *Internet Policy Review*, 9(4).

Prinsloo, D.J., & de Schryver, G.-M. (2005). Managing wordlists for African-Language Lexicography in the electronic age. *Lexikos*, 15(1), 170–188. https://doi.org/10.5788/15-0-990

Quijano, A. (2007). Coloniality and modernity/rationality. *Cultural Studies*, 21(2-3), 168-178. Wikipedia+1SpringerLink+1

Rainie, S.C., Rodríguez-Lonebear, D., & Martinez, A. (2017). Data governance for native nation rebuilding. *Data Science Journal*, 16.

Salami, A.O. (2024). Artificial intelligence, digital colonialism, and the implications for Africa's future development. *Data & Policy*, 6, e3.

Salihu-Lukman, S., Suleiman, M.A., & Yusuf, S.I. (2025). *Unsupervised Exploration of Latent Spaces in Pre-Trained Language Models.* Unpublished (Manuscript drafted).

Sambuli, N., Mare, A., & Udupa, S. (2021). Data justice for the majority world. *Data & Society Report Series*. https://datasociety.net/library/data-justice-for-the-majority-world/

Skutnabb-Kangas, T., & Phillipson, R. (2017). Linguistic human rights. *In:* O. García, N. Flores, & M. Spotti (eds.), *The Oxford Handbook of Language and Society* (pp. 235–257). Oxford University Press.

Spivak, G.C. (1988). Can the subaltern speak? In: C. Nelson & L. Grossberg (eds.), *Marxism and the Interpretation of Culture*. University of Illinois Press.

Walter, D., & Suina, M. (2019). Indigenous data, indigenous methodologies and the concept of sovereignty. In: T. Kukutai, & J. Taylor (eds.), *Indigenous Data Sovereignty*. ANU Press.

Zuboff, S. (2019). *The Age of Surveillance Capitalism: The Fight for a Human Future at the New Frontier of Power*. PublicAffairs.

Index

F

G

H

I

L

M

N

P

R

S

T

U

W

Y

About the Editors

Dr. Sanjay Misra is a Senior Scientist at the Institute for Energy Technology (IFE), Halden, Norway. He holds a Ph.D. in Information and Knowledge Engineering (University of Alcala, Spain) and an M.Tech. in Software Engineering (MLN NIT, India). His research spans Applied Informatics, Digital Sovereignty, Sustainability, and AI-based Intelligent Systems. Recognized among the top 2% of scientists globally by Stanford University for six consecutive years, he ranked 6th in Norway across disciplines in 2024. A recipient of the 2014 IET Software Premium Award, he was a Senior IEEE Member and ACM Distinguished Lecturer (2021–2024). He has chaired major conferences, including founding General Chair of the first Digital Sovereignty Conference (2024, Oslo; proceedings by Elsevier), edited top journals including Nature: Scientific Reports, and serves as Editor-in-Chief of the International Journal of Human Capital & IT Professionals. With 100+ books and proceedings, and over 100 keynotes in 60+ countries, he is a leading global voice in informatics, Digital Sovereignty, and AI.

Petter Kvalvik is Head of Department for Business Development and a Senior Scientist at the Institute for Energy Technology (IFE). He holds a Master's degree in Applied Computer Science, a Master of Management in Strategy and Project Portfolio Management, a Master's degree in Safety and Security Critical Systems, and a Bachelor's degree in Business Administration. Petter leads the new research area on Digital Sovereignty, which includes, among other things, federated and autonomous systems, data spaces and data products, data governance, decentralized identities, digital trust, and interoperability. He is responsible for following up on the European data strategy, the European technology stack, the Big Data Value Association, and the annual International Conference on Digital Sovereignty. He also heads the My Digital City programme and the Norwegian FIWARE iHub for Iot. Both initiatives play a vital role in piloting a Norwegian data space for smart communities, involving project participants such as Halden Municipality, Østfold University College, and Smart Innovation Norway.

Bjørn Axel Gran is vice president for IFE, Digital Systems in Halden. He has more than 25 years of experience with research and consultant/advisory services in oil & gas, energy, nuclear, railways and air traffic management. Gran was employed with Safetec and ABS Consulting (2010–2017) in different roles, among other group leaders and R&D managers. In the period 2014–2019, Gran was an Adjunct Professor (20% position) at the Department of Mechanical and Industrial Engineering, Norwegian University of Science and Technology. He obtained an MSc in industrial mathematics in 1993 and a Ph.D. in the field of software reliability at NTNU in 2002.

Kai Morgan Kjølerbakken is a physicist, computer scientist, and entrepreneur, with a passion for research, technology, and innovation. He is currently a department lead at the Institute for Energy Technology (IFE), where he leads a team focused on data science and AI. In addition, Kjølerbakken is a dedicated educator and serves as an Associate Professor at the Department of Physics, University of Oslo, Norway. Dr. Kjølerbakken's research interests lie in various fields, including sensor technology, computational physics, audio, electronics, signal processing, and AI. He is an expert in leading interdisciplinary collaborations and contributing to the development of innovative theories and methodologies. Beyond his academic pursuits, Dr. Kjølerbakken brings valuable experience from the industry, having funded and contributed to several successful startups, including Squarehead Technology, Elliptic Labs, and Airmont.

Aida Omerovic is a researcher, leader and practitioner with expertise in security risk management and system architectures. She has a track record of over 20 years in the public and private sectors in Europe. Aida works closely with technology-driven organizations across Europe, from critical domains (energy, communication, transport, finance and media), on enabling their strategic and future-proof digital innovation. She also actively disseminates best practices and research as a speaker/author/educator. She has published a textbook and 40+ peer-reviewed scientific articles, most of which deal with applied research, industrial development and innovation. Aida is a research manager and senior scientist at SINTEF, as well as an associate professor at Norwegian University of Science and Technology. Her previous positions include founder, CEO, consultant, senior scientist and research director. She serves as a director on several boards as well as on international public posts, which foster collaborations between professional and research communities. Aida holds an MSc in Engineering Cybernetics from NTNU and a Ph.D. in Computer Science from the University of Oslo, Norway.

Nadia Saad Noori is an associate professor at the ICT department at the University of Agder, Kristiansand, Norway and a Principal Investigator for the Cyber Resilient Organizations and Societies research group at the Centre of Integrated Emergency Management – University of Agder (CIEM-UiA). Dr. Noori is a Marie Skłodowska-Curie alumna with a background in computer and control systems engineering. She has over 20 years of combined experience between industry and academia. She holds both a BSc and an MSc in Computer Systems Engineering, with a focus on design and development of SCADA systems for the electrical energy sector. Furthermore, holds an MA Sc in Technology Innovation Management with a focus on open-source platforms for real-time communications and collaboration. In 2016, she obtained her Ph.D. title in Electronic and Information Systems Engineering with a focus on applications of graph theory and complex network analysis to understand coordination and resource distribution in complex systems. Her research interests focus on the applications of emerging technologies (i.e. Machine Learning and Artificial Intelligence, IoT, Cloud Computing) to solve problems and challenges related to industrial systems like SCADA systems, and the role of AI/ML methods to enable increased resilience of cyber-physical infrastructure systems.

For Product Safety Concerns and Information please contact our
EU representative GPSR@taylorandfrancis.com Taylor & Francis
Verlag GmbH, Kaufingerstraße 24, 80331 München, Germany